Guidebook 2008

12th Edition

GW00496509

sponsored by

www.daysoutuk.com

DaysOutUK Credits

Days Out UK
PO Box 427
Northampton
NN1 3YN

Telephone:
01604 622445
Fax:
01604 633866 or 629900
Email:
info@daysoutuk.com

Web:
www.daysoutuk.com

ISBN 978-0-9543899-5-6

A catalogue record for this book is available from the British Library.

© Days Out UK 2008

Part of Johnston Press Plc.

Printed and bound by
Cromwell Press, Wiltshire

Managing Editor
Julia J. Smith

Front Cover Design
David Thomas

Graphic Design
Sara Tyler Reese

Copy Editor
Berni Frost

Sales & Administration Co-ordinator
Rob Andrew

Sales
Jan Real

Days Out UK Discount Vouchers

Attractions offering a discount will have their voucher offer highlighted within their listing. At the back of this guide you will find 300+ discount vouchers offering you savings of around £2,000.

These vouchers appear in alphabetical order for ease of use. Simply cut-out the voucher you wish to use and exchange at the ticket booth of your selected attraction. Please ensure you read the full terms and conditions prior to making your journey.

UK Public Holidays 2008

England & Wales

21 Mar:	Good Friday
24 Mar:	Easter Monday
05 May:	May Bank Hol
26 May:	Spring Bank Hol
25 Aug:	Summer Bank Hol
25 Dec:	Christmas Day
26 Dec:	Boxing Day
01 Jan:	New Year's Day

Ireland

17 Mar:	St Patrick's Day
24 Mar:	Easter Monday
05 May:	First Monday in May
02 Jun:	First Monday in Jun
04 Aug:	First Monday in Aug
27 Oct:	Last Monday in Oct
25 Dec:	Christmas Day
26 Dec:	St Stephen's Day
01 Jan:	New Year's Day

Northern Ireland

17 Mar:	St Patrick's Day
21 Mar:	Good Friday
24 Mar:	Easter Monday
05 May:	May Bank Hol
26 May:	Spring Bank Hol
14 Jul:	Battle of the Boyne
25 Aug:	Summer Bank Hol
25 Dec:	Christmas Day
26 Dec:	Boxing Day
01 Jan:	New Year's Day

Scotland

21 Mar:	Good Friday
05 May:	Early May Bank Hol
26 May:	Spring Bank Hol
04 Aug:	Summer Bank Hol
01 Dec:	St Andrew's Day
25 Dec:	Christmas Day
26 Dec:	Boxing Day
01 Jan:	New Year's Day
02 Jan:	2nd January

For more information, or to subscribe to the Days Out UK Club, please visit our website, **www.daysoutuk.com**

DAYSOUTUK Contents

DaysOUtUK Contents

DaysOutUK Key to Facility Symbols

All weather attraction		Haunted / resident ghost/s
Allow 1-2 hours for visit		Historic Scotland
Allow all day for visit		Licensed for alcohol
Allow half a day for visit		Licensed for weddings
Baby changing facilities		National Trust
Beach / coastal area		National Trust for Scotland
Cadw Welsh Preservation		No dogs (except guide dogs)
Café / Restaurant on site		Offering a discount voucher
Celebration catering		Offers corporate facilities
Credit cards accepted		Parking is charged
Disabled access (full)		Parking nearby
Education packs available		Parking on site
English Heritage		Photography is allowed
Family friendly		Picnic areas
Gift Shop and/or shop/s		Pushchair access
Good weather attraction		Recommended for adults
Guided tours available		Refreshments available

Bedfordshire

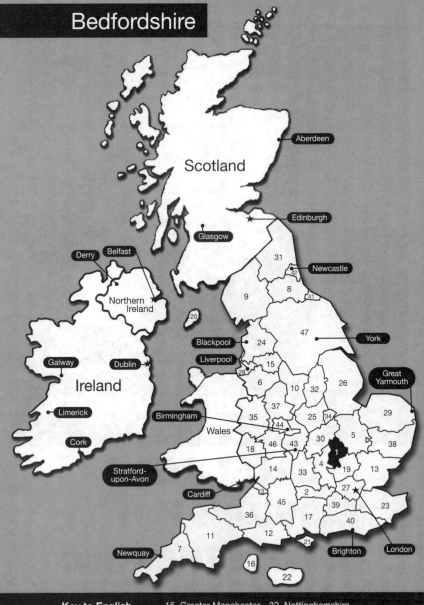

Scotland

Aberdeen

Edinburgh

Glasgow

Derry Belfast

Newcastle

Northern Ireland

Blackpool

Liverpool

York

Galway Dublin

Ireland

Great Yarmouth

Limerick

Birmingham

Cork

Wales

Stratford-upon-Avon

Cardiff

Brighton

London

Newquay

Animal Attractions

Bird of Prey and Conservation Centre

Old Warden Park Biggleswade Bedfordshire SG18 9EA
Tel: 01767 627527
Open all year, the UK's largest Bird of Prey Centre with a collection of 300 birds.

Mead Open Farm

Stanbridge Road Billington Leighton Buzzard Bedfordshire LU7 9HL
Tel: 01525 852954
Cuddle rabbits, bottle feed lambs, milk cows or meet our new baby animals! Plus in Shaggy's PlayWorld, kids can enjoy over 10,000 sq feet of indoor play.

Wild Britain

Bedford Butterfly Park 65a Renhold Road Wilden Bedford Bedfordshire MK44 2PX
Tel: 01234 772770 Fax: 01234 772773
www.wild-britain.com

[From M1, J13 or A1 Blackcat Roundabout. Take A421, exit at Great Barford sliproad. Follow signs for Renhold. After 0.75mi turn R to Wilden. Plenty of on-site parking available]

You are sure to have a great time at Wild Britain. Join in with the adventures of Urchin the hedgehog on our new exploration trail. Meet Urchin or one of his friends in our British Animal Presentation Show. Enjoy tales of butterflies and bugs in our puppet theatre before visiting the childrens' arts and crafts cabin. Enter our tropical butterfly house for a taste of the rainforest. We also have a playground, tea room and souvenir shop.

7 Feb-31 Oct daily 10.00-17.00, 1 Nov-21 Dec Thur-Fri 10.00-16.00
A£6.00, C£4.50

Discount Offer: One Child Free (with a full-paying adult).

Woodside Animal Farm and Leisure Park

Woodside Road Slip End Luton Bedfordshire LU1 4DG
Tel: 01582 841044 Fax: 01582 840626
www.woodsidefarm.co.uk

[From N exit M1 J10, follow dual carriageway to roundabout, take turning for Harpenden (A1081) & follow brown tourist signs for Wildfowl Park. From S exit M1 J9, turning N onto A5 in direction of Dunstable, turn R onto B4540 Luton rd & follow brown tourist signs for Wildfowl Park. Public transport, Rail to Luton main station, then bus service 30, 32, 46 or 231. Plenty of on-site parking available]

Woodside Animal Farm is an exciting and fun filled day out for all the family. With so many farm and zoo animals and birds to see and feed, everyone is encouraged to get "touchy-feely" with many of them in the daily "animal encounter" and handling sessions. The farm also allows visitors to feed a lot of the animals by selling special pots of feed for them.

Included in the price are animal encounter sessions, tractor rides, reptile encounter session, rabbit cuddling, cow milking and egg collecting sessions. As well as bouncy castles and trampolines, visit our traditional country fun fair, rides include helter skelter, teacups and saucers ride, carousel, coconut shy, basketball throw and hook a duck. There are also outdoor play areas and the brand new large heated indoor play area. Farmer Woods 18 hole crazy golf course, a huge sandpit, electric tractors and "hook-a-duck", plus special event days throughout the year, please see the website for further details. Large coffee shop, farm shop and pet store. Please note that some activities are seasonal and/or dry weather activities.

All year Mon-Sat 08.00-18.00, Sun 10.00-18.00. In the winter the Playbarn and shop will remain open until 18.00, the farm park will close at dusk. Please contact farm office for details of Christmas & New Year opening times

A£6.95 C&OAPs£5.95 C(1 yr old)£2.95 C(under1)£Free. Disabled visitors £2.95, accompanying carers £3.95. Group rates (for 20+) available on request

Country Parks & Estates

Dunstable Downs, Chilterns Gateway Centre and Whipsnade Estate

Dunstable Road Whipsnade Bedfordshire
LU6 2GY
Tel: 01582 500920
Commands excellent views over the Vale of Aylesbury and Chiltern Ridge. Kite-flying hotspot with views of gliders and paragliders.

Marston Vale Millennium Country Park

Station Road Marston Moretaine Bedford Bedfordshire MK43 0PR
Tel: 01234 767037
Stretching over 250 hectares, the park has a mosaic of habitats from wetlands to woodlands - lakes and lagoons.

Priory Country Park

Bedford Bedfordshire
Tel: 01234 211182
The park covers over 300 acres including two large lakes, flower grassland and wooded areas. There are riverside walks and beautiful views over water and meadows. The landscape is maintained for the benefit of both wildlife and people and the Park is always open.

Festivals & Shows

Bedfordshire Steam and Country Fayre

Old Warden Park nr Biggleswade Bedfordshire SG18 9EP
Tel: 01462 851711
www.bseps.org.uk

[2mi W on A1 Biggleswade. Plenty of free on-site parking available]

Admission includes entrance to The Shuttleworth Collection. See steam, tractor and heavy horse working demonstrations, steam ploughing, miniature steam, fairground organs, aerobatic display, working crafts, trade and market stalls, how clay pigeon shooting, archery, working dog demonstrations, vintage vehicles, old time fairground and Morris dancing. Plus licensed bar and refreshments.

13-14 September 2008 (09.00-18.00)

Sat & Sun A£12.00 C(5-16)£5.00 OAPs£8.00. Includes free admission to The Shuttleworth Collection, the Bird of Prey Centre & Swiss Garden

Folk & Local History Museums

Bedford Museum

Castle Lane Bedford Bedfordshire MK40 3XD
Tel: 01234 353323 Fax: 01234 273401
www.bedfordmuseum.org

[A short walk from Allhallows Bus Station & Midland Rd Railway Station. Limited on-site parking available]

Embark on a fascinating journey through the human and natural history of North Bedfordshire, pausing briefly to glimpse at wonders from more distant lands. Go back in time to visit the delightful rural room sets and the Old School Museum, where Blackbeard's sword, 'Old Billy' the record breaking longest-lived horse and numerous other treasures and curiosities can be found. Housed in the former Higgins and Sons Brewery, Bedford Museum is situated within the picturesque gardens of Bedford Castle, beside the Great Ouse embankment. The charming courtyard and well laid out galleries provide an excellent setting for the rich and varied nature of the collections. Family activities on selected days. There is a charge for guided tours which must be booked in advance. Facilities available for people with disabilities. Museum shop and coffee shop. Rooms available for hire.

All year Tue-Sat 11.00-17.00, Sun & Bank Hol Mon 14.00-17.00. Closed Mons, Good Fri, Christmas and New Year

Admission Free

Historical

Moggerhanger Park

Park Road Moggerhanger Bedford Bedfordshire MK44 3RW
Tel: 01767 641007 Fax: 01767 641515
www.moggerhangerpark.com

[A1, A603 1.5mi or M1(A421), J13, A603. Rail: Bedford or Sandy. Plenty of on-site parking available]

The Grade 1 listed Georgian Country House has recently been restored in keeping with the original design of its architect, Sir John Soane and is set in 33 acres of parkland originally landscaped by Humphry Repton. Restaurant and tea rooms open throughout the year. Do visit the first restaurant to be awarded a Bedfordshire 'Food Mark'! Guided tours daily throughout the summer. Functions and conference facilities available. Moggerhanger House has 3 executive conference suites making it an ideal venue for conferences, promotions and corporate entertainment.

Restaurant & Tea Rooms: All year daily 11.00-16.00 & Fri-Sat evenings. Guided Tours of Historic Rooms: 14 June-12 Sept daily 12.00 & 14.30. Pre-booked group tours are also available

Guided Tours of Historic Rooms: A£6.00 Concessions£5.00 C(under16)£Free. Group rates available on request.

Discount Offer: Two for the Price of One (full-paying adult).

Moot Hall

Elstow Green Church End Elstow Bedfordshire
MK42 9XT
Tel: 01234 266889/304640
[Off A6 signposted off Elstow Road]
This restored medieval timber-framed market
hall has a collection of 17th-century furniture
and items relating to the life and times of John
Bunyan.

Military & Defence Museums

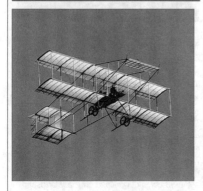

Shuttleworth Collection

Old Warden Aerodrome Biggleswade
Bedfordshire SG18 9EP
Tel: 01767 627927 Fax: 01767 627949
www.shuttleworth.org

*[2mi W of A1 Biggleswade. Plenty of on-site park-
ing available]*

A traditional grass aerodrome, with a world
famous collection of aircraft from a 1909 Bleriot
to a 1942 Spitfire, plus veteran and vintage
motor vehicles and a coachroom of nineteenth-
century, horse-drawn vehicles all displayed
indoors. The aircraft and the vehicles are kept in
working order. Please allow a minimum of two
hours for your visit.

*All year daily, 1 Apr-31 Oct 10.00-17.00, 1 Nov-
31 Mar 10.00-16.00. Closed Christmas and New
Year week*

A£10.00 Accompanied C(0-16)£Free
OAPs£9.00. Group rate (20+): £6.50, School
Parties £3.50. Prices on flying days A£20.00

Places of Worship

Bushmead Priory

Little Staughton Road Colmworth Bedford
Bedfordshire MK44 2LD
Tel: 01234 376614
A rare survival of the medieval refectory of an
Augustinian priory.

John Bunyan Museum

Bunyan Meeting Free Church Mill Street
Bedford Bedfordshire MK40 3EU
Tel: 01234 213722
The John Bunyan Museum opened its new
building in 1998, giving a fascinating and vivid
insight into the life of John Bunyan.

Railways

Leighton Buzzard Railway

Page's Park Station Billington Road Leighton
Buzzard Bedfordshire LU7 4TN
Tel: 01525 373888 (24hours)
Fax: 01525 377814
www.buzzrail.co.uk

*[On A4146 Hemel Hempstead rd, near J with
A505 Dunstable / Aylesbury rd. Rail: Leighton
Buzzard station 2mi. Bus: Arriva service 31 (Luton
Airport) links Leighton Buzzard Station, canal &
town centre with Stanbridge Road, which is a
short walk from Page's Park station along
Billington Rd. Plenty of on-site parking available]*

The Leighton Buzzard Railway lets you experience public transport as it was in the early part

of the twentieth century, and discover the line's unique history, dating back over 85 years. The 70-minute return journey takes you through the edge of the town and out into the countryside, and features level crossings, sharp curves and steep gradients. Most trains are hauled by an historic steam engine from one of Britain's largest collections of narrow-gauge locomotives.

Single Train Service: 16, 21-22, 26 & 30 Mar; 6, 13, 20 & 27 Apr; 3, 11, 18, 24 & 28 May; 1, 8 & 22 Jun; 13, 20, 23, 29, 30 & 31 Jul; 6, 12, 13, 16, 19, 20, 21 & 23 Aug; 14 & 28 Sep; 4, 5, 12, 19, 22 & 29 Oct. Two Train Service: 23 & 24 Mar; 4, 5, 25 & 26 May; 15 & 29 Jun; 27 Jul; 3, 10, 17, 24, 25 & 31 Aug; 21 Sep; 26 Oct. Term Time Specials: 4, 11, 18 & 25 Jun; 2, 9 & 16 Jul. Intensive Service: 6 & 7 Sep. Christmas Specials in Dec. Check website for latest information, including train times

A£7.00 C(2-15)£3.00 C(0-2)Free OAPs£6.00, Family Ticket (A2+C1) £16.00, Family Ticket (A2+C2) £19.00. Day Rover: £13.00

Discount Offer: Two for the Price of One (adult paying full-fare).

Stately Homes

Woburn Abbey

Woburn Bedfordshire MK17 9WA

Tel: 01525 290333

Set in a beautiful 3,000-acre deer park, Woburn Abbey has been the home of the Dukes of Bedford for nearly 400 years.

Wildlife & Safari Parks

Woburn Safari Park

Woburn Park Woburn Bedfordshire MK17 9QN

Tel: 01525 290407

Award winning Woburn Safari Park is set in 350 of the 3,000 acres of parkland surrounding Woburn Abbey.

ZSL Whipsnade Zoo

Whipsnade Dunstable Bedfordshire LU6 2LF

Tel: 01582 872171 Fax: 01582 872649

www.zsl.org

[Located off the M1, J9. Plenty of on-site parking available]

Escape with your family on a big animal adventure for a day out full of excitement and fun at ZSL Whipsnade Zoo. Set in the beautiful Chiltern Hills, ZSL Whipsnade Zoo is home to over 2,500 rare and exotic animals. Don't miss the chance to visit our new Cheetah Rock exhibit where you can view our cheetahs from an African style hut with floor to ceiling glass being the only thing separating you from the animals. Be amazed by our spectacular free-flying bird displays, sealion demonstrations and witness the strength of an elephant's trunk in our Elephantastic demonstration. Take a ride on the wild side on the Jumbo Express and let the fun-packed commentary entertain you! With 600 spectacular acres to explore ZSL Whipsnade Zoo turns a day out into a big animal adventure for the whole family. Book online at zsl.org.

All year daily from 10.00. Closed Dec 25

Please see website for details

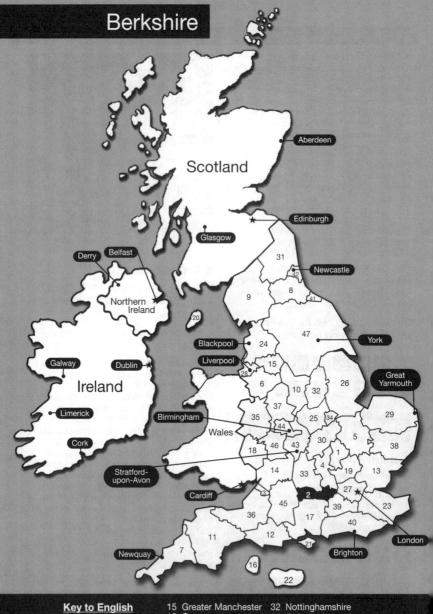

Berkshire

Aberdeen

Scotland

Edinburgh

Glasgow

Newcastle

31

42

Derry
Belfast

Northern
Ireland

8

9

41

47

York

20

Blackpool

24

Liverpool

15

Galway

Dublin

28

6

10

32

26

Great
Yarmouth

Ireland

37

29

Limerick

35

25

34

5

38

Birmingham

44

Cork

Wales

18

46

43

30

1

19

13

Stratford-
upon-Avon

14

33

4

Cardiff

13

2

27

23

45

39

40

London

36

17

Brighton

11

12

Newquay

7

21

16

22

Animal Attractions

Lambourn Trainers Association

Windsor House Crowle Road Lambourn
Hungerford Berkshire RG17 8NR
Tel: 01488 71347 Fax: 01488 72664
www.lambourntraining.org

[M4 J14. Rail: Newbury. Plenty of on-site parking available]

Lambourn Trainers Association will escort visitors around their stables, giving a fascinating insight into the racing world not seen by the public before. Lambourn - Valley of the Racehorse, is highly respected for its enviable record for success, including the winners of the Cheltenham Gold Cup in 2000 and last 2 years of 2000 Guineas and Champion Stakes. Lambourn Trainers Open Day on 21 March 2008.

All year Mon-Sat 10.00-12.00 by appointment. Open Day: 6 Apr 08.30-17.00. Closed Bank Hols & Sun

Tours £7.00+vat C£Free

Country Parks & Estates

Cliveden

Taplow Maidenhead Berkshire SL6 0JA
Tel: 01628 605069
Magnificent formal gardens overlooking the River Thames, once the exclusive haunt of the rich and famous. Sculpture collection, plus spectacular views and enchanting walks.

Wellington Country Park

Odiham Road Riseley Reading Berkshire
RG7 1SP
Tel: 0118 932 6444 Fax: 0118 932 6445
www.wellington-country-park.co.uk

[Signposted off A33. Plenty of on-site parking available]

Wellington Country Park, Riseley, near Reading, has 350 acres of wonderful parkland within the Duke of Wellington's estate, providing an ideal venue for a family outing. Explore the nature trails round the lakes. Play in the adventure playground, and explore our fantastic new play areas. Younger children will enjoy the lovely sandpit, toddlers area and miniature railway. Finish off with a family tournament on the crazy golf course! Acres of space for your own picnics and barbecues, with areas provided. Camping and caravanning site in the park. An ideal touring site for Winchester, Salisbury, Legoland, Windsor and Oxford. Dogs welcomed. Special events throughout the year. Please call for further information.

Feb-Nov daily 10.00-17.30

A£6.00 C(under3)£Free C(3-15)£5.00
OAPs£5.00, Family Ticket (A2+C2) £19.50.
Group rates (for 20+) available on request.
Season tickets: £45.00 for first family member, £30.00 for subsequent family member

Discount Offer: Two for the Price of One.

Historical

Windsor Castle

Windsor Berkshire SL4 1NJ
Tel: 020 7766 7304
Official residence of Her Majesty The Queen.

Science - Earth & Planetary

Look Out Discovery Centre, The

Nine Mile Ride Bracknell Berkshire RG12 7QW
Tel: 01344 354400 Fax: 01344 354422
www.bracknell-forest.gov.uk/be

[J10 M4, J3 M3 off A322 on B3430. Rail: Bracknell. Plenty of on-site parking available]

The Look Out Discovery Centre in Bracknell is a great day whatever the weather. The main attraction is an exciting hands on, interactive science and nature exhibition that offers over 70 bright and fun filled exhibits within five themed zones; Light and Colour, Sound and Communication, Forces and Movement, Woodland and Water and Body and Perception. Come and launch the hot air balloon, freeze your shadow on the wall or climb through a giant mole hole. In the surrounding 2,600 acres of Crown Estate woodland, visitors can enjoy nature walks, cycle trails, a picnic area and a child's play area. With child and adult mountain bike hire (or bring your own), coffee shop, gift shop and Tourist Information Centre. This offers an action packed day for the whole family at reasonable prices. Birthday parties catered for.

All year daily 10.00-17.00. Closed Christmas

A£5.70 Concessions£3.80, Family Ticket £15.30

Discount Offer: One Child Free.

Spectator Sports

Ascot Racecourse

High Street Ascot Berkshire SL5 7JX
Tel: 0870 727 1234 Fax: 0870 460 1238
www.ascot.co.uk

[Rail: Reading, London Waterloo. Plenty of on-site parking available]

The highlight of our year is Royal Ascot which takes place from Tuesday 17th to Saturday 21st June inclusive. The quality of racing at the Royal Meeting is simply outstanding with over £4 million in prize money on offer and a total of seventeen pattern races (the UK's top rated races) over the five-day meeting. Outside Royal Ascot we have 20 other racedays that offer something for everyone. Each of our racedays offers its own unique atmosphere and entertainment programme. Highlights include seven Family Days, a Countryside Day, a Wine Tasting Day, a Beer Festival in association with the Campaign for Real Ale, a Motor Show, a Firework Display as well as some of the best racing action in the UK. Children aged 16 and under are admitted FREE on all racedays. For further information or to book tickets go to www.ascot.co.uk or call 0870 727 1234.

Jan-Dec
From A£10.00 C(0-16)£Free. Restaurant packages start from £65.00 plus VAT

Discount Offer: £5.00 off per ticket on all Family Days.

Sport & Recreation

Coral Reef Water World

Nine Mile Ride Bracknell Berkshire RG12 7JQ
Tel: 01344 862525 Fax: 01344 869146
www.bracknell-forest.gov.uk/be

[From J3 M3, follow A322 to Bracknell for 3.7mi, from J10 M4 follow A329 to Bracknell, then follow A322 to Bagshot for 4.1mi. Plenty of on-site parking available]

Fun at Coral Reef - so let the water excitement start here. Coral Reef Bracknell's Water World is a tropical paradise providing fun for all the family. There are three giant water slides and other water features including the wild water rapids, erupting volcano, firing cannons, squirting snakes and bubbling spas. After all this fun why not visit our air-conditioned restaurant on the first floor with views over the pool. Sauna World is available to over 18s only so you can relax in the tranquil surroundings of a Saunarium (a mix of dry and wet heat), two saunas and our two tier steam room. There is a cool pool and footspa to invigorate the whole body. Light refreshments are also available in Sauna World. Coral Reef is open all year round. Please note that at all times there is a maximum of two children under 8 years to one adult (over 18).

All year Mon 10.30-21.00, Tue-Fri 10.30-21.45, Sat & Sun 09.00-17.45. Please note Wed & Fri 19.00-21.45 over 21's only. Early Bird sessions Mon-Fri 06.30-9.30 excluding Bank Hol. Term Time Only: Mon-Fri 10.30-15.30 are special Parent & Toddler Sessions

Off peak times: Mon-Fri 10.30-15.30 (term time): A&C£3.80 C(0-4)£Free, Peak times: Mon-Fri 15.30-21.00/21.45 & Sat & Sun 09.00-17.45 A£6.65 C£4.60 C(0-4)£Free. Disabled, over 50s and party rates available. Please telephone

venue for price change after Apr 2008

Discount Offer: £5.00 off One Full-Priced Family Ticket.

Stately Homes

Frogmore House

Windsor Berkshire SL1 1SL
Tel: 020 7321 2233

[J6 M4 / J3 M3]

Set amid the extensive Home Park of Windsor Castle, Frogmore House is surrounded by fine and picturesque gardens.

Theme & Adventure Parks

Go Ape! High Wire Forest Adventure (Swinley Forest, Berkshire)

The Look Out Nine Mile Ride Swinley Forest Bracknell Berkshire RG12 7QW
Tel: 0845 643 9245
www.goape.co.uk

[M3 J3 or M4 J10, off A322 on B3430. Plenty of on-site parking available]

Take to the trees and experience an exhilarating course of rope bridges, Tarzan swings and zip-slides up to 40 feet above the ground! Share approximately three exciting hours of fun and adventure, which you'll be talking about for days. Book online and watch people Go Ape! at www.goape.co.uk. Minimum height 1.4m. Maximum weight 130 kg (20.5 stone). Under-18s must be accompanied by a participating adult. One adult can supervise either two children (where one or both of them is under 16 years old) or up to five 16-17 year olds. Pre-booking is essential to avoid disappointment. Book online or by telephone (there is a £1.00 booking fee on all telephone bookings).

18-22 Feb, 14 Mar-31 Oct daily, Nov Sat-Sun. Dec Sat-Sun TBC please visit www.goape.co.uk. Closed Jan

Gorillas (18yrs+) £25.00, Baboons (10-17yrs) £20.00

Discount Offer: £5.00 off per person.

LEGOLAND Windsor
Winkfield Road Windsor Berkshire SL4 4AY
www.legoland.co.uk

[On B3022 Windsor-Ascot road, well signposted from M4 & M3. Plenty of on-site parking available]

LEGOLAND Windsor has over 50 rides, live shows and attractions in 150 acres of beautiful parkland - they're designed to provide exciting, active fun for the whole family, and let you be whatever you want to be! The brand new Land of the Vikings features the huge new Vikings' River Splash ride - take a wild, wet voyage through a world of beasts and barbarians built from millions of LEGO bricks. But before you set sail, find your sea-legs on the hilarious Longboat Invader, new for 2008!

15 Mar-2 Nov. Opening times vary, for more information please visit our website

Discount Offer: Save up to £25.00! Voucher entitles a maximum of 5 people to £5.00 off full admission price per person at LEGOLAND Windsor.

Wildlife & Safari Parks

Beale Park
Lower Basildon Reading Berkshire RG8 9NH
Tel: 0870 777 7160 Fax: 0870 777 7120
www.bealepark.co.uk

[Signposted from J12 M4, follow brown tourist signs. Plenty of on-site parking available]

This glorious Thameside Wildlife and Leisure Park has something for everyone. Unique collection of rare and endangered birds, pets corner, deer park, paddling pools, adventure playground, gardens, trails, narrow gauge railway, picnic areas, shop, restaurant, fishing, little tikes village and jubilee gardens by Pantiles Nurseries and much more.

Mar-end Oct daily 10.00-18.00 (or dusk)
High Season: A£8.50 C£6.00 OAPs£7.00. Low Season: A£6.00 C£4.00 OAPs£5.00

Discount Offer: One Child Free.

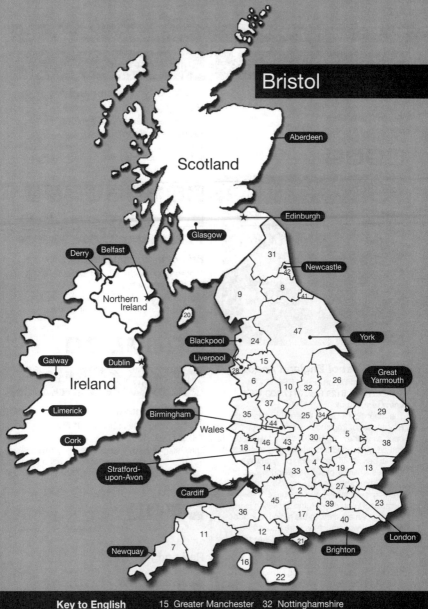

Bristol

Aberdeen

Scotland

Edinburgh

Glasgow

Derry Belfast

Newcastle

Northern
Ireland

31

42

9

8

41

20

Galway Dublin

Blackpool

47

York

Liverpool

24

Great
Yarmouth

Ireland

15

Limerick

6

10

32

26

37

29

Birmingham

35

25

34

Cork

Wales

44

30

5

38

18

46

43

1

Stratford-
upon-Avon

14

4

19

13

Cardiff

33

2

27

23

45

39

40

London

36

17

Newquay

11

12

21

Brighton

7

16

22

Key to English Counties:

1 Bedfordshire
2 Berkshire
3 Bristol
4 Buckinghamshire
5 Cambridgeshire
6 Cheshire
7 Cornwall
8 County Durham
9 Cumbria
10 Derbyshire
11 Devon
12 Dorset
13 Essex
14 Gloucestershire

15 Greater Manchester
16 Guernsey
17 Hampshire
18 Herefordshire
19 Hertfordshire
20 Isle Of Man
21 Isle Of Wight
22 Jersey
23 Kent
24 Lancashire
25 Leicestershire
26 Lincolnshire
27 London
28 Merseyside
29 Norfolk
30 Northamptonshire
31 Northumberland

32 Nottinghamshire
33 Oxfordshire
34 Rutland
35 Shropshire
36 Somerset
37 Staffordshire
38 Suffolk
39 Surrey
40 Sussex
41 Tees Valley
42 Tyne & Wear
43 Warwickshire
44 West Midlands
45 Wiltshire
46 Worcestershire
47 Yorkshire

Airfields / Flight Centres

Concorde at Filton
Filton Bristol BS99 7AR
Tel: 0117 936 5485
Guided tours of Concorde 216.
All year Wed-Sun, visits must be pre-booked

Exhibition & Visitor Centres

Royal West of England Academy
Queens Road Clifton Bristol BS8 1PX
Tel: 0117 973 5129 Fax: 0117 923 7874
www.rwa.org.uk
The magnificent Grade II listed building of the
Royal West of England Academy of Art (RWA) is
open all year round. Built in 1844 it was Bristol's
first art gallery and boasts stunning architecture
of this period. The exhibition programme
includes a variety of shows, which appeal to all
tastes from digital and new media to painting,
drawing, printmaking and sculpture. The
increasingly popular Autumn Exhibition is the
largest open art show in the region. It includes
all types of work, such as portraits, still life,
abstracts and landscapes most of which are for
sale. The RWA has its own collection of fine art,
which it displays in free exhibitions throughout
the year. The New Gallery has free entry and
hosts 12 exhibitions a year with works for sale,
often by artists from the South West region. For
an up to date preview of what's on visit the
RWA website. There is disabled access to the
1st and ground floors but not the basement.
*All year daily Mon-Sat 10.00-17.30, Sun 14.00-
17.00. Closed Easter Sun & 25 Dec-3 Jan*
A£4.00 Concessions£2.50 C£Free

Folk & Local History Museums

Bristol City Museum and Art Gallery
Queens Road Clifton Bristol BS8 1RL
Tel: 0117 922 3571
The museum has regional and international col-
lections representing ancient history, natural sci-
ences, and fine and applied arts.

Heritage & Industrial

Bristol Industrial Museum
Princes Wharf Wapping Road Bristol BS1 4RN
Tel: 0117 925 1470
Motor and horse-drawn vehicles from the Bristol
area are shown, with locally built aircraft and
aero-engines.

Historical

Georgian House
7 Great George Street Bristol BS1 5RR
Tel: 0117 921 1362
The Georgian House is presented as it might
have looked in the eighteenth century and provides an insight into life above and below stairs.

Closed Thursdays & Fridays

Red Lodge
Park Row Bristol BS1 5LJ
Tel: 0117 921160 Fax: 0117 922 2047
The Red Lodge is often described as Bristol's
'hidden treasure' because of its magnificent
Tudor rooms. It was built in 1580 as a lodge for
a Great House, which once stood on the site of
the present Colston Hall. It was subsequently
added to in Georgian times. It has had several
uses in its past, including a reform school for
girls.

Closed Thursdays & Fridays

Maritime

Brunel's SS Great Britain
Great Western Dockyard Gas Ferry Road Bristol
BS1 6TY
Tel: 0117 926 0680 Fax: 0117 925 5788
www.ssgreatbritain.org

[Rail: Temple Meads]

Brunel's SS Great Britain is the world's first
great ocean liner. Launched in 1843 to provide
luxury travel to New York, the iron-hulled
steamship revolutionised travel and set new
standards in engineering, reliability and speed.
Today Brunel's SS Great Britain is a thrilling,
daring, surprising visitor attraction and museum
re-telling the true stories of those who travelled
onboard. Winner of 18 top national and international awards including 'England's Large Visitor
Attraction 2007' and UK Museum of the Year
2006. School workshops allow children to handle and investigate real and replica artefacts, to
help bring the history of the ship to life. Special
events including murder mysteries, historic re-
enactments and Victorian banquets run
throughout the year. See website for details.

*Open daily Apr-Oct 10.00-17.30 (last entry
16.30). 26 Jul-2 Sept 10.00-18.00 (last entry
17.00). Nov-Mar 10.00-16.30 last entry 15.30).
Closed 24 & 25 Dec*

A£10.95 C(4 & under)Free C£5.65
Concessions£8.25, Family Ticket (A2+C3)
£29.95. Tickets allow free unlimited return visits
for 12 months. Membership: A£24.00
Concessions£20.00 Joint Adult£45.00 Joint
Concessionary£37.00, Family£49.00

Multicultural Museums

British Empire and Commonwealth Museum
Station Approach Temple Meads Bristol
BS1 6QH
Tel: 0117 925 4980
Using authentic objects, rare film, photographs,
sound recordings and costumes, visitors jour-
ney through British and world history.

Nature & Conservation Parks

Cabot Tower and Brandon Hill Nature Reserve
Brandon Hill off Great George Street Bristol
BS1 5RR
Tel: 0117 922 3719
Enjoy great views over the city and harbour
from Brandon Hill Park, the oldest park in
Bristol. There's a children's play area, beautiful
paths and a nature conservation area. The
Cabot Tower monument provides panoramic
views of the city.

Places of Worship

Bristol Cathedral
College Green Bristol BS1 5TJ
Tel: 0117 926 4879
Founded as an abbey in 1140, it became a
cathedral in 1542 and developed architecturally
throughout the ages.

John Wesley's Chapel (The New Room)
36 The Horsefair Broadmead Bristol BS1 3JE
Tel: 0117 926 4740
[Central Bristol. Rail: Temple Meads]
This is the oldest Methodist chapel in the world.
Both chapel and living rooms above are pre-
served in their original form.

Science - Earth & Planetary

Explore-At-Bristol
Anchor Road Harbourside Bristol BS1 5DB
Tel: 0845 345 1235 Fax: 0117 915 7200
www.at-bristol.org.uk

[M5 J18 follow A4 (Portway) to The Centre. M4 J19, M32 to city centre where signposted. Entrance located on Canons Way, off Anchor Rd. Rail: GWR, Wales & West or Virgin trains to Bristol Temple Meads - 20min walk, 10min bus (8, 508, 9, 509), or 5min taxi. Bus: all buses stop at The Centre which is 5min walk away. Plenty of on-site parking available (06.30-00.30)]

Explore-At-Bristol...an amazing world of hands-on discovery. With action-packed exhibits, live shows and the iconic Planetarium, Explore really is one of the UK's most exciting interactive science centres. Find out about your amazing brain and body, have a game of virtual volleyball or climb inside the giant hamster wheel! With over 170 interactive experiences there is something to intrigue every member of the family. And that's not forgetting the presenter-led live science shows, 'meet the expert' events, special toddler sessions and a changing programme of exhibitions - from DNA to sport, fossils and animation! The chrome-plated, futuristic sphere in Millennium Square is the Planetarium, where you can sit back and take a trip to the stars beneath an immersive domed screen in our daily seasonal star shows. There's always something new to discover in Explore - so see our website to find out what's on now!

Daily 10.00 - 17.00

Explore: A£9.90 C(under3)£Free C(3-15)&Concessions£7.70, Family Ticket (A2+C2) or (A1+C3) £30.00. All prices include an optional Gift Aid donation

Zoos

Bristol Zoo Gardens
Clifton Bristol BS8 3HA
Tel: 0117 974 7399 Fax: 0117 973 6814
www.bristolzoo.org.uk

[Follow brown tourist signs from J17 M5 or J18 or city centre. Rail: from Bristol Temple Meads take No. 8 or 9 bus to Zoo gates. Limited on site-parking available]

Go wild at Bristol Zoo with over 400 exotic and endangered species to experience plus daily shows, trails and activities. Visit the primates in the new Monkey Jungle and take a stroll through the barrier-free lemur garden. What ever the weather there is something for everyone to enjoy, including the award-winning Seal and Penguin Coast, which allows South American Fur Seals and African Penguins to be watched both above and below the water, gorilla island, an Asiatic lion enclosure, Pygmy hippos, Bug World, Twilight World, the Reptile House and the children's play area.

All year daily: Summer 09.00-17.30, Winter 09.00-17.00. Closed 25 Dec

Please see website for details

Discount Offer: One Child Free.

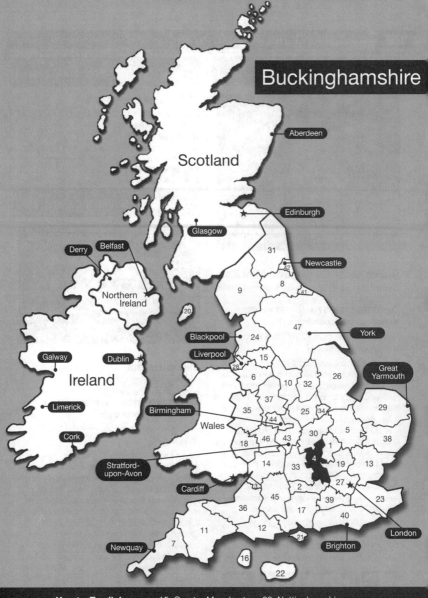

Buckinghamshire

Aberdeen

Scotland

Edinburgh

Glasgow

Derry | Belfast

Northern
Ireland

Galway | Dublin

Ireland

Limerick

Cork

31

Newcastle

42

9

8

41

20

Blackpool

24

47

York

Liverpool

15

28

Great
Yarmouth

6

10

32

26

Birmingham

37

35

44

25

34

29

Wales

18

46

43

30

5

38

Stratford-
upon-Avon

14

33

4

1

19

13

Cardiff

13

2

27

23

45

39

London

36

17

40

Newquay

12

Brighton

7

11

21

16

22

<u>Key to English Counties:</u>

1 Bedfordshire	15 Greater Manchester	32 Nottinghamshire
2 Berkshire	16 Guernsey	33 Oxfordshire
3 Bristol	17 Hampshire	34 Rutland
4 Buckinghamshire	18 Herefordshire	35 Shropshire
5 Cambridgeshire	19 Hertfordshire	36 Somerset
6 Cheshire	20 Isle Of Man	37 Staffordshire
7 Cornwall	21 Isle Of Wight	38 Suffolk
8 County Durham	22 Jersey	39 Surrey
9 Cumbria	23 Kent	40 Sussex
10 Derbyshire	24 Lancashire	41 Tees Valley
11 Devon	25 Leicestershire	42 Tyne & Wear
12 Dorset	26 Lincolnshire	43 Warwickshire
13 Essex	27 London	44 West Midlands
14 Gloucestershire	28 Merseyside	45 Wiltshire
	29 Norfolk	46 Worcestershire
	30 Northamptonshire	47 Yorkshire
	31 Northumberland	

Animal Attractions

Bucks Goat Centre and Mini Zoo

Layby Farm Stoke Mandeville Buckinghamshire
HP22 5XJ
Tel: 01296 612983 Fax: 01296 613663
www.bucksgoatcentre.co.uk

*[3mi outside Aylesbury, on A4010. Plenty of free
on-site parking available]*

A children's miniature zoo that features a wide
range of animals from all over the world, including llamas, wallabies, birds, reptiles, pigs, donkeys and every breed of domestic goat native to
the UK. Visitors are invited to hand-feed our animals. Animal Handling session in the afternoons
- 14.30 to 15.30 (days can vary) i.e Snakes,
Lizards etc. Other facilities include a toyshop, a
picnic lawn, a children's play area (featuring a
giant trampoline) and the Naughty Nanny Café.
Tractor rides are available throughout the summer (weather permitting). Children's parties are
catered for, please call for more information. All
attractions have easy disabled access.

*All year daily: Summer 10.00-17.00, Winter
10.00-16.00*
A£5.25 C(2-16)£4.25 C(under2)£Free
OAPs£4.75. Group rates available on request

Odds Farm Park Rare Breeds Centre

Wooburn Common High Wycombe
Buckinghamshire HP10 0LX
Tel: 01628 520188
With plenty of furry friends to meet and feed.

Country Parks & Estates

Willen Lakeside Park

V10 Brickhill Street Milton Keynes
Buckinghamshire MK15 0DS
Tel: 01908 691620
With a huge variety of activities and leisure facili-
ties there really is something for everyone.

Exhibition & Visitor Centres

thecentre:mk

24 Silbury Arcade Milton Keynes
Buckinghamshire MK9 3ES
Tel: 0870 890 2530 Fax: 01908 604306
www.thecentremk.com

*[J13 / J14 (M1), or follow signs for 'Central
Shopping' from A5]*

thecentre:mk is a regional shopping centre situated in the heart of Milton Keynes. With over
230 stores, cafés and restaurants (all under one
roof), it is anchored by John Lewis, House of
Fraser, Marks & Spencer and Next. As the premier shopping destination in the region between
London and Birmingham, Cambridge and
Oxford, it hosts a varied programme of free
events throughout the year, including bridal
shows, fashion events, motor shows and the
award-winning Christmas display. All this is easily accessible because it's all on one level. the-
centre:mk has unrivalled customer service and
provides excellent facilities for families, the disabled and children in a safe, clean, all-weather
environment.

*All year daily: Mon-Wed 09.30-18.00, Thu-Fri
09.30-20.00, Sat 09.00-18.00, Sun 11.00-
17.00. Extended shopping hours at Christmas.
Closed Easter Sun & 25 Dec*

Folk & Local History Museums

Bucks County Museum and the Roald Dahl Children's Gallery
Church Street Aylesbury Buckinghamshire
HP20 2QP
Tel: 01296 331441
Awaken your senses at this award-winning
Museum with its innovative touchable displays.

Cowper and Newton Museum
Orchard Side Market Place Olney
Buckinghamshire MK46 4AJ
Tel: 01234 711516 Fax: 0870 1640 662
www.cowperandnewtonmuseum.org.uk
[N of Newport Pagnell (via A509)]
John Newton was a former slaver turned evan-
gelical preacher who also wrote world-famous
hymns, including 'Amazing Grace'. He was a
close friend of the poet who lived in the present
buildings of the Cowper and Newton Museum.
William Cowper, a leading poet of this time, was
a major influence on Jane Austen and
Wordsworth. The museum also has a nationally
renowned lace collection, dinosaur bones, a
costume gallery and trade rooms housing a collection of Olney's social history from the early
eighteenth century. Another bonus is the extensive gardens which are home to eighteenth-
century (or earlier) plants. The museum is of
early Georgian origins.

*1 Mar-23 Dec Tue-Sat 10.30-16.30. Also open
Bank Hol Mons & Shrove Tue. Closed Good Fri*
Museum & Gardens: A£3.00 C(under12)£Free
Concessions£2.00. Group rates (for 12+) avail-
able on request. Gardens Only: £1.00

**Discount Offer: Two for the Price of
One (full-paying adult).**

Gardens & Horticulture

Stowe Landscape Gardens
Buckingham Buckinghamshire MK18 5DQ
Tel: 01280 822850/01280 818825
Fax: 01280 822437
www.nationaltrust.org.uk/stowegardens

*[3mi NW of Buckingham via Stowe Ave, off A422
Buckingham - Banbury rd. Plenty of on-site parking available]*

Be inspired by the extraordinary, living, breath-
ing work of art that is Stowe Landscape
Gardens. With its ornamental lakes, glorious
open spaces, wooded valleys and adorned with
over 40 monuments and temples, this magnificent landscape is one of the supreme creations
of the Georgian era. Given to the National Trust
in 1989, the gardens, Stowe House (opened to
the public by Stowe House Preservation Trust)
and the surrounding 750 acres of parkland have
been undergoing an ambitious programme of
restoration to recapture their former unparalleled
magnificence. Described as a 'work to wonder
at' Stowe Landscape Gardens explores ideas
about love, liberty, virtue and politics, inspiring
writers, artists and visitors for over three centuries. Today, the splendour and magic of
Stowe can be enjoyed by all. Whether you want
to enjoy the peace and tranquillity of beautiful
surroundings, an unspoilt setting for a family
picnic or an invigorating walk in the parkland,
Stowe is the perfect place for a day out. A full
programme of fun and educational events for
children and adults is available.

*1 Mar-31 Oct Wed-Sun 10.30-17.30, 4 Nov-28
Feb Sat-Sun 10.30-16.00. Closed 24 May*
Gardens: A£6.90 C£3.50, Family Ticket £17.10.
Group rate (15+): 15% discount

Historical

Bletchley Park Museum
Wilton Avenue Bletchley Milton Keynes
Buckinghamshire MK3 6EB
Tel: 01908 640404
Bletchley Park was home to the WW2 code-
breakers that cracked the Nazi Enigma code.

Claydon House
Middle Claydon Buckingham Buckinghamshire
MK18 2EY
Tel: 01296 730349

[13mi NW of Aylesbury. Rail: Aylesbury]

Lavishly decorated in intricately carved white
woodwork covered with motifs based on oriental birds, pagodas and summer houses.

Chiltern Open Air Museum
Newland Park Gorelands Lane Chalfont St.
Giles Buckinghamshire HP8 4AB
Tel: 01494 871117 Fax: 01494 872774
www.coam.org.uk

*[From J17 M25, follow signs to Maple Cross &
then brown tourist signs. Also signposted from
A413 at Chalfont St Giles & Chalfont St. Peter.
Plenty of on-site parking available]*

Chiltern Open Air Museum is an independent
charity that's open to the public every day from
21st March to 31st October (2008 season).
Now the biggest tourist attraction in Southern
Buckinghamshire, the museum was established
32 years ago in Chalfont St Giles with the aim of
preserving some of the historic buildings that
are unique examples of the heritage of the
Chilterns. Visitors can explore more than 30 historic buildings (that span 2000 years of history)
all rescued from demolition and re-erected on
the museum's beautiful 45-acre woodland and
parkland site. Lots to see and do for all the family, please visit www.coam.org.uk for more
details.

21 Mar-31 Oct daily 10.00-17.00

A£7.50 Concessions£6.50 C(5-16)£5.00
C(under5)£Free, Family Ticket (A2+C2) £22.00

Nether Winchenden House
Aylesbury, Buckinghamshire HP18 0DY
Tel: 01844 290101
Nether Winchendon House is a unique
Strawberry Hill Gothick medieval Manor House
situated in a beautiful valley at the foot of the
Chilterns. It has passed by family descent for
over 400 years and remains a family home.

*3-31 May & 14 Jun. Groups at any time by prior
written agreement, minimum charge £100.00*

Stowe House
Buckingham Buckinghamshire MK18 5EH
Tel: 01280 818166 / 818229
Fax: 01280 818186
www.shpt.org

*[4mi N of Buckingham town. Plenty of on-site
parking available]*

As the most important temple set in the
Landscape Gardens (now owned by the
National Trust), Stowe House is recognised as
one of the most influential neo-classical palaces
in Europe. The House and its contents were

sold off separately in 1922, when the last member of the Temple-Grenville family could no longer maintain it. It has been owned by Stowe School (a major public school) since 1923, and in 1997, it was passed into the care of Stowe House Preservation Trust, which was established to restore and preserve the House, and to open it up to the public. Phase 2 of a six-phase restoration plan was completed in 2005, restoring the magnificent Marble Saloon and South Front Portico. An Interpretation Centre chronologically explains the rise of the family and the evolution of the House. Stowe House is licensed for civil weddings and is also available for private and corporate functions.

Open during term-time for 14.00 tours only, open from 12.00-17.00 (last admission 16.00) in holiday times. For dates and times please visit our website www.shpt.org or call our 24hr info line on 01280 818166. Group visits are available by arrangement throughout the year- please call 01280 818229 during office hours

Admission & Tour A£4.00 C£2.50 C(under 5)£Free. NT member A£3.40 C£2.00. Groups (15+) £3.40 pp

Waddesdon Manor

Aylesbury Buckinghamshire HP18 0JH
Tel: 01296 653211 / 653226
Fax: 01296 653212
www.waddesdon.org.uk

[At W end of Waddesdon village, 6mi NW of Aylesbury on Bicester Rd A41. Bus: Red Rover 1, 15, 16 from Aylesbury. Plenty of on-site parking available]

Waddesdon Manor was built (1874-89) for Baron Ferdinand de Rothschild to display his vast collection of eighteenth-century art treasures, which include French Royal furniture,

Savonnerie carpets and Sèvres porcelain as well as important portraits by Gainsborough and Reynolds. It has one of the finest Victorian gardens in Britain, a fully stocked Rococo-style aviary, wine cellars, shops and licensed restaurants. Many events are organised throughout the year. For more information please call the Booking Office.

Gardens, Aviary, Children's Woodland Playground, Restaurant & Shops: 5 Jan-16 Mar Sat-Sun, 19 Mar-21 Dec Wed-Sun, 27-31 Dec 10.00-17.00 open Bank Hols. House & Wine Cellars: 19 Mar-26 Oct & 12 Nov-23 Dec Wed-Fri 12.00-16.00 Sat-Sun 11.00-16.00 Open Bank Hols. Bachelors' Wing 19 Mar-26 Oct Wed-Fri 12.00-16.00

Gardens, Aviary, Children's Woodland Playground, Shops & Restaurants:5 Jan-16 Mar A£5.50 C(5-16)£2.75 Family Ticket£13.75 19 Mar-31 Dec Wed-Fri A£5.50 C£2.75 Family Ticket£13.75 Sat-Sun & Bank Hols A£7.00 C£3.50 Family Ticket£17.50. House & Gardens, Wine Cellars, Aviary, Children's Woodland Playground, Shops & Restaurants: 19 Mar-26 Oct Wed-Fri A£13.20 C£9.35 Sat-Sun & Bank Hols A£15.00 C£11.00, 12 Nov-23 Dec Wed-Fri A10.00 C£5.00 Sat-Sun A£12.00 C£6.00. Bachelors' Wing 19 Mar-26 Oct: A£3.30 C£3.30. NT Members £Free. Timed tickets to House can be bought up to 24hrs in advance, £3.00 per transaction, please call 01296 653226 Mon-Fri 10.00-16.00. Children welcome under parental supervision in House, babies must be carried in front sling

Literature & Libraries

Milton's Cottage

Deanway Chalfont St. Giles Buckinghamshire HP8 4JH
Tel: 01494 872313
The four ground-floor museum-rooms contain important editions of Milton's poetry, together with many prose writings that were published during his lifetime and shortly after. Hear of the extraordinary career of this blind genius vividly described, in his refuge from the plague where he wrote some of the finest poetry and feel the ambience of the setting.

Model Towns & Villages

Bekonscot Model Village and Railway

Warwick Road Beaconsfield Buckinghamshire HP9 2PL
Tel: 01494 672919 Fax: 01494 675284
www.bekonscot.com

[2.7mi from J2 M40, signposted, 4mi from J16 M25. Free car park nearby]

Good things do come in small packages! BE A GIANT in this miniature wonderland where nobody grows up. Established in 1929 Bekonscot Model Village captures a delightful and timeless image of a lost age, depicting rural England in the 1930s. An unforgettable day out for everyone and all profits are donated to charity! There are six charming little villages in a 1.5 acre miniature landscape of farms, fields, castles, churches, woods and lakes. Walking around you'll tower over the tiny population enjoying the fun of the fair, the zoo or lazily watching a cricket match. Interesting buildings including castles, a Tudor house, thatched cottages, and a replica of Enid Blyton's 'Green Hedges'. There are also moving models, such as a coal mine, nodding donkey and the fun fair. Bekonscot boasts the ultimate train set, and its historic Gauge 1 line has been famous since 1929 for being one of the largest, most exciting and complex in Great Britain. The busy railway race between the villages, over bridges and under your feet. There is a full-size signal box in control of ten scale miles of track, seven stations and often more than eight trains. There is also a sit-on railway running at weekends and school holidays and remote control boats. Bekonscot has a refreshment Kiosk, souvenir shop, playground, picnic areas and free parking. Our log cabin is a fun place to hold a children's birthday party.

16 Feb-2 Nov daily 10.00-17.00

A£7.00 C£4.50 Concessions£5.00. Special rates for school groups £3.60

Discount Offer: One Child Free Per Family (with one full-paying adult).

Sport & Recreation

XScape: Milton Keynes

602 Marlborough Gate Milton Keynes Buckinghamshire MK9 3XS
Tel: 0871 200 3220 Fax: 01908 680834
www.xscape.co.uk
Features real snow slopes, an indoor skydiving tunnel, rock climbing walls, bowling, a multiplex cinema, gym and fitness centre, plus numerous bars and restaurants and urban retail outlets. For events at Xscape visit our website www.xscape.co.uk.

Stately Homes

Claydon House

Middle Claydon Buckingham Buckinghamshire MK18 2EY
Tel: 01494 730349 755561

[13mi NW of Aylesbury. Rail: Aylesbury]

Splendid eighteenth-century country house with with fine Chinoiserie and rococo decorations. Intricate wood carvings and spectacular parquetry staircase. Mementoes of Florence

Nightingale, who was once a regular visitor. All Saints' Church in the grounds is also open to the public. New for 2008: Exhibition of papers from the Verney archives, focusing on 'Household Management' across four centuries.

15 Mar-2 Nov: Mon-Wed & Sat-Sun (13.00-17.00)

Hughenden Manor Estate
Hughenden Manor High Wycombe Buckinghamshire HP14 4LA
Tel: 01494 755573 Fax: 01494 474284
www.nationaltrust.org.uk

[1.5mi N of High Wycombe. Rail: High Wycombe. Plenty of on-site parking available]

A hidden gem nestled amongst the Chiltern Hills, Hughenden Manor was the home of Benjamin Disraeli, the most charismatic of Queen Victoria's prime ministers. Discover more about the private world of a famous Victorian, enjoy lunch in the Stables Restaurant, spend time browsing in the National Trust shop and take a refreshing walk in the beautiful surrounding woodlands.

Mar-Oct Wed-Sun 11.00-17.00 (plus some days in December - please call for details)
A£7.00 C£3.50

Go Ape! High Wire Forest Adventure (Wendover Woods, Buckinghamshire)
Wendover Woods St Leonards Road Aston Clinton Aylesbury Buckinghamshire HP22 5NF
Tel: 0845 643 9245
www.goape.co.uk

[From the A41: take B4009 (Wendover) towards Tring. Wendover Woods are signposted. Entrance is 250yds along St Leonards Rd (on the R). Plenty of on-site parking available]

Take to the trees and experience an exhilarating course of rope bridges, Tarzan swings and zip-slides up to 40 feet off the ground! Share approximately three exciting hours of fun and adventure, which you'll be talking about for days. Book online and watch people Go Ape! at www.goape.co.uk. Minimum height 1.4m. Maximum weight 130 kg (20.5 stone). Under-18s must be accompanied by a participating adult. One adult can supervise either two children (where one or both of them is under 16 years old) or up to five 16-17 year olds. Pre-booking is essential to avoid disappointment. Book online or by telephone (there is a £1.00 booking fee on all telephone bookings).

14 Mar-31 Oct daily, (Closed Mon during term-time). Nov Sat-Sun. Dec Sat-Sun TBC visit www.goape.co.uk. Closed Jan

Gorillas (18 yrs+) £25.00, Baboons (10-17yrs) £20.00.
(Two for the Price of One until 2nd May 2008)
Discount Offer: £5.00 off per person.

Gulliver's Eco Park

Livingstone Drive Newlands Milton Keynes
Buckinghamshire MK15 0DT
Tel: 01908 609001
Whether it's exploring the world of the dinosaurs
or discovering where our food comes from, Eco
Park offers a family experience of fun and
excitement where learning happens naturally
through hands-on activities.

Gulliver's: Milton Keynes

Livingstone Drive Newlands Milton Keynes
Buckinghamshire MK15 ODT
Tel: 01908 609001
From the hustle and bustle of Main Street to the
minature world of Lilliput Land to the excitement
of Adventure Land and Discovery Bay. Enjoy the
delights of Lilliput Castle and treats of Toyland.

Transport Museums

Buckinghamshire Railway Centre

Quainton Road Station Quainton Aylesbury
Buckinghamshire HP22 4BY
Tel: 01296 655450 Fax: 01296 655720
www.bucksrailcentre.org

*[6mi N of Aylesbury, 15mi from Milton Keynes,
10mi from Bicester, 20mi from Oxford & Watford
& 25mi from Luton. Off A41 Aylesbury / Bicester
Rd signposted from A41 at Waddesdon & A413
at Whitchurch. Plenty of free on-site parking avail-
able]*

Buckinghamshire Railway Centre is a working
steam museum where you can step back in
time to the golden age of railways. The centre
has one of the largest private railway collections
in the country with many steam locomotives
from express passenger types to the humble
shunting engine. The museum's interesting
items of rolling stock on display include a coach
from the Royal Train of 1901 and another used
by Winston Churchill and General Eisenhower
for wartime planning meetings. On Steaming
Open Days visitors can take a steam hauled
train ride in vintage carriages and on our extensive miniature railway system whilst on certain
days you can also ride in open wagons. The
centre's new visitor centre is housed in the 1851
former Oxford Rewley Road Station moved from
the centre of Oxford. In its new location it provides the perfect setting for displays of historic
locomotives, carriages and smaller items. Also
included are refreshment rooms and a gift shop.
The centre is fully disabled accessible.

*Mar-Oct Wed-Sun & Bank Hol Mons 10.30-
17.30 (16.30 weekdays) for viewing. Train rides
available on Sun & Bank Hol Mons plus Wed in
School Hols*

Special Events: A£8.00 C(5-15)£5.00
OAPs£6.50, FamilyTicket (A2+C4) £23.00.
Steaming Days: A£7.00 C(5-15)£4.50
OAPs£6.00 Family Ticket (A2+C4) £21.00.
Static Viewing: A£5.00 C(5-15)£2.50
OAPs£4.00 Family Ticket (A2+C4)£14.00. "Day
Out With Thomas": Please apply for details

**Discount Offer: Two for the Price of
One.**

Chiltern Museum of Motoring

Chiltern House Ashendon Aylesbury
Buckinghamshire HP18 0HB
Tel: 01296 651283
Located in the main street of Chiltern, tucked in
behind the only garage or petrol station in the
town, is a unique and extensive museum of
petrol bowsers or pumps, and of vintage motor
bikes, cars and petrol driven engines.

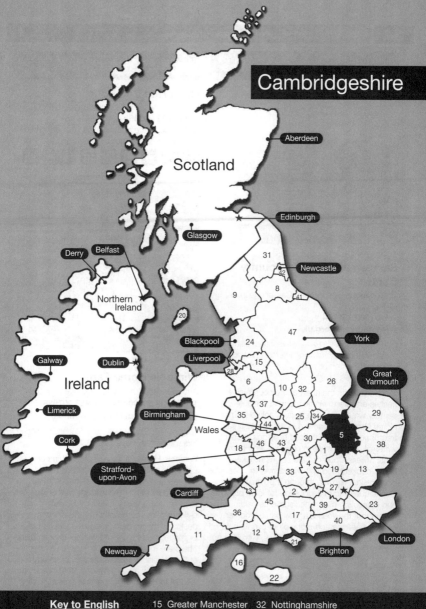

Cambridgeshire

Aberdeen

Scotland

Edinburgh

Glasgow

Derry   Belfast

Newcastle

Northern
Ireland

Blackpool

Liverpool

York

Great
Yarmouth

Galway   Dublin

Ireland

Limerick

Birmingham

Wales

Cork

Stratford-
upon-Avon

Cardiff

Newquay

Brighton

London

Key to English Counties:

1	Bedfordshire	15	Greater Manchester	32	Nottinghamshire
2	Berkshire	16	Guernsey	33	Oxfordshire
3	Bristol	17	Hampshire	34	Rutland
4	Buckinghamshire	18	Herefordshire	35	Shropshire
5	Cambridgeshire	19	Hertfordshire	36	Somerset
6	Cheshire	20	Isle Of Man	37	Staffordshire
7	Cornwall	21	Isle Of Wight	38	Suffolk
8	County Durham	22	Jersey	39	Surrey
9	Cumbria	23	Kent	40	Sussex
10	Derbyshire	24	Lancashire	41	Tees Valley
11	Devon	25	Leicestershire	42	Tyne & Wear
12	Dorset	26	Lincolnshire	43	Warwickshire
13	Essex	27	London	44	West Midlands
14	Gloucestershire	28	Merseyside	45	Wiltshire
		29	Norfolk	46	Worcestershire
		30	Northamptonshire	47	Yorkshire
		31	Northumberland		

Agriculture / Working Farms

Sacrewell Farm and Country Centre

Thornhaugh Peterborough Cambridgeshire
PE8 6HJ
Tel: 01780 782254
www.sacrewell.org.uk

*[Situated just E of A1/A47 intersection, clearly
signposted on approaching intersection from
either direction on both A1 & A47. Plenty of on-
site parking available]*

Hidden deep in the heart of the countryside
nestles an award winning farm and eighteenth-
century watermill. Friendly farm animals, Shire
Horse Centre, indoor and outdoor play areas,
tractor rides, range of listed buildings, working
watermill, gardens, farm bygones, and farm
trails. Miller's Country Café serves delicious
home-cooked food with views over the beautiful
countryside. Browse through the Three Little
Ducks quality farm & gift shop for local produce
and interesting gifts. Special events held
throughout the year. Birthday parties, conferences, meetings and many other events catered
for. Camping and caravan facilities, with electric
hook-ups, toilets and showers. Dogs allowed.

*All year daily, Mar-Sept 09.30-17.00, Oct-Dec
10.00-16.00. Closed 24 Dec-2 Jan*

A£6.00 C£4.50 OAPs£5.00, Family Ticket
£18.50. Prices may vary for special events.
Group rates (for 10+) available on request, pre-
booking is essential

Discount Offer: One Child Free.

Animal Attractions

Hamerton Zoo Park

Hamerton Nr Sawtry Cambridgeshire PE17 5RE
Tel: 01832 293362
Dedicated to the conservation of endangered
species, including gibbons and wildcats.

Wimpole Home Farm

Arrington Royston Cambridgeshire SG8 0BW
Tel: 01223 206000 Fax: 01223 207838
www.nationaltrust.org.uk/wimpole

*[A603, A1198, J12 M11. 8mi SW of Cambridge
(A603) 6mi N of Rayston (A1198)]*

Wimpole Home Farm, part of the Wimpole
Estate, is still a working farm and is East
Anglia's largest rare breeds centre. With its history as a model farm and many rare breeds of
farm animal, it has something for adults and
children alike.The historic Great Barn was
designed by architect Sir John Soane in the late
eighteenth-century, along with a Victorian dairy.
There are modern farm buildings too - take one
of the special tours with the stockman and
you'll see how a real farm operates. Home Farm
is ideal for families, with regular animal feeding,
egg collecting and daily demonstrations. The
Adventure Playground and Tiny Tots outside
play area will keep the children entertained and
the Farm Kitchen is the ideal spot to take time
out for light refreshments and lunch. Don't miss
the lambing in April! New in 2008 - stockman
tours on Saturdays in June and September.

*1 Jan-12 Mar Sat & Sun 11.00-16.00. 15 Mar-
16 Jul Sat-Wed 10.30-17.00. 19 Jul-31 Aug Sat
to Thur 10.30-17.00. 1 Sept-29 Oct Sat-Wed
10.30-17.00. 1 Nov-21 Dec Sat & Sun 11.00-
16.00. 27 Dec-1 Jan 09 Sat-Thur 11.00-16.00.*

3-31 Jan 09, Sat & Sun 11.00-16.00. Open BH Mons 10.30-17.00 & Good Fri. Closed every Fri except Good Fri. Open Sat-Thur during local school hols

Gift Aid admission*: Farm only: A£6.95 C£4.70 Family Ticket £21.50. Farm (NT members): A£3.50C £2.35 Family Ticket £11.00. Hall & Farm A£12.60 C£6.80 Family Ticket £33.00. *Including a voluntary donation of at least 10%; visitors can, however, choose to pay the standard admission prices which are displayed at the property and at www.nationaltrust.org.uk

Discount Offer: One Child Free.

Wood Green Animal Shelters (HQ)

King's Bush Farm London Road
Godmanchester Cambridgeshire PE29 2NH
Tel: 08701 904090
Europe's most progressive shelter for unwanted animals.

Archaeology

Flag Fen Archaeology Park

The Droveway Northey Road Peterborough
Cambridgeshire PE6 7QJ
**Tel: 0844 4140646 Fax: 0844 4140647
www.flagfen.org**

[E of Peterborough. A1 N/S Take Junction for A1139 signed Fengate/ Eastern Industries. Follow brown signs. From Whittlesey take B1040 & turn L at Dog in the Doublet pub]

What will you discover? Flag Fen is one of the finest Bronze Age archaeological sites in Europe, with the oldest wheel in England and an ancient ritual causeway stretching across the Fens. With over 29 acres of parkland and historic reconstructions, you can discover how people lived 4000 years ago. Take a walk on the wild side around the mere and the fields, marvel at the ancient tools, jewellery and woodwork. Special events run monthly throughout the summer (highlights include pond-dipping, artefact-handling, enactments and experimental archaeology). Guided tours available subject to volunteer availability. Hands-on activities for all the family are run on selected days during the school holidays.

Mar-Oct: Tue-Sun & Bank Hols 10.00-16.00. Closed Nov-Feb

A£5.00 C£3.75 OAPs£4.50, Family Ticket (A2+C3) £13.75. Group rates: A&C£4.25 No Guide, A&C£5.00 with guide

Arts, Crafts & Textiles

Fitzwilliam Museum

Trumpington Street Cambridge Cambridgeshire CB2 1RB
Tel: 01223 332900
Houses a fine collection of antiquities, manuscripts, sculpture, furniture and pottery.

Kettle's Yard

Castle Street Cambridge Cambridgeshire CB3 0AQ
Tel: 01223 352124
Kettle's Yard Gallery is a major centre for contemporary art.

Stained Glass Museum

The South Triforum Ely Cathedral Ely Cambridgeshire CB7 4DL
Tel: 01353 660347
Features 100+ stained glass panels rescued from redundant churches.

Birds, Butterflies & Bees

Raptor Foundation
The Heath St Ives Road Woodhurst
Cambridgeshire PE28 3BT
Tel: 01487 741140 Fax: 01487 841140
www.raptorfoundation.org.uk

[From A14 exit at St. Ives follow ring road, follow signs to Industrial Estate, R turn onto B1040 to Somersham follow brown tourist sign. From A1 exit at Huntingdon, follow signs to St. Ives, then B1040 to Somersham, follow brown tourist signs. Plenty of on-site parking available]

Come visit a unique and exciting place for children and adults alike and meet and learn about owls, hawks, falcons, buzzards, eagles and vultures. Located in 30 acres, home to over 210 raptors and more than 44 species, many of whom are threatened or endangered. We hold special events including: Twilight Flying - guest receives a meal. Over half term we will have children's activity days, where they can make an owl design for a t-shirt or make an owl out of feathers. Refreshments are available from our "Silent Wings" restaurant/tearoom. Gifts are also available from "Mad About Owls" and "Raptor Krafts". We have a large children's play area and educational room. Ask about out "Lullabye of Birdland". Stay with us at the "Falcon's Nest", a 3-star Visit Britain B&B featured in BBC2s "B&B the Best". Fall asleep with soft hooting of owls. Wake up to the song of the Lark. Cast your "eagle eye" over beautiful, historic Cambridgeshire.

All year daily 10.00-17.00. Flying displays at 12.00, 14.00 & 16.00

A£4.50 C(5-14)£2.75 C(2-4)£1.25 OAPs£3.50, Family Ticket £12.50. Private groups welcome. Registered Charity No. 1042085. All proceeds contribute to the care and rehabilitation of injured birds of prey

Discount Offer: Two for the Price of One (full-paying adult).

Country Parks & Estates

Milton Country Park
Cambridge Road Milton Cambridgeshire CB4 6AZ
Tel: 01223 420060
A mixture of woodland, grass and water areas.

Wimpole Hall
Arrington Royston Cambridgeshire SG8 0BW
Tel: 01223 206000 Fax: 01223 207838
www.nationaltrust.org.uk/wimpole

[8mi SW of Cambridge A603. Rail: Shepreth]

Quite simply, Wimpole is one of the best days out you can have in the East of England. From an adventure woodland to a working walled garden and farm, one day won't be long enough! Wimpole gives you a real 'upstairs, downstairs' experience. Wander through the staterooms and admire the beautiful interiors, stunning collections of art and furniture; then find your way downstairs to peek into the daily life of the servants that kept this grand house going. Outside, there are 60 acres of garden to explore and over 350 acres of landscaped parkland and woodland walks, including a 2¼-mile long South Avenue, Gothic Folly and serpentine lakes. See a working walled kitchen garden, which includes 50 varieties of tomato - don't miss the festival in August! New for 2008 - a celebration of wildlife and food - look out for our discovery walks and seasonal food events.

Hall: 15 Mar-16 Jul Sat-Wed 13.00-17.00. 19 Jul-31 Aug Sat-Thur 13.00-17.00. 1 Sept-29 Oct Sat-Wed 13.00-17.00. 2-30 Nov Sun only 13.00-16.00.

Garden/Shop Restaurant: 2 Feb-12 Mar Sat-Wed 11.00-16.00. 15 Mar-16 Jul Sat-Wed 10.30-17.00. 19 Jul-31 Aug Sat-Thur 10.30-17.00. 1 Sept-29 Oct Sat -Wed 10.30-17.00. 1 Nov-23 Dec Sat-Wed 11.00-16.00. 27 Dec-1 Jan 09 Sat-Thur 11.00-16.00. 3-31 Jan 09 Sat-Wed 11.00-16.00. Bookshop: as Hall and Winter Sat & Sun. Park open all year, dawn to dusk. Open BH Mons 10.30-17.00 (Hall 11.00-17.00) & Good Fri. Closed every Fri except Good Fri. Hall, Farm & Garden open Sat-Thur during local school hols (Hall closed in Feb half-term)

Gift Aid admission*: Hall A£8.40 C£4.70 Family Ticket £24.00. Hall & Farm A£12.60 C£6.80 Family Ticket £33.00. Garden only A£3.50 C£1.85. *Including a voluntary donation of at least 10%; visitors can, however, choose to pay the standard admission prices which are displayed at the property and at www.national-trust.org.uk

Discount Offer: One Child Free

Folk & Local History Museums

Cromwell Museum
Grammar School Walk Huntingdon Cambridgeshire PE29 6LF
Tel: 01480 375830
A restored Norman building that was attended by Oliver Cromwell and Samuel Pepys.

Heritage & Industrial

Prickwillow Drainage Engine Museum
Main Street Prickwillow Ely Cambridgeshire CB7 4UN
Tel: 01353 688360
Engines and artifacts associated with land drainage of the Fens.

Historical

Anglesey Abbey, Gardens and Lode Mill
Quy Road Lode Cambridge Cambridgeshire CB25 9EJ
Tel: 01223 810080 Fax: 01223 810088
www.nationaltrust.org.uk/angleseyabbey

[6mi NE of Cambridge on the B1102]

Explore the golden age of English country house living, created by the first Lord Fairhaven and his brother between 1926 and 1966. Wander the rooms and corridors of this luxurious country house and imagine yourself as a guest in the 1920s.Outside, discover the year-round delights of the 114-acre garden. See how many mythical beasts, Greek gods and other statues you can spot - there are more than 100 pieces of classical sculpture in the formal and landscape gardens. Be sure to explore the wildflower meadows, the Hoe Fen Wildlife Discovery area and the attractive Winter Garden, with its stunning year-round displays of colour. There was a mill at Anglesey listed in the Domesday Book and the present watermill, Lode Mill, dates from the eighteenth century. Restored in 1982, it is in full working order. Come and feel the power of water in action! New in 2008 - recommended RHS garden.

House/Garden/Restaurant/Shop/Plant Sales: 19 Mar-2 Nov, Wed to Sun, 10.30-5.30 (House 13.00-17.00). Winter Garden: 1 Jan-16 Mar, 5 Nov-21 Dec, 31 Dec-31 Jan 09, Wed-Sun, 10.30-4.30. Lode Mill: 19 Mar-2 Nov, Wed-Sun, 13.00-17.00. Open BH Mon & Good Fri. The Gallery: 19 Nov 08-18 Jan 09 - a display of silver from the collection. 11.00am to 15.30 Wed to Sun. Snowdrop seasons: 15 Jan-24 Feb 08. 21 Jan-22 Feb 09, times and days as Winter Garden. Summer late night openings: Restaurant & Gardens only. 5 Jun-1 Aug, Thurs & Fri until 21.00

Gift Aid admission*: House, Garden & Mill: A£9.25 C£4.65. Garden & Mill: A£5.50 C£2.75. Winter Garden (1 Jan-16 Mar): A£4.40 C£2.20, (5 Nov-31 Dec): A£4.75 C£2.40. *Including a voluntary donation of at least 10%; visitors can, however, choose to pay the standard admission prices which are displayed at the property and at www.nationaltrust.org.uk.

Discount Offer: One Child Free.

Oliver Cromwell's House

29 St. Mary's Street Ely Cambridgeshire CB7 4HF
Tel: 01353 662062
Experience what domestic life would have been like in the seventeenth century.

Peckover House and Garden

North Brink Wisbech Cambridgeshire PE13 1JR
Tel: 01945 583463 Fax: 01945 583463
www.nationaltrust.org.uk/peckover

[On N bank of River Nene. Rail: March]

Explore the history of this elegant Georgian town house in the heart of Wisbech and the family that once lived there. Once home to the Peckover's, a family of Quaker bankers, collectors and philanthropists, the house is a cabinet of curiosities! Discover life 'below stairs' in the intriguing Old Kitchen, Servants' Hall and Butler's Pantry and find out what life was like to be a servant! Behind the elegant façade of this Georgian house lies an outstanding two-acre Victorian garden - an oasis of colour and scent. Explore what is surely one of the finest walled town gardens in the country. Stroll outside to

find the unusual summerhouses and Victorian glasshouses. Enjoy the herbaceous borders and see and smell over 60 species of rose in summer and 300-year-old orange trees. New for 2008 - 60th anniversary of National Trust ownership and virtual tour of the show rooms.

House/Shop/Bookshop: 15 Mar-2 Nov Sat-Wed 13.00-16.30 Garden/Tea room: 15 Mar-2 Nov Sat-Wed 12.00-17.00

House & garden: A£5.50 C£2.75 Family Ticket (A2+C2) £14.00. Garden only: A£3.50 C£1.75

Discount Offer: One Child Free.

Imperial War Museum, Duxford

Duxford Cambridgeshire CB2 4QR
Tel: 01223 835000
Duxford is Europe's premier aviation museum - as well as having one of the finest collections of tanks and military vehicles in the country.

Mills - Water & Wind

Houghton Mill

Houghton near Huntingdon Cambridgeshire PE28 2AZ
Tel: 01480 301494
www.nationaltrust.org.uk

[Signposted off A1123 Huntingdon to St Ives]

Full of hands-on exhibits for all the family, and with most of its machinery still intact, this five-storey weatherboarded mill is the last working watermill on the Great Ouse. Today wheat is still for sale, ground by a pair of millstones on

Sundays and Bank Holiday Mondays. Close by, some parts of the river are so clear you can see fish darting about and you may even be lucky enough to spot a heron or a kingfisher. Across from the mill island, the river meadows offer marvellous walks under the willows. Along with a special family trail, there is a second-hand bookshop and tea room. New in 2008 - virtual tour and interactive model of water use in the landscape

22 Mar-27 Apr Sat 11.00-17.00 Sun 13.00-17.00. 3 May-27 Sep Sat 11.00-17.00 Sun 13.00-17.00. 28 Apr-28 Sep Sun-Wed 13.00-17.00. 4 Oct-26 Oct Sat 11.00-17.00 Sun 13.00-17.00. Open BH Mons & Good Fri: Mill 13.00-17.00 Tea room 11.00-17.00. Caravan & campsite open Mar-Oct. Groups & school parties at other times by arrangement with Property Manager

Gift Aid admission*: A£3.70 C£1.70 Family Ticket £8.50. *Including a voluntary donation of at least 10%; visitors can, however, choose to pay the standard admission prices which are displayed at the property and at www.nationaltrust.org.uk.

Discount Offer: One Child Free.

Nature & Conservation Parks

Wicken Fen (NT) Nature Reserve
Lode Lane Wicken Ely Cambridgeshire CB7 5XP
Tel: 01353 720274
www.nationaltrust.org.uk/wickenfen

[Signed from A1123, 3mi W of Soham A142, 9mi S of Ely. Rail: Ely]

Explore one of England's most diverse wetland sites - one of the very few surviving remnants of the Great Fen of East Anglia and one of the oldest nature reserves in the country. Wicken Fen is a haven for birds, plants, insects, mammals and humans alike. Take in the wide droves, lush green paths and boardwalk nature trail and take a walk on the wild side! Visit Fen Cottage and discover what life was like as a fen labourer, or enjoy a relaxing journey through the Fen by boat (summer weekends). The new all-weather boardwalk allows you to enjoy the site all year round and with over 550 hectares to explore, nine bird hides, wild Konik ponies and over 7,000 species of wildlife, you are sure to have a wild adventure! New in 2008 - displays of reed, sedge and peat tell the story of the fen's social history before the onset of industrial-scale fenland drainage.

18 Feb-23 Mar Tue-Sun 10.00-17.00. Open daily 24 Mar-31 Oct 10.00-17.00. 1 Nov-31 Jan 09 Tue-Sun 10.00-16.30. Café closed Tuesdays between 1 Nov-31 Jan 09. Reserve: closed 25 Dec. Some paths are closed in very wet weather. Fen Cottage open 30 Mar-19 Oct Sun & BH Mons 14.00-17.00

Gift Aid admission*: A£5.25 C£2.65 Family Ticket £13.15. Pay and display car park £2.00 per car (NT members free - please display car sticker). *Including a voluntary donation of at least 10%; visitors can, however, choose to pay the standard admission prices which are displayed at the property and at www.nationaltrust.org.uk

Discount Offer: One Child Free.

Places of Worship

Ely Cathedral
Cambridgeshire CB7 4DL
Tel: 01353 667735
Dominating the skyline, Ely is one of England's largest (and most beautiful) cathedrals.

King's College Chapel
Cambridge Cambridgeshire CB2 1ST
Tel: 01223 331212
One of the finest examples of late English Gothic or Perpendicular-style.

Peterborough Cathedral

Minster Precincts Peterborough Cambridgeshire
PE1 1XS
Tel: 01733 355300 Fax: 01733 355316
www.peterborough-cathedral.org.uk
*[A1 on J with A605 / A47, follow City Centre
signs]*
Peterborough Cathedral "an undiscovered
gem". With one of the most dramatic West
Fronts in the country, it's three arches an extraordinary creation of medieval architecture, it
would be easy for the interior to be an anticli-
max, but it is not. The dramatic Romanesque
building is little altered since its completion 800
years ago and it has recently undergone extensive cleaning and restoration following the serious fire of November 2001. Highlights include
the unique painted nave ceiling, elaborate fan
vaulting in the 'new' building, Saxon carvings
from an earlier church, elaborately carved
Victorian Choir stalls and the burial place of two
queens. An excellent exhibition tells the
Cathedral's story. Freshly prepared meals and
snacks are available at Beckets restaurant
opposite the West Front and the Cathedral
shop is next door. Disabled access to most
areas. A range of tours can be booked in
advance: please contact the Cathedral Office for
details.

*All year Mon-Fri 09.00-18.30 Sat 09.00-17.00,
Sun 12.00-17.00. Some access restricted during
services*

Donations are politely requested

Railways

Nene Valley Railway

Wansford Station Stibbington Peterborough
Cambridgeshire PE8 6LR
Tel: 01780 784444 Fax: 01780 784440
www.nvr.org.uk

*[Turn off the A1 at the new Stibbington fly over,
which is 1mi S of the A1 / A47 and 4mi N of the
end of the A1(M). Look for the large brown "Nene
Valley Railway" signs on both the A1 and A47]*

Full steam ahead for a great day out at Britain's
only International Steam Railway with 7.5 miles
of track through the picturesque Nene Valley.
See website for information on events throughout the year.

Please visit our website for details
Please visit www.nvr.org.uk for details

Science - Earth & Planetary

Cambridge Museum of Science and Technology

The Old Pumping Station Cheddars Lane
Cambridge Cambridgeshire CB5 8LD
Tel: 01223 368650
A preserved Victorian Pumping Station and
working museum the Cambridge Museum of
Science and Technology.

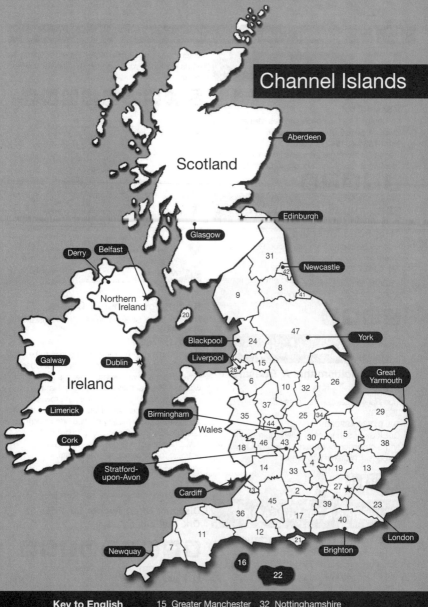

Channel Islands

Aberdeen
Scotland
Edinburgh
Glasgow
Derry
Belfast
Northern Ireland
31
Newcastle
42
9
8
41
20
Blackpool
24
47
York
Liverpool
Galway
Dublin
28
15
Ireland
6
10
32
26
Great Yarmouth
Limerick
37
29
Birmingham
35
44
25
34
Wales
46
43
30
5
38
Cork
18
4
Stratford-upon-Avon
14
33
19
13
Cardiff
13
2
27
23
45
39
London
36
17
40
11
12
Brighton
Newquay
7
21
16
22

Arts, Crafts & Textiles

Jersey Woollen Mills: Home of the Jersey

Le Château La Grande Route des Mielles
St Ouen Jersey Channel Islands JE3 2FN
Tel: 01534 481342
Traditional sweaters, all made from 100% pure oiled wool. Lovely gift shop with unusual gifts.

Communication Museums

Telephone Museum

Hermes House La Planque, Cobo Road Castel
Guernsey Channel Islands
Tel: 01481 257904
Telephones, switchboards and other equipment.

Apr-Oct Mon-Sat 14:00-17:00

Costume & Jewellery Museums

Jersey Goldsmiths: A Treasure Park

Lion Park St Lawrence Jersey Channel Islands
JE3 1GX
Tel: 01534 482098
Quick Silver school of jewellery, gold-panning and a collection of celebrity jewellery. Lake and gardens. Children's play areas.

Exhibition & Visitor Centres

Eric Young Orchid Foundation

La Rue du Moulin du Ponterrin Trinity Jersey
Channel Islands JE3 5HH
Tel: 01534 861963
One of the finest collections of orchids in the world is to be found at the Eric Young Orchid Foundation, housed in a purpose-built nursery and exhibition complex.
All year Wed-Sat

Jersey's Living Legend Village

La Rue du Petit Aleval St. Peter Jersey
Channel Islands JE3 7ET
Tel: 01534 485496

Enter the unforgettable Jersey Experience and let us introduce you to some famous island residents.

Kempt Tower Visitor Centre

Five Mile Road St Ouen Jersey Channel Islands
JE3 2FN
Tel: 01534 483651
One of the most imposing fortifications to be seen along Jersey's Five Mile Road in St Ouen's Bay is Kempt Tower. Kempt Tower is buzzing with hands on activities for all ages. Natural History, agriculture, wildlife films, the tower is packed with enviromental information. There is a surfing exhibition, military section and breathtaking views from the roof of a genuine Martello Tower. Please check our website www.eco-active.je for details on special events.

1 May-30 Sept daily 14.00-17.00

A£2.00 Concessions£1.00. All accompanied school children free during school holidays

Discount Offer: Two for the Price of One (full-paying adult).

New Strawberry Farm (The)

Les Issues St Saviours Guernsey Channel
Islands GY7 9FS
Tel: 01481 264428
Features hand-made chocolates, Guernsey Fudge, silversmiths, crazy golf, pottery, craft and gift shops, children's play area, 200-seat restaurant and (of course) strawberries.

Factory Outlets & Tours

Jersey Pottery
Gorey Village Main Road Gorey Jersey
Channel Islands JE3 9EP
Tel: 01534 850850
Showroom, museum, a 'do-it-yourself' painting
studio and a restaurant.

Folk & Local History Museums

Alderney Museum
High Street Alderney Channel Islands GY9 3TG
Tel: 01481 823222
Collections consist largely of objects that reveal
a small community surviving over the centuries
on subsistence agriculture, fishing and trading.

German Occupation Museum
Les Houards Forest Guernsey Channel Islands
GY8 0BG
Tel: 01481 238205
The Channel Islands' largest collection of
authentic Occupation-related items.
Tue-Sun

Guernsey Museum and Art Gallery
Candie Gardens St Peter Port Guernsey
Channel Islands GY1 1UG
Tel: 01481 726518
Set in attractive Victorian Gardens, the main
exhibition in the Museum tells the story of
Guernsey from Neolithic times.
Feb-Dec daily

Jersey Museum
Weighbridge St. Helier Jersey Channel Islands
JE2 3NF
Tel: 01534 633300
The Jersey Museum, winner of the Museum of
the Year Award 1993, is a specially designed
purpose-built venue.

Heritage & Industrial

Quétivel Mill
Le Mont Fallu St Peter Jersey Channel Islands
Tel: 01534 745040/483193
There has been a mill on this site since 1309.

Historical

Elizabeth Castle
La Rue de la Patente St Helier Jersey
Channel Islands JE2 3NF
Tel: 01534 723971
Elizabeth Castle is a spacious fortress built on a
islet in St. Aubin's Bay.

Little Chapel
Les Vauxbelets College Complex Les
Vauxbelets St. Andrew Guernsey
Channel Islands GY6 8XY
Tel: 01481 237200
Possibly the smallest chapel in the world, the
Little Chapel is beautifully decorated with
seashells, pebbles and pieces of broken china.

Sausmarez Manor
St. Martin Guernsey Channel Islands GY4 6SG
Tel: 01481 235571
Enjoy guided tours of the historic manor, a
miniature railway, a mini golf course, a sub-tropical garden and a tea room. Also on the
grounds are children's play areas, a silversmiths
and a sculpture park.

Maritime

Maritime Museum
New North Quay St. Helier Jersey
Channel Islands JE2 3ND
Tel: 01534 811043
Through specially-designed exhibits, visitors can
explore the maritime forces which have shaped
the experience of life in Jersey.

Military & Defence Museums

German Military Underground Hospital and Ammunition Store

Rue Des Buttes St. Andrew Guernsey
Channel Islands GY6 8XR
Tel: 01481 239100
This is the largest structure created during the
German Occupation of the Channel Islands.

Jersey War Tunnels

Les Charrieres Malorey St Lawrence Jersey
Channel Islands JE3 1FU
Tel: 01534 863442
An exhibition housed in an underground hospital
tunnel complex known as 'HO8.'

Places of Worship

St Matthew's Church

La Grande Route de St Aubin St Lawrence
Jersey Channel Islands JE3 1LN
Tel: 01534 720934
Known as 'the Glass Church' because of the
unique art deco interior decorations made of
glass by Rene Lalique.

Sealife Centres & Aquariums

Guernsey Aquarium

La Vallette St Peter Port Guernsey
Channel Islands GY1 1AX
Tel: 01481 723301
45+ displays, ranging from local sea fish to
tropical marine fish.

Theme & Adventure Parks

aMaizin

La Hougue Farm La Grande Route de St Pierre
St Peter Jersey JE3 7AX
Tel: 01534 482116
Crazy golf, three go-kart tracks, aMaizin
Barnyard, Maze Experience, tractor rides, water
pistol area and Craft Centre.

Zoos

Les Augrès Manor - Durrell Wildlife Conservation Trust

La Profonde Rue Trinity Jersey Channel Islands
JE3 5BP
Tel: 01534 860000 Fax: 01534 860001
www.durrell.org

[4mi N of St Helier. Bus: 3a 3b & 23]

Durrell Wildlife Conservation Trust was founded
by author and naturalist Gerald Durrell nearly
fifty years ago with a mission to save species
worldwide, and it has a proven track record of
doing just that. Species that have been pulled
back from the brink include the Mauritius
kestrel, pink pigeon, echo parakeet and
Mallorcan midwife toad, and our dedicated con-
servationists are hard at work in threatened
habitats around the world continuing the battle
to protect and conserve many more. Durrell has
built up a worldwide reputation for its pioneering
conservation techniques and continues to
develop its overseas work in new areas of the
world, with a particular focus on vulnerable
communities of endemic animals, which make
such a valuable contribution to global biodiversi-
ty. Marvel at 130 species. Walk, look, listen and
play in 32 acres of incredible parkland.
Entertainment and education - Durrell is an
experience for all the family.

*All year. Summer 09.30-18.00, Winter 09.30-
17.00. Closed 25 Dec*

A£11.90 C&OAPs£8.40
Students(NUS/USI)£9.50, Family Ticket £36.00

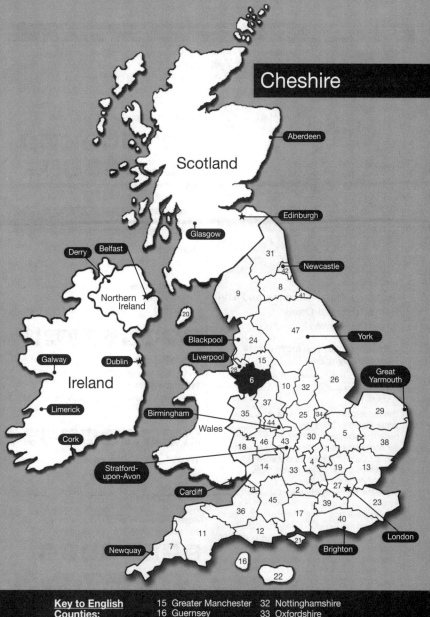

Cheshire

Aberdeen

Scotland

Edinburgh

Glasgow

31

Newcastle

Derry   Belfast

42

8

9

41

Northern
Ireland

20

Blackpool

47

York

24

Galway   Dublin

Liverpool

15

28

Great
Yarmouth

Ireland

6

10

32

26

Limerick

37

29

Birmingham

35

25

34

Wales

44

Cork

30

5

18

46

43

1

38

Stratford-
upon-Avon

14

33

4

19

13

Cardiff

13

2

27

23

45

39

London

36

17

40

Brighton

11

12

Newquay

7

21

16

22

Animal Attractions

Stapeley Water Gardens and The Palms Tropical Oasis

London Road Stapeley Nantwich Cheshire
CW5 7LH
Tel: 01270 623868 Fax: 01270 624919
www.stapeleywg.com

[J16 M6, 1mi S of Nantwich on A51 to Stone follow brown tourist signs. Plenty of on-site parking available]

There's something for everyone at Stapeley Water Gardens. The Palms Tropical Oasis is the perfect destination whatever the weather! With tamarin monkeys, toucans, piranhas, sharks and a crocodile, the Palms provide a unique experience of being in a tropical rainforest with all its fascinating and intriguing plants and animals. There's plenty of exciting areas to explore; from the humid setting of the Tropical House to the creepy Jungle Floor. There's also the Zoo Room and the Tunnel of Underwater Life to discover. The Palms also have a range of children's activities during school holidays and "Meet the Keeper" sessions every Saturday plus Mondays and Wednesdays throughout school holidays. Not only can you visit the Palms, there are fabulous selections of plants, gifts, pets, fish and water gardening at the Garden Centre, plus large Angling and Camping Centres.

Summer (Mid Mar-Mid Sept): Garden & Angling Centres: Mon-Sat 09.00-18.00, Wed open until 20.00. Bank Hol 10.00-18.00, Sun 10.00-16.00, Palms Tropical Oasis: daily 10.00-17.00. Winter: Garden & Angling Centres: Mon-Fri 09.00-17.00, Sat 09.00-18.00, (Angling Centre: Wed open till 20.00), Bank Hol 10.00-17.00, Sun 10.00-16.00. Palms Tropical Oasis: daily 10.00-17.00. Closed 25 Dec except for booked lunches.

Garden & Angling Centres also closed Easter Sunday

The Palms Tropical Oasis: A£4.95 C£2.95 OAPs£4.45. Group rates (15+): A£3.95 C£2.35 OAPs£3.55

Discount Offer: One Child Free.

Arts, Crafts & Textiles

Blakemere Craft Centre

Chester Road Sandiway Northwich Cheshire
CW8 2EB
Tel: 01606 883261
Blakemere's 30 craft shops offer individually handcrafted items within an Edwardian stable block.

Silk Museum

Park Lane Macclesfield Cheshire SK11 6TJ
Tel: 01625 612045
Three distinct galleries: the first charts the history of the Macclesfield School of Art and the Technical School.

West Park Museum

Prestbury Road Macclesfield Cheshire
SK10 3BJ
Tel: 01625 619831
West Park Museum's Collections comprise a wide range of fine and decorative art material and objects relating to local history.

Country Parks & Estates

Marbury Country Park

Comberbach Northwich Cheshire CW9 6AT
Tel: 01606 77741
Marbury Country Park is the parkland of Marbury Hall, which was demolished in 1968. The park is set in 200 acres of woodland, and ideal for walkers and picnickers.

Tatton Park
Knutsford Cheshire WA16 6QN
Tel: 01625 374400
Fax: 01625 374403
www.tattonpark.org.uk

[2mi NE of Knutsford]

Tatton Park is a historical estate set within a country park of 1000 acres. It is home to two herds of deer and a variety of wildlife throughout the year including birds which are attracted by the two meres, or lakes. Tatton is the venue for over 100 events each year including festivals and shows, and it features performing arts including outdoor theatre, classical and popular concerts. The 4 attractions to visit are the Mansion, Farm, Gardens and Old Hall.

High Season: 10.00-19.00 parkland only. Low season: 11.00-17.00 (Tue-Sun) parkland only. Please see website for full details

Car entry £4.20. Attractions: A£3.50 C£2.00 Family Ticket £9.00. Discovery Saver Ticket (any 2 attractions) A£5.00 C£3.00 Family£13.50

Walton Hall and Gardens
Walton Hall Gardens Walton Lea Road
Higher Walton Warrington Cheshire WA4 6SN
Tel: 01925 602336/601617
Set amidst beautiful Chesire countryside, attractions include a heritage centre, children's zoo, crazy-golf, pitch 'n' putt, bowls, coffee shop and much more.

RHS Flower Show at Tatton Park
Tatton Park Grounds Knutsford Cheshire
Tel: 0870 842 2229
www.rhs.org.uk/flowershows

[Plenty of on-site parking available]

Whether you are a first time gardener wanting to learn how to get started, or if you have more seasoned green fingers but are itching for some inspiration, then the RHS Flower Show at Tatton Park is the place to be. The show Gardens are where the crème de la crème of gardening talent push the boundaries of both planting and landscaping design, while small and innovative Back to Back gardens champion the delights of urban gardening. Tatton also plays host to some unique and exciting competitions that you will not see elsewhere. In the RHS / Ball Colegrave National Flower Bed Competition, local authorities and colleges from across the UK use bedding plants to create 3D sculptures and will also crown the National Young florist of the Year.

23-27 July 2008 (Thur-Sat 10.00-18.30, Sun 10.00-17.00).

£23.00 (£21.00 if booked in advance) C(5-15)£5.00 C(under5)£Free

Chester History and Heritage
St Michael's Church Bridge Street Row Chester Cheshire CH1 2HJ
Tel: 01244 402110
Local history study and temporary exhibitions.

Warrington Museum and Art Gallery

Museum Street Warrington Cheshire WA1 1JB
Tel: 01925 442733
Collections of Egyptology, ethnology, geology, archaeology and natural history,

Food & Drink

Cheshire Ice Cream Farm

Drumlan Hall Farm Newton Lane Tattenhall Chester Cheshire CH3 9NE
Tel: 01829 770446
A working dairy farm open to the public.

Salt Museum

162 London Road Northwich Cheshire CW9 8AB
Tel: 01606 41331
Britain's only Salt Museum tells the fascinating story of Cheshire's oldest industry.

Heritage & Industrial

Macclesfield Silk Museums

Heritage Centre Roe Street Macclesfield Cheshire SK11 6UT
Tel: 01625 612045
A visit to our 3 Silk Museums offers you the chance to explore the history of a silk town.

Historical

Adlington Hall

Mill Lane Adlington Macclesfield Cheshire SK10 4LF
Tel: 01625 829206
Adlington Hall is one of England's most beautiful country homes.

Tabley House

Knutsford Cheshire WA16 0HB
Tel: 01565 750151 Fax: 01565 653230
www.tableyhouse.co.uk

[J19 M6 A556, 2mi W of Knutsford, entrance on A5033. Plenty of on-site parking available]

The only Palladian Mansion in the North West, Tabley comprises an extraordinary collection of family memorabilia. The First Lord de Tabley was a distinguished patron of the arts and the house comprises works by Reynolds, Fuseli, Turner and Lawrence, to name a few. Furniture by Bullock and Gillow. Knowledgeable and helpful stewards ensure an enjoyable afternoon out.

Apr-end Oct Thur-Sun & Bank Hol 14.00-17.00. Tea Room: 12.00-17.00
A£4.00 C&Students(NUS/USI)£1.50

Military & Defence Museums

Hack Green Secret Nuclear Bunker

Nantwich Cheshire CW5 8AQ
Tel: 01270 629219
For over 50 years this vast underground complex remained a secret.

On the Water

Anderton Boat Lift

Lift Lane Anderton Northwich CW9 6FW
Tel: 01606 786777
Built in 1875 it was the world's first (and is currently the UK's only) Boat Lift.

Places of Worship

Chester Cathedral

St Werburgh Street Chester Cheshire CH1 2HU
Tel: 01244 324756
An unusually well-preserved example of a medieval monastic complex.

Science - Earth & Planetary

Catalyst: Science Discovery Centre

Mersey Road Widnes Cheshire WA8 0DF
Tel: 0151 420 1121 Fax: 0151 495 2030
www.catalyst.org.uk

[Rail: Runcorn then bus or taxi across bridge. By car J7 M62 0r J12 M56 follow brown & white tourism signs. Plenty of on-site parking available]

Experience an amazing journey of discovery in Catalyst's brand new Interactive Theatre and enter a colourful world of science and technology in our three interactive galleries. Visit our shop or café and travel 30 metres above the River Mersey in our external glass lift to marvel at the views from our glass-walled rooftop gallery. Science has never been so much fun!

All year Tue-Sun & Bank Hol Mons and most Mons during school hols. Closed 24-26 Dec, 31 Dec & 1 Jan
A£4.95 C&Concession£3.95 C(under4)£Free
Family Ticket£15.95

Discount Offer: One Child Free.

Jodrell Bank Visitor Centre

Jodrell Bank Lower Withington Macclesfield Cheshire SK11 9DL
Tel: 01477 571339 Fax: 01477 571695

[Plenty of on-site parking available]

The Visitor Centre stands at the feet of one of the largest radio telescopes in the world, the Lovell telescope, a landmark in both Cheshire and in the world of astronomy.

All year daily 10.30-17.30 (subject to change). Closed 25 Dec, 6 July & 4 Oct
A&C£1.50

Discount Offer: Two for the Price of One (full-paying adult).

For great hotel deals call Superbreak on 01904 679999 or visit www.superbreak.com

Sealife Centres & Aquariums

Blue Planet Aquarium

Longlooms Road Cheshire Oaks Ellesmere Port Cheshire CH65 9LF
Tel: 0151 357 8804 Fax: 0151 356 7288
www.blueplanetaquarium.com

[J10 M53, signposted. Easy to find from M6 & M56. Plenty of on-site parking available]

Blue Planet Aquarium is an experience you'll never forget. A fascinating underwater world of colours and close encounters. A voyage of discovery through rivers and reefs to where our divers hand feed the sharks. Glide through the most spectacular safari and be surrounded by a carnival of Caribbean fish, including one of the largest collections of sharks in Europe!!! Special events held throughout the year, please call for details.

All year daily from 10.00. Please call to check closing times as these may vary. Closed 25 Dec

Please check website for latest information on prices

Stately Homes

Arley Hall and Gardens

Arley Nr Great Budworth Northwich Cheshire CW9 6NA
Tel: 01565 777353
Early Victorian Jacobean-style mansion with private chapel and cruck barn.

Bramall Hall

Bramhall Park Bramhall Cheshire SK7 3NX
Tel: 0161 485 3708 Fax: 0161 486 6959
www.bramallhall.org.uk

[4mi S of Stockport off A5102, 10min from Stockport Town Centre. Plenty of on-site parking available]

Magical Tudor House set in 70 acres of parkland. House contains sixteenth-century wall paintings, Elizabethan plaster ceilings, Victorian kitchens and Servants' quarters. Available for civil marriages and corporate entertaining. Wheelchair access limited to ground floor only. Photography not permitted. You can view the hall by guided tour or self-guided tour.

1 Apr-end Sept Sun-Thur 13.00-17.00, Fri-Sat 13.00-16.00, Bank Hols only 11.00-17.00, 1 Oct-1 Jan Tue-Sun 13.00-16.00, 2 Jan-31 Mar Sat-Sun 13.00-16.00 Guided Tours at 15 mins past the hour

A£3.95 C&OAPs£2.95

Discount Offer: Two for the Price of One (full-paying adult).

Dunham Massey

Altrincham Cheshire WA14 4SJ
Tel: 0161 941 1025
Mansion with important collections and fascinating 'below stairs' area, set in a large country estate and deer park, with a rich and varied garden.

Theme & Adventure Parks

Go Ape! High Wire Forest Adventure (Delamere Forest, Cheshire)

Delamere Forest Park Linmere Visitor Centre
Northwich Cheshire CW8 2JD
Tel: 0845 643 9245
www.goape.co.uk

[10mi outside Chester, close to M56. Plenty of on-site parking available]

Take to the trees and experience an exhilarating course of rope bridges, Tarzan swings and zip-slides up to 40 feet above the ground! Share approximately three exciting hours of fun and adventure, which you'll be talking about for days. Book online and watch people Go Ape! at www.goape.co.uk. Minimum height 1.4m. Maximum weight 130 kg (20.5 stone). Under-18s must be accompanied by a participating adult. One adult can supervise either two children (where one or both of them is under 16 years old) or up to five 16-17 year olds. Pre-booking is essential to avoid disappointment. Book online or by telephone (there is a £1.00 booking fee on all telephone bookings).

9-11 & 14-17 Feb, 14 Mar-31 Oct daily. Nov Sat-Sun. Dec Sat-Sun please visit www.goape.co.uk. Closed Jan

Gorillas (18yrs+) £25.00, Baboons (10-17yrs) £20.00

Discount Offer: £5.00 off per person.

Gulliver's: Warrington

Warrington Cheshire WA5 9YZ
Tel: 01925 444888/230088
From the tumbling and juggling fun of Circus World, mosey on down to High Noon in Western World, walk with dinosaurs in the pre-historic Lost World, feel your knees tremble in Count's Castle and shiver your timbers in Smugglers Wharf.

Transport Museums

Griffin Trust

The Hangars South Road Hooton Park Airfield Ellesmere Port Cheshire CH65 1BQ
Tel: 0151 327 4701
This historic site was one home to many aircraft and airmen during its life both as a civil and operational RAF aerodrome.

Mouldsworth Motor Museum

Smithy Lane Mouldsworth Chester Cheshire CH3 8AR
Tel: 01928 731781
Housed in a large Art Deco building close to Delamere Forest, a collection of over 60 motor cars, motorcycles and early bicycles.

National Waterways Museum, Ellesmere Port

South Pier Road Ellesmere Port South Wirral Cheshire CH65 4FW
Tel: 0151 355 5017
Come and explore the story of the waterways at our historic seven-acre dock complex.

Zoos

Chester Zoo

Upton-by-Chester Chester Cheshire CH2 1LH
Tel: 01244 380280
With over 7,000 animals and over 400 species, Chester Zoo is an exciting, fun day out for all the family.

Cornwall

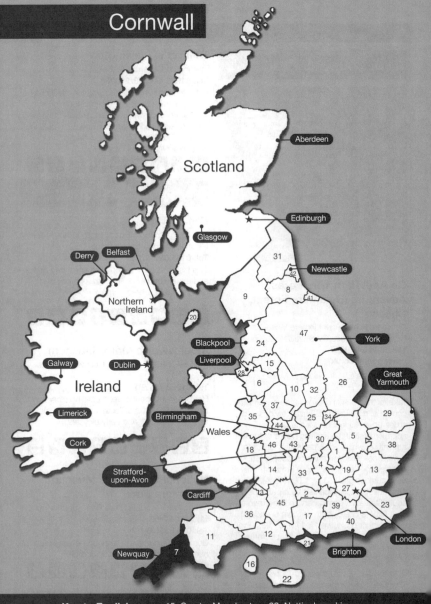

Scotland

Aberdeen

Edinburgh

Glasgow

Newcastle

31

42

9   8

41

Derry   Belfast

Northern
Ireland

20

Blackpool

24   47   York

Galway   Dublin

Liverpool

15

28

Ireland

6   10   32   26   Great
Yarmouth

Limerick

37   29

Cork   Birmingham

35   25   34

Wales   44

18   46   43   30   5   38

Stratford-
upon-Avon   14   4   19   13

33   27   London

Cardiff   13   2   39   23

45   17   40

36

Newquay   7   11   12   21   Brighton

16

22

Animal Attractions

National Seal Sanctuary
Gweek Helston Cornwall TR12 6UG
Tel: 01326 221874 Fax: 01326 221210
www.sealsanctuary.co.uk

[Follow signs to Helston then to Gweek. Plenty of on-site parking available]

Witness animal welfare work at its finest in Europe's busiest seal rescue centre. The Sanctuary extends a vital lifeline every winter to dozens of abandoned, stranded and injured grey seal pups. You will also encounter resident adult seals and sea lions, and even playful otters. Daily talks and feeding presentations ensure a memorable day out for all the family. Californian sea lion, Rocky is a firm favourite and nearby you will also find Patagonian sea lion, Boadicea. Meal times are (without doubt) the sea lions' favourite events, and its also the best times to find out more about these gentle giants. The whole Seal Rescue operation is under a fresh spotlight this year, with new developments that give a deeper insight into the whole process…from rescue and recovery right through to release. Don't miss the underwater observatory where you can watch seals beneath the waves, where they are at their most graceful.

All year daily from 10.00. Closed Christmas Day

Please call for admission prices

Discount Offer: One Child Free

Monkey Sanctuary
St. Martin Murrayton Looe Cornwall PL13 1NZ
Tel: 01503 262532 Fax: 01503 262532
www.monkeysanctuary.org

[Plenty of on-site parking available]

The Monkey Sanctuary near Looe had been home to a colony of Amazonian Woolly monkeys since 1964. Visitors can watch them in their extensive territory of interlinked enclosures, watch them scale trees, forage and socialize. Keepers are on hand daily to give talks and introduce you to the monkeys; their personality, likes and dislikes. The Monkey Sanctuary is also home to a small group of rescued capuchin monkeys brought to the Sanctuary from lives as isolation as pets. Visitors can learn about the problems of keeping intelligent and social monkeys in captivity, and learn about projects in South America working for monkeys in the wild. Visitors are also invited to get a closer look at a colony of lesser horseshoe bats who roost in our cellar courtesy of a CCTV link. There are beautiful gardens overlooking Looe bay for visitors to explore and follow the nature trail. Children can make Amazonian face masks in the activity room, and enjoy a bit of bouncing about of their own in the play area. The Monkey Sanctuary offers a gift shop, vegetarian café, ample parking and free picnic areas. Dogs are allowed in the car park but no dogs at all (inc. guide dogs) are allowed inside the Monkey Sanctuary.

1 Apr-28 Sep Sun-Thur 11.00-16.30. Closed Fri-Sat

Please call for admission prices

Porfell Animal Land
Herodsfoot Liskeard Cornwall PL14 4RE
Tel: 01503 220211
Exotic and farmyard animals to be seen within beautiful countryside.

Art Galleries

Falmouth Art Gallery
Municipal Buildings The Moor Falmouth
Cornwall TR11 2RT
Tel: 01326 313863
The Gallery's art collection is one of the most
important in Cornwall, and features works by
major British artists.

Tate St Ives
Porthmeor Beach St. Ives Cornwall TR26 1TG
Tel: 01736 796226
International modern and contemporary art in
the unique cultural context of St Ives, including
works from the Tate Collection.

Arts, Crafts & Textiles

Barbara Hepworth Museum and Sculpture Garden
Barnoon Hill St. Ives Cornwall TR26 1AD
Tel: 01736 796226
Sculptures in wood, stone and bronze can be
seen in the late Dame Barbara Hepworth's
house, studio and sub-tropical garden.

Birds, Butterflies & Bees

Porteath Bee Centre
St. Minver Wadebridge Cornwall PL27 6RA
Tel: 01208 863718
A small bee keeping business with a shop, exhi-
bition and café.

Communication Museums

Porthcurno Telegraph Museum
Porthcurno Penzance Cornwall TR19 6JX
Tel: 01736 810966
This fascinating museum tells the story of the
origins of today's Internet and the history of
world communications.

Country Parks & Estates

Cotehele
St Dominick Nr Saltash Cornwall PL12 6TA
Tel: 01579 351346/352739
Tudor house with a superb collections of tex-
tiles, armour and furniture, all set in extensive
grounds.

Folk & Local History Museums

Smugglers at Jamaica Inn
Jamaica Inn Complex Bolventor Launceston
Cornwall PL15 7TS
Tel: 01566 86250 Fax: 01566 86177
www.jamaicainn.co.uk

*[On A30 Launceston / Bodmin rd. Plenty of on-
site parking available.]*

An attraction in three parts, designed to appeal
to all the family. Employing the latest digital
technology with traditional methods of interpretation. Visitors are first welcomed with a theatrical presentation of the Jamaica Inn story told in
tableaux, light and sound, then on to see one of
the finest collections of smuggling relics, dating
from past to present. And finally, on to Dame
Daphne Du Maurier's life and works including
her Sheraton writing desk where she wrote so
many of her famous novels.

*Mid season daily 10.00-17.00, Summer daily
10.00-19.00, Part Winter 11.00-16.00*
Museum Passport: A£3.95
C(under16)&OAPs£3.45, Family Ticket (A2+C2)
£9.95. Parties/Groups: £2.50 per person

Food & Drink

Cornish Cyder Farm
Penhallow Truro Cornwall TR4 9LW
Tel: 01872 573356
Makes over forty varieties of delicious fruit products including farm scrumpy, sparkling cyder, country wines, jam, chutneys and spirits.

Gardens & Horticulture

Lost Gardens of Heligan
Pentewan St. Austell Cornwall PL26 6EN
Tel: 01726 845100
World-renowned restored productive gardens and pleasure grounds.

Trelissick Garden
Feock Nr Truro Cornwall TR3 6QL
Tel: 01872 862090
Tranquil varied garden in fabulous position, with a superb collection of tender and exotic plants. Features Roundwood Iron Age Fort and a gallery displaying work by local craftsmen.

Heritage & Industrial

Land's End Visitor Centre
Sennen Penzance Cornwall TR19 7AA
Tel: 0870 458 0044
Come and see the natural beauty or tickets can be purchased for any or all of our 5 exhibitions.

Historical

King Arthur's Great Halls
Fore Street Tintagel Cornwall PL34 0DA
Tel: 01840 770526
Built by a philanthropist millionaire in the 1930's, the building houses round tables, granite thrones and 72 stained glass windows. The shop stocks an array of Arthurian products.

Mount Edgcumbe House
Cremyll Torpoint Cornwall PL10 1HZ
Tel: 01752 822236
Tudor mansion with family treasures.

Prideaux Place
Padstow Cornwall PL28 8RP
Tel: 01841 532411 Fax: 01841 532945
www.prideauxplace.co.uk

[From A30 signposted Wadebridge/Padstow. Plenty of on-site parking available]

Situated above the picturesque port of Padstow is the Elizabethan mansion Prideaux Place. Completed in 1592 by Nicholas Prideaux and still lived in by the family who can trace their ancestry back to William the Conqueror. Surrounded by 40 acres of landscaped gardens and overlooking its ancient Deer Park this splendid house contains a wealth of family and royal portraits, an exquisite collection of porcelain, a growing Teddy Bear collection and a magnificent sixteenth-century plaster ceiling, the crowning glory of the Great Chamber with its stunning views across the Cornish countryside to distant Bodmin Moor. The gardens are undergoing extensive restoration, the family being helped by Tom Petherick who has been instrumental in the restoration of the gardens at Heligan. Visitors can enjoy woodland walks, a formal garden, a garden Temple and Roman antiquities. There is a fully licensed tearoom offering light lunches and renowned Cornish Cream Teas, on warm sunny days one can enjoy refreshments on the Terrace, a haven of peace away from the bustle of Padstow.

Easter Sun-27 Mar & 11 May-9 Oct Sun-Thur, House: 13.30-16.00, Grounds & Tearoom: 12.30-17.00. Group bookings open all year by appointment
A£7.50 C£2.00

St Michael's Mount

West End Marazion Cornwall TR17 0EF
Tel: 01736 710507/710265
[0.5m S of A394]

Originally the site of a Benedictine priory and approached by a causeway at low tide, this dramatic castle dates from the twelfth century.

Tintagel Castle

Tintagel Head Cornwall PL34 0HE
Tel: 01840 770328

With its spectacular location on Cornwall's dramatic Atlantic coastline, this thirteenth-century ruin is a place of myth and magic.

National Maritime Museum Cornwall

Discovery Quay Falmouth Cornwall TR11 3QY
Tel: 01326 313388 Fax: 01326 317878
www.nmmc.co.uk

[At SE end of Falmouth's harbour front, nr docks, car parking & railway station. Rail: Falmouth]

Located on the edge of Falmouth's stunning harbour, the National Maritime Museum Cornwall is a hand-on, twenty-first-century, new generation of visitor attraction that will appeal to landlubbers and sailors alike. More than just a museum about boats, it's all about the sea, boats and Cornwall itself. Experience breathtaking views from the 29m tower, see the only natural underwater tidal zone in Europe and a stunning flying display of boats. Enjoy hand-on activities, an audio-visual immersive experience, talks, special exhibitions, and cruises. The National Maritime Museum Cornwall has something for everyone and is the perfect day out.

The best way to get here is by boat! Use the 'Park & Float' and sail to the museum in a classic ferry (running May-September).

All year daily 10.00-17.00. Closed 25-26 Dec
A£7.95 C(under5)£Free C£5.25 OAPs£6.25, Family Ticket (A2+C3) £21.00

Discount Offer: One Child Free

Nature & Conservation Parks

Eden Project

Bodelva Parr St Austell Cornwall PL26 2SG
Tel: 01726 811911

A large-scale environmental complex.

Performing Arts

Minack Theatre and Exhibition Centre

Porthcurno Penzance Cornwall TR19 6JU
Tel: 01736 810694

Views from the theatre are spectacular, overlooking the Atlantic Ocean.

Places of Worship

Truro Cathedral

Truro Cornwall TR1 2AF
Tel: 01872 276782

The largest UK example of the Gothic Revival architectural style.

Police, Prisons & Dungeons

Bodmin Jail

Berrycoombe Road Bodmin Cornwall PL31 2NR
Tel: 01208 76292

Find out just some of the crimes and punishments of our unfortunate ancestors.

Railways

C(3-16)£6.00, Family Ticket (A2+C4) £28.00.
Bodmin General & Boscarne Junction

Science - Earth & Planetary

Goonhilly Satellite Earth Station Experience

The Visitor Centre Goonhilly Downs Helston
Cornwall TR12 6LQ
Tel: 0800 679593
With over 60 huge dishes, Goonhilly is the
largest satellite earth station in the world.

Stately Homes

Lanhydrock House
Bodmin Cornwall PL30 5AD
Tel: 01208 265950
Magnificent late Victorian country house with
extensive servants' quarters, gardens and
wooded estate.

Sealife Centres & Aquariums

Bodmin and Wenford Railway

Bodmin General Station Lostwithiel Road
Bodmin Cornwall PL31 1AQ
Tel: 0845 125 9678 Fax: 01208 77963
www.bodminandwenfordrailway.co.uk

*[Free parking available at Bodmin General Station,
situated on B3268 Lostwithiel Rd nr Bodmin centre. From A30/A38 follow signs to Bodmin town
centre then brown tourist signs to steam railway.
Car parking NOT available at other stations. Rail:
Mainline rail services operate to Bodmin Parkway.
Through tickets to Bodmin & Wenford Railway are
available tel: 08457 484950. Bus: Western
Greyhound, 01637 871871. Limited on-site parking available]*

The Bodmin and Wenford Railway offers a trip
into nostalgia with steam trains operating from
the historic town of Bodmin through scenic
countryside along the preserved six-mile Great
Western Railway branch line to Bodmin
Parkway (for walks to Lanhydrock House) and
Boscarne Junction (for the Camel Trail footpath).
There are now three ex G.W.R. Locomotives in
steam on different days the oldest of which
dates back to 1916; we are also custodians of
the Beattie Well Tank No.30587 built in 1874
and steamed for special events. The line is
Cornwall's only standard-gauge steam railway -
located about eight miles from the Eden Project.
Bodmin General station (in Bodmin town centre)
offers a refreshment room and souvenir shop.
Evening specials offer a variety of music, brake
van rides and Murder Mystery! Come and enjoy
Sunday lunch in our First Class Dining Coaches,
also available for private hire.

*Opening times: June-Sept daily, also some days
in Mar, Apr, May, Oct, Nov, Dec, please call for a
timetable*

All Line Ticket (Return): A£10.00 C(under3)£Free

Blue Reef Aquarium (Cornwall)
Towan Promenade Newquay Cornwall TR7 1DU
Tel: 01637 878134 Fax: 01637 872578
www.bluereefaquarium.co.uk

*[Follow brown tourist signs to car parks in town
centre, Blue Reef is situated on Towan beach]*

Take the ultimate undersea safari at the award winning Blue Reef Aquarium where there's a world of underwater adventure just waiting to be discovered. Over 30 living displays reveal the sheer variety of life in the deep; from native sharks and lobsters to seahorses and amazing jellyfish. At the aquarium's heart is a giant ocean tank where an underwater walkthrough tunnel offers incredibly close encounters with the stunning beauty of a tropical coral reef - home of hundreds of colourful fish. Blue Reef is a great place for visitors of all ages to discover more about the wonders of the deep. There's a full programme of entertaining, informative talks and feeding displays throughout the day. Learn more about native sea creatures including crabs, anemones and starfish at our popular Rockpool Encounters where our experts will be on hand to answer all your questions. A spectacular experience whatever the weather.

All year daily from 10.00. Closed 25 Dec

A£8.50 C(3-16)£6.00 OAPs&Students(NUS/USI)£7.50. Discounted rates for groups and disabled visitors - please call for details

Discount Offer: One Child Free.

Cornwall's Crealy Great Adventure Park

Tredinnick Newquay Cornwall PL27 7RA
Tel: 01841 540276 Fax: 01395 233211
www.crealy.co.uk

[From A30: off A39 nr Wadebridge, fully signposted. Plenty of free on-site parking available]

Visit Cornwall's Crealy for maximum fun guaranteed at the county's biggest family attraction. NEW for 2008! Brave the real Beast of Cornwall! At 15 metres tall and frighteningly fast, The Beast towers high in the sky, looming above those too scared to ride! Venture into the Realms of Magic, Action, Wild Water, Enchantment, Nature. Climb aboard the Viking Warrior Ship, swinging high through the air, slide down the Raging Rivers raft ride to the biggest splash of your life and whoosh down the rapids of Thunder Falls - Cornwall's only doubled drop log flume! Explore 40,000 sq. ft. of indoor action to discover dragons, ghosts and surprises! Sneak into the darkness of the Haunted House but watch out for ghouls hiding in the corners! Drop into blackness of the Slide of Doom and creep through the shadows... With courage as your armour, climb, swing, slide and leap your way through the Dragon's Kingdom! Outside, scale the heights of the aerial walkways and climbing nets, glide down the bumpy slides and zip along on the super fast cable wire! Now fun never stops with Holiday Tickets at Cornwall's Crealy - seven days of fun for the price of one! For more information and to book tickets in advance visit www.crealy.co.uk.

15 Mar-4 Nov: open daily. Winter: Closed 5 Nov-31 Mar. Reopens 1 Apr 2009

Low season: A&C£9.95, OAPs£6.95, C(under92cm)£Free, Family Ticket (4 people) £9.95 per person. High season: A&C£10.95 C(under92cm)£Free OAPs£7.95, Family Ticket (4 people) £10.50 per person. Crealy Club Membership: £35.00. Cornwall Family Passports: £75.00 (for up to 5 people, valid for entire 2008 season). Explorers: (between 92cm-100cm) £9.95 per-person (return FREE to Devon's Crealy all this year for the price of just one day ticket)

Discount Offer: One FREE tub of Candy Floss.

Flambards Experience

Helston Cornwall TR13 0QA
Tel: 01326 573404 Fax: 01326 573344
www.flambards.co.uk

[0.5mi S of Helston on A3083 towards Lizard. Plenty of on-site parking available]

The secret of Flambards' appeal is its huge variety; there is so much to do and see and so many places where all ages can enjoy themselves together inside and out. Inside, let your imagination lead you through the award winning Flambards Victorian Village, a compelling life-size re-creation of a lamp-lit village of bustling streets and alleyways with more than 50 shops, traders and homes. Or move forward to the Second World War in Britain in the Blitz, an undercover, authentic life-size re-creation of a World War II blitzed street. Then, enjoy the fascinating exhibitions, step into Concorde, enjoy the Wildlife Experience or just let the children play in the Cool Zone undercover play area. And, outside, let rip on the best thrill rides in Cornwall, and children can play to their hearts' content in Ferdi Funland and the children's' ride area. With award winning gardens, top quality entertainment in the high season, a wide choice of picnic areas, catering and gift shops, every visitor can be confident of a superb full day out.

18 Mar-1 Nov daily 10.00/10.30-17.00/17.30 depending on season. Closed some Mon & Fri in low & shoulder season, please call for details
A(11-59)£13.50 C(under3)£Free C(3-10)£8.75 OAPs(60-79)£7.25 OAPs(80+)£Free, Family Ticket (4 people)£42.40, (£10.60 per person) with top ups: C(3-10)£7.25 each, A(11-59) £12.25 each, OAPs(60-79) £6.25 each

Discount Offer: One Child Free

Zoos

Newquay Zoo

Trenance Gardens Newquay Cornwall TR7 2LZ
Tel: 01637 873342 Fax: 01637 851318
www.newquayzoo.org.uk

[A30 Indian Queens, A392 to Newquay, turn R into Trevemper Rd, follow brown & white signs]

Silver Visitor Attraction of the Year 2007-2008 Newquay Zoo is set amongst exotic lakeside gardens with animals from all around the world ranging from the smallest monkey the Pygmy Marmoset to 'Kabir' and 'Connie' the African Lions. Enjoy talks, animal encounters and feeding times throughout the day. See the very popular otter family playing in the stream in the Oriental Garden, Owston's Civets from Vietnam and stunning Hornbills from Asia. Look out for meerkats on sentry duty, penguins playing in their pool and the beautiful Red Pandas. Newquay Zoo is fun for all age groups with plenty of delights for children including the Tarzan trail, a children's play area, the village farm and the dragons maze. Face painting and a 'Wild Times' creative club are also available on most days during the summer. Events run throughout the year. The site is mainly level and is wheelchair friendly.

Apr-Sep daily 09.30-18.00, Oct-Mar daily 10.00-dusk. Closed 25 Dec

Prices change from summer to winter. Please call or check the website for details

Discount Offer: One Child Free.

County Durham

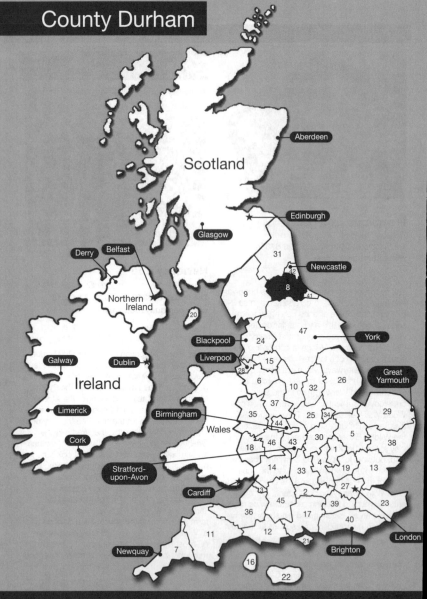

Aberdeen

Scotland

Edinburgh

Derry
Belfast

Glasgow

31

Newcastle

9
8
41

Northern
Ireland

20

Blackpool
47
York

Galway
Dublin

24

Liverpool
15

Great
Yarmouth

Ireland

28
6
10
32
26

Limerick

37

29

Birmingham
35
44
25
34

Cork

Wales
18
46
43
30
5
38

Stratford-
upon-Avon
14
4
1
19
13

Cardiff
33
27

2
39
23

45
17
40
London

36

Brighton

11
12

Newquay
7
21

16

22

Arts, Crafts & Textiles

Bowes Museum, The

Barnard Castle County Durham DL12 8NP
Tel: 01833 690606 Fax: 01833 637163
www.thebowesmuseum.org.uk

[Historic Market Town of Barnard Castle. Plenty of free on-site parking available]

Spend a day at the magnificent Bowes Museum. The first site of the impressive French style chateau never ceases to amaze and with its wonderful history and outstanding treasures there is something to inspire and entertain everyone. The collections of European fine and decorative arts is regarded as one of the greatest in the UK, with thousands of objects offering an intriguing story, including the famous Silver Swan automaton which delights visitors of all ages. You can find out more about the collections and how they are conserved through lots of hands on activities ranging from dressing up to fun interactives. Set within beautiful gardens and parkland, there is plenty to do outside too. The Museum also curates an acclaimed exhibition programme throughout the year and presents a series of events for all the family. Don't miss 'Alfred Sisley: Impressionist Landscapes' running from 17 May-21 Sept. The fabulous building is also home to the popular Café Bowes and gift shop, offering the perfect end to your visit.

All year daily 1 Nov-29 Feb 10.00-16:00, 1 Mar-31 Oct 10.00-17.00. Closed 25-26 Dec & 1 Jan
A£7.00 C(under16)£Free Concessions£6.00 (includes Gift Aid donation)

Discount Offer: Two for the Price of One (full-paying adult).

Folk & Local History Museums

Beamish, The North of England Open Air Museum

Beamish County Durham DH9 0RG
Tel: 0191 370 4000
Beamish is set in over 300 acres of beautiful countryside, and vividly recreates life in the North of England in the early 1800s and 1900s.
Summer: daily. Closed Mon & Fri in Winter

DLI Museum and Durham Art Gallery

Aykley Heads Durham County Durham DH1 5TU
Tel: 0191 384 2214
Occupying the entire top floor of a purpose-built modern building that it shares with the regimental collections of the Durham Light Infantry, the Gallery offers a programme of exhibitions.

Gardens & Horticulture

Botanic Garden University of Durham

Hollingside Lane Durham County Durham DH1 3TN
Tel: 0191 334 5521
18-acre garden set in mature woodland with exotic trees from America and the Himalayas.

Heritage & Industrial

Killhope The North of England Lead Mining Museum

Cowshill Weardale County Durham DL13 1AR
Tel: 01388 537505
Experience the living conditions of Victorian lead miners, and walk the woodland trail. The Park Level Mine is an exciting trip deep underground.

Locomotion: The National Railway Museum at Shildon

Shildon County Durham DL4 1PQ

Tel: 01388 777999

Provides an enjoyable visit telling local, regional and international stories involving social and railway history.

Historical

Auckland Castle

Bishop Auckland County Durham DL14 7NR

Tel: 01388 601627

The largest private chapel in Europe and a fine collection of paintings.

Crook Hall and Gardens

Frankland Lane Sidegate Durham
County Durham DH1 5SZ

Tel: 0191 384 8028

Described by the Sunday Telegraph as "stunning," this house and its gardens can be found on the banks of the River Wear.

Durham Castle

Palace Green Durham County Durham
DH1 3RW

Tel: 0191 334 3800

Dating from 1072, Durham Castle forms part of Durham's World Heritage Site along with Durham Cathedral.

Monks Dormitory

Durham Cathedral The College Durham
County Durham DH1 3EH

Tel: 0191 386 4266

Timber Roof 1398-1404 AD. Anglo-Saxon sculptured stones. Book exhibitions.

Raby Castle

Staindrop Darlington County Durham DL2 3AH
Tel: 01833 660202 Fax: 01833 660169
www.rabycastle.com

[On A688, 1mi N of Staindrop. Plenty of on-site parking available]

This dramatic mediaeval castle built by the mighty Nevills has been home to Lord Barnard's family since 1626. Set within a large deer park with walled gardens and a delightful rolling landscape, it is one of the most impressive castles in England. Discover the fine collections of furniture, impressive artworks and elaborate architecture. Highlights include the vast Baron's Hall, where it's rumoured that in 1569, 700 knights gathered to plot the doomed overthrow of Elizabeth I, a splendid Victorian octagonal drawing room that has emerged as one of the most striking interiors from the nineteenth century. And in contrast, a cavernous mediaeval kitchen that was used right up to 1954. There is an events programme that runs throughout the summer.

Easter (Sat-Mon), May-June & Sep (Sun-Wed, guided tours Mon to Wed), July-Aug (Sun-Fri): Castle 12.30-17.00, Park & Gardens 11.00-17.30. Open BH Sats. Closed Oct-Mar
A£9.50 C£4.00 Concessions£8.50, Family Ticket (A2+C3) £25.00

Places of Worship

Durham Cathedral

The College Durham County Durham DH1 3EH
Tel: 0191 386 4266
A remarkable example of Norman architecture set within an imposing site.

Theme & Adventure Parks

Diggerland (County Durham)
Langley Park County Durham DH7 9TT
Tel: 08700 344437 Fax: 09012 010300
www.diggerland.com

[From A1(M) J62 head W, following signs to Consett, after 6mi turn L at roundabout signed to Langley Park, turn R into Riverside Industrial Estate. Rail: Durham (approx 5mi). Bus: 54 from station. Plenty of on-site parking available]

Diggerland is the best activity day out for all the family with all activities based around construction machinery. With over 15 rides and drives positioned in an adventure park situation. Experience the thrill of riding in Spindizzy and enjoy the view from the Sky Shuttle. Drive across rough terrain in the Super Track and enjoy a mystery ride in the Land Rover Safari. Test your co-ordination in the JCB Challenges and fasten your seat belt for the drive of your life in the Robots. A full day of fun can be had by all ages with everything onsite including refuelling at The Dig Inn and shopping at the Goodie store. Birthday parties are catered for, so if you fancy a party with a difference then contact us for details. Diggerland welcomes its 4th park in Yorkshire for 2008. Please see our website for more information.

Feb 9-Nov 2, Weekends & Bank Hols plus daily during half-term & school hols 10.00-17.00
A&C£15.00 C(under3)£Free OAPs£7.50. Group rates (10+) 10% discount, (50+) 25%

Discount Offer: 10% off Admission.

Transport Museums

Darlington Railway Centre and Museum
North Road Station Station Road Darlington
County Durham DL3 6ST
Tel: 01325 460532 Fax: 01325 287746
www.drcm.org.uk

[1mi from Darlington town centre on A167. Plenty of on-site parking available]

Darlington Railway Centre and Museum reopens in April 2008 with brand new displays, shop, café, learning and activity room and research facilities. One of the world's oldest railway stations has lots to see, touch hear and smell to help everyone to explore their railway heritage. Come and see one of the worlds most famous railway engines - Locomotion No 1. Whether you are interested in how things work or where they were made there's something here for everyone, whatever the weather! Children can enjoy the hands on activities and family friendly events like 'Santa at the Station' and the 'Great Railway Easter Egg Hunt'. For those who want to find out more there's information galore and also improved facilities in the Ken Hoole Study Centre. Why not stop for a break in our new café and browse in our gift shop for a memento of the day, something for the children or a postcard to send to a friend.

Seasonal & event opening times vary. Please see website or contact museum for details
Please see website or contact museum for details of admission prices.

Discount Offer: Two for the Price of One (full-paying adult).

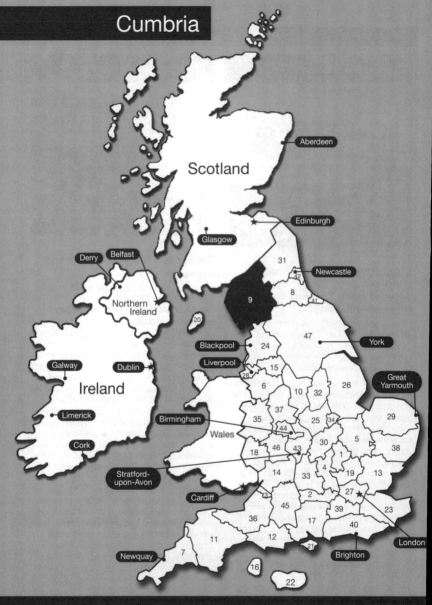

Cumbria

Aberdeen

Scotland

Edinburgh

Glasgow

31

Newcastle

42

Derry   Belfast

8

Northern
Ireland

9

41

20

47

York

Blackpool   24

Liverpool

28   15

Galway

6   10   32   26

Great
Yarmouth

Dublin

Ireland

Limerick

37

35   44   25   34   29

Birmingham

18   46   43   30   5   38

Wales

Cork

Stratford-
upon-Avon

14   33   4   1   19   13

Cardiff

13   2   27   23

45   39

36   17   40   London

Newquay   11   12

7   21   Brighton

16

22

Abbeys

Shap Abbey
Shap Cumbria
Tel: 0191 261 1585
[1.5mi W of Shap on bank of River Lowther]
Shap Abbey was founded by the
Premonastratensian order in 1199 and dedicated to St Mary Magdalene.

Animal Attractions

Lakeland Sheep and Wool Centre
Egremont Road Cockermouth Cumbria
CA13 0QX
Tel: 01900 822673
The Lakeland Sheep and Wool Centre is a purpose built centre, which houses and demonstrates a variety of sheep.

Art Galleries

Abbot Hall Art Gallery
Kendal Cumbria LA9 5AL
Tel: 01539 722464
One of Britain's finest small art galleries showing changing displays of contemporary art and touring exhibitions.

Beatrix Potter Gallery
Main Street Hawkshead Cumbria LA22 0NS
Tel: 015394 36355
An annually-changing exhibition of original sketches and watercolours painted by Beatrix Potter for her children's stories.

Arts, Crafts & Textiles

Lakes Glass Centre
Oubas Hill Ulverston Cumbria LA12 7LB
Tel: 01229 581385
Visit the Lakes Glass Centre, Ulverston, to view the skilled glassblowers of Heron Glass.

Wetheriggs Craft Centre
Clifton Dykes Penrith Cumbria CA10 2DH
Tel: 01768 892733 Fax: 01768 892722
www.wetheriggs-pottery.co.uk
Wetheriggs Pottery is the only remaining steam powered pottery in Britain. Visitors can see all the old workings, the restored steam engine and the potters at work. There's a tea room and shops selling pottery and other crafts. In the seven acres of beautiful surroundings, there is much to observe of the natural world, including a newt pond and collection of rare pigs! There are also children's play areas and a 'have a go' facility, where children can throw thier own pots or paint models.

Sun & Bank Hols 10.00-17.00

Birds, Butterflies & Bees

Eden Ostrich World
Langwathby Hall Farm Langwathby Penrith Cumbria CA10 1LW
Tel: 01768 881771
African Black Ostrich, rare farm animals, adventure and pre-school playgrounds, giant maze, tractor rides and indoor heated soft-play area.

Exhibition & Visitor Centres

Rheged - The Village in the Hill
Redhills Penrith Cumbria CA11 0DQ
Tel: 01768 868000
Named after Cumbria's ancient Celtic Kingdom and recently voted Cumbria's best large visitor attraction 2002.

Festivals & Shows

Grasmere Lakeland Sports and Show

Grasmere Sportsfield Grasmere Ambleside Cumbria LA22 9PZ
Tel: 015394 32127
www.grasmeresportsandshow.co.uk
[M6 then A592. Rail: Windermere 8mi. Plenty of free on-site parking available]
The world famous lakeland heritage and cultural event. Celebrating 800 years of history. Features Cumberland and Westmorland Wrestling inc. 11 stone World Championship. Also includes Inter Family Fun Pull Tug-o-War, Fell Races, Mountain Bike Races, The Scottish Terrier Racing Team, Eagle and Vulture Show, The Adamson Military Band, Elaine Hill Sheepdog Demonstrations, Terrier Show, Trail Hound Puppy Show, Pet Dog Show, Gundog Displays, Soaring Displays and The Wordsworth Trust. Plus Made in Cumbria Marquee, Crafts Marquee, Fairground, 150+ Trade Stands, Beer Tent and Catering. A great family fun day out.
24 August 2008
A£7.50 C(5-14)£2.50
Discount Offer: Two for the Price of One.

Folk & Local History Museums

Dock Museum

North Road Barrow-In-Furness LA14 2PW
Tel: 01229 876400
Built over an historic graving dock, the museum is home to a wealth of objects and information.

Tullie House Museum and Art Gallery

Castle Street Carlisle Cumbria CA3 8TP
Tel: 01228 534781
Discover the tales of the "Border Reivers" (robbers or bandits), walk along a replica of Hadrian's Wall and sit on a Roman saddle!

Forests & Woods

Grizedale Forest Park Visitor Centre

Grizedale Forest Park Grizedale Cumbria LA22 0QJ
Tel: 01229 860010
Several waymarked walks include the Silurian Way (9 mile trail) and the wheelchair friendly Ridding Wood trail, both feature sculpture.

Whinlatter Forest Park

Braithwaite Keswick Cumbria CA12 5TW
Tel: 017687 78469
A network of forest walks for all ages and abilities, cycling, the Rabbit Run and Foxtrot children's trails, adventure playground and Giant Badger Sett.

Heritage & Industrial

Cumberland Pencil Museum

Southey Works Great Bridge Keswick Cumbria CA12 5NG
Tel: 01768 773626
Following the discovery of graphite in nearby Seathwaite Valley, Keswick became the site of the world's first pencil factory. This museum explores the history of the pencil and pencil making. Exhibits include the world's largest coloured pencil and pencil making machinery.

Sellafield Visitors Centre

Sellafield Seascale Cumbria CA20 1PG
Tel: 019467 27027
Designed to inform and entertain the whole family, the Centre features 'hands-on' interactive scientific experiments, intriguing shows and fascinating displays of technology.

Historical

Brougham Hall
Brougham Penrith Cumbria CA10 2DE
Tel: 01768 868184
This thirteenth century historic home features
craft workshops, a tea room and a gift shop.

Carlisle Castle
The Castle Carlisle Cumbria CA3 8UR
Tel: 01228 591922
A massive Norman keep contains an exhibition
on the history of the castle.
1 Mar-30 Sept daily

Isel Hall
Isel Cockermouth Cumbria CA13 0QG

[3.5mi NE of Cockermouth]

Isel Hall is an Elizabethan Range, on a Norman
foundation with a fortified Pele Tower. The whole
dominates the landscape in its magical setting
above the river Derwent. The gardens drop
down to the river and beyond is the eleventh-
century Church, with Skiddaw behind. The site
has been continuously occupied since Norman
times and was passed from the original owners
the Engaynes to the present owner through the
Leigh and Lawson families. The last male
Lawson, Sir Wilfrid, died in 1936 when it passed
to his nephew and then cousin Mrs Margaret
Austen-Leigh and then the present owner.

*Mon only. Last Mon Mar-first Mon Oct 14.00-
16.00. Parties other times by arrangement*
A£4.00 C£2.00. Free to HHA members

Mirehouse Historic House and Gardens
Keswick Cumbria CA12 4QE
Tel: 017687 72287
Mirehouse is a family run historic house open to
visitors to enjoy its strong literary connections,
live piano music and children's activities.

Literature & Libraries

Wordsworth House
Main Street Cockermouth Cumbria CA13 9RX
Tel: 01900 824805
The Georgian town house where William
Wordsworth was born in 1770. Several rooms
contain some of the poet's personal effects.

Wordsworth Trust
Dove Cottage Grasmere Ambleside Cumbria
LA22 9SH
Tel: 015394 35544
Award-winning museum which displays the
Wordsworth Trust's unique collection of manu-
scripts, books and paintings interpreting the life
and work of Wordsworth.

Music & Theatre Museums

Laurel and Hardy Museum
4c Upper Brook Street Ulverston LA12 7BH
Tel: 01229 582292
The world famous museum devoted to Laurel
and Hardy in Ulverston, the town where Stan
was born on 16th June 1890.

Nature & Conservation Parks

Lake District Visitor Centre at Brockhole
Windermere Cumbria LA23 1LJ
Tel: 01539 446601
Outstanding setting on the shores of Lake
Windermere. 30 acres of award-winning gar-
dens and grounds.

68 England: Cumbria

On the Water

Ullswater 'Steamers'
The Pier House Glenridding CA18 1SW
Tel: 017684 82229
[15min from M6 J40 to Pooley Bridge. Piers at Pooley Bridge, Howtown and Glenridding]
Undoubtedly the best way to enjoy 'England's most beautiful lake',

Windermere Lake Cruises
Bowness Promenade (also at Ambleside & Lakeside) Bowness-on Windermere LA23 3HQ
Tel: 015394 43360
Vessels take you to local visitor attractions and most vessels have bars and coffee shops.

Places of Worship

Carlisle Cathedral
7 The Abbey Castle Street Carlisle CA3 8TZ
Tel: 01228 548151
Founded in 1122 as a Norman Priory for Augustinian canons. The chancel roof is magnificent & the cathedral features an exquisite east window.

Railways

South Tynedale Railway
The Railway Station Hexham Road Alston Cumbria CA9 3JB
Tel: 01434 381696
See the South Tyne valley. Spend a little time at Kirkhaugh.

Sealife Centres & Aquariums

Aquarium of the Lakes
Lakeside Newby Bridge Cumbria LA12 8AS
Tel: 015395 30153
Uncover the secret world of the lakes at Britain's unique freshwater aquarium.

Theme & Adventure Parks

Go Ape! High Wire Forest Adventure (Whinlatter Forest, Cumbria)
Whinlatter Forest Park Whinlatter Braithwaite Keswick Cumbria CA12 5TW
Tel: 0845 643 9245
www.goape.co.uk

[From Keswick take the A66 W towards Cockermouth. At Braithwaite turn W onto the B5292 for Lorton follow the visitor centre sign-posts]

Take to the trees and experience an exhilarating course of rope bridges, Tarzan swings and zip-slides up to 40 feet above the ground! Share approximately three exciting hours of fun and adventure, which you'll be talking about for days. Book online and watch people Go Ape! at www.goape.co.uk. Minimum height 1.4m. Maximum weight 130 kg (20.5 stone). Under-18s must be accompanied by a participating adult. One adult can supervise either two children (where one or both of them is under 16 years old) or up to five 16-17 year olds. Pre-booking is essential to avoid disappointment. Book online or by telephone (there is a £1.00 booking fee on all telephone bookings).

14 Mar-31 Oct. (Closed Mons during term-time). Nov Sat-Sun Dec Sat-Sun TBC please visit www.goape.co.uk. Closed Jan

Gorillas (18yrs+) £25.00, Baboons (10-17yrs) £20.00

Discount Offer: £5.00 off per person.

Go Ape! High Wire Forest Adventure (Grizedale Forest, Cumbria)

Grizedale Forest Visitor Centre Grizedale Hawkshead Cumbria LA22 OQJ
Tel: 0845 643 9245
www.goape.co.uk

[Nr Hawkshead on Satterthwaite Rd. Plenty of on-site parking available]

Take to the trees and experience an exhilarating course of rope bridges, Tarzan swings and zip-slides up to 40 feet above the ground! Share approximately three exciting hours of fun and adventure, which you'll be talking about for days. Book online and watch people Go Ape! at www.goape.co.uk. Minimum height 1.4m. Maximum weight 130 kg (20.5 stone). Under-18s must be accompanied by a participating adult. One adult can supervise either two children (where one or both of them is under 16 years old) or up to five 16-17 year olds. Pre-booking is essential to avoid disappointment. Book online or by telephone (there is a £1.00 booking fee on all telephone bookings).

9-11, 14-18 & 20-24 Feb; 14 Mar-31 Oct daily. Nov Sat-Sun. Dec Sat-Sun TBC please visit www.goape.co.uk. Closed Jan

Gorillas (18yrs+) £25.00 (£27.00 Saturdays), Baboons (10-17yrs) £20.00

Discount Offer: £5.00 off per person.

World of Beatrix Potter

The Old Laundry Crag Brow Bowness-On-Windermere Windermere Cumbria LA23 3BX
Tel: 015394 88444
In an indoor recreation of the Lakeland country-side, complete with sights, sounds and smells. Learn the story of Beatrix Potter's life.

Transport Museums

Cars of the Stars Motor Museum
Standish Street Keswick Cumbria CA12 5LS
Tel: 01768 773757
Film set displays and vehicles from Mad Max, Magnum, Batmobiles, Noddy, Postman Pat, The A Team, FAB1, James Bond, Chitty Chitty Bang Bang and Del Boy's Van.
Feb-Dec

Wildlife & Safari Parks

Trotters World of Animals
Coalbeck Farm Bassenthwaite Keswick Cumbria CA12 4RD
Tel: 017687 76239
Trotters World of Animals is home to hundreds of friendly animals including lemurs, wallabies and other exotic animals.

Zoos

Lakeland Wildlife Oasis
Hale Milnthorpe Cumbria LA7 7BW
Tel: 015395 63027
Educational, yet great fun, our exhibits range from chameleons to computers; from microscopes to meerkats and include creatures rarely seen in captivity, such as flying foxes and poison arrow frogs.

South Lakes Wild Animal Park
Crossgates Dalton-in-Furness Cumbria LA15 8JR
Tel: 01229 466086
The rolling 17 acres of South Lake Wild Animal Park are home to some of the rarest animals on earth.

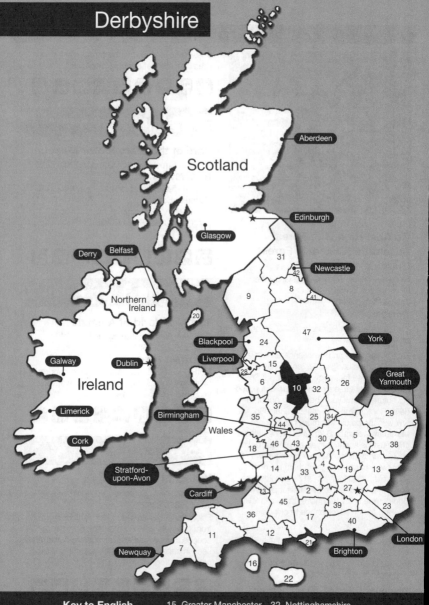

Derbyshire

Scotland

Aberdeen

Edinburgh

Glasgow

Newcastle

Derry

Belfast

Northern
Ireland

31

42

8

41

9

Blackpool

47

York

Liverpool

24

Galway

Dublin

15

Great
Yarmouth

Ireland

28

6

10

32

26

Limerick

37

29

Birmingham

35

44

25

34

Cork

Wales

18

46

43

30

5

38

Stratford-
upon-Avon

14

33

4

1

19

13

Cardiff

13

2

27

London

45

39

23

36

17

40

11

12

21

Brighton

Newquay

7

16

22

Animal Attractions

Chestnut Centre, Otter, Owl and Wildlife Park
Castleton Road Chapel-en-le-Frith High Peak Derbyshire SK23 0QS
Tel: 01298 814099
One of Europe's largest collections of multi-specied otters and owls, plus other wildlife.

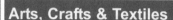

Arts, Crafts & Textiles

Derwent Gallery
Main Road Grindleford Hope Valley Derbyshire S32 2JN
Tel: 01433 630458
The gallery displays fine art in a well-lit, open plan space with a mixture of paintings, sculpture and ceramics.

Arts, Crafts & Textiles

Derby Museum and Art Gallery
The Strand Derby Derbyshire DE1 1BS
Tel: 01332 716659
The museum has a wide range of displays, notably of Derby porcelain and of paintings by the local artist Joseph Wright (1734-97).

On a Wick and a Prayer
The Candle Workshop Tissington DE6 1RA
Tel: 01335 390639
An exciting range of candles and other wax artefacts, individually manufactured by hand in a workshop at Tissington in the Peak District.

Rookes Pottery
Mill Lane Hartington Buxton Derbyshire SK17 0AN
Tel: 01298 84650
An original range of terracotta garden pots and planters.

Caverns & Caves

Heights of Abraham - Cable Cars, Caverns and Hilltop Park
Matlock Bath Matlock Derbyshire DE4 3PD
Tel: 01629 582365
Hilltop Park set at a limestone gorge and reached by cable cars.

Peak Cavern
Peak Cavern Road Castleton Hope Valley Derbyshire S33 8WS
Tel: 01433 620285
www.peakcavern.co.uk
[On A625, 15mi W of Sheffield, 25mi E of Manchester, in centre of Castleton village. Plenty of on-site parking available]
The Peak Cavern is the largest natural cavern in Derbyshire, and has the largest entrance to any cave in Britain. A village once existed inside the cave entrance, built and inhabited by rope makers, who carried out their craft in the cave for over 300 years. Today, ropemaking demonstrations are an integral part of every tour. Find out why it is called the devils arse!
All year, 1 Apr-31 Oct daily 10.00-17.00. Nov-Mar Sat & Sun 10.00-17.00 weekdays two tours per day (call for details). Open daily for school holidays
A£7.25 C(under5)£Free C(5-15)£5.25 Concessions£6.25, Family Ticket (A2+C2) £20.00 - extra C£4.50. Joint ticket with Speedwell Cavern: A£12.00 C£8.50 Concessions£10.25, Family Ticket (A2+C2) £40.00 - extra C£8.00. Group rates available on request

Poole's Cavern and Buxton Country Park

Green Lane Buxton Derbyshire SK17 9DH

Tel: 01298 26978 Fax: 01298 73563

www.poolescavern.co.uk

[Just off A515 Ashbourne rd or A53 Leek rd 15min walk from Buxton town centre. Plenty of on-site parking available]

Discover the secret world of caves Limestone rock, water and millions of years created this magnificent natural cavern. Our expert guides will escort you back in time through vast chambers and incredible stalactite formations on a one-hour tour, comfortable pathways with partial disabled access (contact us for details) and lighting throughout. Set in 100 acres of beautiful woodland. Trails lead towards to Solomon's temple, a panoramic viewpoint tower at the summit of Grin Low hill with spectacular peakland views. New visitor centre, shop, exhibition and restaurant open. Also GO APE high wire forest adventure aerial rope course. Fun for all the family. For bookings see www.goape.co.uk.

Open Mar-Nov 9.30-17.00 Weekends in Winter contact us for variations.

A£7.00 C£4.00 OAPs£5.50, Family Ticket £20.00. Group rates & joint Go Ape & Cavern visit discounts. Contact us for more details

Discount Offer: 20% off Adult Admissions (A£5.40).

Speedwell Cavern

Castleton Hope Valley Derbyshire S33 8WA

Tel: 01433 620512 Fax: 01433 621888

www.speedwellcavern.co.uk

[Off A6187, 0.5mi W of Castleton Village. Plenty of on-site parking available]

Visited by boat, this cavern is a vast natural cave and an old lead mine worked in the early eighteenth century. Parties are taken by guides, who explain the full history and mysteries of this subterranean world 840 feet below the surface.

All year daily, 10.00-17.00

A£7.75 C£5.75 Concessions£6.75. Family Ticket (A2+2C) £26.00 (extra C£5.50). Joint ticket with Peak Cavern: A£12.00 C£8.50 Concessions£10.25, Family Ticket (A2+C2) £40.00 (extra C£8.00). Group rates available on request

Treak Cliff Cavern

Buxton Road Castleton Hope Valley Derbyshire
S33 8WP
Tel: 01433 620571 Fax: 01433 620519
www.bluejohnstone.com

[Castleton is situated at centre of Peak National Park on A6187. 16mi from Sheffield & 29mi from Manchester within easy reach of M1 & M6. Plenty of on-site parking available]

Treak Cliff Cavern at Castleton has been a working Blue John mine since 1750 and open to the public as a visitor attraction since 1935. Visitors can see some of the finest stalactites and stalagmites in the Peak District whilst also experiencing the beauty of Blue John Stone. The largest areas of Blue John Stone ever revealed can be fully appreciated by the light of newly installed spotlights. The largest single piece ever discovered can still be seen in situ. This underground wonderland also contains thousands of stalactites and stalagmites plus all kinds of rocks, minerals and fossils. Multi coloured flowstone covers the walls of Aladdin's cave, whilst the most famous formation is The Stork, standing on one leg. The Cavern is enjoyed by visitors of all ages from all over the world. No wheelchair access - walking disabled only. Facilities for partially deaf visitors.

All year, Mar-Oct daily 10.00, last tour 16.20, Nov-Feb daily 10.00, last tour 15.20. Closed 24-26 Dec. Please call for further details of holiday opening times

A£7.00 C(5-15)£3.60 Concessions£6.00 OAPs&Students(NUS/USI)&YMA £6.00, Family Ticket (A2+C2) £19.00

Discount Offer: 10% off Adult Admissions (A£6.30).

Denby Pottery Visitor Centre

Derby Road Denby Ripley Derbyshire DE5 8NX
Tel: 01773 740799 Fax: 01773 740749
www.denbyvisitorcentre.co.uk

[Next to Pottery on B6179, off A38, 2mi S of Ripley & 8mi N of Derby. Plenty of on-site parking available]

A warm welcome awaits you at Denby Visitor Centre. The centre has an attractive cobbled courtyard with shops, restaurant and play area. Activities include free cookery demonstrations, glass blowing studio and pottery tours. There are lots of bargains on offer in the seconds shop; other shops include gifts, Cookshop, garden centre, new Denby Home Store and Dartington Crystal. Factory tours are fully guided which gives a refreshing personal touch to the experience. Tours of the working factory and also a Craftroom Tour available. Here you find out about Denby stoneware past and present then have a go at painting a Denby plate with glaze and making a clay souvenir to take home. This tour is suitable for all ages and can accommodate wheelchairs. Please contact us for information on school holiday activities, special events and factory shop offers.

All year. Factory Tours: Mon-Thur 10.30 & 13.00 (excluding factory hols). Craftroom Tour daily 11.00-15.00. Centre open: Mon-Sat 9.30-17.00, Sun 10.00-17.00. Closed 25-26 Dec

Factory Tour: A£5.95 C&OAPs£4.95. Craftroom: A£4.50 C&OAPs£3.50

Discount Offer: Two for the Price of One (full-paying adult).

Peak Village Outlet Shopping Centre

Chatsworth Road Rowsley Derbyshire DE4 2JE
Tel: 01629 735326 Fax: 01629 735128
www.peakvillage.co.uk
Nestling in the hills of Derbyshire's Peak District, the Peak Village Shopping Centre is a great place to spend some time browsing and enjoying the atmosphere. It offers full ranges of children's, ladies' and men's fashions, plus shoes, luggage, accessories, textiles, homewares, toys, cards, sweets, gifts, sportswear, books, and much more. Enjoy up to 70% off brands like Ben Sherman, French Connection, Farah, Wolsey, Adidas, Reebok, Nike, Ecco, Scholl, Clarks, Timberland and Caterpillar in more than 26 great shopping outlets! The Peak Village Shopping Centre also features the 'Toys of Yesteryear Museum,' (where you can re-visit your childhood with old friends), the 'Woodlands Fitness and Beauty Centre' and Massarella's restaurant and coffee shop.

Open daily 09.30-17.30 (Closed 25 Dec)
Admission Free

Royal Crown Derby Visitor Centre

194 Osmaston Road Derby Derbyshire DE23 8JZ
Tel: 01332 712800
The only factory allowed to use the words 'Crown' and 'Royal', a double honour granted by George III and Queen Victoria.

Folk & Local History Museums

Buxton Museum and Art Gallery

Terrace Road Buxton Derbyshire SK17 6DA
Tel: 01298 24658
Journey through time into the geology and history of the Peak District in sevenl settings.

Eyam Museum

Hawkhill Road Eyam Hope Valley Derbyshire S32 5QP
Tel: 01433 631371 Fax: 01433 631371
www.eyam.org.uk

[Off A623 signed R to Eyam on B6521, follow white & brown signs]

Bubonic Plague! Our main theme is the famous outbreak in Eyam in 1665-1666. You will see the world-wide spread of plague, leading to its arrival from London in 1665 in a fatally infected bundle of cloth. The awful symptoms are described, and some very strange ancient cures! Carefully researched stories of individual families are graphically told. You see the Rectors Mompesson and Stanley discussing the quarantining of the village, and the dreadful last days of Plague victim John Daniel. We go on to show how the village recovered. Silk, cotton, agriculture, shoes, lead and fluorspar mining, and quarrying played their part in Eyam's subsequent history. We end with a display of fine local minerals and fossils. A 30 seat lecture room is available for talks to pre-booked parties. There is wheelchair access to the ground floor, and a stairlift is available.

18 Mar-2 Nov Tue-Sun & Bank Hol 10.00-16.30
A£1.75 C&OAPs£1.25, Family Ticket £5.00.
Group rates available on request

Sir Richard Arkwright's Masson Mills

Working Textile Museum Derby Road Matlock Bath Derbyshire DE4 3PY
Tel: 01629 581001 Fax: 01629 581001
www.massonmills.co.uk

[On A6 0.5mi S of Matlock Bath. Rail: 1mi. Bus stop directly outside. Plenty of on-site parking available]

Sir Richard Arkwright's Masson Mills were built in 1783 on the banks of the River Derwent at Matlock Bath, Derbyshire. These beautifully restored mills are recognised as the best surviving example of an eighteenth-century cotton mill and are the finest and best preserved example of one of the Arkwright's mills. They now house a shopping village and a fascinating Working Textile Museum illustrating Arkwright's Legacy, where you can experience the genuine atmosphere of Masson Mills and see authentic historic textile machinery spinning yarn and weaving cloth. Masson Mills form the Northern Gateway to the Derwent Valley Mills World Heritage Site.

Working Textile Museum: All year Mon-Fri 10.00-16.00 Sat 11.00-17.00 Sun 11.00-16.00. Closed Christmas Day & Easter Day

A£2.50 C(5-16)£1.50 Concessions£2.00, Family Ticket £6.50. School Groups C£1.00. Group rate (30+): A£2.00

Discount Offer: Two for the Price of One (full-paying adult).

Strutt's North Mill Museum and Visitor Centre

Derwent Valley Visitor Centre North Mill Bridgefoot Belper Derbyshire DE56 1YD
Tel: 01773 880474 Fax: 01773 880474
www.belpernorthmill.org.uk

[Centre of Belper at " The Triangle" Junction of A6 and A517 (Ashbourne) roads. Plenty of on-site parking available]

Strutt's North Mill and Visitor Centre is the gateway to the Derwent Valley Mills World Heritage Site. Built in 1804, William Strutt's technologically advanced 'fire-proof' mill shows by displays and original machinery the history and process of cotton spinning, the story of framework knitting, 'Brettles' renowned silk and cotton hosiery collection, Derbyshire's unique chevening and nailmaking. Leaders of the Industrial Revolution, the Strutt family changed Belper into a thriving industrial town. Our trained guides provide entertaining and informative tours, or we have self-guided audio handsets. Children can count the 'mill mice' and earn a certificate and a treat. The mill shop has books, gifts, drinks and snacks, and the adjacent renowned River Gardens has a playground, boating on the river and a bandstand.

All year Mar-Oct Wed-Sun & Bank Hol Mons 13.00-17.00, Nov-Feb Sat-Sun, 26 Dec & 1st Jan. Pre-booked groups at other times
A£3.00 C(7-16)£2.00 Concessions£2.50, Family Ticket £8.50

Discount Offer: Two for the Price of One (full-paying adult).

Historical

Chatsworth House
Bakewell Derbyshire DE45 1PP
Tel: 01246 582204/565300
Chatsworth is the palatial home of the Duke and
Duchess of Devonshire and has one of the rich-
est collections of fine and decorative arts in pri-
vate hands.

Eyam Hall
Eyam Hope Valley Derbyshire S32 5QW
Tel: 01433 631976
Seventeenth-century house with collections of
portraits, tapestries, costumes and family mem-
orabilia.

Hardwick Hall
Doe Lea Chesterfield Derbyshire S44 5QJ
Tel: 01246 850430
One of Britain's greatest (and most complete)
Elizabethan houses. With sixteenth and seven-
teenth-century tapestries, parkland, herb gar-
dens and rare breeds of cattle and sheep.

Sudbury Hall and the National Trust Museum of Childhood
Sudbury Ashbourne Derbyshire DE6 5HT
Tel: 01283 585305
Late seventeenth-century house with sumptu-
ous interiors and the Museum of Childhood,
where you can take a fresh look at childhood.
You can also uncover life 'below stairs' with
'Meet the Butler' tours.

Mining

Peak District Mining Museum and Temple Mine
The Pavilion Matlock Bath Matlock Derbyshire
DE4 3NR
Tel: 01629 583834
Museum explains the history of Derbyshire's
lead industry from Roman times to present.

Nature & Conservation Parks

Upper Derwent Reservoirs
Fairholmes Visitor Centre Bamford Hope Valley
The Peak District Derbyshire S33 0AQ
Tel: 01433 650953
Ladybower, Derwent and Howden reservoirs
with woodland and lakeside walks.

On the Water

Carsington Water Reservoir
Carsington Ashbourne Derbyshire DE6 1ST
Tel: 01629 540696
A local centre for outdoor activities.

Places of Worship

Derby Cathedral
Derby Derbyshire DE1 3DT
Tel: 01332 341201
The current building is the smallest cathedral in
England.

Sealife Centres & Aquariums

Matlock Bath Aquarium and Hologram Gallery
110 North Parade Matlock Bath Matlock
Derbyshire DE4 3NS
Tel: 01629 583624
An aquarium, hologram gallery, a petrifying well
and a gemstone and fossil collection.

Sporting History Museums

Donington Grand Prix Collection
Donington Park Castle Donington Derby
Derbyshire DE74 2RP
Tel: 01332 811027
The world's largest collection of Grand Prix rac-
ing cars, with 130 exhibits within five halls.

Theme & Adventure Parks

Go Ape! High Wire Forest Adventure (Buxton, Derbyshire)
Poole's Cavern Park Green Lane Buxton Derbyshire SK17 9DH
Tel: 0845 643 9245
www.goape.co.uk

[On Green Lane (0.5mi from Buxton town centre). From A6 & A53 follow brown signs to B5059/A515 J & follow Green Lane for 0.5mi. Plenty of on-site parking available]

Take to the trees and experience an exhilarating course of rope bridges, Tarzan swings and zip-slides up to 40 feet above the ground! Share approximately three exciting hours of fun and adventure, which you'll be talking about for days. Book online and watch people Go Ape! at www.goape.co.uk. Minimum height 1.4m. Maximum weight 130 kg (20.5 stone). Under-18s must be accompanied by a participating adult. One adult can supervise either two children (where one or both of them is under 16 years old) or up to five 16-17 year olds. Pre-booking is essential to avoid disappointment. Book online or by telephone (there is a £1.00 booking fee on all telephone bookings).

16-17 & 23-24 Feb, 14 Mar-31 Oct daily, (Closed Mon during term-time). Nov Sat-Sun. Dec Sat-Sun TBC please visit www.goape.co.uk. Closed Jan

Gorillas (18yrs+) £25.00, Baboons (10-17yrs) £20.00

Discount Offer: £5.00 off per person.

Gulliver's: Matlock Bath
Temple Walk Matlock Bath Derbyshire DE4 3PG
Tel: 01925 444888

Offers everything from from Alpine joy in Little Switzerland to high noon in Western World.

Transport Museums

Crich Tramway Village
Crich Matlock Derbyshire DE4 5DP
Tel: 01773 854321 Fax: 01773 854320
www.tramway.co.uk

[J28 M1, signs from A6 & A38, off B5035. Plenty of on-site parking available]

Crich Tramway Village, offers a family day out in the relaxing atmosphere of a bygone era. Explore the recreated period street with its genuine buildings and features, fascinating exhibitions and most importantly, its trams. Unlimited tram rides are free with your entry fee, giving you the opportunity to fully appreciate Crich Tramway Village and the surrounding countryside. Journey on one of the many beautifully restored vintage trams, as they rumble through the cobbled street past the Red Lion pub and restaurant, exhibition hall, workshops, viewing gallery, children's play and picnic area, before passing beneath the magnificent Bowes-Lyon Bridge. Next it's past the bandstand, through the woods, and then on to Glory Mine taking in spectacular views of the Derwent Valley. New Woodland Walk and Sculpture Trail.

9-24 Feb daily 10.30-16.00, Mar Sat-Sun 10.30-16.00, 21 Mar-02 Nov daily 10.00-17.30

A£10.00 C(3-15)£5.00 OAPs£9.00, Family Ticket £28.00. Group rates (10+): A£8.50 C£4.50 OAPs£7.50

Discount Offer: One Child Free.

Devon

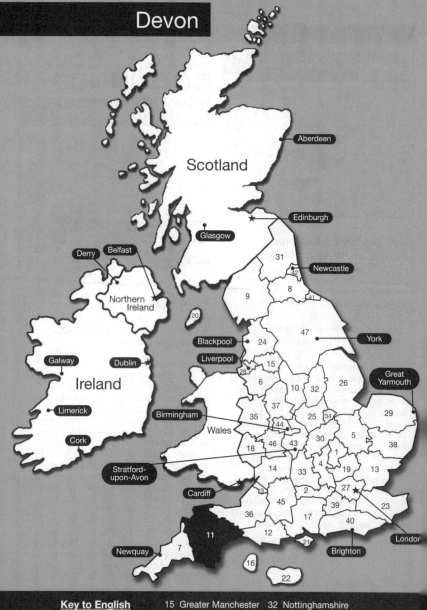

Aberdeen

Scotland

Edinburgh

31

Glasgow

Newcastle

42

Derry Belfast

8

9

41

Northern
Ireland

20

47

York

Blackpool

24

Galway Dublin

Liverpool

15

Great
Yarmouth

Ireland

28

6

10

32

26

29

Limerick

37

Birmingham

35

44

25

34

5

38

Cork

Wales

18

46

43

30

Stratford-
upon-Avon

14

4

19

13

Cardiff

13

33

2

27

London

45

39

23

36

17

40

11

12

Newquay

7

21

Brighton

16

22

Animal Attractions

Donkey Sanctuary, The
Slade House Farm Sidmouth Devon EX10 ONU
Tel: 01395 578222 Fax: 01395 579266
www.thedonkeysanctuary.org.uk

*[At Slade House Farm, nr Salcombe Regis. Do
not drive into Sidmouth or Salcombe Regis, but
look for brown tourist information signs on A3052
between Sidford & turning for Branscombe.
Plenty of on-site parking available]*

The Donkey Sanctuary was founded in 1969 by
Dr. Elisabeth Svendsen MBE. In the United
Kingdom and Ireland, The Donkey Sanctuary
has taken over 12,000 donkeys and also has
major overseas projects in Egypt, Ethiopia,
India, Italy, Kenya, Mexico, and Spain. It aims to
prevent the suffering of donkeys worldwide
through the provision of high quality, professional advice, training and support of donkey welfare. In the UK and Ireland, permanent sanctuary is provided to any donkey in need of refuge.

All year daily, 09.00-dusk
Admission Free

Hedgehog Hospital at Prickly Ball Farm
Denbury Road East Ogwell Newton Abbot
Devon TQ12 6BZ
Tel: 01626 362319
Hedgehog hospital open to the public. A busy
'hands on' and educational farm experience.
Mar-Oct daily

Miniature Pony and Animal Farm
Wormhill Farm North Bovey Newton Abbot
Devon TQ13 8RG
Tel: 01647 432400
See, meet and touch more than 150 animals,
including our famous miniature ponies and don-
keys that foal throughout the spring.

Arts, Crafts & Textiles

Allhallows Museum of Lace and Antiquities
High Street Honiton Devon EX14 1PG
Tel: 01404 44966
The museum has a wonderful display of
Honiton lace, and there are lace demonstrations
from June to August.

Cardew Teapottery
Newton Road Bovey Tracey Devon TQ13 9DX
Tel: 01626 832172 Fax: 01626 834773
The UK's largest ceramic playground attraction
where almost anything "potty" is possible with a
little expert tuition! Crafty gift shop, "seconds"
bargains and home-made Devon food served at
the licensed restaurant. Ten-acre woodland
playground.

Plymouth City Museum and Art Gallery
Drake Circus Plymouth Devon PL4 8AJ
Tel: 01752 304774
Art collection of paintings, prints and Reynolds
family portraits, silver and Plymouth China and
Cottonian Collection of Drawings.

Birds, Butterflies & Bees

Quince Honey Farm
North Road South Molton Devon EX36 3AZ
Tel: 01769 572401
Largest Bee Farm in Britain. View honey bees
without disturbing them in a specially designed
building with glass booths and tunnels.

For great hotel deals call Superbreak on 01904 679999 or visit www.superbreak.com

Caverns & Caves

Exeter's Underground Passages

2 Paris Street Exeter Devon EX1 1GF
Tel: 01392 665887 Fax: 01392 265625
www.exeter.gov.uk/passages

[J30 M5, follow signs for Exeter, use city centre car parks or park and ride scheme]

Exeter's Underground Passages were originally constructed in medieval times, and were built so that underground drinking water pipes could be repaired without digging up the roads and causing disruption to the crowded city. Today visitors can see an interpretation centre with fun and interactive exhibits, a high-speed passages fly through, and full scale passages model. The visitor centre also features the story of water in Exeter and information about the archaeological dig that took place on the Princesshay site, including displays of some of the main finds. The tour starts with a video introduction to the passages, followed by a 25 minute guided tour accompanied by a tour guide. The passages are constricted, and have low vaults, rough floors and dark areas. For this reason they are not suitable for anyone with claustrophobia or for children under 5 years. Wheelchair access is to the visitor centre only.

Low Season, Oct-May (excluding school hols) Tue-Fri 11.30-17.30, Sat 09.30-17.30, Sun 11.30-16.00. High Season June-Sept (incl school hols outside this period) Mon-Sat 09.30-17.30 Sun 10.30-16.00

A£5.00 C£3.50 Concessions £4.00, Family Ticket(A2+C3) £15.00

Country Parks & Estates

Escot Gardens, Maze and Fantasy Woodland

Escot Fairmile Nr Ottery St Mary Devon EX11 1LU
Tel: 01404 822188 Fax: 01404 822903
www.escot-devon.co.uk

[0.5mi off A30 Exeter to Honiton Rd. From Exeter exit at Pattesons Cross & follow signs. From Honiton, exit at Iron Bridge & follow 'Fairmile' signs. Plenty of on-site parking available]

Originally laid out in the eighteenth century as 220 acres of Capability Brown parkland and gardens, here you'll find an ark-full of animals with woodland paths and trails and everywhere beautiful flowers, shrubs and magnificent champion trees. A free visitor map will guide you to the 4,000-Beech Hedge Maze, a real challenge with its five hedge-leaping bridges and stunning central look-out tower. Then on to the birds of prey with their summertime displays, the otters in their holt, the Pirates Playground, the pets and the red squirrels, and the Aquatic Centre housing one of the best collections of tropical and pond fish in the West Country. At the Coach House you'll find the Seahorse Trust, a gift shop, and the restaurant serving delicious home-cooked meals and cream teas using the very best local produce. We even offer free Escot letter-boxing, an unforgettable nature-based treasure hunt. Escot is unique!

All year daily from 10.00. Closed 25-26 Dec
A£5.95 C(0-2)£Free C(3-15)&OAPs£4.95, Family Ticket (A2+C2) £18.50

Discount Offer: One Child Free

Northam Burrows Country Park

Northam Bideford Devon EX39 1LY
Tel: 01237 479708
A 254-hectare country park consisting of
coastal grasslands, sand dunes and salt marsh.
The Burrows Centre has a small shop and a
exhibition area.

Exhibition & Visitor Centres

House of Marbles

The Old Pottery Pottery Road Bovey Tracey
Newton Abbot Devon TQ13 9DS
Tel: 01626 835358
Museums of glass, games, marbles and Bovey
Pottery. See glass blowing.

Quay House Visitor Centre

46 The Quay Exeter Devon EX2 4AN
Tel: 01392 271611 Fax: 01392 265625
www.exeter.gov.uk/visiting
Exeter's Historic Quayside described in lively
displays and illustrations. Also see 'Exeter:
2000 Years of History', an exciting audio-visual
presentation of the City from Roman times to
the present day. Partial disabled and pushchair
access, please call for further details.

*1 Apr-end Oct daily 10.00-17.00, Nov-Mar Sat-
Sun 11.00-16.00. Group visits welcomed by prior
arrangement*
Admission Free

Yelverton Paperweight Centre

4 Buckland Terrace Leg O'Mutton Corner
Yelverton Devon PL20 6AD
Tel: 01822 854250

A permanent exhibition of hundreds of glass
paperweights. With a range on sale.
Apr-Oct daily

Factory Outlets & Tours

Dartington Crystal

Linden Close Torrington Devon EX38 7AN
Tel: 01805 626242 Fax: 01805 626263
www.dartington.co.uk

*[At intersection of routes between Barnstaple,
Plymouth, Bideford, Exeter & South Molton, in
centre of Torrington. Follow brown tourist signs.
Rail: Exeter St. Davids change for Barnstaple,
taxis available from here. Plenty of on-site parking
available]*
Dartington Crystal is internationally famous for
it's beautiful, handmade glassware. Visitors to
the factory will be fascinated to watch the highly
skilled craftsmen blowing and shaping crystal,
perfecting an art form of 3,000 years in the
making. Discover the history of glass and the
unique Dartington story in the popular visitor
centre, or have fun and get hands-on in the
family activity area. You can also visit our glass,
gift and Edinburgh Woollen Mill shops for great
bargains at factory prices or simply relax in our
Café.
*All year Visitors Centre and Shops: Mon-Fri
09.30-17.00,Sat 10.00-17.00, Sun 10.00-16.00.
Factory Tour: Mon-Fri 09.30-17.00 (last tour
15.15) Restaurant: Mar-Oct 09.30-16.00, Nov-
Feb 10.30-15.30. *Tour times, opening times and
demonstrations may be subject to change without
notice, please call for Bank Hols opening times*
A£5.00 C(0-16)£Free OAPs£4.00

**Discount Offer: Two for the Price of
One**

Folk & Local History Museums

Sidmouth Museum

Hope Cottage Church Street Sidmouth Devon
EX10 8LY
Tel: 01395 516139
Situated in the Hope Cottage by the Parish
Church, the museum portrays the rich and varied history of this lovely regency town.
Highlights of the collection include Regency
prints, old photographs, Victoriana, costume,
lace and artefacts of famous residents. A new
land and man room depicts the geology and
archaeology of the area. The world heritage
coast is fully explained in these exhibits.
Museum staff lead guided tours of the town on
Tuesdays and Thursday leaving the museum at
10.15 and Jurassic Coast on Wednesday at
10.15. Please call the museum for more info.
*22 Mar-25 Oct, Mon 14.00-16.30, Tues-Sat
10.00-12.30 & 14.00-16.30*
A&OAPs£1.50 C£Free

Food & Drink

Pack O' Cards Family Pub and Museum

High Street Combe Martin Ilfracombe Devon
EX34 0ET
Tel: 01271 882 300
Built in the seventeenth-century using the win-
nings of a card game, this Grade II Ancient
Monument was constructed to resemble a deck
of cards. Selection of real ales and food.

Forests & Woods

Becky Falls Woodland Park

Manaton Bovey Tracey Devon TQ13 9UG
Tel: 01647 221259
A unique mix of animals and adventure, world
famous waterfalls and ancient woodland.

Gardens & Horticulture

RHS Garden Rosemoor

Great Torrington Devon EX38 8PH
Tel: 01805 624067 Fax: 01805 624717
www.rhs.org.uk/rosemoor
*[1mi SE of Great Torrington on A3124 (formerly
B3220)]*
Come and see this enchanting 65 acre garden
set in the beautiful Torridge Valley. Whatever the
season, Rosemoor is a unique place that people return to time and again for ideas, inspiration or simply to enjoy a relaxing day out. From
the Formal Garden to Lady Anne's original
Garden, there is something for everyone.
Rosemoor also holds over 80 exciting events
throughout the year. Licensed Restaurant, Tea
Room, Plant Centre and Shop on site. No dogs
except guidedogs allowed.
*All year: Gardens & Visitor Centre Apr-Sept
10.00-18.00, Oct-Mar 10.00-17.00. Closed 25
Dec*
A£6.00 C(6-16)£2.00. C(under 6)£Free. RHS
Members + 1 guest £Free. Companion/carer of
a disabled visitor £Free. Pre-booked Groups
10+ £5.00

Discount Offer: One Child Free

Guided Tours

Red Coat Guided Tours

Exeter Devon EX1 1JJ
Tel: 01392 265203 Fax: 01392 265260
www.exeter.gov.uk/guidedtours
Discover one of the oldest cities in England with one of Exeter's Red Coat Guides. Why did the Romans come to Exeter and why is Exeter reported to be one of the most haunted cities in England? There are 18 exciting tours to choose from on your visit to Exeter. All tours are 90mins and free of charge.

Tours held all year daily, except 25-26 Dec
Tours £Free. Charge made for group bookings

Historical

A La Ronde

Summer Lane Exmouth Devon EX8 5BD
Tel: 01395 265514
This quirky, 16-sided house with its fascinating interior decoration and collections was built by two spinster cousins in 1796.

Closed Thu & Fri

Castle Drogo

Drewsteignton Nr Exeter Devon EX6 6PB
Tel: 01647 433306
The 'last castle to be built in England', set above the Teign Gorge with views of Dartmoor.

Clovelly Village

Clovelly Visitor Centre Bideford Devon EX39 5TA
Tel: 01237 431781
Unspoilt fishing village with steep cobbled streets. Donkeys and sledges are the only means of transport. Visitor centre and Kinsley Museum.

Elizabethan House

32 New Street The Barbican Plymouth Devon PL1 2NA
Tel: 01752 304380
A rare, surviving typical Tudor sea captain's timber-framed house, in the heart of Plymouth's historic Barbican.

Hound Tor Deserted Medieval Village

Dartmoor Devon
Tel: 0117 975 0700

[1.5m S of Manaton off Ashburton road. Park in Hound Tor car park 0.5m walk.]

Remains of three or four medieval farmsteads, first occupied in the Bronze Age. Dogs permitted on leads only.

Killerton House and Garden

Killerton House Broadclyst Exeter EX5 3LE
Tel: 01392 881345
Fine eighteenth-century house with costume collection, hillside garden and estate. With tea room, restaurant and plant centre.

Ugbrooke House

Ugbrooke Chudleigh Newton Abbot TQ13 0AD
Tel: 01626 852179
Ugbrooke contains fine furniture, paintings, embroideries, porcelain and an extremely rare family military collection.
Mid July-mid Sept Sun Tue-Thur

Living History Museums

Morwellham Quay

Morwellham near Tavistock Devon PL19 8JL
Tel: 01822 832766 Fax: 01822 833808
www.morwellham-quay.co.uk

[4mi W of Tavistock. Plenty of on-site parking available]

In the heart of the spectacular Tamar Valley, amidst towering cliffs and gently rolling farmland, a lost world lives again. Costumed staff welcome visitors to the bustling 1860s port where history comes alive. All human life is here as you explore their cottages, gardens and workshops, or stroll along the riverside quays, which once housed vessels from all over the world. For many the highlight of a visit to Morwellham is the trip into the George and Charlotte mine. A small tramway follows the riverside before diving into the workings of a nineteenth-century copper mine. An experienced guide and son et lumiere presentations tell the fascinating story of the men who toiled deep underground to extract the valuable minerals that made the Tamar Valley rich. Young or old, there's something for everyone at Morwellham, peace and tranquillity, a beautiful landscape and intriguing glimpses of a bygone age.

All year daily 10.00-17.30. Closed 24 Dec- 31 Jan

Passport Ticket for Mine Train & other activities; A£8.50 C£6.00 OAPs£7.50, Family Ticket (A2+C2) £22.00

Model Towns & Villages

Babbacombe Model Village

Hampton Avenue Babbacombe Torquay Devon TQ1 3LA
Tel: 01803 315315
Set in four acres of beautifully maintained, miniature landscaped garden, the village contains 400 models and 1200ft of model railway.

Natural History Museums

Torquay Museum

529 Babbacombe Road Torquay Devon TQ1 1HG
Tel: 01803 293975 Fax: 01803 294186
www.torquaymuseum.org

[On B3199]

Ranked among the finest in South West England, Torquay Museum is a journey of discovery for everyone. The new interactive Explorers Gallery takes you on a journey around the world to discover cultures, objects and artefacts from the past and present. Experience the sights and sounds of country living in our reconstructed Devon farmhouse, wonder at prehistoric artefacts excavated from nearby Kent's Cavern and detect the real life story behind Agatha Christie, the world famous crime writer born in Torquay. With a programme of temporary exhibitions, events and school holiday activities and workshops there's always plenty to see and do.

All year Mon-Sat 10.00-17.00, Mid July-Sep Sun 13.30-17.00

From 1st April 08: A£4.35 C£2.75 Concessions&NUS/US£3.25, Family Ticket

(A2+C3) £13.50. Group discounts available

Discount Offer: Two for the Price of One (full-paying adult).

Nature & Conservation Parks

Gnome Reserve and Wildflower Garden

West Putford Bradworthy Devon EX22 7XE
Tel: 0870 845 9012
Over 1,000 gnomes and pixies in woodland garden with stream. Wild flower garden with 250 species of wild flowers.

On the Water

Dart Pleasure Craft Ltd

5 Lower Street Dartmouth Devon TQ6 9AJ
Tel: 01803 834488
Five pleasure boats cruising on River Dart. Services operating between Paignton and Totnes.

Stuart Line Cruises

Exmouth Marina Exmouth Docks Exmouth Devon EX8 1DU
Tel: 01395 222144
Sail from Exmouth and enjoy relaxing River Exe cruises along the beautiful East Devon coastline. Sailing throughout the year.

Places of Worship

Exeter Cathedral

1 The Cloisters Exeter Devon EX1 1HS
Tel: 01392 285973
Exeter Cathedral, the 'jewel of the West', is one of England's most beautiful churches.

Railways

Paignton and Dartmouth Steam Railway

Queens Park Station Torbay Road Paignton Devon TQ4 6AF
Tel: 01803 555872 Fax: 01803 664313
www.paignton-steamrailway.co.uk

[Off M5 follow either A380 to Newton Abbot then follow signs for Paignton OR take A379 coastal rd to Paignton]

The holiday line with steam trains running for seven miles in Great Western tradition along the spectacular Torbay Coast to Kingswear, with ferry crossing to Dartmouth. Combined river excursions available 'The Round Robin' and 'Boat Train'. Special trains run for Dartmouth Regatta and the Red Arrows.

Mar, Apr, May & Oct. June-Sept daily

Train only Paignton-Kingswear: Return Fare: A£8.00 C(5-15)£5.50 OAPs£7.50, Family Ticket (A2+C2) £25.00. Train & Ferry to Dartmouth: A£10.00 C£6.50 OAPs£9.50, Family Ticket £30.00. Train, Ferry & 'Boat Train' Cruise: A£14.75 C£9.50 OAPs£13.75, Family Ticket £44.00. Train, Ferry, Cruise & Bus: Circular Trip: A£15.25 C£10.50 OAPs£14.25, Family Ticket £46.00

Pecorama

Underleys Beer Seaton Devon EX12 3NA
Tel: 01297 21542
Includes a display of model railways, a shop, and the Beer Heights Light Railway.

Seaton Tramway

Harbour Road Seaton Devon EX12 2NQ
Tel: 01297 20375 Fax: 01297 625626
www.tram.co.uk

[20mi SE of Taunton. Plenty of on-site parking]

Seaton Tramway runs for three miles through East Devon's glorious Axe Valley. Views of the estuary and its wading birds are unrivalled from the popular open toppers, whilst enclosed saloons maintain comfort during bad weather. The Tramway originated from a miniature system in 1949, which evolved into Eastbourne Tramway (1954-1969). The move to Seaton occurred in 1970, after the company purchased the trackbed of the ex-BR branch. The terminus is in Harbour Road Car Park, Seaton, from where the trams take you through the Axe Valley to Colyton. You can break your journey at the station shop and restaurant, which offer a range of souvenirs, hot and cold food, and of course cream teas! The town centre is a short walk; sights include the twelfth-century church, with its unusual lantern tower. Special events include a Vintage Vehicle Rally, Bird Watching Trips, Santa Specials - and you can even learn to drive a tram!

9-24 Feb, 15 Mar-2 Nov, Weekends 1-9 Mar, 8 Nov-24 Dec

Return Journey A£8.35 OAPs£7.50 C£5.85
Single Journey A£5.55 OAPs£5.00 C£3.90

Discount Offer: One Child Free

Barometer World and Museum

Quicksilver Barn Merton Okehampton Devon EX20 3DS
Tel: 01805 603443

The only barometer museum in the country, with over 300 exhibits dating from 1680 to the present day.

Sealife Centres & Aquariums

National Marine Aquarium

Rope Walk Coxside Plymouth Devon PL4 0LF
Tel: 01752 600301

Discover Britain's Biggest Aquarium with Europe's Deepest Tank! You'll see jewel-bright tropical fish and other marine life around every corner.

Theme & Adventure Parks

Big Sheep

Abbotsham Bideford Devon EX39 5AP
Tel: 01237 472366

A working family farm turned wacky tourist attraction.

Devon's Crealy Great Adventure Park

Sidmouth Road Clyst St Mary Exeter Devon EX5 1DR

Tel: 01395 233200 Fax: 01395 233211
www.crealy.co.uk

[Crealy is Easy to Find - Hard to Leave! 4min from J30 M5, on Sidmouth Rd nr Exeter. Approximate driving times: Birmingham 2h 30min, Bournemouth 2h, Bristol 1h 30min, London 3h, Plymouth 40min, Taunton 30min, Torbay 30min, Weymouth, 1h 25min. Plenty of free on-site parking available]

Devon's Crealy is the South West's favourite family attraction with 3 new ride experiences for 2008 plus free Next-Day Returns throughout the Devon School Holidays! Standing 20ft tall the NEW Meteorite indoor ride will shoot you up in the air, then send you bouncing down to the ground! Prepare for a soaking on the Tidal Wave Terror log flume with NEW dark tunnel to send you zooming through darkness into the water below! Duck, dive and dodge the flying molten-lava-balls of the NEW Battle of the Bears! Explore 100 acres of countryside at Devon's Crealy, with a Coaster, Pirate Ship, Victorian Carousel, Bumper Boats, Summer Soak Zone, River Raiders trail and 75,000 sq. ft of indoor slides and adventures. Maximum Fun is guaranteed at Devon's Crealy where the fun never stops! NOW with free Next-Day Returns throughout the Devon school holidays, you can get twice the excitement from every ticket, plus all kids under 100cms return free all year for the price of 1-day admission! For more information and to book tickets in advance visit www.crealy.co.uk.

15 Mar-4 Nov: Open daily. 5 Nov-31 Mar: Thu-Sun & daily during Devon school holidays. Closed 24-26 Dec & 01 Jan. Reopens 1 Apr 2009

Low season: A&C£9.95, OAPs£6.95, C(under92cm)£Free, Family Ticket (4 people) £9.95 per person. High season: A&C£10.95 C(under92cm)£Free OAPs£7.95, Family Ticket (4 people) £10.50 per person. Winter: A&C£7.95, OAPs£5.95, C(under92cm)£Free. Crealy Club Membership: £35.00. Explorers: (between 92cm-100cm) £9.95 per-person (return FREE to Devon's Crealy all this year for the price of just one day ticket)

Discount Offer: One FREE Go-Kart Ride.

Diggerland (Devon)

Verbeer Manor Cullompton Devon EX15 2PE

Tel: 08700 344437 Fax: 09012 010300
www.diggerland.com

[Exit M5 J27. Head E on A38 towards Wellington for 0.5mi turn R at roundabout onto B3181. Diggerland is 3mi on L-hand side. Rail: Tiverton Parkway (approx 4mi). Bus: 373 From Station to Willand. Plenty of on-site parking available]

Diggerland is the best activity day out for all the family with all activities based around construction machinery. With over 15 rides and drives positioned in an adventure park situation. Experience the thrill of riding in Spindizzy and enjoy the view from the Sky Shuttle. Drive across rough terrain in the Super Track and enjoy a mystery ride in the Land Rover Safari. Test your co-ordination in the JCB Challenges and fasten your seat belt for the drive of your life in the Robots. A full day of fun can be had by all ages with everything onsite including refuelling at The Dig Inn and shopping at the Goodie store. Birthday parties are catered for, so if you fancy a party with a difference then contact us for details. Diggerland welcomes its 4th park in Yorkshire for 2008. Please see our website for more information.

Feb 9-Nov 2, Weekends & Bank Hols plus daily during half-term & school hols 10.00-17.00

A&C£15.00 C(under3)£Free OAPs£7.50. Group rates: (10+) 10% discount, (50+) 25% discount

Discount Offer: 10% off Admission Prices.

Go Ape! High Wire Forest Adventure (Haldon Forest, Devon)

Haldon Forest Park Bullers Hill Kennford Exeter Devon EX6 7XR
Tel: 0845 643 9245
www.goape.co.uk
[On A38, take Exeter Racecourse exit & follow signs for Haldon Forest Park. Plenty of on-site parking available]
Take to the trees and experience an exhilarating course of rope bridges, Tarzan swings and zip-slides up to 40 feet above the ground! Share approximately three exciting hours of fun and adventure, which you'll be talking about for days. Book online and watch people Go Ape! at www.goape.co.uk. Minimum height 1.4m. Maximum weight 130 kg (20.5 stone). Under-18s must be accompanied by a participating adult. One adult can supervise either two children (where one or both of them is under 16 years old) or up to five 16-17 year olds. Pre-booking is essential to avoid disappointment. Book online or by telephone (there is a £1.00 booking fee on all telephone bookings).
14 Mar-31 Oct daily, (Closed Mon during term time). Nov Sat-Sun. Dec Sat-Sun please visit www.goape.co.uk. Closed Jan
Gorillas (18yrs+) £25.00, Baboons (10-17yrs) £20.00. Two for the Price of One until 23rd July 2008

Discount Offer: £5.00 off per person.

Milky Way Adventure Park

Clovelly Bideford Devon EX39 5RY
Tel: 01237 431255
All-weather attraction mix of sheer fun, rides, education and live shows.

Watermouth Castle

Berrynarbor Ilfracombe Devon EX34 9SL
Tel: 01271 867474
Attractions and entertainment for all ages - a unique family day out.
Easter-Oct

Woodlands Leisure Park

Blackawton Dartmouth Devon TQ9 7DQ
Tel: 01803 712598 Fax: 01803 712680
www.woodlandspark.com
[On A3122 8mi from Totnes. Plenty of on-site parking available]
All weather fun - Guaranteed! A full day packed with variety for all the family at one inclusive cost. New Sea Dragon Swing Ship, it's big, it's white knuckle, it's awesome and dynamic. 16 family rides including exhilarating water coasters, Toboggan Run, Avalanche & Bumper Boats. Shout on Dizzy Dune Buggies, Polar Pilots and soft play, big style play zones to entertain big & small kids for hours. Rainy days are great with 100,000 sq.ft of indoor fun. Experience The Empire with 5 floors of challenging tower climbs, rides & slides, hang on to the Trauma Tower as it shoots up and drops down 50 feet! Play the Master Blaster, the zippiest game on the planet, blasting foam balls at buddies. Excitingly different Big Fun Farm - discover amazing night time & day time creatures, insects & birds. Get close to animals, ride big U-Drive tractors while toddlers have fun tractoring round Pedal Town. Live Entertainers everyday in summer holidays.
15 Mar-2 Nov daily 09.30-17.00. Nov-Mar Sat & Sun plus Devon School Hols
A&C£9.75

Discount Offer: 12% off Admissions (makes admissions £8.58).

Victorian Era

Bygones

Fore Street St. Marychurch Torquay Devon
TQ1 4PR

Tel: 01803 326108

Victorian Street, model railway, 'Fantasy Land,'
WW1 trench and a real Anderson Shelter.

Wildlife & Safari Parks

Combe Martin Wildlife and Dinosaur Park

Combe Martin Ilfracombe Devon EX34 0NG
Tel: 01271 882486 Fax: 01271 883869
www.dinosaur-park.com

*[J27 M5. Go W on A361 towards Barnstaple.
Turn R onto A399 following signs for Ilfracombe &
Combe Martin. Plenty of on-site parking available]*

Come and see the UK's only full-size animatronic Tyrannosaurus Rex, along with a pair of vicious interacting Meglosaurs, a Velociraptor and Dilophosaurus 'the Spitting Dinosaur'. Watch out you may get wet! Explore 26 acres of stunning gardens with cascading waterfalls and 100's of exotic birds and animals. Daily sea lion shows, falconry displays, lemur encounters and new for summer 2008 swim the sea lions! Spectacular lightshow, Earthquake Canyon Train ride, Tropical House, Wolf Research and Education Centre, Dinosaur Museum and Cinema and Tomb of the Pharaohs. A great day out for all the family. As seen on T.V.

15 Mar-2 Nov
Please call for prices

Discount Offer: One Child Free (with every two full-paying adults).

Dartmoor Zoological Park

Sparkwell Plymouth Devon PL7 5DG
Tel: 01752 837645 Fax: 01752 837209

Big cat collection, Bears, Wolves, Tapirs, Seal, Llama and various Deer.

Exmoor Zoological Park

South Stowford Bratton Flemming Barnstaple
Devon EX31 4SG
Tel: 01598 763352 Fax: 01598 763352

Covering an area of 12 and a half acres with a waterfall, streams and a lake with penguins.

Zoos

Living Coasts

Beacon Quay Torquay Devon TQ1 2BG
Tel: 01803 202470

Living Coasts features a range of fascinating coastal creatures from wading birds and puffins to penguins and fur seals. There are reconstructed beaches, cliff-faces and an estuary.

Paignton Zoo, Environmental Park

Totnes Road Paignton Devon TQ4 7EU
Tel: 01803 697500

Meet some of the animal kingdom's most fantastic inhabitants. Set in 75 spectacular acres of natural setting.

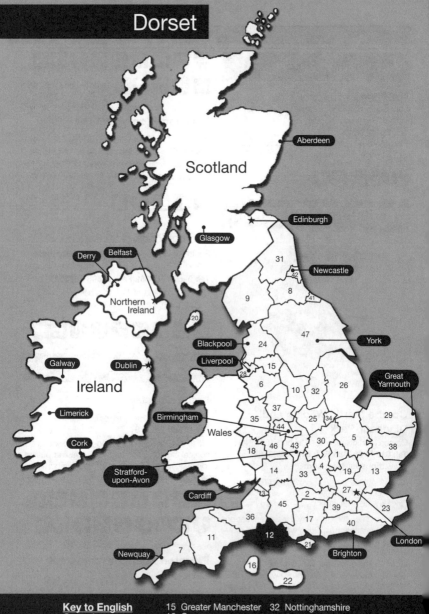

Dorset

Aberdeen

Scotland

Glasgow

Edinburgh

Derry   Belfast

Newcastle

Northern
Ireland

Galway   Dublin

Ireland

Blackpool

Liverpool

York

Great
Yarmouth

Limerick

Birmingham

Wales

Cork

Stratford-
upon-Avon

Cardiff

Newquay

Brighton

London

Key to English Counties:

1 Bedfordshire
2 Berkshire
3 Bristol
4 Buckinghamshire
5 Cambridgeshire
6 Cheshire
7 Cornwall
8 County Durham
9 Cumbria
10 Derbyshire
11 Devon
12 Dorset
13 Essex
14 Gloucestershire

15 Greater Manchester
16 Guernsey
17 Hampshire
18 Herefordshire
19 Hertfordshire
20 Isle Of Man
21 Isle Of Wight
22 Jersey
23 Kent
24 Lancashire
25 Leicestershire
26 Lincolnshire
27 London
28 Merseyside
29 Norfolk
30 Northamptonshire
31 Northumberland

32 Nottinghamshire
33 Oxfordshire
34 Rutland
35 Shropshire
36 Somerset
37 Staffordshire
38 Suffolk
39 Surrey
40 Sussex
41 Tees Valley
42 Tyne & Wear
43 Warwickshire
44 West Midlands
45 Wiltshire
46 Worcestershire
47 Yorkshire

Abbeys

Milton Abbey

Milton Abbas Blandford Dorset DT11 0BZ
Tel: 01258 880489
A fine Abbey Church (Salisbury Diocese) partially completed 15th century on site of 10th century Abbey.

Animal Attractions

Farmer Palmer's Farm Park

Wareham Road Organford Poole Dorset
BH16 6EU
Tel: 01202 622022
Designed for families with children up to 8 years, this award-winning farm park offers a timetable of fun and educational hands-on experiences.

Monkey World Ape Rescue Centre

Near Wareham Dorset BH20 6HH
Tel: 01929 462537 Fax: 01929 405414
www.monkeyworld.org

[Between Bere Regis & Wool off A35, signposted from Bere Regis. Ample on-site parking available]

Since its establishment in 1987, Monkey World - Dorset's internationally-acclaimed ape rescue centre - has helped change the lives of hundreds of primates from around the world. Combining fun with education on primate rescue and conservation, Monkey World works with foreign governments to prevent the illegal trade of primates from the wild. Set in 65 acres of beautiful woodland, Monkey World provides a stable, permanent home for over 160 primates including the largest group of chimpanzees outside Africa, the most important group of orangutans outside Borneo, woolly monkeys, gibbons and many more. Featured in the TV programme 'Monkey Business', the primates live naturally in large enclosures with the companionship of their own kind - a unique opportunity to see these fascinating creatures close up. Keepers hold half-hourly talks with a chance to ask questions. Monkey World also has the South's largest Great Ape Play Area for Kids, woodland walks, a pets corner, café, picnic areas and full facilities for the less-abled.

All year daily 10.00-17.00, July & Aug 10.00-18.00. Closed 25 Dec

A£10.00 C£7.00 Concessions£7.00, Family Ticket (A1+C2) £21.00 or (A2+C2) £30.00. Group rates available on request. School Parties C£5.50, Teacher £Free on (1:6) ratio

Putlake Adventure Farm

Langton Matravers Swanage Dorset BH19 3EU
Tel: 01929 422917
Visitors are encouraged to explores and make contact with a variety of friendly animals in a relaxed atmoshpere.

Archaeology

Dinosaurland

Coombe Street Lyme Regis Dorset DT7 3PY
Tel: 01297 443541
Jurassic Museum, free fossil clinic where visitors can bring in fossils for identification and further information. Guided Fossil Hunting Walks.

Terracotta Warriors Museum

High Street East/Salisbury Street Dorchester
Dorset DT1 1JU

Tel: 01305 266040 Fax: 01305 268885

www.terracottawarriors.co.uk

[At lower end of High St, only 2mins from Dinosaur Museum]

This is the only museum devoted to the terracotta warriors - now regarded as the 8th Wonder of the Ancient World - outside of China. The terracotta warriors created worldwide fascination when 6,000 of them were discovered in a pit in 1974 guarding the First Emperor of China's tomb. The terracotta warriors are unique being life-size and individually modelled in clay to astounding detail. See a unique selection of museum replicas of the terracotta warriors from China, plus reconstructions of costumes and armour and multimedia presentations.

All year daily 10.00-17.00 (closes at 16.30 Nov-Mar). Closed 24-26 Dec

A£5.50 C£3.75 OAP£5.00 Family Ticket £17.00

Tutankhamun Exhibition

High West Street Dorchester Dorset DT1 1UW
Tel: 01305 269571 Fax: 01305 268885
www.tutankhamun-exhibition.co.uk

[On main High Street]

Experience the magnificence and wonder of the world's greatest discovery of ancient treasure. Be there at the discovery, explore the antechamber filled with its treasures, and witness Howard Carter raising the golden coffins in the burial chamber. Marvel at the superb facsimiles of some of Tutankhamun's greatest golden treasures, including the famous golden funerary mask. Finally come face to face with Tutankhamun's mummified body. Featured in numerous television documentaries this internationally renowned exhibition is an amazing experience - spanning time itself. See it now in Dorchester.

All year daily 09.30-17.30. Closed 24-26 Dec
A£6.75 C(under5)£Free C£4.95
Concessions£5.75 Family Ticket (A2+C2)
£21.00

Arts, Crafts & Textiles

Broadwindsor Craft and Design Centre

Broadwindsor Beaminster Dorset DT8 3PX
Tel: 01308 868362
Home to a design led gift shop which houses a selection of gifts and home accessories.

Birds, Butterflies & Bees

Abbotsbury Swannery

New Barn Road Abbotsbury Weymouth Dorset
DT3 4JG
Tel: 01305 871858/871130
For over 600 years this colony of friendly mute
swans has made its home at the Abbotsbury
Sanctuary.

Country Parks & Estates

Durlston Country Park

Lighthouse Road Swanage Dorset BH19 2JL
Tel: 01929 424443
Durlston is a 280-acre countryside paradise,
consisting of sea-cliffs, coastal limestone downland, haymeadows, hedgerows and woodland.

Kingston Lacy

Wimborne Minster Dorset BH21 4EA
Tel: 01202 883402/880413
Elegant country mansion with important collections, set in attractive formal gardens and extensive parkland. With 'Old-Master' paintings,
adventure playground and an Iron Age hill fort.

Moors Valley Country Park Visitor Centre

Ashley Heath Horton Dorset
Tel: 01425 470721
Steam through the park in a traditional way,
explore over 12 miles of tracks on foot or hire a
bike.

Upton Country Park

Upton Poole Dorset BH17 7BJ
Tel: 01202 672625
Upton House was given to Poole by the
Llewellin family in 1957.

Exhibition & Visitor Centres

Streetwise Safety Centre

Unit 1 Roundways Elliot Road Bournemouth
Dorset BH11 8JJ
Tel: 01202 591330
A life-size village built to raise awareness of
everyday safety and good citizenship issues.

Festivals & Shows

Christchurch Food and Wine Festival

Christchurch Dorset
www.christchurchfoodfest.co.uk
Christchurch Food and Wine Festival (running
from the 9th to the 18th of May 2008) is now in
its ninth year. The first weekend of the festival
(9th to the 11th of May) sees the 'Rangemaster'
demonstration kitchen in Saxon Square, with
demonstrations from celebrity chefs Lesley
Waters, Brian Turner and Nick Nairn, plus several chefs from the local area. On Saturday 10th
May and Sunday 11th May, the 'International
Food Market' takes over Christchurch High
Street with hundreds of stalls. There will also be
a 'Kids' Kitchen' in Druitt Hall, with food-tast-
ings, competitions, and quizzes for 5-11 year-
olds. For a full programme of meals and special
events hosted by local restaurants, pubs and
cafés (and details of how to become a 'Friend
of the Festival'), please visit our website.

9-18 May 2008

Cookery demonstrations are free of charge and
prices vary for other events. VIP tickets (including ringside seats and lunch at a local restaurant) are available for some events

Tolpuddle Martyrs Festival

Main Road Tolpuddle Dorchester Dorset
DT2 7EH
Tel: 01305 848237 Fax: 01305 848237
www.tolpuddlemartyrs.org.uk

[Tolpuddle Martyrs Museum & Grounds]

Every summer, the weekend of the third Sunday
in July, the museum hosts the Tolpuddle Martyrs
Festival. This FREE annual family festival combines celebration and tradition, offering both
contemporary and traditional music. Join the
famous 'Parade of Banners,' debates and dis-
cussions, or join thousands of others and listen
to the guest speakers, bands and solo-artists
on stage. On site there are stalls, a children's
fun area, refreshments and beer tents. Festival
Weekend camping is available by pre-booking
only. The main Festival day is Sunday. Please
visit our website for more information.

18-20 July 2008 (Sat&Sun 10.00-18.00)
Admission Free. £5.00 Parking

Folk & Local History Museums

Harbour Life Exhibition

West Bay Bridport Dorset DT6 4SA
Tel: 01308 420997
Located in a converted salt house, the museum
tells the story of Bridport's rope and net trade
and the history of Bridport harbour.

Red House Museum and Gardens

Quay Road Christchurch Dorset BH23 1BU
Tel: 01202 482860
Houses a multitude of fascinating objects which
reflect the social and natural history of the area,
its geology and archaeology.

Tolpuddle Martyrs Museum

Main Road Tolpuddle Dorchester Dorset
DT2 7EH
Tel: 01305 848237 Fax: 01305 848237
www.tolpuddlemartyrs.org.uk

*[Off A35. From Dorchester, Tolpuddle signposted
at Troytown turn off. Continue along old A35
(C34), follow signpost. From Poole/Bournemouth
take A31 then A35 to Dorchester then follow
brown heritage signpost]*

One dawn, in the bitter February of 1834, six
Tolpuddle farm labourers were arrested after
forming a trade union. A frightened Squire's
trumped up charge triggered one of the most
celebrated stories in the history of human rights.
Packed with illustrative displays, this exhibition
tells the Tolpuddle Martyrs story. Discover why
the Judge and Squire were so vindictive - learn
who betrayed the Martyrs in the company of
Death and the Skeleton - hear about their struggle for survival after transportation to Australia -
share the relief of freedom and the pleasure of
the homecoming. Call now for a FREE colour
brochure, or email tolpuddle@tuc.org.uk.

*All year, Summer: Tue-Sat 10.00-17.00, Sun
11.00-17.00. Winter: Thur-Sat 10.00-16.00, Sun
11.00-16.00. Open Bank Hols. Closed Mons &
Dec 18 - Jan 4 incl*
Admission Free

Gardens & Horticulture

Blue Pool
Furzebrook Road Furzebrook nr Wareham
Dorset BH20 5AR
Tel: 01929 551408
The Blue Pool at Furzebrook was once a claypit, which accounts for a rare phenomenon that has attracted visitors from across the world.

Compton Acres Gardens
164 Canford Cliffs Road Poole Dorset
BH13 7ES
Tel: 01202 700778 Fax: 01202 707537
www.comptonacres.co.uk

[On B3065. Plenty of on-site parking available]

Compton Acres - the South's finest privately owned gardens. Spectacular gardens, fine food and drink and a fantastic shopping experience. Compton Acres invites you to escape to a different world. In addition to ten acres of themed gardens, there are exciting shopping opportunities, restaurants, and a host of exhibitions and events happening throughout the year. You'll experience a day to remember, and there's something for everyone to enjoy - plus free parking.

All year daily. Summer: 09.00-18.00. Winter: 10.00-16.00. Closed 25 & 26 Dec. Last Admission: Summer 17.00, Winter 15.00
A£6.95 C£3.95 Concession£6.45, Family Ticket (A2+C3) £17.00

Discount Offer: Two for the Price of One (full-paying adult).

Heritage & Industrial

Mill House Cider Museum and Dorset Clock Collection
Moreton Road Owermoigne Dorchester Dorset DT2 8HZ
Tel: 01305 852220
The Cider Museum traces the heritage of cider-making in Dorset, with displays of antique presses and other traditional equipment dating as far back as the eighteenth century. The clock collection focusses on the "Golden Age" of clock making in Dorset, from the late seventeenth to the nineteenth century.

Historical

Chettle House
Chettle Blandford Forum Dorset DT11 8DB
Tel: 01258 830858
This small country house was designed by Thomas Archer, and is praised as a fine example of the English Baroque.

Corfe Castle
The Square Corfe Castle Wareham Dorset BH20 5EZ
Tel: 01929 481294
A thousand-year-old castle (an iconic survivor of the English Civil War) rising above the Isle of Purbeck. With visitor centre and country estate.

Hardy's Cottage
Higher Bockhampton Dorchester Dorset DT2 8QJ
Tel: 01305 262366
The small cob and thatch cottage where novelist and poet Thomas Hardy was born in 1840.

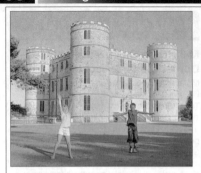

Lulworth Castle and Park

East Lulworth Wareham Dorset BH20 5QS
Tel: 0845 4501054 Fax: 01929 400563
www.lulworth.com

[Off B3070. Plenty of free on-site parking available]

A wonderful seventeenth-century Castle and eighteenth-century Chapel set in extensive parkland. Following a devastating fire in 1929, the castle exterior has been restored to its former glory whilst the bare walls of the interior and many displays reveal past secrets and history. Stunning views across the World Heritage Jurassic Coast from the Castle Tower and Castle lawn. Indoor children's activity room, Courtyard Shop, licensed Stable Café. Adventure playground and Animal Farm. Packed programme of events throughout the year including the Knights of Lulworth in Spectacular Summer Jousting Shows, archery and concerts. See our website for more details.

All year Sun-Fri 1 Jan-28 Mar 10.30-16.00; 30 Mar-26 Sep 10.30-18.00; 28 Sep-31 Dec 10.30-16.00. Closed Sat (except Easter Sat & some special events) Closed 17 Jul & 24-25 Dec 08

Peak (23 Jul-25 Aug): A£9.50 C(4-15)£4.50 OAPs£8.00, Family Ticket (A2+C3)£28.00 or (A1+C3)£18.50 (includes Jousting Shows). Off Peak: A£8.00 C(4-15)£4.00 OAPs£6.00, Family Ticket (A2+C3) £24.00 or (A1+C3) £16.00. Season tickets also available; group rates available on request.

Discount Offer: One Child Free.

Sherborne Castle

off New Road Sherborne Dorset DT9 5NR
Tel: 01935 813182 / 812072
Fax: 01935 816727
www.sherbornecastle.com

[From Bristol & W via Yeovil & A30; from Bournemouth & S via Blandford or Dorchester (A352); from Salisbury & E via A30. The Castle lies off New Rd about 0.75mi to E of centre of town. Plenty of on-site parking available]

Built by Sir Walter Raleigh in 1594 and stately home to the Digby family since 1617, the castle's state rooms reflect a glorious variety of decorative styles, with splendid collections of art, furniture and porcelain. The castle's cellars display Raleigh's original kitchen and a collection of finds from the castle grounds. No photography allowed inside the castle. Capability Brown created the lake in 1753 to give Sherborne the very latest in landscape gardening and today, 30-acres of beautiful lakeside gardens with sweeping lawns, borders and magnificent specimen trees extend around the 50-acre lake in a perfect lakeland setting. Come and explore this peaceful and natural landscape - bring a picnic, walk the dogs, watch the wildlife around the lake. There is disabled access in the gardens and ground floor of the castle. Make a day of Sherborne with its historic abbey and town close by. Enjoy morning coffees, light lunches and afternoon teas plus friendly gift shop. There is partial disabled access in the Castle.

22 Mar-30 Oct Tue-Thur & Sat-Sun 11.00-16.30, (Castle Interior opens later on Sat, 14.00). Open Bank Hol Mons

Castle & Gardens: A£9.00 C(0-15)£Free*
OAPs£8.50. Gardens only: A£4.50 C£Free*. Group rates available for Castle & Gardens only. Private views also available. * a maximum of 4 children can be admitted per paying adult

Natural History Museums

Dinosaur Museum
Icen Way Dorchester Dorset DT1 1EW
Tel: 01305 269880 Fax: 01305 268885
www.thedinosaurmuseum.com

[Off main High East Street]

The only museum on mainland Britain solely devoted to dinosaurs, the award-winning Dinosaur Museum is a treat, especially for children. The museum combines life-sized reconstructions of dinosaurs with fossils and skeletons to create an exciting hands-on experience. Multimedia displays tell the story of the giant prehistoric animals and their enthralling world many millions of years ago. The Dinosaur Museum has twice been voted one of Britain's Top Ten Hands On Museums and is a former winner of the Dorset Family Attraction of the Year. It is frequently featured on national television including Blue Peter, The Tweenies and Tikkabilla. 'Fleshed-out' dinosaur reconstructions - including Tyrannosaurus rex, Stegosaurus and Triceratops - beg to be touched by little hands - and that's encouraged. New reconstructions include the 'sickle claw' Deinonychus and two troodons with feathers. The Dinosaur Museum is part of any Jurassic Coast experience. Its individual and exciting approach has made it extremely popular with visitors.

All year daily Apr-Oct 09.30-17.30, Nov-Mar 10.00-16.30. Closed 24-26 Dec

A£6.75 C(under4)£Free C£4.95 OAPs£5.75, Family Ticket (A2+C2) £21.00

Nature & Conservation Parks

Brownsea Island
Poole Harbour Poole Dorset BH13 7EE
Tel: 01202 707744
Peaceful island of woodland, wetland and heath with a wide variety of wildlife - famous for being the birthplace of Scouting and Guiding.

Police, Prisons & Dungeons

Old Crown Courts and Cells
Dorchester Dorset DT
Tel: 01305 251010
On a visit to the Old Crown Court and Cells you will experience two hundred years of gruesome crime and punishment in a setting little changed over the years. You can stand in the dock and sit in the dimly lit cells where prisoners waited for their appearance before the judge.

Railways

Swanage Railway
Station House Railway Station Approach
Swanage Dorset BH19 1HB
Tel: 01929 425800 Fax: 01929 426680
www.swanagerailway.co.uk
The Swanage Railway runs for six miles from
Swanage to Norden via the historic village of
Corfe Castle. Park and ride facilities available at
Norden.

*Apr-Oct & 22 Dec-1 Jan daily, Feb-Dec Sat &
Sun. Closed 25 Dec*

A£8.00 C(5-15)&OAPs£6.00, Family Ticket
(A2+C3) £21.00

Science - Earth & Planetary

Bournemouth Camera Obscura
The Square Bournemouth Dorset BH2 6EG
Tel: 01202 314231
See the town from a different perspective
through a massive viewing cameras.

Discovery
Brewers Quay Old Harbour Weymouth Dorset
DT4 8TR
Tel: 01305 789007
An independent, self-financed, hands-on
Science Centre. Discovery has over 60 exhibits
covering a wide variety of experiences.

Sealife Centres & Aquariums

Oceanarium
Pier Approach West Beach Bournemouth
Dorset BH2 5AA
Tel: 01202 311993
Explore the secrets of the ocean in an adven-
ture that take you from the flesh-eating piranhas
of the Amazon to the eerie depths of Abyss.

Weymouth Sea Life Park and Marine Sanctuary
Lodmoor Country Park Weymouth Dorset
DT4 7SX
Tel: 01305 788255 Fax: 01305 760165
www.sealifeeurope.com

[On A353]

Weymouth Sea Life Park is unique among the
network of Sea Life attractions in that its numerous marine life exhibitions are not housed under
one roof. They are housed, instead, in separate
pods within a luscious landscape that also
hosts a number of outdoor features. The latter
include otter and seal sanctuaries and the
Park's resident colony of Humboldt penguins.
Indoor displays include the 'Tropical Shark
Nursery,' teeming with black-tip, bonnet head
and other species of sharks, and the spectacular 'Turtle Sanctuary,' with its walkthrough
underwater tunnel. Four amazing children's
rides (a drop ride, a tugboat, a pirate ship and a
seal-themed roundabout) form the core of a
brand new children's play zone, 'Adventure
Island.'

All year daily from 10.00. Closed Christmas Day
Please call for admission prices

Discount Offer: One Child Free

Social History Museums

Dorset County Museum
High West Street Dorchester Dorset DT1 1XA
Tel: 01305 262735
A visit to the museum is a must for anyone interested in the Dorset area and its fascinating archaeology. Over 20 interactives for children.

Museum of Electricity
The Old Power Station Bargates Christchurch Dorset BH23 1QE
Tel: 01202 480467
Set in a genuine Edwardian power station there's fun, interest, nostalgia and novelty for all ages at Britain's premier electricity museum.

Sport & Recreation

Tower Park Entertainment Centre
Yarrow Road Poole Dorset BH12 4NY
Tel: 01202 723671 infoline
Fax: 01202 722087
www.towerparkcentre.co.uk

[Follow signs for town centre, then brown & white signs for Tower Park, just off A3049. Plenty of on-site parking available]

Tower Park in Poole is the south coast's biggest leisure complex offering entertainment for all the family throughout the year. Tower Park has something for everyone whatever the weather.

Tower Park includes; Splashdown - the area's only water flume attraction, tel. 01202 716123; Empire 10 screen cinema, tel. 0871 4714714; Bowlplex - with 24 computerised ten-pin bowling lanes, tel. 01202 715907; Gala Clubs - free membership, tel. 01202 739989; take on the latest Reeltime challenges in video game technology and fruit machines, tel. 01202 716604; Exchange Bar & Grill - offers an extensive American style menu, tel. 01202 738308; Pizza Hut - provides the best pizzas and pastas, tel. 01202 718717; Burger King - restaurant and Drive Thru with varied menu and Kids Club meals, tel. 01202 736761; KFC - serves up the freshest chicken burgers and meal deals, tel. 01202 717173. Nandos 01202 718923, TGI Friday's 01202 746654 Flame Oriental 01202 718615, LA Fitness Gym and Pool 01202 714920 and Chiquitos Mexican Restaurant 01202 711680; Monkey Bizness Opening 18 February 2008 The UK's premier indoor childrens activity centre 0845 8739645.

All year daily. Closed 25 Dec. Opening times of individual attractions do vary, please call for further information

Admission price vary according to season and attraction, please call for more information

Theme & Adventure Parks

Adventure Wonderland
Merritown Lane Hurn Christchurch Dorset BH23 6BA
Tel: 01202 483444
Dorset's number one family theme park is brimming with over 27 rides and attractions.

Deep Sea Adventure and Sharky's Play and Party Warehouse
9 Custom House Quay Old Harbour Weymouth Dorset DT4 8BG
Tel: 0871 222 5760
Family attraction telling the story of underwater exploration and marine history.

Go Ape! High Wire Forest Adventure (Moors Valley, Dorset)

Moors Valley Country Park Horton Road Ashley Heath Nr. Ringwood Dorset BH24 2ET
Tel: 0845 643 9245
www.goape.co.uk

[Follow brown tourist signs to Moors Valley Country Park from A31. Plenty of on-site parking available]

Take to the trees and experience an exhilarating course of rope bridges, Tarzan swings and zip-slides up to 40 feet above the ground! Share approximately three exciting hours of fun and adventure, which you'll be talking about for days. Book online and watch people Go Ape! at www.goape.co.uk. Minimum height 1.4m. Maximum weight 130 kg (20.5 stone). Under-18s must be accompanied by a participating adult. One adult can supervise either two children (where one or both of them is under 16 years old) or up to five 16-17 year olds. Pre-booking is essential to avoid disappointment. Book online or by telephone (there is a £1.00 booking fee on all telephone bookings).

16-18 & 21-24 Feb, 14 Mar-31 Oct daily, Nov Sat-Sun. Dec Sat-Sun TBC please visit www.goape.co.uk Closed Jan

Gorillas (18yrs+) £25.00, Baboons (10-17yrs) £20.00

Discount Offer: £5.00 off per person.

Dorset Teddy Bear Museum

High East Street/Salisbury Street Dorchester Dorset DT1 1JU
Tel: 01305 266040 Fax: 01305 268885

[Corner of High East St & Salisbury St, centre of Dorchester]

See Edward Bear and his people size family of bears in their unique Teddy Bear House. This enchanting family museum has displays from the first teddies to today's T.V. favourites.

All year daily 10.00-17.30 (16.30 Winter). Closed 25-26 Dec

A£5.50 OAPs£5.00 C£3.75 Family Ticket £17.00

Purbeck Toy and Musical Box Museum

Arne House Arne Wareham Dorset BH20 5BJ
Tel: 01929 552018
Set in the grounds on Arne House, a country estate set on the peninsular of Arne on the western shores of Poole Harbour.

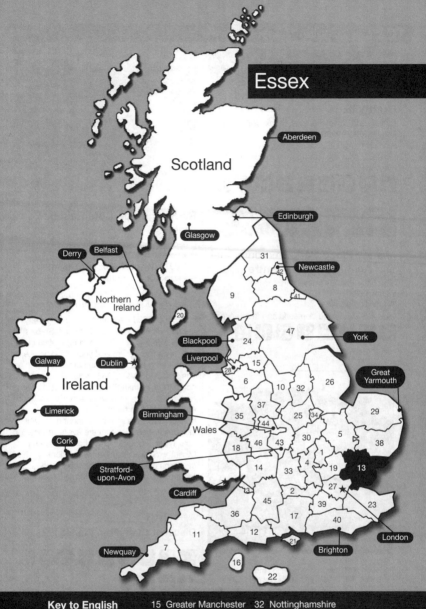

Essex

Aberdeen

Scotland

Edinburgh

Glasgow

Newcastle

Derry

Belfast

31

42

Northern
Ireland

9

8

41

20

Galway

Dublin

Blackpool

24

47

York

Ireland

Liverpool

15

28

6

10

32

26

Great
Yarmouth

Limerick

Birmingham

35

37

44

25

34

29

Wales

18

46

43

30

5

38

Cork

Stratford-
upon-Avon

14

33

4

1

19

13

Cardiff

13

2

27

23

36

45

39

London

11

12

17

40

Newquay

7

21

Brighton

16

22

Agriculture / Working Farms

Barleylands Farm Centre and Craft Village

Barleylands Road Billericay Essex CM11 2UD
Tel: 01268 290229
Animals include a donkey, sheep, cows, goats, pigs, ponies, rabbits, and an array of small furry friends.

Animal Attractions

Mistley Place Park Environmental and Animal Rescue Centre

New Road Mistley Manningtree Essex
CO11 1ER
Tel: 01206 396483
Over 1,500 rescued domestic and farm animals.

Redwings Ada Cole Rescue Stables

Broadlands Epping Road Broadley Common
Waltham Abbey Essex EN9 2DH
Tel: 0870 040 0033 Fax: 0870 458 1942
www.redwings.org.uk

[Off B181 in Broadley Common, nr Nazeing. Plenty of on-site parking available]

In October 2005 Redwings Horse Sanctuary merged with the Ada Cole Memorial Stables, a charity with a long established reputation in the field of equine welfare and years of expertise in rehabilitating and re-homing horses and ponies. The Redwings Ada Cole Rescue Centre is home to more than 50 horses, ponies, donkeys and mules, many of which are being rehabilitated with a view to finding them caring foster homes. There is also a permanent herd, which includes five equines that are available for adoption. These include Boo the handsome Arab, Misfit the Shetland and Louie the donkey. The centre has pleasant paddock walks and guided tours plus a gift shop and information centre.

All year daily 10.00-17.00. Closed 25-26 Dec & 1 Jan

Admission Free

Discount Offer: Free Poster.

Tropical Wings

Wickford Road South Woodham Ferrers Essex
CM3 5QZ
Tel: 01245 425394
Tropical Wings is set in acres of attractive gardens and features one of the largest butterfly houses in the country. Many different species of birds, insects and animals.

Archaeology

Colchester Castle Museum

Castle Park Colchester Essex CO1 1TJ
Tel: 01206 282939
www.colchestermuseums.org.uk
See, hear, touch and discover 2000 years of history in this award-winning Museum. Interactive displays and a year round programme of events make learning fun, bringing history to life. Colchester Castle Museum is the largest keep ever built by the Norman's. This beautiful castle is built on the Roman foundations of the Temple of Claudius over a thousand years ago. The Roman vaults can still be visited today as part of a behind the scenes guided tour, available all year round. The museum is unique and extensive, boasting one of the finest collections of Roman archaeology in Europe. Please visit our website for events.

Mon-Sat 10.00-17.00, Sun 11.00-17.00. Textphone users dial 18001 followed by the full phone number you wish to call.

A£5.20 C£3.40 Concessions£3.40 Saver Ticket(A2+C2)£13.90, tours of the Roman vaults and castle roof are available after admission to the castle, A£2.10 C£1.10, prices valid until 31 December 2008

Art Galleries

Beecroft Art Gallery

Station Road Westcliff-On-Sea Essex SS0 7RA
Tel: 01702 347418
Houses a varied collection, ranging from seven-teeth-century Dutch paintings to contemporary works, as well as a fine collection of local views.

Arts, Crafts & Textiles

Blake House Craft Centre

Blake End Nr Braintree Essex CM77 6RA
Tel: 01376 344123
www.blakehousecraftcentre.co.uk

[Follow brown tourist signs from A120. Plenty of on-site parking available]

The carefully preserved farm buildings at Blake House Craft Centre are centered around a courtyard, which was previously the Blake House farmyard. Wander around the fine variety of art and craft shops in a friendly, relaxed atmosphere, where there really is something for everyone! From antique clothing to animal toys, from Steiff bears to stuffed olives and from electric guitars to elegant fabrics, you can treat yourself or find the perfect gift. Once you've looked around the shops, enjoy a bite to eat, challenge your friends to a round of crazy golf on our new minigolf course and then test your wits against the maize maze challenge! Our licensed restaurant "Timbers" is housed in an eighteenth-century listed corn barn. For coffee, lunchtime snack, full restaurant meal, live band, or private venue, visit Timbers Restaurant. Open 7 days a week and Wednesdays - Saturday evenings! Please call 01376 552553 for bookings.

All year Tue-Sun 10.00-17.00. Individual shop times vary

Admission Free

Country Parks & Estates

Lee Valley Regional Park
Myddelton House Bulls Cross Enfield Middlesex
London EN2 9HG
Tel: 01992 702200 Fax: 01992 719937
www.leevalleypark.org.uk

[Plenty of on-site parking available]

If you enjoy wildlife, sport, countryside, heritage, fantastic open spaces with great places to stay, then the Lee Valley Regional Park is for you. The Park is the regional destination for sport and leisure and stretches for 4,000 hectares between Ware in Hertfordshire, through Essex to the river Thames, and provides leisure activities to suit all ages, tastes and abilities. For more information about the Park and what you can do - please phone 01992 702200 or visit www.leevalleypark.org.uk

Please call for details

Admission price increase from 1 April 2008. See website for details

Discount Offer: One Child Free at the Lee Valley Park Farms.

Weald Country Park
Weald Road South Weald Brentwood Essex
CM14 5QS
Tel: 01277 261343
Features a visitor centre, gift shop, light refreshments, deer paddock, country walks, lakes, horse riding and cycling.

Folk & Local History Museums

Chelmsford Museum and Essex Regiment Museum
Oaklands Park Moulsham Street Chelmsford
Essex CM2 9AQ
Tel: 01245 605700
Local and social history from prehistory to present day, plus temporary exhibitions.

Prittlewell Priory Museum
Priory Park Southend-On-Sea Essex
Tel: 01702 434449
Originally a Cluniac monastery, now a museum of local history and natural history.
Please telephone for opening times before visit

Saffron Walden Museum
Museum Street Saffron Walden Essex
CB10 1JL
Tel: 01799 510333
This friendly museum lies near the castle ruins in the centre of town. Its collections include local archaeology and ceramics.

Southchurch Hall Museum
Southchurch Hall Gardens Southchurch Hall
Close Southend-On-Sea Essex SS1 2TE
Tel: 01702 467671
Moated, timber-framed manor house, 13th-14th century, with small Tudor wing, the open hall furnished as a Medieval hall

Tymperleys Clock Museum
Trinity Street Colchester Essex CO1 1JN
Tel: 01206 282939
Relax in the garden, an oasis of peace in the heart of the town. Tymperleys now houses part of the famous Bernard Mason Collection, one of the largest collections of clocks in Britain. All were made in Colchester between 1640 and 1840 and give a fascinating insight into this specialist trade.

Forests & Woods

Epping Forest Information Centre

Epping Forest Centre High Beach Loughton
Essex IG10 4AF
Tel: 020 8508 0028
Built in 1993 by the Corporation of London, this
attractive brick building provides the visitor to
Epping Forest with an opportunity to see attrac-
tive informative displays relating to the Forest,
and to purchase books, maps and souvenirs.

Hatfield Forest

Takeley Bishops Stortford Essex CM22 6NE
Tel: 01279 870678/874040 info
Fax: 01279 871938
www.nationaltrust.org.uk/hatfieldforest

*[Exit 8 M11, take B1256 towards Takely, sign-
posted from B1256]*

Take a trip back to an age of chivalry, royal
hunts and rebellion! Hatfield Forest is a rare surviving example of a Medieval Royal Hunting
Forest with over 1,000 acres of ancient woodland and pasture to explore. Hatfield Forest is a
Site of Special Scientific Interest and a National
Nature Reserve. If you are looking for unspoilt
open spaces to enjoy then Hatfield is the place
for you. Whether it's the pollarded hornbeams
and oaks, the abundance of wildlife, the nature
trails or a gentle stroll you are looking for,
Hatfield provides it and more! Don't miss the
eighteenth-century 'Shell House', built by previous owners as a magical place to enjoy the
splendour of the Forest. New in 2008 - interpretation at the site of the Doodle Oak.

*Hatfield Forest - All year, dawn to dusk.
Refreshments: 21 Mar-31 Oct, every day 10.00-
16.30. 1 Nov-31 Jan 09, Sat & Sun 10.00-
15.30. Refreshments available daily in School
Hols: Summer 10.00-18.00 Winter 10.00-15.30*

Car park charge for non-members £4.50 (NT
members free - please display car sticker)

Gardens & Horticulture

Cottage Garden

Langham Road Boxted Colchester Essex
CO4 5HU
Tel: 01206 272269
Over 400 varieties of hardy perennials, alpines,
herbs, trees, shrubs, conifers and hedging.

Gnome Magic

New Dawn Old Ipswich Road Dedham
Colchester Essex CO7 6HU
Tel: 01206 231390
Gnome Magic is an unusual treat. Enjoy the
delightful garden which blends into an amazing
wood where the growing number of 500
gnomes and their friends live.

Original Great Maze
Blake House Craft Centre Blake End Rayne Nr. Braintree Essex CM77 6RA
Tel: 01376 553146
www.greatmaze.info

[Follow brown tourist signs from A120 to Blake House Craft Centre. Plenty of on-site parking available.]

The Original Great Maze returns for 2008, but this year it's bigger, better and harder! Sown from over half a million maize seeds, the chal-lenge is on! So come and get lost for a fun fam-ily day out of adventure or a competitive chal-lenge for the experienced maze enthusiast. Many have turned their visit to the maze into an annual event, but don't worry if you are new to one of the greatest maze challenges in the world, there is a lost souls map available and a viewing platform to help you find your way out! When you have conquered the maze, why not take a look around the Blake House Craft Centre, have a round of crazy golf or enjoy a meal in our licensed restaurant, housed in an eighteenth-century listed corn barn. Fun for everyone, whatever the weather.

5 July-7 Sept daily 10.00-16.30
A£4.50 C£2.50 OAPs£3.50 Pushchairs & Wheelchairs Free

Discount Offer: One Child Free.

RHS Garden Hyde Hall
Buckhatch Lane Rettendon Chelmsford Essex CM3 8ET
Tel: 01245 400256 Fax: 01245 402100
www.rhs.org.uk

[A130 follow tourist signs. Plenty of on-site park-ing available]

RHS Garden Hyde Hall provides an oasis of peace and tranquillity far removed from the urbanisation sometimes associated with Essex. Perched on a hilltop, the 360-acre estate inte-grates fluidly into the surrounding farmland, meadows and woodland, providing a gateway to the countryside where you can watch the changing seasons and get closer to nature. Hyde Hall offers a safe, clean environment for children and adults alike providing a fabulous day out whatever the weather! We offer free children's garden trails aimed at encouraging children to learn about nature by going on a treasure hunt around the garden or why not hire a 'Garden Explorers' rucksack at £3.00 (or two packs for £5.00) and you can get digging and discovering with our hands-on activity pack. We also run a number of specific events for children so visit the website for further information: www.rhs.org.uk/hydehall. You can then round off your visit with a well-earned break in our family-friendly restaurant or treat yourself to a little retail therapy in the well-stocked plant centre and shop. Alternatively pack some lunch and relax in our shady picnic area.

All year daily from 10.00. Closing times vary with the season. Closed 25 Dec

A£5.00 C(6-16)£1.50 C(0-5)£Free. Parties 10+ special rates available-booking essential. Carer for disabled visitor and blind visitors free

Discount Offer: Two for the Price of One (full-paying adult).

Heritage & Industrial

Royal Gunpowder Mills

Beaulieu Drive Waltham Abbey Essex EN9 1JY
Tel: 01992 707370 Fax: 01992 707372
www.royalgunpowdermills.com

[Follow A121 (M25 J26) towards Waltham Abbey. Royal Gunpower Mills is straight ahead at crossroads with McDonald's on the L. Plenty of on-site parking available]

Set in 175 acres, the Royal Gunpowder Mills presents its 300-year history to the world. Listed structures and canals combine with extensive woodland, creating a hidden world with a thriving ecology. Take our self-guided nature walk with our map and information sheet, or (if you're feeling less energetic!) take the land train with our knowledgeable guide. For children, there's a special version of our nature walk with animals to spot and games to play that will introduce them to wildlife. Our interactive exhibition is a fun way to learn about history and our 1940s toyshop, general store, and kitchen will show them how children used to live. Our events programme includes the popular 'VE Weekend,' a mix of re-enactments, living history and the legendary Spitfire (performing an aerobic display on the final day). Other family-themed weekends include 'Rocket and Space Event', 'Classic Car Show', 'Jousting Tournament' and the 'Legend of Robin Hood'.

Every Sat-Sun & Bank Hol Mon from 26 Apr-28 Sept 11.00-17.00

A£6.50 C(5-16)£4.00 Concessions£5.50, Family Ticket £21.00

Historical

Hadleigh Castle

off Chapel Lane Hadleigh Essex SS7 2PP
Tel: 01760 755161
A familiar sight from Constable's paintings, this thirteenth-century castle was first built by Hubert de Burgh and has fine views of the Thames estuary. It is defended by ditches on three sides, and the north-east and south-east towers are still impressive.

Hedingham Castle

Bayley Street Castle Hedingham Halstead Essex CO9 3DJ
Tel: 01787 460261 Fax: 01787 461473
www.hedinghamcastle.co.uk

[On B1058 1mi off A1017 (between Colchester & Cambridge), close to Constable country. Easy reach of London and M11. Plenty of on-site parking available]

Hedingham Castle was built in 1140 by Aubrey de Vere II and was the home of the the de Veres, Earls of Oxford for 550 years. The Castle was besieged by King John in 1216, and attacked by the Dauphin of France in 1217. Hedingham has welcomed many royal visitors including King Henry VII, King Henry VIII and Queen Elizabeth I. The Keep stands over 110 feet high with walls 12 feet thick. Most of the Norman architectural features remain around the Keep - especially the chevron stone carvings and the splendid arch, which spans the entire width of the Banqueting Hall and is the widest Norman arch in Western Europe. There are beautiful woodland and lakeside walks and areas where visitors can enjoy a picnic. Unfortunately, disabled access is limited to the grounds. Dogs are

allowed in the grounds if kept on leads. Member of the Historic Houses Association.

23 Mar-26 Oct Sun-Thurs 10.00-17.00. Closed Fri-Sat throughout
A£5.00 C£3.50 Concessions£4.50, Family Ticket £17.00

Discount Offer: One Child Free.

Hylands House

Hylands Park London Road Chelmsford Essex CM2 8WQ
Tel: 01245 605500 Fax: 01245 605510
www.chelmsford.gov.uk/hylands

[Nr Chelmsford, J28 M25 then J15 A12. Follow signposts for Hylands. For House: Use entrance on dual carriageway section of A414 (car park next to house). For Park: use other entrances. Plenty of on-site parking available]

Hylands House is a beautiful grade II* listed building, set in 574 acres of parkland. Visitors can enjoy all of the spectacular rooms in the house, ranging from the exquisitely gilded Drawing Room, to the sumptuously ornate Banqueting Room. The Repton Room on the first floor provides stunning views over the landscaped parkland. The final stages of restoration on the Stable Block (incorporating a gift shop, restaurant, arts and crafts centre and visitor centre) was completed and opened February 2007. Hylands House is also licensed for Civil Ceremonies and can also be hired for Wedding Receptions, Corporate Functions and Private Hire. Hylands Estate is open throughout the year and is a wonderful surrounding for a pleasant walk. Dogs and photography allowed in the park.

House: All Year Sun & Mon. 1 Apr-30 Sept: 10.00-17.00. 1 Oct-31 Mar: 10:00-16:00. Available for hire for weddings, corporate or private functions Tue-Sat. Stables Centre: daily
A£3.50 C(under16)£Free OAPs£2.50

Discount Offer: Two for the Price of One (full-paying adult).

Maritime

National Motorboat Museum

Wat Tyler Country Park Pitsea Hall Lane Pitsea Basildon Essex SS16 4UH
Tel: 01268 550077
The museum documents the history of motorboating concentrating on sports and leisure.
School hols daily

Military & Defence Museums

Kelvedon Hatch Secret Nuclear Bunker

Brentwood Essex CM14 5TL
Tel: 01277 364883
Step inside the door of this rural bungalow nestling in the Essex countryside and discover the twilight world of the Government Cold War.

Natural History Museums

Central Museum and Planetarium

Victoria Avenue Southend-On-Sea Essex SS2 6EW
Tel: 01702 434449
A fine Edwardian building housing displays of archaeology, natural history and local history.

On the Water

Clacton Pier

Clacton-on-Sea Essex CO15 1QX
Tel: 01255 421115

A major entertainment centre with rides, arcades, reptile house and fairground.

Southend Pier

Western Esplanade Southend-On-Sea Essex SS1 1EE
Tel: 01702 215620
Following the tragic fire in 2005, Southend Pier walkway and railway is once again fully open to the public.

Railways

Colne Valley Railway and Farm Park

Castle Hedingham Station Yeldham Road Castle Hedingham Essex CO9 3DZ
Tel: 01787 461174
Housing the largest collection of operational vintage steam and diesel locomotives, carriages and wagons in Essex.

Sealife Centres & Aquariums

Sealife Adventure

Eastern Esplanade Southend-On-Sea Essex SS1 2ER
Tel: 01702 442211 Fax: 01702 462444
www.sealifeadventure.co.uk

[On seafront 0.5mi E of pier]

Just along the seafront from Adventure Island, the Sea Life Adventure themed aquarium is bursting with a unique mixture of education and fun tfor families. Journey through the Sea

Cavern, and the Seahorse Rodeo, wander around the Ray Bay, walk under the waves in Deepwater World, and examine the Sea Nursery. On your journey you will enjoy a wealth of marine marvels from starfish to sharks, piranhas to stingrays and two new attractions 'tottally turtles' and 'Frog fanatical' everyday there is a full programme of demonstrations, talks and presentations. Also, 'Adventure Towers' children's activity centre and Waves Café.

All year daily from 10.00 closing at either 17.00 or 19.00 depending on time of year.

Please see our website for prices

Discount Offer: Two for the Price of One (full-paying adult).

Adventure Island

Western Esplanade Southend-On-Sea Essex SS1 1EE
Tel: 01702 443400 Fax: 01702 601044
www.adventureisland.co.uk

[1hr from central London, on both sides of Southend Pier. M25 J29 then A127 or M25 J30 then A13]

Adventure Island on both sides of Southends pier, is the number one 'fun park' in the south of England, and with over 60 rides and attractions, there's something for the whole family to enjoy. There are four roller coasters including 'Rage' the biggest new coaster to be built in the UK in 2007, with it's 23 metre vertical lift, drop and loop, together with a 360 degree barrel roll. Admission to Adventure Island is FREE 'you only pay if you play' and the best way is with an 'all day wristband' and with a 'band by height' pricing system, Adventure Island is the fairest fun park in the UK, as you only pay for the rides

your height allows you to go on.

Easter Weekend, 29 Mar-7 Sept daily from 11.00, Sept-Mar Sat-Sun & school half-terms. Closing times vary between 18.00 & 23.00.

Please see www.adventureisland.co.uk for Peak and Off-Peak dates. Peak: Riders 1.2m & taller, All-Day Big Adventure Bands (33 rides) £22.00. Riders 1m-1.2m, Junior-Bands (22 rides) £15.00. Riders under 1m, Mini-Bands (14 rides, accompanying adults ride free) £10.00. Off-Peak: Riders 1.2m & taller, All-Day Big Adventure Bands (33 rides) £18.00. Riders 1m-1.2m, Junior-Bands (22 rides) £12.00. Riders under 1m, Mini-Bands ((14 rides, accompanying adults ride free) £7.00. Wristbands are half-price after 18.00 during school holidays, weekends throughout Apr-Oct, and Fri-Sat in Sep-Oct. Book online at www.adventureisland.co.uk to save up to £5.00 off a wristband.

Toy & Childhood Museums

House on the Hill Toy Museum
Grove Hill Stansted Essex CM24 8SP
Tel: 01279 813567
One of the largest toy museums in Europe, housed on two floors.

Wildlife & Safari Parks

Mole Hall Wildlife Park
Mole Hall Widdington Saffron Walden Essex CB11 3SS
Tel: 01799 540400
Set within the grounds of a fully moated Manor house (private) - this wildlife park and butterfly pavilion offers a relaxing day out.

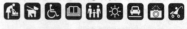

Zoos

Colchester Zoo
Maldon Road Stanway Colchester Essex CO3 0SL
Tel: 01206 331292
Colchester Zoo has over 200 species of animals.

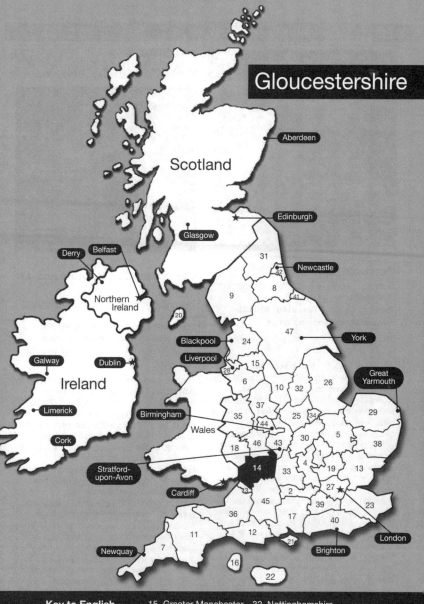

Gloucestershire

Aberdeen

Scotland

Edinburgh

Glasgow

Newcastle

Derry — Belfast

Northern
Ireland

31

42

9

8

41

Galway — Dublin

Ireland

20

Blackpool

24

47

York

Liverpool

28

15

Limerick

6

10

32

26

Great
Yarmouth

Cork

37

29

Birmingham

35

44

25

34

Wales

18

46

43

30

5

38

Stratford-
upon-Avon

14

33

4

1

19

13

Cardiff

13

2

27

23

45

39

London

36

17

40

Newquay

11

12

21

Brighton

7

16

22

Animal Attractions

Cotswold Farm Park

Guiting Power Stow on the Wold Cheltenham
Gloucestershire GL54 5UG
Tel: 01451 850307 Fax: 01451 850423
www.cotswoldfarmpark.co.uk

[J9 M5 off B4077 Tewkesbury/Stow rd. Plenty of free on-site parking available]

At Guiting Power, in the heart of the Cotswolds, lies the Cotswold Farm Park, Britain's first ever Rare Breeds farm to open to the public. Alongside its serious aims of conservation and education, the whole family will find themselves easily entertained whatever the weather. Very much a working farm, there is a comprehensive collection of rare breeds of British farm animals as well as lots of activities for the youngsters; rabbits and guinea pigs to stroke, lambs and calves to bottle feed, tractor and trailer rides, battery powered tractors and good safe rustic-themed play areas both indoors and outside. There is also a gift shop and Cotswold Kitchen. Audio tours are available for adults; a wildlife walk and plenty of space for a picnic. The Cotswold Farm Park also has its own 40-pitch camping and carvanning site, with electric hook-up, toilets and showers, so visitors never have to leave!

15 Mar-7 Sept daily, then Sat-Sun only to end Oct & Autumn Half Term (25 Oct-2 Nov inc) 10.30-17.00

A£6.50 C£5.25 OAPs£6.00, Family Ticket £21.25. Group rates available on request

Discount Offer: One Child Free.

Arts, Crafts & Textiles

Gloucester City Museum and Art Gallery

Brunswick Road Gloucester Gloucestershire
GL1 1HP
Tel: 01452 396131 Fax: 01452 410898
www.gloucester.gov.uk/citymuseum

[Centre of Gloucester, 5min walk from Railway Station]

There is something for everyone with impressive collections. These include a wide range of Roman artefacts such as the Rufus Sita tomb-stone; the amazing Iron Age Birdlip Mirror; one of the earliest backgammon sets in the world; dinosaur fossils; wildlife from the City and the Gloucestershire countryside; and paintings by famous artists such as Turner and Gainsborough. The first floor has been completely re-displayed. The Time Gallery has a range of clocks from the 1680s to the twentieth century, with everything from sand glasses to sun dials. There are fine examples of eigh-teenth-century furniture and ceramics and one of the best collections of eighteenth-century glass in the country. Coins include a rare Viking ingot and a sensational seventeenth-century hoard. There are various interactive activities, including the opportunity to test bank notes and to use the Furniture Explorer to find some of the hidden secrets of the furniture. There is an exciting range of exhibitions throughout the year along with children's holiday activities and spe-cial events.

All year Tue-Sat 10.00-17.00
Admission Free

Nature in Art

Wallsworth Hall Twigworth Gloucester
Gloucestershire GL2 9PA
Tel: 01452 731422 Fax: 01452 730937
www.nature-in-art.org.uk
[On A38, 2mi N of Gloucester. Plenty of free on-site parking available]

Nature in Art is unique. It is the world's only museum and art gallery dedicated to all kinds of art inspired by nature. As well as organising a vibrant programme of temporary exhibitions, we regularly create new displays of our own exhibits. Our collection embraces two and three-dimensional work in all mediums and styles ranging from Picasso to Shepherd. Spanning 1500 years, it contains work by 600 artists from over 60 countries. So whether you prefer exotic oriental treasures or watercolour landscapes, the Flemish masters or contemporary glass, modern abstract interpretations or bronze sculpture - there will be something here for you.You are likely to make some discoveries too! You can also meet an artist as they demonstrate their skills - which could be painting, sculpting, woodcarving or many other art forms (February-November). Homemade snacks and cakes are served in the coffee shop overlooking the sculpture gardens. There are also indoor and outdoor activity areas for children and a well-stocked gift shop with souvenirs and artists materials.

All year Tue-Sun & Bank Hol 10.00-17.00, Mon by arrangement. Closed 24-26 Dec
A£4.50 C&OAPs&Students(NUS/USI)£4.00 C(0-8)£Free, Family Ticket £13.00

Discount Offer: Two for the Price of One (full-paying adult).

Birdland

Rissington Road Bourton on the Water
Cheltenham Gloucestershire GL54 2BN
Tel: 01451 820480 Fax: 01451 822398
www.birdland.co.uk

Birdland is a natural setting of woodland, river and gardens, which is inhabited by over 500 birds; Flamingos, pelicans, penguins (the only group of King Penguins in England, Wales and Ireland), cranes, storks, cassowary and water-fowl can be seen on various aspects of the water habitat. Over 50 aviaries of parrots, falcons, pheasants, hornbills, touracos, pigeons, ibis and many more. Tropical and Desert Houses are home to the more delicate species. Take time out to wander, relax and learn in this tranquil environment and watch the activities of the birds on and around the River Windrush as it meanders through the Park on its journey to the Thames. Dogs are allowed, but must be kept on a lead at all times. Disabled access throughout and toilet facilities. The Penguin Café offers a range of food and beverages in comfortable surroundings; Play area, Picnic areas, Information Centre, Birds of Prey Encounters and much more. Also available Family Ticket, Season Ticket, Bird Adoptions and Educational sheets. See our website for more details e.g. 'Keeper for a Day' or 'Feed the Penguins'.

All year daily Apr-Oct 10.00-18.00, Nov-Mar 10.00-16.00. Closed 25 Dec
A£5.25 C(4-14)£3.25 OAPs£4.25, Family Ticket (A2+C2) £15.50

Discount Offer: One Child Free.

Cotswold Falconry Centre

Batsford Park Moreton-in-Marsh
Gloucestershire GL56 9QB
Tel: 01386 701043
Housing 80-100 individual birds of prey at any
given time, the Cotswold Falconry Centre aims
to be one of the friendliest and most informative
raptor centres in the country. Daily flying displays. Browse one of the many breeding
aviaries, see owls, caracara vultures, eagles and
much more. Tearoom and gift shop.

National Birds of Prey Centre

Great Boulsdon Newent Gloucestershire
GL18 1JJ
Tel: 01531 820286
With over 160 birds of prey, the National Birds
of Prey Centre features 50 different species,
including owls and eagles.

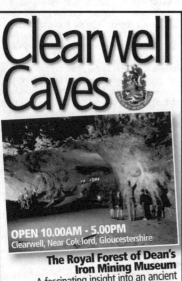

Caverns & Caves

Clearwell Caves Ancient Iron Mines

Royal Forest of Dean Coleford Gloucestershire
GL16 8JR
Tel: 01594 832535 Fax: 01594 833362
www.clearwellcaves.com

*[1.5mi S of Coleford town centre on B4228 sign-
posted from Coleford town centre. Plenty of on-
site parking available]*

Selected as the 'Family Attraction for
Gloucestershire for 2003' by the Good Britain
Guide you will see why when you enjoy a journey of discovery to see how ochre and iron ore
have been 'won' here for over 5,000 years -
from the Neolithic period through to the present
day. The mines were famous for their ochre produced to make pigments for artist's and other
natural paints; red, yellow, brown and purple
ochre is still produced today and sold in the
mine shop. There are nine impressive caverns
to discover, with mining and geological displays
throughout. Visitors will also see the ochre
preparation area and blacksmith's workshop.
Excellent gift shop and tempting tearoom to visit
afterwards. Picnic area. Ample free parking. For
the more adventurous, 'Deep Level' visits can
be arranged for small groups.

*1 Mar-31 Oct daily 10.00-17.00. Christmas
Fantasy; 1-24 Dec 10.00-17.00*

A£5.50 C£3.50 Concessions£4.50, Family
Ticket £16.00

**Discount Offer: One Child Free (with a
full-paying adult).**

Country Parks & Estates

Robinswood Hill Country Park
Reservoir Road Gloucester GL4 6SX
Tel: 01452 303206
Explore the flora, fauna, footpaths and nature trails, then visit the on-site Rare Breeds Farm.

Festivals & Shows

Greenbelt Festival
Cheltenham Racecourse Cheltenham Gloucestershire
Tel: 020 7374 2760 (Tickets)
Fax: 020 7374 2731
www.greenbelt.org.uk
[M5 J10, A435 towards Bishops Cleeve & Evesham, within easy reach of M5 & A40/M40. Rail: Cheltenham Spa. Bus: Stagecoach 01242 522021]
Greenbelt is an all-age Arts Festival with its roots in the Christian faith and a welcome that's wide and inclusive. It's a place to learn, to experience, to be. It's like nothing else in the world, and that's what keeps thousands of people keep coming back year after year. Greenbelt features a great range of music on 5 stages showcasing brand new artists and bands. In addition, the Festival hosts a dynamic, incredibly rich and varied selection of talks, workshop and debates; exploring contemporary issues, faith, social justice, politics - and more. Greenbelt also has a visual and performing arts programme, exploring a variety of alternative worship styles, and runs a daily Children's Festival.

August Bank Holiday Weekend (22-25 Aug 2008)
A£90.00 Concessions£60.00 C(13-17)£50.00, C(4-12)£45.00 C(0-3)£Free, Family Ticket £235.00. Day Tickets available from May 2008 call 01242 227979 or go to cheltenhamtown-hall.org.uk

Royal International Air Tattoo
RAF Fairford Gloucestershire GL7 4RB
Tel: 0870 758 1918 Fax: 01285 713268
www.airtattoo.com

[RIAT 2008 rd signs will direct traffic to main designated entry routes, A417, A419. Rail: Swindon. Shuttle Buses from Swindon Bus Station. Plenty of free on-site parking available]

For one of the UK's most exciting family days out next summer, visit the Royal International Air Tattoo at RAF Fairford in Gloucestershire on July 12-13. See hundreds of incredible aeroplanes from around the world, ranging from fast jets and giant transporters to helicopters and unmanned aircraft plus top international aerobatic display teams including the breath-taking Red Arrows. There will also be the opportunity to marvel at a variety of special tributes - both in the air and on the ground - marking the 90th anniversary of the Royal Air Force. Throughout the day, youngsters will also have the chance to enjoy the critically acclaimed Tri@RIAT attraction, which brings together a feast of entertaining and interactive activities specifically designed to inspire and excite young people. Add this to a rousing outdoor evening concert, and free entry for accompanied under-16's, and it's clear that Europe's largest airshow, held in support of the Royal Air Force Charitable Trust, offers unbeatable value for money. For more details, visit www.airtattoo.com or call the Box Office on 0870 7581918.

12-13 July 2008

In Advance: A£32.50 for specific day ticket, A£37.50 for either day ticket. Tickets can be bought online or by telephone. On the day: A£45.00 C(under16)£Free

Folk & Local History Museums

Gloucester Folk Museum
99-103 Westgate Street Gloucester
Gloucestershire GL1 2PG
Tel: 01452 396868 / 396869
Fax: 01452 330495
www.gloucester.gov.uk/folkmuseum

*[10min walk from railway station. By rd from W
A40 & A48, from N A38 & M5, from E A40 &
B4073, from S A4173 & A38]*

Three floors of attractive Tudor and Jacobean II
listed timber-framed buildings along with new
buildings housing the Dairy, Ironmonger's shop
and Wheelwright and Carpenter workshops.
Displays feature a wide range of local history,
domestic life, crafts, trades and industries from
1500 to the present. The making of brass pins
by hand was once carried out in the original
buildings and a Protestant martyr, Bishop John
Hooper, is said to have lodged here. There is
something for all the family, including a Toys and
Childhood gallery with hands-on toys and a
puppet theatre, the Siege of Gloucester of
1643, a Victorian Class Room, a Victorian
kitchen and laundry equipment. A wide range of
exhibitions, children's activities, events, demonstrations and role-play sessions are held
throughout the year. There is an atmospheric
cottage garden and courtyard for events, often
with live animals, and outside games.

All year Tue-Sat 10.00-17.00
Admission Free

Tewkesbury Borough Museum
64 Barton Street Tewkesbury Gloucestershire
GL20 5PX
Tel: 01684 292901
Social history and archaeology collections illus-
trating the history of Tewkesbury and its people.

Mar-Oct, closed Sun & Mon

Gardens & Horticulture

Hidcote Manor Garden
Hidcote Bartrim Chipping Campden
Gloucestershire GL55 6LR
Tel: 01386 438333
A celebrated twentieth-century garden in the
beautiful north Cotswolds. Considered an Arts &
Crafts masterpiece, with a series of outdoor
rooms.

Painswick Rococo Garden
Gloucester Road Painswick Stroud
Gloucestershire GL6 6TH
Tel: 01452 813204
This beautiful Rococo garden is the only one of
its period to survive completely. It consists of
contemporary buildings, woodland walks, and
magnificent vistas.
Jan-Oct daily

Westbury Court Garden
Westbury-On-Severn Gloucestershire
GL14 1PD
Tel: 01452 760461/ 01684 855377
A formal water garden with canals and yew
hedges, laid out between 1696-1705.

Westonbirt - The National Arboretum
Tetbury Gloucestershire GL8 8QS
Tel: 01666 880220
Spectacular tree gardens with over 3,000 differ-
ent trees and shrub species, many of which are
rare or endangered in their native lands.

Heritage & Industrial

Dean Heritage Centre

Camp Mill Soudley Cinderford Gloucestershire GL14 2UB
Tel: 01594 822170 / 824024
Fax: 01594 823711
www.deanheritagemuseum.com

[On B4227. Plenty of on-site parking available]

The Dean Heritage Centre is set in beautiful Soundley valley on 5 acres of natural woodland. The centre is the only Heritage Centre for the Forest of Dean and tells the story of this unique area through 5 museum galleries, outdoor display, Forester's Cottage with livestock, re-constructed mine and charcoal burners hut and area. The children will be entertained with the adventure playground, Gloucester Old Spot pigs, children's activities and gift shop. Demonstrations and events are organised at the Centre throughout the year, with increased activities during the summer holidays. With an on site café, changing art exhibition room and nearby woodland walks there is plenty to see and do for any visitor for any weather. Disabled access and parking is available, no smoking or dogs allowed on site (guide dogs only). Open daily, free parking and group bookings welcome with possible discount.

Mar-Oct: daily 10.00-17.00. Nov-Feb Sat-Sun 10.00-16.00. Open Bank Holidays

A£4.90 C£2.50 Concessions£4.20, Family Ticket(A2+C4) £14.00

Historical

Berkeley Castle

Berkeley Gloucestershire GL13 9BQ
Tel: 01453 810332 Fax: 01453 511915
www.berkeley-castle.com

[On B4509 (1.5mi W of A38). Plenty of on-site parking available]

Simon Jenkins, in 'England's Thousand Best Houses' describes Berkeley Castle as 'Britain's rose red city half as old as time'. Visit this gemstone of England's ancient past for a unique experience of architectural history - a living home reflecting a thousand years of habitation. In an amazing state of preservation and bursting with stories of an eventful past, Berkeley Castle is a treasure not to be missed. The Berkeley family is one of England's best untold stories: powerful players through turbulent centuries who influenced the course of history while managing to keep both their property and their lives intact. Their influence can be seen throughout a millennium and across the world, from the founding of Berkeley Square in London to the founding of the American colonies. Visit and you will encounter the murder of a King, a struggle with a Queen, a butcher's daughter who became a Countess... and much, much more.

21 Mar-26 Oct open Sun & Bank Hols. Jul-Aug open daily 11.00-17.30

A£7.50 C(under5)£Free C(5-16)£4.50 OAPs£6.00, Family Ticket (A2+C2) £21.00. Gardens only: A£4.00 C£2.00. Group rates (25+) A£7.00 C£3.50 OAPs£5.50 (must be pre-booked)

Discount Offer: One Child Free (with a full-paying adult).

Sudeley Castle, Gardens and Exhibitions

Winchcombe Cheltenham Gloucestershire
GL54 5JD
Tel: 01242 602308 Fax: 01242 602959
www.sudeleycastle.co.uk

[On B4632. Plenty of on-site parking available]

Sudeley Castle sits against the backdrop of the beautiful Cotswold Hills and is steeped in history. With many royal connections, the Castle has played an important role in the turbulent and changing times of England's past. Sudeley is perhaps best known as the home of Queen Katherine Parr, who is entombed in St Mary's Church, situated in the grounds. The 14 acres of magnificent, award-winning gardens are a delight throughout the seasons and are managed on organic principles. The Pheasantry was established in 2004 and the collection includes 15 species of rare and endangered pheasants. Sudeley Castle Country Cottages are located midway between the Castle and the historic town of Winchcombe, they're available all year round for short or long stays. Please visit the website for details of the historic exhibitions and our exciting new events programme! Connoisseur tours of the Castle Apartments take place every Tuesday, Wednesday and Thursday. We have disabled and pushchair access in the garden only.

15 Mar-31 Oct daily 10.30-17.00.
A£7.20 C£4.20 Concessions£6.20

Discount Offer: One Child Free.

Woodchester Mansion

Nympsfield Stonehouse Gloucestershire
GL10 3TS
Tel: 01453 861541 Fax: 01453 861337
www.woodchestermansion.org.uk

[From M5 J13 follow directions for Stroud, at roundabout turn R onto B4066 for Selsey, Follow for 4mi, take L turn signposted Nympsfield. From M4 J18 take A46 signposted Stroud, at crossroads turn L until side road forks R to Nympsfield. At junction (don't go into village) turn R onto B4066 and take next R. Gates to Mansion are then on your L]

Woodchester Mansion is an architectural masterpiece of the Victorian age that was abandoned by its builders before it could be completed. It's remained virtually untouched by time since the mid-1870s, and today it offers visitors a unique opportunity to explore a Gothic building in mid-assembly. The mansion is hidden in a secluded 400-acre landscape park of great beauty, sheltering an abundance of wildlife and rare-breed grazing stock. Enchanting woodland walks snake around its five man-made lakes. The mansion and its park are reputed to be haunted and regular events are held throughout the year for those who want to hunt our ghosts. Facilities for visitors include a tearoom (serving drinks, cakes and snacks) and a gift shop. Volunteers from the Woodchester Mansion Trust conduct guided tours of the house on a regular basis. The park (owned by the National Trust) is open to all.

Easter-Oct, Sun & First Sat Every Month & Bank Hol Weekends inc. Mon. July-Aug Sat & Sun

A£5.50 C(under14)£Free Concessions£4.50
Group rates available.

Living History Museums

Village Life Exhibition
The Old Mill Bourton-on-the-Water
Gloucestershire GL54 2BY
Tel: 01451 821225
A complete Edwardian village shop is displayed
with bathroom, kitchen and bedroom above.

Music & Theatre Museums

Keith Harding's World of Mechanical Music
Oak House High Street Northleach Cheltenham
Gloucestershire GL54 3ET
Tel: 01451 860181
A collection of antique clocks, musical boxes,
automats and mechanical musical instruments.

Nature & Conservation Parks

WWT Slimbridge Wetlands Centre
Slimbridge Gloucester Gloucestershire GL2 7BT
Tel: 01453 891900
One of the finest collections of water-birds in
the world.

Places of Worship

Gloucester Cathedral
Gloucester Gloucestershire GL1 2LR
Tel: 01452 528095
This magnificent 900-year-old Norman
Cathedral lies at the heart of the city.

Police, Prisons & Dungeons

Crime Through Time Museum
Littledean Jail Littledean GL14 3NL
Tel: 01594 826659
A controversial private collection of items asso-
ciated with crimes and punishment, sleaze and
scandals over the centuries.
Easter-Oct, Thu-Sun only

Railways

Dean Forest Railway
Norchard Station Forest Road Lydney
Gloucestershire GL15 4ET
Tel: 01594 843423 info line
www.deanforestrailway.co.uk

*[B4234 N of Lydney. Plenty of on-site parking
available]*

"The Friendly Forest Line" Standard gauge
steam (plus occasional diesel) passenger trains
from Norchard to Lydney Junction and on the
newly opened extension through the medieval
forest to the delightful village of Parkend, for real
ale pubs, forest walks and nature reserve. Also
lake and children's park at Lydney. At Norchard
there is a museum of railway relics, which
includes the history of the Severn and Wye
Railway from 1809. Special events include Days
out with Thomas, Halloween Ghost trains,
Santa specials, Sunday lunch dining car trains
etc. Also steam and diesel locomotive driving
courses.

*Trains Run: Mid Mar-May Sun, June-July Wed,
Sat-Sun, Aug Wed-Thur & Sat-Sun, Sept Wed &
Sat-Sun, Oct Sun. Also Bank Hols & selected
dates in Oct & at Christmas/New Year*

A£9.00 OAPs£8.00 C£5.00 C(under5)£Free,
Family Ticket (A2+C2) £26.00. Pay once & ride
all day! (Different prices apply for special events)

**Discount Offer: One Child Free (with
full-paying adult).**

Gloucestershire Warwickshire Railway

The Railway Station Toddington Cheltenham
Gloucestershire GL54 5DT
Tel: 01242 621405
www.gwsr.com

[J between B4632 / B4077 on Stow Rd (8mi from J9 M5). Plenty of on-site parking available]

The 'Friendly Line in the Cotswolds', offers a 20 mile round trip between Toddington and Cheltenham Racecourse. The views of The Cotswolds, Malverns and The Vale of Evesham are superb, since most of the line runs along embankments. The exciting 693-yard 'Greet Tunnel' is one of the longest on a preserved railway and surely the darkest! Pop along and see the driver and fireman. Break your journey at picturesque Winchcombe Station with its tree lined picnic area or sample the delicious home-made cakes in the 'Flag & Whistle' tearooms at Toddington Station. Refreshments are also available from the buffet car on most trains. A well-stocked station shop sells a variety of 'railway' gifts. Special events are held throughout the year. Visiting locomotives. Wheelchairs can be catered for. Tickets give unlimited travel on the day of purchase. Special group rates available.

Mar-Dec Sat Sun & Bank Hol Mon & selected weekdays

Return tickets: A£10.00 C(0-4)£Free C(5-15)£6.00 OAPs£8.50, Family Ticket (A2+C3) £27.00. Group rates (for 20+) available on request

Discount Offer: Two for the Price of One (full-paying adult).

Jenner Museum

Church Lane High Street Berkeley
Gloucestershire GL13 9BH
Tel: 01453 810631 Fax: 01453 811690
Beautiful Georgian home of Edward Jenner, discoverer of vaccination against smallpox. The displays record Jenner's life as an 18th century country doctor and his work on vaccination.

Sport & Recreation

Cotswold Water Park and Keynes Country Park

Spratsgate Lane Shorncote Cirencester
Gloucestershire GL7 6DF
Tel: 01285 861459 Fax: 01285 860186
www.waterpark.org

[Please see www.waterpark.org for a map]

The Cotswold Water Park and Keynes Country Park is Britain's largest water park. It's 50% larger than the Norfolk Broads AND it's even bigger than the Isle of Jersey! Surprised? The area is a secret known only to local residents and the privileged few who have chosen to buy second homes here. Why not share in the beauty and excitement that is the Cotswold Water Park and Keynes Country Park? We can provide leisure facilities such as boating, canoeing, water-skiing and 4x4 vehicle courses for adrenaline-seekers. We also offer advice on quiet walks, incredible bird-watching opportunities and beautiful picnic spots to those seeking peace and tranquillity. Indeed, the area caters for all tastes - from those seeking solitude, to families looking a fun and safe environment, and to those who are on the lookout for sport and adventure. Just 90mins from London, the Cotswold Water Park and Keynes Country Park is THE place to go!

All year daily

Stately Homes

Dyrham Park

Dyrham Nr Bath Gloucestershire SN14 8ER
Tel: 0117 937 2501
Baroque country house with 'below stairs' area, landscaped garden and deer park.

Theme & Adventure Parks

Cattle Country Adventure Park

Berkeley Heath Farm Berkeley Gloucestershire GL13 9EW
Tel: 01453 810510
Farm Park displaying exotic cattle including a herd of American Bison.

Go Ape! High Wire Forest Adventure (Forest of Dean, Gloucestershire)

Mallards Pike Lake Forest of Dean Lydney Gloucestershire GL15 4HD
Tel: 0845 643 9245
www.goape.co.uk

[From A48 at Blakeney, take Nibley-Parkend Rd, Mallards Pike is signposted. Plenty of on-site parking available]

Take to the trees and experience an exhilarating course of rope bridges, Tarzan swings and zip-slides up to 40 feet above the ground! Share approximately three exciting hours of fun and adventure, which you'll be talking about for days. Book online and watch people Go Ape! at www.goape.co.uk. Minimum height 1.4m. Maximum weight 130 kg (20.5 stone). Under-18s must be accompanied by a participating adult. One adult can supervise either two children (where one or both of them is under 16 years old) or up to five 16-17 year olds. Pre-booking is essential to avoid disappointment. Book online or by telephone (there is a £1.00 booking fee on all telephone bookings).

16-18 & 21-24 Feb, 14 Mar-31 Oct daily, Nov Sat-Sun. Dec Sat-Sun TBC please visit www.goape.co.uk. Closed Jan

Gorillas (18yrs+) £25.00, Baboons (10-17yrs) £20.00

Discount Offer: £5.00 off per person.

Transport Museums

Cotswolds Motor Museum and Toy Collection

The Old Mill Sherbourne Street Bourton-on-the-Water Gloucestershire GL54 2BY

Tel: 01451 821255
Located in the beautiful village of Bourton on the Water, the Cotswold Motor Museum is a veritable treasure chest of yesteryear.

National Waterways Museum

Llanthony Warehouse Gloucester Docks Gloucester Gloucestershire GL1 2EH
Tel: 01452 318200
In this revitalised museum you will be able to discover what it would have been like to live and work on our waterways through the new Water Lives exhibition.
Reopens May 2008 - please call in advance

Greater Manchester

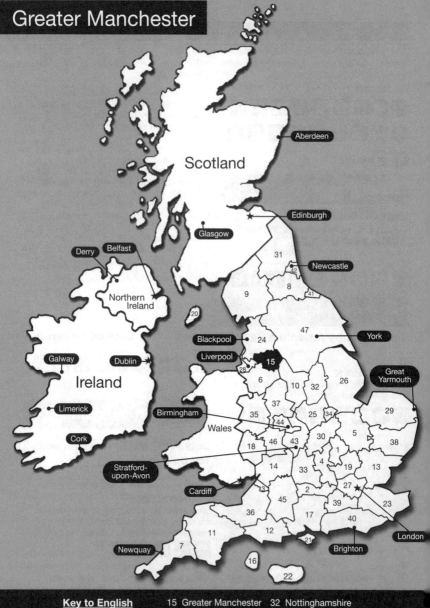

Aberdeen

Scotland

Glasgow

Edinburgh

Newcastle

Derry

Belfast

Northern
Ireland

Galway

Dublin

Ireland

Limerick

Cork

Blackpool

Liverpool

York

Great
Yarmouth

Birmingham

Wales

Stratford-
upon-Avon

Cardiff

Newquay

Brighton

London

Airfields / Flight Centres

Manchester Airport Aviation Viewing Park

Wilmslow Old Road Manchester Airport
Ringway Greater Manchester M90 1QX
Tel: 0161 489 3000
The purpose-built viewing park has a visitor
centre and a growing collection of aircraft
exhibits. Three raised viewing platforms offer
good views of the active runways.

Arts, Crafts & Textiles

Gallery Oldham

Greaves Street Oldham Cultural Quarter
Oldham Greater Manchester OL1 1AL
Tel: 0161 770 4653 Fax: 0161 770 4669
www.galleryoldham.org.uk

*[In Oldham town centre just off Union Street,
10min walk from railway station. Rail: Oldham
Mumps]*

Gallery Oldham is an award winning landmark
building, opened in 2002, which forms part of
Oldham's new Cultural Quarter. Changing exhibitions at the gallery incorporate Oldham's
extensive art, social and natural history collections alongside touring shows, newly commissioned art, international art and work produced
with local communities. Regular events take
place and include family activities, exhibition
talks, live music and a comprehensive schools
programme.

All year Mon-Sat 10.00-17.00
Admission Free

Manchester Art Gallery

Mosley Street Manchester Greater Manchester
M2 3JL
Tel: 0161 235 8888 Fax: 0161 235 8899
www.manchestergalleries.org

*[Corner of Mosley St & Princess St nr Manchester
Town Hall]*

Manchester Art Gallery houses the city's magnificent art collection and hosts a lively programme
of exhibitions and events in stunning Victorian
and contemporary surroundings. The gallery is
located in the heart of the city centre, easily
accessible by tram, bus, train, car and coach.
Family favourites are available in the gallery's
self-service, family style cafe. Choose chef's
special hot pasta with sauces, pasta salad
served with fresh bread or pick and mix your
own Hungry Monkey Lunchbox! Hot food
served daily from 12.00-14.00 plus sandwiches,
salads and delicious cakes. Children's menu
available. High chairs, baby bottle warmers and
baby changing facilities available. The gallery
shop stocks an impressive range of art books,
prints, postcards and gifts inspired by the collection and a variety of children's products
including the best selling, award winning book
'The Gallery Cat'. Families can enjoy a programme of events including hands-on activities
in the Clore Interactive Gallery, family trail activity
packs, story bags and the family audio tour, and
can follow Tony Ross's humorous children's picture labels.

*All year Tue-Sun 10.00-17.00. Closed Mon
except Bank Hols, Good Fri, 24-26 & 31 Dec.*
Admission Free

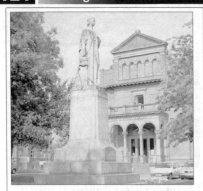

Salford Museum and Art Gallery

Peel Park The Crescent Salford
Greater Manchester M5 4WU
Tel: 0161 778 0800 Fax: 0161 745 9490
[A6 in front of Salford University to end of M602 signposted. Plenty of on-site parking available]
Discover the past at Salford Museum and Art Gallery! Visit Lark Hill Place - our fascinating reconstructed Victorian Street where you will find many shops and houses including a toy shop, chemist, grocer, blacksmith and a cottage. Our Spectacular Victorian Gallery compliments this with a display of Victorian sculpture and paintings. The lifetimes Gallery interprets different aspects of Salford's fascinating history whilst two temporary exhibition spaces present a varied programme of exhibitions. The Local History Library is also in the building and a must for anyone researching the area or their Salfordian relatives. The venue is family friendly and has a programme of activities for all ages.
All year Mon-Fri 10.00-16.45, Sat & Sun 13.00-17.00. Closed Good Fri & Easter Sat 2008 Christmas Opening 2008 to be confirmed.
Admission Free

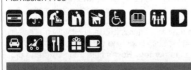

Country Parks & Estates

Etherow Country Park

George Street Compstall Stockport Greater Manchester SK6 5JD
Tel: 0161 427 6937
Covers an area of 240 acres at the heart of the Etherow-Goyt Valley, and offers a variety of leisure pursuits.

Haigh Hall and Country Park

Copperas Lane Haigh Wigan
Greater Manchester WN2 1PE
Tel: 01942 832895
Miles of parkland with a model village, a miniature railway, crazy golf, tea room and art gallery.

Heaton Park

Prestwich Manchester Greater Manchester M25 2SW
Tel: 0161 773 1085 Fax: 0161 798 0107
www.heatonpark.org.uk

[4mi from Manchester City Centre, close to J19 of M60. Plenty of on-site parking available]

Heaton Park is one of the biggest public parks in Europe, and offers a great day out for all ages with most activities free of charge. The magnificent Heaton Hall is open throughout the summer months, with beautifully restored interiors and collections of furniture, paintings, musical instruments and an exhibition celebrating the park's rich history. In the Animal Centre you can watch alpacas, goats, sheep, pigs and cows. There is a Transport Museum with working vintage trams and rowing boats can be hired at the lake. For the more energetic there are bowling greens, horse riding, an 18 hole golf course and a Pitch and Putt course. The park hosts a range of exciting events throughout the year, including outdoor theatre, concerts, themed family fun days and a bonfire night, as well as sponsored walks and runs. No dogs except guide dogs in buildings.

Park: All year daily 08.00-dusk. Hall: 22 Mar-31 Aug Thurs-Sun & Bank Hols 11.00-17.30
Admission Free

Exhibition & Visitor Centres

Lowry, The

Pier 8 Salford Quays Greater Manchester
M50 3AZ
Tel: 0870 111 2000
Arts, entertainment and acitivites, all under one
roof! Two theatres, galleries, cafes, restaurants
and shops.

Folk & Local History Museums

Ordsall Hall Museum

Ordsall Lane Ordsall Salford Greater Manchester
M5 3AN
Tel: 0161 872 0251 Fax: 0161 872 4951

*[The hall is situated 1mi from end of M602.
Disabled access in some areas. Plenty of on-site
parking available]*

Ordsall Hall Museum is a magnificent black and
white half-timbered manor house located in the
heart of Salford. It is fully furnished with seventeenth-century furniture and exhibits, and
stands in its own grounds. The Hall is rumoured
to be haunted - see if you can find the ghosts
that reside there! The Great Hall, kitchen and
Star Chamber take you back in time whilst galleries upstairs show a variety of temporary exhibitions of art, history and hands-on fun. Ordsall
Hall Museum has a full programme of family
friendly events - why not make a trip on the first
Sunday of the month and enjoy the family fun-
day!

*All year Sun-Fri. Mon-Fri: 10.00-16.00. Sun:
13.00-16.00. Closed Easter Sat & Easter Sun.
Christmas opening 08 to be confimed*
Admission Free

Heritage & Industrial

Hat Works - The Museum of Hatting, Stockport

Wellington Mill Wellington Road South
Stockport Greater Manchester SK3 0EU
Tel: 0161 355 7770 Fax: 0161 480 8735
www.hatworks.org.uk
*[Wellington Mill's landmark chimney is highly visible
from all main routes into Stockport & is located on
main throughfare, A6 Wellington Road South.
Opposite bus station, close to railway station, only
2min walk from Merseyway Shopping Centre &
other town centre shops. Parking: Inexpensive
parking facilities available in & around Stockport
town centre. Nearest car parks are: Heaton Lane,
Mersey Way & Grand Central]*

The UK's first and only museum dedicated to
the exciting world of hats and hat-making.
Learn about Stockport's historic links with hatting and how the industry flourished employing
over 4,500 people by the end of the nineteenth
century. Take a step back in time to Hope
Street with a glimpse into a Hatter's Cottage,
marvel at the machines restored to full working
order - giving a noisy and thrilling encounter
with the town's industrial past. Interactive
demonstrations reveal the art and mystery of
hat making. The stunning display of hats from
the early 1800s to modern day. There's so
much to see and do, it is simply brimming over!
Educational sessions: linked to Key Stages 1 &
2 with a dedicated Education Suite, details
available upon request. The Level 2 internet
café is open to all, visitor to the museum or not!
Relax in stylish surroundings and choose from a
range of coffees, pastries or light lunches.
*All year daily Mon-Fri 10.00-17.00, Sat-Sun (and
all Bank Holidays) 13.00-17.00. Please call for
Christmas & New Year opening times*
Admission Free. Guided Tour: £2.50, Family
Ticket £7.00

Staircase House

30-31 Market Place Stockport Greater
Manchester SK1 1ES
Tel: 0161 480 1460 Fax: 0161 474 0312
www.staircasehouse.org.uk

*[In centre of Stockport. 5min walk from bus &
train stations, follow signs to market place.
Parking within short walking distance, follow car
park signs to Merseyway]*

This award-winning attraction invites you to time
travel through the history of Staircase House
from 1460 to WWII. With the help of a state-of-
the-art audio guide, the fascinating history of
the house will unfold on a fun, accessible and
informative journey. The entire 18-room town
house is fully interactive. You are invited to
smell, touch and listen as you relive its history
by pulling back the bedclothes on the four-
poster bed, peeling rush lights, and trying your
hand at seventeenth-century quill pen writing.
Perfect for a family day or simply to enjoy a
unique hands on historical experience. Staircase
House has an intriguing array of rooms linked
by narrow passages and the beautifully restored
Jacobean cage newell staircase - one of only
three surviving examples in Britain. Events
throughout the year. Visit on the last Saturday of
every month and meet characters from the past
in various rooms.

*Mon-Fri 12.00-17.00. Sat-Sun 10.00-17.00.
Group bookings welcome both inside & outside
normal opening hours by special arrangement*

A£3.95 Concessions(under16's & over
60's)£2.95, Leisure key: £2.00. Family Ticket
(A2+C2) £12.00. Prices may very

Manchester Museum, The

The University of Manchester Oxford Road
Manchester Greater Manchester M13 9PL
Tel: 0161 275 2634
15 galleries bring you face-to-face with live reptiles, let you admire ancient art from Egypt, see
a helmet made from a porcupine fish and much
more besides.

Railways

East Lancashire Railway

Bolton Street Station Bolton Street Bury Greater
Manchester BL9 0EY
Tel: 0161 764 7790 Fax: 0161 763 4408
www.east-lancs-rly.co.uk

*[M66 J2. Railway is signposted from all major
roads. Plenty of on-site parking available]*

A mainly steam hauled train service between
Bury to Ramsbottom, Rawtenstall and
Heywood. This popular steam railway offers a
day out for all the family with all the trimmings
you expect on a railway (tunnels, level crossings
etc). You can break your journey at any station
to visit the shops at Dickensian Ramsbottom
with its Farmers and Sunday markets. A riverside picnic area allows you to view the trains.
Then, rejoin the train, and complete your journey with views of the Pennine Moors - an ideal
day out for the family whatever the weather.
Special events are held throughout the year and
include a Day Out with Thomas, Teddy Bears
Picnic, 1940s weekend and Santa Specials to
name just a few. The Railway also runs Sunday
Lunch and Diners trains and Drive a Steam
Engine makes an ideal present.

Weekend service & Bank Hol also May-Sept Wed, Thur, Fri. Dec Santa specials. Closed 25 Dec

Full Line Return Ticket: A£11.40 C£7.60

Discount Offer: Two for the Price of One (full-paying adult).

Science - Earth & Planetary

Museum of Science and Industry in Manchester

Liverpool Road Castlefield Manchester Greater Manchester M3 4FP

Tel: 0161 832 2244

See the wheels of industry turning in the Power Hall and planes that made flying history. Follow textile history and discover technology.

Social History Museums

Bolton Museum and Art Gallery

Le Mans Crescent Bolton Greater Manchester BL1 1SE

Tel: 01204 332190

Collections of archaeology, local and industrial history, Egyptology, natural history, geology.

Bury Art Gallery, Museum and Archives

Moss Street Bury Greater Manchester BL9 0DR

Tel: 0161 253 5878

At Bury Art Gallery, Museum and Archives you'll find world-famous Victorian paintings, challenging contemporary art, mysterious objects and fascinating documents from Bury's past housed in a distinctive Edwardian building.

Closed Mon & Sun

Imperial War Museum North

The Quays Trafford Wharf Road Trafford Park Manchester Greater Manchester M17 1TZ

Tel: 0161 836 4000

A range of innovative displays, exhibitions and events work together to bring the past to life.

Stockport Air Raid Shelters

61 Chestergate Stockport Greater Manchester SK1 1NE

Tel: 0161 474 1940 Fax: 0161 474 1942

www.stockport.gov.uk

[M60, J1, A6. Rail: Stockport, 10min]

First-hand experience of daily life in 1940s, wartime Britain. A labyrinth of tunnels under part of the town centre provided shelter - and a way of life - for Stockport and Manchester families through the dark days of the Blitz. Take time to wonder how everyone managed with those bunks and benches; lights and sounds; toilet arrangements and Red Cross facilities. Explore authentic reconstructions in a core area of sandstone tunnels. Sense the immense network of structure; the thousands of people; their concern and determination. Hear the sounds of 1940 - the historical context, the songs and the reminiscences. Reflect on the complexities of conflict in the 'Web of War' exhibition. Admire the contributions of Wardens, WVS and other volunteers, experience the atmosphere and respect the memories as you stroll through the tunnels.

All year daily 13.00-17.00. Open Bank Hols except 25-26 Dec & 1 Jan times are subject to change please call before visiting

A£3.95 C&Concessions£2.95, Family Ticket (A2+C2) £11.75. (Subject to change)

Stockport Story

30/31 Market Place Stockport Greater
Manchester SK1 1ES
Tel: 0161 480 1460 Fax: 0161 474 0312
www.stockportstory.org.uk
*[In centre of Stockport. 5min walk from bus &
train stations, follow signs to market place.
Parking within short walking distance, follow car
park signs to Merseyway]*
Stockport Story Museum is a local history
museum set in the heart of Stockport's historic
market place. Visitors are invited to experience
10,000 years of history as they travel from prehistoric to present day Stockport. Explore the
Origins gallery and see the fantastic finds from a
local archaeological dig including original flint
tools of the hunter-gatherers. Then travel
through medieval Stockport in the Making of the
Town gallery and find out about Stockport's
once thriving textile industry. Journey on to the
Work and Play gallery where you'll learn about
Victorian Stockport and the industries of the
town. Conclude your journey in the Changing
Lives gallery where you can learn of the impact
of the wars on Stockport, and how the town is
shaping up today. There's also a temporary
exhibition gallery with four exhibitions per year.
The museum is family friendly with interactives
and activities for all ages. Make a day of it by
visiting Staircase House.. it's right next door!
All year daily 10.00-17.00
Admission Free

Urbis: The Museum of Urban Living

Cathedral GardensM4 3BG
Tel: 0161 605 8200/605 8209
An exhibition-centre of city life, featuring interactive exhibits that offer unique insights into the
culture of the modern city.

Sporting History Museums

Manchester United Museum and Tour Centre

Sir Matt Busby Way Old Trafford Manchester
Greater Manchester M16 0RA
Tel: 0870 442 1994 Fax: 0161 868 8861
www.manutd.com
[2mi from city centre off A56. Ample parking]
Manchester United is the world's most famous
football club and the award winning Museum &
Tour Centre at Old Trafford hosts over 230,000
visitors annually. The Museum tracks the history
of the Club from its humble beginnings in 1878,
showcases the silverware collected along the
way, along with the key administrators,
Managers and Players both past and present
who have helped to create the legend that is
Manchester United. The Museum is educational,
interactive and regularly updated with visitors of
all ages sure to find something of interest. And
for those who want to delve behind the scenes
even further at the Theatre of Dreams, the stadium tour allows visitors to stand in Fergie's spot
in the dug, sit at their favourite players peg in
the dressing room and experience what it feels
like to emerge from the player's tunnel to the
roar of 76,000 fans. For further information or to
book a tour please telephone 0870 442 1994 or
email tours@manutd.co.uk
*Museum-all year daily 09.30-17.00. Tours-all year
daily 09.40-16.30. Tours are not available on
match days and museum opening times may
vary. Closed 25 Dec*
Tour & Museum: A£10.00 Concessions£7.00,
Family Ticket £30.00, Group rates (15+):
A£8.50 Concessions£6.00. Museum only:
A£6.50 Concessions£4.75, Family Ticket
£20.00, Group rates (15+): A£5.00
Concessions£3.75

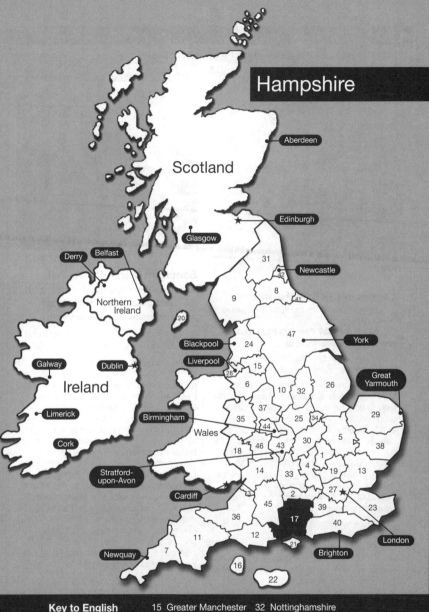

Hampshire

- Aberdeen
- Scotland
- Edinburgh
- Glasgow
- Newcastle
- Derry
- Belfast
- Northern Ireland
- Blackpool
- Liverpool
- Galway
- Dublin
- Ireland
- York
- Great Yarmouth
- Limerick
- Birmingham
- Wales
- Cork
- Stratford-upon-Avon
- Cardiff
- London
- Newquay
- Brighton

31
42
9
8
41
24
47
15
28
6
10
32
26
37
29
35
44
25
34
46
43
30
5
38
18
1
14
33
4
19
13
2
27
45
39
23
17
40
36
12
21
7
16
22

Key to English Counties:

1 Bedfordshire
2 Berkshire
3 Bristol
4 Buckinghamshire
5 Cambridgeshire
6 Cheshire
7 Cornwall
8 County Durham
9 Cumbria
10 Derbyshire
11 Devon
12 Dorset
13 Essex
14 Gloucestershire
15 Greater Manchester
16 Guernsey
17 Hampshire
18 Herefordshire
19 Hertfordshire
20 Isle Of Man
21 Isle Of Wight
22 Jersey
23 Kent
24 Lancashire
25 Leicestershire
26 Lincolnshire
27 London
28 Merseyside
29 Norfolk
30 Northamptonshire
31 Northumberland
32 Nottinghamshire
33 Oxfordshire
34 Rutland
35 Shropshire
36 Somerset
37 Staffordshire
38 Suffolk
39 Surrey
40 Sussex
41 Tees Valley
42 Tyne & Wear
43 Warwickshire
44 West Midlands
45 Wiltshire
46 Worcestershire
47 Yorkshire

Animal Attractions

Longdown Activity Farm

Longdown Ashurst Southampton Hampshire
SO40 7EH
Tel: 023 8029 2837 Fax: 023 8029 3376
www.longdownfarm.co.uk

*[Off A35 between Lyndhurst & Southampton.
Plenty of on-site parking available]*

Meet lots of friendly farm animals, and join in
our range of daily activities - for example bottle-
feeding goat kids or calves, small animal handling and goat feeding. Enjoy a tractor and trailer ride, weather permitting. Farmer Bryan can
arrange a birthday party with a difference, for a
minimum of 10 children. We have indoor and
outdoor play areas where children can let off
steam, in safe surroundings. We also have both
outdoor and under-cover picnic areas. NEW
FOR 2008 - Longdown farm shop, a large
range of delicious local produce.

*16 Feb-2 Nov daily, Nov-Dec Sat-Sun 10.00-
17.00, 13-21 Dec daily*

A£6.75 C(3-14)&OAPs£5.75, Family Ticket
(A2+C2) £23.00. Season tickets and group discounts available, groups of 15+ are given a fully
guided tour at no extra charge. Tours are tailored to suit the age range or particular interest
of the group and must be pre-booked

Discount Offer: One Child Free.

Arts, Crafts & Textiles

Sandham Memorial Chapel

Harts Lane Burghclere Hampshire RG20 9JT
Tel: 01635 278394 Fax: 01635 278394
www.nationaltrust.org.uk/sandham

*[4mi S Newbury, 0.5mi E of A34. Rail: Newbury
4mi. Limited parking nearby]*

This red brick chapel was built in the 1920s for
the artist Stanley Spencer to fill with paintings of
his experiences in the First World War. Inspired
by Giotto's Arena Chapel in Padua, Spencer
took five years to complete what is arguably his
finest achievement. This extraordinary project
illustrates the artist's experiences as a medical
orderly and as a soldier in Macedonia. He celebrates the everyday routine of a soldier's life
with an intensely personal religious faith, reaching its triumphant climax with the huge
Resurrection of the Soldiers, which completely
fills the east wall and dominates the entire
chapel. The chapel is set amidst lawns and
orchards with views across to Watership Down.
Photography allowed in orchard. Note: There is
no lighting in the chapel, it is best to view the
paintings on a bright day. Wheelchair access via
portable ramps. Dogs on leads in grounds.

*5-30 Mar 11.00-15.00 Wed-Sun, 2 Apr-28 Sept
11.00-17.00 Wed-Sun, 1-31 Oct 11.00-15.00
Wed-Sun, 1 Nov-21 Dec 11.00-15.00 Sat-Sun.
Also open Bank Hol Mon. Other times by
appointment only, and groups must book in
advance*

A£3.50 C£1.75 NT Members £Free

Birds, Butterflies & Bees

Hawk Conservancy Trust

Sarson Lane Weyhill Andover Hampshire
SP11 8DY
Tel: 01264 773850 Fax: 01264 773772
www.hawkconservancy.org
[Signposted from A303. On-site parking available]
The Hawk Conservancy Trust, Andover, is a
national award-winning family tourist attraction.
Set in 22 acres of grounds (including woodland
and a wildflower meadow), there is plenty to do
for the whole family. There are three Bird-of-Prey
flying displays every day (including the spectacular 2pm 'Valley of the Eagles' display), each
featuring a different team of birds. Children can
complete our 'Raptor Passport Trail' and nature
trail, and enjoy the fun of ferret and runner duck
racing. All visitors can hold a British Bird-of-
Prey, and either walk or take a tractor ride
around our beautiful wildflower meadow. Adults
also have the opportunity to fly a Harris Hawk.
Our facilities include: Gift Shop, Coffee Shop
(serving light lunches and snacks throughout
the day), BBQ (weekends and school holidays,
when weather permits), Education Centre and
Bird-of-Prey hospital. For more information
please call or visit our website.
*16 Feb-2 Nov daily 10.30-17.30. Nov-Feb 2008
Sat-Sun 10.30-16.30*
A£9.75 C£6.25 OAPs£9.00 Students£8.75,
Family Ticket (A2+C2) £31.00

**Discount Offer: £1.00 off Child
Admission.**

Liberty's Raptor and Reptile Centre

Crow Lane Ringwood Hampshire BH24 3EA
Tel: 01425 476487
www.libertyscentre.co.uk

*[5 min from Ringwood: take the Poulner exit off
the A31 (Signposted Hightown and Crow) and
follow the brown tourist signs.]*

Liberty's Raptor and Reptile Centre is home to
large collection of birds of prey including Eagles,
Owls, Hawks and Vultures. We also house a
number of reptiles and other creepy crawlies
such as Snakes, Lizards and Spiders and
Spiders in our indoor reptile house. Enjoy a visit
that will be fun, exciting and educational for all
ages. Observe these magnificent birds flying
free and the reptiles up close and personal
through various spectacular displays held
throughout the day. We have indoor flying facilities in the event of poor weather. We are also a
rescue centre for wild birds of prey that have
become injured or are in need of care before
being released back to the wild. All medical and
rehabilitation costs for these wild birds are fund-
ed through our entry tickets sales and public
donations.

*Open Daily 1 Mar-31 Oct 10.00-17.00.
Weekends and School Hols Only Nov-Feb 10.00-
16.00 Not Christmas or New Year.*

A£6.50 C£4.95 OAPs£5.50 Family
Ticket(A2+C2)£19.95

Discount Offer: One Child Free.

Hawk Conservancy Trust

National Award Winning Visitor Attraction

✿ 22 acres of grounds

✿ Over 100 birds on show

✿ 3 exciting flying displays daily including the spectacular Valley of the Eagles and unique Woodland Hawks and Owls

✿ Fly a Hawk and hold a British Bird of Prey

✿ Children complete our Raptor passport trail and visit our children's bird hides and much much more!

**So much to do for all the family
See how fun learning about nature can be!**

Call 01264 773850 *or visit*
www.hawkconservancy.org

Itchen Valley Country Park

Allington Lane West End Eastleigh Southampton Hampshire SO30 3HQ
Tel: 023 8046 6091
Itchen Valley Country Park is a large area of unspoilt countryside beside the River Itchen, managed for public enjoyment and wildlife.

Queen Elizabeth Country Park

Gravel Hill Horndean Waterlooville Hampshire PO8 0QE
Tel: 023 9259 5040
Hampshire's biggest country park. 1,400 acres of open access woodland and downland within the East Hampshire Area of Outstanding Natural Beauty.

Staunton Country Park

Middle Park Way Havant Hampshire PO9 5HB
Tel: 023 9245 3405

1,000 acres of landscaped parkland with an ornamental lake, woodland and follies. Children's play areas and petting zoo.

Watercress Festival 2008

Broad Street Alresford Hampshire
www.watercress.co.uk
For all things green and healthy, head to the beautiful Georgian town of Alresford, in Hampshire, on Sunday 11 May for the 6th annual Watercress Festival which kicks off National Watercress Week to celebrate the start of the British watercress season. 2008 marks the bi-centenary of the British watercress industry and the town will be pulling out all the stops to make it a day to remember. Celebrity chef Antony Worrall Thompson will be carrying out free cookery demonstrations in Broad Street and signing copies of a new anniversary watercress recipe book. Hampshire Fare will once again be organising a fabulous food market of local producers, many of whom will be competing in The Watercress Food Awards with new and innovative products. Watercress pesto, watercress scones, watercress quiche, countless variations of watercress soup and even a watercress trifle and watercress ice cream were among the entries last year. There will be live music, street theatre, face painting and a bouncy castle. For more information, visit www.alresford.org and www.watercress.co.uk.
Sunday 11 May 2008, 10.00-16.00
Admission Free

City Museum and Records Office

Museum Road Portsmouth Hampshire PO1 2LJ

Tel: 023 9282 7261 Fax: 023 9287 5276

www.portsmouthmuseums.co.uk

[M27/M275 into Portsmouth, follow museum symbol then City Museum on brown signposts. Rail: Harbour Station, 10min walk. Bus: No. 6. Limited on-site parking available]

The museum is dedicated to local history and fine and decorative art. 'The Story of Portsmouth' displays room settings showing life in Portsmouth from the seventeenth century to the 1950s using modern audio-visual techniques. Experience the different life-styles of the Victorian working poor in the 'Dockyard Workers Cottage' and the affluent 'Victorian Parlour'. A 1930s kitchen with everything including the kitchen sink! A 1930s 'Art Deco' dinning room and a 1950s front room complete with flying ducks on the wall and early television showing "Listen With Mother". The 'Portsmouth at Play' exhibition looks at all aspects of leisure pursuits from the Victorian period to the 1970s. "What the Butler Saw" machines on the pier, a "Pennyfarthing" cycle and film archive's from the 1930s and 1960s.The museum has a temporary exhibition gallery with regular changing exhibitions. New for 2007 - 'The World of Sherlock Holmes, Sir Arthur Conan Doyle and the creation of a hero exhibition.

All year Apr-Sept daily 10.00-17.30, Oct-Mar daily 10.00-17.00. Closed 24-26 Dec

Admission Free

Winchester Hat Fair

Winchester Hampshire SO23 8RZ

Tel: 01962 849841

www.hatfair.co.uk

[Various venues. Winchester is 70mi from London & 9mi from Southampton. M3, J9/10 (Park & Ride service at J) & follow signs to Winchester City Centre. Rail: Winchester]

Hat Fair is England's longest running free festival of street theatre. More than 40 theatre companies from all over the world will perform in and around the city, alongside workshops, large scale theatre performances, pyrotechnic shows and late night cabaret. Hat Fair is a FREE event; it gets its name from the traditional voluntary contribution of money in the hat to street performers. It draws an audience of around 50,000 people of all ages from all over Britain.

3 June - 6 July 2008, 11.00-Late

Admission Free, donations welcome

Folk & Local History Museums

Breamore House and Countryside Museum

Breamore Fordingbridge Hampshire SP6 2DF

Tel: 01725 512468

Breamore House is set in its own beautiful parkland amid surrounding farms and fields.

Forests & Woods

New Forest Museum and Visitor Centre

Main Car Park High Street Lyndhurst Hampshire
SO43 7NY
Tel: 023 8028 3444
The New Forest Museum and Visitor Centre
brings to life the Forest's history, traditions,
characters and wildlife.

Gardens & Horticulture

Exbury Gardens and Steam Railway

The Estate Office Exbury Southampton
Hampshire SO45 1AZ
Tel: 023 8089 1203/8089 9422
Fax: 023 8089 9940
www.exbury.co.uk

*[3mi from Beaulieu off B3054, 20min from J2
M27. Plenty of on-site parking available]*

Natural beauty is in abundance at Exbury
Gardens, a 200 acre woodland garden on the
east bank of the Beaulieu River. Created by
Lionel de Rothschild in the 1920s, the Gardens
are a stunning vision of his inspiration. The
spring displays of rhododendrons, azaleas,
camellias and magnolias are world famous. The
daffodil meadow, rock garden, sundial garden,
herbaceous borders, ponds, river walk and cas-
cades ensure year round interest, and why not
'let the steam train take the strain' on a 1 1/4
mile journey over a bridge, through a tunnel
across a pond in the Summer Lane Garden

planted with bulbs, herbaceous perennials and
grasses? Then travel along the top of the rock
garden and across a viaduct into the American
Garden. Fun for all the family and a day out at
Exbury that the weather cannot spoil. Dogs
allowed on short lead. Neighbouring 'Maize
Maze' open Summer Holidays.

*8 Mar-9 Nov daily 10.00-17.30 (dusk in Nov).
Please call for winter opening arrangements and
Santa Special dates*

A£7.50 C(under3)£Free C(3-15)£1.50 OAPs
£7.00, Family Ticket (A2+C3) £17.50. Railway
an additional £3.00 per person. Rover ticket
(unlimited daily travel) £4.50. Buggy tours
+£3.00/£3.50. Group Rates: Min size 15:
A£7.00. Season Ticket: Gardens Only £29.00,
Family Gardens only £55.00. Gardens & Steam
Railway £39.00. Family Gardens & Steam
Railway £74. For more info visit
www.exbury.co.uk

Petersfield Physic Garden

16 The High Street Petersfield Hampshire
GU32 3JJ
Tel: 01730 269060
Set in an ancient walled plot, the garden has
been planted in a seventeenth-century style.

Spinners

School Lane Boldre Lymington Hampshire
SO41 5QE
Tel: 01590 673347
The garden has been entirely created by the
owners since 1960. It has azaleas, rhododen-
drons, camellias and magnolias.

West Green House Gardens

West Green Thackhams Lane Hartley Witney
Hampshire RG27 8JB
Tel: 01252 844611
Four walled gardens, fruit cages, Orangery,
parterres are surrounded by informal gardens.
Easter, May-Aug Thur-Sun, Sept weekends only

Heritage & Industrial

Beaulieu

John Montagu Building Beaulieu Brockenhurst
Hampshire SO42 7ZN

Tel: 01590 612345 Fax: 01590 612624

www.beaulieu.co.uk

[Follow brown signs from J2 (M27). Plenty of on-site parking available]

Come to Beaulieu in the heart of the new forest
and visit the world famous National Motor
Museum with over 250 vehicles from the World
Land-Speed Record Breakers and F1 racers to
family cars of the 70's, a ride on 'Wheels' will
take on a fascinating journey through 100 years
of motoring history. New exhibition for 2008,
The Art of Custom. Don't miss the James Bond
Experience featuring the Lotus Submarine Car
(twice voted the nations favourite on-screen
car). In Palace House (home of the Montagu
family since 1538) tales from the Butler, Cook
and housemaids give a fascinating insight into
the workings of a Victorian household. The thirteenth-century abbey features and exhibition
and film about the life of its Cistercian monk
founders, while the Secret Army Exhibition tells
the story of wartime Beaulieu and the training of
secret agents.

*Winter 10.00-17.00, Summer 10.00-18.00,
Closed 25 Dec*

Please call or visit website for admission prices

Hollycombe Steam Collection

Midhurst Road Liphook Hampshire GU30 7LP

Tel: 01428 724900 Fax: 01428 723682

www.hollycombe.co.uk

*[Off A3 (2mi SE). Follow brown tourist signs or
local signs for Milland. Plenty of on-site parking
available]*

Britain's largest collection of working steam,
Hollycombe is much more than an enthusiast's
museum. Rather than just studying engines
from the past, there is a complete, working
Edwardian fairground and three different railways, all of which visitors can ride on. The
emphasis is on enjoyment while recreating the
golden age of steam, from a time when Britain
was great. In addition, there are rides behind a
steam traction engine, old film shows in the
Bioscope, the forerunner of town cinemas, agricultural machinery and a whole lot more, all set
in acres of historic woodland gardens. A new
visitor centre brings the experience up to date
while information signs and a brand new gallery
around the site explain what is on show. While
there are special events throughout the season,
late May brings out the best in the gardens
when the azaleas and rhododendrons are in
flower.

*22 Mar-12 Oct Sun & Bank Hols, 26 July-25 Aug
daily 12.00-17.00, rides from 13.00*

Please visit www.hollycombe.co.uk for prices

**Discount Offer: One Child Free (with a
full-paying adult).**

Historical

Mottisfont Abbey Garden, House and Estate
Mottisfont Nr Romsey Hampshire SO51 0LP
Tel: 01794 341220
Historic house set in atmospheric gardens and grounds in the River Test Valley.

Southsea Castle
Clarence Esplanade Southsea Hampshire PO5 3PA
Tel: 023 9282 7261 Fax: 023 9287 5276
www.portsmouthmuseums.co.uk

[M27/M275 into Portsmouth, or A3(M), A27, A2030 follow Seafront symbol then Southsea Castle on brown signposts. Rail: Harbour Station. Bus: No. 6 to Palmerston Rd (shopping area) then 7min walk. Plenty of on-site parking available]

This castle was built in 1544 as part of Henry VIII's national coastal defences. In our amazing Time Tunnel Experience, the ghost of the castle's first Master Gunner guides you through dramatic scenes from the castle's eventful history. Tudor, Civil War and Victorian history. Audiovisual presentation and underground passages.

Apr-Sept daily 10.00-17.30
A£3.50 Concessions£2.50 OAPs£3.00, Family Ticket (A2+C2) £9.50. Two free children under 13 free with full paying adult. Group rates available on request.

Discount Offer: 20% off Adult Admissions.

St Cross Hospital
St Cross Road Winchester Hampshire SO23 9SD
Tel: 01962 851375 Fax: 01962 878221
www.stcrosshospital.co.uk

[J11 M3]

A beautiful group of historical medieval buildings in the water meadows alongside the river Itchen. The hospital was founded in 1132 for the benefit of 13 poor men and is one of England's oldest continuing Almshouses. Travellers can still ask for the Wayfarer's Dole - a horn of beer and a morsel of bread. Free guided tours by prior arrangement.

1 Apr-31 Oct Mon-Sat 9.30-17.00, Sun 13.00-17.00. 1 Nov-31 Mar Mon-Sat 10.30-15.30, Closed Sun

A£3.00 C£1.00 Concessions£2.50

The Vyne
Vyne Road Sherborne St. John Basingstoke Hampshire RG24 9HL
Tel: 01256 883858
With over 500 years of history and 1000 acres of beautiful gardens and parkland to explore, The Vyne has something for everyone to enjoy.

Winchester College

College Street Winchester Hampshire
SO23 9HA
Tel: 01962 621209 Fax: 01962 621166
www.winchestercollege.org

[From N J9 M3, from S J10 M3. Limited on-site parking available]

Founded in 1382, Winchester College is believed to be the oldest continuously running school in the country. Concentrating on the medieval heart of the College, guided tours last approximately 1 hour and include Chamber Court (which takes its name from the Scholars' and Fellows' chambers which surround it), the Gothic Chapel (whose fourteenth-century vaulted roof is one of the earliest examples constructed from wood rather than stone), College Hall (the original Scholars' dining room), the School (a seventeenth-century red-brick schoolroom), and the original Cloister, which contains a memorial to Mallory the mountaineer.

Guided Tours: All year daily except Christmas & New Year. For individuals and small groups - walk in tours Mon, Wed, Fri & Sat 10.45, 12.00, 14.15, 15.30; Tue & Thur 10.45, 12.00; Sun 14.15, 15.30. Group tours for parties of 10+ people can be arranged at times to suit but must be booked in advance

A£4.00 Concessions£3.50

Landmarks

Spinnaker Tower

Gunwharf Quays Portsmouth PO1 3TT
Tel: 023 9285 7520
Soaring 170 metres above Portsmouth Harbour, The Spinnaker Tower (built in 2005) offers visitors uninterrupted panoramic views across the city, harbour, sea and coastline.

Literature & Libraries

Charles Dickens' Birthplace

393 Old Commercial Road Portsmouth
Hampshire PO1 4QL
Tel: 023 9282 7261 Fax: 023 9287 5276
www.portsmouthmuseums.co.uk
[From M275 turn L at 'The News' roundabout, follow signpost for Charles Dickens Birthplace]

Built in 1805, this is Dickens' birthplace and early home. Restored and furnished to illustrate middle-class taste of the early nineteenth century, the museum displays items pertaining to Dickens' work and the couch on which he died. There are Dickens' readings at 15.00 on the first Sunday of each month.
Apr-Sept daily 10.00-17.30, Charles Dickens Birthday 7 Feb 10.00-17.00
A£3.50 Concessions£2.50 OAPs£3.00 Family Ticket (A2+C2) £9.50. Two free children under 13 free with full paying adult. Group rates available on request

Discount Offer: 20% off Adult Admissions.

Living History Museums

Milestones, Hampshire's Living History Museum

Leisure Park Churchill Way West Basingstoke
Hampshire RG22 6PG
Tel: 01256 477766 Fax: 01256 477784
www.milestones-museum.com

[J6 (M3): take ringway W & follow brown signs for Leisure Park. Plenty of on-site parking available]

Milestones brings Hampshire's recent past to life all under one roof, inside one of the biggest buildings in Basingstoke. Set within a recreated town that encompasses houses, shops, factories and even a pub, a network of streets take the visitor back in time, and on a journey through the changing conditions and changing technologies from the late Victorian era to 1940s Britain. Using the free audio guides, discover how a blacksmith turned car repairer, visit a workshop with working machinery, learn how different forms of transport were developed. See how local industrialists responded to the changing technologies of the twentieth century and world events in the nationally important collections of Thornycroft, Tasker and Wallis and Steven's industrial vehicles all set in a realistic context. Historical characters and for families, hands-on activities, all add to the special atmosphere of a visit to Milestones. Special events and exhibitions throughout the year.

All year Tue-Fri 10.00-17.00, Sat & Sun 11.00-17.00, Bank Hol 10.00-17.00. Closed Mon, 25-26 Dec & 1 Jan

A£7.50 C(under5)£Free C(5-15)£4.50 Concessions£6.75, Family Ticket (A2+C2) £22.00. Schools Visit C£3.70. Group rates: (15+) A£5.00

Discount Offer: Two for the Price of One (full-paying adult).

Maritime

Portsmouth Historic Dockyard

Visitor Centre Victory Gate Portsmouth
Hampshire PO1 3LJ
Tel: 023 9283 9766 Fax: 023 9283 8228
www.historicdockyard.co.uk

[5mi from M27 J12. M275 into Portsmouth & follow 'Historic Waterfront' signs]

Portsmouth Historic Dockyard is home to three famous warships, Admiral Lord Nelson's HMS Victory, the first iron hulled armoured battleship HMS Warrior 1860 and King Henry VIII's favourite warship the Mary Rose which sank in 1545. Attractions also include Action Stations, which provides interactive displays and simulators on the modern day Navy, the Royal Naval Museum, Harbour Tours cruises and not to forget a range of retail and catering outlets. A great day out for all the family at Portsmouth Historic Dockyard. There will be a full calendar of events happening throughout the year so be sure to visit our website for more information.

All year daily Apr-Oct 10.00-18.00, last ticket sold 16.30. Nov-Mar 10.00-17.30, last ticket sold 16.00. Closed 24-26 Dec

A Standard Annual Admission gives one entry to each attraction: A£18.50 C£14.00 OAPs£16.50 Family Ticket (A2+C3) £51.50. Savings can be made with gift aid

Discount Offer: 20% off all Annual Admission Tickets.

Royal Marines Museum

Eastney Esplanade Southsea Hampshire
PO4 9PX
Tel: 023 9281 9385 Fax: 023 9283 8420
www.royalmarinesmuseum.co.uk

[M27, M3, A3M to Portsmouth Southsea front, at Eastney follow brown tourist signs. Plenty of on-site parking & dog 'park' available]

At this award winning museum, in what was one of the most stately Officers Messes in England you can discover the exciting 340 year story of the Royal Marines brought to life through dramatic and interactive displays and tour its world famous medal collection. Come and find out for yourself how Hannah Snell posed as a man and served as a marine in India in 1740. Explore the Jungle warfare room but watch out for the live snake and scorpion! Find out how the elite troops of the Royal Marines were closely involved in both World Wars, Battle of Trafalgar, Falklands War - the list goes on. Every year the Royal Marines play a key part in resolving conflicts and keeping peace around the world - here's your chance to see it all under one roof. It's the closest you'll get to experiencing life as a Royal Marine without joining up!

All year daily 10.00-17.00 Closed 24-26 Dec

A£5.25 C&Students(NUS/USI)£3.25 OAPs£4.25. Disabled£3.00. Group rates (10+): 10% discount (organiser & coach driver £Free) Schools Parties£Free, Cadets £1.00 per head

Discount Offer: Two for the Price of One (full-paying adult).

Royal Navy Submarine Museum

Haslar Jetty Road Gosport Hampshire
PO12 2AS
Tel: 023 9252 9217 Fax: 023 9251 1349
www.rnsubmus.co.uk

[Plenty of on-site parking available]

Dive into the past and the future and explore the challenges of the deep! Discover all about submarines and the men who sailed and fought in them. It's a story of remarkable bravery and exciting adventures, revealing how we grew to understand the science and dangers of the sea. Enjoy a guided tour of our World War 2 vintage submarine HMS Alliance, step onboard the fully restored Holland 1 (from 1901) and see inside X24, the only surviving WW 2 midget submarine. Command your own submarine and discover the power of the ocean and the secrets of the deep in our six interactive zones, or re-live life under the sea in our four History Galleries, which contain the personal belongings of submariners and a fascinating collection of photographs, artefacts and archive material. If you are feeling hungry, visit the Jolly Roger Café or take home a souvenir from our gift shop.

All year daily 10.00-17.30 (16.30 Nov-Mar). Closed 24-25 Dec

A£8.00,C&OAPs£6.00 Family Ticket (A2+C4) £20.00

Discount Offer: Two for the Price of One (full-paying adult).

Military & Defence Museums

Army Medical Services Museum

Keogh Barracks Ash Vale Aldershot Hampshire
GU12 5RQ
Tel: 01252 868612 Fax: 01252 868832
Some 2500 items related to the work of the
Army Medical Services are displayed.

All year Mon-Fri, closed Bank Hols

Army Physical Training Corps Museum

Fox Lines Queens Avenue Aldershot Hampshire
GU11 2LB
Tel: 01252 24431 (x 2168)
Pictorial records, militaria and gymnastic equip-
ment used from the very first Army Physical
Training Course held in 1860 to the present day.

D-Day Museum and Overlord Embroidery

Clarence Esplanade Southsea Hampshire
PO5 3NT
Tel: 023 9282 7261 Fax: 023 9287 5276
www.portsmouthmuseums.co.uk

*[M27/M275 into Portsmouth, follow museum
symbol then D-Day Museum on brown signposts.
Rail: Harbour Station. Bus: No. 6 to Palmerston
Rd (shopping area) then 7min walk. Plenty of on-
site parking available]*

Visit this year and see the Faces of History
(Winston Churchill, Montgomery and
Eisenhower) come alive in the magnificent 83
metre 'Overlord Embroidery' depicting scenes
of 'Operation Overlord' - 6 June 1944. The
Museum's unique and dramatic film show,
which includes original, historic footage and
archive film bringing this period of the Second
World War alive to the visitor. Experience life on
the 'Home Front' in an Anderson Shelter and
the period front room of the ARP Warden.
'Listen While You Work' in the factory scene;
keep vigil with the troops camped in the forest
waiting their time to embark; eavesdrop on
communications in 'The Map Room', Southwick
House. Listen to the story behind the crashed
Horda Glider; pass through the German pillbox
to the 'Beach Landing' gallery with video /
archive film of the landings and interactive touch
screens. Tanks, jeep, Dingo Scout Car, anti-aircraft gun, military equipment, models, photographs, uniforms and veteran's memories,
make this museum a necessity for military history enthusiasts.

*All year daily Apr-Sept 10.00-17.30, Oct-Mar
10.00-17.00. Closed 24-26 Dec. Cafe facilities
available May-Sept only*

A£6.00 Concessions£4.20 OAPs£5.00, Family
Ticket (A2+C2) £16.20. Group rates available on
request

**Discount Offer: 20% off Adult
Admissions.**

Explosion! The Museum of Naval Firepower

Priddy's Hard Heritage Way Gosport Hampshire
PO12 4LE
Tel: 023 9250 5600 Fax: 023 9250 5605
www.explosion.org.uk

[J11 (M27), Follow A32 to Gosport & brown tourist signs to Explosion! at Priddy's Hard. Rail: mainline route London to Portsmouth Harbour. Take ferry to Gosport (3min) then turn R & follow brown tourist signs (20min walk) or taxi to Forton Lake Bridge (3min). Plenty of on-site parking available]

Explosion! the Museum of Naval Firepower, is a hands on, interactive Museum set in the historic setting of a former gunpowder and munitions depot at Priddy's Hard, on the Gosport side of Portsmouth Harbour. Priddy's Hard was once a busy Naval Armament supply depot that provided the Royal Navy with its ammunition for over two hundred years. Telling the story of naval warfare from the gunpowder days to modern missiles, the two hour tour of the museum includes a stunning multi media film show set in the original eighteenth-century gunpowder vault, with the latest technology and interactive touch screens that bring the presentations to life. There's a fascinating social history too, including the story of how 2,500 women worked on the site during its peak in World War II. The Museum describes the role that Priddy's Hard played in naval operations worldwide for over 200 years, as well as its importance to the local Gosport community, which not only armed the Navy but also fed and watered it. Explosion! has a gift shop and the Waterside Coffee Shop (that are both open to non-visitors) so please feel free to stop by and enjoy the Camber Dock with its stunning views of the harbour.

All year (weekends only), 10.00-16.00

A£4.00 C(under5)£Free C(5-16)&Concessions£2.00 OAPs£3.00, Family Ticket (A2+C4) £10.00

Discount Offer: Two for the Price of One (full-paying adult).

Royal Armouries, Fort Nelson
Down End Road Fareham PO17 6AN
Tel: 01329 233734
Housed in an 1860's Palmerston Fort overlooking Portsmouth Harbour, the Royal Armouries (Fort Nelson) displays the nation's collection of artillery through the ages.

Nature & Conservation Parks

New Forest Otter, Owl and Wildlife Conservation Park
Deerleap Lane Longdown Nr Ashhurst
Southampton Hampshire SO40 4UH
Tel: 023 8029 2408 Fax: 023 8029 3367
www.ottersandowls.co.uk
[From M27 take exit 3 onto M271 signposted to Southampton Docks. At roundabout turn R onto A35 to Lyndhurst & Bournemouth. Follow brown tourist signs through two roundabouts then turn L into Deerleap Lane. We are just a mile down this rd. Plenty of on-site parking available]

An acknowledged Conservation Park set in 25 acres of ancient woodland within the New Forest National Park. Here you will find one of Europe's largest gathering of otters, owls and other indigenous wildlife all in their natural surroundings including pine martens, badgers, polecats, mink, foxes, Scottish wildcats, deer, lynx, wallabies and wild boar. Stroll through the animal house and watch otters swimming under water, ferrets chasing their tails and harvest mice building their homes on the top of corn stooks. Then take the Wildlife Walkabout past more otters to the Owlery and to all the other interesting animals. Throughout the day there are Keeper Sessions where you can learn more about them.

All year daily 10.00-17.30, weekends only in Jan
A£7.50 C£5.50 OAPs£6.95, Family Ticket (A2+C2) (A1+C3) £23.50. Season Ticket: A£30.50 C£22.50, Family Ticket (A2+C2) (A1+C3) £102.00. Pre-Organised School Educational Visits: A£Free (on a 1:5 ratio) C£5.25

Discount Offer: One Child Free (with a full-paying adult).

For great hotel deals call Superbreak on 01904 679999 or visit www.superbreak.com

Places of Worship

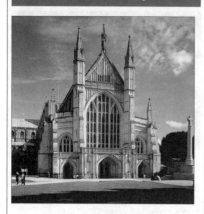

Winchester Cathedral

1 The Close Winchester Hampshire SO23 9LS
Tel: 01962 857200 Fax: 01962 857201
www.winchester-cathedral.org.uk

Explore more than 1000 year's of England's past. Walk in the footsteps of kings, saints, pilgrims, writers and artists in Europe's longest medieval cathedral. Uncover the secrets of how a diver saved the cathedral from collapse and learn why Jane Austen was buried in the nave. There's also a free children's trail available for families. The Cathedral Café (with its open-air terrace and spectacular views) has won awards for its architecture and food. The Cathedral Shop has a unique range of gifts and souvenirs, including CDs of the Cathedral Choir. A wide range of events take place throughout the year including exhibitions, markets, outside theatre, concerts and much more. Please visit our website for more information.

All year daily: Mon-Sat 08.30-18.00, Sun 08.30-17.30. Opening times may vary for services and special events

A£5.00 C(under16)£Free Concessions£4.00. Group rate: £4.00 (please call 01962 857225)

Railways

Watercress Line

The Railway Station Alresford Hampshire SO24 9JG
Tel: 01962 733810 Fax: 01962 735448
www.watercressline.co.uk

[Alresford & Alton stations are signposted off A31 Guildford to Winchester rd, follow brown tourist signs. Leave J9 or J10 M3]

Experience history in motion at the Mid-Hants Railway 'Watercress Line'. Travel by steam or heritage diesel train through 10 miles of beautiful Hampshire countryside between Alresford and Alton. Many of our locomotives have been fully restored by the engineering skills of volunteers. You can either join the line at the Georgian town of Alresford (near Winchester) or Alton, a bustling market town. On your journey you can stop at Ropley and Medstead and Four Marks stations and marvel at their preserved history. We hold special events. We also run pre-booked luxury dining trains, refreshments, picnic areas, gift shops and children's play area.

Jan-end Oct Sat-Sun & Bank Hols plus Tue-Thur May-Sept

Unlimited All-Day Travel: A£12.00 C(2-16)£6.00, Family Ticket (A2+C2) £30.00

Discount Offer: Two for the Price of One (full-paying adult).

Roman Era

Rockbourne Roman Villa
The Roman Villas Rockbourne Fordingbridge Hampshire SP6 3PG
Tel: 0845 603 5635
The Roman villa once stood in the centre of a large farming estate, and is the largest known villa in the area. Walk around the remains and visit the museum that shows what life was like for Roman Britons over 1600 years ago.

Silchester Roman City Walls and Amphitheatre
Silchester Hampshire
Originally a tribal centre of the Iron Age Atrebates, Silchester became the large and important Roman town of Calleva Atrebatum. It's third-century walls are amongst the best-preserved Roman town defences in England.

Science - Earth & Planetary

Intech Science Centre
Telegraph Way Morn Hill Winchester Hampshire SO21 1HX
Tel: 01962 863791 Fax: 01962 868524
www.intech-uk.com

[2mi from M3 J10 (from S) or J9 (N). A31]

90 hands-on exhibits about science and technology. Ideal for families with 5-11 year olds. Holiday activities, see website for details. New for March 2008, UK's biggest Planetarium amazing shows on giant domed screen with surround sound.

All year daily. Closed 24-26 Dec
A£6.75 C£4.50 OAPs£5.25, Family Ticket(A2+C2) £20.25

Discount Offer: One Child Free (with full-paying adult).

Natural History Museum and Butterfly House
Cumberland House Eastern Parade Portsmouth Hampshire PO1 3JN
Tel: 023 9282 7261 Fax: 023 9287 5276
www.portsmouthmuseums.co.uk

[M27/M275 into Portsmouth, follow Seafront symbol then Southsea Castle on brown signposts. Or A3(M), A27, A2030, follow Seafront then Castle signposts. Rail: Harbour Station. Bus: No. 6 to Festing Road]

The geology and natural history of the area are explained, with a full-size reconstruction of a dinosaur, a fresh water aquarium and British and European free-flying butterflies. There are seasonal displays of woodland, downland and marshland ecology. New displays explore the redisplayed area to discover more about dinosaurs, butterflies and wildlife in our area. Visit our new hands-on activities.

Mar 10.00-17.00, Apr-Sept daily 10.00-17.30, Oct-Mar 10.00-17.00. Closed 24-26 Dec

Admission free. Children under 13 must be accompanied by an adult

Sealife Centres & Aquariums

Blue Reef Aquarium (Hampshire)

Clarence Esplanade Southsea Portsmouth
Hampshire PO5 3PB
Tel: 023 9287 5222 Fax: 023 9229 4443
www.bluereefaquarium.co.uk

[Situated on seafront road midway between two piers. Signposted]

Take the ultimate undersea safari at the award winning Blue Reef Aquarium where there's a world of underwater adventure just waiting to be discovered. Over 40 living displays reveal the sheer variety of life in the deep; from native sharks, lobsters and adorable otters to seahorses, fascinating frogs and exotic fish. At the aquarium's heart is a giant ocean tank where an underwater walkthrough tunnel offers incredibly close encounters with the stunning beauty of a tropical coral reef - home of hundreds of colourful fish. Blue Reef is a great place for visitors of all ages to discover more about the wonders of the deep. There's a full programme of entertaining, informative talks and feeding displays throughout the day. Learn more about native sea creatures including crabs, anemones and starfish at our popular Rockpool Encounters where our experts will be on hand to answer all your questions. A spectacular experience whatever the weather.

All year daily from 10.00. Closed 25 Dec only
A£8.75 C(3-16)£6.75 Concessions£7.75
Discount Offer: One Child Free.

Zoos

Marwell Zoological Park

Colden Common Winchester Hampshire
SO21 1JH
Tel: 01962 777407 Fax: 01962 777511
www.marwell.org.uk

[J5 M27, J11 M3. Rail: Eastleigh/ Winchester. Plenty of free on-site parking available]

Beautiful Marwell is six miles southeast of Winchester in Hampshire and makes a wonderful day out for all the family. There are over 250 species of rare animals including tigers in a magnificent enclosure. Don't miss the snow leopards, rhino and hippo! Marwell has one of Europe's largest collections of rare hoofed animals including zebra and antelope and is dedicated to the conservation of endangered species. There are many popular favourites such as giraffe, meerkats, kangaroos and gibbons. Enjoy the World of Lemurs, Into Africa, Tropical World, Penguin World, the Fossa Exhibit, Aridlands and the Bat House. Road train, gift shop and adventure playgrounds. Special activity days held throughout the year. Marwell offers a day full of fun for all ages.

All year daily from 10.00. Closed 25 Dec
Please visit website for admission prices

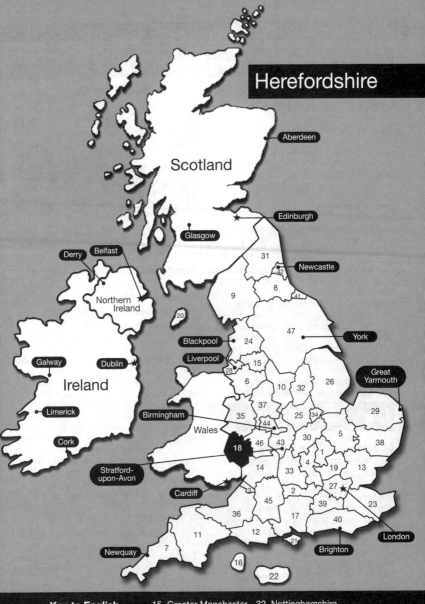

Herefordshire

Aberdeen

Scotland

Edinburgh

Glasgow

Newcastle

Derry • Belfast

Northern
Ireland

31

32

8

41

9

Blackpool

20

24

47

York

Liverpool

15

Great
Yarmouth

Galway

Dublin

Ireland

28

6

10

32

26

29

Limerick

37

25

34

Birmingham

35

44

30

5

38

Wales

46

43

1

Cork

18

14

33

4

19

13

Stratford-
upon-Avon

Cardiff

2

27

London

45

39

23

36

17

40

12

11

21

Brighton

Newquay

7

16

22

Animal Attractions

Small Breeds Farm Park and Owl Centre
Kington Herefordshire HR5 3HF
Tel: 01544 231109
Discover lots of miniature, rare and unusual animals and birds. Enjoy interacting with the birds. The Owl Centre has a superb variety of owls which are beautifully displayed in the intimate garden setting.
Daily Easter-Nov

Arts, Crafts & Textiles

Hereford Museum and Art Gallery
Broad Street Hereford Herefordshire HR4 9AU
Tel: 01432 260692
Housed in a spectacular Victorian gothic building, Hereford Museum and Art Gallery, has been exhibiting artefacts and works of fine and decorative art connected with the local area since 1874. The museum is full of interesting local history with hands-on elements for all the family.
Closed Mondays

Folk & Local History Museums

Ledbury Heritage Centre
The Old Grammar School Church Lane Ledbury Herefordshire HR8 1DN
Tel: 01531 636147
This small museum tells the story of Ledbury's past in the surroundings of a fine timber-framed building situated at the top of the picturesque Church Lane. You can learn about the poets John Masefield and Elizabeth Barrett-Browning, who both lived in Ledbury.

Market House Heritage Centre
Market Place Ross-on-Wye Herefordshire HR9 7BZ
Tel: 01432 260675
Offers a history of the town on panels, in photographs, by computer slide-show and video. It also hosts a range of community exhibitions and craft workshops. There are hands-on elements for younger visitors and an excellent gift shop.

Food & Drink

Westons Cider Visitors Centre
The Bounds Much Marcle Ledbury Herefordshire HR8 2NQ
Tel: 01531 660108 Fax: 01531 660619
www.westons-cider.co.uk

[Plenty of on-site parking available]

Nestling on a gentle hillside amongst apple and perry pear orchards 'Westons Cider' with its 400 year old farmhouse is the centre piece to a unique day out for all the family. Join a tour around our cider mill and hear how cider is produced, from the planting of the orchards to the moment it is poured into a glass. Sample our ciders and perries free in our shop (adults only). With our award winning Henry Weston Courtyard Garden, Bottle Museum Tea Room, Shire Horse Dray Rides, a Traditional and Rare Breeds Farm Park, a children's playground, a cider and gift shop and the award winning Scrumpy House restaurant and bar, there is something for everyone.

All year Mon-Fri 9.00-16.30, Sat & Sun 10.00-16.00, Cider Tours: daily 11.00 & 14.30, Farm Park: Easter-end Sept Mon-Fri 9.00-16.30, Sat & Sun 10.00-16.00 Christmas hol times may differ please check our website for details

Farm Park: A£3.00 C£2.00, Cider Tours: A£5.00 C£3.00, Dray rides A£2.50 C£1.50 (phone for availability), Children's play area & Henry Weston Courtyard Garden £Free

Discount Offer: One Child Free (with a full-paying adult).

Gardens & Horticulture

Hampton Court Gardens
Hope-Under-Dinmore Leominster HR6 0PN
Tel: 01568 797777
Walled flower garden, herbaceous borders,
canals, follies, maze and secret tunnel, hermit's
grotto, waterfalls and sunken garden.

Heritage & Industrial

Bromyard Heritage Centre
Rowberry Street Bromyard HR7 4DU
Tel: 01885 482038
Extensive exhibition on hop growing, both past
and present. Also aspects of Bromyard's local
history are on display.

Historical

Berrington Hall
Leominster Herefordshire HR6 0DW
Tel: 01568 615721
This seventeenth-century mansion is perfectly
situated with stunning views to the Black
Mountains and the Brecon Beacons.

Old House (The)
High Town Hereford Herefordshire HR1 2AA
Tel: 01432 260694
Fascinating museum giving an insight into daily
life in Jacobean times. There are hands-on
activities for children.

Places of Worship

Hereford Cathedral
5 College Cloisters Cathedral Close Hereford
Herefordshire HR1 2NG
Tel: 01432 374200
Hereford's beautiful Romanesque Cathedral
dates from 676, and contains the famous
Mappa Mundi & Chained Library.

Stately Homes

Eastnor Castle
Eastnor Ledbury Herefordshire HR8 1RL
Tel: 01531 633160 Fax: 01531 631776
www.eastnorcastle.com

*[2mi E of Ledbury on A438 Tewkesbury Rd.
Alternatively, J2 M50 then A449/A438 to Eastnor.
Plenty of on-site parking available]*

Fairytale Georgian castle in magical surroundings, with Deer Park, Lake and Arboretum,
which contains the finest collection of Cedars in
Britain. Inside this family home you'll find richly
decorated Gothic interiors by Pugin, Fine Art,
Armour and much more. Adventure Playground
and Assault Course, Knight's Maze, Children's
Fun sheets, Tree trail, Lakeside and Woodland
Walks, tearoom serving light snacks and afternoon tea and Special Events programme.
Disabled access, groups welcome. Member of
the Historic Houses Association.

*Easter Weekend, Thursday 20-24 Mar, Every
Sunday & Bank Holiday Monday from 30 Mar-28
Sept, Every Day from 14 Jul-29 Aug except Sat.
11:00-16:30*

Castle & Grounds: A£8.00 C(5-15)£5.00, OAPs
£7.00 Family Ticket £21.00. Grounds: A£4.00
C(5-15)£2.00 OAPs £10 Family Ticket (2A+3C)
£10.00. Guided tours for groups can be pre-
booked on Mon and Thurs throughout the year
subject to availability. Please see our website for
our Special Events Programme 2008 www.east-
norcastle.com

**Discount Offer: Two for the Price of
One (full-paying adult).**

Hertfordshire

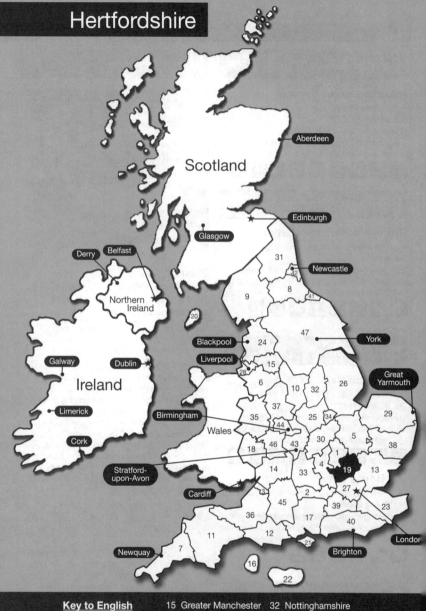

Key to English Counties:

1 Bedfordshire	15 Greater Manchester	32 Nottinghamshire
2 Berkshire	16 Guernsey	33 Oxfordshire
3 Bristol	17 Hampshire	34 Rutland
4 Buckinghamshire	18 Herefordshire	35 Shropshire
5 Cambridgeshire	19 Hertfordshire	36 Somerset
6 Cheshire	20 Isle Of Man	37 Staffordshire
7 Cornwall	21 Isle Of Wight	38 Suffolk
8 County Durham	22 Jersey	39 Surrey
9 Cumbria	23 Kent	40 Sussex
10 Derbyshire	24 Lancashire	41 Tees Valley
11 Devon	25 Leicestershire	42 Tyne & Wear
12 Dorset	26 Lincolnshire	43 Warwickshire
13 Essex	27 London	44 West Midlands
14 Gloucestershire	28 Merseyside	45 Wiltshire
	29 Norfolk	46 Worcestershire
	30 Northamptonshire	47 Yorkshire
	31 Northumberland	

Animal Attractions

Willows Farm Village

Coursers Road London Colney St Albans
Hertfordshire AL2 1BB
Tel: 0870 129 9718
Farmyard favourites, special events and demonstrations plus enjoy fun and adventure activities.

Arts, Crafts & Textiles

Henry Moore Foundation

Dane Tree House Perry Green Much Hadham
Hertfordshire SG10 6EE
Tel: 01279 843333 Fax: 01279 843647
www.henry-moore-fdn.co.uk
The annual visitors' season at Perry Green, where Henry Moore lived and worked for much of his life, offers a privileged insight into the working practices and prodigious output of the artist. The 2008 programme includes an arresting new exhibition, Henry Moore Textiles, which illuminates Moore's little-known work with fabrics, while Hoglands, Henry and Irina Moore's home - meticulously restored and only opened to the public for the first time last year -reveals how the artist lived through his most prolific period. Visitors can also enjoy the grounds set with Moore's impressive monumental sculptures and take a tour of the studios where he worked.
1 Apr-19 Oct Tue-Sun, visits must be booked.
Closed Bank Hols & Tues following Bank Hols
Tour of Studios Gallery & Grounds: A7.00 Concessions £5.00 C(Under 18)&Students(NUS/USI) £Free. Hoglands Tours: A£5.00 Concessions £4.00. Combined Ticket: A£10.00 Concessions £7.00

Country Parks & Estates

Knebworth House, Gardens, Adventure Playground and Park

Knebworth Hertfordshire SG3 6PY
Tel: 01438 812661 Fax: 01438 811908
www.knebworthhouse.com

[Direct access from J7 A1(M) at Stevenage South. Plenty of on-site parking available]

Originally a Tudor manor house this magnificent stately home with Victorian Gothic decoration is set in 250 acres of parkland. There is also a British Raj display on India. The 25 acres of formal gardens include the Jekyll Herb Garden and re-instated Victorian Maze. A self-guided Monsters and Mazes trail leads you to discover more about the gardens including the 72 life size models of dinosaurs in the Wilderness Garden. Outdoor adventure playground and miniature railway. No dogs permitted in House or Gardens except guide dogs, dogs permitted with leads in the Park.

Daily 21 Mar-6 Apr, 24 May-1 June, 30 June-3 Sept. Sat, Sun & Bank Hols 15-16 Mar, 12 Apr-18 May 7-29 June, 6-28 Sept. Park, Playground & Gardens: 11.00-17.00. House & Exhibition: 12.00-17.00 Last Admission 16.15
Including House: A£9.50 Concessions£9.00, Family Ticket £33.00. Excluding House: A£7.50 Concessions£7.50, Family Ticket £26.00. Group rates (for 20+) available for pre-booking

Discount Offer: Two for the Price of One (full-paying adult).

For great hotel deals call Superbreak on 01904 679999 or visit www.superbreak.com

Stanborough Park

Stanborough Road Welwyn Garden City
Hertfordshire AL8 6DQ
Tel: 01707 327655 Fax: 01707 393281
126 acres of parkland with two lakes, a sailing
centre, rowing boats, and a nature reserve.

Folk & Local History Museums

Hertford Museum

18 Bull Plain Hertford Hertfordshire SG14 1DT
Tel: 01992 582686
Fine collections from Hertford, Hertfordshire and
beyond; archaeology, social history, natural history, geology, fine art and photographs.

Hitchin Museum and Art Gallery

Paynes Park Hitchin Hertfordshire SG5 1EQ
Tel: 01462 458406
The gallery houses displays on local, domestic
and working life. The costume gallery covers
two centuries of fashion.

Museum of St Albans

Hatfield Road St Albans Hertfordshire AL1 3RR
Tel: 01727 819340 Fax: 01727 837472
The history of St Albans is traced from the
departure of the Romans up to the present day.
Special exhibitions and wildlife garden.

Gardens & Horticulture

Scott's Grotto

Scotts Road Ware Hertfordshire SG12 9JQ
Tel: 01920 464131
Recently restored by the Ware Society, it consists of underground passages and chambers
decorated with flints, shells, minerals and
stones.

Historical

West Garden at Hatfield House

Hatfield Hertfordshire AL9 5NQ
Tel: 01707 287010 Fax: 01707 287033
www.hatfield-house.co.uk
*[7mi from J23 M25 & 2mi from J4 A1(M), oppo-
site Hatfield railway station. Plenty of free on-site
parking available]*
Where Elizabethan history began. Celebrated
Jacobean House and Tudor Old Palace steeped
in Elizabethan and Victorian political history in a
spectacular countryside setting. Built in 1607
and home of a Cecil family for 400 years. The
Royal Palace of Hatfield (c1485) in the West
Garden is where Elizabeth I spent her childhood
and held her first council in 1558. Enjoy the
scented garden; Knot garden, elegant parterres
and borders. Picnic tables and children's play
area in the extensive park. Dogs welcome in the
Park. Licensed restaurant and gift shop open
daily. Unique venue for weddings, parties and
corporate hospitality in the Old Palace and
Riding School conference centre. The Hatfield
Banquet with costumed players is held most
Friday evenings throughout the year. Plenty of
free parking. Entrance opposite Hatfield Station.
Special events programme. Full information on
the website.
*Easter Sat 22 Mar-end Sept. House: Wed-Sun &
Bank Hols 12.00-16.00. Guided tours: weekdays
except Aug. Park & Garden: daily 11.00-17.30
throughout season. East Garden: Thurs only*
House, Park & West Garden: A£10.00 C(5-
15)£4.50 OAPs£9.00, Family Ticket (A2+C4)
£26.00. Park & West Garden: A£5.50 C£4.00,
Park only: A£2.50 C£1.50. East Garden: £3.50

**Discount Offer: Two for the Price of
One (full-paying adult).**

Literature & Libraries

Shaw's Corner

Ayot St. Lawrence Welwyn Hertfordshire
AL6 9BX
Tel: 01438 820307 Fax: 01438 820307
www.nationaltrust.org.uk/shawscorner

[A1 (M) J4, follow B653 signed to
Wheathamstead Rail: Welwyn Garden City]

Step inside the home, and mind, of the famous
Irish playwright George Bernard Shaw. The
atmospheric rooms in the house remain much
as he left them, evoking the feeling that the
great man has just gone out for the afternoon.
George Bernard Shaw lived in this cosy and
attractive Edwardian house for nearly 50 years.
As you walk through the rooms you can imagine
that he has just stepped out. See Shaw's study,
complete with typewriter, spectacles, pens,
inkwell and pocket dictionaries. Look out for
Shaw's Oscar - awarded for Best Screenplay for
the film 'Pygmalion' in 1938. Outside, relax in
the tranquil 3¼-acre garden, complete with
orchard, flower meadow, rose dell and richly
planted herbaceous borders. Enjoy beautiful
views of the garden and Hertfordshire countryside and find Shaw's revolving writing hut - so
he could catch the light to work.

House: 15 Mar-2 Nov Wed-Sun 13.00-17.00.
Garden: 15 Mar-2 Nov Wed-Sun 12.00-17.30.
Open BH Mons & Good Fri. May close earlier
when evening events occur

A£4.95 C£2.50 Family Ticket £12.40

Discount Offer: One Child Free.

Mills - Water & Wind

Mill Green Museum and Mill

Mill Green Hatfield Hertfordshire AL9 5PD
Tel: 01707 271362
This fully restored, eighteenth-century, water-
powered corn mill, adjacent to the museum, is
in regular use grinding corn in the traditional
way.

Music & Theatre Museums

St Albans Organ Theatre

320 Camp Road St Albans Hertfordshire
AL1 5PE
Tel: 01727 869693
www.stalbansorgantheatre.org.uk/index.ht
ml

[2mi from St Albans city centre. Buses: S2 & C2
come from city centre and railway station.
Located next to Camp School. Plenty of on-site
parking available]

A permanent playing exhibition of mechanical
musical instruments. Dance Organs by Decap,
Bursens, and Mortier; Mills Violano-Virtuoso self
playing violin and piano; reproducing pianos by
Steinway, Weber and Marshall & Wendell; musical boxes. Wurlitzer and Rutt theatre pipe
organs. Regular monthly theatre organ concerts. Disabled access and toilet.

Every Sun 14.00-16.30. Other times by arrange-
ment for groups. Closed 25 Dec

A£4.50 C£2.50 OAPs£3.50, Family Ticket
£10.00

Natural History Museums

Natural History Museum at Tring
Akeman Street Tring Hertfordshire HP23 6AP
Tel: 020 7942 6171

Discover the fascinating range of animals collected by Lionel Walter Rothschild in a beautiful Victorian Museum. It is also home to the research and collections of the Natural History Museum's Bird Group.

Nature & Conservation Parks

Aldenham Country Park
Dagger Lane Elstree Borehamwood
Hertfordshire WD6 3AT
Tel: 020 8953 9602

The park consists of 175 acres of woodland and parkland set around a large reservoir.

Fairlands Valley Park and Sailing Centre
Six Hills Way
Stevenage Hertfordshire SG2 0BL
Tel: 01438 353 241

120-acre park with watersports, paddling-pools and childrens play area.

Wildlife & Safari Parks

Paradise Wildlife Park
White Stubbs Lane Broxbourne Hertfordshire
EN10 7QA

Tel: 01992 470490 Fax: 01992 440525

Paradise Wildlife Park is a fantastic place to discover wonderful exotic animals including tigers, lions, monkeys and zebras.

Shepreth Wildlife Park
Willersmill Station Road Shepreth Nr Royston
Hertfordshire SG8 6PZ
Tel: 01763 262226 Fax: 01763 260582
www.sheprethwildlifepark.co.uk
[Just off A10 between Cambridge & Royston, next to train station. Ample on-site parking]
Established in 1979 the sanctuary has evolved from a quiet refuge for small and domestic animals into a remarkable and peaceful safe haven for all creatures great and small! This popular attraction boasts a cathouse, overhead walkway allowing fantastic photographic opportunities of the tigers. It also offers a tropical pavilion where exotic birds and reptiles reside and where the new tortoise house and capybara houses can be found. The gift shop remains home to Waterworld and Bug City - an indoor fish and insect house that lays claim to being the inspiration behind the National Geographic Channel's series, 'Insects from Hell'. The most recent additions are our new toddlers soft playroom and an impressive new nocturnal house with a colony of flying fox fruit bats and more. When all the animals have been enjoyed and the fish and ponies fed, there remains one last place to take pleasure in, the Wild Sea Monkey! A pirate ship marooned in the children's play area.
All year daily 10.00-18.00 (10.00-dusk during Winter months). Closed 25 Dec
Park: Summer (20 Mar-30 Nov) A£8.95 C£6.95 C(under2)£Free Concessions£6.95. Water World & Bug City only: A£2.50 C£1.75 C(under2)£Free Concessions£1.75. Water World & Bug City (when combined with park) Combined Ticket: A£1.95 C£1.50 Concessions£1.50. Group rates (for 20+): 10% discount on the day, 20% if booked & paid for 3 weeks in advance. Prices as those ruling on day of visit
Discount Offer: Free guide map with voucher.

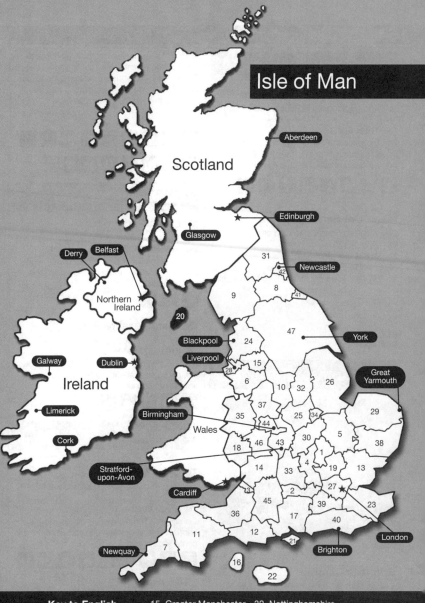

Isle of Man

Scotland

Aberdeen

Edinburgh

Glasgow

Derry

Belfast

Newcastle

31

42

Northern
Ireland

9

8

41

20

Blackpool

24

47

York

Liverpool

15

Galway

Dublin

Great
Yarmouth

Ireland

28

6

10

32

26

29

Limerick

37

Birmingham

35

25

34

44

5

38

Wales

46

43

30

Cork

18

1

Stratford-
upon-Avon

14

33

4

19

13

Cardiff

3

2

27

London

45

39

23

36

17

40

Newquay

11

12

21

Brighton

7

16

22

Key to English Counties:

1 Bedfordshire	15 Greater Manchester	32 Nottinghamshire
2 Berkshire	16 Guernsey	33 Oxfordshire
3 Bristol	17 Hampshire	34 Rutland
4 Buckinghamshire	18 Herefordshire	35 Shropshire
5 Cambridgeshire	19 Hertfordshire	36 Somerset
6 Cheshire	20 Isle Of Man	37 Staffordshire
7 Cornwall	21 Isle Of Wight	38 Suffolk
8 County Durham	22 Jersey	39 Surrey
9 Cumbria	23 Kent	40 Sussex
10 Derbyshire	24 Lancashire	41 Tees Valley
11 Devon	25 Leicestershire	42 Tyne & Wear
12 Dorset	26 Lincolnshire	43 Warwickshire
13 Essex	27 London	44 West Midlands
14 Gloucestershire	28 Merseyside	45 Wiltshire
	29 Norfolk	46 Worcestershire
	30 Northamptonshire	47 Yorkshire
	31 Northumberland	

Animal Attractions

Home of Rest for Old Horses

Bulrhenny Richmond Hill Douglas Isle of Man
IM4 1JH
Tel: 01624 674594
Visit the wonderful Retirement Home for the Ex-Douglas Tram Horses and their friends, set in over 90 acres of glorious countryside.

Mann Cat Sanctuary

Ash Villa Main Road Santon Isle of Man
IM4 1EE
Tel: 01624 824195
Many rescued cats and kittens (including Manx variety) in pleasant country setting. Also rabbits, a sheep, ducks and goats.

Apr-Sep Wed & Sun; Mar-Oct Sun only. 14.00-17.00

Arts, Crafts & Textiles

Erin Arts Centre

Victoria Square Port Erin Isle of Man IM9 6LD
Tel: 01624 832662 Fax: 01624 836658
www.erinartscentre.com
The entertainment hub of the Isle of Man is Douglas but for visitors to the South the spotlight is on the Erin Arts Centre, Port Erin. It serves the fit and well, the young, the elderly, disadvantaged and disabled. This has been a centre of excellence for more than thirty years, hosting regular concerts, plays and exhibitions to cater for all tastes, and is hired by many local organizations including the Rushen Players. The centre was founded in 1971 and since then has received international recognition as home to major cultural events, see section Festivals and Shows, and a great deal more, from instrumental and vocal competitions to visual arts and a film club. It is well worth a visit.

Exhibition Gallery:Tue-Fri 13.30-16.30

Country Parks & Estates

Mooragh Park

Ramsey Isle of Man
Tel: 01624 810100
This large municipal park offers bowling, putting, tennis, a 12-acre boating lake, children's playground and BMX track.

Onchan Pleasure Park

Onchan Isle of Man
Tel: 01624 675564
Motor boats, go-karts, crazy golf, tennis, bowling, pitch and putt, children's playground and amusement arcade.

Exhibition & Visitor Centres

Tynwald Craft Centre

Tynwald Mills St. Johns Douglas Isle of Man
IM4 3AD
Tel: 01624 801213
Country retail and leisure centre including 20+ shops, two cafés, art gallery, garden centre and conference centre.

Villa Marina and Gaiety Theatre Complex

Harris Promenade Douglas Isle of Man IM1 2HH
Tel: 01624 694555
Once a private estate, this site hosts entertainment, film, art and music performances. The complex includes Villa Marina, the Royal Hall, the Gaiety Theatre, 'Dragons' Castle' soft-play area and extensive gardens.

Festivals & Shows

Mananan International Festivals of Music and the Arts

Erin Arts Centre Victoria Square Port Erin
Isle of Man IM9 6LD
Tel: 01624 832662 Fax: 01624 836658
www.erinartscentre.com/events/mananan_
festival.html

[Signposted from Promenade]

The Celtic Sea God Mananan presides over this cornucopia of events in Port Erin in 2008. Its special blend of the very best of recitals, jazz, lectures, opera, theatre and cabaret promises a certain delight for those who venture to dip in. Includes Young Singer and Young Musician of Mann Competitions. The Erin Arts Centre also hosts the annual Mananan Summer Festival and Opera Festival and the Lionel Tertis International Viola Competition and Workshop and The Barbirolli International Oboe Festival and Competition which are held triennial.

Summer Festival: 15-29 Jun 2008. Opera Festival: 7-11 Sept 2008. Next Barbirolli event 28 Mar-2 April 2009 & next Tertis event 20-27 Mar 2010

Prices vary according to event, please call for details or visit the website

Folk & Local History Museums

House of Manannan

Mill Road Peel Isle Of Man IM5 1TA
Tel: 01624 648000 Fax: 01624 648001

[Bus: Douglas to Peel]

This new £6 million centre is an unforgettable experience. A visit will leave you in awe of the diversity of Manx Heritage and eager to learn more.

Manx Museum

Kingswood Grove Douglas Isle Of Man IM1 3LY
Tel: 01624 648000 Fax: 01624 648001
The Island's treasure house provides an exciting introduction to the 'Story of Mann' .

Historical

Peel Castle

Mill Road Peel Isle Of Man IM5 1TB
Tel: 01624 648000
One of the Island's principle historic centres, this great natural fortress with its imposing curtain wall set majestically at the mouth of Peel Harbour.

Mining

Laxey Wheel and Mines Trail

Laxey Isle of Man
Tel: 01624 648000
Built in 1854 the Great Laxey Wheel is the largest working water wheel in the world at 22 metres in diameter.

Railways

Isle of Man Transport

Banks Circus Douglas Isle of Man IM1 5PT
Tel: 01624 662525
The Isle of Man has a public transport system that includes modern buses, steam trains, an electric mountain railway and vintage trams.

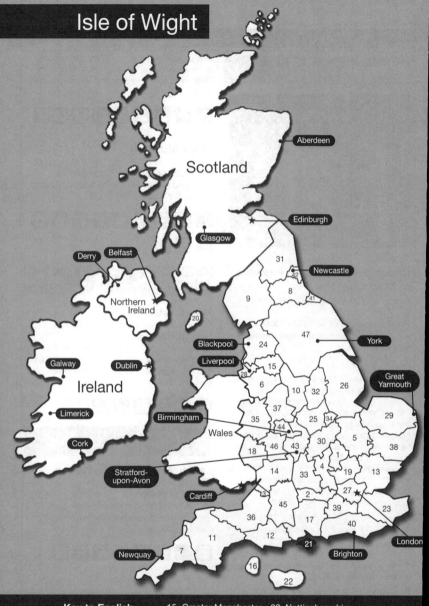

Isle of Wight

Aberdeen

Scotland

Edinburgh

Glasgow

Derry

Belfast

Northern Ireland

Newcastle

31

42

8

9

41

Blackpool

Liverpool

24

47

York

Galway

Dublin

20

Ireland

28

15

Great Yarmouth

6

10

32

26

Limerick

37

29

Cork

35

44

25

34

5

38

Birmingham

Wales

18

46

43

30

Stratford-upon-Avon

14

33

4

19

13

Cardiff

2

27

London

45

39

23

36

17

40

Newquay

11

12

21

Brighton

7

16

22

Agriculture / Working Farms

Colemans Animal Farm
Colemans Lane Porchfield Newport
Isle Of Wight PO30 4LX
Tel: 01983 522831
Friendly, family run open farm with lots of animals to feed and cuddle. Daily activities plus straw fun barns and play areas.

Animal Attractions

Amazon World Zoo Park
Watery Lane Newchurch Sandown Isle of Wight
PO36 0LX
Tel: 01983 867122
Animals, birds, reptiles, fish and insects in recreated habitats.

Brickfields Horse Country
Newnham Road Binstead Ryde Isle of Wight
PO33 3TH
Tel: 01983 566801/615116
A unique family attraction with shire horses, miniature ponies, farm animals and donkeys.

Isle of Wight Donkey Sanctuary
Lower Winston Farm St. Johns Road Wroxall
Ventnor Isle of Wight PO38 3AA
Tel: 01983 852693
The Isle of Wight Donkey Sanctuary was established in 1987 to provide a safe, permanent home for any donkey in distress.

Art Galleries

Wight Light Gallery
1a High Street, Ventnor Isle of Wight PO38 1RY
Tel: 01983 857097
Art cards, coasters, pottery, ceramics, gifts, traditional art for sale, scanning, reproduction, framing, photography courses, conference venue and licensed bar.

Tue-Fri, 09.00-17.00

Arts, Crafts & Textiles

Arreton Old Village and Barns
Main Road Arreton Newport Isle of Wight
PO30 3AA
Tel: 01983 539360
Craft Village, Pub, Lavender Herbal Craft Shop and twelfth-century church.

Quay Arts Centre
Sea Street Newport Isle of Wight PO30 5BD
Tel: 01983 528825
The Quay Arts Centre is the Isle of Wight's leading art gallery and venue for live arts events.

Birds, Butterflies & Bees

Butterfly World and Fountain World
Staplers Road Wooton Isle of Wight PO33 4RW
Tel: 01983 883430
A beautifully landscaped indoor garden with hundreds of exotic butterflies on the wing.

Country Parks & Estates

Robin Hill Country Adventure Park
Down End Nr Arretons Newport Isle of Wight
PO30 2NU
Tel: 01983 730052
The biggest rides, loads of children's play features and areas of space to run free.
Mar-Nov

Factory Outlets & Tours

Garlic Farm
Newchurch Isle of Wight PO36 0NR
Tel: 01983 865378
Learn about garlic and growing your own, plus there's a wide range of Island products.

Folk & Local History Museums

Museum of Island History

Guildhall High Street Newport Isle of Wight
PO30 1TY
Tel: 01983 823366
A new museum presenting the story of the Isle
of Wight from the time of the dinosaurs to the
present day.

Gardens & Horticulture

Ventnor Botanic Garden

Undercliffe Drive Ventnor Isle of Wight
PO38 1UL
Tel: 01983 855397
New state-of-the-art Visitor Centre includes two
exhibitions: The Green Planet and The History
of Ventnor Botanic Garden.

Historical

Appuldurcombe House

Appuldurcombe Road Wroxall Ventnor Isle of
Wight PO38 3EW
Tel: 01983 852484
Set in the imaginatively restored servants' quar-
ters and visit the owl and falconry centre.

Carisbrooke Castle

Newport Isle of Wight PO30 1XY
Tel: 01983 522107
The Isle of Wight's royal castle is remarkably
complete, with battlements to march across, a
keep to climb and a museum to explore.

Dimbola Lodge

Terrace Lane Freshwater Bay Isle of Wight
PO40 9QE
Tel: 01983 756814
The former home of Julia Margaret Cameron (a
Victorian portrait photographer) is now a her-
itage arts and photographic study centre.
Tue-Sun

Needles Old Battery

West Highdown Alum Bay Isle of Wight
PO39 0JH
Tel: 01983 754772
www.nationaltrust.org.uk/isleofwight/

*[At Needles Headland (B3322). Rail: Ferry
Yarmouth. No vehicular access to site. Car park
nearby at Alum Bay, (not NT, chargeable), disabled visitors should contact us in advance for
information]*

This spectacularly sited cliff top fort in the care
of the National Trust has the best views of the
Needles Rocks. Built in 1862 following the
threat of a French invasion, the Old Battery has
a fascinating military history which is brought to
life in a child-friendly way using cartoon displays
by Geoff Campion, leading comic book artist of
the 1950s. Discover the parade ground with its
two original gun barrels and the underground
tunnel leading to a unique view of the Needles.
Enjoy our fascinating exhibitions and then relax
in our tearoom. Families can explore the site
with a Discovery Pack, free to borrow for the
duration of your visit. The Needles New Battery
contains an exhibition about the secret rocket
tests carried out there in the 1950s and 60s as
part of Britain's race for space and there is also
a small refreshment kiosk - opening times vary.

*Needles Old Battery: 15 Mar-2 Nov 10.30-17.00.
Tues-Sun, Jul-Aug daily, Easter Mon & both May
Bank Hol Mons. Needles New Battery: 15 Mar-2
Nov 11.00-16.00. Tues, Sat & most Suns plus
most days during School Hols (but please phone
to check)*

*Closes in high winds (please phone in advance to
check)*

*Gift Aid Admission A&OAPs£4.65 C£2.35,
Family Ticket £11.55, NT Members: Free.
*Including a voluntary 10% donation; visitors
can however choose to pay the standard
admission prices which are displayed at the
property and at www.nationaltrust.org.uk

Maritime

Dinosaur Isle

Culver Parade Sandown Isle of Wight
PO36 8QA
Tel: 01983 404344 Fax: 01983 407502
www.dinosaurisle.com

[Follow brown signs to Dinosaur Isle in Sandown area. Plenty of on-site parking available]

Dinosaur Isle is Britain's first purpose built dinosaur attraction just over the sea wall in Sandown where in a spectacularly shaped building reminiscent of a Pterosaur flying across the Cretaceous skies you can walk back through fossilised time to the period of the Dinosaurs a 120 million years ago. Set in amongst a recreated landscape you will meet life sized models of the Isle of Wight's famous five dinosaurs - Neovenator, Eotyrannus, Iguanadon, Hypsilophodon and Polacanthus. Flying above you, amongst the haunting sounds of a long lost forest, are pterodactyls. You will see dinosaur skeletons as they are found by the fossil hunters and can watch our volunteers preparing the latest exciting finds. At Dinosaur Isle there are many hands on activities to try and you will be able to encounter the lost world of Dinosaurs that once roamed freely across the Isle of Wight.

All year daily, Apr-Sept 10.00-18.00, Oct-Mar 10.00-16.00. Closed 24-26 Dec & 1 Jan. Please call to confirm opening times in Jan.
A£4.95 C£2.95, Family Ticket (A2+C2) £13.95

Discount Offer: One Child Free (with every full-paying adult).

Classic Boat Museum

Sea Close Wharf Newport Harbour Newport Isle of Wight PO30 2EF
Tel: 01983 533493 Fax: 01983 533505
www.classicboatmuseum.org

[Easy access by bus from Ryde, East & West Cowes ferry terminals. Free parking at the door via Seaclose Park]

This Maritime Heritage Museum exhibits 60 small, attractive and unique water craft, both power and sail. Each craft is displayed with well-researched historic notes and with all appropriate gear. An example is 'Flying Spray' a beautiful 1912 Thames pleasure launch shown with velvet upholstery and portable gramophone! The topical displays are changed each year and restoration of historic boats by volunteers is always on view. Research is undertaken from the large archives and enquiries are welcome. The museum is open, daily in the summer and two days a week in winter, all being undercover. Facilities are provided for all abilities and there is a gift shop, and second-hand nautical books for sale. Tea and coffee are available. Group visits welcomed by prior arrangements. Parking is free via Seaclose Park with level access everywhere. Buses from Ryde and Newport stop 2 mins away.

29 Mar-2 Nov daily
A£3.00 C(6-16)&Students(NUS/USI)£1.00
OAPs£2.50. Groups welcome by prior arrangement

Nature & Conservation Parks

Shanklin Chine

The Esplanade Shanklin Isle of Wight
PO37 6BW
Tel: 01983 866432 Fax: 01983 866145
www.shanklinchine.co.uk

[Signposted on A3055. Entrance from Shanklin Esplanade or Shanklin Old Village]

Part of our national heritage, this scenic gorge at Shanklin, Isle of Wight, is a magical world of unique beauty and a rich haven of rare plants, woodland, wildlife, including red squirrels and enchanting waterfalls. A path winds through the ravine with overhanging trees, ferns and other flora covering its steep sides. The exhibition 'The Island - Then and Now' is housed in the Heritage Centre and features "Flora of the Island, new for 2008 - The Histree Trail Project, also PLUTO (Pipe Line Under The Ocean) which carried petrol to the Allied troops in Normandy, and local history displays. The Memorial to 40 Royal Marine Commando, who trained here during the war in preparation for the Dieppe Raid of 1942, can be seen at the lower entrance. After dusk, during the main summer months, subtle illuminations create a different world. Gift shop and tea room. On the beach below, Fisherman's Cottage, built by William Colenutt in 1817, offers a choice of excellent food and real ale, which can be enjoyed on the sun terrace.

20 Mar-26 Oct daily, illuminated 23 May-14 Sept
A£3.75 C(5-14incl)£2.00 C(0-4)£Free,
OAPs£2.75, Disabled/Carer£1.50, Family Ticket
(A2+C2) £9.50 or (A2+C3) £11.50. Group rate
(10+): 10% discount (excluding schools)

Railways

Isle of Wight Steam Railway

The Railway Station Havenstreet Village Ryde
Isle of Wight PO33 4DS
Tel: 01983 882204
A 10 mile 'round trip' through glorious Island countryside in Victorian and Edwardian carriages often hauled by Victorian Locomotives.
May-Sep

Stately Homes

Osborne House

East Cowes Isle of Wight PO32 6JY
Tel: 01983 200022
Queen Victoria's palace by the sea boasts extravagant interiors, jaw-dropping Indian décor, a Swiss Cottage (with child-size furniture) and a children's play area. There are also acres of gardens, carriage rides and a restaurant.

Science - Earth & Planetary

Island Planetarium

Fort Victoria Westhill Lane Norton Yarmouth Isle of Wight PO41 0RR
Tel: 0800 1958295
Planetarium theatre and astronomy centre with fascinating multimedia shows. Astronomy lectures/shows. Stargazing evenings and courses.

Shows Mon-Fri in school hols & some evenings. Term time some shows on Tues, Weds & Thurs

Sealife Centres & Aquariums

Marine Aquarium

Fort Victoria Yarmouth Isle of Wight PO41 0RR
Tel: 01983 760283
Be amazed by the variety of bizarre creatures found in our local waters.

Theme & Adventure Parks

Blackgang Chine Fantasy Park

Blackgang Ventnor Isle of Wight PO38 2HN
Tel: 01983 730330
Set in Over 40 acres of spectacular cliff-top gardens - you will find a magical mix of fantasy, legend and heritage!

Mar-Oct

Needles Park

Alum Bay Isle of Wight PO39 0JD
Tel: 0871 720 0022 Fax: 01983 755260
www.theneedles.co.uk
[Signposted on B3322. Plenty of on-site parking available]

Set in heritage coastline, offering a range of attractions for all; the spectacular chairlift to the beach provides marvellous views of the Island's famous landmark and naturally coloured sand-cliffs. On the beach there's the opportunity to take a boat trip for a closer look at the dramatic rocks and lighthouse and another chance to view the unique sandcliffs. Back at the cliff top, visit the Sand shop and create your own unique sand souvenir. At Alum Bay Glass you can watch skilled glassblowers making beautiful glassware and for those with a sweet tooth, master sweetmakers demonstrate the art of traditional sweetmaking at the Isle of Wight Sweet Manufactory. Junior Driver has proved popular with children as they learn about road safety, whilst driving an electric car and hopefully obeying road signs and working traffic lights! The Park has full catering and retail facilities including a licensed bar. Brand new is the Pier Head shopping emporium.

Easter-end Oct 10.00-17.00, hours extended on event days. Certain facilities open during winter please call for details

Admission free, all day parking £3.00 per car. Plus a range of Pay-as-you-Go Attractions Supersaver ticket provides great discounts. Facilities subject to availability and certain attractions have age/height restrictions

Discount Offer: Three for the Price of Two (Super-Saver ticket books).

Toy & Childhood Museums

Lilliput Antique Doll and Toy Museum

High Street Brading Sandown Isle of Wight PO36 0DJ
Tel: 01983 407231
Contains one of the finest collections of dolls and toys in Britain.

Wax Works

Brading The Experience

High Street Brading Sandown Isle of Wight PO36 0DQ
Tel: 01983 407286
A wax works museum, animal world, and world of wheels. Also offers a themed café, a discount factory outlet store, and a gift shop.

Zoos

Isle of Wight Zoo

Yaverland's Seafront Sandown Isle of Wight PO36 8QB
Tel: 01983 403883
Some of the planet's most endangered creatures. Tigers, lions, jaguars, leopard, black panther, monkeys, birds, snakes, lizards and insects.
Mar, Easter-Sept, Oct.

Kent

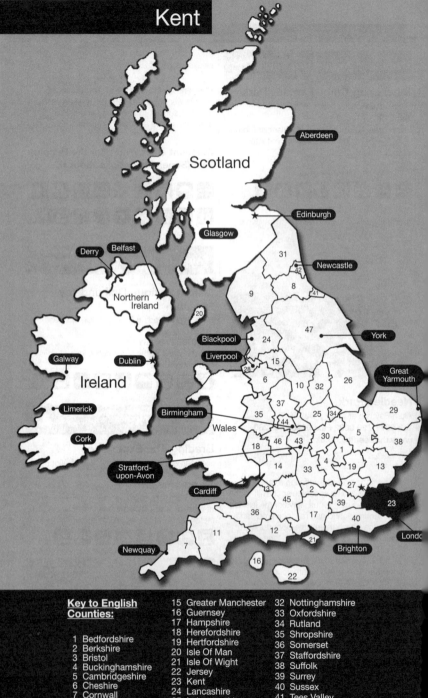

Aberdeen

Scotland

Edinburgh

Glasgow

Newcastle

31

42

8

9

41

York

Blackpool

24

47

Liverpool

15

Great Yarmouth

Derry

Belfast

28

29

Northern Ireland

20

6

10

32

26

Galway

Dublin

Birmingham

37

25

34

38

Ireland

35

44

Limerick

18

46

43

5

Cork

Wales

30

1

19

13

Stratford-upon-Avon

14

33

4

27

23

Cardiff

13

2

39

London

36

45

17

40

11

12

Newquay

7

21

Brighton

16

22

Agriculture / Working Farms

Farming World
Nash Court Boughton Faversham Kent
ME13 9SW
Tel: 01227 751144
Meet the naughty piglets, newly born lambs and
make friends with playful kids.
Feb-Nov

Hop Farm at the Kentish Oast Village
Beltring Maidstone Road Paddock Wood
Tonbridge Kent TN12 6PY
Tel: 01622 872068 Fax: 01622 872630
www.thehopfarm.co.uk

*[On A228. M25 J5 on to A21 S & 15min from
M20 J4. Plenty of on-site parking available]*

Based in the Heart of Kent, the Hop Farm at the
Kentish Oast Village includes Exhibitions, Animal
Farm and Shire Horses, indoor and outdoor
play areas and restaurant providing a great day
out for all ages and interests. The Hop Farm
also hosts a number of special events throughout the year, from Motor Shows, the 'War and
Peace Show' the largest Military Vehicle
Extravaganza in the world, to garden shows
and craft shows. Picnic areas indoor and out.

All year daily 10.00-17.00
Prices vary, please see website for details
www.thehopfarm.co.uk

Discount Offer: One Child Free.

Animal Attractions

South of England Rare Breeds Centre
Woodchurch Ashford Kent TN26 3RJ
Tel: 01233 861493
You can see the reconstruction of a historic
Georgian farmstead.

Wingham Wildlife Park
Rusham Road Shatterling Canterbury Kent
CT3 1JL
Tel: 01227 720836
Walk through the Tropical House, covered
Parrot House and Pet Village. Visit a variety of
small mammals and birds, then let off steam in
the adventure playground.

Arts, Crafts & Textiles

Canterbury Royal Museum Art Gallery
High Street Canterbury Kent CT1 2RA
Tel: 01227 452747
Magnificent Victorian building with fine porcelain
and art collections, notably by TS Cooper.
Gallery for special exhibitions.

Metropole Galleries
The Leas Folkestone Kent CT20 2LS
Tel: 01303 244706
Outstanding artists are invited to create ambi-
tious, thought-provoking exhibitions and pro-
jects.

Tunbridge Wells Museum and Art Gallery
Civic Centre Mount Pleasant
Royal Tunbridge Wells Kent TN1 1JN
Tel: 01892 554171
From Tunbridge-ware caskets, Victorian oil
paintings and archaeology to historic fashions
and dolls.

Birds, Butterflies & Bees

MacFarlane's World of Butterflies

Canterbury Road Swingfield Folkestone Kent
CT15 7HX
Tel: 01303 844244
www.macfarlanesgardens.co.uk
[From A2, take A260 Folkestone exit. From M20, take A260 Hawkinge exit. Rail: Folkestone Central Station. Bus: 16 & 16A to Canterbury service, alight at Robert's Corner. Plenty of free on-site parking available]
Where can you see the world's largest moth? Or discover a butterfly with the 'feathers' and 'eyes' of an owl? And where will you find a butterfly with wings so delicate you can see through them? Surprisingly, in a quiet corner of Kent, and it's the only place of its kind for miles around. Watch the kids' eyes light up as they stroll in a tropical 'rainforest' setting. Here you will discover swallow tails, fritillaries, dainty heliconids and the giant Atlas moth as they flutter freely among hibiscus, lantana and giant fruiting banana plants, feeding on the nectar. We welcome school and adult groups, individuals and families, and offer free guided tours with one of our expert staff. After admiring the butterflies, why not visit our gift shop or browse our Nursery and Plant Centre or relax in the Red Admiral Restaurant and sample mouth-watering home cooking. Visit and open your eyes to the wonderful world of butterflies!
31 Mar-30 Sept daily 10.00-17.00. Closed Easter Sun
A£3.00 C£2.00 Concessions£2.50, Family Ticket (A2+C2) £8.50. Group rates available on request
Discount Offer: One Child Free.

Exhibition & Visitor Centres

Canterbury Tales
St. Margaret's Street Canterbury Kent CT1 2TG
Tel: 01227 479227
Step back over 500 years to join Geoffrey Chaucer (England's finest poet) and his colourful characters on their journey to Canterbury.

Festivals & Shows

Canterbury Festival 2008
Festival Office Christ Church Gate The Precincts Canterbury Kent CT1 2EE
Tel: 01227 452853 Fax: 01227 781830
www.canterburyfestival.co.uk
[Various venues around Canterbury]
The historic setting of Canterbury provides a unique location for the largest festival of arts and culture in the region. This year's festival has over 200 events in two weeks. Working with world-renowned musicians, international companies and local artists, the festival offers an exciting programme with something for everyone, including classical concerts in the Cathedral, dance, theatre, opera, comedy, talks and debate, walks and family events in venues around the city and surrounding area. The popular and intimate festival club features an eclectic mix of jazz, folk, blues and world music.
11-25 October 2008
Prices vary, call 01227 378188 to book your tickets or online at www.canterburyfestival.co.uk. Free brochure available from July, please call 01227 452853 to request

Folk & Local History Museums

Dover Museum
Market Square Dover Kent CT16 1PB
Tel: 01304 201066
History and archaeology of Dover on two floors with models and original objects including Roman, Saxon and medieval archaeology.

Guildhall Museum
High Street Rochester Kent ME1 1PY
Tel: 01634 848717
The Guildhall Museum contains many important and varied items of interest from Pre-history to Victorian times.

Herne Bay Museum And Gallery
12 William Street Herne Bay Kent CT6 5EW
Tel: 01227 367368
Bright and modern in design this museum highlights the history of the Victorian seaside resort of Herne Bay and its surrounding area.

Museum of Canterbury with Rupert Bear Museum
Stour Street Canterbury Kent CT1
Tel: 01227 475202
Come and join Rupert and his Chums in their very own museum - full of adventure and surprises!

Museum of Kent Life
Lock Lane Sandling Maidstone Kent ME14 3AU
Tel: 01622 763936
At the Museum of Kent Life you can discover the rich and vibrant history of the people who lived and worked in The Garden England over the past 150 years.

Old Town Hall Museum
Market Place Margate Kent CT9 1ER
Tel: 01843 231213
Housed in the Grade II listed original 1690 Town Commissioners building with the 1820 Police Station and Court Room extension. The museum depicts various aspects of local history and maritime interests.

Tenterden and District Museum
Station Road Tenterden Kent TN30 6HN
Tel: 01580 764310
www.tenterdentown.co.uk

[On A28 (between Ashford & Hastings)]

Opened in 1976, the Tenterden Museum is housed in an attractive weatherboard building originally built in 1850 as a stable and store. The collections are broad in type, ranging from agriculture and industry to textiles and archives, with very strong potential as a learning resource. The six rooms on two floors house all aspects of the town's social, commercial and agricultural history. Following the Charter Exhibition commemorating the incorporation of Tenterden into the Confederation of Cinque Ports in 1449, the museum now houses a diorama replicating medieval shipbuilding at Small Hythe. To compliment exhibit, the entrance room houses the artefacts found by the 'Channel 4' TimeTeam when they excavated a site establishing that ships were built there for the medieval Royal fleet. Visitors are surprised how extensive and diverse the collection is with artefacts ranging from a 1500 BC flint axe head to the reproduction of a typical Victorian kitchen.

Easter-Oct Tue-Sun (& Bank Hols). Apr-June & Oct 13.30-16.30, July-Sep 11.00-16.30
A£1.00 C(under18)£0.25 C(under5)£Free OAPs£0.75. Group rates available on request

Food & Drink

Biddenden Vineyards and Cider Works

Gribble Bridge Lane Biddenden Kent TN27 8DF
Tel: 01580 291726 Fax: 01580 291933
www.biddendenvineyards.com

[1.5mi outside Biddenden Village on A262, bear R at Woolpack Corner. Plenty of on-site parking available]

Biddenden Vineyards and Cider Works is Kent's oldest family owned vineyard and the County's largest producer of ciders and apple juice. So why not visit us and enjoy a tranquil walk through 22 acres of vines. The grapes are grown on shallow sheltered slopes and the soil and climate is ideal for producing fresh fruity wines, which reflect the richness of the region. Biddenden Vineyards produce White, Red, Rosé and sparkling wines of the highest quality, which is reflected in the awards, received each year. Traditional strong still Ciders are also produced on site, including Monks Delight, a mulling cider and our Special Reserve, a cider oaked in whisky casks. Pure farm pressed apple juice with no added sugar is also an extremely popular product. Dogs on leads are welcome but not in the shop. Please note although our venue is recommended for adults we are also family friendly.

Mon-Sat 10.00-17.00. Sun & Bank Hols 11.00-17.00. Closed Sundays in Jan-Feb. Closed 24 Dec-Jan 1. Guided Tours for 15+ adults only, subject to prior booking

Free Admission and Tastings

Discount Offer: One Free Cup of Tea or Coffee in the Café.

Gardens & Horticulture

Emmetts Garden

Ide Hill Sevenoaks Kent TN14 6AY
Tel: 01732 868381/750367 Fax: 01732 868193
www.nationaltrust.org.uk

[4mi from M25, J5. 1.5mi S of A25 on Sundridge-Ide Hill rd. 1.5mi N of Ide Hill off B2042. Rail: Sevenoaks (4.5mi) or Penshurst (5.5mi). Bus: JRS Traveline 404 from Sevenoaks, alight Ide Hill (1.5mi). Plenty of on-site parking available]

Influenced by William Robinson, this charming and informal garden - with the highest treetop in Kent - was laid out in the late nineteenth century, with many exotic and rare trees and shrubs from across the world. There are glorious shows of daffodils and bluebells, azaleas, rhododendrons in spring and acers and cornus in autumn. There is also a rose garden and rock garden. Volunteer driven buggy can take visitors and one folded wheelchair from car park to ticket hut. Garden, shop and tearoom largely accessible and wheelchairs available. Note: there is a sheer drop at the end of the shrub garden. Occasional guided tours available.

15 Mar-1 Jun Tue-Sun & Bank Hols, 4 Jun-29 Jul Wed-Sun, 2 Jul-2 Nov Wed, Sat-Sun, 11.00-17.00

A£5.90 C£1.50, Family Ticket (A2+C3) £13.30 NT Members £Free. Group rates (15+): £4.45, must be booked in advance

Groombridge Place Gardens and Enchanted Forest

Groombridge Place Groombridge
Tunbridge Wells Kent TN3 9QG
Tel: 01892 861444 Fax: 01892 863996
www.groombridge.co.uk

[Off A264 on B2110. Plenty of on-site parking available]

Experience magic and mystery, history and romance at these beautiful award winning gardens - such an unusual mix of traditional heritage gardens with the excitement, challenge and contemporary landscaping of the ancient forest - appealing to young and old alike. Set in 200 acres of wooded parkland, the magnificent walled gardens are set against the romantic backdrop of a seventeenth-century moated manor and include herbaceous borders, white rose garden, drunken topiary, secret garden and more. Wonderful colour through the seasons. In ancient woodland there's an 'Enchanted Forest' with quirky and mysterious gardens developed by innovative designer, Ivan Hicks, to excite and challenge the imagination. Children love the Dark Walk, Tree Fern Valley, the Groms Village, Romany Camp and the Giant Swings. Also Birds of Prey flying displays, canal boat cruises and a great programme of special events.

21 Mar-8 Nov daily 10.00-17.30 (or dusk if earlier)

A£8.95 C(3-12)&OAPs£7.45, Family Ticket (A2+C2) £29.95. Prices are subject to a 0.50p increase on event days. Season tickets and group rates available

Sissinghurst Castle Garden

Biddenden Road Sissinghurst Cranbrook Kent TN17 2AB
Tel: 01580 710700/1 Fax: 01580 710702

[1mi E of Sissinghurst. Rail: Staplehurst]

One of the world's most celebrated gardens, the creation of Vita Sackville-West and her husband Sir Harold Nicolson. This internationally renowned garden was developed by Vita Sackville-West and Sir Harold Nicolson around the surviving parts of an Elizabethan mansion. It comprises small enclosed compartments, with colour throughout the season, resulting in an intimate and romantic atmosphere. Enjoy the unique ambience of this wonderful historic garden and submerge yourself in peace and tranquillity. The library and study, where Vita worked are open to visitors. Explore the wider estate and Wealden landscape with lake and woodland walks. Children's quizzes, painting and discovery packs are available free of charge. There is a large self-service restaurant, coffee shop, gift shop, plant shop and a full and varied events programme throughout the season, please telephone for more details.

15 Mar-2 Nov: Mon, Tue & Fri 11.00-18.30, Sat-Sun 10.00-18.30

A£9.00 C£4.50, Family Ticket £22.50

Historical

Fleur de Lis Heritage Centre

10-13 Preston Street Faversham Kent ME13 8NS
Tel: 01795 534542
The Centre traces the history of one of Britain's most historic and attractive towns.

Belmont

Belmont Park Throwley Faversham Kent
ME13 0HH
Tel: 01795 890202
This unique Georgian house is set in beautiful
gardens and surrounded by classical English
country parkland.

Cobham Hall

Cobham Gravesend Kent DA12 3BL
Tel: 01474 823371 Fax: 01474 825904
www.cobhamhall.com

*[Adjacent to A2 / M2 between Gravesend /
Rochester. 8mi from J2 M25, 27mi from London.
Plenty of on-site parking available]*

Cobham Hall is an outstandingly beautiful, red
brick mansion in Elizabethan, Jacobean,
Carolian and eighteenth-century styles. This former home of the Earls of Darnley is set in 150
acres of parkland and is now an Independent
international boarding and day school. The
Gothic Dairy and some of the classical garden
buildings are being renovated. The grounds
yield many delights for the lover of nature, especially in spring, when the gardens and woods
are resplendent with daffodils, narcissi and myriad of rare bulbs. The House is open for guided
tours Wednesdays and Sundays with delicious
cream teas available in the Gilt Hall.

*Mar, Apr Wed, Sun & Easter Weekend 14.00-
17.00, July-Aug Wed & Sun 14.00-17.00.
Guided Tours: Weds & Sun 14.00-17.00*
A£4.50 C&OAPs£3.50

Chartwell

Mapleton Road Westerham Kent TN16 1PS
Tel: 01732 868381/866368
Fax: 01732 868193
www.nationaltrust.org.uk/chartwell

*[2mi S of Westerham. Rail: Edenbridge, Oxted or
Sevenoaks. Plenty of on-site parking available
(Free to NT members)]*

Home of Sir Winston Churchill. With pictures,
maps, documents and personal mementoes.
The gardens contain the lakes he dug, the
water garden where he fed his fish and his garden studio. Chartwell has partial disabled
access.

*House: 15 Mar-29 Jun Wed-Sun, 2 July-3 Sept
Tue-Sun, 3 Sept-2 Nov Wed-Sun 11.00-17.00*
A£11.20 C£5.60 Pre-booked Groups£9.00,
Family Ticket £28.00. NT Members free

Chiddingstone Castle

Chiddingstone Edenbridge Kent TN8 7AD
Tel: 01892 870347
Set in 35 acres of woodland and formal gardens, this beautiful house dates back to the sixteenth century and is home to an impressive
collection of art and antiquities.
Thu-Sun

Deal Castle

Victoria Road Deal Kent CT14 7BA
Tel: 01304 372762
Deal Castle was built by Henry VIII as an artillery
fortress. Its huge, rounded bastions, designed
to deflect shot, once carried 66 guns.

Dover Castle and the Secret Wartime Tunnels

Dover Castle Dover Kent CT16 1HU
Tel: 01304 201628
One of the largest castles in the country, Dover Castle's origins lie in the Iron Age. However, it retained a military role right up to twentieth century - an underground hospital and command centre (used for the Dunkirk evacuation) are a legacy from WWII.

Down House - Home of Charles Darwin

Luxted Road Downe Orpington Kent BR6 7JT
Tel: 01689 859119
Visit the family home of Charles Darwin and see the very chair in which he sat to write the scientific masterpiece that first scandalised and then revolutionised the Victorian world.

Godinton House and Gardens

Godinton Park off Godinton Lane Ashford Kent TN23 3BP
Tel: 01233 620773
A superb ancient estate in a magnificent park with formal gardens.
Mar-Oct, Fri-Sun

Hever Castle and Gardens

Hever Castle Hever Edenbridge Kent TN8 7NG
Tel: 01732 865224
This romantic thirteenth-century moated Castle was the childhood home of Anne Boleyn.

Ightham Mote

Mote Road Ivy Hatch Sevenoaks Kent TN15 0NT
Tel: 01732 810378/811145
Superb fourteenth-century moated manor house, with features including the Great Hall, chapels, extensive garden and interesting walks in the surrounding woodland.
Mar-Oct, Thu-Mon

Leeds Castle

Maidstone Kent ME17 1PL
Tel: 01622 765400 Fax: 01622 735616
www.leeds-castle.com
[J8 of M20/A20. Ample on-site parking]
Listed in the Domesday Book, Leeds Castle was originally the site of a manor for the Saxon royal family. It has been a Norman stronghold, a royal residence for six of the medieval queens of England, the palace of Henry VIII and a 1920s country retreat. Today, visitors can journey through 1,000 years of fascinating history as they explore the castle - a treasure house of furnishings, paintings, tapestries and antiques. Discover 500 acres of parkland and woodland walks, watch magnificent falconry displays, see the birds of the aviary, have fun in the 'Knight's Realm' playground or spend time relaxing and picnicking in the gardens. Open all year daily from 10am, Leeds Castle is a guaranteed great day out for all the family.

All year daily: Apr-Sept 10.00-17.00 (last admission), Oct-Mar 10.00-15.00 (last admission). Closed 8-9 Nov and 25 Dec. Please see website for up-to-date opening times
Castle & Grounds: A£15.00 C(under4)£Free C£9.50 Concessions£12.50. Group rates available for 15+ people

Lullingstone Castle

Lullingstone Park Eynsford Dartford DA4 0JA
Tel: 01322 862114
A family mansion and church that was frequented by Henry VIII and Queen Anne. The house contains fine state rooms, portraits and armour.
Mar-Sep, Wed-Sun

Maidstone Museum and Bentlif Art Gallery

St. Faiths Street Maidstone Kent ME14 1LH
Tel: 01622 602838
www.museum.maidstone.gov.uk

[Close to Maidstone East Station in Town Centre]

An absolute must-see, this exceptionally fine regional museum houses a number of intriguing collections in an Elizabethan manor house. Collections range from natural history to military memorabilia and the costume gallery. Look out for the life-size dinosaurs and the fossils under your feet in the Earth Heritage Gallery, and don't miss the real Egyptian Mummy! Interactive areas and an exciting programme of temporary exhibitions, workshops and children's activities mean that there is something to capture everybody's imagination. Limited disabled access. Special workshops for children during half term and school holidays.

All year Mon-Sat 10.00-17.15, Sun 11.00-16.00. Closed 25-26 Dec & 1 Jan
Admission Free

Milton Chantry

Gravesend Kent
Tel: 01474 321520

Mainly encased in brick but still retaining its fourteenth-century timber roof, this building has served as a leper hospital, a chantry chapel, a public house, and Georgian barracks, before its basement became a World War II gas decontamination chamber. The building now gives visitors an insight into the heritage of Gravesham.

Apr-Sep, Sat, Sun & Bank Hols

Penshurst Place and Gardens

Penshurst Tonbridge Kent TN11 8DG
Tel: 01892 870307 Fax: 01892 870866
www.penshurstplace.com

[Car: From M25, J5, follow A21 to Tonbridge, leaving at HILDENBOROUGH exit; then follow brown tourist signs. From M20/M26, J2a, follow A25 (Sevenoaks) then A21 for HILDENBOROUGH, then follow brown tourist signs. Plenty of on site free car and coach parking. Special arrangements can be made for those with disabilities. Please contact us for further information. Rail: Train from London Charing Cross to Tunbridge Wells or London Victoria station to Edenbridge then bus (231 & 233 excl. Sundays) see www.arrivabus.co.uk.Train from London Charing Cross to Tonbridge, then taxi to Penshurst (approx. 6 mi). Or why not leave the car at home and cycle to Penshurst Place via Tonbridge on the newly opened cycle path route no 12]

Ancestral home of the Sidney family since 1552, with a history going back six and a half centuries, Penshurst Place has been described as 'the grandest and most perfectly preserved example of a fortified manor house in all England'. At the heart of this medieval masterpiece is the Barons Hall, built in 1341, and the adjoining Staterooms contain a wonderful collection of tapestries, furniture, portraits and armour. The ten acres of gardens are as old as the original house - the walls and terraces were added in the Elizabethan era - which ensures a continuous display from spring to autumn. There is also a toy museum, venture playground, gift shop and garden tea room.

1-16 Mar Sat-Sun, 21 Mar-2 Nov open daily. House: 12.00-16.00. Grounds: 10.30-18.00

House, Gardens & Grounds: A£8.50 C(5-16)£5.50, Family Ticket (A2+C2) £23.00. Grounds inc gardens : A£7.00 C£5.00, Family Ticket £20.00. Groups (15+) freeflow (non guided) House and gardens: prices frozen for 2008, A£7.00 C(5-15)£4.00. Garden and House Tours for groups (15+) available. House tours A£8.50, C£4.50. Garden Tours A£8.50, C£5.00. Combined tours: A£12.00 C£7.50. Contact our Visitor Coordinator for further information. NEW Garden Family season ticket (A2+C2) £60.00 (each additional child £6.00). Garden Season ticket (A2) £37.50. Group Enquiries: Maryann Webster 01892 870307 groups@penshurst-place.com

Discount Offer: One Child Free.

Quebec House

Quebec Square Westerham Kent TN16 1TD
Tel: 01892 866368 (Infoline)
www.nationaltrust.org.uk

[J5 or J6 (M25)]

A Grade I listed gabled house of significant architectural and historical interest, situated in the centre of the beautiful village of Westerham. Quebec House was the childhood home of General James Wolfe (victor of the Battle of Quebec 1759), and the house contains family and military memorabilia. The Tudor stable block houses an exhibition about the Battle of Quebec. Make a day of it by adding a visit to nearby Emmetts Garden with its idyllic views, spring flowers, autumn colours and rare trees and plants.

15 Mar-2 Nov, Wed-Sun & Bank Hols (13.00-17.00)

A£4.00 C£1.50, Family Ticket £9.50

Quex Museum, House and Gardens - The Powell Cotton Collection

Quex Park Birchington Kent CT7 0BH
Tel: 01843 842168 Fax: 01843 846661
www.quexmuseum.org
[In Birchington 0.5mi S of Birchington Square, SW of Margate, 13mi E of Canterbury. Signposted. Rail: Birchington. Plenty of on-site parking available]

Quex House is one of Kent's loveliest Regency Houses and has been home to five generations of the Powell-Cotton family. It sits at the heart of the fifteenth-century Quex Estate. Rooms in the House are open to the public on summer afternoons. Quex was the home of Major P.H.G. Powell-Cotton, the intrepid nineteenth-century explorer, collector and conservationist. His world-famous collections of African zoology are displayed in stunningly impressive dioramas and his ethnographic collections provide unique insights into the diversity of that continent. Further galleries in the museum contain fine examples of European and Chinese porcelain, Japanese, netsuke, an extensive series of weapons from all over the world and local archaeology. The gardens reward exploration: lawns, fountains, a woodland walk, Victorian walled garden, peacocks, dovecote and wildlife pond. The site has free parking, a shop (including plants for sale) a large licensed tea room and good access for disabled visitors.

16 Mar-30 Oct Sun-Thur 11.00-17.00, House:14.00-16.30. Winter, Sun 13.00-15.30 except Christmas and New Year

A£7.00 C(5-16)&OAPs£5.00, Family Ticket (A2+C3) £18.00. Group rates (for 20+) available on request

Shell Grotto

Grotto Hill Margate Kent CT9 2BU
Tel: 01843 220008
Accidentally discovered in 1835 by schoolboys digging in the fields adjacent to their school, the Grotto's origin is still a mystery. Includes cafe, museum and gift shop.
Good Friday - Halloween

Squerryes Court

Squerryes Westerham Kent TN16 1SJ
Tel: 01959 562345
A beautiful seventeenth-century manor house surrounded by 20 acres of attractive historic gardens, which include a lake, restored parterres and an eighteenth-century dovecote.
Apr-Sep, Wed, Sun & Bank Hols

Tonbridge Castle

Castle Street Tonbridge Kent TN9 1BG
Tel: 01732 770929
Reputedly England's finest example of a Motte and Bailey Castle with a splendid thirteenth-century gatehouse.

Landmarks

Gateway to the White Cliffs

Langdon Cliffs Dover Kent CT16 1HJ
Tel: 01304 202756
Enjoy spectacular views and discover five miles of coast and countryside through imaginative displays at the new Gateway Visitor Centre.

Living History Museums

Canterbury Roman Museum

Butchery Lane Longmarket Canterbury Kent CT1 2RA
Tel: 01227 785575
Underground, at the level of the Roman town, you will find this famous Roman house with its mosaic floors.

Maritime

Historic Dockyard Chatham, The

Chatham Kent ME4 4TZ
Tel: 01634 823807 Fax: 01634 823801
www.thedockyard.org.uk
[Rail: Chatham]
Costumed guides bring this spectacular maritime heritage site alive! Discover over 400 years of maritime history as you explore the world's most complete dockyard of the Age of Sail and 'meet' characters from the past. Set in a stunning 80 acres, our maritime galleries and attractions will excite and entertain you - whatever your age! Make rope in our Victorian Ropery as part of the "Ropery Experience" new for 2008; be gripped by stories of life aboard the three Historic Warships, experience the dockyard of 1758 recreated in the 'Wooden Walls' gallery and be inspired by the museum of the Royal Dockyard and Lifeboat! Opening in 2008 is the wonderful No. 3 Slip - one of many architectural treasures on site. Plus the beautiful Commissioner's garden and the children's indoor and outdoor play areas. Special events take place throughout the year - visit www.thedockyard.co.uk for information on all the galleries, attractions and events.
Open daily from Feb 9-Nov 2, Feb 9-Mar 20 10.00-16.00, Mar 21-Oct 25 10.00-18.00, Oct 26 onwards 10.00-16.00. Open Weekends in Nov
A£13.50 Concessions£11.00 C£9.00, Family Ticket (A2+C3) or (A1+C3) £38.00. Additional Family Child £6.00. Full price tickets are valid from 12 months from the date of first visit allowing return visits for a year, except on specified event days. Terms & conditions apply - see website for details. Subject to confirmation at end of Jan 08

Ramsgate Maritime Museum

Clock House Pier Yard Royal Harbour
Ramsgate Kent CT11 8LS
Tel: 01843 570622
www.ekmt.fogonline.co.uk

[Follow A299 to Ramsgate. Follow signs to harbour]

The museum is housed in Ramsgate Harbour's historic Clock House, a Grade II* listed building. Its five galleries explore the maritime heritage of the Isle of Thanet and East Kent from ancient times up to the present day. Subjects covered include: the construction and history of the country's only Royal Harbour; the fishing and shipbuilding industries; maritime navigation and the search for longitude; the Royal Navy and Ramsgate's role in times of war; the lifeboat service, the Great Storm of 1703; and the dangers to shipping posed by the notorious Goodwin Sands. The museum also houses a fascinating marine archaeological collection composed of artefacts raised from vessels lost on the sands - including a unique Prince Rupert Patent Demi-Cannon, recovered complete with it's original wooden carriage from the wreck of the late Stuart warship Stirling Castle.

All year, Easter-Sept: Tue-Sun 10.00-17.00, Closed Mon (except Bank Hol) .Oct-Easter: Thur-Sun 11.00-16.30. Closed Mon-Wed (except Bank Hol)

A£1.50 C£0.75 OAPs£0.75, Family Ticket £4.00

Discount Offer: Two for the Price of One (full-paying adult).

Mills - Water & Wind

Crabble Corn Mill

Lower Road River Dover Kent CT17 0UY
Tel: 01304 823292
www.ccmt.org.uk

Crabble Corn Mill is run by volunteers from the local community. Since its restoration in 1989, it has won several awards including the Community Enterprise Award. The Mill is one of the finest working watermills in Europe and it is the only working watermill in Kent. This is a must-see visitor attraction and one of Dover's hidden gems.

Apr-Sep Tue-Sun. Feb-Apr & Oct-20 Dec Sundays only. 11.00-17.00

A£5.00 Concessions£3.50, Family Ticket £13.00

Discount Offer: One Child Free With A Paying Adult on Guided Tours of The Mill

Music & Theatre Museums

Finchcocks Living Museum of Music

Riseden Goudhurst Kent TN17 1HH
Tel: 01580 211702
Contains a collection of keyboard instruments from the seventeenth century onwards.

On the Water

Bewl Water

Bewlbridge Lane Lamberhurst Tunbridge Wells
Kent TN3 8JH
Tel: 01892 890661
Watersports, fly fishing, walks and rides, boat
trips, visitor centre, restaurant and conference
facilities plus summer events.

Places of Worship

Canterbury Cathedral

The Precincts Canterbury Kent CT1 2EH
Tel: 01227 762862
One of the oldest and most famous Christian
structures in England, Canterbury Cathedral
forms part of a World Heritage Site and is the
cathedral of the Archbishop of Canterbury.

Friars, The

Aylesford Priory Aylesford Kent ME20 7BX
Tel: 01622 717272 Fax: 01622 715575
An ancient religious house of the Order of
Carmelites dating back to the thirteenth-century.
It is a blend of medieval and modern and its
chapels contain some outstanding modern
works of religious art.

Railways

Romney Hythe and Dymchurch Railway

New Romney Station Littlestone Road New
Romney Kent TN28 8PL
Tel: 01797 362353 Fax: 01797 363591
www.rhdr.org.uk

*[M20, J11 signposted, Hythe station, other sta-
tions on A259. Plenty of on-site parking available]*

The Romney, Hythe & Dymchurch Railway, is
one of the world's unique railways running for
nearly 14 miles across Kent's historic Romney
Marsh, linking the Cinque Ports towns of Hythe
and New Romney via the children's paradise of
Dymchurch and St Mary's Bay, and on to the
lighthouses at Dungeness, this is an ideal day
out for all the family. Take a ride behind one of
the superb fleet of one-third scale Steam and
Diesel locomotives on rails just 15 inches
(381mm) apart as they relive the days of the
express locomotive. There are cafés at New
Romney and Dungeness, gift shops at all major
stations and a real gem is to be found at New
Romney, above the Heywood Buffet is the
Model Railway Exhibition, with a massive working model railway layout depicting scenes from
mountains to the coast, there is also another
working layout plus toys and models which

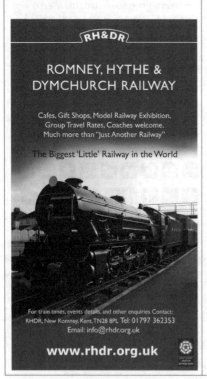

bring back happy memories of yesteryear. The history of the line is featured in words and pictures telling the story of this, the worlds only mainline in miniature, which is still being kept alive by dedicated staff and volunteers. Opened in July 1927, The RH&DR was the brainchild of two former racing drivers, Captain J.E.P Howey and Count Louis Zborowski - who was perhaps better known as the driver of the original Chitty bang bang, (the second 'Chitty' was added for the film) unfortunately Count Louis was killed in a car racing accident before the RHDR was finished but Captain Howey with the help of world renowned model maker Henry Greenly kept the dream alive to build the biggest little railway in the world.

Regular services Easter-Sept daily also weekends in Mar & Oct, Feb-Oct half-terms daily

Fares depend on length of journey, C£half-price, discount for pre-booked parties of 20+. OAP concessions available

Discount Offer: One Child Free (with a full-paying adult).

Spa Valley Railway

West Station Nevill Terrace Tunbridge Wells Kent TN2 5QY
Tel: 01892 537715
The heritage railway, primarily operating Steam hauled passenger trains, runs from the historic town of Royal Tunbridge Wells, via High Rocks, to the charming village of Groombridge.

Theme & Adventure Parks

Dickens World

Leviathan Way Chatham Maritime Kent ME4 4LL
Tel: 0870 241 1415
An indoor visitor complex themed around the life, books and times of one of Britain's best loved authors.

Diggerland (Kent)

Medway Valley Leisure Park Roman Way Strood Kent ME2 2NU
Tel: 08700 344437 Fax: 09012 010300
www.diggerland.com

[M2 J2, A228 towards Rochester. At roundabout turn R, we are on R. Rail: Strood & Rochester. Bus: Arriva 151. Plenty of on-site parking available]

Diggerland is the best activity day out for all the family with all activities based around construction machinery. With over 15 rides and drives positioned in an adventure park situation. Experience the thrill of riding in Spindizzy and enjoy the view from the Sky Shuttle. Drive across rough terrain in the Super Track and enjoy a mystery ride in the Land Rover Safari. Test your co-ordination in the JCB Challenges and fasten your seat belt for the drive of your life in the Robots. A full day of fun can be had by all ages with everything onsite including refuelling at The Dig Inn and shopping at the Goodie store. Birthday parties are catered for, so if you fancy a party with a difference then contact us for details. Diggerland welcomes its 4th park in Yorkshire for 2008. Please see our website for more information.

Weekends & Bank Hols plus daily during half-term & school hols 10.00-17.00

A&C£15.00 C(under3)£Free OAPs£7.50. Group rates: (10+) 10% discount, (50+) 25% discount

Discount Offer: 10% off Admission Prices.

Go Ape! High Wire Forest Adventure (Bedgebury Forest, Kent)

Bedgebury Forest Visitor Centre Bedgebury Road Goudhurst Kent TN17 2SJ

Tel: 0845 643 9245

www.goape.co.uk

[Bedgebury is signposted off A21on B2079. Approx. 12mi SE of Tunbridge Wells & 16mi NW of Hastings. Plenty of on-site parking available]

Take to the trees and experience an exhilarating course of rope bridges, Tarzan swings and zip-slides up to 40 feet above the ground! Share approximately three exciting hours of fun and adventure, which you'll be talking about for days. Book online and watch people Go Ape! at www.goape.co.uk. Minimum height 1.4m. Maximum weight 130 kg (20.5 stone). Under-18s must be accompanied by a participating adult. One adult can supervise either two children (where one or both of them is under 16 years old) or up to five 16-17 year olds. Pre-booking is essential to avoid disappointment. Book online or by telephone (there is a £1.00 booking fee on all telephone bookings).

16-17 & 23-24 Feb, 14 Mar-31 Oct daily, Nov Sat-Sun. Dec Sat-Sun TBC please visit www.goape.co.uk. Closed Jan

Gorillas (18yrs+) £25.00, Baboons (10-17yrs) £20.00

Discount Offer: £5.00 off per person.

Go Ape! High Wire Forest Adventure (Leeds Castle, Kent)

Leeds Castle Maidstone Kent ME17 1PL

Tel: 0845 643 9245

www.goape.co.uk

[M20 J8, follow signs for Leeds Castle. Plenty of on-site parking available]

Take to the trees and experience an exhilarating course of rope bridges, Tarzan swings and zip-slides up to 40 feet above the ground! Share approximately three exciting hours of fun and adventure, which you'll be talking about for days. Book online and watch people Go Ape! at www.goape.co.uk. Minimum height 1.4m. Maximum weight 130 kg (20.5 stone). Under-18s must be accompanied by a participating adult. One adult can supervise either two children (where one or both of them is under 16 years old) or up to five 16-17 year olds. Pre-booking is essential to avoid disappointment. Book online or by telephone (there is a £1.00 booking fee on all telephone bookings).

14 Mar-31 Oct daily, (Closed Mon during term-time). Nov Sat-Sun. Dec Sat-Sun TBC please visit www.goape.co.uk. Closed Jan

Gorillas (18yrs+) £25.00, Baboons (10-17yrs) £20.00. Two for the Price of One until 23rd May 2008

Discount Offer: £5.00 off per person.

Wildlife & Safari Parks

Howletts Wild Animal Park

Bekesbourne Lane Bekesbourne Canterbury
Kent CT4 5EL
Tel: 01227 721286 Fax: 01227 721853
www.totallywild.net

[Signposted off A2 (3mi S of Canterbury). Plenty of on-site parking available]

At Howletts Wild Animal Park, you can see world conservation in action in the heart of Kent. Set in 90 acres of beautiful ancient parkland, Howletts is home to the world's largest family of gorillas in captivity and the UK's biggest African elephant herd. Rare and endangered species include black rhino, Indian and Siberian tigers, clouded leopards, Brazilian tapirs, African hunting dogs, servals, lynx and bongo. You can walk alongside amazingly agile and inquisitive lemurs in their special open enclosure and enjoy one of the world's best vantage points for observing exceptionally rare Javan langurs. Recent additions include gelada baboons, rare Sumatran tigers and wild wolves from Iberia. Summer evening shuttle and walking safaris are available - booking essential. Hot and cold dishes served all day in the Pavilion Restaurant and Pizzeria. No dogs allowed (including Guide Dogs).

Daily, Summer 10.00-18.00, Winter 10.00-17.00. Closed 25 Dec

A£14.45 C(under4)£Free C(4-16)£11.45
OAPs£12.45

Discount Offer: Kid for a Quid.

Port Lympne Wild Animal Park

Aldington Road Lympne nr Ashford Kent
CT21 4PD
Tel: 01303 264647 Fax: 01303 264944
www.totallywild.net

[J11 M20. Park is 5min away, signposted from J. Plenty of on-site parking available]

Port Lympne Wild Animal Park opens up an amazing world of exploration where many endangered and rare animals live in a sweeping 600-acre estate of woodland, hills and grassland. One minute you could be on the plains of Africa - the next, in the heart of the jungle or rainforest. Magnificent views over Romney Marsh remind you that you are in one of the most picturesque corners of the Kent countryside. The 16-acre beautifully landscaped gardens surrounding Port Lympne Mansion are an additional attraction. Recent new arrivals include a 'dancing' sifaka lemur, coatis, and baboons in an open-topped enclosure. There are also Barbary Lions, red pandas, 'flying' monkeys, the world's largest gorilla house, tigers, African hunting dogs and African elephants. You can enjoy a real safari in the 'African Experience'* where giraffe, black rhino, Zebra, ostrich, wildebeest and antelope roam free. Unique Overnight Safaris now available at Livingstone Lodge Camp (booking essential). N.B. Dogs (including Guide Dogs) are not allowed. *Small additional charge

Summer 10.00-18.00. Winter 10.00-17.00. Closed 25 Dec

A£14.45 C(under4)£Free C(4-16)£11.45
OAPs£12.45

Discount Offer: Kid for a Quid.

Lancashire

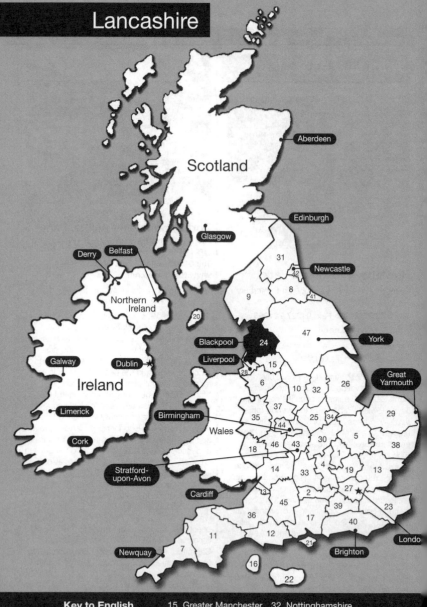

Aberdeen

Scotland

Edinburgh

Glasgow

Newcastle

Derry | Belfast

Northern
Ireland

Blackpool

Liverpool

Galway | Dublin

Ireland

Limerick

Cork

Birmingham

Wales

Stratford-
upon-Avon

Cardiff

Newquay

York

Great
Yarmouth

Brighton

London

Abbeys

Whalley Abbey

The Sands Whalley Clitheroe Lancashire
BB7 9SS
Tel: 01254 828400 Fax: 01254 825519
www.whalleyabbey.org

[J36 M6 Whalley A59 to village. Plenty of on-site parking available]

The ruins of a thirteenth-century Cistercian Abbey are set in the delightful gardens of a sixteenth-century manor house with gardens reaching down to the River Calder. On site facilities include a picnic area within the kitchen garden, a coffee shop, gift shop and small exhibition area plotting the history of the Abbey. The conference house offers Bed and Breakfast accommodation, with a 4* Quality in Tourism rating, weddings, celebration functions and conferences.

All year daily 10.00-16.30. Limited opening over Christmas & New Year

A£2.00 C£0.50 OAPs£1.25 FamilyTicket £4.00

Discount Offer: Two for the Price of One (full-paying adult).

Agriculture / Working Farms

Bowland Wild Boar Park

Chipping Preston Lancashire PR3 2QS
Tel: 01995 61554
View Wild Boar, Longhorn cows and deer in our scenic Ribble Valley Park.

Animal Attractions

Docker Park

Farm Visitor Centre Arkholme Carnforth
Lancashire LA6 1AR
Tel: 015242 21331
Come and see all the animals at Docker Park Farm - stroke the calves and piglets, cuddle baby rabbits and bottle feed the lambs.

ILPH Penny Farm

Preston New Road Peel Blackpool Lancashire
FY4 5JS
Tel: 01253 766983
www.ilph.org/pennyfarm

[On A583 a short distance from M55. Plenty of on-site parking available]

ILPH Penny Farm was opened to the public in June 2001 by HRH the Princess Royal. It is home to around 50 horses and ponies in over 100 acres and has many specialist facilities to allow us to rehabilitate horses and ponies giving them the chance of a new life through our loan scheme. Our volunteers undertake guided farm tours, relating the histories and progress of those equines on view in the yard and surrounding paddocks. Penny Farm has an informative visitor centre, which shows the work of the ILPH both at home and abroad. The coffee shop offers traditional, home made food fayre and occasionally plays host to children's' birthday parties 'with a difference'. Penny Farm is a great day out for all the family.

All year Wed, Sat-Sun & Bank Hols 11.00-16.00. Closed 25 Dec-1 Jan

Admission Free

For great hotel deals call Superbreak on 01904 679999 or visit www.superbreak.com

Birds, Butterflies & Bees

WWT Martin Mere
Fish Lane Burscough Ormskirk Lancashire
L40 0TA
Tel: 01704 895181 Fax: 01704 892343
www.wwt.org.uk

[Only 6mi from Ormskirk & 10mi from Southport. Situated off A59, signposted from M61, M58 & M6. Rail: Burscough (Southport - Manchester line) 1mi. Bus: 3 from Ormskirk (except Sun). Cyclists welcome. Plenty of on-site parking available]

Visit WWT Martin Mere at any time of year and you are guaranteed a great day out. Discover over a thousand ducks, swans, geese and flamingos in our 26 acre waterfowl gardens. Visit themed areas such as the South American Lake, the Oriental Pen and the African area, where you can see our African crowned cranes. As you wander around the waterfowl gardens feeding the waterfowl, bear in mind that your entrance fee has helped WWT to restore habitats and undertake captive breeding programmes for many of the rare birds that you have been feeding. After your walk around the waterfowl garden have lunch or a snack in the Pinkfoot Pantry and visit our gift shop for souvenirs.

All year daily Mar-Oct 09.30-17.30, Nov-Feb 09.30-17.00. Closed 25 Dec

A£8.25 C(4-16)£4.10 Concessions£6.20, Family Ticket (A2+C2) £22.25. (Prices include a voluntary donation of at least 10%, visitors can choose to pay standard admission price)

Exhibition & Visitor Centres

Botany Bay
Canal Mill Botany Brow Chorley PR6 9AF
Tel: 01257 261220
With two licensed restaurants and five floors of shops, all housed within a converted Victorian spinning mill.

Factory Outlets & Tours

Lancaster Leisure Park and GB Antiques Centre
Wyresdale Road Lancaster Lancashire LA1 3LA
Tel: 01524 68444
The complex includes a designer outlet shop, a large antiques centre, a model shop, a restaurant and café/bar, plus children's play areas.

Gardens & Horticulture

Williamson Park
Quernmore Road Lancaster LA1 1UX
Tel: 01524 33318
The Park includes the Ashton Memorial, a Tropical Butterfly House, a Mini-Beast Centre, a Foreign Bird House and a Conservation Garden.

Heritage & Industrial

British Commercial Vehicle Museum
King Street Leyland Preston PR25 2LE
Tel: 01772 451011
Illustrates the history of Britain's road transport industry through a collection of exhibits.

British Lawnmower Museum
106-114 Shakespeare Street Southport
Lancashire PR8 5AJ
Tel: 01704 501336 / 535369
Boasts a massive and unique collection of restored garden machinery and memorabilia.

Gawthorpe Hall

Padiham Burnley Lancashire BB12 8UA
Tel: 01282 771004
Elizabethan house with rich interiors and an important textile collection set in tranquil grounds in the heart of urban Lancashire.

Lancaster Castle

Shire Hall Castle Parade Lancaster Lancashire LA1 1YJ
Tel: 01524 64998 Fax: 01524 847914
www.lancastercastle.com
[Follow brown signs from A6 to the City Centre]
One of the country's hidden gems, Lancaster Castle still serves as a prison and crown court, but it is still possible to visit this intriguing place by joining one of our celebrated guided tours. From the imposing beauty of the Shire Hall to the grim reality of the Old Cells and the Drop Room, the castle reflects a thousand years of history and tells the story of the many people who have passed through its gates. Witches and martyrs, kings and queens, heroes and villains: they all have their place here against a unique setting. The castle is open daily for guided tours (except for Christmas/New Year period), but as well as that we offer regular musical and theatrical events, talks and themed tours. Telephone or visit our website for more information.

All year daily 10.00-17.00, tours 10.30-16.00. Closed Christmas & New Year
A£5.00 C&OAPs£4.00, Family Ticket £14.00

Leighton Hall

Carnforth Lancashire LA5 9ST
Tel: 01524 734474 Fax: 01524 720357
www.leightonhall.co.uk

[J35 M6. Plenty of on-site parking available]

Award-winning Leighton Hall is the lived-in house of the famous furniture-making Gillow dynasty. Unravel the fascinating past of this ancient Lancashire family and wander through the spectacular grounds. Leighton also has a caterpillar maze, plant conservatory and charming tea rooms. Children can run wild in the play area or explore a woodland trail; they're encouraged to get involved - there are no roped off areas! Leighton Hall is very much a 'lived in' house, brought to life by the enthusiasm of its guides. Leighton Hall can be found nestling in a bowl of parkland in the north of Lancashire, a few miles from the city of Lancaster. It's open to the public from May to September, pre-booked groups are welcome all year round and parking is free.

May-Sep, Tue-Fri & Bank Holiday Sun & Mons, 14.00-17.00. Open on Sundays in Aug. Groups of 25+ welcome all year round by prior arrangement.

Hall & Gardens: A£6.00 C£4.00 OAPs£5.00, Family Ticket (A2+C3) £18.00. Gardens Only: £2.00 (for all)

Discount Offer: Two for the Price of One (full-paying adult).

Rufford Old Hall

Liverpool Road Rufford Ormskirk Lancashire
L40 1SG
Tel: 01704 821254
One of the finest sixteenth-century buildings in
Lancashire with a magnificent hall, built in 1530.
Mar-Nov, Sat-Wed

Landmarks

Blackpool Tower and Circus

Central Promenade Blackpool Lancashire
FY1 4BJ
Tel: 01253 622242
Famous Victorian landmark that features a com-
prehensive entertainment programme.

Literature & Libraries

Ruskin Library

Lancaster University Lancaster Lancashire
LA1 4YH
Tel: 01524 593587 Fax: 01524 593580
www.lancs.ac.uk/depts/ruskinlib
Designed by the architect Richard MacCormac,
the dramatic new Ruskin Library features in dictionaries of contemporary world architecture,
and is worth a visit in itself. It houses an outstanding collection of watercolours, books and
manuscripts relating to the great winter and
artist John Ruskin (1819-1900). Public galleries
open daily, shows changing displays from the
collection along with occasional loan exhibitions.
These give a fascinating insight into nineteenth-
century Britain and Ruskin's continuing influence
today.
Mon-Sat 11.00-16.00, Sun 13.00-16.00
Admission Free

Model Towns & Villages

Blackpool Model Village

East Park Drive Stanley Park Blackpool
Lancashire FY3 9RB
Tel: 01253 763827
An enchanting attraction set in 2.5 acres of
landscaped gardens. Marvel at the hand-crafted
models and figures.
Mar-Nov

Performing Arts

Doctor Who Museum

The Golden Mile Centre Central Promenade
Blackpool Lancashire FY1 5AA
Tel: 01253 299982
The all-new Doctor Who Museum boasts the
largest collection of programme exhibits ever,
charting the history of the cult science-fiction
series (from 1963 to present).

Winter Gardens Blackpool

97 Church Street Blackpool Lancashire
FY1 1HL
Tel: 01253 625252
A large complex of theatres and conference
facilities.

Sealife Centres & Aquariums

Blackpool Sea Life Centre

Golden Mile Centre Promenade Blackpool
Lancashire FY1 5AA
Tel: 01253 621258 Fax: 01253 751647
www.sealifeeurope.com

[M55, signposted to venue]

One of the UK's best-known aquariums, the
Blackpool Sea Life centre houses Europe's
most comprehensive collection of tropical

sharks. It also features literally dozens of displays of all conceivable shapes and sizes, showcasing native and tropical marine life, plus a superb Amazon exhibition, complete with piranhas and poison dart frogs. Our latest attraction 'Suckers' is dedicated to octopuses and their relatives. Colour shifting cuttlefish and primitive Nautilus also star, along with a giant Pacific octopus, the largest species in the world.

All year daily from 10.00. Closed Christmas day
Please call for admission prices

Discount Offer: One Child Free.

Social History Museums

Judges' Lodgings
Church Street Lancaster Lancashire LA1 1YS
Tel: 01524 32808
Displays include a gallery featuring the history of Gillows of Lancaster together with a reconstructed cabinet makers' workshop.

Sport & Recreation

Sandcastle Waterworld
South Promenade Blackpool Lancashire FY4 1BB
Tel: 01253 343602
An indoor leisure complex built around a huge water complex.

Sporting History Museums

National Football Museum
Sir Tom Finney Way Preston PR1 6RU
Tel: 01772 908442
'The First Half' is a journey through football's history. 'The Second Half' is a themed, hands-on exhibition, examining different facets within the world of football.
Tue-Sun. Open Bank Hol Mon

Theme & Adventure Parks

Camelot Theme Park
Park Hall Road Charnock Richard Chorley Lancashire PR7 5LP
Tel: 08702 204820 Fax: 01257 452320
www.camelotthemepark.co.uk

[J27 N on M6, J28 S on M6, J8 M61. Plenty of on-site parking available]

Camelot Theme Park is a land of great knights and Amazing days where you can meet Merlin, King Arthur and his brave Knights of the Round Table and explore 5 magical lands filled with thrilling rides, spectacular shows and many more attractions. Thrill seekers will enjoy the mighty Whirlwind, and the scarey 'Knightmare' two terrifying roller coasters, designed to whip you into a frenzy, when you catch your breath dare to try the torturous Rack or brave the waters of Pendragon's Plunge. There's also a great selection of rides for our younger bravehearts. Be amazed at the spectacular horsemanship of the Knights of the Round Table and cheer for your favourite Knight as they perform in a medieval Jousting Tournament or brush up on your magic skills by joining Camelot's grand weaver of spells for a master class in conjuring and magic at Merlin's School of Wizardry. It really is an amazing family day out!

21 Mar-2 Nov Please call 24hr info line to check specific days and times

A&C£19.00 OAPs£12.50, Family Ticket (4 Guests) £64.00. Children under 1 metre in height £Free. Group rates (for 12+) available on request

Discount Offer: Two for the Price of One (full-paying adult).

Pleasure Beach, Blackpool

Blackpool Lancashire FY4 1EZ
Tel: 0871 222 1234 Fax: 01253 336618
www.pleasurebeachblackpool.com

[M6 J32 then take M55, follow brown tourist signs. Plenty of on-site parking available]

There's something for everyone at Pleasure Beach with over 125 rides and attractions plus spectacular shows including the world-renowned dancing on ice spectacular Hot Ice at the Arena and the glamorous and exotic show Forbidden at the Globe. New for 2008, get ready to tee off on the 12 hole Adventure Golf Course with water holes and a figure eight spectacular - a first to the UK. Brace yourself for Infusion - a whirlwind water experience with 5 incredible loops and rolls plus a double line twist all in one suspended looping coaster. Sample the Pepsi Max Big One, Pleasure Beach's biggest and fastest rollercoaster at 235 ft high. Don't miss Bling, a real diamond knuckle experience for riders as you're lifted a whopping 100 ft above the ground and spun through the air in giant glittering gondolas. Plus lots more for thrill seekers and all the family, including Beaver Creek, a unique children's theme park.

Pleasure Beach opens for Thrill Weekends 9 Feb-16 Mar. Open Easter to November. Reduced opening midweek early season. Please call or visit website for details

Please call or visit website for admission prices

Discount Offer: Three Wristbands for the Price of Two Wristbands.

Louis Tussauds Waxworks

87/89 Central Promenade Blackpool FY1 5AA
Tel: 01253 625953
With Celeb City and Chamber of Horrors.

Zoos

Blackpool Zoo

East Park Drive Blackpool Lancashire FY3 8PP
Tel: 01253 830830 Fax: 01253 830800
www.blackpoolzoo.org.uk

[Close to M55. Plenty of on-site parking available]
Over 1500 animals live in our 32-acre zoo, including big cats, elephants, gorillas, orang-utans, sea lions and many more! The Dinosaur Safari comprises 32 life-size dinosaurs on a fun time trail. Realistic sounds, and an erupting volcano, complete this amazing experience. There are two excellent catering facilities serving a full range of meals and snacks. Three retail outlets offer gifts from pocket-money prices to quality collectables such as the Diane Fossey range of gorillas. We also have a free exhibition area, a state-of-the-art conference facility, and an outdoor theatre arena with sheltered seating for events and shows. The entire site is fully accessible to wheelchair users. We also pride ourselves on offering "talking tours" for the blind, and signing for the deaf. No dogs allowed on site. Our superb education team provide talks and presentations for all ages and abilities and can be contacted on 01253 830805.
Daily from 10.00. Closed Christmas Day
Prices to be arranged - please see website

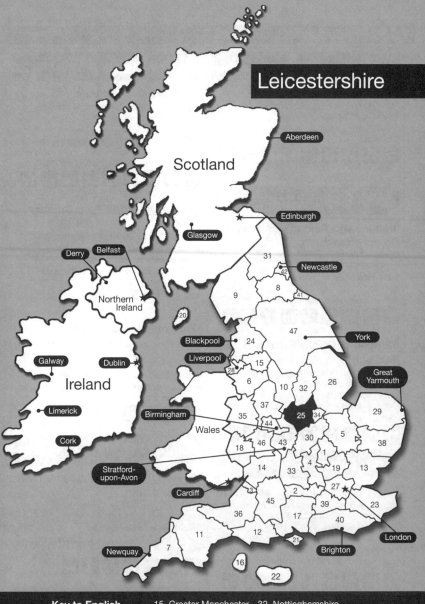

Leicestershire

Scotland

Aberdeen

Edinburgh

Glasgow

Derry
Belfast

Newcastle

Northern
Ireland

Galway
Dublin

Blackpool
Liverpool

York

Great
Yarmouth

Ireland

Limerick

Birmingham

Wales

Cork

Stratford-
upon-Avon

Cardiff

London

Newquay

Brighton

Agriculture / Working Farms

Gorse Hill City Farm

Anstey Lane Leicester Leicestershire LE4 0FL
Tel: 0116 253 7582
A community working farm in the City of
Leicester.

Animal Attractions

Manor Farm Animal Centre and Donkey Sanctuary

Castle Hill East Leake Loughborough
Leicestershire LE12 6LU
Tel: 01509 852525
Set in 100 acres with over 200 tame animals,
children's play areas and quad rides.

Stonehurst Family Farm and Museum

Bond Lane Mountsorrel Loughborough
Leicestershire LE12 7AR
Tel: 01509 413216
Kids can wander amongst and cuddle small
sheep, pigs, rabbits, hens, horses and more.

Arts, Crafts & Textiles

Ferrers Centre for Arts and Crafts

Melbourne Road Staunton Harold Ashby-de-la
Zouch Leicestershire LE65 1RU
Tel: 01332 865408
Set in the grounds of the Staunton Harold
country estate, the Centre is home to 15 high
quality individual craft workshops and studios.

Birds, Butterflies & Bees

Tropical Birdland

Lindridge Lane Desford Leicestershire LE9 9GN
Tel: 01455 824603
Over 85 species, with walk through aviaries,
chick room, woodland walk and koi ponds.
Easter-Oct daily

Country Parks & Estates

Bradgate Country Park

Bradgate Road Newtown Linford Leicester
Leicestershire LE6 0HE
Tel: 0116 236 2713
850 acres of parkland surrounding the ruins of
the fifteenth-century Bradgate House (where
Lady Jane Grey lived for most of her life).

Market Bosworth Park Country Park

The Park Market Bosworth Leicestershire
Tel: 01455 290429
87 acres of rural park, including an 11-acre
arboretum and kids' adventure playground.

Watermead Country Park

off Wanlip Road Syston Leicester Leicestershire
LE7 8PF
Tel: 0116 267 1944
230 acres of country park, with lakes, nature
reserve, woodland walks, footpaths. Access to
River Soar and canal.

Factory Outlets & Tours

Ye Olde Pork Pie Shoppe and the Sausage Shop

8-10 Nottingham Street Melton Mowbray
Leicestershire LE13 1NW
Tel: 01664 482068
Melton Mowbray's oldest and only remaining
bakery producing authentic Melton Pork Pies.

Gardens & Horticulture

Whatton Gardens

Whatton Estate Long Whatton Loughborough
Leicestershire LE12 5BG
Tel: 01509 842302 / 842268
25 acre garden containing formal and wilderness acres, including rock pools with fish and
unusual plants.

Heritage & Industrial

National Gas Museum
195 Aylestone Road Leicester LE2 7QH
Tel: 0116 250 3190
Traces the story of gas - right up to the discovery of natural gas.

Snibston
Ashby Road Coalville Leicestershire LE67 3LN
Tel: 01530 278444 Fax: 01530 813301
www.snibston.com
[10min from J22 of M1. Plenty of on-site parking available]
Visit Snibston and lift a Mini Cooper in our hands on gallery Extra Ordinary, which shows how technology has affected our every day life. Come and see the amazing selection of historic and contemporary costumes in the Fashion Gallery. Join real life miners on a tour of the colliery and experience what it was like to work underground. Take a ride on our diesel locomotive and get creative with our school holiday craft activities. Explore our nature reserve and hunt for local wildlife or let off some steam in our outdoor play area. Please see our website for further details. Some activities incur an additional charge.
All year Apr-Oct daily 10.00-17.00, Nov-Mar Mon-Fri 10.00-15.00, Sat, Sun & School hols 10.00-17.00

A£6.40 C£4.20 Concessions£4.50, Family Ticket (A2+C2) £19.20 or (A2+C3) £21.30
Discount Offer: One Child Free.

Historical

Bosworth Battlefield Visitor Centre and Country Park
Ambion Hill Sutton Cheney Market Bosworth Leicestershire CV13 0AD
Tel: 01455 290429
Gives a comprehensive interpretation of the battle by means of exhibitions.

Stanford Hall
Lutterworth Leicestershire LE17 6DH
Tel: 01788 860250
Beautiful William and Mary (1690s) house set in an attractive Park besides the River Avon.

Mills - Water & Wind

Wymondham Windmill
Butt Lane Wymondham Melton Mowbray Leicestershire LE14 2BU
Tel: 01572 787304
One of only four six-sailed windmills left in the country. Children's outdoor play area. Craft units and workshops.

Multicultural Museums

Guru Nanak Sikh Museum
9 Holy Bones Leicester Leicestershire LE1 4LJ
Tel: 0116 262 8606
Dramatic paintings, coins, hand written manuscripts and spectacular models of shrines.

Railways

Battlefield Line Railway
Shackerstone Station Shackerstone Nuneaton Warwickshire CV13 6NW
Tel: 01827 880754
Runs from Shackerstone Station, which features a small railwayana museum.

Great Central Railway

Great Central Road Loughborough
Leicestershire LE11 1RW
Tel: 01509 230726
Great Central Railway, Britain's only double
track main line heritage railway.

Science - Earth & Planetary

Challenger Learning Centre

Exploration Drive Leicester Leicestershire
LE4 5NS
Tel: 0116 261 0261
Groups take part in realistic simulated space
missions, with crew members becoming astro-
nauts, engineers and researchers.

National Space Centre

Exploration Drive Leicester Leicestershire
LE4 5NS
Tel: 0116 261 0261 Fax: 0116 258 2100
www.spacecentre.co.uk

*[Located just off A6, 2mi N of Leicester City
Centre, midway between Leicester's inner and
outer ring roads. Follow brown rocket signs from
all arterial routes around Leicester. Bus: First Bus
54 runs every 10 min throughout the day (Mon-
Sat) from Charles St and every 20 min on Sun.
First Bus 70 runs from Belgrave Gate to Abbey
Lane every 20 min (Mon-Sat). The Space Centre
is a short walk away, along Corporation Rd and
onto Exploration Dr. Onsite car parking available]*

The UK's largest attraction dedicated to space.
From the minute you catch sight of the Space
Centre's futuristic Rocket Tower, you'll be treat-
ed to hours of breathtaking discovery and interactive fun. Large Visitor Attraction of the Year

2007 and home of the UK's largest planetarium,
the National Space Centre is a hands-on, interactive journey through 6 stunning galleries,
Rocket Tower, S.I.M ride and an experience that
really is out of this world. 2008 welcomes
'Space Now' - a brand new gallery that takes
you on a journey of the exploration of the universe using the latest multimedia technology.
Visit the Human Spaceflight: Lunar Base 2025
and become an astronaut and get ready to
blast off on a stunning 3D SIM journey to the
ice moon Europa. The National Space Centre
hosts many exciting events throughout the year,
these include Movie Mania Weekend, Rise of
the Robots, Astronomy Night and many
more...see the website for full details.

*All year Tue-Sun 10.00-17.00. During
Leicestershire Schools Holidays also Mon 10.00-
17.00*

A£12.00 C(4-16)£10.00 Concessions£10.00
Family Ticket (A2+C2) £38.00 or (A2+C3)
£47.00. All children under the age of 14 must
be accompanied by an adult. All tickets valid for
12 months with gift aid for UK taxpayers.
Parking is charged at £1.00 per day

Theme & Adventure Parks

Twinlakes Park

Melton Spinney Road Melton Mowbray
Leicestershire LE14 4SB
Tel: 01664 567777
Twinlakes Park is set in beautiful countryside
and has 14 family rides, 10 play zones and
100,000 sq.ft. of indoor play.

Transport Museums

Foxton Canal Museum and Inclined Plane Trust

Middle Lock Gumley Road Foxton
Market Harborough Leicestershire LE16 7RA
Tel: 0116 279 2657
Victorian steam-powered boat lift with pub,
shop, museum, boat trips and a working boat-
yard.

Lincolnshire

Scotland

Aberdeen

Edinburgh

Glasgow

Newcastle

Derry
Belfast

Northern Ireland

Blackpool

Liverpool

Galway
Dublin

Ireland

Birmingham

Limerick

Wales

Cork

Stratford-upon-Avon

Cardiff

Newquay

Brighton

London

Great Yarmouth

York

Key to English Counties:

1 Bedfordshire
2 Berkshire
3 Bristol
4 Buckinghamshire
5 Cambridgeshire
6 Cheshire
7 Cornwall
8 County Durham
9 Cumbria
10 Derbyshire
11 Devon
12 Dorset
13 Essex
14 Gloucestershire

15 Greater Manchester
16 Guernsey
17 Hampshire
18 Herefordshire
19 Hertfordshire
20 Isle Of Man
21 Isle Of Wight
22 Jersey
23 Kent
24 Lancashire
25 Leicestershire
26 Lincolnshire
27 London
28 Merseyside
29 Norfolk
30 Northamptonshire
31 Northumberland

32 Nottinghamshire
33 Oxfordshire
34 Rutland
35 Shropshire
36 Somerset
37 Staffordshire
38 Suffolk
39 Surrey
40 Sussex
41 Tees Valley
42 Tyne & Wear
43 Warwickshire
44 West Midlands
45 Wiltshire
46 Worcestershire
47 Yorkshire

Animal Attractions

Rand Farm Park
Rand Lincoln Lincolnshire LN8 5NJ
Tel: 01673 858904 Fax: 01673 858514
Rand Farm Park provides a high quality "hands on" learning and fun experience for visitors of all ages.

Skegness Natureland Seal Sanctuary
North Parade Skegness Lincolnshire PE25 1DB
Tel: 01754 764345
A specialised collection of animals including seals, penguins, tropical butterflies and birds, sea life, reptiles and many more.

Arts, Crafts & Textiles

20-21 Visual Arts Centre
St John's Church Church Square Scunthorpe North Lincolnshire DN15 6TB
Tel: 01724 297070
The centre boasts a wide range of facilities including three excellent spaces for a regularly changing programme of art and craft exhibitions.

Country Parks & Estates

Skegness Water Leisure Park
Walls Lane Ingoldmells Skegness Lincolnshire PE25 1JF
Tel: 01754 899400
Water leisure park with cable-tow water-skiing and coarse fishing, narrow-gauge railway, caravans, tent park and a children's playground. There is also a licensed coffee shop and the Barn Inn (which are open to non-residents).

Exhibition & Visitor Centres

Cleethorpes Humber Estuary Discovery Centre
Lakeside Kings Road Cleethorpes North East Lincolnshire DN35 0AG
Tel: 01472 323232
Cleethorpes Discovery Centre - interactive exhibition - learn more about Cleethorpes history, industry and nature.

Folk & Local History Museums

Alford Manor House
West Street Alford Lincolnshire LN13 9HT
Tel: 01507 463073
Built in 1611, the house is reputedly the largest thatched manor house in the country. Following a major restoration project the house is now open to visitors. Gardens, ongoing exhibitions and special events.

Apr-Sep: Tue-Fri & Sun. Oct-Mar: Tue, Fri & Sun

Baysgarth House Museum and Leisure Park
Caistor Road Barton-Upon-Humber North Lincolnshire DN18 6AH
Tel: 01652 637568
Situated in an attractive Georgian House, set in a delightful 30 acre park, the museum illustrates the area's historical developments.

Church Farm Museum
Church Road South Skegness Lincolnshire PE25 2HF
Tel: 01754 766658
Traditional farmhouse and outbuildings restored to show way of life on a Lincolnshire farm at the end of the 19th century.

Stamford Museum and Nature Centre
Broad Street Stamford Lincolnshire PE9 1PJ
Tel: 01780 766317
See our unique Stamford Tapestry, fascinating local history collections and chat to our enthusiastic and knowledgeable staff - there is something for everyone!

Gardens & Horticulture

Springfields Outlet Shopping and Festival Gardens

Camelgate Spalding Lincolnshire PE12 6EU
Tel: 01775 760909 Fax: 01755 724495
www.springfieldsshopping.com

[1mi E of Spalding signposted off A16. Plenty of on-site parking available]

Springfields Outlet Shopping and Festival Gardens in Spalding offers over 40 factory outlet stores, themed educational gardens, celebrity designed showcase gardens by Charlie Dimmock, Kim Wilde and Chris Beardshaw, striking water features and woodland walks. There is also a children's Play Barn and Adventure Golf along with places to eat and drink. The outlet stores sell well known brands all retailing at up to 75% off high street prices and brands include Marks and Spencer, Clarks, Reebok, Game and many more. There is also the Festival Garden Centre, which houses Springfields Restaurant. New for Summer 2008, 12 new outlets stores, 43 room hotel and more attractions in the gardens.

All year Mon-Wed & Fri 10.00-18.00, Thur 10.00-20.00, Sat 09.00-18.00, Sun 11.00-17.00. Bank Hols 10.00-18.00

Admission free

...time for ...time for ...time for
Shopping Leisure Family

New for 2008
12 new retail stores
43 room feature hotel
New gardens

- 25 acres of beautiful Festival Gardens
- Over 40 Outlet stores with up to 75% off high street prices
- Superb Festival Garden Centre
- Restaurants, cafes and a family pub
- Childrens Play Barn & Mini Golf
- Free Fenscape Museum

A16 Spalding... closer than you think Call **(01775) 760909** for more information or visit www.springfieldsshopping.com

Springfields
OUTLET SHOPPING • FESTIVAL GARDENS

Heritage & Industrial

National Fishing Heritage Centre
Alexandra Dock Grimsby DN31 1UZ
Tel: 01472 323345
Witness first hand the endurance, dangers and disasters that imperilled Grimsby fishermen.
Apr-Oct daily

Historical

Belton House
Grantham Lincolnshire NG32 2LS
Tel: 01476 566116 Fax: 01476 542980
[40 min from Nottingham, Leicester & Lincoln, Belton House is on A607 Grantham / Lincoln Rd easily reached & signposted from A1. Rail: Grantham. Plenty of on-site parking available]
One of the finest examples of Restoration architecture, Belton was built in 1965-68 for 'Young' Sir John Brownlow. Stunning interiors, with fine furnishings, tapestries, paintings and period style. Delightful gardens and Orangery, lakeshore walk with restored Boat House and magnificent parkland. Adventure playground and miniature train rides. Braille, audio guides and Hearing Scheme. Family trails. Children's menu available in restaurant. Front baby slings on loan. Dogs on leads only in parkland.
House: 15 Mar-2 Nov Wed-Sun & Bank Hol Mon 12.30-17.00. Open Good Fri. Garden & Park 11.00-17.30, Shop & Restaurant 11.00-17.00. (Park sometimes closed for special events)
House & Garden: A£9.50 C(under5)£Free C(5-16)£5.50, Family Ticket (A2+C3) £25.00. Grounds only: A£7.50 C£4.50, Family Ticket £20.00. Reductions for pre-booked groups (15 minimum)

Gainsborough Old Hall
Parnell Street Gainsborough Lincolnshire DN21 2NB
Tel: 01427 612669
A stunning fifteenth-century manor house built containing a Great Hall and original kitchens.

Lincoln Castle
Castle Hill Lincoln Lincolnshire LN1 3AA
Tel: 01522 511068
An eleventh-century earthwork motte and bailey fortress, founded by William the Conqueror. Features a Magna Carta exhibition and a Prison Chapel reconstruction.

Tattershall Castle
Tattershall Lincoln Lincolnshire LN4 4LR
Tel: 01526 342543
Fortified and moated red-brick tower, built in medieval times for Ralph Cromwell, Lord Treasurer of England. Explore its six floors, from the cellar to the battlements.

Military & Defence Museums

Battle of Britain Memorial Flight Visitor Centre
Coningsby Lincolnshire LN4 4SY
Tel: 01526 344041
View the aircraft of the Battle of Britain Memorial Flight, comprising the only flying Lancaster in Europe, five Spitfires and two Hurricanes.

Mills - Water & Wind

Waltham Windmill
Brigsley Road Waltham Grimsby Lincolnshire
Tel: 01472 822236
This six sailed windmill was the last to be built in Lincolnshire. Today hosts a variety of attractions and craft units including herb garden.

Places of Worship

Lincoln Cathedral

Minster Yard Lincoln Lincolnshire LN2 1PX
Tel: 01522 561600 Fax: 01522 561634
www.lincolncathedral.com

[Uphill Lincoln]

Lincoln Cathedral is one of the finest medieval buildings in Europe. It has been a major focus of worship for over 900 years and it is a centre of excellence for art, conservation, music and architecture. Find Katherine Swynford's tomb, St Hugh's Shrine and the famous Lincoln Imp. Take a guided tour or explore at your own pace; spend an afternoon browsing in the historic libraries; join us for worship or one of our events. Please see website for details of events.

All year daily summer; Mon-Sat 07.15-20.00, Sun 07.15-18.00, winter; Mon-Sat 07.15-18.00, Sun 07.15-17.00

A£4.00 C(under5)£Free C(5-16)£1.00 Concessions£3.00, Family Ticket £10.00. Annual visitor pass £15.00

Social History Museums

Museum of Lincolnshire Life

Burton Road Lincoln Lincolnshire LN1 3LY
Tel: 01522 528448
The region's largest and most varied social history museum.

Theme & Adventure Parks

Butlins Skegness

Skegness Lincolnshire PE25 1NJ
Tel: 01754 762311
For a great day out, come on holiday for the day! With 70 years experience entertaining holidaymakers, it's no wonder we know what makes the perfect holiday.

Magical World of Fantasy Island

Sea Lane Ingoldmells Skegness Lincolnshire PE25 1RH
Tel: 01754 874668 Fax: 01754 874668
www.fantasyisland.co.uk

[Off A52. Plenty of on-site parking available]

Britain's first themed indoor family resort with traditional family fun to theme park thrills. Europe's largest 7 day open air market, over 30 rides to choose from, both inside and out including 2 of Europe's largest Coasters 1500 seater Show bar with acts showing from midday through till 2am, kiddies characters fun for all the family, Woodys Wine Bar for the younger generation with guest DJs nightly.

Mar-April weekends only. Easter daily. May-Oct daily. Market: Nov & Dec weekends only. (not theme park)

Admission free. Rides charged - tokens needed

Discount Offer: Spend £18.00 on Ride Tokens, get another £18.00 worth free.

For great hotel deals call Superbreak on 01904 679999 or visit www.superbreak.com

Pleasure Island Theme Park

Kings Road Cleethorpes Lincolnshire DN35 0PL
Tel: 01472 211511 Fax: 01472 211087
www.pleasure-island.co.uk

[M180 A180 to Cleethorpes or A46 A16 for scenic route. Rail: Cleethorpes bus runs from Railway to Park. Plenty of on-site parking available]

With oodles of great rides and attractions at Pleasure Island, where else can all the family have so much fun? There's 6 white knuckle rides including, the top spinning HydroMax. Youngsters are not forgotten in Tinkaboo Town with Kiddies' roundabouts and slides. One of the best things about Pleasure Island however, is the number of rides that can be enjoyed by all the family such as the themed water rides, the mini mine train and everyone's favourite, the dodgems, plus so much more. Don't forget that there are 6 fabulous family shows to see also, including Basil Brush during the Summer.

16 Mar-3 Sept. Closed Mon & Tue during quiet times, Sept-Oct Sat & Sun, 25 Oct-2 Nov daily
A&C£15.50 C(0-3)£Free OAPs£8.50, Family Ticket £56.00 (admits any 4 people). Group rates available on request

Discount Offer: Two for the Price of One (full-paying adult).

Trolleybus Museum at Sandtoft

Belton Road Sandtoft Doncaster North Lincolnshire DN8 5SX
Tel: 01724 711391 (24hr info) Fax: 01724 711846
www.sandtoft.org.uk

[J2 M180 (A161) to Belton, R at roundabout & travel approx. 2.5mi. Free bus from Doncaster interchange most open days (call info line for details). Plenty of on-site parking available]

The Trolleybus Museum at Sandtoft (designated as a Registered Museum) houses the largest collection of preserved trolleybuses in the World (49). It is situated on a former aerodrome on the Isle of Axholme, North Lincolnshire, and is located between Doncaster and Scunthorpe. It has more than 60 vehicles in total, including some from the continent. Motorbuses plus other vehicles and associated equipment from the trolleybus era are also represented. The museum's overhead wiring circuit allows operation of the trolleybuses on advertised open days (Trolleydays). Other attractions include an audio-visual theatre, recreated 1950's prefab bungalow and an ever-expanding collection of old cycles and lawnmowers. There is a children's adventure playground and drawing area plus the Axholme Stores with its 1950s/60s shop window displays and a trolleybus-driving simulator. For 2008, a full programme of themed events has been arranged. There is a café (which is normally open on all Trolleydays) and also a museum shop. Much of the museum is accessible to disabled persons, although access within the main vehicle depot is restricted (width-wise) for wheelchairs. We also regret that wheelchairs cannot be accommodated on most trolleybuses. The operating company, Sandtoft Transport Centre Ltd is a Registered Charity (no. 514382), and is run by volunteer members. It was established to preserve the trolleybus as part of Britain's Transport Heritage.

Trolleydays: 22-24 Mar, 12-13 Apr, 24-26 May, 7-8 Jun, 21-22 Jun, 27-28 Sep (11.00-17.00). Trolleybus Extravaganza Weekend: 3-5 May (11.00-17.00). Huddersfield Weekend: 12-13 Jul (11.00-17.00). Sandtoft Gathering Preview: 26 Jul (11.00-22.00). Sandtoft Gathering 2008: 27 Jul (10.00-18.00). Blues and Twos Weekend: 9-10 Aug (11.00-17.00). European Weekend: 23-25 Aug (11.00-17.00). Model Weekend: 13-14 Sep (11.00-17.00). St Leger Rally: 19 Oct (11.00-17.00). Twilight Trolleys: 16 Nov (11.00-18.00). Santa Days: 13-14 Dec (11.00-16.00)

Trolleydays (and pre-booked parties): A£5.00 Concessions£3.00 C(under5)£Free, Family Ticket (A2+C4) £15.00. Annual Tickets (includes quarterly magazine, 'Sandtoft Scene'): A£15.00 C£9.00. Sandtoft Gathering 2008: A£7.00 Concessions£4.00 C(under5)£Free. Santa Days: A£3.50 C£5.00 (includes gift), Concessions£3.00

Discount Offer: One Adult Admitted at the Concession Rate.

out. One of the largest tropical houses in Great Britain has hundreds of colourful butterflies flying freely in a rainforest setting. There are also crocodiles, snakes, water dragons an ant room and an insectarium. Outdoors The Lincolnshire Birds of Prey Centre has eagles, owls, falcons, hawks and vultures and fly them at 12 noon and 3pm everyday (subject to the weather and one display at 2pm during September and October). You can see everything from racoons to water buffalo in the exciting new animal collection. Included within the 20 acre park is an adventure playground with an activity castle, 40m aeriel zipline, toddler's area, ride-on tractors, and lovely gardens. The award winning tea rooms and gift shop compliment this quality assured visitor attraction.

Open daily, Mar-July 10.00-17.00, Aug 10.00-17.30, Sept-Oct 10.00-16.30, Open 2008 - 15 Mar-2 Nov

A£6.50 C£4.95 OAPs£5.95, Family Ticket (A2+C2)£20.00

Wildlife & Safari Parks

Butterfly and Wildlife Park

Long Sutton Spalding Lincolnshire PE12 9LE
Tel: 01406 363833 Fax: 01406 363182
www.butterflyandwildlifepark.co.uk

[A17. Plenty of on-site parking available]

The Butterfly and Wildlife Park voted Lincolnshire's Family Attraction of the Year 2003 by The Good Britain Guide has something to offer all age groups and is a very popular day

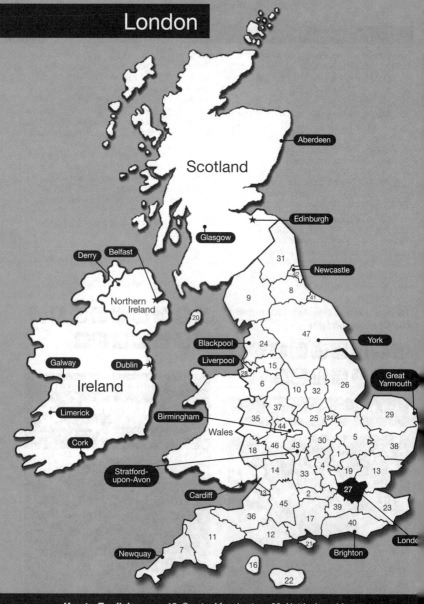

London

Aberdeen

Scotland

Edinburgh

Glasgow

Derry   Belfast   Newcastle

Northern   31
Ireland   42
                9   8   41
                            47   York
                20
Galway   Blackpool   24
              Liverpool   15   Great
Ireland   28   6   10   32   26   Yarmouth
Dublin   37   29
Limerick   Birmingham   35   44   25 34
              Wales   30   38
Cork   18 46 43   5
              Stratford-   14   33   4   1   13
              upon-Avon   19
Cardiff   13   2   27
                        45   39   23
              36   London
                    12   17   40
Newquay   11   21   Brighton
              7   16
                        22

Abbeys

Westminster Abbey: Museum, St. Margarets Church, Chapter House and Pyx Chamber

Broad Sanctuary London SW1P 3PA
Tel: 020 7222 5152
[Tube: Westminster]
A large, mainly Gothic church that serves as the traditional place of coronation.

Art Galleries

Cartoon Museum

35 Little Russell Street Camden WC1A 2HH
Tel: 020 7580 8155
[Tube: Tottenham Court Road]
Combining art with humour, this recent addition to London's gallery scene is refreshingly vibrant.

Dali Universe

County Hall Gallery Riverside Building London SE1 7PB
Tel: 0870 744 7485
[Tube: Westminster & Waterloo]
A 3000 square metre permanent exhibition in central London dedicated to Salvador Dali.

Dulwich Picture Gallery

Gallery Road Dulwich London SE21 7AD
Tel: 020 8693 5254 Fax: 020 8299 8700
www.dulwichpicturegallery.org.uk
[Just off A205 South Circular. Rail: Victoria / West
Dulwich. Plenty of on-site parking available]

Dulwich Picture Gallery is the oldest public art gallery in England is also one of the most beautiful, situated in picturesque Dulwich Village - a mere 12 minutes by train from Victoria Station. Housed in a building designed by Sir John Soane in 1811, displaying a fine cross-section of Old Masters including works by Rembrandt, Rubens, Poussin, Van Dyck, Gainsborough and Reynolds. The Gallery runs events for its visitors and for families and children, including art classes, lectures, film shows, quizzes and parties. But perhaps the Gallery is best known for its three critically acclaimed international loan exhibitions each year.

All year Tue-Fri 10.00-17.00, Sat-Sun & Bank Hol 11.00-17.00. Closed Mon except Bank Hols. Guided tours Sat & Sun at 15.00. Closed Good Friday, 24-26 Dec & 1 Jan

A£5.00 C(0-16)&Disabled&JobSeekers£Free OAPs£4.00

Discount Offer: Two for the Price of One (full-paying adult).

National Gallery

Trafalgar Square London WC2N 5DN
Tel: 020 7747 2885
[Tube: Leicester Square]
Houses one of the greatest collections of Western European painting in the world.

National Portrait Gallery

St Martins Place London WC2H 0HE
Tel: 020 7306 0055
[Tube: Charing Cross / Leicester Square]
The largest collection of portraiture in the world.

Royal Academy of Arts

Burlington House Piccadilly London W1J 0BD
Tel: 020 7300 8000
[Tube: Piccadilly Circus / Green Park]
Famous for its exhibition programme, this is the oldest arts institution in Britain.

Serpentine Gallery

Kensington Gardens Kensington W2 3XA
Tel: 020 7298 1515
[Tube: Lancaster Gate]
Provides a platform for contemporary artists,
with changing exhibitions.

Somerset House

Strand London WC2R 1LA
Tel: 020 7845 4600
[Tube: Temple or Embankment]
Gallery and former Tudor palace. Now a magnif-
icent eighteenth-century art gallery housing cel-
ebrated art collections.

Tate Britain

Millbank London SW1P 4RG
Tel: 020 7887 8888
www.tate.org.uk/britain
*[Located on the N bank of the Thames between
Vauxhall Bridge and Lambeth Bridge. Tube:
Pimlico or Vauxhall. Train: Vauxhall]*
Tate Britain is the original Tate Gallery and holds
the largest collection of British art in the world.
Tate's collection of British art contains iconic
masterpieces by artists including Hogarth,
Gainsborough, Constable, Whistler, Sargent,
Hepworth and Bacon. The gallery has a highly-
acclaimed restaurant and the Tate Boat takes
visitors between Tate Britain, Tate Modern and
the London Eye. Pre-booking recommended for
major exhibitions. For what's on now, please
visit www.tate.org.uk/britain.

Daily 10.00 - 17.50. Closed 24-26 December
Admission Free (charges for major exhibitions)

Tate Modern

Bankside London SE1 9TG
Tel: 020 7887 8888
www.tate.org.uk/modern

*[On the South Bank of the Thames facing the
Millennium Bridge and a short walk from
Blackfriars bridge. Tube: Southwark/Blackfriars,
Train: London Bridge/Blackfriars]*

Britain's national museum of modern and contemporary art from around the world is housed
in the former Bankside Power Station on the
banks of the Thames. The awe-inspiring Turbine
Hall runs the length of the entire building and
you can see amazing work by artists such as
Cezanne, Bonnard, Matisse, Picasso, Braque,
Giacometti, Rothko, Dali, Pollock and Warhol.
Pre-booking is recommended for major exhibitions. For what's on now, please visit
www.tate.org.uk/modern.

Daily 10.00 - 17.50. Closed 24-26 December
Admission Free (charges for major exhibitions)

Victoria Miro

16 Wharf Road Hackney London N1 7RW
Tel: 020 7336 8109

[Tube: Angel or Old Street]

This commercial gallery of contemporary art is
housed in an 8,000 square-foot converted
Victorian furniture warehouse and features work
by Peter Doig, Chris Ofili and Grayson Perry.

Closed Mondays

Wallace Collection

Hertford House Manchester Square London
W1U 3BN
Tel: 020 7563 9500 Fax: 020 7224 2155
www.wallacecollection.org

[Tube: Bond St / Baker St. Off Oxford St, behind Selfridges]

The Wallace Collection is one of the finest collections of art ever assembled by one family and became a national museum in 1897.Today the eclectic, wondrous collection is shown in the family home, a tranquil oasis just minutes from the bustle of London's Oxford Street. Be amazed by the fantastic Old Master paintings by Titian, Canaletto, Rembrandt, Velázquez and Gainsborough amongst others. Be transported to eighteenth-century France, surrounded by the world's greatest selection of eighteenth-century paintings, furniture and Sèvres porcelain. Imagine Queen Marie-Antoinette and Madame de Pompadour sashaying down the staircase as you enjoy the splendour of the family's home. Relish the world-class armouries, perfect for both young boys and overgrown ones! Relax in the serenity of the glazed Courtyard, home to our restaurant The Wallace. Enjoy free exhibitions, family activities and public events throughout the year. Join our mailing list for up to date details.

Open daily 10.00 - 17.00 closed 24 - 26 December

Admission Free

British Museum

Great Russell Street London WC1B 3DG
Tel: 020 7323 8000 Fax: 020 7323 8616
www.britishmuseum.org

[Tube: Holborn, Tottenham Court Rd, Russell Sq, Goodge St]

Founded in 1753, the British Museum's remarkable collections span over two million years of human history. Visitors enjoy a unique comparison of the treasures of world cultures under one roof, centred around the Great Court and the historic Reading Room. World-famous objects such as the Rosetta Stone, Parthenon Sculptures and Egyptian mummies are visited by up to 5 million visitors per year. In addition to the vast permanent collection, the museum's special exhibitions, displays and events are all designed to advance understanding of the collections and cultures they represent. Highlights of the exhibitions programme for 2008 include Hadrian: Empire and Conflict and Babylon.
Galleries: All year daily Sat-Wed 10.00-17.30, Thur-Fri 10.00-20.30 Closed Good Fri, 24-26 Dec & 1 Jan. Certain Galleries are subject to different opening times. Full details are available from the Box Office/Information Desk or please check the web site
Admission Free

Design Museum

Butler's Wharf 28 Shad Thames SE1 2YD
Tel: 0870 833 9955
[Tube: Tower Hill]
The world's leading museum of twentieth and twentyfirst-century design.

Museum of Brands, Packaging and Advertising

2 Colville Mews Lonsdale Road Notting Hill London W11 2AR
Tel: 020 7908 0880
[Tube: Notting Hill Gate]
Unique museum charting British consumerism, From Cornflakes to Ker-plunk.

Victoria and Albert Museum

Cromwell Road South Kensington SW7 2RL
Tel: 020 7942 2000
[Tube: South Kensington]
Holds one of the world's largest and most diverse collections of decorative arts.

Communication Museums

Discover

1 Bridge Terrace Stratford London E15 4BG
Tel: 020 8536 5555 Fax: 020 8522 1003
www.discover.org.uk
Come to Discover, the children's story making centre in London. Visit us for amazing adventures through secret caves, sparkling rivers, magic parcels and flying pages making up stories along the way! Discover is designed especially for children aged 0-8 and their families. You can also now enjoy our new Story Den which hosts an amazing exhibition programme aimed at 5-11 year olds.

All year daily 10.00-17.00 except Mons during School Term

A&C£4.00, Family Ticket £14.00. Concessions available

Costume & Jewellery Museums

Fan Museum

12 Crooms Hill Greenwich London SE10 8ER
Tel: 020 8305 1441
[DLR: Cutty Sark for Maritime Greenwich]
The world's only Fan Museum with its unsurpassed collections of more than 4,000 fans and fan leaves dating from the eleventh century is housed in listed Georgian houses.

Country Parks & Estates

Lee Valley Regional Park

Myddelton House Bulls Cross Enfield Middlesex London EN2 9HG
Tel: 01992 702200 Fax: 01992 719937
www.leevalleypark.org.uk

[Plenty of on-site parking available]

If you enjoy wildlife, sport, countryside, heritage, fantastic open spaces with great places to stay, then the Lee Valley Regional Park is for you. The Park is the regional destination for sport and leisure and stretches for 4,000 hectares between Ware in Hertfordshire, through Essex to the River Thames, and provides leisure activities to suit all ages, tastes and abilities. For more information about the Park and what you can do - please phone 01992 702200 or visit www.leevalleypark.org.uk

Please call for details

Admission price increase from 1 April 2008. See website for details

Discount Offer: Save £3.50! One Child Free at the Lee Valley Park Farms.

Exhibition & Visitor Centres

Central Hall Westminster

Storey's Gate Westminster London SW1H 9NH
Tel: 020 7222 8010 Fax: 020 7222 6883
www.c-h-w.com

Opened in 1912, this unique historic Edwardian building is situated in the heart of Westminster London, just adjacent to Westminster Abbey. Central Hall was designed by Lanchester & Richards in Viennese Baroque style, and the ceiling of the Great Hall is reportedly the second largest of its type in the world. Many events of national importance and eminent speakers have been welcomed, perhaps the most famous event being the Inaugural General Assembly of the United Nations in 1946. Today Central Hall offers a wide variety of event space, from a fine wood panelled boardroom to the Great Hall, which seats over 2,000 people theatre style. The finest in cuisine is offered, together with the latest in audio visual and technical support. One of our events team will be dedicated to your needs. Methodist Church only weddings are available through the church.

All year daily 07.00-18.00 or as required

Earls Court Exhibition Centre

Warwick Road London SW5 9TA
Tel: 020 7385 1200
[Tube: Earls Court]
Earls Court hosts many shows and exhibitions throughout the year, including the Ideal Home Show and the Brit Awards.

Festivals & Shows

City of London Festival

12-14 Mason's Ave London EC2V 5BB
Tel: 020 7796 4949 Fax: 020 7796 4959
www.colf.org

[Numerous venues & open spaces in the City, all of which are within easy walking distance of London Underground, mainline stations & bus routes. Please see www.colf.org for full venue details]

In 2008 the City of London Festival's annual 'Trading Places' theme will be bifocal: a cultural exchange with India on the one hand and Switzerland on the other. Both are places which have inspired artists, travellers and traders, and with which London has deep historic and modern links. Taking place through June and July, in some of the City's most beautiful and historic buildings and open spaces, the Festival celebrates music of all types, contemporary, classical, jazz and world, along with visual arts, film, architecture and an ever growing free, open-air programme. Please call the box office on 0845 120 7502.

20 June-10 July 2008, various times
Free - £65.00

Notting Hill Carnival

Notting Hill London
Tel: 020 7730 3010
[Tube: Westbourne Park]
A huge multi-cultural arts festival attended by over a million revellers every year. The Sunday is traditionally reserved as Children's Day with the emphasis on family and young festivalgoers.
24-25 August 2008

Food & Drink

Hard Rock Café
150 Old Park Lane London W1K 1QZ
Tel: 020 7514 1700
[Tube: Hyde Park Corner]
Still housing the first ever piece of memorabilia donated to the Hard Rock Café (Eric Clapton's Lead II Fender, originally donated to reserve a space at the busy bar), the London Café is as charming and authentic now as it was 35 years ago.

Planet Hollywood
13 Coventry Street London W1D 7DH
Tel: 020 7437 7639
[Tube: Piccadilly Circus]
The world's only restaurant inspired by the glamour of Hollywood was launched with the backing of Hollywood stars Sylvester Stallone, Bruce Willis, Arnold Schwarzenegger and Demi Moore.

Rainforest Café
20-24 Shaftesbury Avenue Westminster London W1D 7EU
Tel: 020 7434 3111

[Tube: Piccadilly Circus]

A tropical paradise for kids, at this buzzy café you can enjoy organic food in the company of animatronic animals and with all the sounds of the rainforest.

Gardens & Horticulture

Kew Gardens (Royal Botanic Gardens)
Kew Richmond London TW9 3AB
Tel: 020 8332 5655

[Tube: Kew Gardens. Rail: Kew Bridge]

The world famous visitor attraction houses more than 40,000 different kinds of plants in the 121 riverside hectares.

All year daily. Closed 24 & 25 Dec

Guided Tours

BBC Tours
BBC Television Centre Wood Lane London W12 7RJ
Tel: 0870 60 30 304
Fax: 020 8576 7466
www.bbc.co.uk/tours

[BBC TELEVISION CENTRE-Tube: White City (Central Line). Bus: 72, 95, 220 all stop opposite Television Centre.There is metered parking in nearby streets & a NCP car park off Rockley Rd, Shepherd's Bush. BROADCASTING HOUSE-Tube: Oxford Circus (Central Line and Bakerloo line) Broadcasting House is a 5 min walk, straight up Regent Street going N towards Regent Street. Bus: 88, 453 and C2. There are a limited number of metered parking spaces on Portland Place and on nearby side streets. There is a small pay & display car park on Chandos Street. There is no coach parking at either BBC building, however, please consult our booking line for further information on coach parking and pick up/ drop off points]

TELEVISION CENTRE: On a tour of London's BBC Television Centre, you will see behind the scenes of the most famous TV centre in the world. On the award winning tour, you may experience areas such as the News Centre, Weather Centre, dressing rooms and studios. Television Centre is a working building so we plan your exact itinerary around what is happening on the day. Please note that visitors must be 9 years and over. Television Centre is a large complex and tours involve a lot of walking. We also offer a CBBC Experience aimed at children 7 - 12 years old. Children may visit the Blue Peter Garden, have fun making a TV programme in our interactive studio, take part in our very own Raven challenge, become 'Diddy Dick and Dom', peek into a dressing room and look down on some of our famous studios. BROADCASTING HOUSE: (Broadcasting

House, Portland Place, London W1A 1AA) New for 2008 - tours of the UK's first ever purpose-built broadcast centre! It has been undergoing a major restoration and modernisation as part of a ten-year development plan which will be completed in 2012. Tours are tailored around the working building's activity and you are likely to see a range of areas such as the newly restored radio theatre, the council chamber, radio studios and from Spring 2008, an interactive drama experience. Tours of Broadcasting House are suitable for children 12 years and over. Tours last approximately 1 1/4 hours and will be initially one Sunday per month.

Tours run regularly throughout the week at Television Centre. Tours of Broadcasting House will run initially one Sunday per month. Please call for further details.

TELEVISION CENTRE & CBBC EXPERIENCE: A£9.50 C(over7)&Students (NUS/USI)£7.00 Concessions£8.50, Family Ticket £27.00. Group rate (15+): A£8.50 C&Students (NUS/USI)£6.00 Concessions£7.50 School Group(under16)£5.00, Teacher£7.00. Please note, the maximum number on each tour is 22 people. BROADCASTING HOUSE: A£6.50 Concession£5.50 C(12-15)&Students(NUS/USI)£4.50 Family Ticket £15.00. Group rates: A£5.50 Concession£4.50 Students£3.50 School Group£3.50.Group rates apply for all BBC Tours for parties of 15 or more. 1 free place for every 15 people. Pre-booking is essential for all BBC Tours

Harrow School Tours
15 London Road Harrow-on-the-Hill Harrow Middlesex HA1 3JJ
Tel: 020 8423 1524
[Tube: Harrow on the Hill]
Fascinating tour of one of Britain's finest public schools. Three types of tour available.

London Walks
Various Locations London NW6 4LW
Tel: 020 7624 3978
www.walks.com
[Walks depart from various London Underground stations, please call or see website for details]

Market-leading tour operator with eccentric guides and around 300 different walks to choose from.

The Original Tour - London Sightseeing
Jews Row Wandsworth London SW18 1TB
Tel: 020 8877 2120 Fax: 020 8877 1968
www.theoriginaltour.com
[Original London Visitor Centre, Embankment Pier, Piccadilly Circus, Victoria, Trafalgar Square & Marble Arch]

Enjoy a capital day out in London aboard The Original Tour's traditional open-top buses. The world's first and largest sightseeing operator offers a flexible 'Hop-on Hop-off' service, with over 90 stops, delivering guests to the door of London's most famous sights and attractions. This entertaining and informative guide to London is presented by English-speaking Tour Hosts or a choice of seven digitally recorded language commentaries plus a children's channel. Children also receive a Kids' Club activity pack. The 24-hour tickets include a fantastic free Thames cruise and free walking tour.
Daily 08.30-17.00, with buses operating until 20.00 July-Aug
For further information please call or visit website

Discount Offer: Save Money when you book in advance.

Heritage & Industrial

Kew Bridge Steam Museum
Green Dragon Lane Brentford TW8 0EN
Tel: 020 8568 4757
[Rail: Kew Bridge Railway Station]
The Museum is housed in a magnificent nineteenth-century pumping station near the river at Kew and features the world's largest collection of steam pumping engines.

Bank of England Museum

Bartholomew Lane London EC2R 8AH
Tel: 020 7601 5545 Fax: 020 7601 5808
www.bankofengland.co.uk/museum
The Bank of England Museum tells the story of
the Bank from its foundation in 1694 to its role
in today's economy. Interactive programmes
with graphics and video help to explain its many
and varied roles. Popular exhibits include a
unique collection of banknotes, a genuine gold
bar which can be handled and free holiday
events, please ring for details.

*All year Mon-Fri 10.00-17.00, closed Weekends,
Public & Bank Hols*
Admission Free

Historical

Alexandra Palace Ice Rink

Alexandra Palace Way Wood Green N22 7AY
Tel: 020 8365 2121
[Tube: Wood Green]
Opened in 1873, this majestic building is one of
London's most famous landmarks and is
renowned as the birthplace of television. It's
now home to the biggest permanent ice rink in
London, and is a great place to go skating.
There are a wide range of activities on offer suit-
able for all ages and covering every aspect of
ice sports.

Apsley House (Wellington Museum)

Hyde Park Corner 149 Piccadilly W1J 7NT

Tel: 020 7499 5676
[Tube: Hyde Park Corner]
Apsley House (No. 1 London) was home to the
great 'Iron' Duke of Wellington and contains his
magnificent art collection.
Closed Mondays

Dennis Severs' House

18 Folgate Street London E1 6BX
Tel: 020 7247 4013
[Tube/Rail: Liverpool St]
This restored red-brick Georgian terraced
house, built in 1724, was owned by American-
born Dennis Severs, who died in 1999. The
eccentric designer and performer recreated a
historical interior that takes the visitor on a journey from 1685-1919.
1st & 3rd Sunday of each month, 12.00-16.00

Fenton House

Windmill Hill Hampstead London NW3 6RT
Tel: 020 7435 3471
[Tube: Hampstead]
Handsome seventeenth-century merchant's
house with walled garden. With a fine collection
of porcelain, early keyboard instruments and
needlework. The garden boasts a 300-year-old
orchard and bees producing honey for sale.
19 Mar-31 Oct: Wed-Fri (Nov-Mar: Sat-Sun only)

Freud Museum

20 Maresfield Gardens Hampstead NW3 5SX
Tel: 020 7435 2002/435 5167
[Tube: Finchley Road]
Papers, books and notes, photos and home
movies combine to create a sensitive and wholly
personal Freud exhibition.
Closed Mon & Tue

Hogarth's House

Hogarth Lane Great West Road Chiswick
London W4 2QN
Tel: 020 8994 6757
[Tube: Turnham Green]
Small Georgian house once the home of William
Hogarth, now a print gallery and has on view
many of his famous engravings.

Houses of Parliament

Westminster London SW1A 0AA

Tel: 0870 906 3773

www.parliament.uk

Once again this year, Parliament will be opening its doors to allow visitors the opportunity to tour this unique building. Visitors will be led by a specially qualified Blue Badge Guide. The tour through the Palace allows visitors to see the Chamber of the House of Lords, Central Lobby, The Chamber of the House of Commons and St Stephen's Hall and Westminster Hall. Tours takes approximately 75 minutes, allowing you to plan your itinerary around them. Tours are available in French, German, Italian and Spanish at specific times. Parliament remains a working building making tours subject to changes and cancellations.

Aug Mon-Tue & Fri-Sat 09.15-16.30, Wed-Thur 13.15-16.30, Sept-Oct Mon & Fri-Sat 09.15-16.30, Tue-Wed & Thur 13.15-16.30

A£12.00 C&Concessions£5.00 Others£8.00, Family Ticket £30.00

Kenwood House

Hampstead Lane London NW3 7JR

Tel: 020 8348 1286/7

[Tube: Golders Green]

Set in tranquil parkland with panoramic views over London, Kenwood House boasts sumptuous interiors and important paintings by many great artists.

Old Royal Naval College

2 Cutty Sark Gardens Greenwich London SE10 9LW

Tel: 020 8269 4747 Fax: 020 8269 4757

www.oldroyalnavalcollege.org

[J2, M25 then A2 & follow signs for Greenwich. Rail: Greenwich. Tube: from Canary Wharf, take the Docklands Light Railway to Cutty Sark. River: Greenwich Pier]

The Old Royal Naval College is one of London's most famous riverside landmarks, and it stands on the site of the former Tudor Palace where both Henry VIII and Elizabeth I were born. The buildings were planned and designed by some of the greatest architects of the seventeenth and eighteenth centuries (including Christopher Wren, Nicholas Hawksmoor, and James "Athenian" Stuart). Originally a hospital for wounded seamen, it became a training college for the Royal Navy in 1873. The site was first opened to the public in 1997, and today visitors can enjoy free entry to its magnificent Painted Hall where Nelson laid in state, the Chapel and café. Guided tours run daily with exclusive access to areas of the site not generally open to the public, including the Nelson Room exhibition, and the Victorian Skittle Alley. Please visit the website for more details and information on the events programme. For disabled access please phone ahead.

All year daily 10.00-17.00. Closed 24-26 Dec

Admission Free

Queen's House

Romney Road Greenwich London SE10 9NF
Tel: 020 8858 4422 Fax: 020 8312 6522
www.nmm.ac.uk

[J2 M25 then A2 & A206, follow signposts into central Greenwich. Rail: Greenwich. DLR: Cutty Sark]

The first Palladian-style villa in England, designed by Inigo Jones for Anne of Denmark and completed for Queen Henrietta Maria, wife of Charles I. Includes a loggia overlooking Greenwich Park. Now the home of the fine art collection of the National Maritime Museum with additional displays on historic Greenwich.

All year daily 10.00-17.00. Closed 24-26 Dec
Admission Free

Royal Hospital Chelsea

Royal Hospital Road Chelsea London SW3 4SR
Tel: 020 7881 5305 Fax: 020 7881 5319
www.chelsea-pensioners.org.uk

[Entrance London Gate. Tube: Sloane Square. Coach party parking can be arranged if pre-booked]

The Royal Hospital Chelsea was established by King Charles II for soldiers who were disabled or worn out by long service. The buildings were constructed by Sir Christopher Wren and the first 'In-Pensioners' admitted in 1692. Currently there are over 300 Chelsea Pensioners. Figure Court is dominated by a statue of King Charles II. On either side are the 'Long Wards' where the In-Pensioners live (not open to the public). The Great Hall which is used for meals and events is open to the public. It is dominated by a mural commemorating the foundation of the Royal Hospital and on the walls are listed the Battle Honours of the British Army. Copies of captured colours hang from the walls. Opposite is the Chapel, with its original woodwork. Museum, souvenir shop and post office on site. The grounds are open to the public except during April/May when closed for the Chelsea Flower Show.

All year Mon-Sat 10.00-12.00 & 14.00-16.00, Apr-Sept Sun 14.00-16.00. Closed 25, 26 Dec & 1 Jan
Admission Free

Shakespeare's Globe Theatre Tour and Exhibition

21 New Globe Walk Bankside London SE1 9DT
Tel: 020 7902 1500 Fax: 020 7902 1515
www.shakespeares-globe.org

[Tube: London Bridge / Mansion House / Southwark / St Paul's]

The largest exhibition of its kind devoted to the world of Shakespeare, from Elizabethan times to the present day - situated beneath the Globe Theatre itself. Explore Bankside, the Soho of Elizabethan London, follow Sam Wanamaker's struggle to recreate an authentic Globe for the twentieth century and beyond, and take a fascinating guided tour of today's working theatre. Globe Education provides workshops, lectures, courses and online learning programmes for students of all ages and nationalities. For further information please call 020 7902 1433.

Performances in the Globe Theatre: Apr-October. Box office 020 7401 9919. The Globe café-bar offers light refreshments and main dishes. The Globe restaurant offers full a la carte dining as well as pre and post performance menus.

Shakespeare's Globe Exhibition: Oct-Apr daily 10.00-17.00, May-Sept (theatre season) 09.00-11.30 exhibition & guided tour into theatre, 12.00-17.00 exhibition, sword fighting & Elizabethan dressing demonstrations. Closed 24-25 Dec

A£9.00 Concessions£7.50 C(5-15)£6.50, Family Ticket £25.00. Admission includes a guided tour of Theatre and demonstrations. Group rates (for 15+) available on request

Discount Offer: One Child Free (with a full-paying adult).

Syon House and Gardens
Syon Park Brentford Middlesex TW8 8JF
Tel: 020 8560 0882
The present house is Tudor in origin but famed for its splendid Robert Adam interiors. The Gardens contain the Great Conservatory.

Landmarks

London Eye
Riverside Building County Hall Westminster Bridge Road London SE1 7PB
Tel: 0870 990 8881
[Tube: Waterloo]
One of the most inspiring and visually dramatic additions to the London skyline.

Tower Bridge Exhibition
Tower Bridge Road London SE1 2UP
Tel: 020 7940 3985
[Tube: Tower Hill / London Bridge]
At the Tower Bridge Exhibition you can enjoy breath-taking views from the high-level walk-ways and learn about how and why the bridge was built.

Literature & Libraries

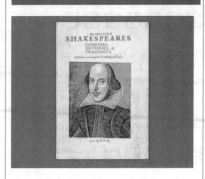

British Library
96 Euston Road London NW1 2DB
Tel: 01937 546060 Fax: 020 7412 7340
www.bl.uk

[Tube: Euston. Next to King's Cross and St Pancras International stations]

The British Library (BL) is the national library of the United Kingdom. It is based in London and is one of the world's most significant research libraries, holding over 150 million items in all known languages and formats; books, journals, newspapers, magazines, sound and music recordings, patents, databases, maps, stamps, prints, drawings and much more, making it the largest collection in the world. The Library's collections include around 25 million books, along with substantial additional collections of manuscripts and historical items dating back as far as 300 BC.

Exhibition Galleries & Shop: Mon-Sat (from 09.30), Sun & Public Holidays (from 11.00). Reader Registration Office: Mon-Sat (from 9.30); Closed Sun & Public Holidays. St Pancras Reading Rooms: Mon (from 10.00), Tue-Sat (from 9.30); Closed Sun & Public Holidays. Restaurant: Mon-Sat (from 09.30); Closed Sun & Public Holidays. Café: Mon-Sat (from 9.30), Sun (from 11.00). Last Word on the Piazza: Mon-Fri (from 08.30), Sat (from 09.15), Sun (from 10.45)

For great hotel deals call Superbreak on 01904 679999 or visit www.superbreak.com

Charles Dickens Museum

48 Doughty Street London WC1N 2LX
Tel: 020 7405 2127

The Charles Dickens Museum in London is the world's most important collection of material relating to the great Victorian novelist and social commentator.

Dr Johnson's House

17 Gough Square London EC4A 3DE
Tel: 020 7353 3745
[Tube: Chancery Lane]

Built in 1700, this museum was once the home and workplace of Samuel Johnson from 1748-1759, and it was here that he compiled the first comprehensive English Dictionary.

Keats' House

Keats Grove Hampstead London NW3 2RR
Tel: 020 7435 2062
[Rail: Hampstead Heath]

Visitors can see Keats's rooms in the house and many of his personal possessions such as his inkstand.

Sherlock Holmes Museum

221b Baker Street London NW1 6XE
Tel: 020 7935 8866
[Tube: Baker Street]

This famous address was opened as a museum in 1990. The first floor rooms contain all the features familiar to the Holmes enthusiast.

Living History Museums

Age Exchange Reminiscence Centre

11 Blackheath Village Blackheath London SE3 9LA
Tel: 020 8318 9105
[Rail: Blackheath]

Small museum depicting everyday life from the 1920s-1940s, with changing exhibitions.

Winston Churchill's Britain at War Experience

64-66 Tooley Street London SE1 2TF
Tel: 020 7403 3171 Fax: 020 7403 5104
www.britainatwar.co.uk
[Close to London Bridge]

A unique museum portraying the life of the British people living through WW2. This is an educational adventure for children and adults and an interesting trip down memory lane for seniors. Take the lift to the London Underground air-raid shelter to see where people spent sleepless nights. Just as they watched films, here visitors can watch a film about those dramatic years. The museum features the BBC radio studio, the dressing room of wartime stars, the Anderson shelter with the air-raid happening overhead, women working for the war effort, rationing, evacuation, the shops of Southwark, the Morrison shelter, bomb disposal, the Rainbow Room for G.I.'s and the full sized recreation of a bombed-out London street with the smouldering remains of a cinema, pub and people's homes. See it, feel it, breathe it!

All year Apr-Sept daily 10.00-18.00, Oct-Mar daily 10.00-17.00. Closed 24-26 Dec

A£9.95 C£4.85 Concessions£5.75, Family Ticket (A2+C2) £25.00 prices subject to change without prior notification

Discount Offer: Two for the Price of One (full-paying adult).

Maritime

Golden Hinde
St Mary Overie Dock Cathedral Street London SE1 9DE
Tel: 020 7403 0123
[Tube: London Bridge]
Full-scale reconstruction of Sir Francis Drake's world-famous, sixteenth-century sailing galleon. The crew (dressed in period costume) talk with visitors and guide groups around the five levels of decks.

National Maritime Museum
Romney Road Greenwich London SE10 9NF
Tel: 020 8858 4422/8312 6565
Fax: 020 8312 6522
www.nmm.ac.uk

[J2 M25 then A2 & A206, follow signposts into central Greenwich. Rail: Greenwich. DLR: Cutty Sark]

See how the sea affects our daily lives in this impressive modern museum. Themes include exploration and discovery, Nelson, passenger shipping and luxury liners, maritime London, costume, art and the sea, the future of the sea and making waves.

All year daily 10.00-17.00. Closed 24-26 Dec
Admission Free

Markets

Camden Lock
Chalk Farm Road London
[Tube: Camden Town]
This is a huge weekend tourist attraction and a great shopping experience, as interesting for the diversity of people as for its mixed bag of stalls and multicultural food on offer.

Portobello Road
Portobello Road London
[Tube: Ladbroke Grove / Notting Hill]

This famous antiques and flea market takes place every Saturday. It's is a colourful, dynamic stretch of London that oozes 'boho' trendiness and fun with over 2,000 stalls.

Medical Museums

Florence Nightingale Museum
St Thomas' Hospital 2 Lambeth Palace Road
London SE1 7EW
Tel: 020 7620 0374
[Tube: Westminster/Waterloo/Lambeth North]
Creates the personal setting in which Florence's
prized possessions, a lamp from the Crimean
War and nursing artifacts are shown.

Museums of the Royal College of Surgeons of England
35-43 Lincoln's Inn Fields London WC2A 3PN
Tel: 020 7869 6560
[Tube: Holborn]
The home of the Royal College of Surgeons
boasts a host of enlightening, permanent and
temporary, galleries and exhibitions.
Closed Mondays.

Old Operating Theatre, Museum and Herb Garret
9a St Thomas Street Southwark London
SE1 9RY
Tel: 020 7188 2679
[Tube: London Bridge]
The oldest surviving operating theatre in Britain.
Provides a fascinating glimpse into the past
using exhibits to tell the story of surgery and
herbal medicine. Functioning before antiseptic
and anaesthetic surgery was invented, the theatre's ominous collection of sawing, cupping,
bleeding, trepanning and childbirth instruments
appear more implements of torture than healing.

Wellcome Collection
183 Euston Road Camden London NW1 2BE
Tel: 020 7611 2222
[Tube: Euston]
The Wellcome Collection combines three galleries, 'Medicine Man', 'Medicine Now' and an
exhibition space. The 1,300 objects on display
include works by Leonardo da Vinci and Andy
Warhol, which sit alongside a range of weird
and wonderful medical devices from the nineteenth-century.

Military & Defence Museums

Firepower! the Royal Artillery Museum
Royal Arsenal Woolwich London SE18 6ST
Tel: 020 8855 7755 Fax: 020 8855 7100
www.firepower.org.uk
*[Rail : Woolwich Arsenal from Cannon Street,
Charing Cross, Waterloo East & London Bridge. 5
min walk from Woolwich Arsenal to Firepower
look for brown Firepower signage. National Rail
Enquiries: 08457 484950. Bus routes 472, 161,
96, 180 stop in Plumstead Road outside the
Royal Arsenal. Bus routes 53, 54,422,380 stop in
Woolwich Town Centre. Tube: Jubilee Line to
North Greenwich, then 15 min bus ride to
Woolwich (161, 422, 472) to stops A & B. Car:
The Royal Arsenal car park entrance is just off
Beresford Street/Plumstead Road A206, E from
the Woolwich Ferry roundabout (A205). Plenty of
on-site parking available]*
Located in the Historic Royal Arsenal, the
world's centre for munitions manufacture,
Firepower takes you from slingshot to supergun,
starting in the Field of Fire; where big screens,
dramatic surround sound and moving eyewit-
ness accounts illuminate the conflicts of the
twentieth century. See and touch artillery from
early cannon to modern missile systems. Learn
how they work with touch-screen interactives.
See the actual guns that provided the metal for
the last 800 Victoria crosses. The Cold War
Gallery section displays large self-propelled
guns, from the Cold War era to the present day.
*Apr-Oct Wed-Sun 10.30 - 17.00, Nov-Mar Fri-
Sun 10.30 -17.00, Open all School & Bank Hols*
A£5.00, C£2.50, Concessions£4.50, Family
Ticket £(A2+C2) or (A1+C3) £12.00. Special
prices for groups (10+)

Guards Museum, The

Wellington Barracks Birdcage Walk London
SW1E 6HQ
Tel: 020 7414 3428/414 3271
Fax: 020 7414 3429
www.theguardsmuseum.com

[Tube: St. James Park. Walk up Queen Anne's Gate, turn L into Birdcage Walk & entrance is by Guards Chapel]

The Guards Museum is a superb facility covering the exciting, entertaining and interesting world of the Five Regiments of Foot Guards. Here you can find everything from the glory days of scarlet and gold to the mud and blood of two devastating World Wars. It traces the dangerous role of present-day soldiering in an increasingly volatile world. The cornucopia of weapons, paintings, uniforms and memorabilia includes personal items, not only of the Dukes of Marlborough and Wellington, but also of the equally heroic men who served them. The collection boasts a large number of artefacts belonged to members of the Royal Family, many of whom served in the Guards. There's also an inspiring exhibition of Victoria Crosses won by Guardsmen since it was first awarded 150 years ago, as well as numerous other gallantry awards. The museum is a hidden gem and well worth a visit.

All year daily 10.00-16.00 (occasionally closed for state ceremonies)
A£3.00 C£Free OAPs£2.00

Discount Offer: Two for the Price of One (full-paying adult).

HMS Belfast

Morgan's Lane Tooley Street London SE1 2JH
Tel: 020 7940 6300 Fax: 020 7403 0719
When you visit HMS Belfast you will have nine decks of living history to explore. The ship has been carefully preserved to reflect the different decades of her service and the campaigns that she served in.

National Army Museum

Royal Hospital Road Chelsea London SW3 4HT
Tel: 020 7730 0717
[Rail: Victoria]
Discover the lives, legends and legacies of the men and women who have served in the British Army.
All year daily. Closed Good Fri, May Day, 24-26 Dec & 1 Jan

Royal Air Force Museum London

Grahame Park Way Hendon London NW9 5LL
Tel: 020 8205 2266
Take off to the Royal Air Force Museum to see our world-class collection of over 100 aircraft, memorabilia and artefacts together with an awe inspiring sound and light show that takes you back in time to the Battle of Britain.

Royal Armouries Museum (London)

HM Tower of London Tower Hill London
EC3N 4AB
Tel: 020 7480 6358
[Rail: Fenchurch Street. Tube: Tower Hill]
The Royal Armouries at HM Tower of London is Britain's oldest museum. Its collection includes royal armour (including that worn by Henry VIII) and an Spanish armoury.
Admission to the Royal Armouries is free to holders of entry tickets to The Tower of London

Mills - Water & Wind

Wimbledon Windmill Museum
Windmill Road Wimbledon Common
Wimbledon London SW19 5NR
Tel: 020 8947 2825
www.wimbledonwindmillmuseum.org.uk

[Windmill Road off Parkside (A219). Plenty of on-site parking available]

Have you ever visited a windmill and not understood how it worked? This is your opportunity to find out. The Windmill Museum is housed in the historic Wimbledon Windmill, built in 1817. It tells the story of windmills and milling in pictures, working models and the machinery and tools of the trade. Children can grind their own flour using a hand quern, saddle stone or mortar and have the working of the millstones explained. We have a collection of over 400 woodworking tools, donated by a millwright, and there are life size displays showing how the mill was built and what it was like to live in the mill after it stopped working in 1864. There is parking space for 300 cars and the mill is surrounded by Wimbledon Common with its 1,100 acres of heath, lakes and woodland. Our shop sells cut out model windmills, books and Wombles!

22 Mar-end Oct Sat 14.00-17.00 Sun & Public Hol 11.00-17.00

A£1.00 C£0.50 Concessions£0.50. Group visits by arrangement only

Multicultural Museums

Horniman Museum and Gardens
100 London Road Forest Hill London
SE23 3PQ
Tel: 020 8699 1872 Fax: 020 8291 5506
www.horniman.ac.uk

[On South Circular Road (A205) Rail: Forest Hill. Bus: 176 / 185 / 122 / P4 / P13 / 356 / 363]

Situated in 16 acres of beautiful gardens, this award winning south London museum has unique exhibitions, events and activities to delight adults and children alike. Housed in Charles Townsend's landmark Arts and Crafts style building, the Museum has outstanding collections that illustrate the natural and cultural world. The museum dramatically doubled the public space with the opening of the Centenary Development in 2002, finally realising founder Frederick Horniman's vision of re-orientating the museum to take in the green oasis of the gardens. Visitors can discover African Worlds showcasing the largest ceremonial mask in Britain, celebrate world cultures in the Centenary Gallery, experience the Victorian time-capsule of the Natural History gallery with original specimens and fossils, sound out the Music Gallery with Britain's largest collection of musical instruments from around the world, or dive into the stunning Aquarium featuring jellyfish, seahorses, coastal rock pools, a mangrove swamp and South American rainforest.

All year daily 10.30-17.30. Closed 24-26 Dec. Gardens close at sunset

Admission Free

Music & Theatre Museums

Handel House Museum

25 Brook Street Mayfair London W1K 4HB
Tel: 020 7495 1685 Fax: 020 7495 1759
www.handelhouse.org

[Tube: Bond Street (entrance to museum at rear in Lancashire Court)]

Home to composer Handel from 1723 until his death in 1759, the Handel House Museum celebrates Handel's music and life, through restored Georgian interiors, special exhibitions, displays, live baroque music and events, portraits of Handel and his contemporaries and eighteenth-century art.

All year Tue-Wed, Fri-Sat 10.00-18.00, Thur 10.00-20.00, Sun 12.00-18.00. Closed Bank Hols & Mon

A£5.00 C£2.00 Concessions£4.50, free entry for children on Saturdays

Discount Offer: Two for the Price of One (full-paying adult).

V and A Theatre Museum

Victoria and Albert Museum Cromwell Road London SW7 2RL
Tel: 020 7942 2000
[Tube: South Kensington]
The V&A Theatre Collections have moved to the Victoria and Albert Museum, South Kensington.

Handel House Museum

25 Brook Street, Mayfair, London W1K 4HB
tel: 020 7495 1685 • www.handelhouse.org

Directions: Tube: Bond Street (entrance to museum at rear in Lancashire Court)

Opening Times:
All year Tue-Wed, Fri-Sat 10.00-18.00,
Thur 10.00-20.00, Sun 12.00-18.00.
Closed Bank Hols & Mon

Admission: Adult £5.00, Child £2.00
Concessions £4.50
(free entry for children on Saturdays)

Handel House Museum was home to the composer Handel from 1723 until his death in 1759 and is where he composed many of his greatest works including 'Messiah'.

The Museum celebrates Handel's music and life through beautifully restored Georgian interiors, 18th-century portraits of Handel and his contemporaries, regular live music, events, displays and exhibitions.

Natural History Museums

Natural History Museum

Cromwell Road London SW7 5BD
Tel: 020 7942 5000
[Tube: South Kensington]
Explore world-class collections, fantastic exhibitions and cutting-edge research.

Nature & Conservation Parks

WWT London Wetland Centre

Queen Elizabeth's Walk Barnes London SW13 9WT
Tel: 020 8409 4400
[Rail: Barnes Bridge]
The Wetland Centre is a major new attraction for London that brings wildlife and wetlands into the heart of the city.

On the Water

Canal Cruises - Jenny Wren
250 Camden High Street London NW1 8QS
Tel: 020 7485 4433/6210
[Tube: Camden Town]
Discover London's fascinating hidden water-ways and enjoy the unique experience of passing through a canal lock.

Canal Cruises - My Fair Lady
250 Camden High Street London NW1 8QS
Tel: 020 7485 4433/6210
[Tube: Camden Town]
Enjoy a leisurely dining experience aboard the luxury Cruising Restaurant, 'My Fair Lady.'

City Cruises
Cherry Garden Pier Cherry Garden Street
London SE16 4TU
Tel: 020 7740 0400 Fax: 020 7740 0495
www.citycruises.com
[Tube: Westminster (for Westminster Millennium Pier), Waterloo (for Waterloo Millennium Pier), Tower Hill (for Tower Millennium Pier) & Cutty Sark (DLR) (for Greenwich Pier)]
City Cruises plc, the largest operator of passenger services on the Thames, carries some 750,000 people annually on its extensive sightseeing, entertainment and charter services. The company offers a variety of boat services during the day and evening to suit all tastes. With City Cruises you can rest assured of a warm welcome and a friendly efficient service.

Westminster/Waterloo/Tower/Greenwich Sightseeing Service; a hop-on hop-off facility between the three major destination piers on the Thames. Passengers are able to travel in comfort on one of four new state of the art luxury Riverliners which offer on-board catering and bar services. A joint ticket is also available with the DLR. London Showboat; a unique floating entertainment experience with dinner and cabaret. Corporate and Private Charters; City Cruises has years of experience hosting important and memorable functions from Christmas and Birthday celebrations to corporate dinners and weddings. Our menus and staff make every occasion special. The company has an extensive fleet of 15 vessels catering for all budgets. City Cruises is the sole company on the Thames to possess its own catering facilities, including a dedicated floating kitchen at Cherry Garden Pier. Baby changing facilities, pushchair access and shelter available on some boats, please specify if you require these services when booking.
Westminster/Waterloo/Tower/Greenwich Sightseeing Service - operates every 40mins from 10.00. Boarding at either Westminster Millennium Pier, Waterloo Millennium Pier, Tower Millennium Pier or Greenwich Pier. London Showboat - Apr-Oct, Wed-Sun and Nov-Mar Thur-Sat. Corporate and Private Charters - please call for Charter information pack and further details
Westminster/Waterloo/Tower/Greenwich Sightseeing Service: A£10.50 C&Concessions£5.25, Family Ticket (A2+C3) £24.00 (these River Red Rover tickets offer unlimited travel throughout the day). Single and return tickets also available. London Showboat: £70.00 (inclusive of welcome drink, half bottle of wine, 4 course meal, cruise, cabaret and dancing). Corporate and Private Charters - please call for Charter information pack and further details

Discount Offer: One Child Free.

London Ducktours
55 York Road London SE1 7NJ
Tel: 020 7928 3132
[Tube: Waterloo]
Not only do you get a guided tour by road, you also get to take a trip along the river, without ever leaving the comfort of your seat.

London Waterbus Company

London NW1 8AF
Tel: 020 7482 2660
www.londonwaterbus.com/

[Camden Lock Location: West Yard, Camden Lock, off Camden High Street, London, NW1, Camden Lock access: Bus: 24 / 27 / 29 / 31 /74 / 88 / 168 / 214 / 253. Tube: Camden Town / Chalk Farm. Little Venice location: Brownings Pool, Little Venice, Warwick Cres/Blomfield Rd, W9,Little Venice access: Bus: 6 / 8 / 16 / 18 / 31 / 46. Tube: Warwick Avenue/ Paddington]

Cruises on traditional canal narrow boats along the historic Regents Canal, through the green and leafy fringes of Regents Park in central London. From the pool at Little Venice where Brownings Island is surrounded by elegant Regency architecture, through the dark and mysterious Maida Hill tunnel, past Marylebone and the park to the lively bustle of Camden Lock Market. On the way the boat stops at our canal gate into London Zoo. Trips one way, either way, or return. Make a stopover for a picnic at Little Venice or to shop and eat at Camden Lock. If you want to visit the Zoo, take the Waterbus from either end and pay our special low prices and miss out the queues at the Main Gate. No bookings necessary just turn up and pay on board. No dogs permitted.

Apr-Sept daily on the hour 10.00-17.00. Oct Thur-Sun 11.00-15.00, Nov - Mar Sat & Sun 11.00-15.00

Camden Lock or Little Venice One-way: A£6.60 C(3-15)&OAPs£5.00. Return: A£9.00 C(3-15)&OAPs£6.00. To London Zoo including admission A£17.70, OAPs£16.70 C(3-15)£14.70. All tickets on board - cash or cheques only. Group rates (for 20+) available on request and pre-booking is essential

Discount Offer: 0.80p off Adult Fares.

Barbican Centre

Silk Street London EC2Y 8DS
Tel: 020 7638 4141
[Tube: Barbican]

Huge, multifaceted arts, entertainment and education centre. Open 363 days a year, it offers the most diverse program of any London venue. Two theatres, three cinemas, the redeveloped Barbican Art Gallery, several exhibition spaces, shops, cafés, restaurants, bars, live music in the foyer and plenty of events for children.

BFI London IMAX Cinema

1 Charlie Chaplin Walk South Bank Waterloo London SE1 8XR
Tel: 0870 787 2525
[Rail/Tube: Waterloo]

Offers the biggest cinema screen in Europe housed inside a spectacular glass building. Showing breathtaking 2D and 3D films.

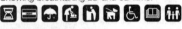

Places of Worship

Southwark Cathedral

London Bridge London SE1 9DA
Tel: 020 7367 6700
[Tube: London Bridge, Monument]

Southwark Cathedral has been a centre for Christian worship for more than 1,000 years.

St Paul's Cathedral

The Chapter House St Paul's Churchyard London EC4M 8AD
Tel: 020 7236 4128
[Tube: St Paul's]

Sir Christopher Wren's architectural masterpiece. Climb to the Whispering Gallery where your whisper can be heard on the other side.

Westminster Cathedral

Clergy House Victoria Street London
SW1P 1QW

Tel: 020 7798 9055 Fax: 020 7798 9090

www.westminstercathedral.org.uk

[300 yards from Rail: Victoria Station. Tube: Victoria]

Called 'A Series of Surprises' because of its architecture, mosaics and marble decorations, Westminster Cathedral was begun in 1895. Its origins go back much further, being designed in the early Christian Byzantine style by the Victorian architect, John Francis Bentley. Appointed by the third Archbishop of Westminster, Cardinal Herbert Vaughan, Bentley took much of his inspiration from the Italian churches and cathedrals he visited during the winter of 1894, particularly those in Ravenna, Pisa, Bologna and Venice where he undertook a detailed study of St Mark's Cathedral. His other inspiration was the Emperor Justinian's great church of Santa Sophia in Istanbul. The Cathedral was conceived to be built quickly with inside decorations added, as funds became available. The structure was completed in 1903. Brick built, the vast domed interior has the widest and highest nave in England and is decorated with mosaics plus 125 varieties of marble from around the world.

Cathedral: All year Mon-Fri 07.00-19.00, Sat 08.00-19.00 Sun closes 20.00. Tower: Apr-Nov daily 09.00-17.00. Dec-Mar Thur-Sun 09.00-17.00

Admission Free, Tower lift charged

Clink Prison Museum

1 Clink Street Bankside London SE1 9DG

Tel: 020 7403 0900

[Tube: London Bridge]

Enter the Clink Prison Museum, on the site of the prison that gave its name to all others.

Roman Era

Crofton Roman Villa

Crofton Road Orpington Kent BR6 8AF

Tel: 01689 873826/020 8460 1442

www.the-cka.fsnet.co.uk

[J4 M25, A232 adjacent Orpington Railway station, signs on cover building. Rail: Orpington. Bus: 61, 208, 353]

The only Roman Villa in Greater London which is open to the public. The Crofton Villa house was inhabited from about AD140 to 400 and was the centre of a farming estate of about 200 hectares. Nearby would have been farm buildings, surrounded by fields, meadows and woods. The house was altered several times during its 260 years of occupation and at its largest probably had at least 20 rooms. The remains of 10 rooms can be seen today, with tiled floors and underfloor heating systems, within a modern cover building. Graphic displays, children's activity corner, schools service.

2 Apr-31 Oct Wed, Fri & Bank Hol Mon 10.00-13.00 & 14.00-17.00, Sun 14.00-17.00
A£1.00 C£0.70

Royal

Banqueting House
Whitehall London SW1A 2ER
Tel: 0870 751 5178
[Tube: Westminster / Embankment]
Whether visiting during the day or enjoying a unique evening event, visitors will be enthralled by the history and splendour of this magnificent building.

Buckingham Palace, Royal Mews
London SW1A 1AA
Tel: 020 7766 7302
[Tube: Victoria, Green Park & Hyde Park Corner]
Houses the State vehicles (both horse-drawn carriages and motor cars) used for official engagements. For most of the year, the stables are home to The Queen's working horses.
15 Mar-30 Oct (Closed: Fridays, plus 21 Mar, 31 May, 7 Jun, 14 Jun & during State Visits)

Joint Ticket available for the State Rooms, Royal Mews and the Queen's Gallery

Buckingham Palace, State Rooms and Gardens
London SW1A 1AA
Tel: 020 7766 7300
[Tube: Victoria, Green Park & Hyde Park Corner]
The State Rooms are used by The Queen and members of the Royal Family to receive and entertain their guests on State, ceremonial and official occasions.
31 Jul-29 Sep 2008

Joint Ticket available for the State Rooms, Royal Mews and the Queen's Gallery

Buckingham Palace, the Queen's Gallery
London SW1A 1AA
Tel: 020 7766 7301
[Tube: Victoria, Green Park & Hyde Park Corner]
A permanent space dedicated to changing exhibitions of items from the Royal Collection.
Open daily (Closed 21 Jan-13 Mar, 21 Mar & 29 Sep-16 Oct)

Joint Ticket available for the State Rooms, Royal Mews and the Queen's Gallery

Changing of the Guard
Buckingham Palace Forecourt London SW1A 1AA
[Tube: Victoria, Green Park & Hyde Park Corner]
The Changing of the Guard is an intricate ceremony that draws millions of tourists every year. The new guards arrive at the forecourt of the Palace at 11:30 from Wellington Barracks and are accompanied by a band. The ceremony takes approximately forty minutes to complete.
May-July daily. Alternate days for the rest of the year (weather permitting): Jan - even numbered dates (2, 4, 6, etc), Feb - odd numbered dates (1, 3, 5, etc), Mar - even numbered dates (2, 4, 6, etc). These dates are subject to change, please see www.army.mod.uk for more details

Clarence House
London SW1A 1AA
Tel: 020 7766 7303
[Tube: Green Park or St James's Park]
The official residence of The Prince of Wales, The Duchess of Cornwall, Prince William and Prince Harry. Visitors are guided around the five ground-floor rooms where the family undertakes official engagements and receives guests.
5 Aug- 28 Sep 2008 (pre-booked guided tours only)

Hampton Court Palace
Hampton Court Palace East Molesey London KT8 9AU
Tel: 0870 752 7777
[Tube: Richmond Rail: Hampton Court Station]
A magical history tour inside and out, with stunning State Apartments, a choice of six individual tours, costumed guides and 60 acres of spectacular riverside gardens including the world famous Maze.

Kensington Palace
Kensington Gardens London W8 4PX
Tel: 0870 751 5170
[Tube: High Street Kensington or Queensway]
A Royal residence since 1689, today visitors can explore the magnificent State Apartments and the Royal Ceremonial Dress Collection.
All year daily. Closed 24-26 Dec

Kew Palace and Queen Charlotte's Cottage

Kew Gardens Richmond TW9 3AB
Tel: 0870 7515178
The intimate Kew Palace, once a merchant's home, was home to George III, Queen Charlotte and some of their daughters from 1801-1818, during the King's bouts of supposed 'madness'. Now, after a ten-year conservation project and with a fascinating new re-presentation, the palace is open to the public.
21 Mar-28 Sep 2008

Tower of London

Tower Hill London EC3N 4AB
Tel: 0870 756 6060
[Tube: Tower Hill]
One thousand year-old prison, palace and place of execution. Includes the Royal Armouries and the Crown Jewels.

Royal Observatory Greenwich

Greenwich Park Greenwich London SE10 8XJ
Tel: 020 8858 4422/8312 6565
Fax: 020 8312 6522
www.rog.nmm.ac.uk

[In Greenwich Park, off A2. Rail: Greenwich. DLR: Cutty Sark]

Stand on longitude zero - the Greenwich Meridian, the home of time itself. See the Astronomer Royal's apartments and Harrison's amazing timekeepers in the charming Wren building. The time ball falls daily at 13.00. See our giant refracting telescope, our new astronomy galleries and the new Peter Harrison Planetarium. No wheelchair access to three rooms.

All year daily 10.00-17.00. Closed 24-26 Dec.
Admission Free. Planetarium Shows: A£6.00
Concessions£4.00

Discount Offer: 20% Off Peter Harrison Planetarium Ticket.

Science Museum

Exhibition Road South Kensington London SW7 2DD
Tel: 0870 870 4868
See, touch and experience the major scientific advances of the last 30 years at the largest Museum of its kind in the world, with over 40 galleries, and 2,000 hands-on exhibits.

London Aquarium

County Hall Westminster Bridge Road London SE1 7PB
Tel: 020 7967 8000
Experience one of Europe's largest displays of aquatic life.

Social History Museums

Churchill Museum and Cabinet War Rooms

Clive Steps King Charles Street London SW1A 2AQ
Tel: 020 7930 6961 Fax: 020 7839 5897
www.iwm.org.uk

[Tube: Westminster or St. James's Park. Bus: 3, 11, 12, 24, 53, 87, 88, 109, 159, 184, 211]

The world's first major museum dedicated to the life of Sir Winston Churchill at the Cabinet War Rooms, the top secret underground command centre that provided shelter for the British Prime Minister and his government during the Second World War. Take a step back in time in the atmospheric rooms, which have been left untouched since August 1945. In contrast, the Churchill Museum is London's most technologically advanced and interactive visitor attraction and explores the character and experiences of the man behind the legend. The museum examines how Churchill achieved his iconic status not just in Britain, but worldwide. It looks at the changing world on which Churchill lived, the successes and controversies of his long career as a soldier, writer, politician, statesman, and the conflicting opinions about him. Free personal sound guides are provided for every visitor.

All year daily 09.30-18.00. Closed 24-26 Dec
A£12.00 C£Free OAPs£9.50 Students(NUS/USI)£9.50 Unemployed (with ES40) £6.00. Group rates available on request

Imperial War Museum

Lambeth Road London SE1 6HZ
Tel: 020 7416 5320
[Tube: Lambeth North]
Exhibitions include WW1 and WW2 Galleries, Conflicts since 1945 and Holocaust Exhibition.

Museum in Docklands

No 1 Warehouse West India Quay Hertsmere Road London E14 4AL
Tel: 0870 444 3855 Fax: 0870 444 3858
www.museumindocklands.org.uk
[Tube: Canary Wharf, DLR: West India Quay]
The Museum in Docklands unlocks the history of London's river, port and people in a nineteenth-century warehouse at West India Quay. Explore London's connections with the world through an epic 2000-year story of trade, expansion and immigration. Please visit our website for events.
All year daily 10.00-18.00. Closed 24-26 Dec
A£5.00 C(under16)&Students(NUS/USI)£Free Concessions £3.00

Discount Offer: Two for the Price of One (full-paying adult).

Museum of London

150 London Wall London EC2Y 5HN
Tel: 0870 444 3850 Fax: 0870 444 3853
www.museumoflondon.org.uk

[Entrance located on pedestrian high walk from Aldersgate St, London Wall or St Martins-le-Grand. Nearest Underground stations: barbican/St Pauls]

Step inside Museum of London for an unforgettable journey through the capital's turbulent past. Journey back in time and discover London before London, see how the city changed as Romans gave way to Saxons, and wonder at the splendour of Medieval London. Museum of London is currently undergoing a major redevelopment, transforming the way it tells London's story from 1666 to the present day. The new galleries will open by 2010 but until then visitors can still enjoy prehistoric, Roman and Medieval London, as well as events and exhibitions including London's Burning, which explores the Great Fire of London. Please visit our website for event details.

All year daily 10.00-18.00, closed 24-26 Dec
Admission Free

Museum of Richmond

Old Town Hall Whittaker Avenue Richmond TW9 1TP
Tel: 020 8332 1141
[Tube: Richmond]
This new independent museum deals with Richmond's rich and colourful history in a lively and informative way.

Spectator Sports

Chelsea Football Club Stadium Tours

Stamford Bridge Ground Fulham Road London SW6 1HS
Tel: 0871 9841955
www.chelseafc.com/tours

[Tube: Fulham Broadway. Plenty of on-site parking available]

The Chelsea FC Stadium Tour and Museum is the perfect football treat for all the family! Tour the home of one of the world's most famous sporting arenas and go behind-the-scenes into areas you'd only ever dreamed of seeing! Your guided tour will include the magnificent Home Dressing Room, the Away Dressing Room, the Press Room, the Players Tunnel, the Manager's Dug-Out and much, much more! After the guided tour, visit the club museum, and see an exhibition documenting the history of football at Stamford Bridge. With sought after artifacts such as trophies, medals, shirts, boots and pennants, the Chelsea FC Museum has something for everybody. Guided tours run throughout the year and can be booked online at www.chelseafc.com/tours or by telephone 0871 9841955. Tours are subject to cancellation and alteration at short notice. Tours do not operate on Chelsea FC home matchdays. It is always advisable to check for availability before your visit.

Tours: All year daily, Mon-Sun 11.00, 12.00, 13.00, 14.00, 15.00. No tours on home match days or the day before home champions league games

A(16-64)£15.00 C(5-15)£9.00 C(under5)£Free OAPs(65+)£9.00, Family Ticket(A2+C2)£42.00

Discount Offer: One Child Free.

Crayford Greyhound Stadium

Stadium Way Crayford Kent DA1 4HR
Tel: 01322 557836 Fax: 01322 559394
www.crayford.com

[Between Bexleyheath & Dartford. M25 J1. Take A2 to London, follow signs for Crayford]

The fully air conditioned modern arena has a capacity of 1,200 and boasts a 250 seated restaurant. One of the most popular tracks in the UK with matinee racing on Tuesday, Thursday & Saturday mornings, which are televised to over 1 million viewers. Crayford is the largest provider of televised racing to the industry.

Sat & Mon (PM): 19.30. Tues:14.08. Thurs: 14.18. Sat (AM) 10.37
A£6.00 C£4.50 Matinee's Free

Sport & Recreation

Crystal Palace Park

Thicket Road Penge London SE20 8UT
Tel: 020 8778 9496
[Rail: Crystal Palace Railway Station]
The extensive grounds contain lakes, ancient oak trees, the National Sports Centre, a maze and the resident life-size (but anatomically inaccurate) dinosaur statues, first built in 1852.

Sporting History Museums

Lord's Tour and MCC Museum

Lord's Ground St John's Wood London
NW8 8QN
Tel: 020 7616 8595/6 Fax: 020 7266 3825
www.lords.org
[Tube: St John's Wood. Limited on-site parking available]
Lord's was established in 1787 and is the home of the MCC and cricket. When you tour this famous arena you follow in the footsteps of the 'greats' of the game, from W G Grace to Ian Botham. Daily guided tours take you behind the scenes at this venue. You will visit the Members' Pavilion including the hallowed Long Room and the Players' Dressing Room, the MCC Museum where the Ashes Urn is on display and many other places of interest including the newly constructed Grand Stand and futuristic NatWest Media Centre.

Tours normally at 10.00, 12.00 & 14.00 (10.00 tour subject to availability during winter)
A£12.00 C£6.00 Concessions£7.00, Family Ticket £27.00

Discount Offer: One Child Free.

Museum of Rugby and Twickenham Stadium Tours

Rugby Football Union Rugby Road Twickenham Middlesex London TW1 1DZ
Tel: 0870 405 2001
[Rail: Twickenham Railway Station]
Home to the world's largest collection of rugby memorabilia.

Wimbledon Lawn Tennis Museum

Church Road Wimbledon London SW19 5AE
Tel: 020 8946 6131
[Tube: Wimbledon Park]
Traces the history of the once-Royal sport, right
through to the modern game.

London Dungeon

28-34 Tooley Street London SE1 2SZ
Tel: 020 7403 7221 Fax: 020 7378 1529
www.thedungeons.com
[Rail/Tube: 100m from London Bridge Station]
The London Dungeon invites you to a feast of
fun with history's horrible bits. Live actors,
shows, rides and interactive special effects take
you back to those black, bleak times. Cower
under the wrath of a vengeful sixteenth-century
judge, face the resident torturer in his dark,
dingy lair and try to find your way through the
terrifying 'Labyrinth of the Lost.' Ninety minutes
of thrills and chills includes two scary rides that
will leave you screaming for more! New for
2008: 'Jack the Ripper.' As you wander the
stinking slums, the true horror of his terrible
crimes is revealed in bloody, graphic detail. And
then a scream, the flash of a cloak and an evil
smile as you come face to face with Jack the
Ripper himself... will you survive?

*All year daily 10.00-17.00. Varies in holiday peri-
ods, please check website*

Please call for admission prices

Discount Offer: One Child Free.

Trocadero Centre

1 Piccadilly Circus London W1V 7DD
Tel: 020 7439 1791
A grand centre of leisure, shopping and enter-
tainment located in the heart of the West End.

V and A Museum of Childhood

Cambridge Heath Road London E2 9PA
Tel: 020 8983 5200 Fax: 020 8983 5225
www.museumofchildhood.org.uk
[Next to Bethnal Green tube station]
Recently transformed, the V&A Museum of
Childhood opened in December 2006 and now
features a stunning new entrance and front
room gallery designed by award-winning architects. Part of the V&A family, the Museum houses the national childhood collection. The galleries are designed to show the collections in a
way which is accessible to adults and children
of all ages. Visitors are encouraged to explore
the themes of childhood past and present
through the displays: Creativity; Moving Toys
and the Childhood Galleries. As well as many
hands-on activities including: dressing-up,
indoor sandpit, Punch and Judy, ride-on rocking
horses and role-play area. Highlights of the collection include the Nuremberg dolls' house, a
rocking horse possibly owned by Charles I and
Princess Daisy. We have a dynamic programme
of temporary exhibitions, daily activities and
seasonal events - please visit our website for
more information.
*All year daily 10.00-17.45. Closed 25-26 Dec, 1
Jan*
Admission free

Transport Museums

London Canal Museum

12-13 New Wharf Road King's Cross London N1 9RT
Tel: 020 7713 0836
[Tube: Kings Cross 5 min walk]

The London Canal Museum is housed in a former ice warehouse built in the nineteenth century. The exhibits are diverse and all-encompassing, spanning the history of the ice trade and ice cream as well as the canals themselves. You can see inside a narrowboat cabin and learn about the history of London's canals.

London's Transport Museum

Covent Garden Piazza Covent Garden London WC2E 7BB
Tel: 020 7379 6344
[Tube: Covent Garden]

Reopening on 22 November 2007 with more exhibition space than before, including a brand new gallery, learning zone and more on the 200 year history of public transport, the refurbished Museum also has several new themes: London Transport's famous design heritage, the poster collection, public transport during both World Wars and plans for the capital's development in the twenty-first century.

Wax Works

Madame Tussauds

Marylebone Road London NW1 5LR
Tel: 020 7487 0200
[Tube: Baker Street]

Mix with celebrities at the world-famous collection of realistic wax figures in specially designed settings.Interactive attractions include 'Sport Zone,' 'World Leaders,' 'Music Zone,' 'Big Brother Diary Room' and the 'Chamber of Horrors.' A visit to The Stardome (which replaced the London Planetarium in 2006) is now part of the Madame Tussaud's experience.

Zoos

Battersea Park Children's Zoo

Battersea Park London SW11 4NJ
Tel: 020 7924 5826 Fax: 020 7350 0477
www.batterseaparkzoo.co.uk
[Rail: Battersea Park or Queenstown Rd. See website for public transport info]

So much to see and so much to do at Battersea Park Children's Zoo! Fun and enjoyment for the whole family… grandparents too! Come and visit the animals down on Barley Mow Farm and wander through the Mouse House with all its secrets. Then round the corner to the monkeys and lemurs who are waiting to show you how they can jump and swing. Say "Hello!" to the Mynah birds. Watch the otters swim and crawl down the tunnel to check on the meerkats. Any energy left? Then on to the Krazy Kids play area and move sand with a digger! Finally, need a drink? The Lemon Tree Café has light refreshments and excellent coffee. Please call to confirm closing times.
Summer 10.00-17.30, Winter 10.00-Dusk. Guided tours by prior arrangement
A£6.50 C(2-15)£4.95, Family Ticket(A2+C2) £20.50

Discount Offer: One Child Free.

ZSL London Zoo

Regents Park London NW1 4RY
Tel: 020 7722 3333
[Tube: Great Portland Street / Regents Park]

Set in the heart of Regent's Park, London Zoo boasts not only a vast array of amazing animals, but also beautiful gardens.

Merseyside

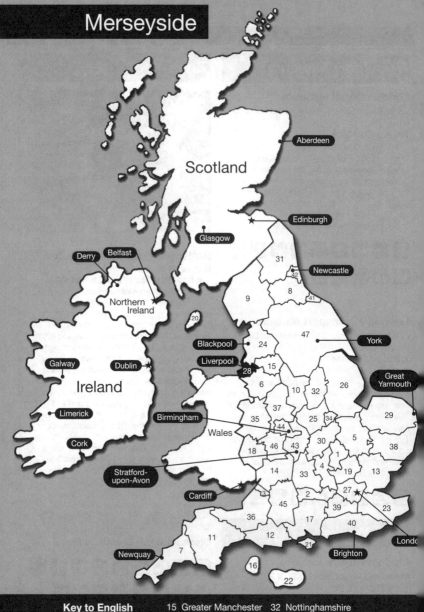

- Aberdeen
- Scotland
- Edinburgh
- Glasgow
- Newcastle
- 31
- 42
- 8
- 41
- 9
- Derry
- Belfast
- Northern Ireland
- 20
- 47
- York
- Blackpool
- 24
- Liverpool
- 28
- 15
- Galway
- Dublin
- Ireland
- 6
- 10
- 32
- 26
- Great Yarmouth
- 37
- 29
- Limerick
- Birmingham
- 35
- 44
- 25
- 34
- Wales
- 30
- 5
- 38
- Cork
- 18
- 46
- 43
- 1
- Stratford-upon-Avon
- 14
- 33
- 4
- 19
- 13
- Cardiff
- 13
- 2
- 27
- 23
- 45
- 39
- Londo
- 36
- 17
- 40
- Newquay
- 11
- 12
- 21
- Brighton
- 7
- 16
- 22

Key to English Counties:

1 Bedfordshire	15 Greater Manchester	32 Nottinghamshire
2 Berkshire	16 Guernsey	33 Oxfordshire
3 Bristol	17 Hampshire	34 Rutland
4 Buckinghamshire	18 Herefordshire	35 Shropshire
5 Cambridgeshire	19 Hertfordshire	36 Somerset
6 Cheshire	20 Isle Of Man	37 Staffordshire
7 Cornwall	21 Isle Of Wight	38 Suffolk
8 County Durham	22 Jersey	39 Surrey
9 Cumbria	23 Kent	40 Sussex
10 Derbyshire	24 Lancashire	41 Tees Valley
11 Devon	25 Leicestershire	42 Tyne & Wear
12 Dorset	26 Lincolnshire	43 Warwickshire
13 Essex	27 London	44 West Midlands
14 Gloucestershire	28 Merseyside	45 Wiltshire
	29 Norfolk	46 Worcestershire
	30 Northamptonshire	47 Yorkshire
	31 Northumberland	

Art Galleries

Lady Lever Art Gallery
Lower Road Port Sunlight Village Wirral
Merseyside CH62 5EQ
Tel: 0151 478 4136
Houses the art collection of soap-magnate,
William Hesketh Lever (the first Lord
Leverhulme). The gallery is famous for its Pre-
Raphaelite paintings.

Tate Liverpool
Albert Dock Liverpool Merseyside L3 4BB
Tel: 0151 702 7400
Tate Liverpool is home to the national collection
of modern art in the North and is housed in a
beautiful converted warehouse in the historic
Albert Dock.

Walker Art Gallery
William Brown Street Liverpool Merseyside
L3 8EL
Tel: 0151 478 4199 Fax: 0151 478 4190
The 'national gallery of the North,' the Walker
Art Gallery is one of the finest galleries in Europe
housing outstanding collections of British and
European art from 1300 to the present day.

Williamson Art Gallery and Museum
Slatey Road Birkenhead Merseyside L43 4UE
Tel: 0151 652 4177
English watercolours and works by the
Liverpool school are an outstanding feature of
the gallery.

Arts, Crafts & Textiles

National Conservation Centre
Whitechapel Liverpool Merseyside L1 6HZ
Tel: 0151 478 4999
This award-winning attraction reveals the delicate work of museum conservators. Everything
from Roman sculpture to Cold War spacesuits
comes here to be preserved and restored.

Country Parks & Estates

Croxteth Hall and Country Park
Muirhead Avenue Liverpool Merseyside
L12 0HB
Tel: 0151 233 6910
Apart from the historic building itself, Croxteth
Hall also features a farm, a Victorian walled gar-
den and a country park.

Festivals & Shows

Southport Flower Show
Victoria Park Southport Merseyside PR8 2BZ
Tel: 01704 547147 Fax: 01704 500750
www.southportflowershow.co.uk
Southport Flower Show is one of the largest,
most diverse and friendliest shows in the country. With up to a million blooms on display and
over 250 trade exhibitors offering an array of
products from plants and gardening equipment
to delicious organic food and local produce, it's
a day out for everyone interested in new ideas
and inspiration for lifestyle, homes and gardens.
Enjoy informative question and answer sessions
with celebrity gardeners and an entertainment
programme which includes live music, exciting
acrobatics and the ever-popular dog and falconry displays. Set in 34 beautiful acres of
Victoria Park, it is easy to stroll around and with
a great deal of the show under cover, is
designed to be enjoyed whatever the weather.
For more information visit our website.

21-24 August 2008

Please call 0844 847 1555 for information and
tickets

Historical

Mr Hardman's Photographic Studio

59 Rodney Street Liverpool Merseyside L1 9EX
Tel: 0151 709 6107
www.nationaltrust.org.uk
[City Centre]

Situated just below the Anglican Cathedral in the centre of Liverpool is this fascinating house, home, between 1947 and 1988, to Edward Chambré Hardman and his wife Margaret. The house contains a selection of photographs, the studio where most were taken, the darkroom where they were developed and printed, the business records and the rooms complete with all their contents and ephemera of daily life. The subject matter of the photographs - portraits of the people in Liverpool, their city and the land-scapes of the surrounding countryside - provide a record of a more prosperous time when Liverpool was the gateway to the British Empire and the world. Parallel to this is the quality of Hardman's work and his standing as a pictorial photographer.

15 Mar-2 Nov Wed-Sun 11.00-16.15. 8 Nov-21 Dec Sat &Sun 11.00-16.15. Open Bank Hol Mons. Admission by timed tickets and guided tour only including NT members, to avoid over-crowding and to preserve the fragile contents, no photography allowed inside property

Gift Aid Prices* A£5.70 C£2.80, Family Ticket (A2+C2) £14.00. NT Members £Free. *Gift Aid: These prices include a voluntary 10% donation. Visitors can, however choose to pay the standard admission price displayed at the property

Discount Offer: One Child Free.

Speke Hall

The Walk Speke Liverpool Merseyside L24 1XD
Tel: 08457 585702/0151 427 7231
Fax: 0151 427 9860

[8mi SE of Liverpool city centre, S of A561. Signposted. Plenty of on-site parking available]

One of the most famous half-timbered houses in the country set in varied gardens and an attractive woodland estate. The Great Hall, Oak Parlour and priest holes evoke Tudor times while the small rooms, some with original William Morris wallpapers, show the Victorian desire for privacy and comfort. Fine plasterwork and tapestries, plus a fully equipped Victorian Kitchen and Servants' Hall. The restored garden has spring bulbs, rose garden, Summer border and stream garden; bluebell walks in the ancient Clough Woodland, rhododendrons, spectacular views of the grounds and Mersey Basin from a high embankment - the Bund. Peaceful walks in the wildlife oasis of Stocktons Wood. 1998 was the 400th anniversary of Speke Hall and this marks the four hundred years since the date of 1598 was carved over the front door during the time of Edward Norris, the first owner of Speke Hall, to mark the completion of the North Range and the building we see today. Events and activities reflect the different eras of the history of Speke, its estate and the families who lived and worked there, including open air theatre, children's activities, and much more. Picnic area by children's play area. Partial disabled access please call before visit, 0151 427 7231.

House: 15 Mar-2 Nov Wed-Sun 13.00-17.30, 8 Nov-14 Dec Sat-Sun 13.00-16.30. Grounds: 15 Mar-2 Nov Tue-Sun 11.00-17.30, 4 Nov-31 Jan 09 Tues-Sun 11.00-dusk. Home Farm/Restaurant/Shop: 15 Mar-13 Jul Wed-Sun 11.00-17.00, 15 Jul-14 Sept Tue-Sun 11.00-17.00, 17 Sept-2 Nov Wed-Sun 11.00-17.00, 8 Nov-14 Dec Sat-Sun 11.00-16.30. Open Bank Hol Mons. Grounds (Garden & Estate) closed 24-

26, 31 Dec, Closed 1 Jan 09

House,Gardens and Grounds: Gift Aid Prices* A£7.50 C£3.80, Family Ticket (A2+C3) £20.50. Gardens & Grounds only:Gift Aid Prices* A£4.50 C£2.50 Family Ticket (A2+C3) £11.50. NT Members £Free.*Gift Aid: These prices include a voluntary 10% donation. Visitors can, however choose to pay the standard admission price displayed at the property

Discount Offer: One Child Free.

Sudley House

Mossley Hill Road Liverpool L18 8BX
Tel: 0151 724 3245
A Victorian shipping merchant's legacy. It contains fabulous works by Gainsborough, Reynolds, Landseer and Turner.

Maritime

HM Customs and Excise National Museum

Merseyside Maritime Museum Albert Dock
Liverpool Merseyside L3 4AQ
Tel: 0151 478 4499
This museum tells the exciting story of the age-old battle between smugglers and duty men, from 1700 to the present day.

Merseyside Maritime Museum

Albert Dock Liverpool Merseyside L3 4AQ
Tel: 0151 478 4499
Liverpool's seafaring heritage is brought to life in the historic Albert Dock.

Multicultural Museums

World Museum Liverpool

William Brown Street Liverpool L3 8EN
Tel: 0151 478 4393
World Museum Liverpool (formerly Liverpool Museum) has collections from the Amazonian rainforest to the mysteries of outer space.

Music & Theatre Museums

Beatles Story

Britannia Vaults Albert Dock Liverpool
Merseyside L3 4AD
Tel: 0151 709 1963 Fax: 0151 708 0039
www.beatlesstory.com

[Road: follow M62 into Liverpool, then follow signs for Albert Dock. Large car park adjacent to Dock. Rail: James Street Station, follow tourist signs to Albert Dock, approx. 10min walk. By foot: 10min walk from City Centre, follow tourist signs. The Beatles Story can be found between the Holiday Inn Express & Premier Travel Inn]

Located within Liverpool's historic Albert Dock, the Beatles Story is a unique day out for all the family! Embark on a dizzying journey and see how four lads from Liverpool became the biggest band in the world. Along the way you'll experience the excitement of the Cavern Club, the hysteria of Beatlemania and the groovy psychedelia of Sgt Pepper, all accompanied by the family-friendly Living History audio tour narrated by John Lennon's sister, Julia. 2008 will also see opening of our interactive, hands on Discovery Zone, an exciting programme of children's workshops, our new Fab4Store gift shop and Beatles themed Starbucks Coffee store. Excellent discounts on family saver tickets make this a truly fab day out for both adults and kids!

All year daily 09.00-19.00. Closed 25-26 Dec

A£12.50 C£6.50 Concessions£8.50. Group rates (for 10+) available on request

Discount Offer: One Child Free.

Mendips and 20 Forthlin Road

Liverpool Merseyside L24
Tel: 0151 4277231 / 0870 9000256
Fax: 0151 4279860
www.nationaltrust.org.uk/beatles

[Scheduled mini-bus tours from Liverpool City Centre in morning or Speke Hall in afternoon. Advance booking recommended. Tickets available on day subject to availability. Book tickets on-line]

Mendips was the childhood home of John Lennon, he lived there with his Aunt Mimi and Uncle George and composed early songs in the front porch and in his bedroom. 20 Forthlin Road is a 1950s terraced house and the former home of the McCartney family, where the Beatles met, rehearsed and wrote many of their earliest songs. Displays include contemporary photographs by Michael McCartney and early Beatles memorabilia. The audio tour features contributions from both Michael and Sir Paul McCartney. We offer visitors a combined trip to both 20 Forthlin Road and Mendips. There is partial disabled access to Ground Floors only.

1 Mar-30 Nov Wed-Sun & Bank Hols. Between 1-14 Mar and during weekdays between 3-28 Nov, tours will operate from Liverpool City Centre, reducing in frequency to 3 tours per day

Joint tour of both houses: A£15.00 C£3.00 NT Members £7.00

Eastham Country Park

Ferry Road Eastham Wirral Merseyside CH62 0BH
Tel: 0151 327 1007
Once a Victorian pleasure garden, now a local beauty spot. Superb views across the Mersey estuary with its abundant birdlife and busy shipping lanes. A network of surfaced paths provide access throughout the woodland.

Formby Point

National Trust Victoria Road Freshfield Formby Liverpool Merseyside L37 1LJ
Tel: 01704 878591 Fax: 01704 835378
www.nationaltrust.org.uk

[15mi N of Liverpool, 2mi W of Formby, 2mi off A565. Rail: Freshfield]

202ha of dunes, sandy beaches and pinewoods between the sea and the town of Formby. Red squirrels can sometimes be seen along the woodland walks, and the site is a good starting point for walks on the Sefton Coastal Path. The shoreline attracts wading birds such as oyster-catchers and sanderlings in the winter. Dogs must be kept on a lead near wildlife, and under control at all times. Learning Office fax/tel: 01704 874949.

Apr-Oct 09.00-17.30, Nov-Mar 09.00-16.30
£3.70 per car. Minibuses £10.00 & Coaches £25.00 all year (must be pre-booked). School groups must book in advance

On the Water

National Wildflower Centre

Court Hey Park Roby Road Liverpool
Merseyside L16 3NA
Tel: 0151 738 1913 Fax: 0151 737 1820
www.nwc.org.uk

[0.5mi from J5 M62. Rail: Broadgreen Station, approx 10min walk. Take Bowring Park Rd exit, follow rd under bridge & straight across traffic lights. Continue down rd (keeping M62 on L) for approx 0.5mi. Bus: Nos. 6 & 61 from Queens Square, Liverpool city centre or Broadgreen Station. Plenty of on-site parking available]

The centre provides a national focus for promoting new wildflower landscapes and the creation of new wildlife habitats. Located in a 35 acre park, once the home of the Gladstone family, a former walled garden now produces the wildflower seeds and plants that help fund the charity. Nearby is a stunning and innovative 150 metre long visitor building, it features a café and shop, outdoor exhibitions, the wildflower garden centre and a children's area, whilst a roof top walkway looks out across the complex. There are seasonal wildflower demonstration areas.

1 Mar-30 Sept daily 10.00-17.00

A£3.50 C&Concessions£1.75, Family Ticket (A2+C2) £9.00. Season Ticket available

Discount Offer: Two for the Price of One.

Mersey Ferries Ltd

Victoria Place Wallasey Merseyside CH44 6QY
Tel: 0151 330 1444 Fax: 0151 639 0578
www.merseyferries.co.uk

[Pier Head via M62 & Liverpool city centre, Wirral via M56 / M53 or A41. Parking on site available at Woodside and Seacombe. Park at Albert Dock for Pier Head]

A River Explorer Cruise on the famous Mersey Ferries is an unforgettable day out for all the family. There's no better way to learn the area's fascinating history, see its spectacular sights and discover its unique character. There's a full commentary, the chance to stop at Seacombe and visit 'Spaceport,' the space-themed visitor attraction or 'Play Planet,' our children's play area. Spaceport is a £10m attraction dedicated to space and space-travel. Visit six differently themed galleries that all feature a variety of interactive, 'hands-on' exhibits and audio/visual experiences. Spaceport also offers a 30min Planetarium show. River Explorer Cruises leave every day from Pier Head, Liverpool and Seacombe or Woodside, Wirral.

All year daily Mon-Fri 07.30-19.30, Sat & Sun 09.00-19.20. Cruise Timetable: See special events guide or call venue. Spaceport open Tue-Sun 10.30-17.30 (open most Bank Hols & Mons during school hols)

Cruise A£5.30 C£2.95, Family Ticket £14.15. Joint Ferry/Spaceport tickets are available (see website)

Discount Offer: Save up to £1.00 off your journey.

Yellow Duckmarine

Unit 32 Anchor Courtyard Atlantic Pavilion
Albert Dock Liverpool Merseyside L3 4AS
Tel: 0151 708 7799
Travel in comfort on one of our converted WWII
DUKW vehicles, which depart daily from the
Albert Dock.

Performing Arts

Cavern Quarter (Mathew Street)

Mathew Street Liverpool Merseyside L2 6RE
Home to the Cavern Club (still a thriving music
venue), the Cavern Club's Wall of Fame, the
Mathew Street Gallery (the art of John Lennon),
and the Liverpool Wall of Fame.

Places of Worship

Birkenhead Priory and St Mary's Tower

Priory Street Birkenhead Merseyside CH41 5JH
Tel: 0151 666 1249
An interpretive centre traces the history and
development of the site. St Mary's tower offers
superb views of the River Mersey.

Liverpool Cathedral

St James Mount Liverpool Merseyside L1 7AZ
Tel: 0151 709 6271 Fax: 0151 702 7292
www.liverpoolcathedral.org.uk
*[Rail: Lime Street. New S1 bus service links Lime
Street and bus station, Albert Dock and the two
cathedrals. Plenty of on-site parking available]*

The largest cathedral in Britain and one of the
great buildings of the twentieth century. See
panoramic views from the famous vestey tower
and 'The Great Space' film and audio tour for
children and adults with computer interactive
stations and a 'music experience' on the high
Nave Bridge. New for 2008, foreign languages
and BSL interpreted tours for deaf people.
Check website for opening times and admission.

*All year daily. New mezzanine café bar and refec-
tory, shop and visitor attractions open daily.
Check website for opening times*

Metropolitan Cathedral of Christ the King

Cathedral House Mount Pleasant Liverpool
Merseyside L3 5TQ
Tel: 0151 709 9222 Fax: 0151 708 7274
www.liverpoolmetrocathedral.org.uk

[Plenty of on-site parking available]

Visit Liverpool's dramatic, modern, circular,
Roman Catholic cathedral with its glorious
multi-coloured windows and many modern art
works, now features magnificent entrance steps
and a visitor centre incorporating the Piazza
Café and cathedral gift shop.

*All year daily 08.00-18.00. Closes at 17.00 on
Sun in winter*

No Admission Charge. A donation of £3.00 per
head is requested

Sporting History Museums

Liverpool Football Club Museum and Tour Centre

Anfield Road Liverpool Merseyside L4 0TH
Tel: 0151 260 6677
Fax: 0151 264 0149
www.liverpoolfc.tv/club/tour.htm

[From all major routes into Liverpool. Ground is 3mi from city centre, 4mi from M62 & 7mi from end of M57 and M58. Well signposted from city centre. Weekday - park in Main Stand or Centenary Stand car parks, (except on mid-week match-days). Rail: Lime Street Railway Station 2mi from Anfield. Match days: use Merseyrail network to link with Soccerbus service from Sandhills Station. Taxis available from Lime Street. Bus: 26 / 27 from Paradise St. bus station or 17B, 17C, 17D, or 217 from Queen Square bus station directly to ground. 68 & 168 operate between Bootle and Aigburth, 14 & 19 stop a short walk away. By Air: Liverpool Airport approx. 10mi from Ground. The Soccerbus Service: Leave The Car At Home On Match Day! A direct bus link from anywhere on Merseyrail Network via Sandhills Station to Anfield. Plenty of on-site parking available]

Liverpool Football Club Museum & Stadium Tour Liverpool's newest Five Star Attraction; England's most successful football club has a record 18 league Championships, 13 League and FA Cups, plus 3 UEFA and European Super Cups apiece. But it's the Five European Trophies that place the club in an exclusive group of just three, who have won the most prestigious prize of all, five times or more. Following "The Greatest football game ever" on the 25th May 2005, Liverpool FC Museum has added to it's collection the beautiful Champions League trophy. Surrounded by the sights and sounds of that night in Istanbul with many witty

banners created by fans, the Trophy has brought in unprecedented numbers of adoring fans. The stadium tour takes you behind the scenes at Anfield, visiting the dressing rooms, down the tunnel to the sound of the crowd, touch the famous "This Is Anfield' sign and sit in the team dug-out. We strongly recommend booking in advance for stadium tours. There is no need to pre-book a museum-only visit.

All year daily 10.00-17.00. Match Days: 10.00-1 hr before kick-off. No stadium tours on Match days. Closed 23 May-4 Jun 2008

Museum Only: A£5.00 C&OAPs£3.00, Family Ticket £13.00. Museum & Tours: A£10.00 C&OAPs£6.00, Family Ticket £25.00. Group rates available on request

Discount Offer: One Child Free (with a full-paying adult).

Transport Museums

Pacific Road

Tram Shed Pacific Road Birkenhead Merseyside CH41 1LJ
Tel: 0151 666 2756
[Off M53 Wallasey All Docks exit, Hamilton Square BR station nearby]
The trams are back at Woodside after 58 years, running between Woodside and Old Colonial Public House. Egerton Bridge is open when the trams operate and features displays tracing the history of Birkenhead Docklands.

Sat-Sun 13.00-17.00

Wildlife & Safari Parks

Knowsley Safari Park

Prescot Merseyside L34 4AN
Tel: 0151 430 9009
A five-mile drive through the reserves enables visitors to see lions, tigers, elephants, rhinos, baboons, and many other animals in spacious natural surroundings.

Norfolk

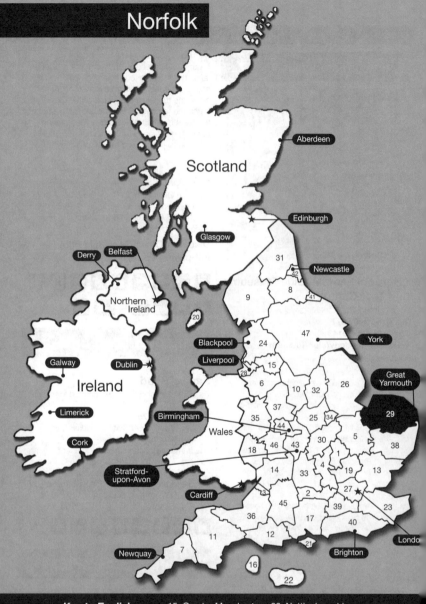

Key to English Counties:

1	Bedfordshire	15	Greater Manchester
2	Berkshire	16	Guernsey
3	Bristol	17	Hampshire
4	Buckinghamshire	18	Herefordshire
5	Cambridgeshire	19	Hertfordshire
6	Cheshire	20	Isle Of Man
7	Cornwall	21	Isle Of Wight
8	County Durham	22	Jersey
9	Cumbria	23	Kent
10	Derbyshire	24	Lancashire
11	Devon	25	Leicestershire
12	Dorset	26	Lincolnshire
13	Essex	27	London
14	Gloucestershire	28	Merseyside
		29	Norfolk
		30	Northamptonshire
		31	Northumberland

32	Nottinghamshire
33	Oxfordshire
34	Rutland
35	Shropshire
36	Somerset
37	Staffordshire
38	Suffolk
39	Surrey
40	Sussex
41	Tees Valley
42	Tyne & Wear
43	Warwickshire
44	West Midlands
45	Wiltshire
46	Worcestershire
47	Yorkshire

Place labels shown on the map: Aberdeen, Scotland, Glasgow, Edinburgh, Newcastle, Derry, Belfast, Northern Ireland, Galway, Dublin, Ireland, Limerick, Cork, Blackpool, Liverpool, Birmingham, Wales, Stratford-upon-Avon, Cardiff, Newquay, York, Great Yarmouth, London, Brighton

Animal Attractions

Animal Ark

Fakenham Road Gt Witchingham Norfolk
NR9 5QS
Tel: 01603 872274

Adventure play and tiny tots adventure play.
Lots of green space to run off that excess ener-
gy. Feed the farm animals and cuddle the pets.
Meet the keepers at 12.00 and 14.30 in the
Pets Pavillion.

Hillside Animal and Shire Horse Sanctuary

Hall Lane Frettenham Norfolk NR12 7LT
Tel: 01603 736200

Hillside Animal Sanctuary is home to hundreds
of rescued animals and campaigns on behalf of
those who suffer in the factory farming industry.

ILPH Hall Farm

Ada Cole Avenue Snetterton Norfolk NR16 2LP
Tel: 01953 499100 Fax: 01953 498705
www.ilph.org/hallfarm

*[0.5mi from A11 between Attleborough &
Thetford. Approx 30min from Norwich &
Newmarket. Plenty of on-site parking available]*

Set in 250 acres of beautiful countryside, you
can take one of the marked walkways around
the paddocks (dogs on leads welcome) where
you will meet some of the 150 or more rescued
horses and ponies. We offer guided tours of
Hall Farm and our visitor centre has information
on the work we do in the UK and overseas. We
also have equine related events on most weekends. You can spend time in our coffee shop,
which provides a good range of hot and cold
snacks and drinks.

*All year Weds, Weekends & Bank Hols 11.00-
16.00. Closed 25 Dec-1 Jan*
Admission Free

Redwings Caldecott Visitor Centre

Caldecott Hall Beccles Road Fritton Great
Yarmouth Norfolk NR31 9EY
Tel: 0870 040 0033 Fax: 0870 458 1942
www.redwings.org.uk

*[1mi NE of Fritton village on A143. Plenty of on-
site parking available]*

Established in 1984, Redwings is now the
largest horse charity in the UK, working to provide and promote the welfare, care and protec-
tion of horses, ponies, donkeys and mules.
Redwings' Norfolk visitor centre has more than
70 acres of paddock and there is plenty for the
whole family to enjoy. Residents include beautiful pony Darcey, Muffin the mule, cheeky donkey Denise and stunning Shire Victor. Visitors
can meet the horses and ponies, watch equine
care demonstrations, take a guided tour, shop
in the gift shop or enjoy a light meal in the
Nosebag café. There is even the chance to
adopt one of the centre's special equines.

1 Apr-28 Oct daily 10.00-17.00
Admission Free

Discount Offer: Free Poster.

Snettisham Park
Snettisham King's Lynn Norfolk PE31 7NQ
Tel: 01485 542425
Safari tours, visitor centre, crafts centre, art gallery, tearoom and souvenir shop. Indoor and outdoor activities include farm animals and pets.

Festivals & Shows

Royal Norfolk Show and Showground
Dereham Road New Costessey Norwich Norfolk NR5 0TT
Tel: 01603 748931 Fax: 01603 748729
www.norfolkshowground.com

[Off A47 southern bypass. Plenty of on-site parking available]

We are looking forward to yet another bumper Royal Norfolk Show for 2008. Major entertainment is planned for the Grand Ring and will be suitable for all age groups. The main attraction this year will be the King's Troop Royal Horse Artillery together with many more events taking place around the showground. The Showground also hosts many other varied shows throughout the year. Please visit our website for details.

25-26 June 2008 08.00

Tickets discounted if purchased in advance. A£16.00 C£5.00 OAP£14.00 Disabled£14.00 Carer£7.00, Family Ticket (A2+C3) £42.00. Group rate (25+): 15% discount

Gardens & Horticulture

Fairhaven Woodland and Water Garden
School Road South Walsham Norwich Norfolk NR13 6DZ
Tel: 01603 270449 Fax: 01603 270449
www.fairhavengarden.co.uk

[9mi E of Norwich at South Walsham signposted on A47 at J with B1140. Plenty of on-site parking available]

This delightful woodland and water garden is a garden for all seasons. Only farmyard manure and the garden's leaf mulch is used to fertilise the soil and the fauna and flora are a testimony to an organic approach. Over three miles of wonderful woodland walks - all easy - with superb views across Fairhaven's private Broad. There are many ancient oaks and beech trees including the 950 year-old King Oak. Boat trips on our private broad, Apr to end of Oct (additional charge) and a children's trail. Dogs on leads allowed. Programme of events throughout the year.

All year daily (except Christmas Day) 10.00-17.00 (10.00-16.00 winter months). Extended opening hours in May, Jun, Jul, & Aug. (Wed &Thu 10.00-21.00)

A£4.75 C(under5)£Free C(5+)£2.25 Concessions£4.25 Dog£0.25. Memberships: Single £17.50 Family £40.00 Dog£2.50

Discount Offer: Two for the Price of One (full-paying adult).

Hoveton Hall Gardens

Hoveton Hall Norwich Norfolk NR12 8RJ

Tel: 01603 782798

Set at the edge of the Norfolk Broads, Hoveton Hall Gardens is a delightful 15-acre garden mixing both formal and informal planting across the seasons. Guided tours and wildlife walks available. Tea room serving light lunches and afternoon tea. Plant sales with hostas and ferns from the water garden and a vast array of herbaceous plants from the 'spider garden.' The hall is not open to the public.

Apr-Sep: Sun, Wed-Fri & Bank Hols

Mannington Gardens and Countryside

Mannington Hall Norwich Norfolk NR11 7BB
Tel: 01263 584175 Fax: 01263 761214
www.manningtongardens.co.uk

[2mi N of Saxthorpe nr B1149, 18mi NW of Norwich, 9mi from coast. Plenty of on-site parking available]

This moated manor house was built in 1460. Gardens to view and lovely countryside. Extensive country walks, Wildflower Meadow, Arboretum, Heritage Rose Gardens, shrubs, trees, scented and sensory gardens and events.

May-Sept Sun 12.00-17.00, June-Aug Wed-Fri 11.00-17.00

A£4.00 Concessions£3.00

Discount Offer: Two for the Price of One (full-paying adult).

Norfolk Lavender

Caley Mill Heacham King's Lynn Norfolk PE31 7JE

Tel: 01485 570384 Fax: 01485 571176

www.norfolk-lavender.co.uk

[On A149 at J with B1454. Plenty of free on-site parking available]

England's premier lavender farm. Home of the National Collection of Lavender. Tea room offering hot lunches from 12.00-15.00, cream teas and snacks, gift shops, conservatory plant sales area, herb garden and fragrant meadow. Tours of grounds (including distillery and drying barn) from May to September. Minibus tours to lavender field and surrounding villages from July to end of harvest (pre-booking advisable). Please phone for more details.

All year daily Apr-Oct 9.00-17.00, Nov-Mar 9.00-16.00. Closed 25-26 Dec & 1 Jan

Admission Free

Priory Maze and Gardens

Cromer Road Beeston Regis Sheringham Norfolk NR26 8SF
Tel: 01263 822986

Ten acres of gardens with natural running water, ponds, wild flower meadows, herb and aromatic gardens, pine walk, seaside garden and herbaceous beds. The Priory Maze is based on the adjacent Beeston Priory with various plant varieties. Plant Centre and tea rooms.

Walsingham Abbey Grounds and Shirehall Museum

Estate Office Common Place Walsingham
Norfolk NR22 6BP
Tel: 01328 824432 Fax: 01328 820098

[On B1105 between Wells / Fakenham]

Set in the picturesque medieval village of Little Walsingham, a place of pilgrimage since the eleventh century, the Abbey Grounds contain the remains of the famous Augustinian Priory. Although little now remains of the priory, the great east window is perhaps the most striking feature and along with the refectory walls, remains of the west tower and monks bath, give an impression of the size and scale of the original building. Visitors can enjoy the tranquil gardens and over the ancient packhorse bridge, the river and woodland walks lead into unspoilt natural woods and parkland. Entrance to the grounds in the summer is through the Shirehall Museum - a Georgian Magistrates court, now a 'hands-on' museum detailing the history of this interesting village. During the snowdrop season the Abbey Grounds are home to one of the most popular and impressive displays of snowdrops in the country. Member of the HHA.

Courthouse & Museum: Easter-end Oct.
Grounds: All year, call for more information

Combined Entrance: A£3.00 C&OAPs£2.00

Discount Offer: Two for the Price of One (full-paying adult).

Heritage & Industrial

Bressingham Steam Museum and Gardens

Bressingham Nr Diss Norfolk IP22 2AB
Tel: 01379 686900 Fax: 01379 686907
www.bressingham.co.uk

[On A1066]

A visit to Bressingham Steam and Gardens is a great way to spend all day! You have to go a long way to beat Bressingham Steam and Gardens for a family day out. For here is where world-renowned horticulturist Alan Bloom combined his passion for plants and gardens with his love of steam to create a truly unique experience for all the family. Whether you choose to explore one of Europe's leading steam collections, take a ride on Bressingham's famous Victorian Gallopers, journey on over five miles of narrow gauge steam railway, wander through beautiful gardens with 6000 varieties or visit the official "Dads Army" exhibition, you will find something for everyone when you arrive at Bressingham! Bring your own picnic and take a break in the gardens, or choose from the café or restaurant within Blooms Centre and you really can make the fun last all day!

20 Mar-2 Nov 10.30-17.30

A£12.00 C£8.00 Concessions£10.75 Family Ticket £35.00

Discount Offer: One Child Free.

Historical

Blickling Hall, Gardens and Park

Blickling Norwich Norfolk NR11 6NF
Tel: 01263 738030 Fax: 01263 738035
www.nationaltrust.org.uk/blickling

[On B1354. Plenty of on-site parking available]

Blickling has so much to offer that you will want to come back time after time. Indoors or outdoors, whatever the weather, however old or young you are, a visit will be a day to remember. Built in the early seventeeth century, Blickling is one of England's great Jacobean houses. The spectacular Long Gallery houses one of the finest private collections of rare books in England and you can view fine Mortlake tapestries, an excellent collection of furniture and paintings as well as the newly restored Hungerford Pollen painted ceiling. The glorious gardens are beautiful all year round, with thousands of spring bulbs, vibrant summer borders and rich autumn colours. It really is a garden for all seasons. New in 2008 - restoration of the kitchen and service areas. Learn about life downstairs in the 1930s and hear stories by the actual people who lived and worked at Blickling.

House: 15 Mar-27 Jul Wed-Sun 11.00-17.00, 28 Jul-31 Aug Wed-Mon 11.00-17.00, 1 Sep-2 Nov Wed-Sun 11.00-17.00.
Garden/Restaurant/Shop/Bookshop: 15 Mar-27 Jul Wed-Sun 10.15-17.15, 28 Jul-31 Aug Wed-Mon 10.15-17.15, 1 Sep-2 Nov Wed-Sun 10.15-17.15, 3 Nov-31 Jan 09 Thurs to Sun 11.00-16.00. Plant centre: 15 Mar-2 Nov Wed-Sun 10.15-17.15. Cycle hire: 21 Mar-2 Nov, Sat & Sun only 10.15-17.00

Gift Aid admission*: Hall & gardens: A£9.10 C£4.50 Family Ticket £24.00 Family Ticket (A1) £14.50 Gardens only: A£6 C£3, Family Ticket £16.00 Family Ticket (A1) £10.00. *Including a voluntary donation of at least 10%; visitors can, however, choose to pay the standard admission

prices which are displayed at the property and at www.nationaltrust.org.uk

Discount Offer: One Child Free.

Felbrigg Hall

Felbrigg Norwich Norfolk NR11 8PR
Tel: 01263 837444 Fax: 01263 837032
www.nationaltrust.org.uk/felbrigg

Wander along to Felbrigg and unravel the history of one of Norfolk's most appealing houses. A house of surprising contrasts, stroll through the hall with its fine seascapes, large collection of Grand Tour paintings and impressive Gothic-style library. Investigate the kitchen with its collection of beautiful copperware, in a domestic wing that would be the envy of any grand house. Outside, Felbrigg is a gardener's delight. Explore the restored Walled Garden with its tranquil pond, working dovecote and colourful potager gardens. Wander in the West Garden, a Victorian pleasure garden of azaleas, rhododendrons and camellias and in September the rich blooming of the national collection of autumn crocus. The rolling landscaped park has magnificent ancient trees as well as newly planted sweet chestnut, beech and oak, a lake and 200 hectares of woods with waymarked trails. New in 2008 - new displays - 'Unseen Felbrigg'.

House: 1 Mar-2 Nov Sat-Wed 11.00-17.00. Gardens: 1 Mar-26 Oct Sat-Wed. Open daily 26 May-1 Jun, 21 Jul-31 Aug, 27 Oct-2 Nov, 11.00-17.00. 27 Dec-31 Dec, Sat-Wed 11.00-16.00. Shop/Refreshments/Bookshop/Plant sales: 1 Mar-2 Nov, Sat-Wed 11.00-17.00. 3 Nov-14

Dec, Thur-Sun 11.00-16.00. 27 Dec-31 Dec, Sat-Wed 11.00-16.00. 5 Jan-31 Jan 09, Sat & Sun 11.00-16.00. Open BH Mons & Good Fri. Estate: All year, dawn to dusk

Gift Aid Admission*: House & Garden: A£7.90 C£3.70 Family Ticket £19.50. Garden only: A£3.70 C£1.60 Parking £2.00 (NT members free - please display car sticker). *Including a voluntary donation of at least 10%; visitors can, however, choose to pay the standard admission prices which are displayed at the property and at www.nationaltrust.org.uk

Discount Offer: One Child Free.

Holkham Estate

Holkham Norfolk NR23 1AB
Tel: 01328 710227

Classic eighteenth-century Palladian-style mansion. Attractions include the Bygones Museum, the 'History of Farming' exhibition, Holkham Pottery, gift shop, art gallery, café, tearooms, lake cruises, hotel, beach and nature reserve.
June-Sep

Oxburgh Hall, Garden and Estate

Oxborough King's Lynn Norfolk PE33 9PS
Tel: 01366 328258 Fax: 01366 328066
www.nationaltrust.org.uk/oxburghhall

[7mi SW of Swaffham. Rail: Downham Market]

Step back in time through the magnificent Tudor gatehouse at Oxburgh Hall, into the dangerous world of Tudor politics. Oxburgh's secret doors and priest's hole make this a house of mystery and history. Home to the Bedingfeld family since 1482 this stunning red-brick house charts their

precarious history from medieval austerity to neo-Gothic Victorian comfort. As well as beautiful early Mortlake tapestries in the Queen's Room, Oxburgh houses beautiful embroidery by both Mary Queen of Scots and the famous Bess of Hardwick. Panoramic views from the roof look out over the estate. Marvel at and explore the Victorian French parterre, walled orchard, kitchen garden and Catholic chapel. New in 2008 - gatehouse showrooms open weekends January to March. External tours of the hall and grounds with guides in Tudor costume. Portrait by Enoch Seeman that once hung at Oxburgh has recently been acquired and will be re-hung for 2008.

Gatehouse: 5 Jan-9 Mar Sat & Sun 12.00-15.00 (Gatehouse open for tours-advance booking is essential on 01366 328258) House: 15 Mar-30 Jul, Sat-Wed 13.00-17.00. Open daily 31 Jul-31 Aug 13.00-17.00. 1 Sep-1 Oct Sat-Wed 13.00-17.00. 4 Oct-2 Nov, Sat-Wed 13.00-16.00.Garden/Tea room/Shop: 5 Jan-9 Mar Sat & Sun 11.00-16.00. 15 Mar-30 Jul Sat-Wed 11.00-17.00. Open daily 31 Jul-31 Aug 11.00-17.00. 1 Sep-1 Oct Sat-Wed 11.00-17.00. 4 Oct-2 Nov Sat-Wed 11.00-16.00 8 Nov-21 Dec Sat & Sun 11.00-16.00. 3-31 Jan 09 Sat & Sun 11.00-16.00. Open BH Mons & Good Fri: 11.00-17.00 (inc. house)

Gift Aid Admission* House & garden: A£7.10 C£3.70 Family Ticket £19.00(A2+C2) Garden & Estate: A£3.70 C£2.10 Garden & Gatehouse: A£5.80 C£2.95, Family Ticket £14.50 *Including a voluntary 10% donation; visitors can, however, choose to pay the standard admission prices which are displayed at the property and at www.nationaltrust.org.uk

Discount Offer: One Child Free (with full-paying adult).

Sandringham Estate

Sandringham Norfolk PE35 6EN

Tel: 01553 772675

Sandringham is the much-loved country retreat of Her Majesty the Queen, and its attractions include the stately home, a museum, gardens, a country park, a visitor centre, a church, gift shops and three restaurants.
22 Mar-25 Jul & 3 Aug-26 Oct 2008

Wolterton Park

Wolterton Hall Erpingham Aylsham Norfolk
NR11 7LY
Tel: 01263 584175 Fax: 01263 761214
www.manningtongardens.co.uk

[Nr Erpingham signposted from A140 Norwich to Cromer rd. Rail: Gunton. Plenty of on-site parking available]

Extensive historic park with lake, orienteering, adventure playground, walks. Hall built by diplomat brother of Sir Robert Walpole. Family portraits, fascinating history, special events; talks, music and textiles. Chair lift for disabled access.

Park: daily 9.00-dusk, Hall mid Apr-end Oct Fri 14.00-17.00

Cars£2.00 Hall£5.00

Discount Offer: Two for the Price of One (full-paying adult).

Military & Defence Museums

City of Norwich Aviation Museum

Old Norwich Road Horsham St. Faith Norwich
Norfolk NR10 3JF
Tel: 01603 893080

The collection features a massive Vulcan bomber and some of the military and civil aircraft which have flown from Norfolk airfields.

Muckleburgh Collection

Weybourne Military Camp Weybourne Holt
Norfolk NR25 7EG
Tel: 01263 588210 Fax: 01263 588425
www.muckleburgh.co.uk
[on A149]

The Muckleburgh Collection has been named after Muckleburgh Hill at the foot of which the former Weybourne Military Camp is situated. Weybourne has been a base for the repulse of invasion from the days of the Spanish Armada in 1588. The site became an anti-aircraft artillery base in 1936 and remained in use until 2nd October 1958. In 1986, work began to demolish nearly 200 old buildings which were beyond repair and 45,000 tons of rubble was removed to make way for the Collection which was opened in 1988 by Berry and Michael Savory. The Collection has grown to over 120 tanks, guns and vehicles in addition to thousands of other items. The vehicles on display have come from as far as Russia, Norway, Czechoslovakia, Belgium, Syria, Kuwait, Israel, USA and Iraq. Over the weekend of 7th & 8th June 2008 the Territorial Army will celebrate its 100th Anniversary at The Muckleburgh Collection with many displays and events. Visitors can see a tank demonstration and enjoy a bumpy coastal ride in an American Gama Goat personnel carrier. A children's play area and picnic site give all the family an exciting day out. Dog kennels are provided and there are facilities for the disabled including use of a wheelchair.

23 Feb-16 Mar Sat-Sun, 21 Mar-2 Nov daily 10am-5pm

A£6.00, C(Over 5)£3.50 C(Under 5) Free, Family Ticket(2A+2C)£17.00, OAPs+HM Forces£5.00, Group rates on application. Gama Goat Rides£2.50, Tank Drives£100.00

Music & Theatre Museums

Thursford Collection

Thursford Fakenham Norfolk NR21 OAS
Tel: 01328 878477 Fax: 01328 878415
www.thursford.com

[1mi off A148 between Fakenham & Holt. Plenty of on-site parking available]

Mechanical organs, Wurlitzer organ, road engines, old-fashioned fairground rides and engines. Musical shows each day. Restaurant / coffee shop, Dickensian styled gift shops, including our famous Christmas shop, all housed in traditional Norfolk farm buildings.

1 Apr-30 Sept 12.00-17.00

A£6.30 C(4-14)£3.80 OAPs£6.00
Students(NUS/USI)&Groups£5.60

Discount Offer: Two for the Price of One (full-paying adult).

Places of Worship

Norwich Cathedral

12 The Close Norwich Norfolk NR1 4DH
Tel: 01603 218321/218324
A beautiful Norman building set in the largest close in England.

Railways

Bure Valley Railway

Aylsham Station Norwich Road Aylsham Norfolk NR11 6BW
Tel: 01263 733858 Fax: 01263 733814
www.bvrw.co.uk

[Mid-way between Norwich & Cromer on A140. Plenty of on-site parking available]

Travel through the Norfolk countryside on the 9 mile long, 15 inch Bure Valley Steam Railway. The Boat Train connects with cruises on the Broads - inclusive fares available. Regular services from Easter to end of September. Steam Locomotive driving courses are also available in off peak periods.

10-18 Feb, 31 Mar-30 Sept, 20-28 Oct (please call or visit website for detailed timetable)

Sample fares from A£10.50 C(5-15)£6.50 OAPs£9.50

Discount Offer: 50p off per Adult on Standard Fares.

Science - Earth & Planetary

Inspire Discovery Centre

St Michael's Church Coslany Street Norwich Norfolk NR3 3DT
Tel: 01603 612612
Promotes and encourage the discovery and enjoyment of science using hands-on exhibits and related activities.

Sealife Centres & Aquariums

Great Yarmouth Sea Life Centre

Marine Parade Great Yarmouth Norfolk
NR30 3AH

Tel: 01493 330631 Fax: 01493 330442

www.sealifeeurope.com

[A47 or A12 to Great Yarmouth, then head towards Sea Front]

Welcome to the magical marine world. Great Yarmouth Sea Life Centre will introduce you to many strange, beautiful and fascinating creatures of the deep. Prepare for astonishing close views of everything from humble starfish to mighty sharks and giant sea turtles, all in displays that carefully recreate their natural habitats. Explore a rich variety of underwater environments, from freshwater streams to the rugged coastline, from the sandy shallows to the darkest depths of the ocean. At every step there are different amazing creatures to find, watch and learn about. Discover the truth about the much-misunderstood shark, the plight of the endangered sea turtle, the remarkable lives of seahorses and countless more surprising facts about these and other incredible creatures. Some of the most beautiful and primitive of the ocean's inhabitants will take centre stage in Great Yarmouth's new feature, 'Jellies.' With recent invasions of tropical jellyfish into British waters, this feature is sure to attract a lot of attention.

All year daily from 10.00. Closed Christmas Day

Please call for admission prices

Discount Offer: One Child Free.

Hunstanton Sea Life Sanctuary

Southern Promenade Hunstanton Norfolk
PE36 5BH

Tel: 01485 533576 Fax: 01485 533531
www.sealsanctuary.co.uk

[On seafront, signposted]

Hunstanton Sea Life Sanctuary will introduce you to many strange, beautiful and fascinating creatures of the deep. Prepare for astonishing close views of everything from humble starfish to mighty sharks, from otters and penguins to rescued and resident seals. Explore a rich variety of underwater environments, from the sandy shallows to the darkest depths. At every step there are different amazing creatures to find, to watch and to learn about. Discover the truth about the much-misunderstood shark, about the lives and trials of our native seals, the remarkable lives of seahorses and countless more surprising facts about these and other incredible creatures. The whole seal rescue operation is under a fresh spotlight this year, with new developments that give a deeper insight into the whole process…from rescue and recovery right through to release. You may be lucky enough to see newly rescued pups being cared for in the indoor hospital, before watching other rescuees and residents in the outdoor pools.

All year daily from 10.00. Closed Christmas Day

Please call for admission prices

Discount Offer: One Child Free.

Sport & Recreation

Sheringham Park

Upper Sheringham Sheringham Norfolk
NR26 8TL
Tel: 01263 820550
www.nationaltrust.org.uk/sheringham

Enjoy a sea of colour at Sheringham Park, the perfect place to escape for a day. With miles of fabulous scenic countryside and spectacular views over the North Sea, climb to the top of the viewing towers and enjoy spectacular views of coast and countryside. This wonderful park was designed in 1812 by the great landscape designer Humphry Repton - he called it 'my most favourite work'. Watch the woodlands, full of oak, ash and sweet chestnut, come alive with birdsong and colour in April, and the magnificent display of rhododendrons and azaleas in late May and June is a sight enjoyed by tens of thousands of visitors each year. Enjoy a gentle stroll and relax in the tranquillity of North Norfolk. In the visitor centre, see displays which explore the life and work of Humphry Repton and the Upcher family who owned the park.

Park: Open all year, dawn to dusk. Visitor centre: 1 Feb-14 Mar Sat & Sun 11.00-16.00. Open daily 15 Mar-30 Sep 10.00-17.00. 1-31 Oct Wed-Sun 10.00-17.00. 1 Nov-31 Jan 09 Sat & Sun 11.00-16.00. Refreshment kiosk opens at 11.00. Sheringham Hall is privately occupied. Visitor centre and kiosk open every day in local Oct half-term holiday

Pay and display £4.00 per car (NT members free, please display membership sticker or card in car)

Theme & Adventure Parks

Dinosaur Adventure Park

Weston Park Lenwade Norwich Norfolk
NR9 5JW
Tel: 01603 876310

Take part in a Scavenger Hunt, Track T-Rex, ride on Raptor Racers, dig for fossils and follow the Dinosaur Trail. Deer park, mini-golf, fun barn and 'creepy crawlies.'

Joyland

Marine Parade Great Yarmouth Norfolk
NR30 2EH
Tel: 01493 844094

Family fun park catering for children up to early teens. Rides include the 'Tyrolean Tub Twist,' the 'Spook Express' and 'Neptune's Kingdom' (an undersea fantasy ride).
Mar-Oct

Pettitts Animal Adventure Park

Camphill Church Road Reedham Norfolk
NR13 3UA
Tel: 01493 700094 Fax: 01493 700933
www.pettittsadventurepark.co.uk

[Off A47 between Norwich / Great Yarmouth, follow brown & white signs from Acle]

Pettitts is the top attraction to visit because it's three parks in one. Superb fun rides includes flying elephants, teacups, runaway train roller coaster, half mile miniature train, Alice In Wonderland, Toad of Toad Hall plus Robin Hoods adventure play area. Animals galore, with reindeer, lemurs, alpacas, racoons, reptile house and a petting area where you can feed the animals and lots more to see. Live shows featuring, Bingo the clown and the park mascots, Maxi mouse and Bobbi rabbit, three times a day. We have large picnic areas as well as three catering units. Palm's café, Maxi Snax and

Express Pizzas where hot and cold food and snacks are available. Our gift and candy shops offer a wide range of souvenirs and crafts. So, spend a day not a fortune at Pettitts.

15 Mar-2 Nov daily 10.00-17.00/17.30. Nov-Dec open Sat & Sun, open everyday in Christmas School Hols. (except 25 Dec)

A&C£8.95 C(under3)£Free
OAPs/Disabled£6.85, Family Ticket (A2+C3) £35.00. Group rates available on request

Discount Offer: Two for the Price of One (full-paying adult).

Pleasure Beach, Great Yarmouth

South Beach Parade Great Yarmouth Norfolk NR30 3EH
Tel: 01493 844585
Situated on the seafront, the Pleasure Beach is a 9-acre leisure park featuring over 70 rides and attractions. Entry is completely free.

The Playbarn

West Green Farm Shotesham Road Poringland Norwich Norfolk NR14 7LP
Tel: 01508 495526
A fun-packed indoor and outdoor centre especially designed for children aged 7 or under.

Caister Castle Car Collection

Caister-on-Sea Great Yarmouth Norfolk
Tel: 01572 787251
The largest private selection of cars in Britain is set in the grounds of a moated castle ruin. The ruin iteslf is about 550 years old and the collection dates from the 1890s right through to the present day.

May-Sep (Closed Saturdays)

Norfolk Motorcycle Museum

Station Yard Norwich Road North Walsham Norfolk NR28 0DS
Tel: 01692 406266
A small but interesting collection of over 80 motorcycles from the 1920's to the 1960's.

Strangers' Hall Museum

Charing Cross Norwich Norfolk NR2 4AL
Tel: 01603 667229
A perfect example of a wealthy merchant's house that dates back to 1320. The museum plots a fascinating journey through time from Tudor to Victorian times and houses a collection of historic toys.

Banham Zoo

The Grove Banham Norwich Norfolk NR16 2HE
Tel: 01953 887771
Set amongst 35 acres of beautiful Breckland countryside, you will discover hundreds of animals ranging from big cats to birds of prey and siamangs to shire horses. Don't miss the daily feeding talks and displays.

Thrigby Hall Wildlife Gardens

Filby Road Thrigby Great Yarmouth Norfolk NR29 3DR
Tel: 01493 369477
Housing animals and birds from around the world, Thrigby Wildlife Gardens also boasts a walk-through aviary, willow pattern garden and lake, swamp house, forest house and tiger tree walk. There are also children's play areas, a café, picnic areas and a gift shop.

Northamptonshire

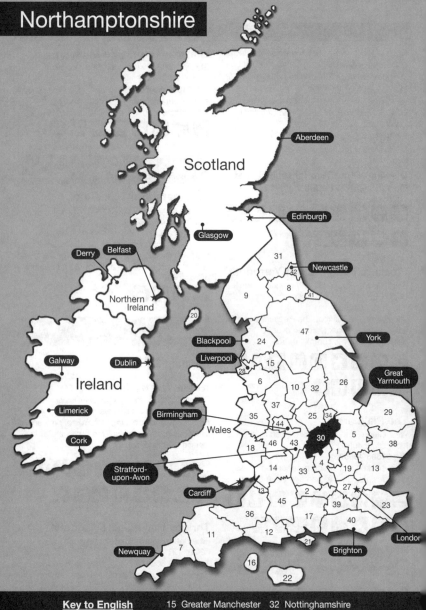

Aberdeen

Scotland

Edinburgh

Glasgow

Newcastle

Derry
Belfast

Northern
Ireland

31

42

9

8

41

Blackpool

20

47

York

Galway
Dublin

Liverpool

24

15

Great
Yarmouth

Ireland

Limerick

28

6

10

32

26

29

Birmingham

37

25

34

5

Cork

35

44

38

Wales

30

18

46

43

1

19

13

Stratford-
upon-Avon

14

4

33

Cardiff

13

2

27

23

London

45

39

36

17

40

11

12

Brighton

Newquay

7

21

16

22

Agriculture / Working Farms

Rookery Open Farm

Rookery Lane Stoke Bruerne Towcester
Northamptonshire NN12 7SJ
Tel: 01604 864855
A safe, clean environment based on this commercial sheep farm for families to enjoy themselves whilst learning.

Animal Attractions

West Lodge Rural Centre

Back Lane Desborough Kettering
Northamptonshire NN14 2SH
Tel: 01536 760552 Fax: 01536 764862
www.westlodgeruralcentre.co.uk
[Signposted off A6 from Desborough & Market Harborough. From Kettering, Wellingborough or Northampton, access A6 from A14 J3A. Plenty of on-site parking available]
One of the most spacious open Family Farms with over 100 acres and 3.5 miles of walks to explore. Encompassing rare breeds, cuddle corner, display barn, tractor rides, fantasy sculpture trail, nature trails, play areas, play barn, licensed restaurant and tea room. Many special events held throughout the year.
All year please call for specific times. Closed 25 & 26 Dec
Open in Jan Sat & Sun only
A£4.95 C£3.95 C(under2)£Free
Concessions£4.45

Art Galleries

Kettering Museum and Art Gallery

The Coach House Sheep Street Kettering
Northamptonshire NN16 0AN
Tel: 01536 534219
www.kettering.gov.uk/museums
[The best routes from the M1 area, N bound - leave at J15 - A45 to Northampton, A43 to Kettering, S bound - leave at J19 - A14 to Kettering, from A1 N bound, A14 (M1/A1 Link Road) to Kettering, from A1 S bound, A43 from Stamford to Kettering. Rail: Kettering is on the main St Pancras to Sheffield line. The Museum and Art Gallery is situated next to the Market Place, by the Parish Church, about 5 mins walk from the railway station and close to a main car park which is accessed via London Rd.]
The Museum has many temporary exhibitions throughout the year, its permanent displays are packed with fascinating objects in a broad range of topics. The current size of the collections is thought to total circa 20,000 artifacts. This includes items which were made or used within the geographical area of Kettering Borough from social and industrial history, geology, natural history and coins. Regular activities and a "hands-on" approach to history make this a lively and vibrant place to visit, appealing to children and adults alike. The Museum shop is well stocked with educational and fun gift items related to the themes of the Museum. A perfect place to buy a unique treat. The Alfred East Art Gallery hosts a continuous series of exhibitions by local and national artists. The permanent exhibition gallery displays, amongst other pieces, important works by Sir Alfred East and Thomas Cooper Gotch, both born in Kettering.
All year Tues-Sat 09.30-17.00
Admission Free
Discount Offer: 10% off in the
Museum gift shop with any purchase.

Arts, Crafts & Textiles

Northampton Museum and Art Gallery

Guildhall Road Northampton Northamptonshire NN1 1DP
Tel: 01604 838111 Fax: 01604 838720
www.northampton.gov.uk/museums

[M1, J15, signposted town centre]

The museum reflects Northampton's proud standing as Britain's shoe capital by housing a collection considered to be the world's finest. Two shoe galleries: 'Life & Sole' focuses on the industrial, commercial and health aspects of footwear giving visitors the opportunity to try out interactive exhibits and enjoy an audio-visual display. 'Followers of Fashion' is an Aladdin's cave of shoe delights spanning the centuries, which looks at shoe fashion and design featuring some of the most influential designers of the last 100 years. Also available is an art gallery featuring permanent and temporary exhibitions of fine art and a stunning display of Oriental and British ceramics. Two galleries show the town's history, from Stone Age times right up to the present day. There is a lively programme of talks, toddler afternoons, school holiday workshops and regular special themed activity days. The galleries and meeting room are available for hire

All year Mon-Sat 10.00-17.00, Sun 14.00-17.00. Closed 25 Dec, 26 Dec & 1 Jan

Admission Free

78 Derngate: The Charles Rennie Mackintosh House and Galleries

78 Derngate Northampton Northamptonshire NN1 1UH
Tel: 01604 603407 Fax: 01604 603408
www.78derngate.org.uk

[Close to town centre nr museum, gallery & Northampton Theatres]

The only house in England designed by Charles Rennie Mackintosh: one of the most individual and creative designers of the twentieth century. Famous for his earlier works including the Glasgow School of Art, The Hill House and the Glasgow Tea Rooms, 78 Derngate features his extraordinarily modern and striking interiors. 'To the great museums of the world, there must now be added one other. No 78 Derngate, Northampton...this is the most delightful museum you will ever see'. Daily Telegraph.

1 Feb-Christmas 2008, Weds-Sun 10.00-17.00, Tues afternoon from 13.00. Closed Mon (Except Bank Hols) & Tues morning. Guided Tours and unaccompanied tours available daily. Booking not essential

A£5.50 Concessions£4.50, Family Ticket £14.50. English Heritage Card holders £Free

Country Parks & Estates

Barnwell Country Park

Barnwell Road Oundle Peterborough
Northamptonshire PE8 5PB
Tel: 01832 273435
[Follow signs off A605 Oundle bypass]
15 hectares of lakes, riverbank and meadows to explore, close to the historic market town of Oundle. With three way marked waterside trails, numerous picnic spots, a wealth of wildlife and facilities, Barnwell Country Park is a great place for a family day out.

Brixworth Country Park

Northampton Road Brixworth Northampton
Northamptonshire NN6 9DG
Tel: 01604 883920
[Located off A508 roundabout near Brixworth village, follow brown and white signs]
Northamptonshire's youngest country park is a patchwork of meadows and newly planted woodland with stunning views over Pitsford Water. Facilities include a sensory garden, scupture trail, pond-dipping, bird hides, mini maze and visitor centre.

Irchester Country Park

Gypsy Lane Little Irchester Wellingborough
Northamptonshire NN9 7DL
Tel: 01933 276866
[On Gypsy Lane (B570) off A509 SE of Wellingborough]
Located in the Nene Valley, this former ironstone quarry has a network of long and short trails through 83 hectares of mixed woodland. The park is home to a wealth of wildlife as well as the Iron Narrow Gauge Railway museum.

Sywell Country Park

Washbrook Lane Ecton Northampton
Northamptonshire NN6 0QX
Tel: 01604 810970
[Off the Northampton to Mears Ashby road, near Earls Barton crossroads on the A4500]
Offers meadowland and lakeside walks, with a small arboretum of exotic trees and Edwardian buildings still surviving from its past role as a water supply reservoir with a water works heritage trail to guide you round.

Festivals & Shows

Castle Ashby Country Fair

Horton Road Brafield on the Green
Northamptonshire NN7 1BJ

Tel: 01604 696521/07791 244161
Fax: 01604 696361

www.castleashbycountryfair.co.uk

[Off A428 nr Northampton. Plenty of on-site parking available]

The 27th Castle Ashby Country Fair has activities and entertainment for all the family with over 100 trade stands, a craft fair, farmers' market and regional food area. Over six hours of Main Arena events include falconry, pig and sheep racing, a heavy horse demonstration, Jez Avery's Mountain Bike Show, Prison dog display team, lorry pulling, Territorial Army displays and classic vehicle parades. Other attractions include animal shows; show jumping; clay shoot and shooting clinic; gundogs; Young Farmers; chain saw carving; helicopter rides; Petting zoo; the Farmyard Experience; model boats and aircraft; archery; off-road course; tractor and trailer rides, Countryside area; plant societies, brass bands and free children's shows. Licensed catering, free car parking, disabled parking and mobility scooters available. Something for everyone!

13 July 2008 (09.30-18.00)

A£7.00 C(5-16)£3.00 OAPs£5.00

Northampton Balloon Festival

The Racecourse Kettering Road Northampton
Northamptonshire NN1 4LG

Tel: 01604 838222 Fax: 01604 838223

www.northamptonballoonfestival.com

*[1mi N of town on Kettering Rd. Park & Ride:
Return from Sixfields Stadium, Delapre Park &
Nene College (Boughton Park). Plenty of on-site
parking available]*

Three action-packed days combining a mix of
hot air ballooning, live music, roadshows, entertainment, displays, exhibitions and trade stands.
The balloon races and evening glows all form
the centrepiece of this annual event that hosts
over 70 balloons of all shapes and sizes.
Alongside the balloons, the event offers all the
fun of the fair as well as a wide variety of food
and beverage and market stalls. Additional
entertainment takes the form of the arena entertainment, stage shows and family entertainment.

15-17 August 2008

A£4.00 C(under16)£Free

Oundle International Festival

The Creed Chapel Ashton Oundle
Northamptonshire PE8 5LD
Tel: 01780 470297 Fax: 01780 470297
www.oundlefestival.org.uk

*[12mi W of Peterborough, 7mi N of A14 (A1-M1
link rd). Rail: Peterborough. Plenty of on-site parking available]*

A chance to hear rising young stars and world-
class musicians performing at historic venues in
an around this lovely Nene Valley market town,
and to join 5,000 others for a massive party
under the stars at the annual festival fireworks
concert on Saturday 12 July. Ten days of classical music, jazz, open-air theatre, celebrity organ
recitals, films, exhibitions, children's events and
more.

11-20 July 2008
£5.00-£22.00

Forests & Woods

Fermyn Woods Country Park
Brigstock Northamptonshire NN14 9HA
Tel: 01536 373625
*[Follow brown and white signs off A6116 -
Brigstock bypass]*
A partnership between Forestry Commission
and Northamptonshire County Council has cre-
ated Fermyn Woods Country Park, the county's
largest park. Situated in the heart of the
Rockingham Forest, the park offers fantastic
woodlands, meadows, thickets, marshes and
ponds to explore.

Salcey Forest

Hartwell Northamptonshire MK16 8LR
Tel: 01780 444394

[Located between Northampton & Milton Keynes, on Quinton to Hanslope rd]

The Royal Forest of Salcey offers excellent walking and opportunities to view an amazing range of wildlife. Trails include the Woodpecker Trail, The Church Path Trail, the Elephant Walk and Treetop Way.

Historical

Althorp

Northampton Northamptonshire NN7 4HQ
Tel: 01604 770107

[M1, J16, A45 to Northampton, A428 Northampton / Rugby Road, approx. 7m NW of Northampton]

Experience 500 years of history at Althorp, home of the Spencer Family. With stately home, stables, lake and gardens, plus an award-winning Diana exhibition.

[1 Jul-30 Aug, 11.00-17.00]

Boughton House

The Living Landscape Trust Kettering Northamptonshire NN14 1BJ
Tel: 01536 515731

A 500-year-old Tudor Monastic building that was gradually enlarged until a French-style addition in 1695 led to the nickname "The English Versailles." Outstanding collection of fine arts, furniture, tapestries, and porcelain. The House is set in extensive parkland with woodlands, lakes and riverside walks.

[1 Aug-1 Sep, daily 14.00-17.00]

Deene Park

Deene Corby Northamptonshire NN17 3EW
Tel: 01780 450223/450278

House of great architectural importance and historical interest. Extensive gardens with old-fashioned roses, rare trees and shrubs.

Mar-Aug: Bank Hols (Sun-Mon), plus Sundays in Jun-Aug (14.00-17.00)

Rockingham Castle

Rockingham Market Harborough LE16 8TH
Tel: 01536 770240

Spectacular castle that boasts architecture, furniture and art from practically every century and is surrounded by 18 acres of gardens.

[23 Mar-30 Jun: Sun & Bank Hols only. Jul-Sep: Tue, Sun & Bank Hol Mons. 12.00-17.00]

Social History Museums

Abington Park Museum

Abington Park Park Avenue South Northampton Northamptonshire NN1 5LW
Tel: 01604 838110
www.northampton.gov.uk/museums

[Plenty of on-site parking available]

Abington Park Museum is a beautiful Grade 1 listed building in a picturesque setting of one of Northampton's popular parks. Gaze at the hammer bean roof in the Tudor hall and the intricate carved panelling. Follow the Northamptonshire Regiment and the Northamptonshire Yeomanry round the world and through two world wars. Look at life as it was for Northampton people around one hundred years ago and stroll around the fashions of the nineteenth century. The museum also houses significant and interesting items from the Museum of Leather craft collection. There is a lively programme of talks at lunchtimes and for the over 60s mornings together with the popular toddler afternoons. In addition, look out for our school holiday workshops and special themed activity days. The atmospheric courtyard and hall are available for hire including wedding receptions.

Mar-Oct Tue-Sun & Bank Hol Mon 13.00-17.00, Nov-Feb Tue-Sun 13.00-16.00. Closed 25 + 26 Dec & 1 Jan

Admission Free

Theme & Adventure Parks

Wicksteed Park

Barton Road Kettering Northamptonshire
NN15 6NJ
Tel: 01536 512475 Fax: 01536 518948
www.wicksteedpark.co.uk

*[On outskirts of Kettering. Follow signs from J10
off A14. Main Gate is on A6. Plenty of on-site
parking available]*

With 147 acres of Parkland and lakes and over
35 rides and attractions including one of the
largest free playgrounds in the UK, a double
pirate ship, roller coasters, bumper boats, fairground rides, outdoor entertainment and an
events programme throughout the year -
Wicksteed Park really is the all round family day
out. The Wicksteed Railway is another major
attraction and the busiest commercial narrow
gauge railway in the UK carrying in excess of
250,000 passengers a year. The Wicksteed
Pavilion hosts 'It's Showtime' daytime entertainment all year round attracting audiences from
across the UK (tickets must be booked in
advance). The pavilion is also licensed for
Wedding ceremonies and is one of the largest
banqueting venues in Northamptonshire making
it the perfect venue for your party, wedding,
conference or corporate event. Wicksteed Park
now offers Caravan and Camping facilities on
site making it 'The coastal experience in the
heart of traditionally landscaped British countryside'.

*21 Mar-30 Sept, inclusive, opening times vary so
please telephone for more details*

No entry fee to the Park, car parking charged
maximum £6.00. Simply buy wristbands/tickets
as required. Wristbands: A£10.00 C£15.00
OAPs£7.50. Tickets: Sheet of 12 £10.00, sheet

of 30 £20.00, single tickets £1.00 each. Where
applicable, children under 0.9m ride free! Buying
a wristband entitles the wearer to unlimited
rides only on the day of purchase. This does
not include coin-operated amusements or
admission to certain special events. In the interests of safety, certain rides have passenger
height restrictions, which are clearly displayed
by means of a colour code

**Discount Offer: Three Wristbands for
the Price of Two (cheapest wristband
free).**

Transport Museums

Canal Museum

Bridge Road Stoke Bruerne Towcester
Northamptonshire NN12 7SE
Tel: 01604 862229
[Off J15 (M1)]

Situated in a beautiful canal-side village and
with a 'living canal' on its doorstep, Stoke
Bruerne is an ideal place to explore the story of
our waterways. Located in a restored corn mill
alongside the Grand Union Canal, you can easily imagine what life was like during the 1840s
when it was a working mill receiving cargo from
boats on the canal. The museum features
examples of canal painted-ware and the type of
clothing work by boat men and women.
Outside the museum you can see a Weighing
Machine, one of only three ever constructed.

Rushden Station Transport
Museum

Rushden Station Station Approach Rectory
Road Rushden Northamptonshire NN10 0AW
Tel: 01933 318988
The Museum, consisting of many pieces of rail
memorabilia and small items linked with road
transport, is housed in the waiting room, ticket
office, parcels office and Stationmaster's office
of Rushden Station.
[Easter-Oct: Sun 10.00-15.00]

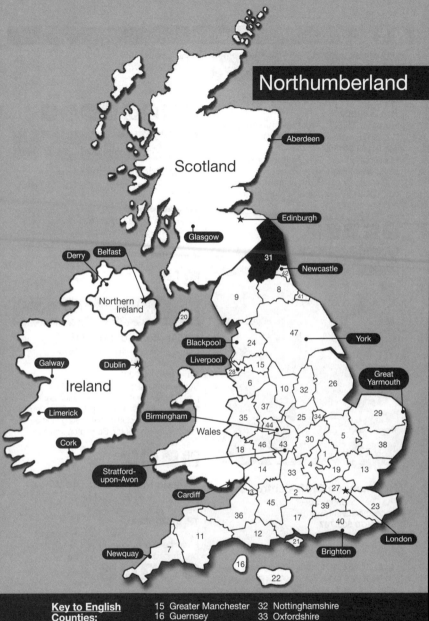

Northumberland

Scotland

Aberdeen

Edinburgh

Glasgow

31

Newcastle

42

Derry

Belfast

9

8

41

Northern
Ireland

Blackpool

24

47

York

Galway

Dublin

20

Liverpool

28

15

Great
Yarmouth

Ireland

6

10

32

26

29

Limerick

37

Birmingham

35

25

34

Cork

Wales

44

30

5

38

18

46

43

Stratford-
upon-Avon

14

1

4

19

13

Cardiff

33

3

27

London

2

39

23

45

36

17

40

11

12

Newquay

7

21

Brighton

16

22

Art Galleries

Berwick Borough Museum and Art Gallery

The Clock Block Ravensdowne Berwick-upon-Tweed Northumberland TD15 1DQ
Tel: 01289 301869
Housed in an early Georgian barrack block, featuring nineteenth-century French paintings and eighteenth-century British portraits. Decorative arts include Venetian glass, Dutch metalwork and oriental ceramics.
Apr-Oct

Arts, Crafts & Textiles

Northumbria Craft Centre

The Chantry Bridge Street Morpeth Northumberland NE61 1PD
Tel: 01670 500 707
www.castlemorpeth.gov.uk

[In Morpeth Town Centre, off A1, on A167]

Northumbria Craft Centre, housed in the medieval splendour of Morpeth Chantry provides a unique opportunity to browse and buy from a huge selection of hand crafted gifts and paintings from the Northumbria region. Northern talent on display includes colourful examples of glass, ceramics and wood sitting side by side with exquisite collections of jewellery to suit all pockets. Knitwear, leather and silk capture the spirit of rural and city life. Black and white Northumberland tartan inspires local pride. Original paintings and prints from Northumbrian artists can be bought at very affordable prices. A glorious profusion of talent to suit all tastes and pockets!

All year opening Mon-Sat 09.30-17.00. Aug & Dec Sun 11.00-16.00. Closed 23-24 Mar & 25-27 Dec

Free admission

Birds, Butterflies & Bees

Chain Bridge Honey Farm

Horncliffe Berwick-upon-Tweed Northumberland TD15 2XT
Tel: 01289 386362
Large family-owned bee farm on the banks of the river Tweed offering interesting displays and a shop with a comprehensive range of home-grown products.

Country Parks & Estates

Bedlington Country Park

Humford Mill Church Lane Bedlington Northumberland NE22 5RT
Tel: 01670 843200
Bedlington Country Park has over 5 miles of pathways and nature trails along the banks of the river Blyth, giving access to some stunning riverside views including the striking Hartford Hall and the site of the Bedlington Iron and Engine Works.

Carlisle Park and Castle Wood

28 Bridge Street Morpeth Northumberland NE61 1NL
Tel: 01670 535000
Formal park, historic architectural remains. Riverside and woodland walks, aviary, tennis courts, paddling pool and boating.

Hulne Park

Alnwick Northumberland NE66 1NQ
Tel: 01665 510777
Parkland, Gothic tower, lovely views and good walking. Hulne Park extends over 3000 acres within a walled enclosure. The Park consists of estate forestry, farm and sawmills. In the midst of Hulne Park there is a Priory (Carmelite), Brizlee Tower built in 1781 and Alnwick Abbey.

Festivals & Shows

Northumberland County Show

Tynedale Park Corbridge Northumberland
NE45 5AY
Tel: 01434 604216 Fax: 01434 609533
www.northcountyshow.co.uk
*[15mi W of Newcastle Upon Tyne & 4mi E of
Hexham. Tynedale Park on S side of river at
Corrbridge. Event AA signposted from A69 & A68
trunk roads. Plenty of on-site parking available]*
The regions single most successful agricultural
event with agriculture remaining firmly at its
heart. With emphasis on tradition e.g. sheep
shearing, heavy horses, parade of the hounds,
grand parade of livestock. Showing classes for
everything from cattle to alpacas attracting
exhibitors from as far as northern Scotland to
Lancashire. Intermingled with some spectacular
main arena acts to thrill and over 300 trade
stands entertain all members of the family.
*Bank Holiday Monday 26 May 2008 (09.00-
18.00)*
A£10.00 C(3-16)£2.50 OAPs£6.00

Food & Drink

Lindisfarne Mead

St.Aidans Winery Holy Island Berwick-upon-
Tweed Northumberland TD15 2RX
Tel: 01289 389230
St Aidan's Winery is the home of the world
famous Lindisfarne Mead and Lindisfarne
Preserves. The Winery Showroom opens to visi-
tors for free sampling daily throughout the sea-
son.

Gardens & Horticulture

Alnwick Garden

Denwick Lane Alnwick Northumberland
NE66 1YU
Tel: 01665 511350
An exciting, contemporary garden with beautiful
and unique gardens, features and structures
brought to life with water. Fantastic eating,
drinking and shopping. Events throughout the
year.

Howick Hall Gardens

Howick Alnwick Northumberland NE66 3LB
Tel: 01665 577285 Fax: 01665 577285
www.howickhallgardens.org

*[6mi NE of Alnwick off B1339 between Boulmer &
Craster. Plenty of on-site parking available]*

Howick Hall Gardens - Stunningly beautiful and
an oasis of tranquillity. Located 6 miles from
Alnwick, Northumberland the gardens are rated
by BBC Gardeners World magazine as "one of
the 'Top 5' coastal gardens in the UK. "The
extensive grounds boast a wealth of plant life to
be explored and wildlife to be discovered. Stroll
along the woodland walks covering some 65
acres, in an entirely wild collected arboretum,
it's unique in the North East. And afterwards
relax in the Earl Grey Tea House serving teas,
coffee and light snacks set in beautiful, stately
surroundings. Howick Hall Gardens - it's
Northumberland's best-kept secret!

Daily 21 Mar-31 Oct 2007 12.00-18.00
A£5.00 OAPs£4.00 C£Free

Historical

Alnwick Castle

Estates Office Alnwick Northumberland
NE66 1NQ
Tel: 01665 510777 Fax: 01665 510876
www.alnwickcastle.com

*[33mi N of Newcastle-upon-Tyne, 30mi S of
Berwick-upon-Tweed & 80mi S of Edinburgh just
off A1 in historic market town of Alnwick]*

Best Large Visitor Attraction of the Year 2007,
Enjoy England Awards for Excellence. A warm
welcome awaits visitors to the mighty medieval
fortress of Alnwick Castle - one of Europe's
finest. Set in a stunning landscape this magnificent castle dominates the skyline and overlooks
the historic market town of Alnwick. Alnwick
Castle is home to the Duke and Duchess of
Northumberland whose family have lived here
for almost 700 years. This glorious castle has a
wealth of history to be explored and treasures in
abundance, a legacy of the Percy family who
have been collecting for generations. Come and
view the recently refurbished Dining Room
which has beautiful silk walls, hand-woven carpet and intricately carved ceiling. This year The
Saloon will be undergoing extensive renovation
and you will be able to see expert craftsmen
restoring this room to its former glory. Whether
you wish to explore the fine collection of paintings and porcelain in the State Rooms or face
the terrifying monster in the exciting and interactive activity area, Dragon's Quest, you are invited to experience the unique delights of Alnwick
Castle for a truly magical visit. Exterior photography only.

*20 Mar-26 Oct 10.00-18.00, (State Rooms
11.00-17.00)*

Day Ticket: A£10.50 Concession£9.00 C£4.50,
Family Ticket £27.50. Weekly Ticket: A£15.00
Concession£15.00 C£6.00, Family Ticket

£37.50. Season Ticket: A£22.50
Concession£22.50, Family Ticket (A1+up to C4)
£52.50

Chillingham Castle and Gardens

Chillingham Alnwick Northumberland NE66 5NJ
Tel: 01668 215359
A remarkable fortress with alarming dungeons
and a torture chamber.

Cragside Estate

Cragside Rothbury Morpeth Northumberland
NE65 7PX
Tel: 01669 620333/620150
Extraordinary Victorian house, gardens and
estate, which features a rock garden, woodland
(with red squirrels), a maze and an adventure
playground.

Housesteads Roman Fort (Hadrian's Wall)

Bardon Mills Haydon Bridge Hexham
Northumberland NE47 6NN
Tel: 01434 344363
Housesteads is located halfway along Hadrian's
Wall in Northumberland. There are magnificent
ruins to explore and a dedicated museum.

Wallington

Cambo Morpeth Northumberland NE61 4AR
Tel: 01670 773600
Magnificent mansion with fine interiors and collections, set in an extensive garden and parkland. Features a 'Cabinet of Curiosities' and a
collection of dolls' houses.

Literature & Libraries

Barter Books

Alnwick Station Wagonway Road Alnwick
Northumberland NE66 2NP
Tel: 01665 604888
The 'British Library of second hand bookshops'

is located in a listed Victorian station. Children's room and light refreshments.

Wildlife & Safari Parks

Chillingham Wild Cattle Park

Wardens Cottage Chillingham Alnwick
Northumberland NE66 5NP

Tel: 01668 215250

www.chillingham-wildcattle.org.uk

[Plenty of on-site parking available]

Of all the 1200 million cattle in the world, the Chillingham Wild Cattle are the only ones to have remained free of any human interference or management, and are closest to their wild prehistoric ancestors in the way they live. They still roam in their natural surroundings, in the 134 hectares of Chillingham Park near Wooler in Northumberland. The existing herd are thought to have been enclosed at Chillingham for over 700 years. In recent years DNA samples have been prepared from hair roots collected from dead animals in the Park and sent to the Roslin Institute and Edinburgh University, which have revealed that the Wild Cattle are a natural clone, and are genetically identical. This is unique among animals, and arises from their very long history of inbreeding, together with occasional periods of very low numbers. No dogs allowed at all.

1 Apr-31 Oct Wed-Mon 10.00-12.00 & 14.00-17.00, Sun 14.00-17.00. Closed Tues

A£4.50 OAPs£3.00 C£1.50

Music & Theatre Museums

Morpeth Chantry Bagpipe Museum

The Chantry Bridge Street Morpeth
Northumberland NE61 1PD

Tel: 01670 500717 Fax: 01670 500710

www.bagpipemuseum.org.uk

[In Morpeth Town Centre, off A1 on A197]

Most people think that all bagpipes are Scottish. They are not. Bagpipes are to be found all over Europe, Asia and North Africa and are one of the most ancient musical instruments. Morpeth Chantry Bagpipe Museum is devoted to bagpipes of all countries, but particularly those of Northumberland and the Borders. The Northumbrian pipes are a light, lilting and melodic instrument, made for playing indoors. They are played by inflating the bag with bellows held under one arm (rather than by blowing into the bag, like the Scottish bagpipes). The museum has a pre-recorded soundtrack, which allows visitors to hear how each set of pipes sounds. Live music is a feature of the museum - the Northumbrian Pipers Society holds Saturday afternoon meetings every month. The museum holds concerts throughout the year, at the Morpeth Northumbrian Gathering in March, and at the Traditional Music Festival every October.

Mon-Sat 10.00-17.00, also Sun in Aug & Dec. Closed 23-24 Mar, 25-27 Dec

Admission Free

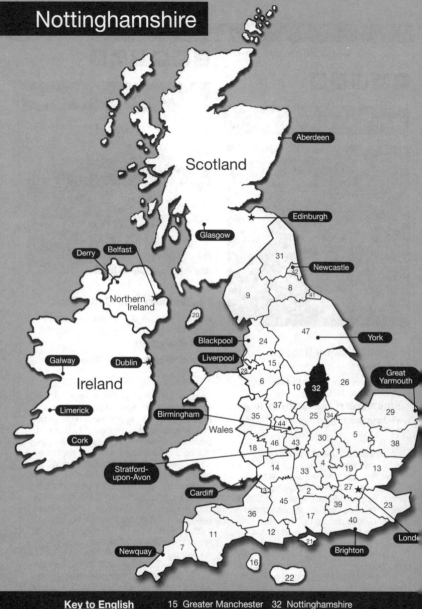

Nottinghamshire

Aberdeen

Scotland

Edinburgh

Glasgow

Newcastle

Derry

Belfast

Northern
Ireland

31

42

9

8

41

20

47

York

Blackpool

24

Liverpool

28

15

Galway

Dublin

26

Great
Yarmouth

Ireland

6

10

32

Limerick

37

29

Birmingham

35

44

25

34

Wales

18

46

43

30

5

38

Cork

14

33

4

1

19

13

Stratford-
upon-Avon

27

Cardiff

13

2

39

23

London

36

45

17

40

11

12

21

Brighton

Newquay

7

16

22

Animal Attractions

Sherwood Forest Farm Park
Lamb Pens Farm Edwinstowe Mansfield
Nottinghamshire NG21 9HL
Tel: 01623 823558
Rare breeds of farm animals are waiting to give
a friendly welcome to visitors of all ages.

White Post Farm
Mansfield Road Farnsfield Newark
Nottinghamshire NG22 8HL
Tel: 01623 882977 Fax: 01623 883499
www.whitepostfarm.co.uk
[Plenty of on-site parking available]
Visit the White Post Farm in 2008 celebrating
our 20th anniversary! We're proud to offer a
great day out with a difference, whatever the
weather. With over 25 acres and over 3,000
animals and lots of indoor activities, a wonderful
day out is guaranteed. With llamas, cows, wallabies, reptiles and special events all-year round,
the White Post Farm is exciting, dynamic and
most of all, fun! A great chance to learn about
farming and interact with a wide range of animals. With indoor and outdoor play areas and a
fantastic go-kart track, there's plenty of time for
play. We cater for groups and offer great deals
on birthday parties and group tours - please call
for details.
All year daily from 10.00
A£7.95 C£7.50 Group rates available on
request

**Discount Offer: Two Free Bags of
Animal Feed.**

Arts, Crafts & Textiles

Longdale Craft Centre
Longdale Lane Ravenshead NG15 9AH
Tel: 01623 794858
Includes workshops, a museum, gallery and first
class restaurant.

Caverns & Caves

City of Caves
Upper Level Broad Marsh Shopping Centre
Nottingham Nottinghamshire NG1 7LS
Tel: 0115 952 0555
www.cityofcaves.com
*[M1 J26 from N, off M1 J25 from Derby & the W.
Situated beneath Broadmarsh Shopping centre.
There is plenty of public car parking nearby]*
Imagine a world that existed under your feet,
which hasn't been seen for centuries. Beneath
the Broad Marsh shopping centre exists a city
of caves where our forefathers lived and worked
in caverns hollowed out of the sandstone.
Guided by our actors from the award winning
Galleries of Justice you will be taken back into
the past to meet the Tanner, pass by an ancient
enchanted well and find safety in a World War 2
Air Raid Shelter. 2008 is your last chance to be
part of Nottingham history by experiencing the
City of Caves before its closure as part of the
redevelopment of the shopping centre.
*All year daily 10.30-16.30. Mon-Sun. Please call
for details of Christmas opening times*
A£5.50 C£4.25 Concessions£4.25, Family
Ticket £16.50. Group rates available on request

Discount Offer: One Child Free.

For great hotel deals call Superbreak on 01904 679999 or visit www.superbreak.com

Country Parks & Estates

Rufford Abbey Country Park

Ollerton Newark Nottinghamshire NG22 9DF
Tel: 01623 822944 Fax: 01623 824840
www.nottinghamshire.gov.uk/ruffordcp
[A614, 2mi S of Ollerton roundabout. 17mi N of Nottingham. For public transport details call Traveline on 0870 608 2 608. Plenty of on-site parking available]

Set in the heart of Robin Hood County and once one of North Nottinghamshire's great private estates, the picturesque remains of Rufford Abbey, founded in the twelfth century by Cistercian monks and later transformed into a grand county house, are at the heart of the Country Park and house an exhibition on Cistercian life in the Undercroft. The craft centre in the former stable block houses a nationally renowned gallery as well as two shops one featuring a selection of quality British crafts and the other a variety of souvenirs and gifts. The nearby Coach House serves drinks and light refreshments while the Savile Restaurant offers traditional lunches. Enjoy the restored orangery and formal gardens before taking a stroll down to Rufford Lakes where you will find both the Lakeside Garden Shop and Outdoor Living store.

All year, High Season (end Feb-end Oct) 10.30-17.00, Low Season (end Oct-end Feb) 10.30-16.30. Closed afternoon 24 Dec & reopens 26 Dec

Admission Free. Car Park charge at various times throughout the year

Sherwood Forest Country Park and Visitor Centre

Edwinstowe Mansfield Nottinghamshire NG21 9HN
Tel: 01623 823202 Fax: 01623 823202
www.nottinghamshire.gov.uk/countryparks
[On B6034, N of Edwinstowe between A6075 & A616. For public transport details to park call Traveline on 0870 608 2 608. Minicom 0870 241 2 216 or email buses@nottscc.gov.uk. Plenty of on-site parking available]

Visit Sherwood Forest, the legendary home of England's most famous outlaw-Robin Hood, and now part of Nottinghamshire's only National Nature Reserve. Over 450 acres of ancient oak woodland, including the mighty Major Oak, known world-wide as Robin Hood's tree. The visitor centre houses the 'Robyn Hode's Sherwode' Exhibition which shows visitors what life was like in medieval times and a video studio where you can find out more about this former Royal Hunting Forest. We have two on-site shops for souvenirs and gifts, and the Forest Table restaurant, where you can relax over a drink or meal. Explore woodland paths, picnic in the forest glades or enjoy the year round programme of events activities- including the Annual Robin Hood Festival which takes place from 28th July-3rd August 2008.

All year, High Season (Easter-Jan) 10.00-17.00, Low Season (Jan-Easter) 10.00-16.30. Closed afternoon 24 Dec & reopens 26 Dec

Admission Free, Car Park charge at various times throughout the year (£3)

Wollaton Hall, Gardens and Deer Park

Wollaton Nottingham Nottinghamshire NG8 2AE
Tel: 0115 915 3900 Fax: 0115 915 3932
www.wollatonhall.org.uk

[10min drive from Nottingham City Centre off A609, also accessible by bus. Plenty of on-site parking available]

Standing on a natural hill 3 miles west of Nottingham city centre, Wollaton Hall is a flamboyant sixteenth-century Robert Smythson building, set in a scenic, 500-acre historic deer park. Wollaton Hall houses a Natural History Museum, an Industrial Museum and the Yard Gallery, which features exhibitions inspired by nature, science and history. Guided tours are available to experience the sights and sounds of an authentic working Tudor kitchen or the Prospect Room at the top of the Hall with its panoramic views. The park is home to herds of free-roaming red and fallow deer. Visitors have the choice of a variety of walks, or they can simply stroll around the lake, or relax in the formal gardens.

Hall: Mar-Oct 11.00-17.00, Nov-Feb 11.00-16.00. Park: Sat-Sun 9.00-dusk, Mon-Fri 8.00-dusk

Admission Free. Charges apply for special events and guided tours only. Car Parking £2.00 per day

Festivals & Shows

Robin Hood Festival

Sherwood Forest National Nature Reserve and Visitor Centre Edwinstowe Nottinghamshire NG21 9HN
Tel: 01623 823202
www.robinhood.co.uk

[Off B6034, between A6075 & A616, 20mi from Nottingham, 35mi from Derby & 32mi from Sheffield. Plenty of on-site parking available]

The 23rd Annual Robin Hood Festival - Nottinghamshire's biggest celebration of the life and times of its legendary hero - will be taking place at Sherwood Forest Country Park this summer. During the week-long extravaganza, costumed entertainers will provide fun for all the family. These include jugglers, jesters, strolling minstrels, street theatre performers, archers and experts in medieval combat. No Robin Hood Festival would be complete without archery and costumed archers will offer visitors the chance to use a longbow. The festival also includes a Medieval Market and weekend jousting tournaments.

28 July-3 Aug 2008

Admission Free, small charge for some events. Parking charge for Cars £3.00

Folk & Local History Museums

Bassetlaw Museum

Amcott House 40 Grove Street Retford
Nottinghamshire DN22 6LD
Tel: 01777 713749
www.bassetlawmuseum.org.uk

[5min walk from Retford Market Place, next to Tourist Information Centre]

Set in the beautiful eighteenth-century Amcott House, the Bassetlaw Museum displays fascinating collections of archaeology, costume, local, social and farming history illustrating the life of Bassetlaw and its people. The Welchman collection of 20,000 images is an invaluable pictorial record of the period 1910-50. Supported by the Heritage Lottery Fund, these photographs, and many others, are available on computer in the museum and on the website. The museum and art gallery is a rich resource for schools, local and family historians. School parties are welcome by appointment. Contact the museum for details of our education service. The gift shop stocks a wide range of books, cards, jewellery and toys with something for every pocket. Please note we have disabled access on the ground floor and in the garden.

Mon-Sat 10.00-17.00. Closed Sun.
Admission Free

D H Lawrence's House

8a Victoria Street Eastwood Nottinghamshire
NG16 3AW
Tel: 01773 717353
Through a guided tour, you will be able to learn about D.H. Lawrence's family life and the type of working class home and mining community that shaped his formative years.

Durban House Heritage Centre

Durban House Mansfield Road Eastwood
Nottinghamshire NG16 3DZ
Tel: 01773 717353
A visit to this thriving heritage centre complements a visit to the D.H. Lawrence Birthplace Museum. Through its permanent exhibition, it depicts community life for the young Lawrence and introduces you to some more of the early influences on his life. The Centre also includes a modern art space and a restaurant on the ground floor.

Gilstrap Centre

Castle Gate Newark NG24 1BG
Tel: 01636 655765
The Gilstrap Centre, located in the Castle grounds, includes an exhibition 'Castle and Conflict' on Newark's historic castle and the civil war, 1642-1646. The Tourist Information Centre is located in the Gilstrap Centre.

Mansfield Museum and Art Gallery

Leeming Street Mansfield NG18 1NG
Tel: 01623 463088
The five galleries of Mansfield Museum contain a fascinating mix of contemporary and modern displays, from the exquisite Buxton watercolours and Pinxton porcelain to the hands-on XplorActive environment gallery.

Millgate Museum

48 Mill Gate Newark NG24 4TS
Tel: 01636 655730
Millgate Museum is housed in a Victorian warehouse in a picturesque setting on the banks of the River Trent. The museum displays are spread over three floors and cover the agricultural, industrial and social history of Newark.

All year daily

Museum of Nottingham Life at Brewhouse Yard

Castle Boulevard Nottingham Nottinghamshire NG7 1FB

Tel: 0115 915 3600

www.nottinghamcity.gov.uk/museums

[A short walk from Nottingham Castle]

Located at the base of the Castle Rock, this museum depicts the social history of Nottingham over the last 300 years. It contains a mixture of reconstructed room and shop settings, and gallery displays. Step into an air-raid shelter, experience being in a Victorian home, see inside a child's bedroom and look through the cupboards in the kitchen. See objects that were made or used by people in Nottingham and learn about the history of the area, through sight, touch and sound. Events are held regularly - from reminiscence sessions, talks and tours, to trails, dressing-up, plus seasonal and school-holiday activities. A 1940s extravaganza held every May Day celebrates the lighter side of WWII with song, dance and games. Schools are always welcome for both teacher-led and freelancer sessions.

All year daily 10.00-16.30

Joint Ticket with Nottingham Castle A£3.50 C&Concessions£2.00, Family Ticket (A2+C3) £8.00. Group rate: 1 Free ticket for every 10 purchased

Tales of Robin Hood

30-38 Maid Marian Way Nottingham Nottinghamshire NG1 6GF

Tel: 0115 948 3284 Fax: 0115 950 1536

www.robinhood.uk.com

[J25 M1 Southbound, J26 M1 Northbound, follow signs for City]

Robin, his merry men and their legendary Tales are brought to life as you join them on our travel back in time themed tour. Young outlaws will love our exciting adventure ride, experiencing the sights and smells of medieval England. Step back in time with Robin, England's best-loved outlaw on his quest to fight his evil archenemy, The Sheriff of Nottingham. Explore the tales behind the folklores, bring the past back to life in our educational living history talks and weapon handling sessions. All this as well whilst trying your hand at sword and shield painting, brass rubbing, and even shoot a few arrows like Robin himself at our archery range. Unwind in Greenwood's Café, then visit Maid Marian gift shop, for that special souvenir to remind you of a magical experience, that'll make all your friends as green as Robin's hat with envy!

All year daily 10.00-17.30. Closed Dec 25-26

A£8.95 C£6.95 OAPs&Student£7.95 Family Ticket (A2+C2) £26.95 (A2+C3) £32.95

Discount Offer: One Child Free.

Heritage & Industrial

Workhouse, The

Upton Road Southwell Nottinghamshire
NG25 0PT

Tel: 01636 817250

Perfectly preserved nineteenth-century workhouse with interactive displays.

Historical

Newstead Abbey

Newstead Abbey Park Ravenshead
Nottinghamshire NG15 8NA
Tel: 01623 455900 Fax: 01623 455904
www.newsteadabbey.org.uk

*[J27 M1 12mi N of Nottingham on A60. Plenty of
on-site parking available]*

Beautiful historic house set in parklands, former
home of the poet Lord Byron. Byron's own
room and mementoes on display, and splendid-
ly decorated rooms from the Medieval to the
Victorian era. 40 acres of formal gardens to
explore. Disabled access limited to ground floor.

*Grounds only: All year daily 9.00-18.00 (except
last Fri in Nov & Christmas Day). House: 1 Apr-30
Sept daily 12.00-17.00*

House & Grounds: A£6.00 C£2.50
Concessions£4.00, Family Ticket (A2+C3)
£16.00. Group rate: £4.00. Grounds only:
A£3.00 C£1.50 Concessions£2.50
Cyclists£0.50 Group£2.50, Family Ticket
(A2+C2) £8.50. Prices are subject to change
from 1 April 2008 - please call for details

Nottingham Castle

Friar Lane Off Maid Marian Way Nottingham
Nottinghamshire NG1 6EL
Tel: 0115 915 3700 Fax: 0115 915 3653
www.nottinghamcity.gov.uk

*[From M1, follow signs for Nottingham City
Centre, then follow tourist signs. 5min walk from
Nottingham City Centre]*

Situated high above the city, Nottingham Castle
is a seventeenth-century mansion built over 300
years ago, on the site of a medieval castle originally built by William the Conqueror. Within the
Castle a vibrant museum that houses a range of
collections including historic and contemporary
fine art, china and silverware can be found. The
Castle also exhibits many contemporary exhibitions ranging from local artist to touring shows.
There are tours available to discover the network of caves and hidden passageways under-
neath the Castle. Located in beautiful Victorian
inspired gardens, the site offers stunning views
across the city and countryside beyond. The
Castle is a great place for children, with interactive displays and an activity - led gallery bringing
paintings to life, specifically for the under 5s,
plus a medieval - style playground with covered
picnic area on the green.

*All year daily Mar-Sept 10.00-17.00 Oct-Feb
10.00-16.00. Closed 24-26 Dec & 1 Jan*

Joint Ticket with Museum of Nottingham Life at
Brewhouse Yard: A£3.50 C&Concessions£2.00,
Family Ticket (A2+C3) £8.00. Group rates: 1
Free ticket for every 10 purchased

Living History Museums

NCCL Galleries of Justice

Shire Hall High Pavement Lace Market
Nottingham Nottinghamshire NG1 1HN
Tel: 0115 952 0555 Fax: 0115 993 9828
www.nccl.org.uk

[City centre, signposted both traffic & pedestrian, multi-storey parking signposted, 5-10min walk]

Let us welcome you to Nottingham's Notorious County Gaol and once behind bars, our resident ghosts won't want you to leave! Learn about heinous crimes, rioting and reform and what would happen if you got caught....Home of HM Prison Service Collection, the award winning Galleries of Justice offers the visitor a unique actor led experience of what it is like to pass through a Victorian court and Georgian prision. New for 2008: the Sheffiff's Dungeon, where Robin Hood escaped by tunnelling through the labyrinth of caves under Nottingham. Mugshots Cafe open for all escaped prisoners. Wheelchair access: 85%. Nottinghamshire's Museum of the Year.

All year Tue-Sun, Bank Hol Mon & Mon throughout school hols, peak times 10.00-17.00, please call to confirm off peak times

A£8.95 C£6.95 Concessions£6.95, Family Ticket (A2+C2) £24.95. Tickets are valid for one visit to each exhibition over 12 months. Group rates available on request

Discount Offer: One Child Free.

Science - Earth & Planetary

Green's Windmill and Science Centre

Windmill Lane Sneinton Nottingham
Nottinghamshire NG2 4QB
Tel: 0115 915 6878 Fax: 0115 915 6875
www.greensmill.org.uk

[1mi outside Nottingham City Centre. Bus: 23 & 24 from King Stree. Plenty of on-site parking available]

Green's Windmill is a working windmill that produces its own organic flour. You can see how the flour is made by climbing the different levels of the windmill. When the wind is blowing the experience is even better, as you watch and hear the machinery turning the millstones. The award-winning organic flour can be bought from the shop. Children and adults can test their minds with fun, hands-on puzzles and experiments in the Science Centre, and for the under-5s, there's a special 'Mini Millers' area, where even the youngest scientists can start learning. Green's Windmill is a grade II listed building set in parkland, with a cobbled courtyard which provides an attractive space to sit and relax. It is the only inner-city working windmill in the UK and the former home of the famous nineteenth-century mathematician George Green.

Wed-Sun 10.00-16.00 & most Bank Hols
Admission Free

Theme & Adventure Parks

Go Ape! High Wire Forest Adventure (Sherwood Pines, Nottinghamshire)

Sherwood Pines Visitor Centre Sherwood Pines Forest Park Nr. Edwinstowe Mansfield Nottinghamshire NG21 9JH
Tel: 0845 643 9245
www.goape.co.uk

[Off B6030 between Old Clipstone & Ollerton. Plenty of on-site parking available]

Take to the trees and experience an exhilarating course of rope bridges, Tarzan swings and zip-slides up to 40 feet above the ground! Share approximately three exciting hours of fun and adventure, which you'll be talking about for days. Book online and watch people Go Ape! at www.goape.co.uk. Minimum height 1.4m. Maximum weight 130 kg (20.5 stone). Under-18s must be accompanied by a participating adult. One adult can supervise either two children (where one or both of them is under 16 years old) or up to five 16-17 year olds. Pre-booking is essential to avoid disappointment. Book online or by telephone (there is a £1.00 booking fee on all telephone bookings).

9-11 &14-17 Feb, 14 Mar-31 Oct daily, Nov Sat-Sun. Dec Sat-Sun TBC please visit www.goape.co.uk Closed Jan

Gorillas (18yrs+) £25.00, Baboons (10-17yrs) £20.00

Discount Offer: £5.00 off per person.

Sundown Adventureland

Treswell Road Rampton Retford Nottinghamshire DN22 0HX
Tel: 01777 248274 Fax: 01777 248967
www.sundownadventureland.co.uk

[6mi from A1 Markham Moor. Plenty of on-site parking available]

The Theme Park especially designed for the under 10s. Your adventure is just beginning the moment you enter the park! Explore the Rodeo Corral indoor play area, Fort Apache & Captain Sandy's play cove, ride aboard the Rocky Mountain Railroad, Santa's Sleigh ride, Robin Hood ride, and the Boozy Barrel Boat ride, a full day of fun awaits you! Adventure play areas Cafés, Shops, plus lots lots more, Also don't forget, we're open at Christmas, so come along and visit Santa in his lovely home and receive a free gift for all children aged 2 to 10 years.

9 Feb-24 Dec daily from 10.00

A&C£8.50 C(under2)£Free. Group rates available on request

Toy & Childhood Museums

Vina Cooke Museum of Dolls and Bygone Childhood

The Old Rectory Great North Road Cromwell Newark Nottinghamshire NG23 6JE
Tel: 01636 821364
A large collection of dolls brought together in a late seventeenth-century building, along with Vina's own handmade portrait dolls.
Mar-Oct (Closed Wed & Fri)

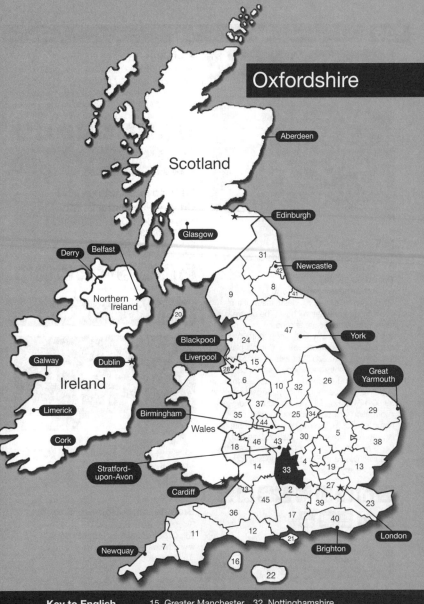

Oxfordshire

Scotland

Aberdeen

Edinburgh

Glasgow

Newcastle

Derry · Belfast

Northern
Ireland

Blackpool

Liverpool

York

Great
Yarmouth

Galway · Dublin

Ireland

Limerick

Cork

Birmingham

Wales

Stratford-
upon-Avon

Cardiff

Newquay

Brighton

London

**Key to English
Counties:**

1 Bedfordshire
2 Berkshire
3 Bristol
4 Buckinghamshire
5 Cambridgeshire
6 Cheshire
7 Cornwall
8 County Durham
9 Cumbria
10 Derbyshire
11 Devon
12 Dorset
13 Essex
14 Gloucestershire

15 Greater Manchester
16 Guernsey
17 Hampshire
18 Herefordshire
19 Hertfordshire
20 Isle Of Man
21 Isle Of Wight
22 Jersey
23 Kent
24 Lancashire
25 Leicestershire
26 Lincolnshire
27 London
28 Merseyside
29 Norfolk
30 Northamptonshire
31 Northumberland

32 Nottinghamshire
33 Oxfordshire
34 Rutland
35 Shropshire
36 Somerset
37 Staffordshire
38 Suffolk
39 Surrey
40 Sussex
41 Tees Valley
42 Tyne & Wear
43 Warwickshire
44 West Midlands
45 Wiltshire
46 Worcestershire
47 Yorkshire

Animal Attractions

Millets Farm Centre

Kingston Road Frilford Abingdon Oxfordshire OX13 5HB
Tel: 01865 392200
www.milletsfarmcentre.com
Millets Farm Centre provides a taste of the countryside at its natural best. The centre is a mixture of retail, leisure and countryside activities with an extensive farm shop, garden centre, restaurants, woodland walk, children's play area and a small farm zoo. Our extensive Oxfordshire site has free entry, including over 800 car-parking places and disabled friendly access throughout. We are open 7 days a week generally from 09.00-17.00. For full opening hours and site information visit our web site on www.milletsfarmcentre.com. We run numerous events during the year including the Maize Maze (July-Sept) and the 'Pick Your Own' season starting in June. The Farm Shop has special product tastings every Thursday.

Archaeology

Museum of Oxford

St. Aldates Oxford Oxfordshire OX1 1DZ
Tel: 01865 252761
Permanent displays depict the archaeology and history of the city.

Arts, Crafts & Textiles

Ashmolean Museum of Art and

Archaeology

Beaumont Street Oxford Oxfordshire OX1 2PH
Tel: 01865 278000 / 278015
The Ashmolean is Oxford University's Museum of Art and Archaeology housing collections of art from Europe, Japan, India and China.

Birds, Butterflies & Bees

Waterfowl Sanctuary and Children's Animal Centre

Wigginton Heath Banbury OX15 4LQ
Tel: 01608 730252
Children are encouraged to handle and feed the animals at this friendly, family-run centre.

Festivals & Shows

Bicester and Finmere Show

Bicester Oxfordshire
Tel: 01869 253566 Fax: 01869 369064
www.bicesterandfinmereshow.co.uk
[1mi from Bicester town on the Buckingham rd A4421. Plenty of on-site parking available]
Raising funds for the Back Up Trust and Spinal Research. Main attractions include: Top class show jumping, featuring the countries leading riders, dog show, classic car display, crafts, trade stands, members tent, bars and refreshments and much more. Trade stand enquiries welcome please call 07973 543516. Horse show schedules please call venue number or see the website.
3 August 2008 (09.00 onwards)
A£7.50 (inc parking) C£Free

Gardens & Horticulture

Brook Cottage Garden

Well Lane Alkerton Banbury Oxfordshire
OX15 6NL
Tel: 01295 670303/670590
Fax: 01295 730362
www.brookcottagegarden.co.uk
[6mi NW Banbury, 0.5mi off A422 Banbury-Stratford upon Avon Rd. Limited on-site parking]
This 4-acre hillside garden is set in exceptionally tranquil countryside. There is a wide variety of plants (some rare) to provide interest throughout the season. From the formal paved terrace (enclosed by weathered stonewalls and sharply symmetrical yew hedges), a wide sweep of steps form the start of a tour of imaginatively and richly planted areas of differing character. There are a water and bog gardens, colour co-ordinating borders with themes of white/silver, purples/magentas and soft pinks/blues, a small gravel garden, handsome species trees andunusual flowering shrubs. There is a profusion of roses (species, old cultivars and modern) and clematis, from atrogenes to late summer flowering. The diversity of planting is supplemented by tender perennials in a variety of ornamental pots; while the handmade, designer wooden furniture offers resting places to pause and contemplate. Plants for sale. Evening, weekend and group visits by appointment only.
Easter Mon-31 Oct Mon-Fri (including Bank Hols) 09.00-18.00
A£5.00 C£Free OAPs£4.00

Historical

Blenheim Palace

Woodstock Oxfordshire OX20 1PX
Tel: 08700 602080

Birthplace of Sir Winston Churchill, with a magnificent collection of paintings, tapestries and furniture. It is set in a landscaped park, with lake and formal gardens.
14 Feb-mid Nov daily

Broughton Castle

Banbury Oxfordshire OX15 5EB
Tel: 01295 276070
www.broughtoncastle.com

[2mi W of Banbury on B4035 Shipston on Stour Rd. Plenty of on-site parking available]

Historic fourteenth-century fortified manor house that was enlarged in the sixteenth century. Home of the family of Lord Saye and Sele for over 600 years, it contains its own medieval chapel, vaulted passages, fine panelling and splendid plaster ceilings and fireplaces. It was a centre of resistance to King Charles I during the Civil War and contains mementos of the period including armour and weapons. There are fine walled gardens with old roses, shrubs and herbaceous borders. The castle is surrounded by a broad moat and set in open parkland. It was a location for the filming of Shakespeare in Love and featured in many other films and TV programmes including the recently shown 'Elizabeth, The Virgin Queen' and Stephen Poliakoff's film 'Friends and Crocodiles.'

1 May-15 Sep Wed, Sun & Bank Hols 14.00-17.00, also Thurs in July-Aug. Groups welcome at any time by appointment

A£6.50 C£2.50 OAPs&Students(NUS/USI)£5.50

Discount Offer: Two for the Price of One (full-paying adult).

Mapledurham House and Watermill

Mapledurham Village Reading Oxfordshire
RG4 7TR
Tel: 0118 972 3350 Fax: 0118 972 4016
www.mapledurham.co.uk

[Off A4074. Plenty of on-site parking available]

Mapledurham House, the historic home of the Blount family is an Elizabethan mansion full of history and intrigue, set in idyllic rural South Oxfordshire. Famous for the film, 'The Eagle has Landed,' the watermill is the last working watermill on the River Thames and still produces flour - excellent for bread making. Cream teas are served in the original Old Manor tea room together with a selection of handmade cakes to tempt you. Visitors may arrive by boat from near Caversham - a delightful cruise along a stunning stretch of river. We also have eleven self-catering cottages for visitors who wish to stay a little longer, full details of which can be found on our website.

Easter-end Sept Sat-Sun & Bank Hols from 14.00. Mid-week parties by arrangement

Please call for prices

Nuffield Place

Huntercombe, Nr Nettlebed Nuffield Henley-On-Thames Oxfordshire RG9 5RY
Tel: 01491 641224
Nuffield Place was the home of William Morris, Lord Nuffield. Built in 1914, it retains the majority of the furniture and contents acquired by Lord and Lady Nuffield.

Pitt Rivers Museum

South Parks Road Oxford Oxfordshire OX1 3PP
Tel: 01865 270927
World-famous museum of anthropology with a unique Victorian atmosphere. Audio tour provided by Sir David Attenborough.

Sulgrave Manor

Manor Road Sulgrave Banbury Oxfordshire OX17 2SD
Tel: 01295 760205
The ancestral home of George Washington's family. Tudor house and gardens with a collection of sixteenth and eighteenth-century furniture and artefacts.

Literature & Libraries

Bodleian Library

Broad Street Oxford OX1 3BG
Tel: 01865 277000
The main research and copyright deposit library of the University of Oxford. The Divinity School and the Bodleian's exhibition room are open to the public, and receive a quarter of a million visitors each year.

Natural History Museums

Oxford University Museum of Natural History

Parks Road Oxford Oxfordshire OX1 3PW
Tel: 01865 272950
The museum in its high-Victorian Gothic building makes freely available to the public the University's very extensive natural history collections.

Performing Arts

Creation Theatre Company
Oxford Oxfordshire OX
Tel: 01865 766266 Fax: 01865 764677
www.creationtheatre.co.uk

[Oxford Castle, (City Centre, Summer). BMW Group Plant Oxford (Winter)]

"If you are a visitor in Oxford and you only have time for one cultural experience, make it this!" (The Oxford Times). Creation Theatre Company produces highly visual, energetic and accessible theatre in unusual spaces. Over the past 12 years, Creation has earned a reputation as Oxfordshire's foremost producing theatre company, with their magical open-air productions of Shakespeare and many popular stories. Previous site-specific venues include an island in the River Cherwell, a ruined abbey, a beautiful arboretum, a car factory and a spectacular Mirror Tent. Following Creation's exciting 2007 with three fantastic open-air shows in the courtyards of Oxford Castle and a return to the BMW Plant in the winter for a fabulous family Christmas show, Creation presents a brand new extraordinary venue, The North Wall for spring 2008. These exceptional spaces provide the backdrop for a unique theatrical experience... come and see for yourself! "Energetic and imaginative" (The Independent).

Summer Season: June-Sept, Winter Season: Nov-Apr. Evenings 19.30/20.00, Matinees 14.30. Please visit website for more details
Prices range from £8.00-£22.50

Places of Worship

University Church of St. Mary the Virgin
High Street Oxford Oxfordshire OX1 4AH
Tel: 01865 279111
One of the oldest university buildings in the world, its tower boasts excellent views of Oxford. On-site cafe and gift shop.

Police, Prisons & Dungeons

Oxford Castle (Unlocked)
44-46 Oxford Castle Oxford OX1 1AY
Tel: 01865 260666
This ex-prison has been redeveloped as a shopping and heritage complex, with open courtyards for markets and theatrical performances, plus a bar/restaurant/venue complex. At the museum ('Oxford Castle - Unlocked') visitors can learn about the castle's dark history.

Railways

Didcot Railway Centre

Didcot Oxfordshire OX11 7NJ
Tel: 01235 817200 Fax: 01235 510621
www.didcotrailwaycentre.org.uk

[On A4130 at Didcot Parkway Station signed from M4, J13 & A34]

Recreating the golden age of the Great Western Railway with a fine collection of over 20 steam locomotives, housed in the original engine shed, together with many passenger coaches and freight wagons. Other locomotives can be seen being overhauled in the Locomotive Works. There is a typical country station and signal box, and a recreation of Brunel's original broad gauge railway together with an impressive display of smaller items in the Relics Display. On Steamdays some of the locomotives come to life and you can ride the 1930s carriages and see the activities of a typical steam age depot.

All year Sat & Sun, daily 16-24 Feb, 5-20 Apr, 24 May-1 Jun, 21 Jun-7 Sept, 25 Oct-2 Nov & 27 Dec-1 Jan 2009. Open 10:30-16:00 (Weekends & Steamdays Mar to Oct 10:30-17:00). Closed Christmas Day & Boxing Day. Steamdays: 2 Mar, Easter 21-24 Mar, 6 Apr, Spring Hol 24-26 May, 31 May-1 Jun, 14-15 Jun, all Sat, Sun & Public Hols 5 Jul-31 Aug, Weds 23 Jul-27 Aug and Half Term 29 Oct, 25-26 Oct. Broad Gauge Fire Fly Steamings: 20 Apr, 3-5 May, 28-29 Jun, 23, 26-27, 30 Jul, 13, 23-25 Aug, 27-29 Sep. Thomas Santa Special: 6-7, 13-14, 19-22 Dec. New Year Steaming: 1 Jan 2009

A£5.00-£9.50 C£4.00-£7.50 OAPs£4.50-£8.00 (depending on event)

Discount Offer: Two for the Price of One (full-paying adult).

Pendon Museum of Miniature Landscape and Transport

High Street Long Wittenham Abingdon Oxfordshire OX14 4QD
Tel: 01865 407365
www.pendonmuseum.com

[Rail: Didcot. Please see website for further details. Limited on-site parking available]

Located in the village of Long Wittenham in Oxfordshire (near Abingdon and Didcot), Pendon portrays parts of rural England as they were in the 1920s and 30s and reflects the transport infrastructure of the period. It achieves this through incredibly detailed models to a scale of 1:76, set out in typical rural landscapes: literally art in three dimensions! The prototypes for many of the model buildings can still be seen in the Vale of White Horse and, at Pendon, you'll find them gathered together in the imaginary but stunning village of Pendon Parva. Are you interested in rural social history? Or model railways? Do you appreciate superb modelling craftsmanship? It's all here, under cover, waiting for your visit and Pendon is open at weekends, bank holidays and some Wednesdays in school holidays. Special exhibitions on normal open days from January 5th to March 30th 'The Letcombe Brook Project' and 'Building in the Vernacular' from April 5th to the end of 2008. Historic Madder Valley Railway operates on Feb 2nd, June 15th and November 15th.

All year 1 Jan-7 Dec Sat & Sun 14.00-17.30. Extended opening 11.00-17.30, 20 Feb, 21-24 Mar, 9 & 16 Apr, 3-5, 10 & 11, 24-26 & 28 May, 30 Jul, 6,13, 20, 23-25 & 27 Aug, 29 Oct. Closed 8-31 Dec

A£5.00 C(7-16)£3.00 C(0-6)£Free OAPs£4.00, Family Ticket (A2+C3) £16.00

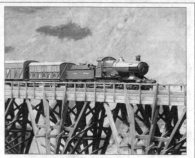

Science - Earth & Planetary

Hands On

Old Fire Station 40 George Street Oxford
Oxfordshire OX1 2AQ
Tel: 01865 728953
Hands-On is a science gallery located at
Science Oxford and is packed with loads of
exciting interactive experiments.

Museum of the History of Science

Old Ashmolean Building Broad Street Oxford
Oxfordshire OX1 3AZ
Tel: 01865 277280
The museum, housed in the oldest public
museum building in the country, opened in
1683 as the original Ashmolean Museum.

Social History Museums

Abingdon Museum

The County Hall Market Place Abingdon
Oxfordshire OX14 3HG
Tel: 01235 523703
A museum showing displays of local history,
crafts and a range of temporary exhibitions and
events.

Banbury Museum

Spiceball Park Road Banbury Oxfordshire
OX16 2PQ
Tel: 01295 259855
Museum on the history of Banbury and district.
Plus innovative temporary exhibitions.

Oxfordshire Museum

Fletcher's House Park Street Woodstock
Oxfordshire OX20 1SN
Tel: 01993 811456
Displayed in Fletcher's House is an exhibition of
the story of Oxfordshire and its people, from
early times to the present day.

River and Rowing Museum

Mill Meadows Henley-on-Thames Oxfordshire
RG9 1BF
Tel: 01491 415600 Fax: 01491 415601
www.rrm.co.uk
*[By Car: follow signs for Henley, then Museum &
Mill Meadows, off A4130 Oxford to Maidenhead
rd in Henley. Bus: regular bus services from High
Wycombe, Marlow, Reading, Thame, Watlington
& Lane End. Hourly X39 service from Oxford to
Heathrow via Wallingford, Henley & Maidenhead.
Rail: hourly services from London (Paddington),
Reading & Maidenhead via Twyford. Henley station 5min walk from museum. By Foot: follow
signposts around town centre]*
Visit the award winning River & Rowing Museum
with its stunning architecture and unique interpretation of the River Thames, the riverside
town of Henley and the sport of Rowing. History
is brought to life with interactive displays and
fascinating exhibits. Special exhibitions, family
activities and events are held throughout the
year and its Terrace Café offers excellent food in
distinctive surroundings. In a spectacular permanent attraction, every one of EH Shepard's
famous illustrations from The Wind in the
Willows is brought to life in an enchanting recreation of the classic English book. You can walk
along the river bank, through the wild wood,
see into Badger's house and visit all 12 chapters of this delightful adventure story. Using theatrical and audio techniques, superb models,
lighting and sets you are magically transported
into the world of Ratty, Mole, Badger and of
course the irrepressible Mr Toad.
*All year 1 May-31 Aug daily 10.00-17.30, 1 Sept-
30 Apr daily 10.00-17.00. Closed 24, 25, 31
Dec & 1 Jan*
Museum Galleries only: A£3.50 C(under3)£Free
C£2.50 Concessions£3.00, Family Ticket (4
people) £11.50, (5 people) £13.00, (6 people)
£14.00. Galleries & Wind in the Willows: A£7.00
C(under3)£Free C£5.00 Concessions£6.00
Family Ticket (4 people) £18.00, (5 people)
£23.00, (6 people) £25.00

Stately Homes

Kingston Bagpuize House

Kingston Bagpuize Abingdon Oxfordshire
OX13 5AX
Tel: 01865 820259
A Family home, this beautiful house originally
built in the 1660s and features well-propor-
tioned panelled rooms with some good furniture
and pictures.

Stonor Park

Stonor Henley-On-Thames Oxfordshire
RG9 6HF
Tel: 01491 638587 Fax: 01491 639348
www.stonor.com

*[Between M4 & M40 on B480 Henley on Thames
to Watlington. Approx 5mi N of Henley. 15min
from M40 & 25min from J8/9 of M4 Rail: Henley
on Thames. Plenty of on-site parking available]*

A hidden treasure near London, "possibly the
best setting for a country house in England".
Take yourself out for a tranquil day in the beautiful Chiltern countryside, visit Stonor, the home
of Lord and Lady Camoys. This magnificent
house set in 200 acres of parkland, has been
home to the Stonor family for 850 years. Tour
the house at leisure where guides will be on-
hand to unravel the fascinating history of this
family, the house and its contents. Full of treasures, wonderful paintings, bronzes, furniture,
tapestries and ceramics. 500 year-old books,
some illegal to own and smuggled into England.
Learn of the family struggle to hold true to the
Catholic faith. Stories of their imprisonment and
fines during the darker days that followed the
reformation. Visit the thirteenth-century chapel
once occupied by some of Cromwell's army.
Take refreshment and visit the souvenir shop in
the medieval hall dating back to 1180. Stroll the
formal Italianate gardens, see the pagan circle,
picnic and walk in the park where fallow deer
roam freely. We are also members of the
Historic Houses Association. Due to the style of
rooms and their location, we are very sorry the
tour is unsuitable for physically disabled visitors.
Dogs are not permitted in the house and formal
gardens; they are permitted in the park providing they are always on a lead.

*23 Mar-14 Sept (Closed Mon-Sat except for
group visits). Also open Bank Hols during the
above dates, Jul-Aug open Weds. Gardens and
Chapel: 13:00-17:30. House, Tea Room and
Shop: 14:00 to 17:30. Pre booked group visits
on Tue, Wed & Thurs during above dates, For the
full details and other events taking place, please
visit our website*

House & Gardens: A£7.00 1st C(5-16yrs)£3.00.
2 or more C£Free.Gardens only: A£3.50 1st
C(5-16yrs)£1.50. 2 or more C£Free.
C(under5)£Free

Transport Museums

Oxford Bus Museum

Old Station Yard Long Hanborough Whitney
Oxfordshire OX29 8LA
Tel: 01993 883617
The museum has a display of over 40 public
transport bus vehicles that have been used
around the Oxfordshire Cotswolds over the past
100 years.

Victorian Era

Cogges Manor Farm Museum

Church Lane Witney Oxfordshire OX28 3LA
Tel: 01993 772602
Cogges is a unique, working museum depicting
Oxfordshire rural life in Victorian times set in an
historic manor house and Cotswold stone farm
buildings.

Wildlife & Safari Parks

Cotswold Wildlife Park
Bradwell Grove Burford Oxfordshire OX18 4JP
Tel: 01993 823006 Fax: 01993 823807
www.cotswoldwildlifepark.co.uk
[2.5mi S of A40 on A361. Plenty of free on-site parking available]
The 160-acre landscaped zoological park, surrounding a Gothic-style Manor House, has a varied collection of animals from around the world. Many of these are endangered in the wild and are part of an international breeding programme, including Asiatic lions, Amur leopards and red pandas. There is a large Reptile House, Tropical House, children's farmyard and the ever-popular penguins and meerkats. Visitors are surprised and delighted at the beautiful gardens and wide range of planting to be seen as they walk around the Park, from the formal herbaceous borders and parterre by the Manor House to the exotic bananas, Daturas and Canna lilies in the walled garden. Other attractions include an adventure playground, animal brass-rubbing centre in the Manor House and the narrow-gauge railway which runs daily during the summer months, limited winter runs. The large self-service cafeteria serves hot and cold meals and snacks. There are also many picnicking areas and a well-stocked gift shop. New in 2008 Madagascar walk-through enclosure with free-roaming lemurs.
All year daily from 10.00. Closed 25 Dec
A£10.00 C(3-16)£7.50 OAPs£7.50. Group rates (20+): A£8.00 C£5.50 OAPs£6.00 (must be pre-booked). Season tickets (valid for 12 months) A£50.00 C£37.50 OAPs£37.50, Family Ticket (A2+C2) £165.00 - extra C£35.50

Rutland

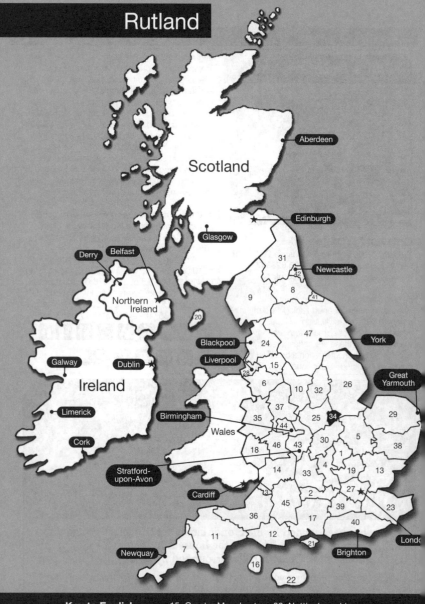

Aberdeen

Scotland

Edinburgh

Glasgow

Derry   Belfast

Northern
Ireland

Galway   Dublin

Ireland

Limerick

Cork

31

42   Newcastle

9   8

41

Blackpool   24   47   York

Liverpool   15

28   Great
Yarmouth

6   10   32   26

37   29

Birmingham   35   44   25   34

Wales   46   43   30   5   38

18   1

14   4   19   13

Stratford-
upon-Avon   33   2   27

Cardiff   13   39   23

45   17   40

36   London

11   12   21

Newquay   7   Brighton

16

22

Birds, Butterflies & Bees

Rutland Water Butterfly Farm and Aquatic Centre

Sykes Lane Car Park North Shore Oakham Rutland

Tel: 01780 460515

5,000 sq. ft. of walk-through jungle with free-flying butterflies and tropical birds. Ponds with Koi carp and terrapins.

Folk & Local History Museums

Rutland County Museum and Visitor Centre

Catmos Street Oakham Rutland LE15 6HW
Tel: 01572 758440 Fax: 01572 758445
www.rutland.gov.uk/museum

[Nr town centre on A6003 signposted]

The perfect introduction to England's smallest county. The "Welcome to Rutland" gallery tells the story of Rutland and leads into displays of archaeology, history and an extensive rural life collection. Family activities are run during every holiday and exhibitions with the work of local artists are run throughout the year. See our website or telephone for further details. Oakham Castle within walking distance. For information on the Castle see www.rutland.gov/castle.

All year Mon-Sat 10.30-17.00, Sun 14.00-16.00. Closed Good Fri, 25-26 Dec & 1 Jan

Admission Free

Gardens & Horticulture

Barnsdale Gardens

The Avenue Exton Oakham Rutland LE15 8AH
Tel: 01572 813200 Fax: 01572 813346
www.barnsdalegardens.co.uk

[Turn off A606 Oakham / Stamford rd at Barnsdale Lodge Hotel, then 1mi on L. Parking for cars & coaches free. Special parking spaces for disabled & people bringing dogs, (dogs not allowed in gardens). In event of car park filling up, spaces allocated for people with dogs will be used if needed. Tell us in advance you are bringing your dog & we will do our best to reserve parking for you]

Barnsdale Gardens are familiar to millions of BBC viewers as the home of Gardeners' World. The Gardens comprise 37 individual smaller gardens and features that all blend together by the linking borders into one 8 acre garden set in the heart of the beautiful Rutland countryside. There is not only a wealth of different plants to come and see in many different combinations but also a wealth of practical ideas for any garden with all gardeners, experienced or novice, leaving totally inspired. After strolling around the garden, why not relax in our friendly, licensed coffee shop that serves a very appetising range of hot and cold food and drink. Our large specialist nursery sells a wide range of choice and unusual garden plants, many initially propagated from the gardens. With our gift shop selling a range of exclusive Barnsdale gifts, all in all this makes for a memorable visit.

Garden, Gift Shop & Nursery: All year daily Mar-May 09.00-17.00, June-Aug 09.00-19.00, Sept-Oct 09.00-17.00, Nov-Feb 10.00-16.00. Closed 23 & 25 Dec. Coffee Shop: Mar-May daily 10.00-17.00 (stop serving 16.30), Jun-Aug daily 10.00-19.00 (stop serving 18.30), Sept-Oct daily 10.00-17.00 (stop serving 16.30) Nov-Feb daily 10.00-16.00 (stop serving 15.30)

A£6.00 Concessions£5.00 C£2.00, Family Ticket (A2+C3) £15.00. Season Tickets A£17.00 A(2) £30.00. Group rate (10+): A£4.50

Historical

Burghley House

Stamford Rutland PE9 3JY
Tel: 01780 752451
A grand sixteenth-century English country
house, with a park laid out by Capability Brown.
With its State Rooms, paintings and sculptures,
Burghley House is a popular location for feature
films.

Normanton Church Museum

Normanton South Shore Rutland Water Rutland
Tel: 01572 653026
Rutland Water's most famous landmark – tells
the story of this ancient valley. Inside the museum you will find Anglo-Saxon discoveries,
including a complete skeleton from the excava-
tion of the reservoir in 1972. Geological finds
even include dinosaur remains.

Apr-Sep, 11.00-16.00

Performing Arts

Stamford Shakespeare Season

Rutland Open Air Theatre Tolethorpe Hall Little
Casterton Stamford Rutland PE9 4BH
**Tel: 01780 754381/756133 Fax: 01780
481954**
www.stamfordshakespeare.co.uk

*[Just off A1, 90mi N of London. From Stamford
take A6121 (Bourne Road), after 2mi take first L
signposted Tolethorpe, follow Heritage & RAC
Shakespeare at Tolethorpe signs. Plenty of on-site
parking available]*

The finest open air theatre venue in Europe with
600 upholstered seats under a permanent covered auditorium, only the stage is in the open air
in an enchanted wooded glade. Described in a
national journal as one of England's premier
alfresco venues. The theatre's historic
Tolethorpe Hall houses a high class pre-perfor-
mance restaurant (advance booking essential),
seating up to 90 in two elegant dining rooms, a
theatre bar, and a large new orangery used for
serving interval coffee. There is a picnic area
overlooking classic English parkland and free on
site coach and car park. All facilities are within a
minutes walk of each other on a compact site in
an outstandingly beautiful garden setting.
Tolethorpe attracts more than 30,000 worldwide
patrons annually, many regular visitors. There is
wheelchair access and disabled toilets. For a full
colour brochure with booking details send SAE
to the above address.

*June-Aug, performances Mon-Sat 20.00,
Grounds open for picnics from 17.00. 2008
Plays: The Wind in the Willows, Romeo and Juliet
and Richard III. Please call box office on 01780
756133 for details/brochure or please visit our
website*

Seat prices: Mon-Tue £11.00, Wed-Thur
£12.00, Fri £14.00, Sat £16.00, Preview Nights
£9.00. Concessions £1.00 off except Fri-Sat.
Group rates available on request

Railways

Rutland Railway Museum

Cottesmore Iron Ore Mines Sidings, Ashwell
Road Cottesmore Oakham Rutland LE15 7BX
Tel: 01572 813203
Run by volunteers, the museum has an exten-
sive collection of industrial locomotives and
rolling stock.

Sport & Recreation

Rutland Water

Sykes Lane Empingham Oakham Rutland
Tel: 01572 653026
Rutland Water is one of the largest man-made
reservoirs in Europe. Set in 3,100 acres of
countryside, the reservoir has somthing for
everyone.

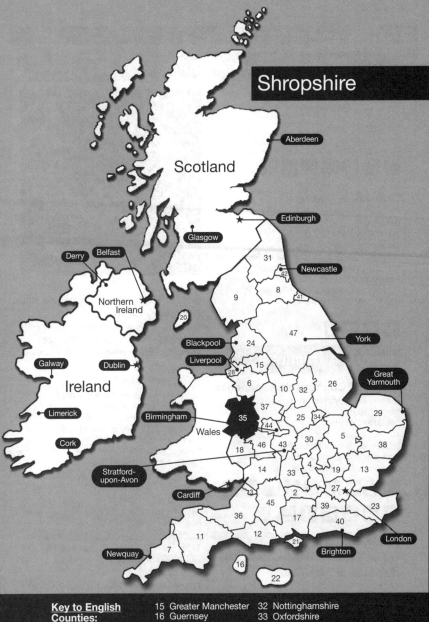

Shropshire

Scotland

Aberdeen

Edinburgh

Glasgow

Newcastle

Derry
Belfast

Northern
Ireland

31

42

41

9

8

Galway

Dublin

Ireland

20

Blackpool

Liverpool

24

47

York

15

28

6

10

32

26

Great
Yarmouth

Limerick

Birmingham

35

37

44

25

34

29

Wales

46

43

30

5

38

Cork

18

Stratford-
upon-Avon

14

33

4

19

13

Cardiff

13

2

27

23

London

45

39

40

Brighton

36

17

Newquay

11

12

21

7

16

22

Key to English Counties:

1	Bedfordshire	15	Greater Manchester	32 Nottinghamshire
2	Berkshire	16	Guernsey	33 Oxfordshire
3	Bristol	17	Hampshire	34 Rutland
4	Buckinghamshire	18	Herefordshire	35 Shropshire
5	Cambridgeshire	19	Hertfordshire	36 Somerset
6	Cheshire	20	Isle Of Man	37 Staffordshire
7	Cornwall	21	Isle Of Wight	38 Suffolk
8	County Durham	22	Jersey	39 Surrey
9	Cumbria	23	Kent	40 Sussex
10	Derbyshire	24	Lancashire	41 Tees Valley
11	Devon	25	Leicestershire	42 Tyne & Wear
12	Dorset	26	Lincolnshire	43 Warwickshire
13	Essex	27	London	44 West Midlands
14	Gloucestershire	28	Merseyside	45 Wiltshire
		29	Norfolk	46 Worcestershire
		30	Northamptonshire	47 Yorkshire
		31	Northumberland	

Agriculture / Working Farms

Rays Farm Country Matters
Rays Farm Billingsley Bridgnorth Shropshire
WV16 6PF
Tel: 01299 841255
Set in the heart of unspoilt Shropshire country-
side, a perfect way to spend a relaxing day.

Thresholds Centre
Picklescott Church Stretton Shropshire
SY6 6NU
Tel: 01694 751411
Thresholds Centre offers a diverse range of
activities from Easter to November. These range
from crafts and creative writing to local history,
exhibitions, landscape appreciation, walking,
guided tours, displays about the area, drama
and murder mystery events.
Easter-Nov

Animal Attractions

Park Hall Countryside Experience
Burma Road Park Hall Whittington Oswestry
Shropshire SY11 4AS
Tel: 01691 671123
40,000 square-feet of indoor attractions, with
regular hands-on animal activities, lots of outdoor play and driving activities. Museums, exhibitions and beautiful countryside.

Country Parks & Estates

Hawkstone Park Follies
Weston-under-Redcastle Near Shrewsbury
Shropshire SY4 5UY
Tel: 01939 200611
With its fairytale landscape and strange follies
rising out of lush woodland, Hawkstone Park is
one of Shropshire's oldest tourist attractions.

Exhibition & Visitor Centres

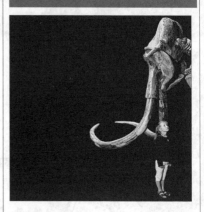

Secret Hills - The Shropshire Hills Discovery Centre
School Lane Craven Arms Shropshire SY7 9RS
Tel: 01588 6760060 Fax: 01588 676030
www.shropshireonline.gov.uk/discover.nsf

*[On A49 in Craven Arms. 20mi S of Shrewsbury,
7mi N of Ludlow. Plenty of on-site parking]*

Unfold the secrets of the Shropshire Hills in an
amazing grass roofed building. Enjoyable and
informative displays explore the heritage, wildlife
and traditions of this special area. Have fun in
the simulated hot air balloon ride and see the
famous Shropshire Mammoth. Admission to the
Centre is free (although there is an admission
charge to the exhibition) and visitors have free
access to 25 acres of attractive meadows slop-
ing down to the River Onny.

*All year Apr-Oct daily 10.00-17.30, Nov-Mar Tue-
Sun 10.00-16.30*

A£4.50 C£3.00 Concessions£4.00, Family
Ticket (A2+C3) £13.50. Group rates: A£4.00
C£1.00 Concessions£3.75. Prices stated are for
exhibition only

**Discount Offer: Two for the Price of
One (full-paying adult).**

Festivals & Shows

West Mid Show

The Showground Berwick Road Shrewsbury
Shropshire SY1 2PF
Tel: 0870 957 6444 Fax: 0870 957 6445
www.westmidshow.co.uk

*[Follow AA signs from any approach road into
Shrewsbury. Free shuttle buses from Shrewsbury
Station. Plenty of free on-site parking available]*

The West Mid Show is one of the major 2-day
shows in the UK. It's an excellent day out for
the whole family, with a varied programme of
events taking place. This year, the headline
attractions in the main ring will be the Devils
Horsemen and the Big Pete and Grim Reaper
Monster trucks. There is an excellent range of
trade stands with something for all the family.
Food Hall, 'Shropshire on Show' and a wide
range of agricultural machinery. There will also
be some of the finest livestock in the UK,
including cattle, horses and sheep. The Red
Devils Parachute Regiment Skydiving team will
also be performing over the weekend.

21-22 June 2008
In Advance A£10.00 C£2.00, Family Ticket
(2A+3C)£20.00

Folk & Local History Museums

Mythstories Museum

The Morgan Library Aston Street Wem
Shropshire SY4 5AU
Tel: 01939 235500
Offers myths legends and fables from around
the world and especially from Shropshire.

Resident storyteller. Reference library.

Shrewsbury Museum and Art Gallery

Barker Street Shrewsbury Shropshire SY1 1QH
Tel: 01743 361196
An impressive timber-framed building and
attached seventeenth-century brick mansion.
Major displays of the archaeology, geology, pre-
history, ceramics and local history of the region.
25 May-14 Sep, Mon-Sat

Heritage & Industrial

Ironbridge Gorge Museums

Coalbrookdale Telford Shropshire TF8 7DQ
Tel: 01952 884391
One of Britain's World Heritage Sites,
Ironbridge Gorge is home to ten superb attrac-
tions set within six square miles of beautiful
scenery.

Whitchurch Heritage and Visitor Information Centre

12 St. Marys Street Whitchurch Shropshire
SY13 1QY
Tel: 01948 665432/664577
Offers a wealth of information on the town's history as well as giving invaluable advice on what
to visit in the area and further afield. Many interactive exhibits suitable for both adults and children.

Historical

Attingham Park

Attingham Park Shrewsbury Shropshire
SY4 4TP
Tel: 01743 708123
Elegant eighteenth-century mansion with
Regency interiors and a deer park. Features
costumed guides.

Dudmaston Hall

Quatt Nr Bridgnorth Shropshire WV15 6QN
Tel: 01746 780866 Fax: 01746 780744
www.nationaltrust.org.uk

[4mi SE of Bridgnorth on A442. Rail: Nearest station Hampton Loade, Severn Valley Railway 1.5mi, Kidderminster 10mi. Bus: 297 Bridgnorth-Kidderminster. Parking available all year at Hampton Loade car park]

Built in the late seventeenth century, Dudmaston Hall is a beautiful mansion house set in a lakeside garden. The house contains a fabulous collection of modern art, Dutch paintings and botanical drawings. Dudmaston Hall and Estate does not stand still, since Charles Babbage created the central heating system, innovation has been part of the character of the estate. More recent innovations include award-winning forestry techniques and environment heating on the estate. There are also miles of walks around the estate through the woods and beside the River Severn. Stiles inspired by modern designs, provide a point of interest throughout several of the walks. There are also links with the Severn Valley Railway at Hampton Loade.

23 Mar-30 Sep: House (14.00-17.30), Garden (12.00-18.00), Shop (13.00-17.30) & Tea Room (11.30-17.30), Tue-Wed & Sun only. Garden & Tea Room also opens Mon

House & Grounds: A£5.50 (Gift Aid £6.10), C£2.75 (Gift Aid £3.05), Family Ticket £13.75 (Gift Aid £15.25). Grounds & Garden Only: A£4.45 (Gift Aid £4.90), C£2.20 (Gift Aid £2.45), Family Ticket £11.00 (Gift Aid £12.20)

Royal Air Force Museum Cosford

Cosford Shifnal Shropshire TF11 8UP
Tel: 01902 376200 Fax: 01902 376211
www.rafmuseum.org.uk

[From the N leave M6 at J12 and follow A5 W. From the S leave M6 at J10a. From A41 less then 1mi from J3 on the M54]

70 Historic aircraft on display in three wartime hangars and within the National Cold War Exhibition. Some aircraft are suspended in flying attitudes with interactive kiosks and audio visuals telling the story in a fun and innovative way.

10.00-18.00
Admission Free

Mickey Miller's Playbarn and Maize Maze

Oakfield Farm Watling Street Craven Arms Shropshire SY7 8DX
Tel: 01588 640403 / 777612
Covering almost six acres, the Maize Maze is located at Oakfield Farm, Craven Arms in the heart of the Shropshire countryside. The Playbarn is Shropshire's new all-weather attraction; a massive indoor play area for the whole family.

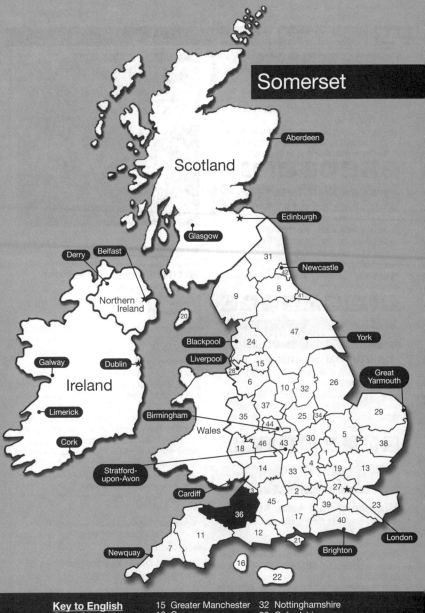

Somerset

Aberdeen

Scotland

Edinburgh

Glasgow

Derry · Belfast

Northern
Ireland

Newcastle

31
42
8
41
9

Blackpool
24
47
York

Liverpool
15
Great
Yarmouth

Galway · Dublin
28
6
10
32
26
29

Ireland
37
35
25
34

Limerick
Birmingham
44
5
38

Wales
46
43
30

Cork
18
4
1
19
13

Stratford-
upon-Avon
14
33
2
27
23

Cardiff
3
39

45
17
40

36
12
21
Brighton

11
London

Newquay
7
16

22

Abbeys

Cleeve Abbey
Washford Watchet Somerset TA23 0PS
Tel: 01984 640377
The picturesque Cistercian abbey boasts the most impressively complete and unaltered set of monastic cloister buildings in England.

Agriculture / Working Farms

Noah's Ark Zoo Farm
Moat House Farm Failand Road Wraxall
North Somerset BS48 1PG
Tel: 01275 852606
Noah's Ark Zoo Farm offers a truly 'hands-on' experience for all the family.

Animal Attractions

Ferne Animal Sanctuary
Wambrook Chard Somerset TA20 3DH
Tel: 01460 65214
51 acres of lovely Somerset countryside with over 300 animals including horses, donkeys, pigs, goats, sheep, cats, dogs, cattle, poultry, ducks, rabbits, guinea pigs and so much more.

Arts, Crafts & Textiles

Museum of East Asian Art
12 Bennett Street Bath Somerset BA1 2QJ
Tel: 01225 464640
This unique museum offers its visitors a wonderful insight into the art and cultures of China, Japan, Korea and South-East Asia.
Tues-Sat 10.00-17.00, Sun 12.00-17.00

Caverns & Caves

Cheddar Caves and Gorge
Cheddar Somerset BS27 3QF
Tel: 01934 742343
Discover Britain's biggest gorge and two beautiful showcaves.

Wookey Hole Caves
Wookey Hole Wells Somerset BA5 1BB
Tel: 01749 672243 Fax: 01749 677749
www.wookey.co.uk

[J22 M5, A39, A38, A371. Plenty of on-site parking available]

Britain's most spectacular caves and legendary home of the infamous Witch of Wookey. The nineteenth-century Papermill houses a variety of fascinating attractions including a Cave Museum, Victorian Penny Arcade, Magical Mirror Maze, Haunted Corridor of Crazy Mirrors and Wizard's Castle play area. See paper being made in Britain's only surviving handmade papermill. Relax in our Enchanted Fairy Garden, visit King Kong or stroll around the Valley of the Dinosaurs. Self-service restaurant, gift shops, picnic areas and ample free parking. Please note, it may sometimes be necessary to close or restrict any attractions without prior notice. Live family shows most weekends and school holidays, please phone for show times and details.

All year daily Apr-Oct 10.00-17.00, Nov-Mar 10.30-16.00. Closed Christmas Day
A£15.00 C£10.00, Family Ticket £45.00

Discount Offer: Two for the Price of One (full-paying adult).

Country Parks & Estates

Ashton Court Estate and Gardens

Ashton Court Long Ashton Somerset BS41 9JN
Tel: 0117 963 9174
A historic park that covers 850 acres of woods and grasslands. Deer park, two 18-hole pitch and putt golf courses, minature railway and visitor centre.

Ham Hill Country Park

Stoke sub Hamdon Yeovil Somerset TA14 6RW
Tel: 01935 823617
Four-hundred acre open access country park. Superb countryside walks with iron age and Roman earthworks. Panoramic views of Somerset.

Yeovil Country Park

Yeovil Somerset
Tel: 01935 462462
88-acre country park including wooded hillsides, wetland habitats, waterfalls, lakes and grassland.

Festivals & Shows

Bath and West Showground

Shepton Mallet Somerset BA4 6QN
Tel: 01749 822200 Fax: 01749 823169
www.bathandwest.com

[A371. Rail: Castle Cary Station. Plenty of on-site parking available]

The Bath and West Showground offers visitors a huge range of events all year round. With several Exhibition Halls ranging from 500 to 2,787 square-metres in size, the showground hosts a wide variety of events from the smallest meeting to major conferences, antique fairs, dog shows, and national exhibitions, with plenty to interest people of all ages. All the facilities are based on the 240-acre showground - complete with car parks, toilets and permanent restaurant facilities. Major events for 2008 include The Royal Bath & West Show May 28th - 31st, The National Amateur Gardening Show 5th, 6th & 7th September, The Dairy Show 1st October, The Royal Smithfield Christmas Fair 5th & 6th December. For full details of all events please call or visit our website.

Please visit our website for opening times

Bridgwater Guy Fawkes Carnival

Bridgwater Somerset TA6 5EJ
www.bridgwatercarnival.org.uk
[Nr J23/24 M5. Procession in Town Centre; Rds closed to traffic from 18.00. Ample parking available, clearly signposted]
Bridgwater Carnival commemorates Guy Fawkes and his failed attempt to blow up the Houses of Parliament, and is commonly referred to as the world's largest illuminated winter carnival. The Carnival procession takes over two hours to pass any one point, and contains over 70 carnival carts - some 100ft long, 17ft high, 11ft wide and lit by over 25,000 light bulbs. Once the procession has finished, the Carnival is brought to a dramatic finale with an amazing squibbing firework display. Seeing is believing - don't miss this amazing Carnival.

Friday 7 November 2008, 19.00 start
Admission Free

Folk & Local History Museums

Shoe Museum

C & J Clark Ltd 40 High Street Street Somerset
BA16 0YA
Tel: 01458 842169 Fax: 01458 842226

[J23 M5. Bus: services run to High St]

The museum is in the oldest part of the shoe
factory set up by Cyrus and James Clark in
1825. It contains shoes from Roman times to
the present, buckles, engravings, fashion plates,
machinery, hand tools and advertising material.
One section illustrates the early history of the
shoe firm and its role in the town. Disabled
access available.

All year Mon-Fri 10.00-16.45. Closed Bank Hols
Admission Free

Food & Drink

Sheppy's Cider Farm Centre

Three Bridges Bradford on Tone Taunton
Somerset TA4 1ER
Tel: 01823 461233
Traditional family run working cider farm. The
Rural Life Museum shows a video of the cider
making year.

Gardens & Horticulture

Prior Park Landscape Garden

Ralph Allen Drive Bath Somerset BA2 5AH
Tel: 01225 833422

A beautiful eighteenth-century landscape garden, set in a sweeping valley with magnificent
views of the City of Bath.

Historical

American Museum in Britain

Claverton Manor Bath Somerset BA2 7BD
Tel: 01225 460503
Learn about the early pioneers in the American
Heritage Exhibition, wonder at the American
quilts, run around the grounds and enjoy an
American cookie.
15 Mar-2 Nov: Tue-Sun, 12.00-17.00

Dunster Castle

Dunster Nr Minehead Somerset TA24 6SL
Tel: 01643 823004 Fax: 01643 823000
Ancient castle with fine interiors and subtropical
gardens. also features the National Collection of
strawberry trees.

Farleigh Hungerford Castle

Farleigh Hungerford Bath Somerset BA3 6RS
Tel: 01225 754026
The ruined fourteenth-century castle has a
chapel containing wall paintings, stained glass
and the fine tomb of Sir Thomas Hungerford
who built the castle.

Lytes Cary Manor

Kingsdon Charlton Mackrell Somerton Somerset
TA11 7HU
Tel: 01458 224471
Intimate manor house with Arts & Crafts-style
garden. Tudor great hall and fourteenth-century
chapel. Herbal gardens and estate walks.
15 Mar-2 Nov, Sat-Wed

Montacute House

Montacute Somerset TA15 6XP
Tel: 01935 823289 Fax: 01935 826921
www.nationaltrust.org.uk
A glittering mansion set in beautiful formal gardens and parkland. Home to over 60 portraits from the National Portrait Gallery. Excellent shop, restaurant and café.

Park: All year daily. 15 Mar-2 Nov, House, Garden/Shop & Restaurant/Café: Wed-Mon (Closed Tue), from 11.00am. 1 & 10-15 Mar, Garden/Shop Only: Wed-Sun (Closed Mon-Tue), from 11.00am. 2-9 Mar, Restaurant/Café & Garden/Shop Only: Sat-Sun (Closed Mon-Fri), from 11.00am. 5 Nov-21 Dec, Restaurant/Café (Sun) & Garden/Shop (Wed-Sun) Only: from 11.00am.

House & Garden: A£8.50 (Gift Aid: A£9.50), C£4.00 (Gift Aid: C£4.50), Family Ticket £21.10 (Gift Aid: £23.50), Group rates A£8.30. Gardens Only: A£5.10 (Gift Aid: A£5.70), C£2.50 (Gift Aid: C£2.80)

Tyntesfield

Wraxall Somerset BS48 1NT
Tel: 0844 800 4966
Spectacular Victorian country house and grounds, with working kitchen garden, chapel and grand Victorian designs. Tyntesfield brings the conservation process to life for its visitors.

15 Mar-2 Nov (Closed Thu-Fri)

Fleet Air Arm Museum

Royal Naval Air Station Yeovilton Yeovil Somerset BA22 8HT
Tel: 01935 840565 Fax: 01935 842630
www.fleetairarm.com

[on B3151, close to J of A37 & A303. 7mi N of Yeovil. Plenty of on-site parking available]

The Fleet Air Arm museum is where Museum meets theatre. You'll be 'transported by helicopter to the replica flight deck of the aircraft carrier HMS ARK ROYAL where you'll see fighter aircraft and two enormous projection screens showing a phantom strike fighter and a Buccaneer fighter-bomber. You'll experience the thrills and sounds of a flight deck, and feel the wind in your hair and will even see a nuclear bomb! The museum has the largest collection of Naval aircraft anywhere in Europe and the first British built Concorde, which you can go on-board, and visit the cockpit. Outside, there is a children's adventure playground, a licensed restaurant and a shop, ample parking and excellent disabled access. The museum is located alongside Europe's busiest military air station RNAS Yeovilton.

All year Apr-Oct daily 10.00-17.30, Nov-Mar Wed-Sun 10.00-16.30. Closed 24-26 Dec, open all public hols

A£10.50 C(under5)£Free C(5-16)£7.50 Concessions£8.50, Family Ticket (A2+C3) £32.00. Reduced rates for service personnel. Group rates available on request

Discount Offer: One Child Free.

Palaces

Bishop's Palace and Gardens
The Bishop's Palace Wells Somerset BA5 2PD
Tel: 01749 678691
www.bishopspalacewells.co.uk
Enjoy the tranquillity of the beautiful gardens in this unique and historic site. Discover the wells from which the city takes it name and the splendid thirteenth-century palace buildings. The Bishop's Palace and Gardens lies in the heart of Wells, within very easy access of the market place and cathedral. Enter the moated and fortified grounds from the gatehouse and discover the splendour of the beautiful medieval Palace. Behind the thirteenth-century building lies 14 acres of gardens, springs and an arboretum, with plenty of space to really relax. Make the most of your day at the Palace by joining one of our knowledgeable tour guides (subject to availability, please call for details) who will really bring the abundant history of the place alive for you. A delicious range of home made lunches, cakes, and cream teas are served in the Undercroft Restaurant, or can be enjoyed on the garden terrace.

21 Mar-31 Oct Sun-Fri 10.30-18.00 Sat 10.30-14.00, 1 Nov-19 Dec Wed-Sun 10.30-15.30 . Guided tours for groups available but must be booked in advance
A£5.50 C(0-12)£Free C(12-18)£1.10 Concessions£4.40 Group rate (10+): £4.40

Places of Worship

Bath Abbey
Abbey Churchyard Bath BA1 1LT
Tel: 01225 422462
Fifteenth-century Abbey Church built on site where Edgar was crowned first King of England in 973.

Wells Cathedral
Chain Gate Cathedral Green Wells Somerset BA5 2UE
Tel: 01749 674483
Dating from the twelfth century and built in the early English Gothic style. Magnificent West Front with 296 medieval groups of sculpture. Chapter House, Lady Chapel, Scissor arches and unique mechanical clock also feature.

Railways

West Somerset Railway
The Railway Station Minehead Somerset TA24 5BG
Tel: 01643 704996 Fax: 01643 706349
www.west-somerset-railway.co.uk

[Leave M5 at J25 (Taunton) & follow brown tourist signs. Plenty of on-site parking available]

The West Somerset Railway recaptures the era of the branch line country railway in the days of steam. Enjoy 20 miles of glorious Somerset scenery as the train gently rolls back the years on its journey beside the Quantock Hills to the Bristol Channel coast. Just sit back in your seat and watch the steam and the countryside drift past the window. The West Somerset Railway is a wonderful day out for all the family, whatever the weather. We look forward to welcoming you.

First train from Bishop Lydeard (3mi from Taunton) at 10.40. First train from Minehead at 10.30
Full Day Ticket: A£13.40 OAPs£11.60 C£6.70

Roman Era

Roman Baths

Abbey Church Yard Bath Somerset BA1 1LZ
Tel: 01225 477785
This Great Roman Temple and bathing complex is one of Britain's most spectacular ancient monuments, built 2000 years ago around the country's only hot springs and still flowing with natural hot water.

Science - Earth & Planetary

Herschel Museum of Astronomy

19 New King Street Bath North East Somerset BA1 2BL
Tel: 01225 311342
Delightful Georgian townhouse, home to astronomer and musician William Herschel during the eighteenth century. Visit the astronomer's workshop where he made his telescopes, and the original kitchen and music room. Star Vault astronomy auditorium and Georgian landscaped garden.

Sealife Centres & Aquariums

SeaQuarium Ltd

Marine Parade Weston-Super-Mare Somerset BS23 1BE
Tel: 01934 613361 Fax: 01934 613371
www.seaquarium.co.uk

[J21 M5 follow A370 to Weston Super Mare & follow rd signs for Aquarium or signs for Beach.

We are situated on beach in front of Beach Lawns]

The SeaQuarium features over 30 displays, from British Marine Sharks and Rays to Tropical Seahorses and Lionfish. Our EvoZone exhibit features creatures that have adapted to new landscapes through evolution! Walk under the waves with our Ocean Depths Tunnel, watch as our resident sharks swim inches above you! Don't miss our successful breeding programme within the Seahorse Family Nursery, the Red-Bellied Piranhas and Puffer Fish within our Rainforest Rivers and the Deadly Stone Fish and Blue Spotted Ray in the Lethal Reef! We have interactive touch-screens throughout the aquarium for further fun and learning. Our daily feeding demonstrations and presentations are not to be missed! Just for kids - our Discovery Trail quiz. Your ticket is valid ALL DAY! Don't forget our tea room for light snacks and gift shop for souvenirs for one and all!

All year daily from 10.00 please call for last admissions. Closed 24-26 Dec

A£6.15 C(4-16)£5.15 C(under4)£Free OAPs£5.15, Family Ticket £22.00. Discounts for groups and school parties (12+) please call for further information

Discount Offer: One Child Free.

Social History Museums

Blake Museum

Blake Street Bridgwater Somerset TA6 3NB
Tel: 01278 456127
Housed in the birthplace of Robert Blake (1598-1657), General at Sea, the museum's displays look at the history and archaeology of Bridgwater and the surrounding area.

Sport & Recreation

Wimbleball Lake

Brompton Regis Dulverton Somerset
Tel: 01398 371372
Lakeside area with picnic areas, play area, cafe, walks and fishing.

Theme & Adventure Parks

Brean Leisure Park

Coast Road Brean Sands Somerset TA8 2QY
Tel: 01278 751595 Fax: 01278 752102
www.brean.com

*[J22 M5, follow brown & white tourist signs from
motorway towards Burnham On Sea & N heading
for Berrow & Brean. Go past Holiday Resort Unity
& at mini roundabout turn R onto Park entrance
Rd. Plenty of on-site parking available]*

The South West's largest Fun Park with over 30
rides and attractions, with something for everyone, from roundabouts to rollercoasters. There's
a choice of roller coasters, a Wild Water flume
ride with two huge drops to get you soaked,
and Wipeout, the 100ft swinging pendulum.
Also the Super Looper Roller Coaster and many
more.

*Mar-Nov Visit www.brean.com or call 01278
751595 for opening times, from 24 Jul-31 Aug
daily 11.00-22.00*

Entrance free, wristband price depends on age,
ranges from £9.99-£18.99. Alternatively, you
can also purchase tokens

**Discount Offer: Three for the Price of
Two (full-paying adults).**

Butlins Minehead

Warren Road Minehead Somerset TA24 5SH
Tel: 0845 070 4795 Fax: 01643 705264
www.butlins.com/dayvisitor
*[Heading S: take J24 (M5) & follow signs on A39.
Heading N: take J26 (M5) & follow signs on
A358/A39. Plenty of on-site parking available]*
For a great day out, come on holiday for the
day! With over 70 years experience entertaining
holidaymakers, it's no wonder we know what
makes the perfect day out. So come and see
how much you can pack in! With wet n wild
Splash Waterworld, adventure fort, indoor soft
play zones, traditional funfair and fantastic
entertainment in the Skyline Pavilion, it's a day
out that will be altogether more fun for everyone!

*Please call 0845 070 4795 for latest opening
times*
A(15+)£12.00 C(under2)£Free C(2-14)£9.00,
OAPs(60+)£9.00. Group rates (20+) £6.00.
School groups (20+) 1 free adult with every 10
children

Discount Offer: Kid For A Quid.

Wildlife & Safari Parks

Wildlife Park at Cricket St. Thomas

Cricket St. Thomas Chard Somerset TA20 4DB
Tel: 01460 30111
This wildlife park has over 600 animals and
birds from around the world and is home to
more than 70 different species.

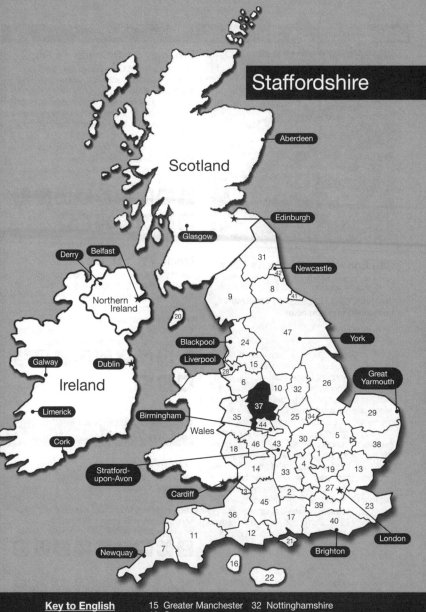

Staffordshire

Scotland

Aberdeen

Edinburgh

Glasgow

Newcastle

Derry
Belfast

Northern
Ireland

31

42

8

9

41

Blackpool

24

47

York

Liverpool

15

28

Galway
Dublin

6

Ireland

10

32

26

Great
Yarmouth

Limerick

37

25

34

29

Birmingham

35

44

Wales

5

38

Cork

18

46

43

30

Stratford-
upon-Avon

14

33

1

19

13

4

Cardiff

13

2

27

London

45

39

23

36

17

40

11

12

Brighton

7

21

Newquay

16

22

20

Animal Attractions

Ash End House Children's Farm

Middleton Lane Middleton Tamworth
Staffordshire B78 2BL
Tel: 0121 329 3240 Fax: 0121 329 3240
www.childrensfarm.co.uk

[Signposted off A4091. Plenty of on-site parking available]

Ash End House Children's Farm is a fun filled family day out. Lots of undercover activities, ideal for rainy days! These include Chick chatting; sit on a pony; help bottle feed a lamb or goat kid (spring/summer); goat kid walking (weather permitting); meet Chirpy; make a memento to take home; Bunny brushing and Guinea pig grooming; Join in one of our Playlets (weekends/school holidays) and lots, lots more. We have three play areas, family games yard, crazy golf, toddler's tractor and trike barn, new gift shop, farmhouse café and picnic barns. Birthday parties are our speciality with 4 different themes to choose from; Traditional, Star in your party, Nursery Rhyme Tractor and Trike and Crafty Party. Come and join in our delightful Nativity Story and "wake up Santa in his cottage" from the last weekend of November until Christmas Eve.

Summer/Autumn 10.00-17.00. Winter 10.00-16.00. Closed 25 Dec until 2nd weekend in January.

A£4.50 C£4.90 (includes animal feed, farm badge & all activities) OAPs£4.50. Group rates available on request

Broomey Croft Children's Farm

Bodymoor Heath Lane Bodymoor Heath Nr Tamworth Warwickshire B76 0EE
Tel: 01827 873844
This award winning farm attraction is a fun family day out and has been laid out and organised to especially suit families with younger children. There are plenty of opportunities to see and feed the friendly farm animals as close quarters. There is a delightful tea shop on site, which serves hot, and cold snacks and has a good children's menu.

Monkey Forest

Trentham Estate, Southern Entrance Stone Road Trentham Staffordshire ST4 8AX
Tel: 01782 659 845
A unique experience for everyone - come to the only place in Britain where you can walk amongst 140 Barbary macaques roaming free in 60 acres of beautiful English Forest.

Arts, Crafts & Textiles

Ceramica

Old Town Hall Market Place Burslem Stoke-on-Trent Staffordshire ST6 3DS
Tel: 01782 832001
See, listen and touch our interactive displays and activities in which we will show you how clay is transformed into ceramic masterpieces.

Curborough Antiques and Crafts Centre

Curborough Hall Farm Watery Lane Lichfield Staffordshire WS13 8ES
Tel: 01543 256395
The Curborough Collection contains many small arts and crafts businesses all set around a working farm.

Bedford Museum

Castle Lane, Bedford, MK40 3XD
Tel: 01234 353323
www.bedfordmuseum.org

Embark on a fascinating
journey through the human
and natural history of North
Bedfordshire, pausing briefly
to glimpse at wonders from
more distant lands.

Wildlife Park & Gardens
Leisure and entertainment for all the family

Beale Park

FREE TRAIN RIDE

£8.50 Adults • £6.00 Children
£7.00 Senior Citizens (High season)
Group booking rates also available

Opening Times: Open daily, from
10am - March 1st until October 31st

Beale Park, Lower Basildon, Reading, Berks RG8 9NH

Tel: 0870 777 7160

www.bealepark.co.uk

The Child-Beale Trust is a registered charity.

The Look Out
Discovery Centre

THE LOOK OUT DISCOVERY CENTRE

A Great Family Day Out,
Whatever the Weather!
Hands on Science and Nature
Exhibition - Over 70 Exhibits
Open Daily 10am - 5pm

- Children's Adventure Playground
- Coffee Shop
- 2,600 Acres of Crown
  Estate Woodland
- Gift Shop
- Mountain Bike Hire
- Free Car Parking

Hands-On Science Fun

HOW TO FIND US
Follow the brown tourist signs:-
Junction 10 off the M4 or Junction 3 off the M3

The Look Out Discovery Centre
Nine Mile Ride, Bracknell,
Berkshire, RG12 7QW

Tel: 01344 354400

www.bracknell-forest.gov.uk/be

for a magical

SAVING OF UP TO £2000
WORTH OF DISCOUNT VOUCHERS

PLEASE SEE THE
GREY SECTION
AT THE BACK OF THE BOOK

Please see the relevant county section for further information on each of these attractions

1

Vikings have invaded LEGOLAND® Windsor!

Vikings have invaded LEGOLAND Windsor! Check out the amazing, humungous and hilarious Vikings' River Splash ride. Take a wild, wet voyage through a Viking world built from thousands of LEGO® bricks but try to avoid a complete soaking!

UP TO £25 OFF

£5 off per person for up to 5 people

Cut out this coupon and take to LEGOLAND Windsor to receive up to £25 discount.

Terms & Conditions:

Up to £25 off entry to LEGOLAND Windsor* - Excluding August

• This voucher entitles a maximum of five people to £5.00 off the full admission price per person at LEGOLAND Windsor. • Entrance for children under three years of age is free. • Voucher must be presented upon entrance into LEGOLAND Windsor and surrendered to the ticket booth operator. Discount vouchers cannot be used for pre-bookings. • Not to be used in conjunction with any other offer, reward/loyalty program, 2 Day Pass, Annual Pass, group booking, on-line tickets, rail inclusive offers. • Guests are advised that not all attractions and shows may be operational on the day of their visit. • Height, age and weight restrictions apply on some rides. Some rides will require guests who only just meet the minimum height requirements to be accompanied by a person aged 16 years or over. • Guests under the age of 14 must be accompanied by a person aged 16 or over. • This voucher is not for re-sale, is non-refundable and non-transferable. • The park opens for the 2008 season on 15 March and closes on 2 November. • This voucher is valid for admissions from 15 March to 2 November 2007, excluding the month of August. • This offer is limited to one per household. • This offer will apply irrespective of the entrance price at the time of use. • LEGOLAND Windsor will be closed on selected weekdays in April, May, September, October and November. • PLEASE visit www.LEGOLAND.co.uk in advance to confirm dates and prices.

For great hotel offers go to www.LEGOLANDhotels.co.uk

2

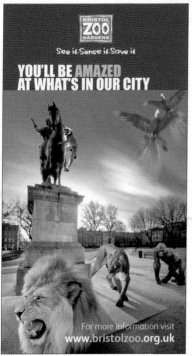
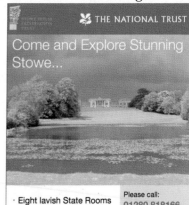

Please see the relevant county section for further information on each of these attractions

Please see the relevant county section for further information on each of these attractions

Please see the relevant county section for further information on each of these attractions

There's nowhere quite like the world famous Jamaica Inn on Bodmin Moor

Along with a good selection of real ales, home cooked food, cosy bedrooms (some with four-posters and all with en-suite facilities) we've a host of other attractions.

Daphne du Maurier's Smugglers at Jamaica Inn Experience in tableaux, light and sound the novel 'Jamaica Inn' then visit one of the world's finest collections of smuggling artefacts at the Smugglers' Museum. There's a souvenir shop, a children's play area and even a pirate ship!

How to find us
Jamaica Inn is located halfway between Bodmin and Launceston, just off the A30 at Bolventor.

BOLVENTOR . LAUNCESTON . PL15 7TS

Tel: 01566 86250 . Fax: 01566 86177
Email: enquiry@jamaicainn.co.uk
www.jamaicainn.co.uk

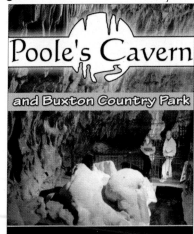

Poole's Cavern
and Buxton Country Park

Deep beneath the Peakland Hills of Buxton is a hidden world of stunning beauty.

Green Lane, Buxton, Derbyshire SK17 9DH
01298 26978
Email: info@poolescavern.co.uk

Exhibition & Visitor Centre • Shop • Play Area
Cafe • Picnic Area • Toilets • Car Parking

www.poolescavern.co.uk

The Devil's Arse! | Speedwell Cavern

PEAK CAVERN

OPEN DAILY: 10.00am to 5.00pm
Last tour leaves at 4.00pm (Times may vary)

NOVEMBER TO MARCH
Weekends 10.00am - 4.00pm
Weekdays 2 Tours per day (Phone for timings)
OPEN DAILY DURING SCHOOL HOLIDAYS

Peak Cavern Ltd, Castleton
Tel: 01433 620285
Email: info@peakcavern.co.uk

www.devilsarse.com

SPEEDWELL CAVERN

OPEN DAILY: 10.00am to 5.00pm
Last tour leaves at 4.00pm (Times may vary)

BOATS DEPART AT REGULAR INTERVALS.

Speedwell Cavern Ltd,
Winnats Pass, Castleton
Tel: 01433 620512
Email: info@speedwellcavern.co.uk

www.speedwellcavern.co.uk

PLEASE ASK ABOUT OUR JOINT TICKET

Please see the relevant county section for further information on each of these attractions

Treak Cliff CAVERN

Home of Blue John Stone

Visit an underground wonderland of Stalactites, Stalagmites, Rocks, Minerals and Fossils

Home of the world famous Blue John Stone
Special Events are held throughout the year.

For further information contact:
T: 01433 620571
F: 01433 620519
E: treakcliff@bluejohnstone.com
www.bluejohnstone.com

Discover East Devon's glorious Axe Valley - from the top of a heritage tram!

Journey from Seaton, gateway town to the World Heritage Jurassic Coast through two nature reserves alongside the Axe estuary to historic Colyton, Devon's most rebellious town.

2008 OPENING TIMES
OPEN DAILY: 9 - 24 Feb & 15 Mar - 2 Nov
OPEN WEEKENDS: 1 - 9 Mar & 8 Nov - 13 Dec

Halloween Tram of Terror: 31st Oct.

Bird Watching: February - May & September - December.

Children's Birthday Parties and Tram Driving Lessons available all year round.

Santa Specials: 14th, 20th, 21st, 23rd & 24th December.

Harbour Rd, Seaton, Devon EX12 2NQ
01297 20375
info@tram.co.uk
www.tram.co.uk

Enclosed saloons operate during bad weather

LULWORTH CASTLE & PARK

The Knights of Lulworth Return!
Spectacular Summer Jousting Battles
23rd July to 25th August
(performed by Jousts Impossible)

PLUS Medieval Village & Fiery Jack Juggling Shows

Stunning 17thC Castle | Adventure Play Area | Licensed Stable Café
18thC Chapel | Animal Farm | Woodland Walks | Courtyard Gift Shop
Indoor Children's Activity Room | OPEN Sun to Fri 10.30am to 6pm
FREE Parking | Under 4's FREE | Special events all year

LULWORTH
0845 450 1054   www.lulworth.com
East Lulworth, Wareham, Dorset BH20 5QS

Make the connection

Special Group & School Rates + Driver & Organiser Incentives!

How does your group match up with our group? The best way to find out just how much we have in common with man's closest living relatives is to visit Monkey World and meet our ever-growing family of rescued and endangered apes and monkeys in our 65-acre park.

● Unique sanctuary with over 160 primates including the largest group of chimps outside Africa, orangutan nursery, rare gibbons & woolly monkeys ● Keeper's talks every half hour ● Primate adoption scheme ● All-day refreshments & gift shop ● Facilities for the less-able ● South's largest Great Ape Play Area for Kids

20 YEARS OF RESCUE

MONKEY WORLD
APE RESCUE CENTRE
Near Wareham, Dorset BH20 6HH   Tel 01929 462537
OPEN EVERY DAY (except Christmas Day) 10am-5pm (6pm July & August)
FREE INFO LINE 0800 456600
www.monkeyworld.org

Please see the relevant county section for further information on each of these attractions

BERKELEY CASTLE
BERKELEY, GLOUCESTERSHIRE

For group bookings, events,
and all openday information:
Tel: 01453 810332
www.berkeley-castle.com

Keynes Country Park

'Under New Management'
Operated and managed by Watermark Investments
Leisure & Developments Ltd.

Facilities include: *fun for all the family*

Bathing beach
Playgrounds   01285 868 096
Picnic & BBQ areas   keynescountrypark.com
Nature Walks
Lakeside cafe and bar
High ropes adventure
Watersports activity centre
Venue for private parties
Shop and information point
and much more to come...

Keynes Park Opening Times:

Watermark
The Cotswolds

October - March	9.00am - 5.00pm daily
April & September	9.00am - 7.00pm daily
May	9.00am - 8.00pm daily
June - August	9.00am - 9.00pm daily

Dean
Heritage Centre

Discover An Inspiring Day Out

Adventure Playground
5 Museum Galleries
Gift Shop & Café
Children's Activities
Monthly Events

Forest of Dean, Gloucestershire, Gl14 2UB
Tel: 01594 822 170   Fax: 01594 823 711
www.deanheritagemuseum.com

THE ROYAL INTERNATIONAL

AIR TATTOO

12 - 13 July 2008
www.airtattoo.com

ROYAL
AIR FORCE Charitable Trust
Enterprises

Please see the relevant county section for further information on each of these attractions

England: Greater Manchester

Hat Works

Discover the UK's only museum
dedicated to the hatting industry,
hats and headwear

*Admission Free Guided tours £2.50 per person

- Guided tours of the cottage industry, original Victorian machinery and the history behind it
- Large display of fascinating hats from around the world
- HOLIDAY FUN! - Kids craft workshops offered daily in the school holidays.
- Group tour visits by arrangement
- Family Fun area
- Level 2 Cafe and museum shop

Wellington Mill, Wellington Road South,
Stockport SK3 0EU.

*Please note that all guided tours, organised group visits and special events are charged for

Manchester Tourism Awards 2006
Winner
Best Small Visitor Attraction

STOCKPORT METROPOLITAN BOROUGH COUNCIL

Tel. 0161 355 7770
www.hatworks.org.uk

Travel Through Time and Touch the Past...

at Staircase House - an exciting new interactive attraction exploring the history of one fascinating house from 1460 to WWII. Smell, touch and listen on a fantastic family day out.

Open 7 days a week.

 **STOCKPORT** METROPOLITAN BOROUGH COUNCIL

Market Place, Stockport, SK1 1ES t. 0161 480 1460
www.staircasehouse.org.uk

Please see the relevant county section for further information on each of these attractions

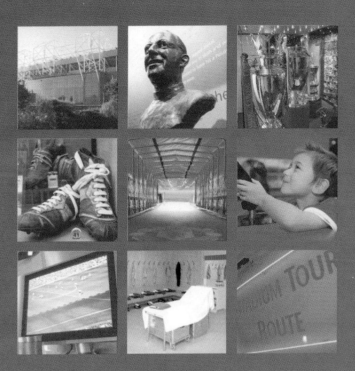

Not what you would expect from a Museum and Tour.

Everything you would expect from UNITED.

The Museum and Tour Centre is open all year round. For more information or to book a tour please call: **0870 442 1994** or email: **tours@manutd.co.uk**

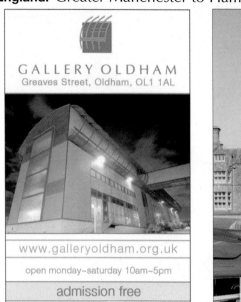

GALLERY OLDHAM
Greaves Street, Oldham, OL1 1AL

www.galleryoldham.org.uk

open monday~saturday 10am~5pm

admission free

for more information call
0161 770 4653

OLDHAM
Metropolitan Borough

Beaulieu
the Heart of the New Forest

National Motor Museum
Palace House
Beaulieu Abbey

OPENING EASTER 2008
A new exhibition in the
National Motor Museum
celebrating the Art of Custom

www.beaulieu.co.uk   01590 612345

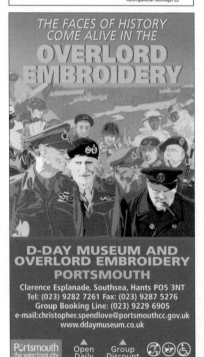

THE FACES OF HISTORY
COME ALIVE IN THE
OVERLORD
EMBROIDERY

D-DAY MUSEUM AND
OVERLORD EMBROIDERY
PORTSMOUTH
Clarence Esplanade, Southsea, Hants PO5 3NT
Tel: (023) 9282 7261 Fax: (023) 9287 5276
Group Booking Line: (023) 9229 6905
e-mail:christopher.spendlove@portsmouthcc.gov.uk
www.ddaymuseum.co.uk

Portsmouth
the waterfront city

Open
Daily

Group
Discount

The all-weather undercover
attraction packed with
hands-on activities

intech
family science centre
& planetarium

FREE
ENTRY
Free entry for one child,
to Science Centre only,
when accompanied by
one full paying adult or
senior on presentation
of this voucher
VALID UNTIL 30/09/2008 - DAYSOUT

NEW FOR 2008
THE UK's LARGEST
planetarium

www.intech-uk.com   01962 863791
Telegraph Way, Morn Hill, Winchester, Hampshire SO21 1HZ
(M3 exits 9 or 10, A31 Alresford) Open every day 10am - 4pm
Seperate entry fees apply to Science Centre and Planetarium

Please see the relevant county section for further information on each of these attractions

Please see the relevant county section for further information on each of these attractions

England: Hampshire to Kent

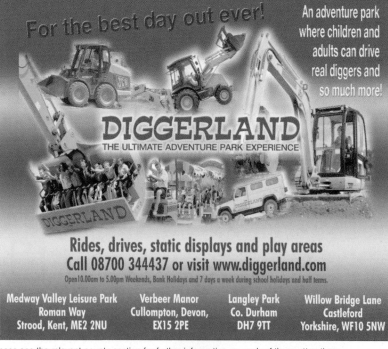

Please see the relevant county section for further information on each of these attractions

Please see the relevant county section for further information on each of these attractions

Please see the relevant county section for further information on each of these attractions

THRILLS & BARGAINS...
one of the UK's most POPULAR Resorts

- **OPEN FROM MARCH ONWARDS**
- Great rides and family fun
- Europe's biggest 7-day, indoor/outdoor market
- Exciting events and celebrity guests
- Home of 'The Big Weekend'
- Group discounts
- Free admission & free coach-parking

THE Market
GOOD VALUE... GREAT VARIETY

A GREAT DAY OUT FOR THE WHOLE FAMILY!
Visit www.fantasyisland.co.uk
Fantasy Island Theme Park, Ingoldmells,
Lincolnshire PE25 1RH Tel: 01754 871 706

Pleasure Island
Family Theme Park
Cleethorpes

HYDROMAX

Basil Brush SHOW

Terroriser
New for 2008

New show for Spring Bank and Summer 2008

Discover the
MAGIC

For Further Information Please call
01472 211 511
www.pleasure-island.co.uk

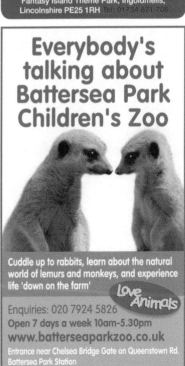

Everybody's talking about Battersea Park Children's Zoo

Cuddle up to rabbits, learn about the natural world of lemurs and monkeys, and experience life 'down on the farm'

Love Animals

Enquiries: 020 7924 5826
Open 7 days a week 10am-5.30pm
www.batterseaparkzoo.co.uk
Entrance near Chelsea Bridge Gate on Queenstown Rd.
Battersea Park Station

discover
amazing
Treasures
marvel
explore
from Magna Carta
shakespeare
MOZART *to the* music
sound Beatles
books
at the British Library
manuscripts

BRITISH LIBRARY

ADMISSION FREE

THE BRITISH LIBRARY
96 Euston Road London NW1 2DB

T +44 (0)20 74127332

⊖⊛ King's Cross St Pancras
and Euston

www.bl.uk/everyone

Please see the relevant county section for further information on each of these attractions

19

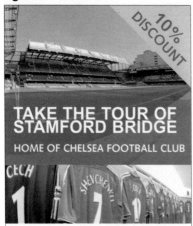

Please see the relevant county section for further information on each of these attractions

Please see the relevant county section for further information on each of these attractions

Please see the relevant county section for further information on each of these attractions

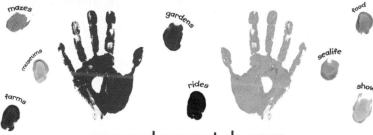

Please see the relevant county section for further information on each of these attractions

England: Nottinghamshire

Take to the trees and experience an exhilarating course of rope bridges, Tarzan swings and zip slides high above the forest floor. Ideal for fun lovers, you'll share around 3 hours of adventure going ape up in the trees.

Book online & watch people Go Ape! at

goape.co.uk
or call 0845 643 9245

Courses nationwide
See our listings in this book under Cheshire, Cumbria, Berks, Bucks, Derbys, Dorset, Devon, Glos, Kent, Notts, Stirlingshire, Suffolk, Surrey and Yorkshire.

BROUGHTON CASTLE

Banbury, Oxfordshire OX15 5EB
Tel: 01295 276070
Email: info@broughtoncastle.com

Civil War armour and weapons, medieval corbel heads, spiral stone staircase and a secret rooftop meeting room used to plot against the King - Just some of the reasons that you should come and discover the wonders of Broughton Castle.

Open from:
1st May until 15th September 2008 on Wednesdays and Sundays and Bank Holiday Mondays 2-5pm. Also Thursdays July and August 2-5pm.

PRIVATE GUIDED TOURS FOR GROUPS ALL YEAR BY APPOINTMENT

www.broughtoncastle.com

COTSWOLD Wildlife Park and Gardens

OPEN DAILY From 10am

from **ANTS** to **WHITE RHINOS** and **BATS** to **BIG CATS** in 160 acres of Landscaped Parkland.

- ADVENTURE PLAYGROUND
- CHILDRENS FARMYARD
- CAFETERIA • PICNIC AREAS
- NARROW GAUGE RAILWAY
(Runs from April to October)

New for 2008 LEMUR Walkthrough

TEL: 01993 823006
BURFORD • OXON OX18 4JP
(Mid-way between Oxford & Cheltenham)

www.cotswoldwildlifepark.co.uk

Mapledurham House & Watermill
Nr. Reading, RG4 7TR

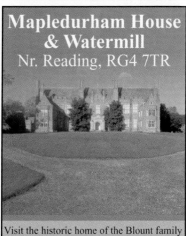

Visit the historic home of the Blount family and the last working watermill on the river Thames. Open Saturdays, Sundays and Bank Holidays from Easter until the end of September 2-5pm. Tea room serving delicious cream teas and cakes. Visitors may arrive by boat from nearby Caversham.

For full details please contact
0118 9723350

www.mapledurham.co.uk

© Estate of E H Shepard 2005
Licensed by ©opyrights Group

The Wind in the Willows

Based on the famous EH Shepard drawings this fantastic permanent exhibition brings the classic story of Mole, Ratty, Badger and the irrepressible Mr Toad to life.

River & Rowing Museum, a great day out

Mill Meadows
Henley on Thames
RG9 1BF
01491 415600
www.rrm.co.uk

THE WIND IN THE WILLOWS
at the River & Rowing Museum

Please see the relevant county section for further information on each of these attractions

Stamford Shakespeare Season 2008

RUTLAND OPEN AIR THEATRE
TOLETHORPE HALL
June 9th – August 30th

The Wind in the Willows
Romeo and Juliet
Richard III

A 600 seat covered auditorium set in stunning grounds. Tolethorpe Hall is situated off the A1 just outside the picturesque town of Stamford.

Come and enjoy a magical evening at one of Europe's finest Open Air Theatres. On-site car park, picnic area, bar and restaurant in historic Tolethorpe Hall.

Box Office: 01780 756133
Brochure: 01780 480216
or book online at:
www.stamfordshakespeare.co.uk

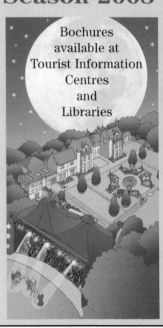

Bochures available at Tourist Information Centres and Libraries

Please see the relevant county section for further information on each of these attractions

Please see the relevant county section for further information on each of these attractions

Please see the relevant county section for further information on each of these attractions

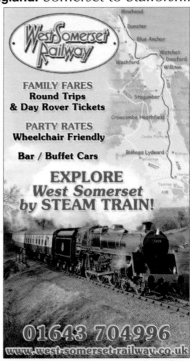

Please see the relevant county section for further information on each of these attractions

England: Staffordshire

Visitors Centre

A wide selection of best-quality fine bone china, giftware & tableware, Seconds & discontinued lines, at discounted prices.

Belleek products & Galway Irish Crystal

Visit our 'Bargain Basement.'

Relax in our 'Pembroke' Coffee Shop

Factory Tours (price: £3.50, welcome beverage included).

All tours must be pre-booked.

For further information on bookings
Please ring Alison Lockett on 01782 339420
Opening Hours:
Mon-Sat: 9.00-5.30
Sun: 11.00-4.00
Bank Hols: 11.00-4.00
Coffee Shop open:
Mon-Sat 10.00-5.00, Sun 1.00-3.00
Aynsley China Ltd, Sutherland Road, Longton, Stoke-on-Trent, Staffordshire ST3 1HS

Aynsley Est 1775

Shugborough > 08

Mansion House, Servants' Quarters, Farm & Mill, Craft Workshops, Gardens

The Complete Working
SHUGBOROUGH
Historic Estate

Near Stafford, only six miles from M6 J13
call 01889 881388 or visit shugborough.org.uk

MOORCROFT
Factory Shop

With a vast selection of handmade Moorcroft giftware and table lamps. All pieces are sold at the factory shop are less than perfect.

With that comes the opportunity to make savings of up to 50% off the usual best quality retail price.

All stock is subject to availability.

Moorcroft Factory Shop
Nile Street, Burslem, Stoke-on-Trent, Staffordshire ST6 2BH
Telephone: 01782 820505 Fax: 01782 820501
Email: factoryshop@moorcroft.com Web: www.moorcroft.com

Open: Mon-Fri 10am-5pm, Sat 9.30am-4.30pm
Closed Sundays. Open for all Bank Holidays.

Made for over 100 years
MOORCROFT
Heritage Visitor Centre

There is something for everyone who comes to Moorcroft

Described as the world's leading art pottery made by the finest craftsmen offering a kaleidoscope of colour and quality

MOORCROFT

Moorcroft Heritage Visitor Centre, Shop, Museum and Bottle Oven
Sandbach Road, Burslem, Stoke-on-Trent, Staffordshire ST6 2DQ
heritagevisitorcentre@moorcroft.com www.moorcroft.com
Telephone: 01782 207943
Open: Mon-Fri 10am-5pm Sat 9.30am-4.30pm
Closed Sundays. Open all Bank Holidays.
Guided Factory Tours: Booking in advance is advisable
Mon, Wed, Thurs (11am-2pm). Fridays (11am only)
Factory Tour Fee: Adults £4.50 Concessions £3.50

Please see the relevant county section for further information on each of these attractions

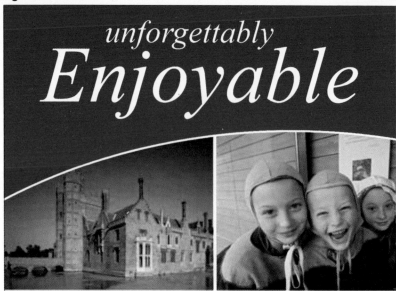

unforgettably
Enjoyable

Great days out - all year round!

There are over 40 fabulous days out for you to choose from in the East of England. From romantic historic houses, inspiring gardens and open spaces, to dramatic coastlines and nature reserves; we look forward to welcoming you time and time again!

For more information, pick up a copy of our Places to Visit in the East of England brochure - available from your local Tourist Information Office or National Trust property. Alternatively, visit the website www.nationaltrust.org.uk

 THE NATIONAL TRUST

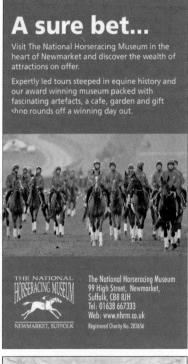

Please see the relevant county section for further information on each of these attractions

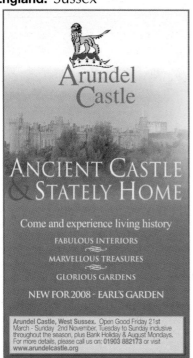

Arundel Castle

ANCIENT CASTLE & STATELY HOME

Come and experience living history

FABULOUS INTERIORS

MARVELLOUS TREASURES

GLORIOUS GARDENS

NEW FOR 2008 - EARL'S GARDEN

Arundel Castle, West Sussex. Open Good Friday 21st March - Sunday 2nd November, Tuesday to Sunday inclusive throughout the season, plus Bank Holiday & August Mondays. For more details, please call us on: 01903 882173 or visit www.arundelcastle.org

Looking for a great day out?

Knockhatch Adventure Park

... so much to see and do!

- **Giant Sky Leap**
- **Trampolines**
- **Birds of Prey**
- **Go-Karts**
- **Adventure Playground**
- **Bouncy Castle**
- **Boating Lake**
and much much more!!

Don't forget to use your **One Child Free** discount voucher from the back of this guidebook!

A fun day out for all the family

www.knockhatch.com

Lancing College Chapel

Lancing, West Sussex
BN15 0RW

01273 465949

Magnificent Gothic chapel set on the South Downs

The chapel is open to visitors every day
Monday-Saturday 10.00-4.00
Sundays & Bank Holidays 12.00-4.00
Closed Christmas Day
Admission is free but donations are welcome

LEONARDSLEE
lakes & gardens

& "Beyond the Dolls House"

Open all week
1 Apr - 31 Oct
Ample parking

Lower Beeding, Horsham,
West Sussex, RH13 6PP
Tel 01403 891212
info@leonardsleegardens.com

www.leonardsleegardens.com

Please see the relevant county section for further information on each of these attractions

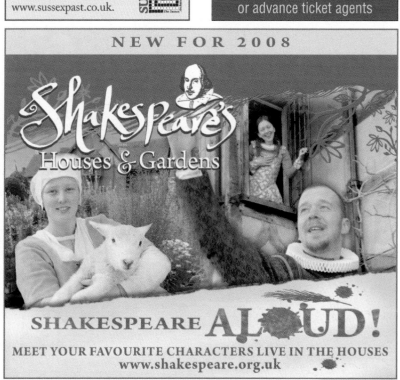

Please see the relevant county section for further information on each of these attractions

Don't worry, he's just a big pussycat.

Set in 50 acres of parkland, Twycross Zoo is alive with rare animals, exotic birds and strange reptiles. Pop in and meet them all in the flesh. For full prices and opening times call 01827 880250 or visit twycrosszoo.org

Atherstone, Warwickshire CV9 3PX

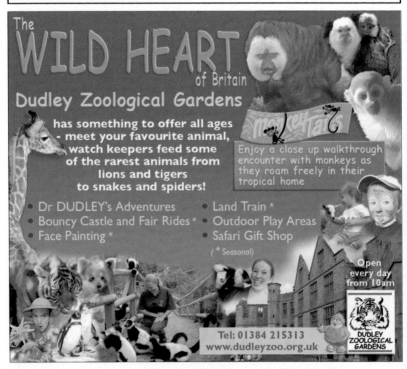

The **WILD HEART** of Britain

Dudley Zoological Gardens

has something to offer all ages - meet your favourite animal, watch keepers feed some of the rarest animals from lions and tigers to snakes and spiders!

Enjoy a close up walkthrough encounter with monkeys as they roam freely in their tropical home

- Dr DUDLEY's Adventures
- Bouncy Castle and Fair Rides *
- Face Painting *
- Land Train *
- Outdoor Play Areas
- Safari Gift Shop

(* Seasonal)

Open every day from 10am

Tel: 01384 215313
www.dudleyzoo.org.uk

DUDLEY ZOOLOGICAL GARDENS

The Birmingham
Botanical Gardens
& Glasshouses

Open Daily (*except Christmas Day*)
9.00am (*10.00am Sundays*) - 7.00pm
(*or dusk if earlier*)

Adults £7.00 Concessions £4.50

Westbourne Road, Edgbaston,
Birmingham B15 3TR
Tel: 0121 454 1860
www.birminghambotanicalgardens.org.uk
admin@birminghambotanicalgardens.org.uk

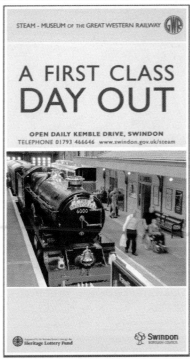

STEAM - MUSEUM OF THE GREAT WESTERN RAILWAY

A FIRST CLASS
DAY OUT

OPEN DAILY KEMBLE DRIVE, SWINDON
TELEPHONE 01793 466646 www.swindon.gov.uk/steam

Heritage Lottery Fund

Swindon
BOROUGH COUNCIL

Please see the relevant county section for further information on each of these attractions

England: Worcestershire

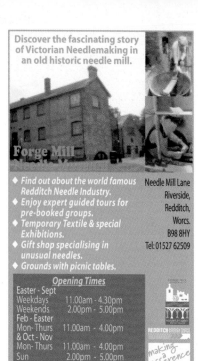

Please see the relevant county section for further information on each of these attractions

38

WHITLENGE GARDENS AND NURSERY

Map Grid Reference:23
Whitlenge House Cottage, Whitlenge Lane,
Hartlebury, Worcestershire DY10 4HD

Tel: 01299 250720 • Fax 01299 251259
www.whit-lenge.co.uk

For the perfect day out,
why not stroll through our 3-acre
inspirational "Show Gardens"

See our Water Features, walk through the brick
Twisted Pillar Pergola, and Living Gazebo, Walk
our Camomile Lawn, enter our Mysterious Cave,
then explore our Labyrinths!

Garden Admission: Adults £1.50 Admission
Free to our well stocked Nursery, with quality
shrubs, trees, and herbaceous, Lastly, why not
pop into our "TEA ROOM" where you can
purchase speciality teas ....and refreshments.

Open: ALL YEAR,
Mon-Sat 9.00am-5.00pm • Sun 10.00-5.00pm
Closed for Two weeks over Christmas,
see our website for more details.

I ♥ Eureka!

And so will you with:
100s of 'must-touch' exhibits

Where children play to
learn... and adults
learn to play!

Visit The
Dinosaur Dig
this Easter
and see The Circus
and Beach this
Summer!

Call 01422 330069

EUREKA!

www.eureka.org.uk

Eureka! The National Children's Museum
Discovery Road, Halifax, HX1 2NE

Action packed value for all the family!

LIGHTWATER VALLEY
THE FAMILY SIZED THEME PARK

www.lightwatervalley.co.uk

NRM
NATIONAL
RAILWAY
MUSEUM

A fantastic free day out

Enjoy action-packed fun
for the whole family!

Open daily 10.00-18.00, closed 24-26 December

National Railway Museum
Leeman Road
York
YO26 4XJ
T: 0844 815 3139

www.nrm.org.uk

*We reserve the right to charge admission for special events

Please see the relevant county section for further information on each of these attractions

England: Yorkshire

North Yorkshire Moors Railway

Pickering - Levisham - Goathland - Grosmont - Whitby

Running Daily:
15 March - 2 November,
plus weekends in
December 2008

Relive the Golden Age of
steam on one of Britain's
most popular heritage railways

Enjoy 21 miles of
spectacular scenery through
the North York Moors
National Park.

FOR A GREAT FAMILY DAY OUT!

Beautifully restored period stations, shops, refreshment rooms, locomotive viewing sheds, historical information, walks in the countryside... whatever you want from a day out, you're sure to find it on the North Yorkshire Moors Railway!

Dining Trains all-year round. Special events include:
Apr: *LNER Festival*, **May:** *Diesel Gala*, **Jun:** *60's Weekend*, **Jul:** *Vintage Vehicles*, **Sep:** *Family Day*, **Oct:** *Wartime Weekend*, **Nov:** *Halloween/Bonfire*, **Dec:** *Santa Specials*

For more information, please contact:
Customer Services: 01751 472508
Talking Timetable: 01751 473535
Email: info@nymr.co.uk

www.nymr.co.uk

QUALITY ASSURED
VISITOR
ATTRACTION

DANGEROUSLY ENTERTAINING

LIVE PERFORMANCES

COMBAT DEMONSTRATIONS

CHILDREN'S ACTIVITY DAYS

FALCONRY DISPLAYS

HORSE SHOWS

JOUSTING TOURNAMENTS

PLUS A WHOLE MUSEUM OF TREASURES TO EXPLORE

www.royalarmouries.org

LEEDS

ROYAL ARMOURIES

The Saltburn Smugglers Heritage Centre

Old Saltburn
Next to The Ship Inn
Saltburn by the Sea
TS12 1HF

Tel:
01287 625252
Fax:
01287 625252

REDCAR & CLEVELAND
RC
BOROUGH COUNCIL

SALTBURN

Discover the sights, sounds and smells of Saltburn.

Its hidden treasures will appeal to everyone old and young!

www.redcar-cleveland.gov.uk/leisure

Opening Times		
21st March-31st May Wed-Sun 10am-6pm, closed Mon & Tues	**Open Spring & Summer Bank Holidays**	
1st June-30th June Tues-Sun 10am-6pm, closed Mon		
1st July-31st Aug daily 10am – 6pm		
1st Sept – 30th Sept Wed-Sun 10am-6pm, closed Mon & Tues	**Last Admission 5.30pm**	

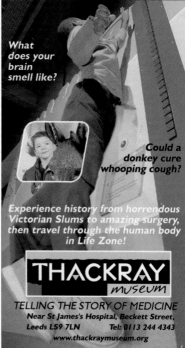

What does your brain smell like?

Could a donkey cure whooping cough?

Experience history from horrendous Victorian Slums to amazing surgery, then travel through the human body in Life Zone!

THACKRAY museum

TELLING THE STORY OF MEDICINE
Near St James's Hospital, Beckett Street, Leeds LS9 7LN   Tel: 0113 244 4343
www.thackraymuseum.org

Please see the relevant county section for further information on each of these attractions

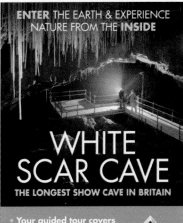
Please see the relevant county section for further information on each of these attractions

Ireland & Northern Ireland

Visit
BUNRATTY
Castle & Folk Park

A Window on the Past

Enjoy A

MEDIEVAL CASTLE BANQUET
OR
TRADITIONAL IRISH NIGHT

Bunratty Castle & Folk Park,
Bunratty, Co. Clare, Ireland
Tel: +353 61 360788
Email: reservations@shannonheritage.com
www.shannonheritage.com

Mizen Head Signal Station
IRELAND'S MOST SOUTHWESTERLY POINT!

In any weather the Mizen is spellbinding.
Keeper's Quarters, The 99 Steps, The famous
Arched Bridge, Navigational Aids Simulator,
Mizen Cafe, Shop@TheMizen.

OPEN DAILY: Mid-march, April, May & Oct Daily 10.30-17.00
June to September Daily 10.00-18.00
OPEN WEEKENDS: November-Mid-March 11.00-16.00

PRICES

Adult	6.00 Euro
OAP/Student	4.50 Euro
Children Under12	3.50 Euro
Children Under 5	Free
Family Ticket: 2 Adults/3 Children	18.00 Euro
Groups 10+	Less 10%

IF YOU MISS THE MIZEN YOU HAVEN'T DONE IRELAND

Mizen Tourism Co-operative Society Ltd 028-35115 Goleen, West Cork, Ireland
www.mizenhead.net www.mizenhead.ie info@mizenhead.ie

Armagh
ancient cathedral city...

Palace Stables Heritage Centre
Based in a Georgian stable block, beside the Primate's Palace.
Experience how the Stables and Kitchen operated in 1786;
visit the walled garden, withdrawing room, experience a Victorian
school room, The Primate's Chapel, Servants Tunnel and Ice House.
Walk in the gardens or on the Demesne.

Saint Patrick's Trian Visitor Complex
Incorporating - The Armagh Story: tracing Armagh's history from
pre Christian times, the coming of Saint Patrick to the modern day.
Patrick's Testament: examining our patron Saint through the
"The Book of Armagh". The Land of Lilliput: Swift's most famous book,
"Gulliver's Travels" is narrated by a 20-ft giant.

The Navan Centre and Fort
Royal seat of the Kings of Ulster. Discover Navan through the
lost myths and legends, archaeology and the history of this
mystical place. Visit the Iron Age/Early Christian period dwelling and,
through Living History, learn about the celtic way of life.

For opening times further information and booking contact:
Armagh Tourism,
40 English Street, Armagh BT61 7BA Tel 028 3752 1801
e: info@saintpatrickstrian.com w: www.visitarmagh.com

Please see the relevant county section for further information on each of these attractions

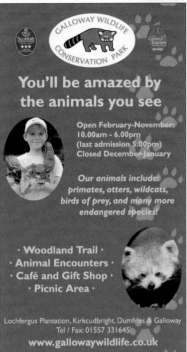

Please see the relevant county section for further information on each of these attractions

- See the crowning place of Scottish kings and the site of the *Stone of Scone*
- Visit the home of the Earls of Mansfield
- Superb collection of furniture, fine art and objets d'art
- The Murray Star Maze, the Pinetum and glorious gardens
- Gift shops, food shops, picnic and play areas, and restaurant
- 45min from Edinburgh Airport and 2 miles north of Perth (A93)

OPEN FROM: 21st March - 31st October 2008
PALACE OPENING TIMES: 9.30–5.30 (last admission 5pm) except Saturday 9.30–4.45 (last admission 4pm)
GROUNDS OPENING TIMES: 9.30–5.45 except Saturday 9.30–5.00
WINTER OPENING TIMES: 21st Nov - 14th Dec (Fri, Sat & Sun only), 11.00 - 4.00
SCONE PALACE, PERTH, SCOTLAND. tel: 01738 552300 e: visits@scone-palace.co.uk
www.scone-palace.co.uk

Please see the relevant county section for further information on each of these attractions

44

what's happening *at* Summerlee?

THE SCOTTISH MUSEUM OF INDUSTRIAL LIFE

Re-opening for Summer 2008

Summerlee Industrial Museum has been closed since 2006 for a major Heritage Lottery Fund supported redevelopment.

The main exhibition hall has had a ground-up rebuild and will reopen for the summer 2008 season with brand-new facilities and displays.

Celebrating the museum's location at the birthplace of Scotland's iron revolution, there will be new interactive displays, working machinery and children's Discovery Zone.

Outside the new hall will be Summerlee's regular attractions – the electric tramway; drift mine (by guided tour) and miners' cottages; timber exhibition and sawmill; and viewing pod and canal walkway by the site of the former Summerlee Ironworks.

– Tour groups are welcome.
– Parking and admission is free.
– Conference and meeting facilities available for hire.
– Open seven days. Closed Dec 25 & 26 and Jan 1 & 2.

For full details on the reopening and events planned for 2008, contact the Duty Manager on (01236) 638460.

Summerlee Heritage Park, Heritage Way,
Coatbridge ML5 1QD

FAMILY ADVENTURE

AT GREENWOOD FOREST PARK SNOWDONIA

GIANT JUMPER
WALES' FIRST GIANT BOUNCING PILLOW

GREEN DRAGON
Family Eco-Coaster

TREETOP TOWERS
WOODEN TOWERS, TUBES AND SLIDES

FANTASTIC ENTERTAINMENT

So much fun for you & your family - rain or shine!
OPEN DAILY MID-MARCH TO END OCT. 10AM - 5.30PM. INFO LINE 01248 670076.
FIND US OFF THE B4366 BETHEL ROAD BETWEEN BANGOR & CAERNARFON.
www.greenwoodforestpark.co.uk

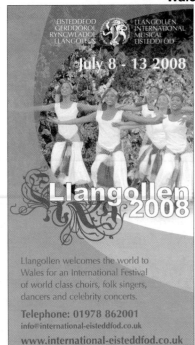

EISTEDDFOD GERDDOROL RYNGWLADOL LLANGOLLEN
LLANGOLLEN INTERNATIONAL MUSICAL EISTEDDFOD

July 8 - 13 2008

Llangollen 2008

Llangollen welcomes the world to Wales for an International Festival of world class choirs, folk singers, dancers and celebrity concerts.

Telephone: 01978 862001
info@international-eisteddfod.co.uk
www.international-eisteddfod.co.uk

Powis Castle & Garden
Nr. Welshpool, Powys, Wales SY21 8RF

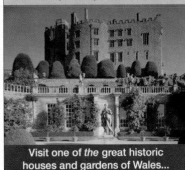

Visit one of *the* great historic houses and gardens of Wales...

Open: 13 March - 2 November,
Thursdays - Mondays only
(also open Wednesdays during July - August)

For information on special events, please visit:
www.nationaltrust.org.uk

For opening times, prices and information on disabled access, please call:
01938 551929

THE NATIONAL TRUST
YR YMDDIRIEDOLAETH GENEDLAETHOL

for further details on how DAYSOUTUK can help advertise YOUR ATTRACTION HERE (or on our website)

PLEASE CALL 01604 622445

www.daysoutuk.com

Please see the relevant county section for further information on each of these attractions

Oriel Ynys Môn
HISTORY AND
ART GALLERY

Rhosmeirch • Llangefni • Anglesey • Wales • LL77 7TQ
01248 724444 • Open Daily: 10.30-17.00

www.angleseyheritage.org

During the Summer of 2008 Oriel Ynys Môn
will proudly open the doors to its new gallery,
Oriel Kyffin Williams - an event eagerly
anticipated by art lovers everywhere.

Oriel Kyffin Williams will be a permanent and fitting tribute
to one of Wales' most celebrated and respected artists.

Oriel Kyffin Williams will have a dynamic and changing programme of exhibitions displaying the artists' work.
This will range from Oriel Ynys Môn's own collection to collections borrowed from institutions and individuals.

Visitors who wish to learn about the cultural history of Anglesey can enjoy the centre's atmospheric **History
Gallery.** One section of the gallery is dedicated to one of the foremost wildlife artists of the twentieth century,
Charles F. Tunnicliffe. This unique collection of paintings records Anglesey's abundant wildlife.

The **Art Gallery** holds up to eight exhibitions every year. It serves to allow artists, sculptors and craftworkers
to present their work on a local, regional and national level.

Boasting an array of unique and exciting gifts (books, toys, prints and much more), the Oriel shop, **Jac Do** is
also home to a superb range of innovative crafts from some of the best craftworkers around.

Oriel Ynys Môn has a newly refurbished café, **BLAS MWY,** where a delicious range of homemade delicacies and
a tempting range of vegetarian and children's meals are available. BLAS MWY is a licensed café.

Please see the relevant county section for further information on each of these attractions

workshops, potters can be found demonstrating traditional pottery skills. There are lots of opportunities for you to have a go at pottery making, throw your own pot on the potters wheel, make china flowers and decorate pottery items to take home. Now open, Flushed with Pride - the story of the toilet - remarkable new interactive galleries dedicated to the development of the humble loo.

All year daily 10.00-17.00. Limited opening Christmas & New Year

A£5.95 C£4.50 Concessions£4.95, Family Ticket (A2+C2) £18.00, Annual museum passport, A£8.50, Concessions£7.50, Family£20.50 (Free entry for a year and other local discounts)

Discount Offer: Two for the Price of One (full-paying adult).

Gladstone Pottery Museum

Uttoxeter Road Longton Stoke-On-Trent Staffordshire ST3 1PQ
Tel: 01782 237777 Fax: 01782 237076
www.stoke.gov.uk/museums

[On A50 signposted from A500 link with M6. Plenty of free on-site parking available]

Located at the heart of the Potteries, Gladstone Pottery Museum is the last remaining Victorian Pottery factory and perfectly presents the fascinating story of the pottery industry. In original

Portmeirion Factory Shop

London Road Stoke-on-Trent Staffordshire
ST4 7QQ
Tel: 01782 749131
Portmeirion produce tableware, giftware, candles, and decorative accessories in glass, metal, textile, and wood.

Potteries Museum and Art Gallery

Bethesda Street City Centre Stoke-on-Trent
Staffordshire ST1 3DW
Tel: 01782 232323 Fax: 01782 232500
www.stoke.gov.uk/museums

[City centre, A50, A52, A53 all meet at Stoke on Trent]

The home of the World's finest collection of Staffordshire Ceramics. A family friendly welcome awaits at one of Britain's leading museums where the unique combination of 'product and place' is celebrated in its outstanding displays. With pottery that will win your heart, galleries that win awards and a Spitfire that won a war. Discover the story of Stoke-on-Trent's people, industry, products and landscapes through displays of pottery, community history, archaeology, geology and wildlife. Explore rich and diverse collections of paintings, drawings, prints, costume and glass. Relax in the tea room with a light lunch or Staffordshire Oatcake. Teas, coffee and pastries. Try the Foyer Shop for unique and quality gifts, stationary and crafts. Ceramic and local history books and souvenirs of the Potteries. Experience our 300 seat Forum Theatre available for hire, for conferences, concerts and talks, not to mention a consistent programme of films for all the family at great prices. There is also lots to learn for all ages in our wide range of educational activities.

1 Mar-31 Oct Mon-Sat 10.00-17.00, Sun 14.00-17.00, 1 Nov-28 Feb Mon-Sat 10.00-16.00, Sun 13.00-16.00. Closed Christmas to New Year,

please call for Christmas opening times
Admission Free

Shire Hall Gallery

Market Square Stafford Staffordshire ST16 2LD
Tel: 01785 278345 Fax: 01785 278156
www.staffordshire.gov.uk/sams

[M6 J13/14]

The Shire Hall Gallery is an exciting and innovative contemporary visual art gallery. It hosts a diverse programme of lively and family friendly temporary art and craft exhibitions throughout the year and has a registered craft shop stocking quality one-off work by British designer-makers as well as a coffee shop serving a range of drinks and snacks. Visitors can also explore the historic Victorian Crown Court which still stands within this listed building, learn about the fate of the people who stood in the dock and see the holding cells where prisoners would await trial. The gallery has a regular programme of activities and events ranging from art for the under fives through to master classes with professional artists. There's also a multi-sensory room, which is available to all visitors free of charge and can be used to stimulate the senses of babies, toddlers and special needs visitors.

All year Mon-Sat. Closed Bank Hol
Admission Free

Factory Outlets & Tours

Aynsley China Factory Shop
Sutherland Road Longton Stoke-on-Trent
Staffordshire ST3 1HS
Tel: 01782 339420 Fax: 01782 339401
[Signposted from Main Rd. Plenty of on-site parking available]
Aynsley China Factory Shop has many attractions including a wide selection of best quality giftware and tableware at reduced prices and also discontinued and seconds ware on two floors, extensive collections of Belleek Parian China and Galway Irish Crystal. Enjoy a snack in the Pembroke Coffee Shop.
All year Mon-Sat 09.00-17.30, Sun 11.00-16.00, Bank Hol 11.00 - 16.00 Closed 25-26 Dec, 1 Jan & Easter Sun

Moorcroft Factory Shop
Nile Street Burslem Stoke-on-Trent Staffordshire ST6 2BH
Tel: 01782 820505 Fax: 01782 820501

www.moorcroft.com
[Plenty of on-site parking available]

The Factory Shop sells a selection of handmade giftware and table lamps, which are all less than perfect. With that comes the opportunity to save up to 30% off the usual best-quality retail price. All stock is subject to availability.

All year Mon-Fri 10.00-17.00, Sat 09.30-16.30. Open Bank Hols. Closed Sundays & 25 Dec.

Moorcroft Heritage Visitor Centre
Sandbach Road Burslem Stoke-on-Trent
Staffordshire ST6 2DQ
Tel: 01782 207943 Fax: 01782 283455
www.moorcroft.com
[Plenty of on-site parking available]

Visit the heritage centre shop where a wide selection of hand made giftware and table lamps awaits you. With a kaleidoscope of colour, all pieces are displayed to breathtaking effect in the shop. Our museum houses fascinating pieces of Moorcroft showing the rich and colourful history of our unique company. Every piece of Moorcroft is made by hand with no two pieces the same. Moorcroft pieces are still made using the traditional techniques, which have remained virtually unchanged for over 100 years.

All year Mon-Fri 10.00-17.00, Sat 09.30-16.30. Open Bank Hols. Closed Sun & 21 Dec-1 Jan incl. Guided Factory Tours: Mon, Wed & Thurs 11.00 & 14.00. Fri, 11.00 only

Admission free (to Shop, Museum & Bottle Oven)

Museum of Brewing and Coors Visitor Centre

Horninglow Street Burton-On-Trent DE14 1YQ
Tel: 0845 600 0598
Offers a unique blend of historic galleries and living heritage.

Spode Visitor Centre

Church Street Stoke-On-Trent Staffordshire
ST4 1BX

Tel: 01782 572598 Fax: 01782 572505
www.spode.co.uk

[Plenty of on-site parking available]

Visit the birthplace of fine bone china. Come with us behind closed doors and see traditional craftsmen at work. Fully guided tours, museum and on site refreshment. There are bargains galore in our Best shop, gift shop, cook shop and Spode factory clearance shops.

All year daily Mon-Sat 09.00-17.30, Sun 10.00-16.00. closed 25-26 Dec, Jan 1 & Easter Sun

Tour of Blue Room £2.50, Tour of Museum £2.50, Combined Tour £4.00

Discount Offer: Two for the Price of One (full-paying adult).

Wedgwood Visitor Centre

Barlaston Stoke-On-Trent Staffordshire
ST12 9ES
Tel: 0870 606 1759 Fax: 01782 223063
www.thewedgwoodvisitorcentre.com

[J15 M6, signposted. Plenty of on-site parking available]

Deciding on a family outing can be tricky. Some people want to delve into history, some want a little culture and for others, only retail therapy will do! The Wedgwood Visitor Centre meets all those needs and many more besides. Set in 200 acres of lush parkland (right in the heart of Staffordshire), visitors can take a fascinating trip behind-the-scenes of one of the world's most famous pottery companies. The award-winning tour allows visitors to enjoy the entire experience at their own pace. Hands-on activities (such as throwing your own pot or painting your own plate) are available in the demonstration area, where individual craft artisans demonstrate their skills, including a Coalport painter, a jewellery maker, a hand-painter and a flower maker. Add to this a superb restaurant, exhibition areas, film theatre, and an exclusive Wedgwood shop, the Wedgwood Visitor Centre offers an all-inclusive day out for all the family.

All year daily Mon-Fri 09.00-17.00, Sat-Sun 10.00-17.00. Exclusive Wedgwood Shop closed 16.00 on Sun. Closed Christmas week

Weekdays: A£8.25 Concessions£6.25, Family Ticket£28.00, Weekends: A£6.25 Concessions£4.25, Family Ticket£20.00

Discount Offer: Two for the Price of One (full-paying adult or concession).

Biddulph Grange Garden

Grange Road Biddulph Staffordshire Moorlands Staffordshire ST8 7SD
Tel: 01782 517999
A rare and exciting example of a high Victorian garden. Tunnels and pathways guide visitors around rare and exotic plantings. Victorian eccentricities such as an upside-down tree, Egyptian architecture and a Chinese garden (complete with temple).
15 Mar-2 Nov: Wed-Sun, 11.00-17.00

Heritage & Industrial

Etruria Industrial Museum

Lower Bedford Street Etruria Stoke-On-Trent Staffordshire ST4 7AF
Tel: 01782 233144 Fax: 01782 233145
www.stoke.gov.uk/museums

[J15 M6 onto A500 then B5045. Free parking off Etruria Vale Road]

The Industrial Museum includes the Etruscan Bone and Flint Mill which was built in 1857 to grind materials for the agricultural and pottery industries. It's Britain's sole surviving, steam-powered potters' mill and contains an 1820s steam-driven beam engine, 1903 coal fired boiler and original grinding machinery. Tea room and shop, children's activities every school holiday, from April to December

26 Mar-7 Dec Wed-Sun 12.00-16.30, Jan-Mar by appointment
A£2.50 Concessions£1.50, Family £5.95

Lichfield Heritage Centre

Market Square Lichfield WS13 6LG
Tel: 01543 256611

'The Lichfield Story' exhibition gives a vivid account of 2,000 years of Lichfield's rich and varied history.

Historical

Ancient High House

Greengate Street Stafford Staffordshire ST16 2JA
Tel: 01785 619131 Fax: 01785 619132
www.staffordbc.gov.uk/heritage

[J13 & J14 M6]

Built in 1595 the Ancient High House is the largest timber framed town house in England. Room settings reflect the various periods in the history of the House; Tudor Bedroom, Civil War Room, Georgian Room and Edwardian Shop, and each has its own story to tell. With educational displays, art gallery with exhibition programme, gift shop and children's activities in each room - there's something for all the members of the family. The top floor houses the museum of the Staffordshire Yeomanry Regiment. Conveniently situated in the centre of Stafford, ideal for shopping, restaurants, theatre and other local attractions, the High House is a 'must visit' destination.

All year Tue-Sat 10.00-16.00

Admission Free. Charges may apply for some events, please call for details

Erasmus Darwin House

Beacon Street Lichfield Staffordshire WS13 7AD
Tel: 01543 306260

Erasmus was a highly regarded doctor, a critically acclaimed poet, a biologist, an inventor and a botanist.

Ford Green Hall

Ford Green Road Smallthorne Stoke-on-Trent Staffordshire ST6 1NG
Tel: 01782 233195 Fax: 01782 233194
www.stoke.gov.uk/museums

[NE of Stoke-on-Trent on B551 between Burslem / Endon. Signposted from A500. Situated next to a Nature Reserve. Ample on-site parking]

Ford Green Hall is a seventeenth-century house, home of the Ford family for almost two centuries. Designated a museum with an outstanding collection the rooms are richly furnished with original and reproduction pieces according to inventories of the seventeenth century. Outside a garden has been reconstructed with Tudor and Stuart features including a knot garden, raised herb beds and a viewing mount. The museum has an award winning education service. Shop and tea room serving light refreshments. Children's activities held every holiday. Wheelchair access limited to ground floor only.
All year Sun-Thur 13.00-17.00 (times subject to change) Please call for details
A£2.50 Concessions£1.50. Wheelchair users & C(0-4)£Free. Groups & coaches by appointment only

Discount Offer: Two for the Price of One (full-paying adult).

Shugborough Estate

Shugborough Milford Stafford Staffordshire
ST17 0XB
Tel: 01889 881388 Fax: 01889 881323
www.shugborough.org.uk

[Off A513, well signed from J13 M6. Plenty of on-site parking available]

Leave the twenty-first century behind and step into the real working environments of The Complete Working Historic Estate of Shugborough, near Stafford. The elegant, eighteenth-century mansion house, Victorian Servants' quarters, homely working farm and walled garden are preserved just as they were centuries ago. At the walled garden meet the character gardeners as they work with authentic tools and seeds. The dairymaids at the farm will show you the very latest technology (early nineteenth-century, of course!) in our dairy where butter and cheese is produced. Our miller will gladly show you his pride and joy - the only working water mill of its kind in the country. After working up an appetite taste the delights of Shugborough's historically inspired dishes in the tea room. Meet Mrs Stearn, the head cook, in the Victorian Servants' Quarters and discover what it was like to be a cook in the eighteenth century. Washdays in the laundry produce a flurry of activity as piles of linen are washed, scrubbed, rinsed, dried and then ironed using flat irons by our costumed laundry maids. Lord and Lady Anson greet visitors in the elegant Mansion House. Set in 900 acres of beautiful countryside with land train, play area, walks and trails there's lots to do for all the family.

14 Mar-29 Oct daily 11.00-17.00, Nov-Mar, Events and pre-booked parties only

A£12.00 C£7.00 Concessions£9.50, Family Ticket(A2+C3) £30.00, (A1+C1) £15.00

Izaak Walton's Cottage

Worston Lane Shallowford Stafford Staffordshire
ST15 0PA
Tel: 01785 760278 Fax: 01785 760278
www.staffordbc.gov.uk/heritage

[Shallowford off A5013 5mi N of Stafford, J14 M6. Plenty of on-site parking available]

Thatched timber-framed sixteenth-century cottage bequeathed to the people of Stafford by Izaak Walton, the celebrated church biographer and author of the 'Compleat Angler'. The cottage is decorated in period style and is home to a small angling museum. An entertaining events programme is available throughout the opening period and staff are on hand to give an insight into both this unique property and the great man himself. Wander around the rose and herb garden or linger over a pot of tea or refreshments from the tea room. A gift shop is available to purchase souvenirs to remind you of your visit.

May-Aug Sat-Sun 13.00-17.00

Admission Free. Charges may apply for some events, please call for details

Samuel Johnson Birthplace Museum

Breadmarket Street Lichfield Staffordshire
WS13 6LG
Tel: 01543 264972
Houses a museum dedicated to this great man and famous writer. With a second-hand bookshop that upholds the tradition of bookselling.

Stafford Castle

off Newport Road Stafford Staffordshire
ST16 1DJ

Tel: 01785 257698 Fax: 01785 257698

www.staffordbc.gov.uk/heritage

[Off A518 Newport Road, SW of Stafford, J13 & 14 M6. Plenty of on-site parking available]

Crowning an important Norman archaeological site, Stafford Castle's ruined Gothic Revival Keep is built on the remains of an earlier medieval structure. The castle site consists of: Keep, motte and inner and outer baileys. The site also boasts commanding panoramic views over the surrounding countryside. The visitor centre, created to represent a Norman guard-house, has an audio-visual display, museum exhibits and a souvenir gift shop. Reproduction period arms and armour is available to try out - a fun hands-on experience for all the family. Limited wheelchair access is available to the visitor centre. A full events programme is planned and coaches and group tours are welcome.

Apr-Oct Tue-Sun & Bank Hol Mon 10.00-17.00, Nov-Mar Sat-Sun 10.00-16.00

Admission Free. Charges may apply for some events, please call for details

Tamworth Castle

The Holloway Ladybank Tamworth Staffordshire
B79 7NA

Tel: 01827 709629 Fax: 01827 709630
www.tamworthcastle.co.uk

[J10 M42, signposted off A51/A5. Rail: Tamworth Station 10min walk away]

Dramatic Norman motte and bailey castle set in attractive town centre park with floral terraces. Fifteen authentically furnished rooms open to the public, including Great Hall, Dungeon and Haunted Bedroom. Living Images of Baron Marmion and the Black Lady ghost. "The Tamworth Story" is a fascinating interactive exhibition telling the market town's history from Roman times to the present day using exhibits from the Museum Collection. Battlement wall-walks, gift shop, interactives and free quizzes.
Spring/Summer: Tue-Sun 12.00-17.15, Autumn/Winter Sat & Sun 12.00-17.15
To Sept 2008: A£5.00 C(under2)£Free C(under5)£1.00 C(5+)£3.00 OAPs£4.00, Family Ticket (A2+C2) £14.50 Specially reduced rate for wheelchair users as access confined to the ground floor

Discount Offer: Two for the Price of One (full-paying adult).

Places of Worship

Lichfield Cathedral
The Close Lichfield Staffordshire WS13 7LD
Tel: 01543 306240
An 800 year old Gothic Cathedral with three spires, dedicated to St Chad.

Railways

Foxfield Steam Railway

Blythe Bridge Road Caverswall Stoke-On-Trent
Staffordshire ST11 9EA
Tel: 01782 396210

Take a nostalgic train journey on this unique
heritage steam railway as it winds you gently
through the beautifully scenic Staffordshire
countryside. With driving experiences and special events.

Sport & Recreation

SnowDome

Leisure Island River Drive Tamworth
Staffordshire B79 7ND
Tel: 08705 000011 Fax: 01827 625490
www.snowdome.co.uk

*[5min from J10 M42. Plenty of on-site parking
available]*

The SnowDome in Tamworth is the ultimate
snow, ice and leisure experience. Whether it's a
fun packed day on the snow, a family outing on
the ice or a dip in the swimming pool, the
SnowDome provides fun for all! The SnowDome
complex houses a 170m indoor slope covered
in real snow all year round and two further nursery slopes, providing the perfect facilities for
learning new skills such as skiing and snowboarding. It's not only skiing and snowboarding
on the main slope, imagine racing your family
and friends down the snow in steerable tobog-
gans! Or hold on tight for the fastest experience
on snow - hurtling down the slope in specially
designed inflatable tubes! The Snow and Ice
Arena features an ice rink, the UK's only Ice
Track and 'mini' rink for first timers, providing an
unparalleled skating facility for all ages and abilities! The children's snow-play area is the place
for children to have fantastic fun with a game of
snowballs and a slide around in the snow. Also
within the complex there is a selection of bars
and restaurants including a Starbucks Coffee
lounge plus the new Swim & Fitness facility
offering a 25m swimming pool with flumes and
inflatable fun plus a brand new 4,000 sq ft gym.
All you need is a sense of adventure!

All year Daily 09.00-23.00

**Discount Offer: Two for the Price of
One.**

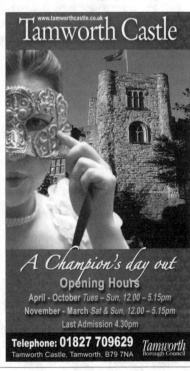

For great hotel deals call Superbreak on 01904 679999 or visit www.superbreak.com

WaterWorld

Festival Park Stoke-on-Trent ST1 5PU
Tel: 01782 205747
The UK's No.1 aqua park.

Theme & Adventure Parks

Alton Towers

Alton Stoke-On-Trent Staffordshire ST10 4DB
Tel: 08705 204060
A family theme park located in the small village of Alton in Staffordshire. Home to many world-famous rides from Nemesis to Oblivion.

Drayton Manor Theme Park

Tamworth Staffordshire B78 3TW
Tel: 08708 725252 Fax: 01827 288916
www.draytonmanor.co.uk

[M42, J9 or J10, M6 toll, exit T2. Plenty of on-site parking available]

For total family entertainment head over to the award-winning Drayton Manor Theme Park, near Tamworth, Staffordshire. Come and experience our brand new attraction - Europe's first Thomas Land, home to Thomas the Tank Engine and all his friends. The magical island of Sodor has been created within the theme park for the enjoyment of the young and young at heart. Thomas Land features 12 wonderful theme rides based on characters, including Cranky the Crane and Harold the Helicopter. There's also a Thomas the Tank Engine train that takes visitors on an enchanting journey around the attraction, as well as a wonderful indoor play area. Drayton Manor Theme Park is also packed with thrilling rides, including the incredible G-Force roller coaster; The Bounty, which swings high, back and forth above the park's lake; Shockwave, Europe's first stand-up roller coaster; and Stormforce 10, one of the wettest rides around. Meanwhile, Drayton Manor Zoo is home to animals including tigers, snakes spiders, exotic birds, monkeys, meerkats and penguins. For special events please visit our website.

The 2008 season runs from 15-March-2 Nov. Rides operate from 10.30-17.30 or 18.00 depending on the time of year. The zoo is open throughout the year, except during certain dates at Christmas and New Year. In the run up to Christmas, Thomas Land will be open on selected dates.

Please call or visit our website for admission prices

Zoos

Blackbrook Zoological Park

Blackbrook Ellaston Road Winkhill Nr Leek Staffordshire ST13 7QR
Tel: 01538 308293 Fax: 01565 308293
www.blackbrookzoologicalpark.co.uk

[A523]

Birds, animals, aquarium, insects, reptiles, mammals, children's play areas, picnic facilities, talks, displays, shop, tea rooms, delicatessen and education room. Group bookings and guided tours available.

All year daily. Closed 25, 26 & 31 Dec & 1 Jan
A£8.50 C(3+)£5.00 C(Under3)£Free
Concessions £6.50

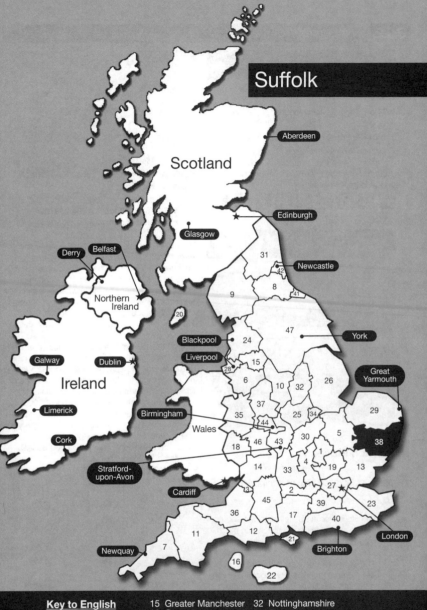

Suffolk

Scotland

Aberdeen

Edinburgh

Glasgow

Derry   Belfast

Northern
Ireland

31

Newcastle

42

8

41

9

Galway   Dublin

Ireland

20

Blackpool

Liverpool

24

47

York

Limerick

28

15

Great
Yarmouth

Birmingham

6

10   32

26

Cork

37

35   44

25   34

29

38

Wales

18   46   43

30

5

Stratford-
upon-Avon

14

4

1

19

13

Cardiff

13

33

2

27

23

Newquay

45

39

London

7

36

17

40

11

12

Brighton

16

21

22

Animal Attractions

Easton Farm Park

Pound Corner Easton Woodbridge Suffolk
IP13 0EQ

Tel: 01728 746475

Educational project to teach children and families about life on the farm. With adventure playground, pony rides, farm animals, Victorian dairy and working blacksmith.

Archaeology

Ipswich Museum

High Street Ipswich Suffolk IP1 3QH
Tel: 01473 433550 Fax: 01473 433558

[Just 5 mins walk from Ipswich Town Centre]

Discover life in Roman Suffolk, find out about the Anglo-Saxon origins of Ipswich and much more, by visiting the fantastic Ipswich Museum. See artefacts from Africa, Asia, North America and the Pacific, plus find out all about the fossils, rocks, and minerals in our region. Enjoy the Victorian Natural History Gallery, where you can see favourites including a woolly mammoth, a rhino, a giraffe and more! Plus discover gods and mummies in the Egyptian gallery.

All year Tues-Sat 10.00-17.00, Closed Good Fri, 24-26 and 31 Dec, 1 Jan

Admission Free

Sutton Hoo

Tranmer House Woodbridge Suffolk IP12 3DJ
Tel: 01394 389700 Fax: 01394 389702
www.nationaltrust.org.uk/suttonhoo
[A12, B1083]

Walk in the footsteps of warriors, pagans and kings at Sutton Hoo. Visit Sutton Hoo and uncover the history of one of this country's most important archaeological sites, the location of a ship burial of an Anglo-Saxon warrior king and his most treasured possessions. This discovery changed perceptions of the Dark Ages, revealing a society rich in wealth and creativity. Take a wander with one of our experienced guides around the atmospheric burial mounds and discover the compelling story of the Anglo-Saxons and their way of life in the Exhibition Hall. Watch history brought to life with costumed characters (daily May - September) and don't miss Sutton Hoo Through The Ages (9 &10 August 2008), a Dark Ages festival with combat, displays, activities and birds of prey - plenty for all the family to see and do. New exhibition for 2008 - Life and Death of a Kingdom: East Anglia 500-869AD, 15 March - 2 November 2008.

1-8 Feb, Sat & Sun 11.00-16.00. Open daily 9-17 Feb 11.00-16.00. 18 Feb-16 Mar Sat & Sun 11.00-16.00. Open daily 19 Mar-6 Apr 10.30-17.00. 7 Apr-20 May Wed-Sun 10.30-17.00. Open daily 21 May-1 Jun 10.30-17.00. 2-24 Jun Wed-Sun 10.30-17.00. Open daily 25 Jun-31 Aug 10.30-17.00. 1 Sep-21 Oct Wed-Sun 10.30-17.00. Open daily 22 Oct-2 Nov 10.30-17.00. 3 Nov-31 Jan 09, Sat & Sun 11.00-16.00.Open BH Mons

Gift Aid Admission*: A£6.20 C£3.20, Family Ticket (A2+C2) £15.70 *Including a voluntary 10% donation; visitors can, however, choose to pay the standard admission prices which are displayed at the property and at www.nationaltrust.org.uk.

Discount Offer: One Child Free.

West Stow Anglo-Saxon Village
West Stow Country Park Icklingham Road West Stow Bury St Edmunds Suffolk IP28 6HG
Tel: 01284 728718
A unique reconstructed Anglo-Saxon village built on an original settlement site.

Art Galleries

Gallery Three at the Town Hall
The Town Hall Galleries Cornhill Ipswich Suffolk IP1 1BH
Tel: 01473 432863

[In Ipswich Town Centre]

Throughout the year Colchester and Ipswich Museum Service hosts a range of events and exhibitions at Gallery 3. Exhibitions and events are linked to community heritage and the town's recent past, allowing visitors to get involved with the history of their community.

All year Tues-Sat 10.00-17.00
Admission Free

Arts, Crafts & Textiles

Bury St Edmunds Art Gallery
The Market Cross Cornhill Bury St. Edmunds Suffolk IP33 1BT
Tel: 01284 762081
Changing exhibitions of painting, sculpture and crafts. Shop with ceramics, glass, jewellery, books and children's gifts.

Birds, Butterflies & Bees

Suffolk Owl Sanctuary
Stonham Barns Pettaugh Road Stonham Aspal Stowmarket Suffolk IP14 6AT
Tel: 01449 711425
Beautiful owls and other birds of prey in spacious aviaries and flying free. Information centre, Raptor Trust Hospital and falconry centre.

Country Parks & Estates

Alton Water
Holbrook Road Stutton Ipswich Suffolk IP9 2RY
Tel: 01473 589105
Water park with sailing, windsurfing, nature reserve, picnic area, footpaths, water sports centre and visitor centre. Cycle hire and catering available.

Clare Castle and Country Park
Visitor Centre Malting Lane Clare Sudbury Suffolk CO10 8NW
Tel: 01787 277491
A 33-acre site fronting the River Stour with the remains of a Norman Motte and bailey castle which overlooks the park.

Factory Outlets & Tours

Henry Watson's Potteries
Wattisfield Bury St Edmunds Suffolk IP22 1NH
Tel: 01359 251239
Produces well-crafted, innovative products that compliment both traditional and contemporary kitchen styles.

Lowestoft Porcelain
Redgrave House 10 Battery Green Road Lowestoft Suffolk NR32 1DE
Tel: 01502 572940
For 200 years, Lowestoft Porcelain collectors have prized this porcelain, and it is now enjoying a historic revival.

TeaPot Pottery

Low Road Debenham Suffolk P14 6QU
Tel: 01728 860475
A visit will show you these world renowned tea pots being made and painted by hand.

Food & Drink

Greene King Brewery

Westgate Street Bury St Edmunds IP33 1QT
Tel: 01284 714382/714297
Start at the museum, tour the brewery then taste the different beers in the Brewery Tap.

Forests & Woods

High Lodge Forest Centre

Santon Downham Brandon Suffolk IP27 0TJ
Tel: 01842 810271/815434
Waymarked walks with extensive facilities.

Gardens & Horticulture

Helmingham Hall Gardens

The Events Office Helmingham Stowmarket Suffolk IP14 6EF
Tel: 01473 890799 Fax: 01473 890776
www.helmingham.com

[9mi N of Ipswich on B1077. Plenty of on-site parking available]

Helmingham Hall Gardens see a wide variety of visitors, groups and clubs, as well as tour operators, from all over the world visiting the captivating gardens each year. The Tollemache family, whose ancestors have lived at Helmingham Hall for the past 500 years, enjoy sharing their passion for the beautiful gardens. The gardens surround the impressive Tudor moated Hall set in a 400 year old ancient deer park. The rich traditional gardens are complimented by a wonderful balance of nature and the modern accents inspired by the current Lady Tollemache, a well-known garden designer and Chelsea Gold Medal Winner. A visit to the gardens makes a perfect afternoon out for everyone. There is a relaxed atmosphere for people to enjoy the serenity and tranquillity of the gardens, to lose themselves in the plethora colour, scents and history. Most visitors take the opportunity to enjoy a delicious lunch or a cream tea in the Coach House and to visit the gift shop, produce and plant stall.

4 May-14 Sept Wed & Sun 14.00-18.00. Sun 25 May: Plant Sale 10.00-16.00, 21 Sept: Autumn Plant Sale 10.00-16.00

A£5.00 Concessions£4.50 C£3.00. Group rate (30+): £4.50

Heritage & Industrial

Long Shop Museum
Main Street Leiston Suffolk IP16 4ES
Tel: 01728 832189
Enjoy a look back at Suffolk's amazing industrial past in this fascinating museum.

Saxtead Green Post Mill
The Mill House Saxtead Green Woodbridge Suffolk IP13 9QQ
Tel: 01728 685789
One of the finest examples of a traditional Suffolk post mill can be seen at Saxtead Green.

Historical

Christchurch Mansion
Soane Street Ipswich Suffolk IP4 2BE
Tel: 01473 433554/433563
Fax: 01473 433564
Discover 500 years of history in the beautiful Christchurch Mansion. See period rooms from the sixteenth through to the nineteenth century and have fun exploring the past. Don't miss the enchanting toys and historic games, as well as beautiful Lowestoft porcelain. Plus you can see the biggest collection of Constable paintings outside of London.

All year daily, 10.00-17.00. Closed Good Friday, 24-26 Dec, 31 Dec & 1 Jan
Free admission

Flatford: Bridge Cottage and Dedham Vale
Flatford East Burgholt Suffolk CO7 6UL
Tel: 01206 298260
www.nationaltrust.org.uk/flatford
This thatched sixteenth-century cottage is at the very heart of Constable Country. Inside, it tells the story of the great painter. Bridge Cottage, Flatford Mill and Willy Lott's House were the subject of several of John Constable's paintings. Today, you can take a tour of the sites of Constable's paintings and enjoy some of the best walks you could wish for in the beautiful unspoilt countryside of the Dedham Vale. Soak up the atmosphere and stand on the spot where Constable stood to sketch his now famous paintings, such as 'The Haywain'. Hire a boat and take in the stunning views along the River Stour or enjoy tasty, seasonal food in the stunning riverside setting of Bridge Cottage tea room (open all year).
2-24 Feb Sat & Sun 11.00-15.30. 1 Mar-30 Apr Wed-Sun 11.00-17.00. Open daily 1 May-28 Sep 10.30-17.30. Open daily 1 Oct-31 Oct 11.00-16.00. 1 Nov-21 Dec Wed-Sun 11.00-15.30. 3-31 Jan 09 Sat & Sun 11.00-15.30. Open BH Mons.
Bridge Cottage: Admission Free. Guided walks (when available: A£2.50 C£Free). When tour guides are not available, audio tapes can be hired (£2.00 per tape, £5.00 deposit)

Framlingham Castle
Castle Street Framlingham Woodbridge IP8 9BT
Tel: 01728 724189
Walk the full length of the remarkable 12th-century battlements that encircle the castle site with their thirteen impressive towers.

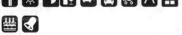

Ickworth House Park and Gardens

Ickworth Bury St Edmunds Suffolk IP29 5QE
Tel: 01284 735270 Fax: 01284 735175
www.nationaltrust.org.uk/ickworth

[2mi SW of Bury St Edmunds on A143, signposted from A14. Plenty of on-site parking available]

Discover the eccentric world of the Hervey family. Whether you step inside the house to be amazed at the central Rotunda and curving corridors or explore the idyllic pleasure grounds outside, you'll never find a day out quite like it! In 1795, the eccentric 4th Earl of Bristol created this equally eccentric Georgian house. Full of internationally important art, Georgian silver and Regency furniture, a visit will transport you back to the days of style, extravagance and excess. Today, visitors can enjoy the splendid Italianate gardens, parkland and woods; with Waymarked walks, tracker packs and children's play area.

House: 15 Mar-30 Sep Fri-Tue 13.00-17.00, 1 Oct-2 Nov Fri-Tue 13.00-16.30. Park & Garden walks: Open daily all year, 08.00-20.00. Italianate Garden: 1-14 Mar, Fri-Tue 11.00-16.00. Open daily 15 Mar-2 Nov, 10.00-17.00. 3 Nov-31 Jan 09, Fri to Tue 11.00-16.00. Shop/Restaurant: Fri-Tue, 1 Mar-14 Mar, 11.00-16.00. Fri-Tue, 15 Mar-2 Nov, 10.00-17.00. Fri-Tue, 3 Nov-31 Jan 09, 11.00-16.00. Park, Gardens, Shop & Restaurant Open daily during Suffolk CC school hols. Open all BH Mons, Good Fri & 1 Jan. Property closed 24, 25, 26 Dec. Park closes at dusk if earlier than 20.00. Italianate Garden closes at dusk if earlier than 17.00

Gift Aid Admission*: House, Park & Gardens: A£8.30 C£3.30, Family Ticket (A2+C2) £19.80, subsequent child £1.80. Park & Gardens only (inc. access to Shop/Restaurant): A£4.20 C£1.10 Family Ticket £9.50, subsequent child 80p. *Including a voluntary donation of at least 10%; visitors can, however, choose to pay the standard admission prices which are displayed at the property and at www.nationaltrust.org.uk.

Discount Offer: One Child Free.

Kentwell Hall and Gardens

Long Melford Sudbury Suffolk CO10 9BA
Tel: 01787 310207 Fax: 01787 379318
www.kentwell.co.uk

[Off Suffolk/Essex border. Ample on-site parking]

Kentwell Hall at Long Melford Suffolk, described by the writer Lucy Norton as 'a little great house of magical beauty, one of the loveliest of the Elizabethan houses that still remain to us, with an exterior that is quite unspoiled, a paradise on earth.' Subject of a unique restoration project since 1972. Extensive gardens, dominated by moats and mellow brickwork, enjoyable in every season. Renowned re-creations of sixteenth-century life. These take place on at least one weekend each month from April to September. Then anything from about 50 to, perhaps, 400 of Kentwell's 'Tudors' re-create aspects of daily life at the Hall over 400 years ago. Also occasional re-creations of WWII daily life. 3 -week season of Open Air Entertainments - Plays, Opera and Concerts (Classical, Jazz or Popular) - in late July/early August. Beautiful, peaceful venue for weddings, dinners, conferences, Tudor banquets and corporate events of all kinds. We do have disabled access but this limited in some areas. Photography within the house is not allowed. Email us on info@kentwell.co.uk

Please call the office for opening dates and times 01787 310207

House, Garden & Farm on non-event days: A£8.50 C(under5)£Free C(5-15)£5.50 OAPs£7.50. Reductions for Gardens and Farm only on all Open Days when no event. Special prices may apply on all events days. Please phone for details

Discount Offer: One Child Free.

Lavenham Guildhall of Corpus Christi

Market Place Lavenham Sudbury Suffolk
CO10 9QZ
Tel: 01787 247646
www.nationaltrust.org.uk/lavenham
Discover one of the finest surviving examples of timber-framed buildings in England. Situated in the Market Place of the historic and picturesque village of Lavenham in Suffolk, the Guildhall was built by the prosperous Guild of Corpus Christi around 1530. Its purpose was religious rather than commercial and it reflects the great wealth generated in Lavenham in the fifteenth and early sixteenth centuries due to the production of woollen cloth, a speciality of this area. Its large rooms now hold a fascinating museum with unique displays on timber-framed buildings, 700 years of the medieval woollen cloth trade, farming and the history of the village. There is a tranquil courtyard garden with dye plants used to colour cloth since medieval times, and a restored Victorian parish lock-up and mortuary. The pretty beamed tea room serves homemade, locally sourced produce, while the gift shop has a range of National Trust and local goods.

Guildhall: 8-31 Mar, Wed-Sun 11.00-16.00. Open daily 1 Apr-2 Nov 11.00-17.00. 8-30 Nov, Sat & Sun 11.00-16.00. Shop/tea room: 8 Mar-31 Oct, as Guildhall. 1 Nov-21 Dec, Thu-Sun 11-4. Shop: 3-31 Jan 09, Sat & Sun 11.00-16.00. Open BH Mons, closed Good Fri. Part of the building may be closed occasionally for community use.

Gift Aid Admission*: A£4.00 C£1.65, Family Ticket £9.65. *Including a voluntary 10% donation; visitors can, however, choose to pay the standard admission prices which are displayed at the property and at www.nationaltrust.org.uk.

Discount Offer: One Child Free.

Melford Hall

Long Melford Sudbury Suffolk CO10 9AA
Tel: 01787 379228
www.nationaltrust.org.uk/melfordhall
Come to Melford Hall and walk in the footsteps of one of the country's best-loved children's writers, Beatrix Potter. The home of the Hyde Parker family since 1786, this mellow, red bricked Tudor mansion appeals to anyone with a sense of romance. Overlooking the green of one of Suffolk's prettiest villages, Melford Hall has welcomed royalty, great authors, sea-faring folk and wartime heroes in its lifetime. Be amazed by the beautifully decorated Regency, Georgian and Victorian interiors, full of maritime related paintings, fine furniture, porcelain and a collection of Beatrix Potter memorabilia. Then explore the garden, with its many specimen trees or enjoy the one-mile circular walk through the park. New in 2008 - new Interpretation Room will allow visitors to find out more about the history of the Hall and the people that have lived there. There will also be new craft displays and events.

22-30 Mar Wed-Mon 13.30-17.00. 5-27 Apr Sat & Sun 13.30-17.00. 1 May-28 Sept Wed-Sun 13.30-17.00. 4-26 Oct Sat & Sun 13.30-17.00. Open BH Mons

House & Garden: A£5.80 C(Under16)£2.90 Family Ticket £14.50

Discount Offer: One Child Free.

Orford Castle and Museum

Castle Terrace Orford Woodbridge Suffolk
IP12 2ND
Tel: 01394 450472
Visit the great keep of Henry II with its three huge towers rising 30 metres and providing commanding views over Orford Ness.

Nature & Conservation Parks

Dunwich Heath Coastal Centre and Beach

The Coastguard Cottages Dunwich
Saxmundham Suffolk IP17 3DJ
Tel: 01728 648501 Fax: 01728 648384
www.nationaltrust.org.uk/dunwichheath
Dunwich Heath is a real glimpse of paradise, with open tracts of heather and gorse, shady woods, sandy cliffs and unspoilt beach, offering you a real breath of fresh air. Situated within an Area of Outstanding Natural Beauty and a designated Site of Special Scientific Interest, Dunwich Heath is the ideal place to enjoy wonderful walks and fabulous views. Immerse yourself in the magnificent display of purple and pink heather and yellow gorse in summer or have fun with the whole family on the beach. Dunwich Heath provides a vital habitat for many rare species such as the Dartford Warbler, Nightjar, Hen Harrier and the curiously named Ant-lion. Don't forget to visit the SeaWatch centre lookouts to see seals and harbour porpoise as well as many seabirds passing offshore. See how many you can spot! Whilst you're there, enjoy some home-cooked food in the National Trust's award-winning Coastguard Cottages tea room.

Heath open dawn-dusk: 5 Mar-20 Jul Wed-Sun, Open every day 24-30 Mar, 26 May-1 Jun, 21 Jul-14 Sept, 17 Sept-21 Dec, Wed-Sun. 27 & 28 Dec, 31 Dec-4 Jan 09, Wed-Sun, 10 Jan-31 Jan 09 Sat & Sun only. Open BH Mons

Pay and display parking. Cars £4.00
Caravans/large vans £5.00 Motorcycles £3.00
Coaches £30.00 (unless booked to use tea room) limited to three coaches. NT members free (please display car sticker)

Orford Ness National Nature Reserve

Orford Quay Orford Woodbridge Suffolk
IP12 2NU
Tel: 01394 450900 Fax: 01394 450901
www.nationaltrust.org.uk/orfordness
[Accessed by ferry only from Orford Quay. Boats cross regularly between 10.00-14.00. Last ferry leaves the Ness at 17.00]
Take a short boat ride out to this wild and remote shingle spit and uncover some of Suffolk's secret past. Known as 'The Island', Orford Ness NNR is the largest vegetated shingle spit in Europe and an internationally important nature reserve. Discover the unusual natural history of the Ness and explore a variety of habitats including shingle, saltmarsh, mudflat, brackish lagoons and grazing marsh. A haven for birdlife and home to a large number of nationally rare species of fauna and flora. From 1913 until the mid-1980s the Ness was used as a secret military test site and today, visitors can walk amongst some of the unusual and intriguing test sites and buildings. Get up close and personal with an atomic bomb!
22 Mar-28 Jun Sat only. 1 Jul-27 Sep Tue-Sat. 4-25 Oct Sat only. The only access is by NT ferry from Orford Quay, with boats crossing regularly from the Quay to the Ness between 10.00 & 14.00 only. Last return ferry 17.00
Admission (including ferry crossing): Non-members £6.50, NT members (ferry only) £3.70.
Children half price (under 3s free)

Discount Offer: One Child Free.

RSPB Minsmere Nature Reserve

Minsmere Nature Reserve Westleton
Saxmundham Suffolk IP17 3BY
Tel: 01728 648281
Includes an RSPB shop and tea room.

Sporting History Museums

National Horseracing Museum and Tours

99 High Street Newmarket Suffolk CB8 8JH
Tel: 01638 667333 Fax: 01638 665600
www.nhrm.co.uk
[On High St in centre of Newmarket off A14. Ample car parking in the town]

The story of horseracing is told through the Museum's permanent collections that feature the horses, people, events and scandals that make the sport so colourful. Highlights include the head of Persimmon (a great Royal Derby winner in 1896, a special display about Fred Archer (a Victorian jockey who committed suicide after losing the struggle to keep his weight down), items associated with Red Rum, Lester Piggott, Frankie Dettori and other heroes of the turf. Learn all there is to know about the horse and jockey and experience the thrill of riding on the horse simulator in The Practical Gallery. Retired jockeys and trainers staff the Practical Gallery and make the world of racing come alive. New for 2008 : Lester - the Legend and Racing Colours both temporary exhibitions for 2008.

Museum: 18 Mar-2 Nov daily including Bank Hols. 11.00-16.30. Café and shop open all year but closed on Sun during winter period. Tours depart at 09.20 on Museum open days (except Sun).

A£5.50 C£3.00 Concessions£4.50 (includes temporary exhibitions), Family Ticket (A2+C2) £12.00. Group rate (20+): 10% discount (must be pre-booked). Pre-booked tours: A£22.00 Concessions£20.00 (includes entry to museum and exhibitions)

Discount Offer: Two for the Price of One (full-paying adult).

Theme & Adventure Parks

Go Ape! High Wire Forest Adventure (Thetford Forest, Suffolk)

High Lodge Forest Visitor Centre Thetford Forest Nr. Brandon Suffolk IP27 0AF
Tel: 0845 643 9245
www.goape.co.uk

[On Norfolk/Suffolk border, off B1107 between Thetford & Brandon. Plenty of on-site parking available]

Take to the trees and experience an exhilarating course of rope bridges, Tarzan swings and zip-slides up to 40 feet above the ground! Share approximately three exciting hours of fun and adventure, which you'll be talking about for days. Book online and watch people Go Ape! at www.goape.co.uk. Minimum height 1.4m. Maximum weight 130 kg (20.5 stone). Under-18s must be accompanied by a participating adult. One adult can supervise either two children (where one or both of them is under 16 years old) or up to five 16-17 year olds. Pre-booking is essential to avoid disappointment. Book online or by telephone (there is a £1.00 booking fee on all telephone bookings).

9-11 & 14-17 Feb, 14 Mar-31 Oct daily, Nov Sat-Sun. Dec Sat-Sun TBC please visit www.goape.co.uk. Closed Jan

Gorillas (18yrs+) £25.00, Baboons (10-17yrs) £20.00

Discount Offer: £5.00 off per person.

Pleasurewood Hills Theme Park

Leisure Way Corton Lowestoft Suffolk
NR32 5DZ
Tel: 01502 586000 Fax: 01502 567393
www.pleasurewoodhills.com

[Off A12 at Lowestoft. Plenty of on-site parking available]

Don't let the year slip by without a visit to the regions biggest and best theme park, Pleasurewood Hills. Set in 50-acres of beautiful coastal parkland just 10 minutes south of Gt. Yarmouth and only 5 minutes north of Lowestoft, Pleasurewood Hills has all the ingredients for a great day out, thrill seekers in your group will be spoilt for choice with plenty of adrenaline fuelled rides including, Wipeout the regions biggest, fastest and most extreme rollercoster along with water drenching rides such as the Mellow Yellow and Wave Breaker. Pleasurewood Hills has so much to offer you! You will come for the rides but you will want to stay for the shows, with a variety of top class entertainment including the awesome Sea Lions, the hilarious Parrots and our breathtaking new thrilling Circus Show. Please see our website for specific opening dates, times and a full price list.

21 Mar-2 Nov (dates not inclusive), please see our website for specific opening dates

Over 1.4m £15.75, 1m-1.4m £13.50, under 1m £Free. OAPs+Special Needs£10.00. Prices will increase during high season

Discount Offer: Three for the Price of Two (full-paying adults).

East Anglia Transport Museum

Chapel Road Carlton Colville Lowestoft Suffolk
NR33 8BL
Tel: 01502 518459

[3mi SW of Lowestoft on B1384. Rail: Oulton Broad South]

At Carlton Colville you will find a unique transport museum, this is the only place in the British Isles where visitors can not only view, but also ride on all three principal forms of public transport from the earlier part of last century - tram, trolleybus and light railway. This collection is one of the finest examples if its kind, and evokes memories for all its visitors.

Apr-Sep

Ipswich Transport Museum

Old Trolleybus Depot Cobham Road Ipswich
Suffolk IP3 9JD
Tel: 01473 715666/832260
The Ipswich Transport Museum has the largest collection of transport items in Britain (devoted to just one town). Everything was either made or used in and around Ipswich, the county town of Suffolk. The collection has been building up since about 1965, and consists of around 100 major exhibits. These include commercial vehicles, trams and trolleybuses, buses, emergency vehicles and horse-drawn vehicles.

23 Mar-30 Nov: Sun & Bank Hols, 11.00-16.00

Wildlife & Safari Parks

Africa Alive

Whites Lane Kessingland Lowestoft Suffolk
NR33 7TF
Tel: 01502 740291
Take your family on a walking safari at one of the UK's largest and most exciting wildlife attractions, set in 80 acres of dramatic coastal parkland. Explore the sights and sounds of Africa and discover, giraffes, rhinos, cheetahs, hyenas and hundreds more African animals.

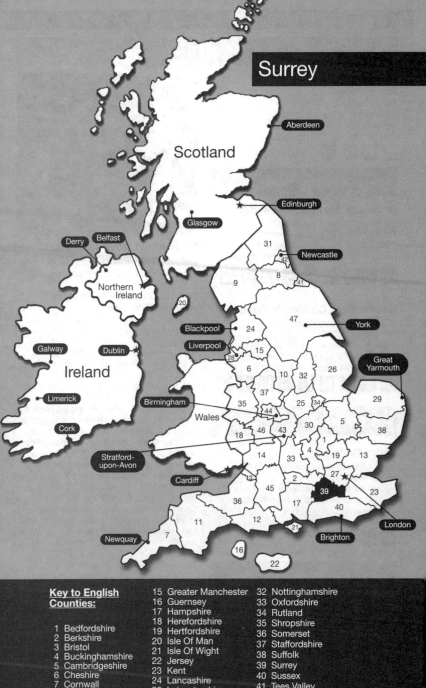

Surrey

Aberdeen

Scotland

Edinburgh

Glasgow

Derry   Belfast

Newcastle

31   42

Northern
Ireland

8   41

9

Galway   Dublin

20

Blackpool   24   47   York

Liverpool   15

Great
Yarmouth

28   6   10   32   26

29

Ireland

Birmingham   35   37   25   34   5   38

Limerick   44   30

Wales   18   46   43

Cork   19   13

Stratford-
upon-Avon   14   1   4

Cardiff   3   33   27

2   39   23

45   40   London

36   17

11   12   21   Brighton

Newquay   7   16

22

**Key to English
Counties:**

1	Bedfordshire	15 Greater Manchester	32 Nottinghamshire
2	Berkshire	16 Guernsey	33 Oxfordshire
3	Bristol	17 Hampshire	34 Rutland
4	Buckinghamshire	18 Herefordshire	35 Shropshire
5	Cambridgeshire	19 Hertfordshire	36 Somerset
6	Cheshire	20 Isle Of Man	37 Staffordshire
7	Cornwall	21 Isle Of Wight	38 Suffolk
8	County Durham	22 Jersey	39 Surrey
9	Cumbria	23 Kent	40 Sussex
10	Derbyshire	24 Lancashire	41 Tees Valley
11	Devon	25 Leicestershire	42 Tyne & Wear
12	Dorset	26 Lincolnshire	43 Warwickshire
13	Essex	27 London	44 West Midlands
14	Gloucestershire	28 Merseyside	45 Wiltshire
		29 Norfolk	46 Worcestershire
		30 Northamptonshire	47 Yorkshire
		31 Northumberland	

Abbeys

Waverley Abbey
Farnham Surrey
[M25 J10, 2mi SE of Farnham off B3001]
Waverley was the first Cistercian Abbey to be established in England. The remaining ruins date from the thirteenth century.

Animal Attractions

Godstone Farm and Play Barn
Tilburstow Hill Road Godstone Surrey RH9 8LX
Tel: 01883 742546
A popular children's farm set in 40 acres of wooded farmland with 3 ponds and a stream.

Horton Park Children's Farm
Horton Lane Epsom Surrey KT19 8PT
Tel: 01372 743984
A friendly children's farm set up for the under 9s. There are lots of different farm animals including cows, sheep, pigs, goats and ponies.

Art Galleries

Watts Gallery
Down Lane Compton Guildford GU3 1DQ
Tel: 01483 810235
Houses the studio collection of G F Watts OM RA, and includes works by his wife and other Victorian artists.
Closed Mondays

Arts, Crafts & Textiles

Toilet Gallery
151 Clarence Street Kingston upon Thames Surrey KT1 1QP
Tel: 07881 832291
The gallery is housed in a converted public loo. Its mission is to provide a free and highly adaptable exhibition space to new artists and provide the community with an alternative art space.

Birds, Butterflies & Bees

Birdworld, Underwater World and Jenny Wren Farm
Farnham Road Holt Pound Farnham Surrey GU10 4LD
Tel: 01420 22140 Fax: 01420 23715
www.birdworld.co.uk
[By road: follow brown & white cockatoo sign boards. 3mi S of Farnham on A325. Well signposted from M3. Easily accessible from M25. Rail: train service runs from Waterloo through to Aldershot & Farnham. Buses run from Farnham Station. Aldershot to Birdworld: 6mi (using bus service). Farnham to Birdworld: 3mi (using a taxi or bus). Plenty of on-site parking available]
28 acres of garden and parkland are home to a wide variety of birds, from penguins to parrots, pelicans to peacocks. Meet some of the birds with their keepers at the Heron Theatre shows and learn more about them. Children will enjoy the special penguin feeding times and animal encounter sessions at the Jenny Wren children's farm. Shop and self-service restaurant. There are play areas and snack bars in the park. Underwater World contains a beautiful collection of marine and freshwater tropical fish, plus the alligators. There is also a link path to award winning Forest Lodge Garden Centre.
16 Feb-end Oct daily, Nov-mid Dec Sat-Sun, mid Dec-early Jan daily, early Jan-mid Feb Sat-Sun. Summer 10.00-18.00, Winter 10.00-16.30. Please call to confirm specific dates
A£12.95 C(3-6)£9.95 C(7-15)£10.95 Concessions£10.95, Family Ticket (A2+C2) £42.00. Group rates available on request

Discount Offer: Two for the Price of One (full-paying adult).

Country Parks & Estates

Box Hill - The Old Fort
Box Hill Road Box Hill Tadworth KT20 7LB
Tel: 01306 885502
An outstanding area of woodland and chalk downland. On the summit there is an information centre, shop, servery and a fort dating from the 1890s.

Festivals & Shows

Hampton Court Palace Flower Show
Hampton Court Palace Grounds East Molesey Surrey
Tel: 0870 842 2227
www.rhs.org.uk/flowershows

[Plenty of on-site parking available]

This year's RHS flower show is set to host an abundance of new and exciting features. In the Growing Tastes Marquee experts will be available for all your questions on growing and cooking fresh produce. Seeing the future is made possible by The Met Office where futuristic gardens will show how climate change will affect horticulture in years to come. The Thai floating market along the Long Water and exciting show gardens with the biggest names in gardening all create a special day out!

8-13 July 2008. Thur-Sat: 10.00-19.30, Sun: 10.00-17.30

10.00-19.30: A£26.00, 15.00-19.30: A£16.50. C(5-15)£5.00 C(under5)£Free

Folk & Local History Museums

Honeywood Heritage Centre
Honeywood Walk Carshalton Surrey SM5 3NX
Tel: 020 8770 4297
Honeywood (a listed building overlooking the picturesque town ponds) houses a heritage centre displaying major themes of the borough's history. Features Tudor Gallery, Edwardian toys, art gallery, tea room and gift shop.

Food & Drink

Denbies Wine Estate
London Road Dorking Surrey RH5 6AA
Tel: 01306 876616
Set in the spectacular scenery of the Surrey Hills, the chateau-style visitor centre offers excellent facilities.

Forests & Woods

Alice Holt Woodland Park
Forestry Commission Bucks Horn Oak Farnham Surrey GU10 4LS
Tel: 01420 23666 / 520212
This ancient forest has a children's playground, the Timberline Trail, the Habitat Trail and an Easy Access Trail.

Gardens & Horticulture

Claremont Landscape Garden
Portsmouth Road Esher Surrey KT10 9JG
Tel: 01372 467806
One of the first gardens of the English Landscape style. With grass amphitheatre, serpentine lake and children's trails.

Painshill Park
Portsmouth Road Cobham Surrey KT11 1JE
Tel: 01932 868113
158 acres of awarding-winning, authentically restored parkland and lake complete with fabulous vistas, unusual follies and a Crystal Grotto.

RHS Garden Wisley

RHS Garden Wisley Woking Surrey GU23 6QB
Tel: 0845 260 9000 Fax: 01483 211750
www.rhs.org.uk

[J10 M25 on A3, London 22mi, Guildford 7mi. Plenty of on-site parking available]

Stretching over 240 acres, Wisley is the flagship of the Royal Horticultural Society demonstrating the very best in gardening practices. Highlights include the magnificent Rock Garden, rock pools and Alpine Houses, glories of the Mixed Borders and Rose Garden and 16 acre Fruit Field containing over 760 apple cultivars. Model Gardens demonstrate design ideas on a realisable scale reflecting changing styles and new techniques. Opened in 2007, The new Wisley Glasshouse shows spectacular exotic plants from around the world. Whatever the season, the Garden serves as a working encyclopedia for gardeners of all levels. Special events and activities take place throughout the year.

All year daily, Mon-Fri 10.00-18.00 (Nov-Feb 16.30), Sat & Sun 09.00-18.00 (Nov-Feb 16.30)
A£8.00 C(0-6)£Free C(6-16)£2.00. Group rate (10+): £6.00

Discount Offer: Two for the Price of One (full-paying adult).

Valley Gardens in Windsor Great Park

Wick Road Englefield Green Surrey SL4 2HS
Tel: 01753 847518
The Valley Gardens, part of the Royal Landscape, is a woodland garden on a grand scale, set beneath majestic trees with delightful views of Virginia Water Lake.

Winkworth Arboretum

Hascombe Road Nr Godalming Surrey
GU8 4AD
Tel: 01483 208477 Fax: 01483 208252
www.nationaltrust.org.uk

[SE of Guilford. Plenty of on-site parking available]

110 acres of native and exotic trees and shrubs. The arboretum is set in a valley in the rolling Surrey hills in an Area Of Oustanding Natural Beauty (AONB). The paths lead down to a lake with a boathouse and newly created wetland area. Winkworth is famous in Spring for its mass of bluebells, and also flowering shrubs such as azaleas and rhododendrons. Autumn, though, is equally impressive as the leaves on the trees and shrubs change colour in a riot of reds and golds and put on a show which is difficult to rival. New planting schemes have ensured year round colour. Dogs on leads are welcome.

Dawn-Dusk

For admission prices and opening times please visit our website www.nationaltrust.org.uk or telephone 01483 208477

Historical

Guildford Castle and Grounds

Castle Grounds Castle Street Guildford Surrey
Tel: 01483 444750
A Norman keep and castle arch, standing high on the castle mound above Guildford. It is surrounded by beautifully-kept castle gardens.

Guildford House Gallery

155 High Street Guildford Surrey GU1 3AJ
Tel: 01483 444740 Fax: 01483 444742
www.guildfordhouse.co.uk

[N side of High St opposite Sainsbury]

Important features of the fascinating building are the finely decorated plaster ceilings, panelled rooms, wrought iron balcony and window catches, together with the richly carved oak and elm staircase. Guildford House dates from 1660 and has been Guildford's art gallery since 1957. Changing art exhibitions throughout the year.

All year Tue-Sat 10.00-16.45

Admission Free

Hatchlands Park

East Clandon Guildford Surrey GU4 7RT
Tel: 01483 222482
[Rail: Clandon or Horsley]
Handsome eighteenth-century mansion set in a beautiful landscaped park. Formal garden designed by Gertrude Jekyll and stunning bluebell woods. The house features the world's largest collection of keyboard instruments and a good collection of fine English, Italian, Flemish and Dutch paintings.
23 Mar-31 Jul: Tue-Thu & Sun (14.00-17.30). 1-31 Aug: Tue-Fri & Sun (14.00-17.30). 2 Sep-30 Oct: Tue-Thu & Sun (14.00-17.30). Also open Bank Hols

Loseley Park

Guildford Surrey GU3 1HS
Tel: 01483 304440 Fax: 01483 302036
www.loseley-park.com

[Leave A3 at Compton on B3000 signposted. Rail: Guildford 2mi. Bus: 1.25mi. Plenty of on-site parking available access via Stakescorner Rd]

Loseley Park, home of the More-Molyneux family for nearly 500 years, is set amid 1,400 acres of glorious parkland and rolling pastures. Built in 1562 by an ancestor of the present owner, the Elizabethan mansion features many fine works of art including paintings, tapestries and panelling from Henry VIII's Nonsuch Palace. The Walled Garden has been carefully restored and includes an award-winning rose garden with over 1,000 old fashioned rose bushes. The herb garden, planted with over 200 herbs (some dating back to ancient times), is divided into 4 separate sections: culinary, medicinal, household and ornamental. Other features include flower and white gardens, organic vegetable garden specialising in companion planting, with an area devoted to producing special seed for the National Seed Library (HDRA), an idyllic moat walk and new wild flower meadow. Member of the Historic Houses Association. Gift shop sells an exciting array of unusual and original gifts based on a gardening and historical theme. Photography permitted outside house only.

Gardens, Grounds, Shop & Tea room: May-Sept Tue-Sun & Bank Hol Mons 11.00-17.00. House: May-Aug Tue-Thur, Sun & Bank Hol Mons 13.00-17.00

House & Gardens: A£7.00 C£3.50 Concessions£6.50. Gardens & Grounds: A£4.00 C£2.00 Concessions£3.50. Group rates available on request, must be pre-booked

Polesden Lacey

Great Bookham Dorking Surrey RH5 6BD
Tel: 01372 458203/452048
Regency country house with renowned
Edwardian interiors and gardens, set in beautiful
downland countryside. Features opulent
Edwardian interiors and a fine collection of 'Old
Masters' paintings.

Royal Logistic Corps Museum

Princess Royal Barracks Deepcut Camberley
Surrey GU16 6RW
Tel: 01252 833371
Tells the story of logistical support to the British
Army from the time of Oliver Cromwell to the
present. Examine how over the last 500 years
the soldier has been transported, fed, supplied
with equipment and kept in touch with loved
ones.

Bockett's Farm Park

Young Street Fetcham Surrey KT22 9BS
Tel: 01372 363764
A working family farm set in beautiful country-
side on the slopes of the North Downs in
Surrey. With plenty of friendly animals.

On the Water

Busbridge Lakes, Waterfowl and Gardens

Hambledon Road Busbridge Godalming Surrey
GU8 4AY
Tel: 01483 421955 Fax: 01483 425903
www.busbridgelakes.co.uk

*[1.5mi from Goldalming off B2130 Bus: to Home
Farm Rd (6min walk). Rail: Milford 2mi, Godalming
1.5mi. Plenty of on-site parking available]*

Busbridge Lakes is situated in a valley of some
forty acres, with three spring fed lakes, home to
over 150 species of wild waterfowl, pheasants,
cranes, peafowl and fancy bantams, from all
over the world, many endangered. It is a
Heritage 2* Garden with follies and grottos; outstanding old specimen trees; nature trails. Much
flora and fauna around the lakes and over the
hills. Wander amongst the birds in the stunning
landscaped gardens, many with their young
babies. An ideal place for photography due to
the wealth of colour and variety of scenery. A
place of outstanding beauty.

*21-30 Mar. 4, 5, 25 & 26 May. 17-25 Aug.
10:30-17:30*
A£6.00 C(3-13)£4.00 OAPs£4.50

Social History Museums

Spectator Sports

Rural Life Centre

The Reeds Tilford Farnham Surrey GU10 2DL
Tel: 01252 795571 Fax: 01252 795571
www.rural-life.org.uk

[Off A287 3mi S of Farnham halfway between Frensham / Tilford follow brown signposts. Plenty of on-site parking available]

The Rural Life Centre is a museum of past village life covering the years from 1750 to 1960. It is set in over ten acres of garden and woodland and housed in purpose-built and reconstructed buildings including a chapel, village hall, cricket pavilion and schoolroom. Displays show village crafts and trades such as wheelwrighting of which the centre's collection is probably the finest in the country. An historic village playground provides entertainment for children as does a preserved narrow gauge light railway which operates on Sundays. There is also an arboretum with over 100 species of tree from around the world. Indoor and outdoor picnic areas.

12 Mar-1 Nov Wed-Sun & Bank Hol Mons 10.00-17.00, Winter Wed & Sun only 11.00-16.00

A£6.00 C(5-16)£4.00 OAPs£5.00, Family Ticket(A2+C2) £18.00

Discount Offer: Two for the Price of One (full-paying adult).

Sandown Park Racecourse

Portsmouth Road Esher Surrey KT10 9AJ
Tel: 01372 470047 /464348 Fax: 01372 470427
www.sandown.co.uk

[SE A3]

Considered the best viewing racecourse and a natural amphitheatre, Sandown Park's exceptional facilities make it one of the top racecourses in the UK. The racecourse has two fantastic areas to watch the racing from - the Premier Enclosure and the Grandstand Enclosure, both of which have convenient Tote betting facilities, bookmakers, bars, and catering facilities. The Premier enclosure gives you direct access to the Winning Post lawn, the famous 'horsewalk' and also the Loch Fyne Seafood restaurant and with a pre-parade ring, parade ring and winners circle, there is no course where you can get closer to the horses. The terrace around the parade ring creates the perfect garden party atmosphere, and is the ideal setting for an evening of racing. There are also 34 private boxes which are spacious, light and bright with balconies, fantastic views of the racecourse, betting and cloakroom facilities. With 30 days of premier racing throughout the year, serious race-goers mingle with those heading for a great day out. For Ticket and Booking hotline call 01372 470047 for Reception call 01372 464348.

A£From 15.00, C(under16)£Free

Sport & Recreation

Campaign Paintball Park

Old Lane Cobham Surrey KT11 1NH
Tel: 01932 865999 Fax: 01932 865744
www.campaignpaintball.com

[Plenty of on-site parking available]

Campaign is situated in 100 acres of ancient forest and has enough space for over ten game zones. Through large investments these areas are not just 'trees and mud' but highly developed themed arenas. These include a film-set designed replica 'wild west' town, a WW2 trench system and 'convoy' scenario with trucks, tanks, jeeps and a scud missile! For those really wet days campaign also has a flood lit all weather speedball arena. Located near Cobham, Surrey, where the A3 meets the M25, Campaign Paintball Park is only 20 minutes from Central London. It is easily reached by train, with direct regular services from Waterloo or Clapham Junction. The site itself is just 5 minutes from Effingham Junction. Opened in 1998, this venue comes highly recommended for birthday parties, school and college trips, stags parties and office outings.

From £12.50

Discount Offer: 100 Free Paintballs.

Theme & Adventure Parks

Chessington World of Adventures

Leatherhead Road Chessington Surrey
KT9 2NE
Tel: 0870 444 7777
A blend of exciting rides, animal encounters, live shows and unrivalled excitement.

Go Ape! High Wire Forest Adventure (Alice Holt, Surrey)

Alice Holt Woodland Park Rucks Horn Oak Nr Farnham Surrey GU10 4LS
Tel: 0845 643 9245
www.goape.co.uk

[Take A325 on A31 (heading S). Turn L after approx. 3mi then follow signs to Woodland Park. Plenty of on-site parking available]

Take to the trees and experience an exhilarating course of rope bridges, Tarzan swings and zip-slides up to 40 feet above the ground! Share approximately three exciting hours of fun and adventure, which you'll be talking about for days. Book online and watch people Go Ape! at www.goape.co.uk. Minimum height 1.4m. Maximum weight 130 kg (20.5 stone). Under-18s must be accompanied by a participating adult. One adult can supervise either two children (where one or both of them is under 16 years old) or up to five 16-17 year olds. Pre-booking is essential to avoid disappointment. Book online or by telephone (there is a £1.00 booking fee on all telephone bookings).

16-17 & 23-24 Feb, 14 Mar-31 Oct daily, Nov Sat-Sun. Dec Sat-Sun TBC please visit www.goape.co.uk. Closed Jan

Gorillas (18yrs+) £25.00, Baboons (10-17yrs) £20.00

Discount Offer: £5.00 off per person.

Thorpe Park

Staines Road Chertsey Surrey KT16 8PN
Tel: 0870 444 4466
With over 25 rides and attractions, Thorpe Park is guaranteed to leave you glowing with energy.

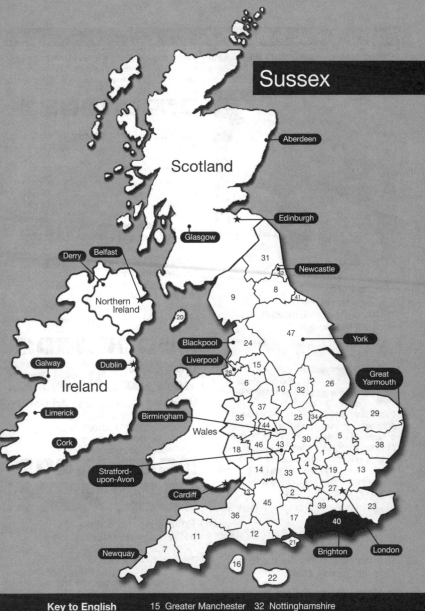

Sussex

Aberdeen

Scotland

Edinburgh

Glasgow

Derry
Belfast

Newcastle

Northern
Ireland

31

32

8

41

9

Galway

Dublin

20

Blackpool

24

47

York

Ireland

Liverpool

15

28

Great
Yarmouth

Limerick

6

10

32

26

29

Cork

37

35

44

25

34

Birmingham

Wales

5

38

18

46

43

30

Stratford-
upon-Avon

14

33

1

19

13

Cardiff

4

27

London

3

2

39

23

45

36

17

40

Newquay

11

12

21

Brighton

7

16

22

Agriculture / Working Farms

Middle Farm

Firle Lewes Sussex BN8 6LJ
Tel: 01323 811411 Fax: 01323 811622
www.middlefarm.com

[On A27 Lewes to Eastbourne rd, between villages of Firle & Selmeston]

See all your farmyard favourites at the Open Farm. Lots of fun indoors and out. Watch our Jersey cows being milked each afternoon from 15.15. Explore the Open Farm Nature Trail and try the scrumptious food and drink from our prize-winning Farm Shop. Enjoy a lovely lunch or tasty tea freshly prepared in the 'Plough Monday' kitchen. Visit the National Collection of Cider and Perry for new seasonal vintages and the freshest apple juice. End your visit browsing in our elegant gift shop for must-have accessories for house and garden.

All year daily, 09.30-17.30. Closed 25-26 Dec & 1 Jan

A&C£3.00 C(under3)£Free, Family Ticket (5 people) £13.00

Discount Offer: Two for the Price of One (full-paying adult).

Animal Attractions

Fishers Farm Park

Newpound Lane Wisborough Green
Billingshurst West Sussex RH14 0EG
Tel: 01403 700063

Meet a great variety of animals to see and enjoy. From chick, piglets and lambs to the mighty Shire Horses. There are soft indoor play zones for toddlers and adventure play areas.

Holmbush Farm World

Crawley Road Faygate Horsham West Sussex RH12 4SE
Tel: 01293 851110
Set in the beautiful Sussex countryside, on the edge of St. Leonards Forest we offer an exciting, fun day out for the whole family with plenty to see and do whatever the weather.

Seven Sisters Sheep Centre

The Fridays Gilberts Drive East Dean
Eastbourne East Sussex BN20 0DG
Tel: 01323 423207
A family run farm for animal lovers of all ages, with over 45 British breeds of sheep and all the other farm favourites.

Archaeology

Worthing Museum and Art Gallery

Chapel Road Worthing West Sussex BN1 1HP
Tel: 01903 239999 / 221067
A particularly rich collection of archaeological finds is displayed in this museum.

Art Galleries

Pallant House Gallery

9 North Pallant Chichester West Sussex PO19 1TJ
Tel: 01243 774557
Pallant House Gallery is a Queen Anne townhouse and a contemporary building holding one of the best collections British art in the country.

Rye Art Galleries

Easton Rooms 107 High Street Rye
East Sussex TN31 7JE
Tel: 01797 222433/223218
Rye Art Gallery has two exhibition areas: The Easton Rooms and The Stormont Studio.

Arts, Crafts & Textiles

Bosham Walk Art and Craft Centre
Bosham Walk Bosham Lane Bosham
West Sussex PO18 8HX
Tel: 01243 572475
Small shops of individual crafts. Glass cabinets with many more interesting crafts displayed. A light and airy gallery with a variety of paintings by local artists.

Brighton Museum and Art Gallery
Royal Pavilion Gardens Brighton East Sussex
BN1 1EE
Tel: 01273 290900
Houses nationally important collections of twentieth-century art and design, fashion, paintings, ceramics and world art.
Closed Mondays

Fabrica
40 Duke Street Brighton East Sussex BN1 1AG
Tel: 01273 778646
Fabrica is an art gallery in the heart of Brighton town centre, committed to promoting understanding of contemporary visual art and craft.

Hove Museum and Art Gallery
19 New Church Road Hove East Sussex
BN3 4AB
Tel: 01273 290200
Displays a collection of toys, films, local history, paintings and contemporary craft.
Closed Mondays

Sculpture at Goodwood
Hat Hill Copse Goodwood Chichester West
Sussex PO18 0QP
Tel: 01243 538449
Sculpture at Goodwood is a changing collection of specially commissioned contemporary British sculpture set in beautiful woodland.
Closed Mondays

Truggery
Coopers Croft Herstmonceux Hailsham
East Sussex BN27 1QL
Tel: 01323 832314
A Sussex Trug is a wooden basket mainly used for gardening. Local craftsmen can be seen in the workshop on weekdays demonstrating preparation of the timber, use of the drawknife and the assembly of a trug.

Birds, Butterflies & Bees

Bentley Wildfowl and Motor Museum
Harveys Lane Halland Lewes East Sussex
BN8 5AF
Tel: 01825 840573
Beautiful Palladian mansion with gardens to match. With a woodland that features reconstructed prehistoric buildings, a wildfowl reserve, a motor museum, children's play areas, miniature railway, gift shop and cafe.
17 Mar-31 Oct, daily

WWT Arundel, The Wildfowl and Wetlands Trust

Mill Road Arundel West Sussex BN18 9PB
Tel: 01903 883355 Fax: 01903 884834
www.wwt.org.uk/visit/arundel

[Close to A27 & A29, at Arundel follow brown signs, 0.75mi along Mill Road on R-hand side. Rail: Arundel 1.5mi. Plenty of on-site parking available]

Set in ancient woodland in the middle of the South Downs, Arundel Wetland Centre holds exotic wildfowl from around the world and much more. Daily fish feeds are held in our Icelandic bird exhibit, and every day Guided Boat Safaris take you deep into the reed beds of Wetland Discovery. Gliding along the waterways keep your eyes open for "Ratty," the water vole and all other amazing wetland wildlife. On Sundays find out about the reserve and who lives there with our Wetland Wildlife Talks. After sauntering around the reserve restore your energies whilst taking in the beautiful scenery in our Waterside Restaurant.

All year daily, Summer: 09.30-17.30, Winter: 09.30-16.30. Closed 25 Dec

Gift Aid Admission: A£8.50 C(4-16)£4.15 Concessions(65+ & students)£7.15, Family Ticket (A2+C2) £22.95, C(under 4)£Free. Group rates (for 12+) available on request and pre-booking is essential

Discount Offer: Two for the Price of One (full-paying adult).

Buchan Country Park

Horsham Road Crawley Sussex RH11 9HQ
Tel: 01293 542088
170 acres of woodland, heath and meadow, with countryside centre and picnic areas.

Southwater Country Park

Cripplegate Lane Southwater Horsham Sussex RH13 7UN
Tel: 01403 731218
90-acre site with adventure-style play area, a beautiful wildlife area, visitor centre and cafe.

Festivals & Shows

Airbourne: Eastbourne's International Airshow

Western Lawns and Seafront King Edwards Parade Eastbourne East Sussex BN21 4BY
Tel: 01323 415442 Fax: 01323 736373
www.visiteastbourne.com

[On Seafront & Western Lawns. A22 from London, A259 from Hastings, A27 from Brighton. Rail: Trains from London & Gatwick half-hourly]

Airbourne is a four-day international air show that takes place along Eastbourne's seafront. There are over 75 flying displays featuring the Red Arrows, the RAF, international aircraft and free-fall parachutists. Also features an RAF ground display, children's entertainment, trade stands, sunset ceremony and fireworks.

14-17 August 2008 10.00-18.00

Brighton Festival

Various Venues Brighton East Sussex BN1 1EE
Tel: 01273 709709
Fax: 01273 707505

[Events take place at various locations throughout Brighton]

Brighton Festival is the largest event of its kind in England. Now in its fifth decade, it has become one of the major milestones in the cultural calendar. This year's Festival features 12 premieres, 9 exclusives and 30 free events in venues, parks and unusual spaces across the city.

3-25 May 2008
Prices vary depending on event

Brighton Festival Fringe

Various Venues Brighton East Sussex BN1 1EE
Tel: 01273 260804 / 260831
Fax: 01273 722996

[Events take place at various locations throughout Brighton]

The biggest open-access mixed arts event in England. Brighton & Hove has held alternative 'Fringe' activity since the Brighton Festivals' creation in 1967. By definition the Fringe can include any art form, from performance to visual arts. Each year the range of events included expands, from circus to exhibition, from classical concerts to club nights and from street theatre to tours.

3-26 May 2008
Prices vary depending on event

Brighton Pride

Pride in Brighton & Hove Various Venues Brighton Sussex BN1 1HG
Tel: 01273 775939 Fax: 01273 775964

[Events take place at various locations throughout Brighton]

The biggest and best free Pride festival in the UK, organised by the Lesbian, Gay, Bisexual and Trans (LGBT) community. Brighton Pride takes over the city for a week in summer, culminating in a flamboyant carnival parade from the seafront to Preston Park on the final Saturday, with street parties on St James's Street.

26 Jul-3 Aug 2008 (various locations). Carnival Parade & Park Event: Sat 2 Aug (Preston Park). The Carnival Parade starts from Maderia Drive at 11.00 and heads towards Preston Park. The Park Event runs 12.00-20.00

Prices vary depending on event

Eastbourne Beer Festival

Winter Garden Compton Street Eastbourne East Sussex BN21 4JJ
Tel: 01323 415442 Fax: 01323 736373
www.visiteastbourne.com

Eastbourne's 6th annual Beer Festival - Eastbourne Borough Council team up with CAMRA's Sussex branch to offer over 120 real ales, ciders, perries, bottled beers and wines. Take your pick from over 120 cask real ales from across the UK. Will your pint be a 'Double Dragon Ale' from Felinfoel (West Wales), a 'Black Gold' from the Scottish Cairngorms or a 'Star of Eastbourne' from Harveys Brewery of Lewes? All weekend there will be live music, pub games and competitions 'on tap.' For further details, check out our website for what promises to be a weekend of fun, music, entertainment and lots of beer.

9-11 October 2008

Tickets available in advance from the Congress Theatre Box Office on 01323 412000 (from July 2008) or online at www.visiteastbourne.com

Discount Offer: £1.00 off individual admissions.

Eastbourne Extreme

Eastbourne Seafront Royal Parade Eastbourne
East Sussex BN21 7LQ
Tel: 01323 415442 Fax: 01323 736373
www.visiteastbourne.com

*[A22 from London; A259 from Hastings; A27
from Brighton. Trains from London & Gatwick half-
hourly. On Eastern Seafront opposite Princes
Park]*

Eastbourne goes 'Extreme' for the 4th time! An
extreme sports event incorporating the land,
sea and air with windsurfing, kite-surfing, thun-
dercat racing, skateboarding, inline skating,
paragliding, sailing and parkour to mention a
few. Check out the UK Windsurfing Association
freestyle and slalom trials. Across the range of
sports there are a variety of demonstrations,
displays and hands on 'have a go' sessions.
Also features a 'Saturday Night Skate'.

19-20 July 2008
Admission Free

Glyndebourne Festival Opera

Glyndebourne Lewes East Sussex BN8 5UU
Tel: 01273 815000 (Box Office)
Held at one of the world's most famous opera
houses, the prestigious summer-long
Glyndebourne Festival aspires to be one of the
biggest and best in the world with a fantastic
programme of performances by world-class
singers. The event is always a lavish affair that
attracts well-heeled crowds where black tie and
evening dress are expected.
18 May-31 Aug 2008
Prices vary depending on event

Horsham Town Centre Festival

Horsham Town Centre The Carfax Horsham
West Sussex RH12 1ER
Tel: 01403 215279 Fax: 01403 215268
www.horsham.gov.uk

[A24 / A264 / A281 all go to Horsham]

The Horsham Town Centre Festival, entering its
17th year, attracts thousands of visitors to the
town centre. Be delighted by a diverse range of
activities including arts workshops, live music,
wacky street entertainment, a traditional fun fair
as well as other fun treats. The feast of activities
will spread throughout the town and as usual,
the majority of entertainment will be absolutely
free, keeping youngsters and adults alike busy
for the latter part of the half-term week.

30 October-1 November 2008 10.00-21.00
Admission Free. Fair rides are charged

Hastings Old Town Week

Various Venues Hastings Sussex
Tel: 0845 274 1001
*[Events take place at various locations throughout
Hastings]*
The Old Town week is officially opened on
Winkle Island and during the week events such
as concerts, street parties, charity races and
Morris Dancing take place. The week ends with
the Old Town Carnival procession, which con-
tains 'floats', dancers, majorettes and marching
bands and ends with a firework display.
2-9 August 2008 (tbc)
Prices vary depending on event

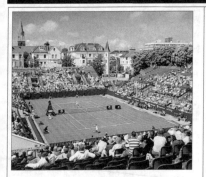

International Women's Tennis Open

Devonshire Park Eastbourne East Sussex
BN21 4JJ
Tel: 01323 415442 Fax: 01323 736373
www.visiteastbourne.com

This major international women's tennis tournament takes place in Eastbourne the week
before Wimbledon. See the world's top female
tennis players compete on the famous grass
courts at Devonshire Park. Last year's thrilling
final saw Justine Henin win against Amelie
Mauresmo and it is anticipated that Justine will
return to defend the title in 2008.

14-21 June 2008

Ground Pass: 14-19 Jun £10.00, 20 Jun £8.00,
21 Jun £6.00, Centre Court: 16-17 Jun Tier 1
£22.00, Tier 2 £20.00, Tier 3 £18.00. 18-19
Jun Tier 1 £30.00, Tier 2 £28.00, Tier 3 £26.00.
20-21 Jun Tier 1 £32.00, Tier 2 £30.00, Tier 3
£28.00. Weekly Pass Tier 1 £150.00, Tier 2
£140.00, Tier 3 £120.00. Tickets are on sale
from : previous customers 25 Feb, general public 10 Mar call box office on 01323 412000

**Discount Offer: Save up to £2.00 off
any full rate price.**

Magners Paramount Comedy Festival

Brighton Sussex BN1 1UG
Tel: 01273 709709
*[Events take place at various locations throughout
Brighton]*
Fresh on the heels of Edinburgh Fringe,
Brighton hosts the Magners Paramount
Comedy Festival, its own homage to all things
funny. The Dome venues play host to perfor-
mances such as Grumpy Old Women, Ross
Noble, Andy Parsons, Jo Caulfield, Lucy Porter
and Sean Hughes.
Various dates in October 2008
Prices vary depending on event

Magnificent Motors

Western Lawns and Seafront King Edwards
Parade Eastbourne East Sussex BN21 4BY
Tel: 01323 415442 Fax: 01323 736373
www.visiteastbourne.com

*[On Seafront & Western Lawns. A22 from
London; A259 from Hastings; A27 from Brighton.
Rail: Trains from London & Gatwick half-hourly]*

Eastbourne's vintage vehicle spectacular, with
over 400 exhibitors. It takes place on the
seafront and includes displays of classic cars,
buses, motorbikes, cycles, cars, military and
commercial vehicles, steam and traction
engines. Vehicles range from 1899-1980 clas-
sics, with vintage vehicle rides, funfair, French
market and cavalcades along the seafront.

3-4 May 2008 (11.00-17.00)
Admission Free

South of England Show
The South of England Centre Ardingly
West Sussex RH17 6TL
Tel: 01444 892700
www.seas.org.uk

[M23, J10 & take A264 towards East Grinstead. At first roundabout, continue straight on along A264. Follow signposts From next roundabout. Rail: East Grinstead & Haywards Heath. Plenty of on-site parking available]

Enjoy the British countryside at its best at the South of England Show. The three-day show is a celebration of rural life and all that it has to offer - from farming and food to crafts and entertainment. For those who live in the town or city it's a chance to enjoy all aspects of the countryside and get back to nature. Children can get close and personal with their favourite farmyard animals - from cute chicks to mighty shire horses - and learn about the environment in a fun way. An action-packed programme of arena events, show jumping competitions, displays, special attractions and amusements means there is always something different to enjoy. New attractions this year include breathtaking motor cycle stunt displays by Jason Smyth's Adrenaline Tour and Titan the robot, which promise thrills, spills and laughs for all ages. And, after browsing the array of attractions and stands, sit back and relax with some of the South East's finest local produced food and drink in the Food Hall and around the showground. Visit www.seas.org.uk - for advance discount tickets.

5,6,7, June 2008, 09.00-18.00

On the gate: Thur A£13.00 C£5.00 Concessions£9.00 Family Ticket (A2+C2)£30.00; Fri-Sat A£12.00 C£5.00 Concessions£9.00 Family Ticket £30.00. In advance: Thurs, Fri & Sat A£11.00 C£4.00 Concessions£8.00 Family Ticket £25.00

Folk & Local History Museums

Horsham Museum
9 The Causeway Horsham RH12 1HE
Tel: 01403 254959
Offers a treasure trove of local history objects stored in over twenty-six galleries.

Marlipins Museum
36 High Street Shoreham-By-Sea West Sussex BN43 5DA
Tel: 01273 462994
www.sussexpast.co.uk
The striking chequerboard facade on Shoreham High Street fronts one of the oldest lay buildings in Sussex, dating originally from the twelfth century. Towards the rear is one of the newest buildings, an award-winning purpose-built extension, with a gallery for temporary displays, education workshops, holiday activities and talks on subjects from Postal History to Pirates. Marlipins Museum (once a Customs House) now holds artefacts from the long history of the Shoreham area and our maritime past. It houses a fine collection of local archaeological material from prehistoric to medieval times. Upstairs are displays on the local silent film industry, the beach and transport from ferries and boat models to Shoreham Airport. Every month sees a new exhibition of paintings and photographs from the Museum's fine collections and temporary shows, including Sussex Sculptors in June and Motor Memories in September. This is also a venue for art demonstrations and seminars.
1 May-1 Nov: Tue-Sat 10.30-16.30. Closed Sun-Mon and Bank Holidays
A£3.00 C£1.75 Concessions£2.50
Discount Offer: Two for the Price of One (full-paying adult).

Forests & Woods

Priest House

North Lane West Hoathly near East Grinstead
West Sussex RH19 4PP
Tel: 01342 810479
www.sussexpast.co.uk/priesthouse

This timber-framed hall house sits on the western edge of Ashdown Forest in the picturesque Wealden village of West Hoathly. Built in the fifteenth century for the Priory of St. Pancras in Lewes, the property was seized by Henry VIII in 1538 and belonged in turn to Thomas Cromwell, Anne of Cleves, Mary I and Elizabeth I. In the sixteenth century, central chimneys and a fine Horsham stone roof were added when it became a substantial yeoman farmer's house. The Priest House celebrates 100 years as a museum in 2008 and contains collections of seventeenth and eighteenth-century country furniture, ironwork, textiles and domestic objects displayed in furnished rooms. Standing in the colourful surroundings of a traditional cottage garden, the house is the only one of its kind open to the public in the Weald. The garden includes borders of herbaceous perennials, shrubs, wild flowers and over 170 culinary, medicinal and household herbs.

1 Mar-2 Nov Tue-Sat (and Bank Hols): 10.30-17.30, Sun 12.00-17.30; 1-31 Aug daily 10.30-17.30

A£3.20 C£1.60 OAPs£2.75, Disabled/Carer £1.60

Discount Offer: £1.00 off each full-priced adult, senior or student ticket.

Pooh Corner

High Street Hartfield East Sussex TN7 4AE
Tel: 01892 770456 Fax: 01892 770872
www.pooh-country.co.uk

[B2110/B2026. Rail: East Grinstead or Tunbridge Wells. Bus: 291 (weekdays)]

The Pooh Corner shop is the 'Gateway' to Pooh Country from where you can explore the settings for the famous Winnie-the-Pooh stories and adventures of Christopher Robin and his nursery toys. The Pooh Corner shop also has the world's largest collection of 'Pooh-phernalia' and was where, back in the 1920's, his nanny brought the young Christopher to buy sweets. Before you start your 'Expotition', to find Poohsticks Bridge, visit Pooh Corner and collect a free map and guide to the real Pooh places. Mike Ridley created the shop in 1978. He met Christopher Robin Milne on a number of occasions and has spent the last 30 years promoting Pooh Country for all Pooh fans so that they can enjoy a visit to this beautiful area. There are no charges to visit Pooh Corner or any of the real Pooh places and they are open to the public throughout the year.

All year Mon-Sat 09.00-17.00, Sun & Bank Hols 10.30-17.00. Closed 25-26 Dec

Admission Free

Discount Offer: 5% discount on all gift shop purchases (when you spend £10.00 or more).

Gardens & Horticulture

Leonardslee Lakes and Gardens

Lower Beeding Horsham West Sussex
RH13 6PP

Tel: 01403 891212 Fax: 01403 891305

www.leonardslee.com

[4mi SW of Handcross via B2110 at bottom of M23. BR: Horsham (5mi). Bus: 107. Plenty of on-site parking available]

Leonardslee, listed Grade 1, has spectacular woodland gardens, containing world renowned Rhododendrons, Camellias, Magnolias and Azaleas. 240 acres nestling in a valley with seven lakes meandering through, Leonardslee provides a paradise for any visitor. In May it is described as one of Europe's most spectacular gardens, when spring flowers blossom they provide an incredible mosaic of colours and reflections. After spring spectacle the gardens calm down to more tranquil environment with softer, subtler, summer flowers, and ending with an exquisite display of autumn shades. There is an abundance of wildlife including wallabies, which help to cut the grass, and various duck, geese and swans. As well as the gardens see the amazing Victorian town in Miniature 1/12 scale called "Beyond the Dolls House"; a fine collection of working Victorian motorcars; and the new Sculpture for the Garden exhibition with exhibits by well known Sussex artists.

1 Apr-31 Oct daily 09.30-18.00

May weekends & Bank Holidays: A£9.00 May weekdays: A£8.00, Apr & June-Oct: A£6.00 C(5-15yrs)£4.00 (all year)

Denmans Garden

Denmans Lane Fontwell West Sussex
BN18 0SU

Tel: 01243 542808 Fax: 01243 544064

www.denmans-garden.co.uk

[5mi E of Chichester on A27. Plenty of on-site parking available]

A beautiful garden designed for year round interest - through use of form, colour and texture. Individual plantings are allowed to self-seed and ramble. Nearly 4 acres in size and owned by Michael Neve and John Brookes MBE, renowned garden designer and writer, it is a garden full of ideas to be interpreted within smaller home spaces. Gravel is used extensively in the garden both to walk on and as a growing medium so that you walk through the plantings rather than past them. A dry gravel 'stream' meanders down to a large natural looking pond. There is a walled garden, a refurbished conservatory and a larger glass area for tender plants. The Plant Centre stocks over 1500 varieties of rare and unusual plants. The award winning Garden Café (Les Routiers Café of the year 2005 for London & South East) serves a selection of light lunches, coffees, teas and a variety of delicious cakes and is fully licensed.

All year daily 09.00-17.00 (dusk in winter)

A£4.50 C(0-4)£Free C(4+)£3.00 OAPs£4.25, Family Ticket £14.00 Group rate (15+): £4.00

Discount Offer: Two for the Price of One (full-paying adult).

Merriments Gardens
Hawkhurst Road Hurst Green East Sussex
TN19 7RA
Tel: 01580 860666 Fax: 01580 860324
www.merriments.co.uk

[On A229 just off A21]

A Unique Experiment in Colour Composition.
Created during the early 1990's the beautiful
gardens at Merriments have quickly developed
into a stunningly beautiful 4 acres of densely
planted borders where the plants grown in the
nursery can be seen in a garden context with a
truly remarkable depth of imagination.

*Easter-30 Sept Daily, Mon-Sat 10.00-17.30 Sun
10.30-17.30*
A£ 4.50 C(5-16)£2.00, Groups 15+ £4.00

Nymans Garden
Handcross Haywards Heath West Sussex
RH17 6EB
Tel: 01444 400321/405250
Outstanding twentieth-century garden with a
collection of rare and important plants, set
around a romantic house and ruins in a beautiful
wooded estate. Nymans House boasts beautiful
family rooms to explore. Outside there are 275
acres of natural woodland with medieval lakes,
seasonal wild flowers and the tallest tree in
Sussex.
19 Mar-2 Nov, Wed-Sun (11.00-16.00)

Pashley Manor Gardens
Pashley Road Ticehurst Wadhurst East Sussex
TN5 7HE
Tel: 01580 200888 Fax: 01580 200102
www.pashleymanorgardens.com
*[On B2099 off A21 follow brown signposts. Plenty
of on-site parking available]*
'One of the finest gardens in England' Pashley
Manor Gardens offer a sumptuous blend of
romantic landscaping, imaginative plantings and
fine old trees, fountains, springs and large
ponds with interest and colour throughout the
season. This is a quintessential English garden
with a very individual character and exceptional
views to the surrounding valleyed fields. Many
eras of English history are reflected here, typify-
ing the tradition of the English Country house
and its garden. Delightful licensed Garden
Room Café offering light lunches and afternoon
teas, which can be enjoyed on the terrace overlooking the moat. Member of the Historic
Houses Association and a winner of the
HHA/Christie's 'Garden of the Year' Award.
*Gardens, Gift Shop & Café: 3 Apr-30 Sep
Tue,Wed,Thu, Sat & Bank Hol Mons 11.00-
17.00. Gardens Only: Oct Mon-Fri 10.00-16.00*
A£7.00 C(under6)£Free C(6-16)£5.00. Season
Tickets: £23.00. Admission for Tulip Festival:
£7.50 (for all). Group rate (15+): £6.50. No
group concessions

Wakehurst Place
Ardingly Haywards Heath West Sussex
RH17 6TN
Tel: 01444 894066
Kew's 'country garden', with 300 acres of
walled and water gardens, plus a woodland and
wetland conservation area.

West Dean Gardens

West Dean Chichester West Sussex PO18 0QZ
Tel: 01243 818210 Fax: 01243 811342
www.westdean.org.uk

[On A286. 6mi N of Chichester & 6mi S of Midhurst. Plenty of on-site parking available]

A place of tranquillity and beauty in the rolling South Downs all year round, the award winning gardens at West Dean feature a restored walled kitchen garden with some of the finest Victorian glasshouses in the country. Over 200 varieties of carefully trained fruit trees, rows of vegetables and an array of exotic flowers and produce are grown in the walled garden. In the extensive grounds visit rustic summerhouses, a 300ft Edwardian pergola, ornamental borders and a pond. A circular walk through a 49-acre arboretum offers breathtaking views of the surrounding countryside and the fine flint mansion of West Dean College in its parkland setting. The visitor centre has a licensed restaurant and a gift shop. The new Sussex Barn Gallery has an exciting programme of art exhibitions which showcase work by internationally renowned and emerging artists as well as students of West Dean College.

Mar-Oct daily 10.30-17.00, Nov-Feb Wed-Sun 10.30-16.00

Mar-Oct A£6.75 C£3.25 OAPs£6.25, Family Ticket (A2+C2) £16.50. Nov-Feb A£4.00 C£2.00 OAPs£3.75, Family Ticket £10.00

Discount Offer: One Child Free (with a paying adult).

Historical

1066 Story in Hastings Castle
Castle Hill Road West Hill Hastings East Sussex
TN34 3RG
Tel: 0845 274 1001
Visit and learn about Britain's first Norman
Castle built by William the Conqueror in 1067.

Anne of Cleves House Museum
52 Southover High Street Lewes East Sussex
BN7 1JA
Tel: 01273 474610 Fax: 01273 486990
www.sussexpast.co.uk/anneofcleves
The oldest part of this lovely timber-framed
house was built in the fifteenth century. It was
given to Henry VIII's fourth wife (Anne of Cleves)
as part of her divorce settlement. The kitchen
and bedroom are furnished in period. The
Lewes Gallery tells the story of Lewes from the
fifteenth century to modern times, the role of
local resident Tom Paine, the Lewes Bonfire traditions and the sad story of the Snowdrop Inn.
A further gallery illustrates the important
Wealden iron industry and there are also displays of everyday domestic objects and children's toys from times past. The historic atmosphere and beautiful enclosed gardens give a
very real feeling of stepping back into an earlier
age. In October 2008, Anne of Cleves House
Museum will host a Tudor Fair that's not to be
missed!

*1 Jan-29 Feb: Tue-Sat 10.00-17.00. 1 Mar-31
Oct: Tue-Sat 10.00-17.00, Sun-Mon & Bank Hols
11.00-17.00. 1 Nov-31 Dec: Tue-Sat 10.00-
17.00. Closed 24-26 Dec*

A£3.65 C£1.70 Disabled/Carer£1.75
OAPs&Students(NUS/USI)£3.25, Family Ticket
(A2+C2) £9.85 or (A1+C4) £8.75. Joint tickets
(with Lewes Castle & Barbican House Museum)
available

**Discount Offer: Buy One Full-Priced
Adult, Senior or Student Ticket and
Get Another Ticket Half-Price.**

Arundel Castle and Gardens
Arundel West Sussex BN18 9AB
Tel: 01903 882173 Fax: 01903 884581
www.arundelcastle.org

[Lower Lodge off Mill Rd]

Set high on a hill in West Sussex this great castle commands the landscape with magnificent
views across the South Downs and the River
Arun. Built at the end of the eleventh century it
has been the home of the Dukes of Norfolk and
their ancestors for nearly 1,000 years. Many of
the original features such as the Crenellated
Norman Keep, Gatehouse, Barbican and the
lower part of the Bevis Tower survive. Between
the 1870s and 1890s the house was almost
completely rebuilt and the magnificent architecture in Gothic style is considered to be one of
the great works of Victorian England. With finely
preserved interiors, fascinating furniture, tapestries, rare art collections by renowned artists,
beautiful well-stocked gardens and the exciting
new Earls' Garden (opens summer 2008)-
Arundel Castle provides the perfect day out.

*21 Mar-2 Nov Tues-Sun 10.00-17.00, (Closed
Mondays except Bank Hols & Aug Mons)*

Castle Keep Gardens & Grounds: All £6.50
(except 2 & 3 Aug) Full Visit: A£13.00 C(5-
16)£7.50 Concessions£10.50, Family Ticket
(A2+C3) £34.00

Battle of Hastings, Abbey and Battlefield

High Street Battle East Sussex TN33 0AD
Tel: 01424 773792

A major new exhibition uses film, computer technology and interactive exhibits to bring to life this bloodiest of conflicts.

Bodiam Castle

Bodiam Robertsbridge East Sussex TN32 5UA
Tel: 01580 830436

A perfect example of a late medieval moated castle. Bodiam Castle is one of Britain's most famous and evocative castles, with medieval battlements, ramparts and moat to explore. Newly refurbished museum with new displays puts the castle in its context.

16 Feb-31 Oct, daily (10.30-18.00)

Boxgrove Priory

Church Lane Boxgrove Chichester West Sussex PO18 0ED
Tel: 01243 774045

This lovely old church is dedicated to St Mary and to St Blaise, and dates from the early twelfth century. From an entry in the Domesday Book, we know that Boxgrove had the status of a parish and that a church existed before the Norman Conquest.

Bramber Castle

Castle Lane Bramber Steyning West Sussex BN44 3FB
[On W side of Bramber village, off A283]
The remains of a Norman castle on the banks of the River Adur, founded by William de Braose c. 1075. The earthworks are dominated by a towering wall of the keep-gatehouse.

Camber Castle

Rye East Sussex TN31 7RS
Tel: 01797 223862
[1mi walk across fields, off the A259. 1mi S of Rye, off Harbour Rd. No vehicle access]
The ruins of an unusually unaltered artillery fort, built by Henry VIII to guard the port of Rye.
1 Jul-30 Sep, Sat & Sun (14.00-17.00)

Charleston

Firle Lewes East Sussex BN8 6LL
Tel: 01323 811265 info line
Fax: 01323 811628
www.charleston.org.uk

[6mi E of Lewes on A27 between Firle & Selmeston. Plenty of on-site parking available]

A seventeenth-century farmhouse, Charleston was transformed from 1916 onwards by the two Bloomsbury artists, Vanessa Bell and Duncan Grant. It is now a place of wonder and inspiration. They took painting beyond the canvas, decorating walls, doors and furniture in their unique style, influenced by post-impressionists like Picasso. They also created a painters' garden, filled with sculptures, mosaics and ponds. The flowers reflect their love of vibrant colour and appear in their still lives. Pioneering thinkers gathered here, like the writer Virginia Woolf, the economist Maynard Keynes, the art critics Roger Fry and Clive Bell and the irreverent biographer Lytton Strachey. Guided tours, on Wednesdays to Saturdays, offer illuminating insights into the bohemian lifestyles and experimental ideals of the Bloomsbury group, as well as the fine and decorative art in this very personal collection. On Sundays and Bank Holiday Mondays visitors can wander freely through this extraordinary house.

Apr-Oct Wed-Sun & Bank Hols. Wed & Sat 11.30-18.00, Thur-Fri 14.00-18.00 (11.30-18.00 July-Aug), Sun & Bank Hols 14.00-18.00

House & Garden: A£7.50 C£5.00 Disabled£5.00, Family Ticket £20.00 Concessions£6.50 Thurs only. Friday themed tour: £9.00. Garden only: A£3.00 C£1.50

Gardens and Grounds of Herstmonceux Castle

Herstmonceux Hailsham East Sussex
BN27 1RN
Tel: 01323 833816 Fax: 01323 834499
www.herstmonceux-castle.com
[Just outside village of Herstmonceux on A271, entrance on Wartling Rd. Ample on-site parking]
Make time to visit this magnificent moated fifteenth-century castle set in beautiful parkland and superb Elizabethan gardens. Built originally as a country home in the mid fifteenth century, Herstmonceux Castle embodies the history of medieval England and the romance of renaissance Europe. Your experience begins with your first sight of the castle as it breaks into view. In the grounds you will find the formal gardens including a walled garden dating from 1570, a herb garden, the Shakespeare Garden, woodland sculptures, the pyramid, the water lily filled moat and the Georgian style folly. The woodland walks will take you to the remains of the three hundred year old sweet chestnut avenue, the rhododendron garden from the Lowther/Latham period, the waterfall (dependent on rainfall), and the 39 steps leading you through a woodland glade. Whilst you are here don't forget to visit the gift shop, tea room, visitor's centre, children's woodland play area and nature trail.
Gardens & Grounds: 12 Apr-2 Nov daily 10.00-18.00 (17.00 Oct). Please call for confirmation of opening times
Gardens & Grounds: A£5.50 C(under15)£3.00 C(under5)£Free Concessions£4.50, Family Ticket (A2+C3 or A1+C4) £13.00. Joint ticket available with the Herstmonceux Science Centre. Castle Tours: A£2.50 C(under15)£1.00 C(under5)£Free. Group rates (for 15+) available on request, please call 01323 834457 for info

Discount Offer: One Child Free (with every full-paying adult).

Lewes Castle and Barbican House Museum

169 High Street Lewes East Sussex BN7 1YE
Tel: 01273 486290 Fax: 01273 486990
www.sussexpast.co.uk/lewescastle

Lewes Castle is one of the oldest castles in England (built shortly after the Norman Conquest) and is one of only two castles in England to be built on two mounds. Although never attacked, Lewes Castle played a part in the Battle of Lewes in 1264 and the Peasant's Revolt in 1381. The panoramic views over the county town of Lewes, the River Ouse and the surrounding Downs are worth the climb up the Keep. The Barbican House Museum (adjacent to the Castle) tells the story of Sussex from the Stone Age to the end of the medieval period. Displays include flint tools, pottery, weapons, jewellery and other archaeological discoveries. It also houses a model of the town of Lewes during the Victorian period at around 1870. Special family sessions on archaeological and historical themes are run throughout the year. Other events include a Medieval Day in May and open-air theatre and music.

All year daily. Tue-Sat 10.00-17.30, Sun-Mon & Bank Holidays 11.00-17.30. Closed Mons in Jan & 24-26 Dec

A£4.90 C£2.55 OAPs&Students(NUS/USI)£4.35 Disabled/Carer £2.45, Family Ticket (A2+C2) £13.55 or (A1+C4) £12.55. Joint tickets (with Anne of Cleves House Museum) available

Discount Offer: Buy One Full-Priced Adult, Senior or Student Ticket and Get Another Ticket Half-Price.

For great hotel deals call Superbreak on 01904 679999 or visit www.superbreak.com

Michelham Priory
Upper Dicker Nr Hailsham East Sussex
BN27 3QS
Tel: 01323 844224 Fax: 01323 844030
www.sussexpast.co.uk

[Plenty of on-site parking available]

The buildings at Michelham Priory have evolved over 800 years. The range of furniture and artefacts on display trace the property's religious origins through its life as a working farm and its development as a country house. Objects include tapestries, furniture (including some made in the 1920s/1930s for the owner at that time), kitchen equipment and a fully furnished eighteenth-century child's bedroom. Seven acres of superb gardens are enhanced by a fourteenth-century gatehouse, fully restored medieval watermill, Kitchen, Physic Herb and Cloister Gardens, a working forge, rope museum and a dramatic Elizabethan Great Barn, now used for weddings, corporate functions and as exhibition space. See our website for special events including the Spring Garden Festival in mid-April, an exciting Celtic Weekend with Iron Age living history activities followed by a new event, an Antiques and Collectors Fair at the end of June. Mid-summer sees three popular events, the Game and Country Fair in July, Sussex Guild's Crafts in Action in August and the Medieval Market weekend held early September. The season ends with the sell-out Christmas Gift and Craft Fair at the end of November. Disabled access and wheelchair loan. Call 01323 849141 for Catering.

1 Mar-2 Nov: Tue-Sun (daily in Aug) and Bank Hols from 10.30

A£6.25 C&Disabled/Carer£3.25 OAPs&Students(NUS/USI)£5.20, Family Ticket (A2+C2) £15.95

Discount Offer: £1.00 off each full-priced adult, senior or student ticket.

Petworth House and Park
Petworth West Sussex GU28 0AE
Tel: 01798 342207 Fax: 01798 342963
www.nationaltrust.org.uk/petworth

[A272 / A283 centre of Petworth. Plenty of on-site parking available]

Magnificent mansion set in 700 acre deer park landscaped by 'Capability' Brown. State rooms contain the largest collection of paintings and sculpture in the care of the National Trust. To include works by Turner, Van Dyck, Blake and Claude. Intricate Grinling Gibbons carving in the Carved Room and beautiful Laguerre murals in the Grand Staircase. Fascinating Servants' Quarters to include Victorian kitchens and ancillary rooms. Guided tours by prior arrangement. Picnics allowed - no special seating or covered area. Events and exhibitions throughout the year.

House: 15 Mar-5 Nov Sat-Wed (open Good Fri) 11.00-16.30. Extra rooms shown weekdays (by kind permission of Lord & Lady Egremont), (not Bank Hol Mons): Mon - White & Gold Room and White Library Tue-Wed three bedrooms on first floor. Pleasure Ground & Car Park: as House but 11.00-18.00. Park: daily 08.00-dusk (closes 12.00 for open air concerts)

House, Pleasure Ground & Servants' Quarters: A£9.50 C(5-17)£4.80, Family Ticket (A2+C2) £23.80. Pleasure Grounds only: A£3.80 C£1.90. Park: Car park £2.00. NT Members £Free. Private Guided Tours for booked groups. Group rate (15+): A£7.50

Pevensey Castle

Castle Road Pevensey East Sussex BN24 5LG
Tel: 01323 762604

With a history stretching back over sixteen centuries, Pevensey Castle chronicles more graphically than any other fortress the story of Britain's south coast defences. An exhibition with artefacts found on site and an audio tour tell the story of the castle.

Royal Pavilion

Brighton East Sussex BN1 1EE
Tel: 01273 290900

Decorated in Chinese taste with an Indian exterior, this Regency palace is quite breathtaking.

Weald and Downland Open Air Museum

Singleton Chichester West Sussex PO18 0EU
Tel: 01243 811348 Fax: 01243 811475
www.wealddown.co.uk

[On A286 between Midhurst & Chichester. Discounted combined ticket on Stagecoach Coastline Bus. Plenty of free on-site parking available]

Situated in a beautiful downland setting, this museum displays more than 45 rescued historic buildings from south-east England. The buildings range from medieval houses to a nineteenth-century schoolhouse and Victorian labourers cottages. There is a medieval farmstead complete with animals, seven period gardens, a lakeside café, indoor and outdoor picnic areas, a working watermill, rural crafts, trade demonstrations and a working Tudor kitchen in an original Tudor service building. Shire horses and working cattle may be seen at seasonal tasks around the site. The first major timber gridshell building in Britain houses a conservation workshop and the Museum's collection of rural artefacts.

2 Jan-27 Feb Wed, Sat & Sun Only, plus daily for half term 18-22 Feb. 1 Mar-23 Dec Open daily. 10.30-18:00 during Bristish Summer Time, 10:30-16:00 rest of year

A£8.50 C(5+)£4.50 OAPs£7.50, Family Ticket(A2+C3) £23.30

Discount Offer: One Child Free.

Maritime

Shipwreck and Coastal Heritage Centre

Rock-A-Nore Road Hastings East Sussex TN34 3DW
Tel: 01424 437452

Tells the unique story of the maritime Hastings area, encouraging visitors to explore the 'maritime park' shore at low tide. They will also discover how to find the two major historic shipwrecks on the beach nearby.

Smugglers Adventure

St. Clements Caves Cobourg Place West Hill Hastings East Sussex TN34 3HY
Tel: 01424 422964

A labyrinth of caverns and passages. Tour a comprehensive exhibition and museum including video presentation, before embarking on the Adventure Walk - a trip through several acres of caves.

Military & Defence Museums

Redoubt Fortress and Military Museum

Redoubt Fortress Royal Parade Eastbourne East Sussex BN22 7AQ
Tel: 01323 410300

Built in the early 1800's, the Redoubt has defended the Eastbourne coast for nearly 200 years. Today this magnificent building houses the rich military collections of The Royal Sussex Regiment, The Queen's Royal Irish Hussars and the Sussex Combined Services.

Nature & Conservation Parks

Pulborough Brooks RSPB Nature Reserve

Wiggonholt Pulborough West Sussex RH20 2EL
Tel: 01798 875851 Fax: 01798 873816
www.rspb.co.uk

[Off A283, follow brown tourist signs from Pulborough. Plenty of on-site parking available]

Set in the sheltered Arun Valley, in the heart of West Sussex, Pulborough Brooks is a fantastic place for a day out for people of all ages. There is a superb nature reserve and trail with bird watching hides and viewpoints, a visitor centre with a gift shop and a tea room with terrace, not to mention the play area! There is something of interest to see and hear throughout the year. Families can come and use the play area, look around the shop and enjoy lunch in the tearoom, without having to pay an entry charge. For those wishing to venture further, the reserve's nature trail offers a gentle walk with lots to see and do for just £7.00 for the whole family. A range of events run throughout the year and many are especially for kids and families.

All year daily. Nature Trail: 09.00-21.00 or dusk if sooner. Visitor Centre: daily 9.30-17.00. Closed 25 & 26 Dec

A£3.50 C£1.00 Concessions£2.50, Family Ticket (A2+C4) £7.00

Discount Offer: 50% off One Family Ticket (A2+C4 £3.50).

Places of Worship

Arundel Cathedral

Parsons Hill Arundel West Sussex BN18 9AY
Tel: 01903 882297
Built for the fifteenth Duke of Norfolk in 1873, the cathedral was constructed in the French Gothic style of 1300, with Romantic features such as pinnacles, flying buttresses and gargoyles.

Chichester Cathedral

West Street Chichester West Sussex PO19 1PX
Tel: 01243 782595 Fax: 01243 812499
www.chichestercathedral.org.uk

[City centre]

In the heart of the city, this fine cathedral has been a centre of worship and community life for 900 years and is the site of the Shrine of St Richard. Its treasures range from Romanesque stone carvings to twentieth-century works of art by Feibusch, Benker-Schirmer, Chagall, Piper, Procktor, Skelton, Sutherland and Jackson. The delightful Cloisters Café on site offering a selection of homemade food, snacks and drinks. Shop situated next to café. Guided tours are available; general or specialist. Loop system during cathedral services; touch and hearing centre and Braille guide for the blind. Assistance dogs only.

End Mar-end Sept daily 07.15-19.00, end Sept-end Mar 07.15-18.00

Admission Free - Donations invited

Railways

Lancing College Chapel

Lancing West Sussex BN15 0RW
Tel: 01273 465949 Fax: 01273 464720

[Midway between Lancing & Shoreham, off A27 N of Shoreham Airport. Plenty of on-site parking available]

Magnificent Gothic Chapel set on the South Downs. Founded in 1868 and dedicated in 1911. Lancing College Chapel is the largest school chapel in the world - the height of the nave is 90ft to the apex of the vault. The out-standing feature is the Rose window, dedicated by Archbishop Coggan in the presence of H.R.H. The Prince of Wales, in 1978 - At 32ft in diameter it is the largest in England. Come and view the many other features of this magnificent building, including the stained glass window dedicated by Archbishop Desmond Tutu on 22nd May 2007 in memory of Bishop Trevor Huddleston, a pupil at Lancing in the late 1920's.The school, founded by Nathaniel Woodward in 1848, is an independent boarding and day school for boys and girls aged 13-18.

Mon-Sat 10.00-16.00, Sundays & Bank Hols 12.00-16.00

Free Admission-Donations welcome

St Mary's Church

Lion Street Rye East Sussex TN31 7LB
Tel: 01797 224935
For 900 years the Parish Church has dominated the hill on which Rye stands. It has the oldest church turret clock in the country (which is still functioning).

Bluebell Railway

Sheffield Park Station Uckfield East Sussex TN22 3QL
Tel: 01825 722370/720800 Fax: 01825 720804
www.bluebell-railway.co.uk

[A275 between Lewes & East Grinstead]

Here you will find the locomotive sheds, shop, museum and restaurant. Trains run between Sheffield Park, Horsted Keynes and Kingscote. An 18 mile round trip between Sheffield Park and Kingscote through open countryside.

All year Sat & Sun, Apr-Oct daily
A10.50 C(3-15)£5.25, Family Ticket(A2+C3)£30.00. Discounts are available for early booking

Eastbourne Miniature Steam Railway Park

Lottbridge Drove Eastbourne Sussex BN23 6NS
Tel: 01323 520229
A railway adventure in Rastbourne. Visitors can take an eighth-scale miniature steam and diesel-hauled passenger train journey for a mile around Southbourne Lake. There is also an 'environmental excursion' nature trail offering an insight into local history, wildlife, flora and fauna. Children's playground and wilow maze. Café and gift shop.

Roman Era

Fishbourne Roman Palace

Salthill Road Fishbourne Chichester West
Sussex PO19 3QR
Tel: 01243 785859 Fax: 01243 539266
www.sussexpast.co.uk/fishbourne

[5 min walk from Train Station. Plenty of on-site parking available]

The remains of the late-first-century palace at
Fishbourne were first discovered in 1960. After
extensive archaeological excavations, a cover
building protects the impressive remains of one
wing. Here you can see Britain's largest collection of in-situ Roman floor mosaics. Other
everyday Roman objects found from the excavations are displayed in the museum gallery. An
audio-visual presentation uses computer-gener-
ated images to explain the site. Outside, the
garden has been replanted to its original plan,
using plants that may have been grown then. A
fascinating 'Collections Discovery Centre' displays and houses yet more artefacts from both
Fishbourne and Chichester district. Join a
behind-the-scenes tour for an opportunity to
handle some of these ancient objects (£2.00).
Special events throughout the year include a
Celtic Spring Festival in April, a Roman
Gladiator re-enactment weekend in September
and a week of Roman army activities for all the
family during October half term.

*22 Jan-15 Dec daily. 22 Jan-Feb 10.00-16.00,
Mar-July & Sep-Oct 10.00-17.00, Aug 10.00-
18.00, 1 Nov-15 Dec 10.00-16.00. Also open
Sat-Sun in Dec 10.00-16.00*

A£7.00 C£3.70 OAPs&Students(NUS/USI)£6.00
Disabled/Carer £5.50, Family Ticket (A2+C2)
£17.90

**Discount Offer: Buy One Full-Priced
Adult, Senior or Student Ticket and**

Get Another Ticket Half-Price.

Science - Earth & Planetary

Observatory Science Centre

Herstmonceux Hailsham East Sussex
BN27 1RN
Tel: 01323 832731 Fax: 01323 832741
www.the-observatory.org

*[2mi E of Herstmonceux village, on Boreham St to
Pevensey Road. Look for sign to 'Herstmonceux
Castle & Science Centre' from A271. Plenty of
on-site parking available]*

The Royal Greenwich Observatory (RGO) was
founded at Greenwich in London in 1675 by
King Charles II but was moved just after the
second world war in order to escape the lights
and pollution of the city. The site at
Herstmonceux was chosen as the most suitable
in the UK. The existing telescopes were aug-
mented in 1967 by the giant 98-inch Isaac
Newton Telescope (INT). The domes, buildings
and telescopes are being renovated and the
centre is a major venue for exhibitions, lectures
and educational programmes. Events and activities programme.

All year daily 26 Jan-30 Nov

A£7.00 C(under4)£Free C(4-15)£5.18
OAPs£5.45, Family Ticket (A2+C2 or A1+C3)
£21.50 or (A2+C3 or A1+C4) £24.50

Sealife Centres & Aquariums

Brighton Sea Life Centre

Marine Parade Brighton East Sussex BN2 1TB
Tel: 01273 604234 Fax: 01273 681840
www.sealifeeurope.com
[A23, M233]
Welcome to the magical marine world. Brighton Sea Life Centre will introduce you to many strange, beautiful and fascinating creatures of the deep. Prepare for astonishing close views of everything from humble starfish to mighty sharks and giant sea turtles, all in displays that carefully recreate their natural habitats. Explore a rich variety of underwater environments, from freshwater streams to the rugged coastline, from the sandy shallows to the dark depths of the ocean. At every step there are different amazing creatures to find, to watch and to learn about. Discover the truth about the much-mis-understood shark, the plight of the endangered sea turtle, the remarkable lives of seahorses and countless more surprising facts about these and other incredible creatures. The oldest aquarium in Britain is inviting visitors to literally get lost this year, with the unveiling of a dizzying mirror maze with a rainforest theme, 'Lost in Amazonia.' There will also be a variety of Amazon creatures to discover as explorers try to navigate from the entrance to the exit.
All year daily from 10.00. Closed Christmas Day
Please call for admission prices

Discount Offer: One Child Free.

Social History Museums

How We Lived Then: Museum of Shops and Social History

20 Cornfield Terrace Eastbourne East Sussex BN21 4NS
Tel: 01323 737143
In this late -Regency town house (built in 1850)

you will see 100 years of shopping and social history, uniquely captured in many old shops, rooms and displays.

Theme & Adventure Parks

Butlins Bognor Regis

Bognor Regis West Sussex PO21 1JJ
Tel: 01243 810005
With 'Splash Waterworld', the 'Skyline Pavilion', a funfair, an indoor soft-play area, go-karts, crazy-golf, a recording studio, plus bars, restaurants, and much more.

Harbour Park

Seafront Arun Parade Littlehampton
West Sussex BN17 5LL
Tel: 01903 721200
Harbour Park is situated right on the sandy beaches and adjacent to the working harbour and marina in Littlehampton, West Sussex.

Knockhatch Adventure Park

Hempstead Lane Hailsham East Sussex
BN27 3PR
Tel: 01323 442051 Fax: 01323 843878
www.knockhatch.com

*[A22, to W of Hailsham. 8mi N of Eastbourne, 30
min from Brighton, Hastings & Tunbridge Wells,
60 min from London. Plenty of on-site parking
available]*

Exciting, yet relaxing - the most varied day out
around. Bird of prey centre, Treetops indoor soft
play, adventure playgrounds, trampolines, crazy
golf, small childrens' area, sandpit, demon drop,
bouncy castle play barn, reptile centre, boating
lake, toboggan slide, ball games, giant astro
slide, bungee trampoline, rock climbing wall
plus for additional cost, burger bars, coffee corner, karting for children aged 3 years and over,
laser adventure game, rodeo bull and corporate
hospitality.

*21-24 Mar, 4 Apr-2 Nov. Some school term days
have limited opening, see website for details*

A£7.99 C(under3)£Free C(3-16) £6.99
Students(NUS/USI)£5.99 OAPs£5.99, Family
Ticket (4 people) £26.00, extra C£5.50. Season
Tickets £20.00 per person. Group rate (16+pay-
ing people): 25% discount. Free pre-school visit
for teachers, pre-booked C£3.99 + vat during
term time through school

Discount Offer: One Child Free.

Paradise Park

Avis Road Newhaven East Sussex BN9 0DH
Tel: 01273 512123 Fax: 01273 616000
www.paradisepark.co.uk

*[A27 Brighton-Lewes bypass & A26 give easy
access to Paradise Park. Rail: regular services to
Newhaven. Bus: regular services to Denton
Corner. Plenty of on-site parking available]*

The Heritage Trail and Gardens at Paradise Park
are the ideal day out for all ages. Discover the
fascinating world of animals and plants from millions of years ago to the present day. An extensive exhibition traces the history of Planet Earth.
See fabulous collections of fossils, minerals and
crystals. The life size moving dinosaurs provide
an unforgettable experience. The Planthouses
have a spectacular collection of the world's
flora. The Dinosaur Garden reveals Sussex life
millions of years ago. The gardens are one of
Newhaven's hidden secrets with paths meandering through exquisite flowering shrubs, trees
and plants that form a backdrop to waterfalls,
fountains and small lakes. Follow the Sussex
Heritage Trail through one of the finest water
gardens in the South, with handcrafted models.
Enjoy children's activities including crazy golf,
miniature railway, indoor and outdoor play areas
and amusements. Visit the unique garden centre with terrace café overlooking the gardens.

*All year daily 09.00-18.00. Closed 25-26 Dec.
Alternative tel no: 01273 616006*

Combined Ticket to all 3 attractions: A£7.99
C£5.99, Family Ticket (A2+C2) £23.99. Any
Pass purchased after 16.00 is valid the follow-
ing day (subject to authorisation upon entry).
Group rates available on request

Discount Offer: One Child Free.

Tulleys Farm

Turners Hill Road Turners Hill Crawley West
Sussex RH10 4PD
Tel: 01342 718472 Fax: 01342 718473
www.tulleysfarm.com

[M23 J10. Rail: Three Bridges. Plenty of on-site parking available]

Tulleys Farm, with its shop stocked with top class food, tea room serving light refreshments and lunches and bistro style Hayrack (open seasonally) is set in acres of outstanding natural beauty. There is much on offer; picnic, play areas and 'animal patch' to amuse the children. Quality bedding plants available from spring to autumn and we have extended our range of garden accessories and general giftware. Our renowned PYO strawberries and other soft fruit are available in season. There are several events during the year, including the Easter Eggstravaganza, a full day's fun for all ages at the A-Maze-ing adventure park from early July to early Sept which now includes Torch light evenings, October Festival packed with spooky goings-on, then finally at Christmas you can select your tree, gifts and produce and visit Santa in his Enchanted Forest. Corporate and children's parties can be booked at certain times. Pushchair access in most areas.

All year daily, Maze Only 10.00-18.00 Early July-mid Sept. Tea room: end Oct-end Mar daily 09.30-16.30, Apr-Sept 09.30-17.00. Shop: end Oct-end Mar daily 09.00-17.00, Apr-Sept 09.00-18.00

Prices vary, please call for further details

Zoos

Drusillas Park

Alfriston East Sussex BN26 5QS
Tel: 01323 874100 Fax: 01323 874101
www.drusillas.co.uk

[Off A27 between Brighton / Eastbourne, 7mi from Seaford beach. Ample on-site parking]

Award winning Drusillas Park is widely regarded as the best small zoo in the country and is fast becoming recognised as one of the most popular places for children in the south east of England. With over 130 animal species in naturalistic environments there is plenty to enthral everyone from the youngest to the oldest visitor. Animals include the popular meerkats where children can climb inside a dome to get really close to the animals, as well as penguins, otters, beavers, lemurs, gibbons, a range of monkeys and a walk-through bat enclosure, to name but a few. However, animals are only half the Drusillas experience. Playland, including Monkey Kingdom, has masses of climbing, sliding, jumping and swinging fun thoughtfully separated for different age groups. Indoors there is Amazon Adventure, a state-of-the-art soft play complex, as well as the Toddler Village and Toy Stables which are a hit with the under 6s. And every day is a Thomas day at Drusillas! So it's all aboard Annie and Clarabel as Thomas takes visitors on a train journey from Tidmouth Hault. In addition to this there is also the Zoolympics Challenge, Animal Spotter Books and Stamping Trail, Jungle Adventure Golf, Panning for Gold, Penguin Plunge, Vertical Limit, the Discovery Centre and Wacky Workshop, Explorers Restaurant, Oasis Café, five shops plus an interesting and varied event diary.

All year daily Summer: 10.00-18.00, Winter: 10.00-17.00. Closed 24-26 Dec. Penguin feeding takes place daily at 11.30 & 16.00.
A&C(13+) from £11.20 C(under2)£Free C(2-12) from £10.20, Family Tickets (2 people) from £20.40, (3 people) from £30.60, (4 people) from £40.80, (5 people) from £51.00

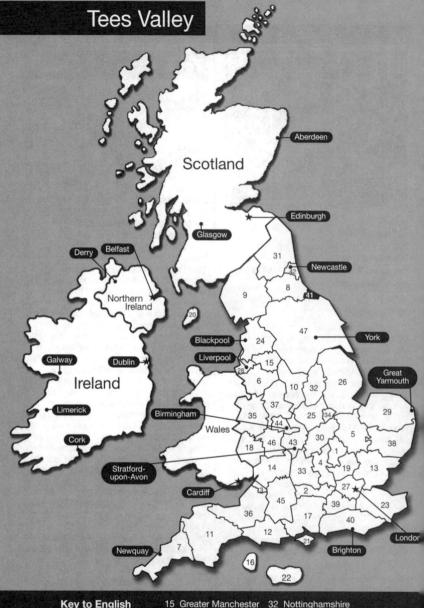

Tees Valley

Aberdeen

Scotland

Edinburgh

Glasgow

31

42 — Newcastle

8

9

41

Derry

Belfast

Northern
Ireland

20

Blackpool

24

47 — York

Galway

Dublin

Liverpool

15

Great
Yarmouth

Ireland

28

6

10

32

26

Limerick

37

Birmingham

35

44

25

34

29

Cork

Wales

18

46

43

30

5

38

Stratford-
upon-Avon

14

33

4

1

19

13

Cardiff

3

2

27 — London

45

39

23

36

17

40

11

12

Newquay

7

21

Brighton

16

22

Agriculture / Working Farms

Newham Grange Leisure Farm

Wykeham Way Coulby Newham Middlesbrough Tees Valley TS8 0TG

Tel: 01642 300202

The farm offers examples of rare cattle, sheep and pig breeds, as well as usual farm animals.

Art Galleries

Hartlepool Art Gallery

Church Square Hartlepool Tees Valley TS24 7EQ

Tel: 01429 869706

Hartlepool Art Gallery, opened in 1996 (the year of Visual Arts), is situated in a stunning and beautifully restored Victorian church and features a 100ft viewing tower and coffee shop.

Tue-Sat

Arts, Crafts & Textiles

MIMA (Middlesbrough Institute of Modern Art)

Centre Square Middlesbrough Tees Valley TS1 2AZ

Tel: 01642 726720

Features the work of internationally acclaimed artists, with programmes includes painting, drawing, ceramics, jewellery design, sound, film, mixed media, photography and sculpture. Exhibitions change every quarter. Café, shop, roof terrace and gardens.

Closed Mondays

Birds, Butterflies & Bees

Butterfly World

Preston Park Yarm Road Stockton-On-Tees Tees Valley TS18 3RH

Tel: 01642 791414

An indoor tropical rainforest populated by exotic free-flying butterflies and birds complemented by a display of fascinating insects.

Kirkleatham Owl Centre

Kirkleatham Old Hall, Kirkleatham Redcar Tees Valley TS10 5NW

Tel: 01642 480512

Kirkleatham Owl Centre is home to one of the UK's largest collection of owls.

Thu-Sun, 11.00-16.30

Country Parks & Estates

Hardwick Hall Country Park

Sedgefield Stockton-on-Tees Tees Valley TS21 2EH

Tel: 0191 383 3594

A former landscape garden designed by James Paine in the eighteenth century. Contains the remains of several follies and a serpentine lake.

Festivals & Shows

Hartlepool Fireworks and Music Spectacular

Seaton Carew Seafront Hartlepool Tees Valley TS24 0JN

Tel: 01429 869706
www.destinationhartlepool.com

[South Shelter/Clock Tower. Park & Ride available]

One of the most popular firework displays in the area. Children's funfair rides and stalls, entertainment and displays. Park and Ride shuttle service available, see press for details or contact the Tourist Information Centre.

1 November 2008 (Sat funfair from 16.00, entertainment from 17.00, displays from 18.30)

Admission Free

Hartlepool Maritime Festival 2008

Hartlepool Marina and Hartlepool's Maritime Experience Hartlepool Tees Valley TS2 0XZ
Tel: 01429 860077 Fax: 01429 867332
www.hartlepoolmaritimefestival.co.uk

[A19: A179 from N or A689 from S]

The Hartlepool Maritime Festival will be set against the background of the Marina and Hartlepool's Maritime Experience. There will be a programme of maritime themed activities including street theatre, music, re-enactments, water sports, crafts, French market, international cuisine and much, much more. Park and Ride available.

4-6 July 2008 (times to be confirmed)
Admission Free

Stockton International Riverside Festival

Stockton-On-Tees Tees Valley TS18 1XE
Tel: 01642 527040 Fax: 01642 527037
www.sirf.co.uk

[Various venues in Stockton. From A1(M) N take A168 / A19 to Teeside leave A19 at A1046 to Stockton. Trans-Penine Express from Manchester, Leeds & York - alight at Thornaby, or East Coast Main Line, change at Darlington. Plenty of on-site parking available]

Stockton International Riverside Festival plans to celebrate its 21st birthday with hundreds of top quality British and international performers on the guest list and an unrivalled atmosphere provided by the whole town. Highlights include the Flying Dragon Circus, a new project specially created in the year of the Beijing Olympics by SIRF and its partner festival in the Chinese capital. There'll be spectacular outdoor shows from Africa, the UK and Europe and a stunning finale from Dutch science fiction fantasists Close Act. All this plus SIRF's joyously diverse Community Carnival and Festival Fringe. We hope you'll join the party from 30th July to 3rd August.

30 Jul-3 Aug 11.00-23.00
Most events are free, check website for up to date details

Heritage & Industrial

Ironstone Mining Museum

Deepdale Skinningrove Saltburn-by-the-Sea Tees Valley TS13 4AP
Tel: 01287 642877
Discover the special skills and customs of the miners who helped make this region the most important ironstone mining district in Victorian and Edwardian England.
1 Apr-31 Oct

Historical

Dorman Museum

Linthorpe Road Middlesbrough Tees Valley TS5 6LA
Tel: 01642 813781
Houses eight permanent galleries to suit every taste, with topics ranging from local history to dinosaurs and Ancient Egypt to Twentieth-Century Woman. The Water Gallery is especially popular with children.

Maritime

Hartlepool's Maritime Experience
Maritime Avenue Hartlepool Tees Valley
TS24 0XZ
Tel: 01429 860077 Fax: 01429 867332
www.hartlepoolsmaritimeexperience.com
*[From N A19 take A179 & follow signs for historic
quay. From S A689 from A19 & follow signs for
quay 1032. Ample free on-site parking]*
The North East's premier maritime attraction. A
voyage back in time to the sights and sounds of
an eighteenth-century quayside. A full day of fun
with loads of themed activities. Take a journey
through an audio / visual tour of a frigate then
board the real thing; the magnificent HMS
Trincomalee, the oldest ship afloat in the UK
where you can explore the decks accompanied
by an audio guide. Skittle Square, the children's
maritime adventure centre, outdoor wooden
playship and a short film presentation
'Pressganged' are just a few of the attractions
to enjoy. Costumed guides and regular sword
fighting, cannon firing, musketry displays and
pirate and marine re-enactors enhance the
experience, please check the website to confirm
details. Visit the free Museum of Hartlepool
which tells the fascinating story of the town,
including the monkey legend. Featuring a year
long programme of exhibitions. Look around the
restored paddle steam ship Wingfield Castle
with coffee shop.
*All year daily, summer 10.00-17.00, Winter Open
daily please check website for times. Closed 25-
26 Dec & 1 Jan*
A£7.75 C£4.75 Over 60's £5.75, Family Ticket
£20.00

Discount Offer: One Child Free.

Nature's World
Ladgate Lane Acklam Middlesbrough
Tees Valley TS5 7YN
Tel: 01642 594895
A pioneering eco-experience, featuring
'Futureworld' and a tropical Hydroponicum.

Sport & Recreation

Stewart Park
Ladgate Lane Marton-in-Cleveland
Middlesbrough Tees Valley TS7 8AR
Tel: 01642 300202/515600
The park has a varied landscape, and includes
the Captain Cook Birthplace Museum.

Victorian Era

Preston Hall Museum and Park
Preston Park Yarm Road Stockton-On-Tees
Tees Valley TS18 3RH
Tel: 01642 527375 Fax: 01642 527571
www.stockton.gov.uk/museums
[On A135. Rail: Eaglescliffe 10m walk]
The museum illustrates Victorian social history,
with reconstructions of period rooms and a
street with working craftsman including black-
smith, farrier and toymaker.
*All year daily, Mon-Fri 10.00-16.30, Weekends
11.00-16.30*
A£1.30, C£0.60, Concessions£0.60

**Discount Offer: Two for the Price of
One (full-paying adult)**

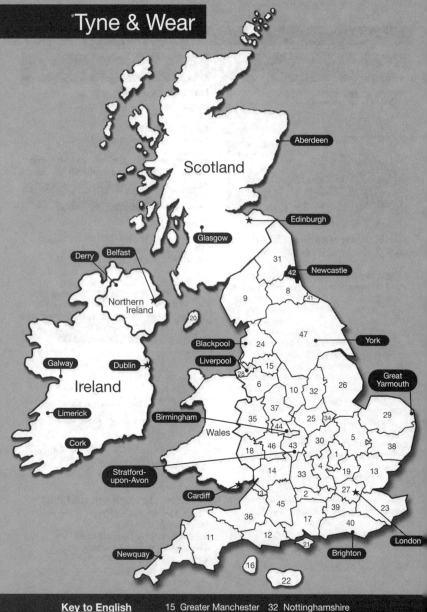

Tyne & Wear

Scotland

Aberdeen

Edinburgh

Glasgow

Derry

Belfast

Newcastle

31

42

Northern
Ireland

9

8

41

20

Blackpool

24

47

York

Galway

Dublin

Liverpool

15

Great
Yarmouth

Ireland

28

6

10

32

26

29

Limerick

37

25

34

Birmingham

35

44

5

38

Cork

Wales

46

43

30

18

1

Stratford-
upon-Avon

14

4

19

13

33

Cardiff

13

2

27

London

45

39

23

36

17

40

11

12

Brighton

7

Newquay

21

16

22

Animal Attractions

Bill Quay Community Farm

Haining Wood Terrace Bill Quay Gateshead
Tyne & Wear NE10 0UE
Tel: 01914 335780
Farm livestock from the traditional to the bizarre,
an abundance of artworks and a green retreat
for wildlife. Panoramic views of Tyne and urban
parkland.

Art Galleries

Baltic Centre for Contemporary Art

South Shore Road Gateshead Tyne & Wear
NE8 3BA
Tel: 0191 478 1810
This converted Rank Hovis grain warehouse is
one of the largest centres for contemporary
visual art in Europe.

Northern Gallery for Contemporary Art

City Library and Arts Centre Fawcett Street
Sunderland Tyne & Wear SR1 1RE
Tel: 0191 514 1235
Presents changing exhibitions of new work by
emerging and established artists from the UK
and abroad, bringing key new works of art of
our time to new audiences. The gallery runs a
programme of talks, tours, education activities,
workshops and artists residencies.

Arts, Crafts & Textiles

Laing Art Gallery

New Bridge Street Newcastle upon Tyne
Tyne & Wear NE1 8AG
Tel: 0191 232 7734
The North of England's premier art gallery dis-
plays a stunning array of watercolours, cos-
tume, silver, glass, pottery and sculpture.

Shipley Art Gallery

Prince Consort Road Gateshead Tyne & Wear
NE8 4JB
Tel: 0191 477 1495
Over the last 25 years, Shipley Art Gallery has
become established as a national centre for
contemporary craft and has built up one of the
best collections outside London, including
ceramics, wood, metal, glass, textiles and furniture.

Country Parks & Estates

Derwent Walk Country Park and Derwenthaugh Park

Lockhaugh Road Rowlands Gill Tyne & Wear
NE39 1AU
Tel: 01207 545212
A mixture of natural woodlands, meadows,
riverside and reclaimed industrial land. 11 mile
track bed of the old Derwent Valley Railway
between Swalwell and Consett suitable for
walking, cycling, horses and wheelchairs.

Rising Sun Country Park and Countryside Centre

Whitley Road Benton Newcastle Upon Tyne
Tyne & Wear NE12 9SS
Tel: 0191 200 7841
Visitor and field study facility, specialising in
cross-curricular countryside and environmental
education. Visitor centre with exhibition, café,
play sculptures and picnic area. Country park
including woodlands, ponds, grassland, an
organic farm and swallow pond local nature
reserve.

Exhibition & Visitor Centres

Life Science Centre

Times Square Newcastle Upon Tyne Tyne &
Wear NE1 4EP
Tel: 0191 243 8210
Life is an exciting place where science comes
alive in a fun and funky environment! We want
to inspire curiosity and encourage you to uncover new things about Life.

National Glass Centre

Liberty Way Sunderland Tyne & Wear SR6 0GL
Tel: 0191 515 5555
Explore the full history of glass making in the UK and see cutting-edge examples of the contemporary glass maker's art. Housed in an innovative glass-roofed building on the north bank of the Wear, the National Glass Centre is a fascinating experience for visitors of all ages.

Folk & Local History Museums

Bedes World: The Museum of Early Medieval Northumbria at Jarrow

Church Bank Jarrow Tyne & Wear NE32 3DY
Tel: 0191 489 2106
Travel back and explore his world and the amazing Golden Age of Northumbria at this exciting museum. See St Paul's Church and the ruins of the monastery where the Venerable Bede lived, the visitor centre, gift shop and restaurant, plus the recreated Anglo-Saxon farm with rare breeds of animals and replica timber buildings.

South Shields Museum and Art Gallery

Ocean Road South Shields Tyne & Wear NE33 2JA
Tel: 0191 456 8740
South Shields Museum and Art Gallery explores the story of South Tyneside through sensational displays, hands-on exhibits and stunning art.

Sunderland Museum and Winter Gardens

Burdon Road Sunderland Tyne & Wear SR1 1PP
Tel: 0191 553 2323
Combines a museum, art gallery, exhibition space and Winter Gardens to create a stunning visitor attraction in the heart of the city centre.

Gibside

Estate Office Gibside Burnopfield Newcastle Upon Tyne Tyne & Wear NE16 6BG
Tel: 01207 541820 Fax: 01207 542741
www.nationaltrust.org.uk

[6mi SW of Gateshead, 20mi W of Durham, on B6314 between Burnopfield & Rowlands Gill, from A1 exit N of Metro Centre & follow brown property signs. Rail: Blaydon 5mi. Bus: Go North East Gateshead 611-3, 621. Newcastle 45,46A, 611. Picnic area adjacent to car park & on many of the walks. Plenty of on-site parking available]

One of the North's finest landscapes, much of which is SSSI (Site of Special Scientific Interest). There is a forest garden embracing many miles of riverside and forest walks, with fine views and abundant wildlife which is currently under restoration. Several outstanding buildings including a Palladian Chapel, Column of Liberty and others. The estate is the former home of the Queen Mother's family, the Bowes-Lyons. Disabled Access; some areas easier than others, please call Visitor Services Manager for details. Braille guide available.

10 Mar-2 Nov daily 10.00-18.00, 3 Nov-31 Jan 2009 10.00-16.00

A£6.00 C(under5)£Free C(5+)£3.50, Family Ticket (A2+C4) £17.50 or (A1+C3) £12.00. NT Members £Free. Group rate (15+): A£4.50 these prices include a voluntary 10% gift aid donation

Washington Old Hall

The Avenue Washington Village Washington Tyne & Wear NE38 7LE
Tel: 0191 416 6879

Manor house associated with the family of George Washington. With mementoes of the American connection and the War of Independence, an impressive Great Hall and an authentic seventeenth-century kitchen. Outside there are attractive gardens and meadows.
Mar-Nov, Sun-Wed (11.00-17.00)

Literature & Libraries

Seven Stories

30 Lime Street Newcastle-upon-Tyne Tyne & Wear NE1 2PQ
Tel: 0845 271 0777 Fax: 0191 261 1931
www.sevenstories.org.uk
Seven Stories is where our rich heritage of children's books is collected, explored and celebrated. A great day out for the whole family; visitors can explore the world of children's books where words and pictures are the inspiration for creative activities, special events and child friendly exhibitions. Browse the specialist children's bookshop and relax in the café. We're open seven days a week, admission charges apply. Find Seven Stories tucked under the Byker Bridge in Newcastle's Ouseburn Valley - the perfect storybook setting! For all the latest news and events log on to www.sevenstories.org.uk.

Open all year daily Mon-Sat 10.00-17.00 Sun 11.00-17.00

A£5.00 C(under 4)£Free Concessions £4.00, Family Ticket £15.00

Discount Offer: One Child Free.

Maritime

Souter Lighthouse

Coast Road Whitburn Sunderland Tyneside SR6 7NH
Tel: 01670 773966
Boldly painted in red and white hoops, Souter lighthouse opened in 1871 and was the first to use alternating electric current. With fantastic views, hands-on activities and a tea room.
22 Mar-2 Nov (Closed Fridays)

Military & Defence Museums

North East Aircraft Museum

Old Washington Road Sunderland Tyne & Wear SR5 3HZ
Tel: 0191 519 0662
The North of England's premier collection of Aviation History and the largest Aviation collection between Yorkshire and Scotland.

Mills - Water & Wind

Path Head Water Mill

Summerhill Blaydon-On-Tyne Tyne & Wear NE21 4SP
Tel: 0191 414 6288
An eighteenth-century watermill being restored as a water-powered joiner's shop, demonstrating early engineering techniques. Interpretation of mill artefacts. Tranquil setting, picnic area, garden, visitor centre and tea room.

Nature & Conservation Parks

Castle Eden Dene National Nature Reserve

Peterlee Tyne & Wear SR8 1NJ
Tel: 0191 586 0004
Picturesque wooded valley. National Nature Reserve with 550 acres of natural woodland and 12 miles of footpaths. Parts of the reserve remain almost unaltered by man since the Ice Age. With wild flowers and woodland birds.

WWT Washington Wetland Centre

Pattinson Washington Tyne & Wear NE38 8LE
Tel: 0191 416 5454
Explore 103 acres of wetland, woodland and wildlife reserve at Washington Wetland Centre.

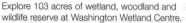

Places of Worship

St Nicholas Cathedral

St. Nicholas Churchyard Newcastle Upon Tyne
Tyne & Wear NE1 1PF
Tel: 0191 232 1939
Mainly fourteenth-century cathedral with a striking Lantern Tower. There is also a fine collection of stained-glass windows.

Railways

Tanfield Railway

Old Marley Hill Nr Stanley Newcastle Upon Tyne
Tyne & Wear NE16 5ET
Tel: 0191 388 7545 Fax: 0191 387 4784
www.tanfield-railway.co.uk

[Off A6076 (J63, A1). Ample on-site parking]

The world's oldest existing railway, originally opened in 1725. Three-mile steam passenger railway between Sunniside, Causey Arch and East Tanfield.

All year daily. Train times: all year Sun, PLUS Summer School Holidays Wed & Thur
A£7.00 C(5-14)£4.00 C(under5)£Free
OAPs£5.00

Discount Offer: Two for the Price of One (full-paying adult).

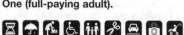

Roman Era

Arbeia Roman Fort and Museum

Baring Street South Shields Tyne & Wear
NE33 2BB
Tel: 0191 456 1369
Built around AD160, Arbeia Roman Fort once guarded the entrance to the River Tyne. Today, the excavated remains, stunning reconstructions of original buildings and finds from the fort show what life was like in Roman Britain.

Segedunum Roman Fort, Baths and Museum

Buddle Street Wallsend Tyne & Wear NE28 6HR
Tel: 0191 295 5757
Today, Segedunum is once again the gateway to Hadrian's Wall. It is the most excavated Fort along the Wall and has a large interactive museum plus a 35-metre high viewing tower.

Sealife Centres & Aquariums

Blue Reef Aquarium (Tyne & Wear)

Grand Parade Tynemouth Tyne & Wear
NE30 4JF
Tel: 0191 258 1031 Fax: 0191 257 2116
www.bluereefaquarium.co.uk

[Signposted from A19/1058]

Take the ultimate undersea safari at the award winning Blue Reef Aquarium where there's a world of underwater adventure just waiting to be discovered. Over 30 living displays reveal the sheer variety of life in the deep; from native sharks, lobsters and adorable otters to seahorses, fascinating frogs and exotic fish. At the aquarium's heart is a giant ocean tank where an underwater walkthrough tunnel offers incredibly close encounters with the stunning beauty of a tropical coral reef - home of hundreds of colourful fish. Blue Reef is a great place for visitors of all ages to discover more about the wonders of the deep. There's a full programme of entertaining, informative talks and feeding displays throughout the day. Learn more about our native sea creatures including crabs, anemones and starfish at our popular Rockpool Encounters where our experts will be on hand to answer all your questions. New 'Seal Cove,' a spectacular experience whatever the weather.

All year daily 10.00. Closed 25 Dec only
A£7.50 C£5.50 OAPs&Students(NUS/USI)£6.50

Discount Offer: One Child Free.

Social History Museums

Discovery Museum
Blandford House Blandford Square Newcastle upon Tyne Tyne & Wear NE1 4JA
Tel: 0191 232 6789
Discover all about local life - from the area's renowned maritime history and world-changing science and technology, right through to 'fashion through the eras' and military history.

Theme & Adventure Parks

New Metroland
39 Garden Walk Metrocentre Gateshead Tyne & Wear NE11 9XY
Tel: 0191 493 2048
Europe's largest indoor funfair theme park offering 12 major attractions.

Ocean Beach Pleasure Park
23 The Foreshore Sea Road South Shields Tyne & Wear NE33 2LD
Tel: 0191 456 1617
www.oceanbeach.co.uk
[Plenty of on-site parking available]
Ocean Beach Pleasure Park is undoubtedly the largest standing Amusement Park on the North East coast, so why not come and join us for a fun filled day out! With free admission, enjoy our attractions all day long. New to Ocean Beach from May 08 is the 'Shark Island' water ride (Europe's first!). Our rides range from the traditional Waltzers and Carousel to the thrilling Rollercoaster and Go-Karts along with much more! For the visitors who like to keep their feet on the ground, there are a number of amusement arcades, restaurants, gift shops and a ten-pin bowling alley to keep everyone happy.

Mar-Nov. Please see website for further details
Free Admission to park, although tokens must be purchased for the rides

Discount Offer: Save £10.00! Get £25.00 worth of tokens for just £15.00 (single tokens cost 50p).

Transport Museums

Monkwearmouth Station Museum
North Bridge Street Sunderland Tyne & Wear SR5 1AP
Tel: 0191 567 7075
Victorian Station and booking office with large collection of railway and second world war memorabilia. Following a redevelopment project, it now houses seven interactive galleries.

Warwickshire

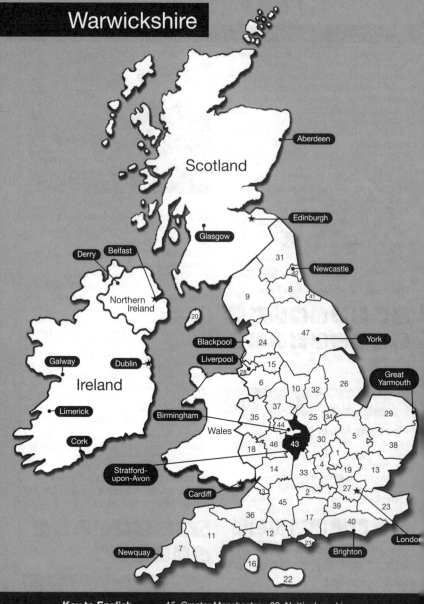

Aberdeen

Scotland

Edinburgh

Glasgow

Newcastle

Derry
Belfast

Northern
Ireland

Blackpool

Liverpool

York

Great
Yarmouth

Galway
Dublin

Ireland

Birmingham

Wales

Limerick

Stratford-
upon-Avon

Cork

Cardiff

Newquay

Brighton

London

Animal Attractions

Hatton Farm Village at Hatton Country World
Dark Lane Hatton Warwick Warwickshire
CV35 8XA
Tel: 01926 843411
Offers a great day for children and families with
a host of farmyard friends and fun adventures.

Redwings Oxhill Rescue Centre
Banbury Road Oxhill Warwickshire CV35 0RP
Tel: 0870 040 0033 Fax: 0870 458 1942
www.redwings.org.uk
*[On A422 between Stratford & Banbury. Plenty of
on-site parking available]*
Established in 1984, Redwings is now the
largest horse charity in the UK, working to provide and promote the welfare, care and protec-
tion of horses, ponies, donkeys and mules.
Redwings Oxhill Rescue Centre is the charity's
first visitor centre established outside East
Anglia. The site is home to more than 50 rescued horses, ponies and donkeys including
cheeky pony Dylan, Will the former Police horse
and dinky Shetland Wensley. There is a brand
new gift shop, information centre and café, and
we hope the centre will serve to make more
people aware of the charity's work and provide
enjoyment and education for a new generation
of supporters.
*All year daily: 10.00-17.00. Closed 25-26 Dec &
1 Jan*
Admission Free

Discount Offer: Free Poster.

Archaeology

Warwickshire Museum
Market Hall Museum Market Place Warwick
Warwickshire CV34 4SA
Tel: 01926 412500 Fax: 01926 419840
www.warwickshire.gov.uk/museum
Wildlife geology, archaeology and history of
Warwickshire including the famous Sheldon
tapestry map and giant fossil plesiosaur.

*10.00-17.00 Tue-Sat, 11.30-17.00 Sun, Apr-
Sept. Also open Bank Hol Mons*
Admission Free

Arts, Crafts & Textiles

Compton Verney
Compton Verney Warwickshire CV35 9HZ
Tel: 01926 645500 Fax: 01926 645501
www.comptonverney.org.uk
*[9mi E of Stratford-upon-Avon, 10 min from M40
(J12). Entrance on B4086 Kineton to
Wellesbourne Rd, just off Fosse Way (B4455).*

Plenty of on-site parking available]

Compton Verney is an award winning art gallery. Voted Visitor Attraction of the year and short-listed for The Guardian Family Friendly Award, it offers a great day out for all ages. Explore our collections of art from around the world with fun family activity packs or relax and picnic in our 120 acres of 'Capability' Brown parkland. Take time out for lunch in our café which has some-thing yummy for everyone including organic baby food, children's lunch boxes and child size portions of all our main meals. There's also a fun programme of drop-in family art and craft activities for all the school holidays, give us a call or check our website for full details.

15 Mar-14 Dec Tue-Sun 11.00-17.00 & Bank Hol Mons

A£7.00 C(under5)£Free C(5-16)£2.00 Concessions£5.00, Family Ticket (A2+C4) £16.00. Membership: A£24.00 Family Ticket £50.00. Group rates available on request

Discount Offer: Get One Family Ticket Half-Price.

Herbert Art Gallery and Museum
Jordan Well Coventry CV1 5QP
Tel: 024 7683 2386
As a focus for the city's heritage and treasures, the Herbert Art Gallery and Museum offers a fascinating visit with international appeal.

Rugby Art Gallery and Museum
Little Elborow Street Rugby CV21 3BZ
Tel: 01788 533201
Rugby's strong cultural heritage and bright artisitic future is celebrated in the Art Gallery and Museum's ever changing display of art & craft exhibitions.

Warwick Arts Centre
University Of Warwick Coventry CV4 7AL
Tel: 024 7652 4524
The largest arts centre in the Midlands, attract-ing around 280,000 visitors a year to over 2,000 individual events embracing music, drama, dance, comedy, literature, films and visual art.

Birds, Butterflies & Bees

Stratford-upon-Avon Butterfly Farm
Swan's Nest Lane Stratford-upon-Avon Warwickshire CV37 7LS
Tel: 01789 299288 Fax: 01789 415878
www.butterflyfarm.co.uk

[S bank of River Avon opposite RSC]

The UK's largest live Butterfly and Insect Exhibit. Hundreds of the world's most spectacular and colourful butterflies. Insect City has a huge col-lection of strange and fascinating animals. Arachnoland features the 'dealers in death'. There is also an outdoor British butterfly garden in the summer.

All year, Summer daily 10.00-18.00, Winter 10.00-dusk. Closed 25 Dec

A£5.50 C£4.50 Concessions£5.00, Family Ticket (A2+C2) £16.00. Special school tours can be arranged

Discount Offer: Two for the Price of One (full-paying adult).

Country Parks & Estates

Coombe Country Park
Brinklow Road Binley Coventry Warwickshire CV3 2AB
Tel: 024 7645 3720
500 acres of historic parkland with a children's playground, an adventure playground, and a visitor centre with restaurant, souvenir shop and exhibitions.

Historical

Anne Hathaway's Cottage

Cottage Lane Shottery Stratford-Upon-Avon
Warwickshire CV37 9HH
Tel: 01789 292100 Fax: 01789 205014
www.shakespeare.org.uk

*[Off A422, 1mi from town centre. Plenty of on-site
parking available]*

Explore the beautiful house where the young
William wooed his future wife at her childhood
home. Enjoy the romantic setting of this quintessential thatched country cottage. Wander
through the stunning grounds overflowing with
beautiful blooms, shrubs and traditional vegetables. Have fun in the Tree Garden and
Elizabethan style yew maze. A virtual reality tour
is available for our visitors with restricted mobility.

*All year daily Apr-May Mon-Sat 09.30-17.00, Sun
10.00-17.00, June-Aug Mon-Sat 09.00-17.00,
Sun 09.30-17.00, Sept-Oct Mon-Sat 09.30-
17.00, Sun 10.00-17.00, Nov-Mar daily 10.00-
16.00. Times listed are opening time to last entry.
Closed 23-26 Dec. Café and refreshment facilities subject to seasonal opening*

A£6.00 C£3.00 Concession£5.00, Family Ticket
£15.50. Multiple House Tickets, All 5 Houses:
A£14.50 C£7.20 Concessions£12.50, Family
Ticket £37.70. 3 In-Town Houses: A10.60
C£5.30 Concession£9.30, Family Ticket
£27.80. Group rates available on request,
please call 01789 201806 for details

**Discount Offer: See Shakespeare's
Birthplace voucher for details.**

Coughton Court

Coughton Alcester Warwickshire B49 5JA
Tel: 01789 400777 Fax: 01789 765544
www.nationaltrust.org.uk
*[On A435, 2mi N of Alcester. Plenty of on-site
parking available]*

Coughton Court is one of England's finest Tudor
houses. Home of the Throckmorton family since
1409, the house is one of the few in the country
to retain its historic treasures including fine collections of furniture, porcelain and family portraits. From the Tudor court of Henry VIII to the
Gun Powder Plot of 1605 this influential family
has witnessed some of the most defining events
in our history, detailed in a fascinating exhibition
on the Gunpowder Plot of 1605. Within the varied grounds is a walled garden containing stunning displays of roses and herbaceous plants,
as well as two churches, one of which was the
first private Roman Catholic Church to be built
in England following a change in the law in the
nineteenth century.

*House: 15 Mar-29 Jun (Wed-Sun), 1 Jul-31 Aug
(Tue-Sun). 3 Sep-28 Sep (Wed-Sun), 4 Oct-2
Nov (Sat-Sun). 11.00-17.00.
Gardens/Restaurant/Shop: As House 11.00-
17.30. Walled Garden: As House11.30-16.45.
Open Bank Hols and Tue.*

House & Garden: A£9.20 C£4.60, Family Ticket
£23.00. Garden Only: A£6.40 C£3.20, Family
Ticket £16.00 (Includes a voluntary 10% donation; visitors can however choose to pay the
standard admission prices which are displayed
at the property and at
www.nationaltrust.org.uk). NT Members £Free
(Walled Garden: £2.50). Group rates (15+):
House & Garden £7.30, Garden Only £5.00
(standard admission prices apply to groups)

Hall's Croft

Old Town Stratford-Upon-Avon Warwickshire
CV37 6BG
Tel: 01789 292107 Fax: 01789 266209
www.shakespeare.org.uk
[Town centre location]
Visit the luxurious home of Shakespeare's
daughter and her husband, John Hall, an emi-
nent physician. Explore the lavish and elegant
rooms with exquisite furnishings and paintings.
Discover John Hall's Consulting Room with
interesting medical artefacts, notes and tools.
Enjoy the tranquil garden, filled with the beautiful
roses, herbs and herbaceous borders. Limited
disabled access, please call for details.
*All year Apr-May daily 11.00-17.00, June-Aug
Mon-Sat 09.30-17.00, Sun 10.00-17.00, Sept-
Oct daily 11.00-17.00, Nov-Mar daily 11.00-
16.00. Times listed are opening times to last
entry. Closed 23-26 Dec*
A£4.00 C£2.00 Concessions£3.50, Family
Ticket £10.50. Multiple Houses, 3 In-Town
Houses: A£10.60 C£5.30 Concessions£9.30,
Family Ticket £27.80. All 5 Houses: A£14.50
C£7.20 Concessions£12.50, Family Ticket
£37.70. Group rates available on request,
please call 01789 201806 for details

**Discount Offer: See Shakespeare's
Birthplace for details.**

Harvard House and the Museum
of British Pewter

High Street Stratford-Upon-Avon CV37 6AU
Tel: 01789 204507
Discover pewter's fascinating history through
the centuries, try your hand at decorative
pewter and take a virtual reality tour.
Jul-Sep, 12.00-17.00

Kenilworth Castle

Castle Green Kenilworth Warwickshire CV8 1NE
Tel: 01926 852078
One of the largest castle ruins in England,
Kenilworth was once a stronghold to the rich
and famous. Today you can visit the Tudor
Gardens and the Great Hall.

Lunt Roman Fort

Baginton Coventry CV1 5QP
Tel: 024 7678 6142
The Lunt, a particial reconstruction of a First
Century Roman Fort, dates from AD60 and is
closely connected with the legendary Boudica.
Visitors are invited to follow in the footsteps of
the Roman army at unique reconstruction of a
first century Roman fort and museum. The
Granary includes a museum, a model of the
Fort in AD64 and gift shop.
*1 Apr-15 Jul: Sat, Sun & Bank Hol Mons (10:30 -
16:30). 16 Jul-18 Sep: Wed-Sun (10:30 - 16:30)*

Middleton Hall

Middleton Nr Tamworth Warwickshire B78 2AE
Tel: 01827 283095
[J9 M42 on A4091 Belfry / Tamworth rd]
Small country house of cultural and historic
interest dating from 1320. Attractions include a
lakeside walk, two walled gardens, a restored
smithy, a courtyard craft centre, café, book
room and souvenir shop. *Hall - 24 Mar-28 Sep:
Sun (14.00-17.00), Bank Hol Mons (11.00-
17.00). Craft Centre & Coffee Shop - all year,
Wed-Sun*

Mary Arden's Farm

Station Road Wilmcote Stratford-Upon-Avon
Warwickshire CV37 9UN
Tel: 01789 293455 Fax: 01789 415404

www.shakespeare.org.uk

[3mi NW off A34 just 3.5mi from town centre. Plenty of on-site parking available]

Experience the sights, sounds and smells of a Tudor farm and marvel as the farmer, maid and labourer bring the farm to life. Watch and help the family with their daily chores of baking bread, lighting fires, making candles, washing clothes and more. Take a walk on the nature trail and track down our Longhorn cattle, Cotswold sheep and other rare breeds. Limited disabled access, please call for details.

All year daily, Apr-May 10.00-17.00, June-Aug 09.30-17.00, Sept-Oct 10.00-17.00, Nov-Mar 10.00-16.00. Times listed are opening time to last entry. Closed 23-26 Dec

A£7.00 C£3.50 Concessions£6.00, Family Ticket £18.00. All 5 Houses: A£14.50 C£7.20 Concessions£12.50, Family Ticket £37.70. 3 In-Town Houses: A£10.60 C£5.30 Concessions£9.30 Family Ticket £27.80. Group rates available on request, please call 01789 201806 for details

Discount Offer: See Shakespeare's Birthplace for details.

Nash's House and New Place

Chapel Street Stratford-Upon-Avon Warwickshire CV37 6EP
Tel: 01789 292325 Fax: 01789 266228
www.shakespeare.org.uk

[Town centre, next door to Shakespeare Hotel & opposite Falcon Hotel]

See where the Shakespeare story ended in 1616. Wander through the picturesque gardens and see the mulberry tree, claimed to be from a cutting planted by Shakespeare himself. Visit Nash's House, once owned by Thomas Nash, a wealthy property owner and first husband of Shakespeare's granddaughter, Elizabeth. Learn about the story of one of the most influential books in the English language. Enjoy the peaceful gardens and sculptures. Limited disabled access, please call for details.

All year Apr-May daily 11.00-17.00, June-Aug Mon-Sat 09.30-17.00, Sun 10.00-17.00, Sept-Oct daily 11.00-17.00, Nov-Mar daily 11.00-16.00. Times listed are opening times to last entry. Closed 23-26 Dec

A£4.00 C£2.00 Concessions£3.50, Family Ticket £10.50. Multiple Houses, 3 In-Town Houses: A£10.60 C£5.30 Concessions£9.30, Family Ticket £27.80. All 5 Houses: A£14.50 C£7.20 Concessions£12.50, Family Ticket £37.70. Group rates available on request, please call 01789 201806 for details

Discount Offer: See Shakespeare's Birthplace for details.

Ragley Hall

Alcester Warwickshire B49 5NJ
Tel: 01789 762090 Fax: 01789 764791
www.ragleyhall.com

The family home of the Marquess and Marchioness of Hertford is one of the earliest and loveliest of England's great Palladian Houses.

Mar-Nov Weekends & School Hols

A£8.50, C£5.00, OAPs£7.00

Shakespeare's Birthplace

The Shakespeare Centre Henley Street
Stratford-Upon-Avon Warwickshire CV37 6QW
Tel: 01789 204016 Fax: 01789 299132
www.shakespeare.org.uk

[J15 M40, A46 to Stratford upon Avon, in town centre]

Discover the exciting story of Shakespeare's childhood and see where he spent the first years with his new wife. Discover what life was like for Shakespeare in the house where he was born and grew up. Watch a glover recreate the trade of Shakespeare's father in the workshop and stroll around the traditional English garden, which features many plants and herbs mentioned in Shakespeare's plays. Limited disabled access, please call for details.

All year daily, Apr-May Mon-Sat 10.00-17.00, June-Aug Mon-Sat 09.00-17.00, Sun 09.30-17.00, Sept-Oct Mon-Sat 10.00-17.00, Nov-Mar Mon-Sat 10.00-16.00, Sun 10.30-16.00. Times listed are opening times to last entry. Closed 23-26 Dec

A£8.00 C£4.00 Concessions£7.00, Family Ticket £21.00. Multiple Houses, 3 In-Town Houses: A£10.60 C£5.30 Concessions£9.30, Family Ticket £27.80. All 5 Houses: A£14.50 C£7.20 Concessions£12.50, Family Ticket £37.70. Group rates available on request, please call 01789 201806 for details

Discount Offer: Two for the Price of One (full-paying adult). Conditions: voucher entitles one adult or one child to be admitted free of charge when accompanied by a full-paying adult to one of the following venues: Shakespeare's Birthplace, Hall's Croft, Mary Arden's Farm, Nash's House and New Place or Anne Hathaway's

Cottage.

Warwick Castle

Warwick Warwickshire CV34 4QU
Tel: 0870 442 2000
The finest medieval fortress in Britain, Warwick Castle is bursting to the towers with tales of treachery, torture and power.

Military & Defence Museums

Midland Air Museum

Coventry Airport Baignton Coventry
Warwickshire CV8 3AZ
Tel: 02476 301033
Displays over 40 aircraft from the Gnat jet fighter to the giant Vulcan bomber.

Stately Homes

Upton House and Gardens

Upton Nr Banbury Warwickshire OX15 6HT
Tel: 01295 670266 Fax: 01295 671144
www.nationaltrust.org.uk
[On A422 between Stratford-upon-Avon & Banbury. Plenty of on-site parking available]
Upton House, together with its magnificent collections and stunning gardens, reflects its 1930s heyday when it was home to millionaire oil magnate, the 2nd Viscount Bearsted. An avid collector of English and Continental Old Master paintings, fine porcelain and tapestries, Lord Bearsted bought and remodelled the seventeenth-century mansion to house his growing collection in the 1930s. Visitors can get close to internationally important works by Hogarth, Stubbs, Guardi, Canaletto, Bosch, Bruegel & El

Greco. Lord Bearsted was Chairman of Shell from 1921-1946, and son of the company's founder. During this time Shell commissioned some of the period's most fashionable artists, including Graham Sutherland and Rex Whistler, to create a unique series of vibrant advertising posters. Stunning colours are abundant in the garden all year round. Principally designed by Kitty Lloyd-Jones with Lady Bearsted in the 1920s, the formal lawns give way to surprise as the land drops away in a dramatic series of terraces and herbaceous borders, descending to a kitchen garden and tranquil water gardens. Upton is also home to the National Collection of Asters.

House: 1 Mar-15 Mar (Sat-Wed, closed Thu-Fri) 13.00-17.00, House Tours - 11.00-13.00; 17 Mar-30 Mar (daily) 13.00-17.00, House Tours - 11.00-13.00; 21 Jul-31 Aug (daily) 13.00-17.00, House Tours - 11.00-13.00; 1 Sep-5 Nov (Sat-Wed, closed Thu-Fri) 13.00-17.00, House Tours - 11.00-13.00; 8 Nov-21 Dec (Sat-Sun only) 12.00-16.00 (with Ground Floor access only). Garden/Restaurant/Shop/Plant Centre: 1 Mar-16 Mar (Sat-Wed, closed Thu-Fri) 11.00-17.00; 17 Mar-30 Mar (daily) 11.00-17.00; 21 Jul-31 Aug (daily) 13.00-17.00; 1 Sep-2 Nov (Sat-Wed, closed Thu-Fri) 11.00-17.00; 3 Nov-21 Dec (Sat-Wed, closed Thu-Fri) 12.00-16.00; 26 Dec-4 Jan 09 (daily) 12.00-16.00. Entry to house is by timed ticket only on Bank Hols. Garden winter route only available Nov-Jan

House & Gardens: A£8.50 C£4.20, Family Ticket £21.00. Gardens only: A£5.00 C£2.50 (includes a voluntary 10% donation; visitors can however choose to pay the standard admission prices which are displayed at the property and at www.nationaltrust.org.uk). NT Members £Free. Group rate (15+): £6.70 (standard admission prices apply to groups). Guided tours available by arrangement. Reduced rates in winter

Coventry Toy Museum

Whitefriars Gate Much Park Street Coventry Warwickshire CV1 2LT
Tel: 024 7623 1331
A collection of toys dating from 1740 to 1980, including trains and games, housed in a fourteenth century monastery gatehouse.

Transport Museums

Coventry Transport Museum

Millennium Place Hales Street Coventry
Warwickshire CV1 1JD
Tel: 024 7623 4270 Fax: 024 7623 4284
www.transport-museum.com

[Follow signs for Coventry City Centre; exit ring rd at J1]
It's hard to find places to visit that offer something that interests the whole family. But Coventry Transport Museum is different. It's full of inspiration, thrills and fun, and everyone in the family will find something to keep them happy. Visitors can explore over 150 years of unique history with something different round every corner. But its not just a place for the past - you can design your own car, feel what it's like to break the sound barrier at 763 miles an hour, and even travel into the future. This is what makes the museum one of the most popular family days out in the West Midlands. What's more admission is free for everyone and as it's open every day of the week there really is no excuse not to visit.
All year daily 10.00-17.00. Closed 24-26 Dec
Admission Free

Discount Offer: 10% discount on all gift shop purchases (when you spend £10.00 or more).

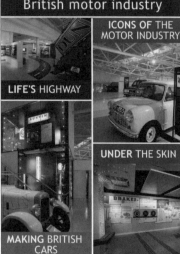

Heritage Motor Centre

Banbury Road Gaydon Warwickshire CV35 0BJ
Tel: 01926 641188 Fax: 01926 645103
www.heritage-motor-centre.co.uk
[J12 M40, 2-3 min away on B4100, follow signs. Plenty of on-site parking available]
The Heritage Motor Centre is home to the worlds largest collection of historic British cars. Following a £1.7million makeover the museum now boasts three new exciting and interactive exhibitions which uncover the story of the British motor industry from the 1890s to the present day. Fun for all the family with free guided tours twice a day, onsite café and gift shop and a selection of outdoor activities including children's play area, picnic site, 4x4 experience, go-karts and children's miniature roadway. Check our website for school holiday activities and special weekend events.
Easter-Oct daily, 3 Nov-Easter Wed-Sun only, 10.00-17.00. Closed 24 Dec-2 Jan
A£9.00 C(0-4)£Free C(5-16)£7.00 Concessions£8.00, Family Ticket (A2+C3) £28.00. Annual passes available

Discount Offer: Two for the Price of One (full-paying adult).

Zoos

Twycross Zoo

Burton Road Atherstone Warwickshire CV9 3PX
Tel: 01827 880250 Fax: 01827 880700
www.twycrosszoo.org
[A444 nr Market Bosworth on Burton to Nuneaton rd, off J11 M42. Ample on-site parking available]
See wildlife from across the world at Twycross Zoo, the centre for conservation, education and fun. 50 acres of parkland housing nearly 1,000 animals, mainly rare and endangered species. Famous primate collection, fascinating new Borneo Longhouse Exhibit, Lions, Giraffes, Elephants and Pets Corner.
All year daily 10.00-17.30 (closes 16.00 in winter). Closed 25 Dec only
Please see our website for ticket prices

Discount Offer: One Child Free.

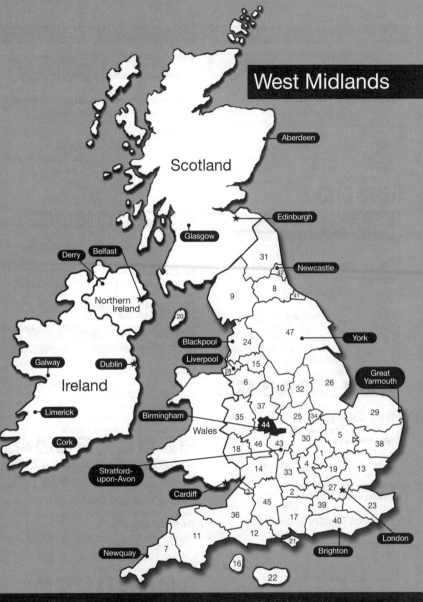

West Midlands

Aberdeen

Scotland

Edinburgh

Glasgow

Derry   Belfast

Newcastle

Northern
Ireland

Blackpool

Galway   Dublin

Liverpool

Ireland

Great
Yarmouth

Limerick

Birmingham

Wales

York

Cork

Stratford-
upon-Avon

Cardiff

London

Newquay

Brighton

Animal Attractions

Sandwell Park Farm
Sandwell Valley Country Park Salters Lane
West Bromwich West Midlands B71 4BG
Tel: 0121 553 0220
Restored nineteenth-century working farm with
livestock breeds of the period, traditional farm-
ing methods, displays and exhibitions. Also tea
rooms and Victorian kitchen garden.

Art Galleries

Birmingham Museum and Art Gallery
Chamberlain Square Birmingham B3 3DH
Tel: 0121 303 2834
Opened in 1885, the collections cover fine art
and applied arts, archaeology and ethnography,
natural history, social history. The Museum has
the largest collection of Pre-Raphaelite works in
the world, as well as Old Masters and
Impressionists.

Ikon Gallery
68-70 Heath Mill Lane Birmingham B9 4AR
Tel: 0121 248 0708
Ikon Gallery is one of Europe's leading venues
for new art. The changing exhibitions programme shows work by artists from Britain.

New Art Gallery Walsall
Gallery Square Walsall West Midlands WS2 8LG
Tel: 01922 654400
With core art collection, the Garman Ryan
Collection, Children's Discovery Gallery, and
world-class exhibition spaces.

Wolverhampton Art Gallery
Lichfield Street Wolverhampton West Midlands
WV1 1DU
Tel: 01902 552055
With its family friendly displays, Wolverhampton
Art Gallery welcomes visitors to explore 300
years of art; from delightful Georgian paintings
to thought provoking contemporary pieces.

Arts, Crafts & Textiles

Broadfield House Glass Museum
Compton Drive Kingswinford West Midlands
DY6 9NS
Tel: 01384 812745
Situated in the historic Stourbridge Glass
Quarter, Broadfield House Glass Museum is one
of the best glass museums in the world. The
Museum has a magnificent collection of British
glass, much of it made locally, dating from the
seventeenth century up to the present day.

Dudley Museum and Art Gallery
St James's Road Dudley DY1 1HU
Tel: 01384 815575
One of the Midland's most exciting exhibition
venues, famous for its temporary exhibitions.

Birds, Butterflies & Bees

Falconry Centre
Kidderminster Road South Hagley Stourbridge
West Midlands DY9 0JB
Tel: 01562 700014
The centre houses some 80 birds of prey
including Hawk, Owls and Falcons.

Country Parks & Estates

Himley Hall and Park
Himley Dudley DY3 4DF
Tel: 01902 326665
Himley Hall is open to the public during the
spring and summer with an exhibitions pro-
gramme. Himley Park includes 180 acres of
'Capability' Brown gardens and woodland.

Lickey Hills Visitor Centre and Country Park
Visitor Centre Warren Lane Rednal Birmingham
West Midlands B45 8ER
Tel: 0121 447 7106
524-acre country park of woodlands, heathland
and amenity grassland giving views over
Birmingham. Golf course and forest.

Exhibition & Visitor Centres

Cadbury World

Linden Road Bournville Birmingham West
Midlands B30 2LU
Tel: 0845 450 3599 Fax: 0121 451 1366
www.cadburyworld.co.uk

[1mi S of A38 Bristol Rd on A4040. Plenty of on-site parking available]

Cadbury World : Where chocolate comes to life!
Cadbury World is a fun day out suitable for all
ages. Uncover a world of chocolate delights as
you tour through the different exhibits and learn
about the history and heritage of the Cadbury
firm. Discover the processes involved in creating
the nation's favourite chocolate, see yourself
moulded in chocolate and excite your senses
choosing your own chocolate concoction in
Essence. With the world's largest Cadbury
shop, a new revamped Cadabra ride and much
more, you couldn't ask for a more scrumptious
day out. The new Bournville Experience focuses
on how the Cadbury brothers created the factory and the Bournville Village. Design a village of
the future and try your hand at producing your
own packaging design for display in the vintage
shop!

Please call for opening times
A£13.00 C(4-15)£9.95 Concessions£10.00
C(under4)£Free, Family Ticket (A2+C2) £40.00
or (A2+C3) £48.50

**Discount Offer: £10.00 off One Family
Ticket (A2+C2) or (A2+C3).**

Gardens & Horticulture

Birmingham Botanical Gardens and Glasshouses

Westbourne Road Edgbaston Birmingham West
Midlands B15 3TR
Tel: 0121 454 1860 Fax: 0121 454 7835
www.birminghambotanicalgardens.org.uk

[2mi W of City Centre. Ample on-site parking]

The lush rainforest vegetation in the Tropical
House includes many economic plants. Palms,
tree ferns, orchids and insectivorous plants are
displayed in the Subtropical House. The
Mediterranean House features a wide variety of
citrus plants, a pelargonium collection and seasonal displays of conservatory plants. A desert
scene, with its giant agaves and opuntias, fills
the Arid House. Outside there is colourful bedding on the Terrace and a tour of the 15 acres
of Gardens includes rhododendrons and azaleas, herbaceous borders, an impressive Rock
Garden and a collection of over 200 trees.
There are Herb and Cottage Gardens, a Water
Garden, Alpine Yard, Historic Gardens, Organic
Garden and the National Bonsai Collection and
Japanese Garden. Ferns, grasses and sensory
plants all have their own areas. There is a children's adventure playground, Discovery garden,
aviaries, gallery and sculpture trail. Shop at the
gardens, plant sales and tea room.

*All year daily Mon-Sat 09.00-19.00 or dusk if
sooner, Sun 10.00-19.00 or dusk if sooner.
Closed 25 Dec*
A£7.00 Concessions£4.50

Discount Offer: One Concession Free.

Castle Bromwich Hall Gardens

Chester Road Castle Bromwich Birmingham
West Midlands B36 9BT
Tel: 0121 749 4100
This rare and enchanting late-seventeenth and
early-eighteenth century walled garden is set
within 10 acres of land, with very fine examples
of period planting.
Closed Mondays

Heritage & Industrial

Birmingham Railway Museum

Warwick Road Tyseley Birmingham B11 2HL
Tel: 0121 707 4696
This is a working railway museum with a fully
equipped workshop.

Red House Glass Cone

High Street Wordsley Stourbridge West
Midlands DY8 4AZ
Tel: 01384 812750
Built at the end of the eighteenth century, it is
one of only four glassmaking cones surviving in
the UK. With the aid of film, audio guides,
exhibits and live glassmaking demonstrations,
you can explore its 200 years of history.

Walsall Leather Museum

Littleton Street West Walsall WS2 8EQ
Tel: 01922 721153
This museum is housed in a former leather
goods factory dating from 1891. In the atmospheric workshops visitors can see how traditional leather goods have been made.

Historical

Baddesley Clinton

Rising Lane Baddesley Clinton Village Knowle
Solihull West Midlands B93 0DQ
Tel: 01564 783294
Picturesque medieval moated manor-house and
garden. With nineteenth-century Catholic
chapel, priest's holes, gardens with lakeside
walks and a nature trail.

Packwood House

Packwood Lane Lapworth Solihull B94 6AT
Tel: 01564 783294
Much-restored Tudor house, park and garden
with notable topiary.

Wightwick Manor

Wightwick Bank Wolverhampton WV6 8EE
Tel: 01902 761400
Victorian manor house with William Morris interi-
ors and colourful garden.
Wed-Sat

Living History Museums

Black Country Living Museum

Tipton Road Castle Hill Dudley West Midlands
DY1 4SQ
Tel: 0121 557 9643
Friendly costumed demonstrations bring recon-
structed, original cottages, shops and work-
shops to life on a 26 acre site.

Nature & Conservation Parks

Cannon Hill Park

The Information Centre 2 Russell Road Moseley
Birmingham B13 8RD
Tel: 0121 442 4226
Ornamental flower beds and shrub areas, tennis, bowls, putting and fishing available. Tropical
plant display house and children's play area
with climbing frames and swings. Boating, picnic areas and nature centre. Nature conservation area with self-guided nature trails available.

Places of Worship

Birmingham Cathedral

Colmore Row Birmingham B3 2QB
Tel: 0121 236 4333
Birmingham Cathedral, designed by Thomas
Archer, is one of the most notable eighteenth-
century church buildings in the country and
stands at the heart of the city.

Science - Earth & Planetary

Thinktank

Millennium Point Curzon Street Birmingham
West Midlands B4 7XG
Tel: 0121 202 2222
Four floors of fun and exploration, 10 themed
galleries containing over 200 interactive games.
Attractions include the IMAX cinema and a
Planetarium.

Sealife Centres & Aquariums

National Sea Life Centre (Birmingham)

The Waters Edge Brindleyplace Birmingham
West Midlands B1 2HL
Tel: 0121 633 4700 Fax: 0121 633 4787
www.sealifeeurope.com

[Rail: New Street Station]

The National Sea Life Centre will introduce you
to many strange, beautiful and fascinating creatures of the deep. Prepare for astonishing close
views of everything from humble starfish to
mighty sharks and playful otters, all in displays
that carefully recreate their natural habitats.
Explore a rich variety of underwater environments, from freshwater streams to the rugged
coastline, from the sandy shallows to the dark
depths of the ocean. At every step there are different amazing creatures to find, to watch and
to learn about. Discover the truth about the
much-misunderstood shark, the plight of the
endangered sea turtle, the remarkable lives of
seahorses and countless more surprising facts
about these and other incredible creatures. Our
new feature, 'Amazon Attack' will turn the spotlight on the more dangerous creatures of the
Amazon River and the surrounding rainforest -
everything from piranhas and dart frogs to sabre
toothed tetras and terrifying tarantulas. A unique
new refuge for endangered freshwater turtles
(which will include a special turtle hatchery) will
soon follow this.

All year daily from 10.00. Closed Christmas Day

Please call for admission prices
Discount Offer: One Child Free.

Sport & Recreation

Blue Ice, Solihull Rink

Hobs Moat Road Solihull West Midlands
B92 8JN
Tel: 0121 742 5561 Fax: 0121 742 4315
www.solihullicerink.co.uk

*[M6 J4/4A take M42 S exit J6, take A45
Birmingham. L lane into Hobs Moat Rd B425.
Follow brown tourist sign. To enter the FREE car
park go past Solihull Ice Rink & turn R into Ulleries
Rd & next R by Fitness First. M42 J5 on A41
Solihull bypass turn R into B425 Lode Lane & fol-
low brown tourist sign. Continue past Land Rover
factory on your R, straight ahead at island into
Hobs Moat Road. Ice rink is second L. R by
Fitness First. Rail: Solihull. Bus: 71, 72 & 57a & to
Coventry Rd 57, 58, 60 & 900. Plenty of free on-
site parking available]*

Welcome to Blue Ice, Solihull Rink @ Blue Ice
Plaza. The venue also incorporates Fitness First
Health Club, Riley's pool and snooker and three
restaurants to include Spicewood's, Pizza by
Goli and Woks Hall. Solihull Ice Rink has its very
own skate shop within the ice rink. The shop
sells a wide variety of recreational ice skates
and skating accessories. Also specialises in ice
hockey equipment and figure skates for both
juniors and adults. We are also proud to offer
cool birthday parties, group visit packages,
skating lessons, café, function rooms for hire as
well as a variety of hockey, figure/dance and
speed skating clubs for adults and children.

*All year round. Sessions: Mon 13.45-15.45; Tue
10.00-12.00 &13.45-15.45 & 19.30-21.30; Wed*

10.00-12.00 & 13.45-15.00 & 19.30-21.30 (speed garage and funky-house disco); Thu 10.00-15.45 & 19.30-21.30; Fri 10.00-12.00 & 13.45-15.45 & 17.00-18.30 & 20.00-22.30 (live DJ); Sat 11.00-16.00 & 20.00-22.30 (live DJ); Sun 11.00-16.00 & 20.30-22.30; Local School Hols (excluding teacher-training days) 11.00-16.00 & evenings as normal

Prices valid until 30 Nov 2008. Spectators £1.60. C(under4)£3.00 A(over60)£3.00. Mon-Fri Daytime Sessions: A(+skate-hire)£6.30 C(+skate-hire)£6.00, Family Ticket(A2+C2) or (A1+C3) (+skate-hire) £18.70. Sat-Sun Daytime Session: A(+skate-hire)£7.60 C(+skate-hire)£7.40, Family Ticket(A2+C2) or (A1+C3) (+skate-hire) £22.60. Local School Holidays (Daytime Sessions): A(+skate-hire)£7.40 C(+skate-hire)£7.20, Family Ticket(A2+C2) or (A1+C3) (+skate-hire) £22.20. Tue -Thu & Sun Evening Sessions: A(+skate-hire)£6.30 C(+skate-hire)£6.00, Family Ticket (A2+C2) or (A1+C3) (+skate-hire) £18.70. Fri & Sat Evening Sessions (Disco): A(+skate-hire)£7.60 C(+skate-hire)£7.40. Group rates, Off Peak: £3.50 Peak: £4.90. Skating lessons available on request

Discount Offer: Save up to £5.00!

Transport Museums

Jaguar Daimler Heritage Trust
Jaguar Cars Ltd Browns Lane Alesbury Coventry West Midlands CV5 9DR
Tel: 02476 203322
Portraying over a century of outstanding automotive design, fine engineering, and world leading car development. The Collection is Jaguar's living heritage, mainly on display under one roof at the JDHT Museum.
Last Sunday of every month (Subject to availability). Other times by appointment only

National Motorcycle Museum
Coventry Road Bickenhill Solihull West Midlands B92 0EJ
Tel: 01675 443311
The National Motorcycle Museum. Is recognized as the finest and largest motorcycle museum in the world. It is a place where 'Legends Live On' and it is a tribute to this once great British Industry that dominated world markets for some sixty years. Encompassing five 400m² exhibition

halls it is record of Britains finest industrial era.

Zoos

Dudley Zoological Gardens
2 The Broadway Dudley West Midlands DY1 4QB
Tel: 01384 215313 Fax: 01384 456048
www.dudleyzoo.org.uk

[Situated on A461 (Castle Hill) 3mi from J2 of M5. Dudley Bus Station is 2 min walk from Zoo entrance. Rail: Dudley Port station 3m. Coseley Station 3mi. Sandwell & Dudley 5m. Frequent bus service from Dudley to both. Disabled parking facilities]

The wooded grounds of Dudley Castle make a wonderful setting for the long-established, traditional zoo, which has animals from every continent. From lions, giraffes, tigers to snakes and spiders. During summer months enjoy animal talks and encounters, fair rides, bouncy castle, adventure playground and face painting.

All year Easter-Sept daily 10.00-16.00, Sept-Easter daily 10.00-15.00. Closed 25 Dec

A£10.95 C(under3)£Free C(3-15)£6.95 Concessions£7.50. Group rates available

Discount Offer: One Child Free.

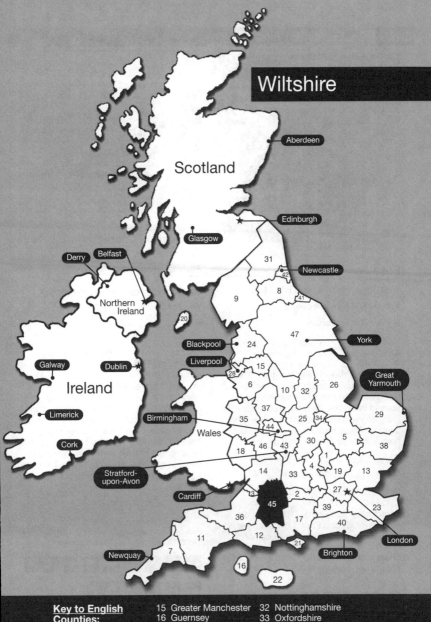

Wiltshire

Aberdeen

Scotland

Edinburgh

Glasgow

Derry | Belfast

Northern Ireland

31

Newcastle

42

8

9

41

Galway | Dublin

Ireland

20

Blackpool

24

47

York

Liverpool

15

Great Yarmouth

Limerick

28

6

10

32

26

Cork

37

35

44

25

34

29

Birmingham

Wales

46

43

30

5

38

Stratford-upon-Avon

18

14

33

4

1

19

13

Cardiff

13

2

27

23

45

39

40

London

36

17

Newquay

7

11

12

21

Brighton

16

22

Animal Attractions

Bush Farm Bison Centre

West Knoyle Mere Wiltshire BA12 6AE

Tel: 01747 830263 phone/fax

www.bisonfarm.co.uk

[Follow the brown signs from A350. 1mi from the A303. Plenty of on-site parking available]

Bush Farm is tucked away in a great Oak Wood. Visitors will see herds of bison, elk and Red deer as they follow the trail through 100 acres of meadows, lakes and woodlands. There is a gallery and shop selling art, native American artefacts, bison meat and venison. We also have a children's farmyard and playground.

19 Mar-26 Sept Wed-Sun 10.00-17.00. Winter months: Shop & Gallery Thur & Fri only

Farmyard & Woodland Walks: A£6.00 C(under4)£Free C£3.00. Camping and Caravanning Club Pitches £8.00 per night, Woodland Camping £8.00 per person per night. 50% discount on Farm Walks for campers

Discount Offer: One Child Free (with a full-paying adult).

Cholderton Charlie's Rare Breeds Farm

Amesbury Road Cholderton Salisbury Wiltshire SP4 0EW

Tel: 01980 629438 Fax: 01980 629594

www.choldertoncharliesfarm.com

[4mi E of Stonehenge. Plenty of on-site parking available]

A farm park set in the Wiltshire countryside close to the A303 and only 4 miles from Stonehenge. We boast a superb collection of rare breed farm animals, education centre, home cooked food in our café, gift shop, undercover picnic area, Rabbitworld, adventure play area and indoor soft play area in a massive play barn. New for 2008 is our refurbished youth hostel accommodation, now comprising of 60 beds - why not extend your stay and soak up the countryside for a few days? Check our website for updates and special activities that we run throughout the year.

All year daily, Summer 10.00-18.00, Winter 10.00-16.00

A£5.50 C(2-16)£4.95 Concessions£4.50 Family Ticket (A2+C2)£19.00, Season Tickets available

Farmer Giles Farmstead

Teffont Salisbury Wiltshire SP3 5QY

Tel: 01722 716338 Fax: 01722 716993

Bottle-feed the lambs and the kid-goats, groom the donkeys, ride the ponies and cuddle the rabbits, before browsing the gift shop and enjoying a tractor-ride.

Roves Farm Visitor Centre

Sevenhampton Nr Highworth Swindon Wiltshire
SN6 7QG
Tel: 01793 763939 Fax: 01793 766846
www.rovesfarm.co.uk

[Off B4000 or A361]

New indoor play area, big bale stack, bouncy
castle and ball pond. Heated indoor soft play for
the under 5's and giant sandpit. Tractor rides
around the 400 acre farm and kids crafts.
Animal racing at weekends and themed activity
weeks in the school holidays.

*Open daily 16 Feb-4 Nov please visit the website
for full details.*

A£6.50 C(3+)£5.50. Group rates available

Archaeology

Wiltshire Heritage Museum

41 Long Street Devizes Wiltshire SN10 1NS
Tel: 01380 727369
World-famous collections from Wiltshire, includ-
ing unique finds from barrows around
Stonehenge, are on display.

Country Parks & Estates

Lackham Country Park

Wiltshire College Lackham Lacock Chippenham
Wiltshire SN15 2NY
Tel: 01249 466800
Set within the grounds of Lackham House,
there is the Museum of Agriculture and Rural

Life, parkland and a miniature railway.

Forests & Woods

Brokerswood Country Park

Brokerswood Westbury Wiltshire BA13 4EH
Tel: 01373 822238
80-acre country park with woodland railway,
Adventureland, play trails, heritage centre,
indoor toddler play area, café and gift shop.

Gardens & Horticulture

Stourton House Flower Garden

Stourton Warminster Wiltshire BA12 6QF
Tel: 01747 840417
Stourton House specialises in unusual plants,
many of which are for sale..

Rare Breed Farm Park
Opening Times:
Summer 10-6 • Winter 10-4

Daily activites all year
round include the famous
pig racing, rabbit
handling, chick handling
and Cholderton Charlie
Tractor rides (peak times).

**New for 2008 is a
family friendly youth
hostel and tipi tents.**

Cholderton Charlie's Farm
Rare Breed Farm Park
Amesbury Road
Cholderton, Salisbury
Wilts SP4 0EW

01980 629438
www.choldertoncharliesfarm.com

Heritage & Industrial

Crofton Beam Engines
Crofton Pumping Station Crofton Marlborough
Wiltshire SN8 3DW
Tel: 01672 870300
Amazing industrial archaeology situated in the
beautiful Wiltshire countryside.

Historical

Avebury Henge
Avebury Nr Marlborough Wiltshire SN8 1RF
Tel: 01672 539250
*[in Avebury, 7m W of Marlborough, Bus: Trans
Wilts Express 49/A, Wilts & Dorset 5/6. Rail:
Swindon 11mi]*
World-famous stone circle (and World Heritage
Site) at the heart of a prehistoric landscape.
Archaeological finds displayed in the on-site
Alexander Keiller Museum.

Bowood House and Gardens
Bowood Calne Wiltshire SN11 0LZ
Tel: 01249 812102
Outstanding eighteenth-century house with
remarkable collection of family heirlooms includ-
ing fine paintings and water-colours. 100 acre
Park landscaped by Capability Brown.

Corsham Court
Corsham Wiltshire SN13 0BZ
Tel: 01249 701610
An Elizabethan Manor House built in 1582 and
home of the Methven family since 1745.
*20 Mar-30 Sep: daily 14.00-17.30 (Closed Mon
& Fri)*

Great Chalfield Manor
Great Chalfield Melksham Wiltshire SN12 8NJ
Tel: 01225 782239
Charming fifteenth-century manor house with an
Arts & Crafts garden.
30 Mar-2 Nov: Tue-Thu & Sun

Lydiard House and Park
Lydiard Tregoze Swindon Wiltshire SN5 3PA

Tel: 01793 770401
Striking Palladian house set in a 260 acres of
eighteenth-century parkland. Features include
lake, coach house, ice house, ornamental fruit
and flower walled garden and St Mary's
Church.
Closed Mondays

Old Wardour Castle
Old Wardour Tisbury Salisbury Wiltshire
SP3 6RP
Tel: 01747 870487
Built in the late fourteenth century for John, fifth
Lord Lovel, this unusual six-sided castle was
unique in medieval English architecture.

Silbury Hill
West Kennet Avebury Wiltshire
Tel: 0117 975 0700
[1mi W of West Kennet on A4]
The largest man-made mound in Europe,
Silbury Hill is comparable in height and volume
to the Egyptian pyramids (which were built
around the same time). However, its purpose
and significance remain a mystery.

Stonehenge
Amesbury Salisbury Wiltshire SP4 7DE
Tel: 01980 624715
*[Monument 2mi W of Amesbury at J of A303 &
A344/A360]*
One of the most famous prehistoric sites in the
world, Stonehenge is a World Heritage Site and
is thought to date back to 2200 BC. It is often
associated with British Druidism, Neo Paganism
and New Age philosophy.

Stourhead
Stourton Warminster Wiltshire BA12 6QD
Tel: 01747 841152
Eighteenth-century landscape garden and
Palladian mansion. Features include temples,
monuments and rare planting around a tranquil
lake, Chippendale furniture and fine paintings,
woodland walks, King Alfred's Tower, and two
Iron Age hill forts.

Westwood Manor

Bradford-On-Avon Wiltshire BA15 2AF
Tel: 01225 863374
A fifteenth-century Wiltshire stone manor house
with gothic and jacobean windows. Modern
topiary garden with attractive views over the
Frome Valley.
23 Mar-30 Sep: Tue-Wed & Sun (14.00-17.00)

Wilton House

Wilton Salisbury Wiltshire SP2 0BJ
Tel: 01722 746720
Built on the site of a "ninth-century abbey" and
set in 21 acres of landscaped parkland, Wilton
House contains a superb art collection, a recreated Tudor Kitchen and a Victorian laundry. With
parkland and an adventure playground.
*5 Apr-28 Aug: Sun-Thu & Bank Hol Sat (12.00-
17.00). 1-28 Sep: Tue-Thu (12.00-17.00)*

Windmill Hill

Avebury Wiltshire
Tel: 0117 975 0700
[1.5m NW of Avebury]
The classic Neolithic 'causewayed enclosure',
with three concentric but intermittent ditches.
Large quantities of animal bones found here
indicate feasting, animal trading or rituals, or
perhaps all three. Part of the Avebury World
Heritage Site.

Military & Defence Museums

Rifles (Berkshire and Wiltshire) Museum, The

58 The Close Salisbury Wiltshire SP1 2EX
Tel: 01722 414536

*[Salisbury Cathedral Close, beneath shadow of
Cathedral spire, within easy walking distance from
City Centre & car parks]*

"The Wardrobe" is now the museum of the
Royal Gloucestershire, Berkshire and Wiltshire
Regiment, with displays telling the absorbing
story of the Royal Berkshire Regiment, the
Wiltshire Regiment and the Duke of Edinburgh's
Royal Regiment. Restaurant and gardens.

Places of Worship

Salisbury Cathedral

33 The Close Salisbury Wiltshire SP1 2EJ
Tel: 01722 555120 Fax: 01722 555116
www.salisburycathedral.org.uk

[A30, M3, M27 signposted locally]

Salisbury is Britain's finest thirteenth-century
Cathedral - with the highest spire (123
metres/404 ft), the best preserved Magna Carta
(AD 1215), a unique thirteenth-century frieze of
bible stories in the octagonal Chapter House
and Europe's oldest working clock (AD 1386).
Boy and girl choristers sing daily services, continuing a tradition of worship that dates back
nearly 800 years. Set within the Cathedral
Close, surrounded by eight acres of lawns and
eight centuries of beautiful houses, Salisbury
Cathedral has been the source of inspiration to
generations of artists and writers. Volunteers
provide guided tours highlighting the Cathedral's
many fine treasures, including tours of the roof
and tower. The city of Salisbury, Stonehenge
and Old Sarum are all within easy reach.

*All year Mon-Sat, 1 Jan-10 June 07.15-18.15,
11 June-24 Aug 07.15-19.15, 25 Aug-31 Dec
07.15-18.15, Sun 07.15-18.15*

Suggested Donations: A£5.00 C(5-17)£3.00
OAPs&Students(NUS/USI)£4.25, Family Ticket
£12.00. Tower Tour: A£6.50 Concessions£5.50

STEAM - Museum of the Great Western Railway

Kemble Drive Swindon Wiltshire SN2 2TA
Tel: 01793 466646 Fax: 01793 466615
www.swindon.gov.uk/steam

[Adjacent to Great Western Designer Outlet Centre. From M4 & other major routes, follow brown tourist signs to 'Outlet Centre' plus M for Museum]

STEAM - Museum of the Great Western Railway tells the story of the men and women who built, operated and travelled on the Great Western Railway. Hands-on displays, world famous locomotives, archive film footage and stories told by ex-railway workers all bring the story of steam to life. A recreated 1930s station platform, posters and holiday memorabillia, together with a brand new interactive working signal box and the amazing train simulator, bring back the glamour and excitement of the golden age of steam. Located next door to the Swindon Designer Outlet Centre, STEAM is a great day out for all. There's a year round programme of special events and exhibitions too, plus gift shop and refreshments. Visit www.swindon.gov.uk/steam for more details.

All year daily 10.00-17.00. Closed 25-26 Dec & 1 Jan

A£6.00 C(under5)£Free C£4.00, Family Ticket (A2+C2) £16.00 or (A2+C3) £19.00. Free family fun trail

Wildlife & Safari Parks

Longleat

Longleat Warminster Wiltshire BA12 7NW
Tel: 01985 844400 Fax: 01985 844885
www.longleat.co.uk
[A36 between Bath & Salisbury, A362 Warminster to Frome. Plenty of on-site parking available]
The star of BBC's hugely popular Animal Park is looking forward to welcoming you in 2008. Discover the magnificent animals which roam the first Safari Park outside Africa from the comfort of your own car... See how you measure up to a giraffe, watch out for the zebra's crossing, wander amongst the wallabies in wallaby wood and be enthralled by the majestic lions and tigers! Continue your adventure aboard the Safari Boats for a sea lion escorted cruise to Gorilla Island, find yourself lost in the Longleat Hedge Maze and enjoy a fun packed railway ride before discovering the treasures and priceless heirlooms within Longleat House and much, much more... Your day at Longleat will never be long enough! The Passport Ticket offers access into over 12 Longleat attractions.
All Attractions: 16 Feb-24 Feb daily, 1 Mar-9 Mar Sat-Sun, 15 Mar-2 Nov daily. Longleat Safari Park:10.00-16.00 (17.00 Sat-Sun, Bank Hols & state school holidays). Other Longleat Attractions: 11.00-17.00 (10.30-17.30 Sat-Sun, Bank Hols & state school holidays). Longleat House: All year daily Easter-Sept 10.00-17.00 (17.30 on Sat-Sun, Bank Hols & state school holidays). Closed 25 Dec, All other times guided tours only 11.00-15.00, subject to change, please call for info.
Make huge savings by purchasing the 'Great Value' Passport and seeing all 12 of the Longleat attractions! Visit Longleat in a day or come back at any time before the end of the season to see those attractions previously missed... the choice is yours! Each attraction may be visited only once. A£22.00 C(3-14)£16.00 OAPs£16.00

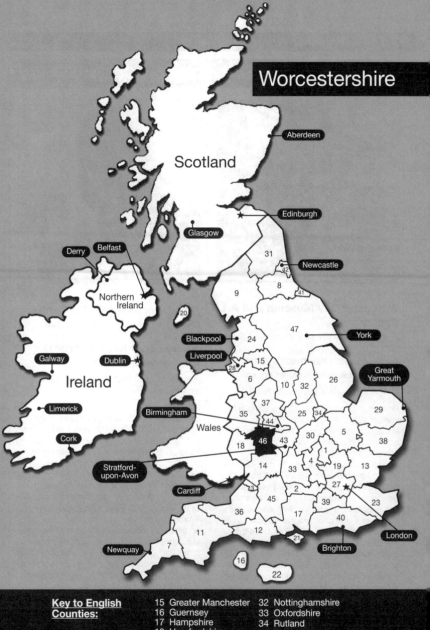

Worcestershire

Scotland

Aberdeen

Edinburgh

Glasgow

Derry · Belfast

Newcastle

31

42

Northern
Ireland

8

41

9

Galway · Dublin

20

47

York

Ireland

Blackpool

24

Liverpool

Great
Yarmouth

Limerick

28

15

6

10

32

26

Cork

37

29

Birmingham

35

25

34

Wales

44

46

43

30

5

38

Stratford-
upon-Avon

18

4

1

19

13

Cardiff

14

33

2

27

London

13

Newquay

36

45

39

23

7

11

17

40

Brighton

12

21

16

22

Arts, Crafts & Textiles

Worcester City Museum and Art Gallery

Foregate Street Worcester Worcestershire
WR1 1DT
Tel: 01905 25371 Fax: 01905 616979
www.worcestercitymuseums.org.uk/

[Worcester City Centre J6 or J7 M5]

Housed in a beautiful Victorian building in the heart of Worcester, the City Art Gallery & Museum runs a lively programme of exhibitions, activities and events for all the family. The gallery presents a changing programme of contemporary art and craft exhibitions. Current displays also include the Spirit of Enterprise tracing the history of Worcester's industrial past, displays of geology and natural history as well as a selection of nineteenth and twentieth-century paintings, prints, and photographs. Visitors can also discover the colourful collections of uniforms, medals and pictures from the independent museums of the Worcestershire Regiment and the Yeomanry Cavalry. The museum has an activity space and runs a regular programme of art and craft workshops for children, as well as artist led events for schools and adults. Visit the gallery shop, which has a superb selection of cards, books and gifts, or relax in the Balcony Café.

All year Mon-Fri 09.30-17.30, Sat 09.30-17.00. Closed Sun & Bank Hols

Admission Free

Factory Outlets & Tours

Royal Worcester Visitor Centre

Severn Street Worcester Worcestershire
WR1 2NE
Tel: 01905 21247 Fax: 01905 619503
www.royalworcester.com

[2 min walk from cathedral/city centre easy access, 3mi from J7 of M5. Plenty of on-site parking available]

Established in 1751 along the banks of the River Severn The Royal Worcester Visitor Centre is a Great Day Out for everyone. Nestles amidst Victorian factory buildings, just 2 minutes walk from the Cathedral & historic city centre, the Royal Worcester visitor centre offers something of interest for everyone whether you take a guided tour and see skilled craftsmen at work or try your hand at Paint a Plate. Our Royal Worcester bestware and seconds shops offer an extensive range of quality bone china, porcelain and giftware with great savings and special offers throughout the year. The Shopping Court, home to a many famous names, offers an unrivalled array of home accessories, cookware, linens, luggage, glassware and cutlery.

Open 7 days Mon-Sat 09.00-17.30, Sun 11.00-17.00)

Guided Tour A£5.00 Concessions£4.25, Family Ticket £12.00

Discount Offer: Two for the Price of One (full-paying adult).

Folk & Local History Museums

Almony Heritage Centre

Abbey Gate Evesham Worcestershire
WR11 4BG
Tel: 01386 446944
This fourteenth-century stone and timber building houses exhibitions relating to the history of Evesham Abbey, the battle of Evesham, and the culture and trade of Evesham.

Avoncroft Museum of Historic Buildings

Redditch Road Stoke Heath Bromsgrove Worcestershire B60 4JR
Tel: 01527 831363/831886
Avoncroft is a fascinating collection of historic buildings, rescued and restored on a scenic 15-acre open-air site in north Worcestershire.

Bewdley Museum

The Shambles Load Street Bewdley
Worcestershire DY12 2AE
Tel: 01299 403573 Fax: 01299 405306
www.wyreforestdc.gov.uk/museum

[4mi W of Kidderminster off A456 on B4190]

This unique Museum is housed in an unusual eighteenth-century 'Butchers Shambles'. Fascinating displays give an insight into the trades and crafts of the town and the surrounding Wyre Forest area. Indoor and outdoor displays feature the work of basket and besom makers, charcoal burning, coracles, the village wheelwright, horn working, pewtering and brass founding. There are daily demonstrations of rope making and claypipe making by traditional methods, and a variety of resident crafts peo-

ple. As well as a lovely herb garden and tea shop there is access to the beautiful adjoining Jubilee Gardens with a wildlife pond. A wide variety of exhibitions, events and children's activities take place through out the season. For full details of the 2008 programme see www.wyreforestdc.gov.uk/museum. Education programmes are available for schools and groups.

21 Mar-Oct daily 10.00-16.30 (11.00-16.00 Oct)
Admission Free

Discount Offer: 10% discount on any purchase in the Museum Tea Shop.

Malvern Museum

Abbey Gateway Abbey Road Malvern
Worcestershire WR14 3ES
Tel: 01684 567811
The local history exhibits range from the story of the Malvern Hills to the Water Cure and the lives of Sir Edward Elgar and G. Bernard Shaw.

Forests & Woods

Wyre Forest Visitor Centre

Wyre Forest Callow Hill Bewdley Kidderminster Worcestershire DY14 9XQ
Tel: 01299 266944
[On A456]
Tranquil woodland walks, deer at dusktime and a colourful array of toadstools in autumn all add to the woodland tapestry that is Wyre through the seasons.

Gardens & Horticulture

Bodenham Aboretum and Earth Centre

Wolverley Kidderminster Worcestershire
DY11 5SY
Tel: 01562 852444
A collection of over 2,700 trees set in 156 acres of Worcestershire countryside with 11 pools, four miles of footpaths and a working farm. There is also an award-winning Visitor Centre set in the hillside overlooking the Big Pool.

Croome Park

National Trust Estate Office The Builders' Yard
High Green Severn Stoke Worcestershire
WR8 9JS
Tel: 01905 371006 Fax: 01905 371090
www.nationaltrust.org.uk

[9mi S of Worcester off A38. 6mi NW of Pershore off B4084. Exit 1 off M50, Exit 7 off M5. Rail: Pershore. Plenty of on-site parking available]

Croome Park was the first commissioned landscape by Capability Brown who went on to revolutionise the world of garden and landscape design. The restoration project, the largest of its kind undertaken by the National Trust, has included the replanting of thousands of trees, creation of wetlands, replacement of shrubberies, the lake and river cleared and re-creation of pastureland. The planting now appears as it would have done in the 1760s. Gentle paths take visitors around the Pleasure Garden, to the river and lake and through the meadows. Be inspired by the Classical Temple Greenhouse or lakeside garden with its bridges, grotto, urn and temple. Or admire the parkland as you walk along the river to the Park Seat. Enjoy refreshments in the restored 1940's-style RAF canteen. A full programme of events takes place year-round.

1 Mar-30 Mar: Wed-Sun 10.00-17.30; 31 Mar-31 Aug: Daily 10.00-17.30; 3 Sep-26 Oct: Wed-Sun 10.00-17.30; 1 Nov-21 Dec: Sat-Sun 10.00-16.00; 26 Dec-1 Jan Daily 10:00-16:00. Open Bank Hol Mon's

A£4.80 C£2.40, Family Ticket £12.00.

Spetchley Park Gardens

Spetchley Worcester Worcestershire WR5 1RS
Tel: 01453 810303 Fax: 01453 511915
www.spetchleygardens.co.uk

[Off A44, 2mi E of Worcester]

The 110-acre deer park and the 30-acre gardens surround an early nineteenth-century mansion (not open), with sweeping lawns and herbaceous borders, a rose lawn and enclosed gardens with low box and yew hedges.

Mar-Sep Wed-Sun & Bank Hols 11.00-18.00
A£6.00 C£(under-16)Free Concessions£5.50

Discount Offer: Two for the Price of One (full-paying adult).

Stone House Cottage Gardens and Nursery

Stone Kidderminster Worcestershire DY10 4BG
Tel: 01562 69902
A romantic garden set in an old walled kitchen garden. The area is only 1 acre but seems much larger- hedges divide it into different compartments and create diverse habitats in which to grow the vast selection of rare and unusual plants that thrive here. Unusual brick follies adorn the walls and these in turn, are covered with a multitude of climbing and twining plants in which the garden specialises. The garden acts as a shop window for the adjoining nursery. Here you can buy plants of almost all that grow in the garden - the list of shrubs and climbers includes many hardly ever seen for sale in this country.
Gardens & Nursery: Mar-Sept Wed-Sat

Whitlenge Gardens and Nurseries

Whitlenge Lane Hartlebury Worcestershire
DY10 4HD
Tel: 01299 250720 Fax: 01299 251259
www.whit-lenge.co.uk

[S of Kidderminster off A442 Kidderminster-Droitwich Road. Look for Brown Whitlenge Garden signs. Plenty of on-site parking available]

Wander through the three-acre show garden of professional designer Keith J Southall, set around his eighteenth-century cottage. Walk the 'Twisted Brick Pergola' with its fan trained apples and pears, sit in the 'Verdigris Gazebo' see the water gardens with their split-level waterfalls. Listen to the 'bubblers' and marvel at the size of the Gunnera in the bog garden, against the compactness of the 'Scree Gardens.' Walk into the manmade cave and fernery, dwell upon the mystic of the 'Green Man' and the 'Sword in the Stone' features. Explore our Labyrinths. A plantsmans delight with over 800 varieties. Come and be inspired.

All year Mon-Fri 09.00-17.00, Sun 10.00-17.00
A£1.50 C£Free

Heritage & Industrial

Transport Museum, Wythall

Chapel Lane Wythall nr Birmingham
Worcestershire B47 6JX
Tel: 01564 826471
Two large halls containing buses and coaches, a Frankfurt tramcar, fire engines and a battery-electric vehicle display.
Apr-Oct Sat & Sun & Bank Hols

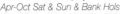

Forge Mill Needle Museum and Bordesley Abbey Visitor Centre

Needle Mill Lane Riverside Redditch
Worcestershire B98 8HY
Tel: 01527 62509
www.forgemill.org.uk

[N side of Redditch off A441 / J2 M42. Plenty of on-site parking available]

Forge Mill Museum is a unique museum about the Redditch needle industry. Redditch supplied the ninety percent of the world's needles in Victorian times. Part of the Museum is a needle scouring mill, which was working until 1958, and still has original water-powered machinery. See how needles were made from the initial metal coil to the packets sold in the shops. The Museum also has fishing tackle displays and holds contemporary textile exhibitions. The Bordesley Abbey Visitor Centre is an archaeo-logical site museum telling the story of the Cistercian Abbey in the meadows next to the Museum. Adult and children's audio tours for both the Needle Museum and Bordesley Abbey. The pleasant grounds with picnic tables enhance the visit.

Easter-Sept Mon-Fri 11.00-16.30, Weekends 14.00-17.00. Feb-Easter & Oct-Nov Mon-Thur 11.00-16.00, Sun 14.00-17.00
A£3.90 C£1.00 OAPs£2.95

Discount Offer: Two for the Price of One (full-paying adult).

Places of Worship

Worcester Cathedral

10a College Green Worcester Worcestershire
WR1 2LH
Tel: 01905 28854 Fax: 01905 611139
www.worcestercathedral.co.uk

[M5 J6/J7, then follow signs to city centre]

Worcester Cathedral is one of England's most
interesting cathedral's, with Royal tombs,
medieval cloisters, an ancient crypt and Chapter
House, and magnificent Victorian stained glass.
The Tower is open in the summer on Saturdays
and school holidays. We welcome families,
groups and individuals, with refreshments, a gift
shop, disabled access and gardens. We also
offer Conference facilities, with rooms catering
for 6-60. There is nearby parking, bus and train
stations. Services three times daily. "Turn up for
a tour" available from May until the end of
October.

*All year daily 07.30-18.00. Tower open in summer
from 11.00-16.00 Sat & School Hols "Turn up for
a tour" Mon-Sat at 11.00 &14.30 May to end Oct*

Admission Free: Invite donation of A£3.00
C£1.50. Guided Tours: A£4.00
Concessions£3.50 C£1.50, Prebooked Group:
£3.00

Railways

Severn Valley Railway

The Railway Station Bewdley Worcestershire
DY12 1BG
Tel: 01299 403816 Fax: 01299 400839
www.svr.co.uk

*[Rail: Kidderminster. Town station is adjacent to
railway station. This in on Comberton Hill on
A448. Plenty of on-site parking available]*

The leading standard gauge steam railway, with
one of the largest collections of locomotives
and rolling stock in the country. Services oper-
ate from Kidderminster and Bewdley to
Bridgnorth through 16 miles of picturesque
scenery along the River Severn. Events through-
out the year include: 1960s Transport Day,
Diesel and Steam Gala Weekends, Day Out
With Thomas Weekends, 1940s Weekends,
Severn Valley in Bloom, Bridgnorth Beer
Festival, Classic Car and Bike Day,
Remembrance Day Service, Santa Specials and
Festive Season Specials. Full details can be
found on the website.

*Weekends throughout year, 3 May-28 Sept daily
plus school holidays*

Prices depend on journey, call for details

Wildlife & Safari Parks

West Midlands Safari and Leisure Park

Spring Grove Bewdley DY12 1LF
Tel: 01299 402114
This extensive Safari and Leisure Park covers an
area of some 200 acres.
Feb-Nov daily

Yorkshire

Scotland

Aberdeen

Edinburgh

Glasgow

Newcastle

Derry

Belfast

Northern
Ireland

31

42

8

41

9

47

York

Blackpool

24

Galway

Dublin

Liverpool

15

28

20

Great
Yarmouth

Ireland

6

10

32

26

Limerick

37

29

Birmingham

35

44

25

34

Wales

46

43

30

5

38

Cork

18

1

Stratford-
upon-Avon

14

33

4

19

13

Cardiff

3

2

27

23

45

39

London

36

17

40

Newquay

11

12

21

Brighton

7

16

22

Abbeys

Fountains Abbey and Studley Royal Water Garden
Ripon North Yorkshire HG4 3DY
Tel: 01765 608888
Yorkshire's first World Heritage Site. It features a twelfth-century Cistercian abbey, a Georgian water garden and a medieval deer park.

Whitby Abbey
Whitby North Yorkshire YO22 4JT
Tel: 01947 603568
High on a cliff above Whitby are the imposing remains of Whitby Abbey. With visitor centre.

Agriculture / Working Farms

Brockholes Farm Visitor Centre
Off Warning Tongue Lane Bessacarr Doncaster South Yorkshire DN3 3NH
Tel: 01302 535057 Fax: 01302 533187
www.brockholesfarm.co.uk
[From M18 - J4: Leave the M18 at J4 and take the A630. At the second roundabout turn L on to Hatfield Lane. At the next mini roundabout, take a L-turn into Nutwell Lane. Follow the road through Old Cantley until you reach the next roundabout, go straight on here and follow Warning Tongue Lane for approx. 0.5mi until you see the entrance to the farm on your L.]
Brockholes Farm has been a working farm since 1759. There are many traditional breeds of farm animals no longer common, such as a variety of goats and sheep plus exotic animals.
All year daily 10.30-17.30 Closed Dec 25
A£5.95 Concessions£5.50

Cruckley Animal Farm
Foston on the Wolds Driffield
East Riding of Yorkshire YO25 8BS
Tel: 01262 488337
Cruckley is a working family farm with many kinds of modern and rare breeds of animals.

Heeley City Farm
Richards Road Sheffield Yorkshire S2 3DT
Tel: 0114 258 0482
Wind and sun powered city farm and education centre with friendly farm animals.

Airfields / Flight Centres

Yorkshire Flight Centre
Moor Lane Arkendale Knaresborough
North Yorkshire HG5 0RQ
Tel: 01423 340664
Offers rides in Boeing 737 and F4 Phantom flight simulators.

Animal Attractions

Ponderosa Rural Therapeutic Centre
Smithies Lane Heckmondwike WF16 0PN
Tel: 01924 235276
Disabled and disadvantaged children of all ages can come to the centre and engage in a variety of interesting and stimulating rural activities.

St Leonard's Farm Park
Chapel Lane Esholt Bradford BD17 7RB
Tel: 01274 598795
Come and meet friendly farmer James and his family, on this award-winning farm.

Staintondale Shire Horse Farm Visitor Centre
Staintondale Scarborough Yorkshire YO13 0EY
Tel: 01723 870458
An award-winning family attraction in an idyllic location, with all-weather facilties.
20 May-5 Sep: Tue, Wed, Fri & Bank Holidays

Archaeology

DIG - An Archaeological Adventure

St Saviour's Church St. Saviourgate York
North Yorkshire YO1 8NN
Tel: 01904 543403 Fax: 01904 627097
www.digyork.co.uk
[M62 / A1041 / A19 to City Centre]
York Attraction of the Year. Never before have you been able to experience an authentic interactive archaeological adventure like this! Visitors of all ages are invited to grab their trowels and go on a fascinating archaeological exploration to unearth the secrets of York's past. This world first offers the latest in 3D audio-visual and IT Interactive experiences! The concept, development and management of DIG are brought to visitors by the team who created JORVIK Viking Centre, The York Archaeological Trust.
Open every day Mon-Fri 10.00-17.00. Opening times may vary over the Christmas period. Please call to check opening and availability and to pre-book your visit
A£5.50 C(5-15)£4.50, Family Ticket (A2+C2) £16.00 or (A2+C3) £19.50

Discount Offer: One Child Free.

Hull and East Riding Museum

36 High Street Hull East Yorkshire HU1 1NE
Tel: 01482 300300
The museum boasts spectacular archaeology and natural history displays.

Art Galleries

1853 Gallery, Salt's Mill
Victoria Road Shipley West Yorkshire BD18 3LA
Tel: 01274 531163
Salt's Mill is an art gallery, shopping and restaurant complex located in Saltaire. It is home to more than 300 pieces of David Hockney's work.

Ferens Art Gallery
Monument Buildings Queen Victoria Square Hull East Riding of Yorkshire HU1 3RA
Tel: 01482 300300 x4
Extensive permanent collection displays are complemented by thriving exhibition and education programmes.

Graves Art Gallery
Surrey Street Sheffield South Yorkshire S1 1XZ
Tel: 0114 278 2600
Home to Sheffield's impressive collection of British and European late nineteenth and twentieth-century art.

Leeds City Art Gallery
The Headrow Leeds West Yorkshire LS1 3AA
Tel: 0113 247 8248
Home to one of the most outstanding collections of twentieth-century British art outside London.

Piece Hall Art Gallery
Halifax West Yorkshire HX1 1RE
Tel: 01422 284412
The gallery is situated in the Piece Hall, a historic Cloth Hall built in 1779 (which now houses a shopping and entertainment complex).

Wakefield Art Gallery
Wentworth Terrace Wakefield West Yorkshire WF1 3QW
Tel: 01924 305796
This art gallery has an important collection of twentieth-century works by local artists including Henry Moore and Barbara Hepworth.

York Art Gallery
Exhibition Square York YO1 7EW
Tel: 01904 687687
700 years of European painting, from early Italian gold-ground panels to the art of the twentieth century.

Arts, Crafts & Textiles

Henry Moore Institute
74 The Headrow Leeds West Yorkshire LS1 3AH
Tel: 0113 246 7467 Fax: 0113 246 1481
www.henry-moore-fdn.co.uk
[In centre of Leeds, adjacent to Leeds City Art Gallery. Rail: approx. 10 min walk from Leeds railway station. Leeds is equidistant from London & Edinburgh & just 2h by train from London King's Cross Station]
The Henry Moore Institute, an award winning, architecturally designed gallery, is a centre for the study of sculpture, with exhibition galleries, a reference library and archive, and an active research programme. The four gallery spaces on the ground floor show temporary sculpture exhibitions of all periods and nationalities. It is advisable to ring the recorded information line (0113 234 3158) prior to a visit for up-to-date information. Wheelchair access is from Cookridge Street and a lift serves all floors. Induction loops are sited at ground floor and library reception areas. Information is available in Braille and large print.
All year daily 10.00-17.30, Wed 10.00-21.00. Closed Bank Hols. Free guided tours require pre-booking (0113 246 7467). Library / Collection enquiries, 0113 246 9469
Admission Free
Discount Offer: 15% discount on all publications, plus a free poster.

Millennium Galleries

Arundel Gate Sheffield South Yorkshire S1 2PP
Tel: 0114 278 2600
With four individual galleries under one roof, there are all sorts of wonderful things to see and enjoy at the Millennium Galleries. Be inspired by treasures from the past, admire masterpieces from Britain's national collections and discover new creations.

University of Hull Art Collection

University of Hull Cottingham Road Hull East Riding of Yorkshire HU6 7RX
Tel: 01482 465192 Fax: 01482 465192
www.hull.ac.uk/artcoll

[Plenty of on-site parking available]

The Hull University Art Collection is a small but outstanding collection specialising in paintings, sculpture, drawings and prints produced in Britain 1890-1940. Displayed in two purpose-built galleries in Sir Leslie Martin's Middleton Hall, it includes works by Beardsley, Sickert, Steer, Lucien Pissarro, Augustus John, Stanley Spencer, Wyndham Lewis and Ben Nicholson as well as sculpture by Epstein, Gill, Gaudier-Brzeska and Henry Moore. The Camden Town Group and Bloomsbury artists are particularly well-represented. Also on display are two collections of Chinese ceramics, on long loan from Dr. & Mrs. Peter Thompson, of Hong Kong. One is an important collection of seventeenth-century works. The second provides choice examples from the Tang to the Qing dynasties (c.618-1850). Regular loan exhibitions are also shown.

Mon-Fri 10.00-16.00 except Bank Hols
Admission Free

Birds, Butterflies & Bees

Tropical Butterfly House, Wildlife and Falconry Centre

Woodsetts Road North Anston Nr Sheffield South Yorkshire S25 4EQ
Tel: 01909 569416 Fax: 01909 564025
www.butterflyhouse.co.uk
[J31 (M1), then A57 towards Worksop & follow brown signs. Ample free on-site parking available]
Discover a wild family day out, catch a glimpse into a faraway world and make friends with creatures great and small. Get close to lots of free-roaming creatures - from amazing leaf-cutter ants and exotic butterflies to goats, ducks and peacocks. Handle exotic snakes, millipedes, lizards and magnificent birds of prey. Feed marmoset monkeys, lorikeets, calves, goats and squirrels. Enjoy spectacular bird of prey displays and noisy parrot shows. New for 2008 is the exciting Meerkat Enclosure - come and see how the inhabitants are settling in. Sip tea in the delightful Patio and Garden or tuck into a freshly prepared meal while the kids dig in the sandpit and take to the wheel of a pedal car. On weekends and during school holidays, hitch a ride aboard the tractor-trailer. The Family Fun House has interactive games, crafts and puzzles for tots, teens and in-betweens. Telephone or visit the website for details of events, birthday parties and Falconry Experience Days.
All year daily. Apr-Sept: Sat-Sun & School Hols. 10.00-17.30, Mon-Fri 10.00-16.30. Oct-Mar: Sat-Sun & School Hols 10.00-17.00/dusk, Mon-Fri 11.00-dusk/16.30 (whichever is earliest) Closed 22-27,31 Dec & 1 Jan 2009
A£6.99 C£5.99 Concessions£6.25, Family Ticket £25.99
Discount Offer: One Child Free.

Yorkshire Dales Falconry and Conservation Centre

Crows Nest Austwick via Lancaster North Yorkshire LA2 8AS

Tel: 01729 822832 / 825164
Fax: 01729 825160
www.falconryandwildlife.com

[A65 bypass from Settle to Kendal, 2nd L after Giggleswick railway station. Plenty of on-site parking available]

Since the Centre's creation in 1991, its role has been to demonstrate birds of prey to the public, while educating the public that many of these birds are now endangered species. To assist the re-population of the birds of prey, the Centre is now part of a worldwide breeding and conservation programme. The displays at the Centre take place in a purpose built display area allowing the public to observe dramatic fly-bys, swoops, and the awesome gracefulness of flight that these birds can achieve. Birds that are not on flying duty are viewable in purpose built aviaries and cave dwellings. Members of staff are on hand to answer any questions that you may have and to make sure your visit is a most enjoyable one. We have a gift shop, a tea room and a video room should the weather turn nasty. There are also picnic area's and a children's play area. All areas are suitable for wheelchair visitors.

Mar-Sept 10.00-17.00, Sept-Feb 10.00-15.30. Mar-Sept three displays during the day at 12.00, 13.30 & 15.00, Sept-Feb two displays during the day at 12.00 & 13.30 Closed 25-26 Dec & 1 Jan

A£5.90 C£3.90 OAPs£4.80, Family Ticket (A2+C2) £18.50. Group rate: A£4.90 C£3.50

Discount Offer: One Child Free.

Caverns & Caves

Mother Shipton's Cave and the Petrifying Well

Prophecy House High Bridge Knaresborough North Yorkshire HG5 8DD
Tel: 01423 864600
Learn about Yorkshire's sixteenth-century prophetess. Features Wishing Well, museum, electronic information points, woodland walk, riverside picnic area, tea rooms and gift shop.

White Scar Cave

Ingleton North Yorkshire LA6 3AW
Tel: 015242 41244 Fax: 015242 41700
www.whitescarcave.co.uk

[1.5mi from Ingleton on B6255 rd to Hawes. Plenty of on-site parking available]

White Scar Cave, in the Yorkshire Dales National Park, is the longest show cave in Britain. There are underground waterfalls and streams, and thousands of stalactites. The curious cave formations include the Devil's Tongue, the Arum Lily, and the remarkably lifelike Judge's Head. Guides lead visitors along the well-lit paths and explain the features. The highlight of the tour is the 200,000-year-old Battlefield Cavern. Over 330 feet long, with its roof soaring in places to 100 feet, this is one of the largest caverns in Britain. The visitor centre has an eco-friendly turf roof, and an alpine-style café with views over the Dales to the sea. The cave shop stocks fine rock and mineral specimens, jewellery, and much more besides.

All year, Feb-Oct daily, Nov-Jan Sat-Sun, from 10.00, weather permitting. Closed 25-26 Dec

A£7.50 C£4.50, Family Ticket (A2+C2) £21.00. Group rate (12+): A£6.20 C£3.50

National Media Museum

Bradford West Yorkshire BD1 1NQ
Tel: 0870 701 0200
Based in Bradford, West Yorkshire, this award-winning museum is home to ten free galleries, two cinemas and an IMAX theatre.

Bolton Abbey Estate

Bolton Abbey Skipton North Yorkshire
BD23 6EX
Tel: 01756 718009 Fax: 01756 710535
www.boltonabbey.com

[On B6160 N from roundabout J with A59 Skipton to Harrogate rd 23mi from Leeds. Plenty of on site parking available]

Bolton Abbey, in the heart of Wharfedale is the Yorkshire estate of the Duke and Duchess of Devonshire. With over 80 miles of moorland, woodland and riverside paths, there are walks to suit all ages and abilities. Follow the nature trails through Strid Wood, established almost 200 years ago by the 6th Duke of Devonshire and Rev. William Carr and visit the spectacular Strid where the water is funnelled through a narrow gorge. Explore the Priory Ruins and Church over looking the River Wharfe. The church guides would be pleased to answer any questions you may have. Below the Priory are the stepping stones, are you brave enough to cross them? On the opposite side of the river is a large beach area, ideal for building sandcastles and the perfect location to enjoy a picnic. Electric wheelchairs are available for visitors to borrow between April to October giving access to the Priory Ruins, riverside, Strid Wood, the Strid and Cumberland Trail.

17 Mar-31 May 09:00-19:00 (last admission 17.30) 1 Jun-31 Aug 09:00-21:00 (last admission 19.00) 1 Sep-31 Oct 09:00 to 19:00 (last admission 17.30) Winter, 09:00-18:00 (last admission 16.00)

£5.50 per day for a group of up to 7 people, 50 pence per person for groups of 12 or more travelling in one vehicle

Bretton Country Park and Yorkshire Sculpture Park

Castle Arch Quarry Street West Bretton
Barnsley Yorkshire S73 4BX
Tel: 01924 830550
Bretton Estate includes the adjoining Yorkshire Sculpture Park, Bretton Hall and Bretton Lakes Nature Reserve. The stunning landscape was designed over 200 years ago as a private pleasure ground.

Goathland and Mallyan Spout

Nr. Whitby Yorkshire
Tel: 01723 383637 (TIC)
A picturesque village in the North Yorkshire Moors National Park. Surrounded by open moorland and farms, the village provides the setting for the television series 'Heartbeat.' During late summer, the heather turns a vivid purple as far as the eye can see. Tame, black-faced sheep roam the village at leisure. The train station is located on the North Yorkshire Moors steam railway line, and was recently used to represent Hogwarts Station in a recent Harry Potter film. There are several waterfalls around Goathland, the best known is Mallyan Spout. There are interesting walks in virtually every direction that will take you through some stunning scenery.

Highfields Country Park

Doncaster South Yorkshire
Tel: 01302 737411
This beautiful lake and grounds are a haven for wildlife. Ideal for strolls and feeding the ducks including several exotic varieties.

Humber Bridge Country Park and Local Nature Reserve

Ferriby Road Hessle Hull Yorkshire
Tel: 01482 395207 Fax: 01482 393445

[Access is via 3 paths leading from entrances at Hessle Foreshore, Little Switzerland and the Bridge Car Park]

The Humber Bridge Country Park Local Nature Reserve is a haven for people and wildlife set amongst woods, meadows and ponds. The tree covered cliff terraces of this old chalk quarry offer dramatic views over the River Humber and towering Humber Bridge. Follow the nature trails around the reserve or explore the Phoenix Sculpture Trail.

Rother Valley Country Park

Mansfield Road Wales Bar Sheffield South Yorkshire S26 5PQ
Tel: 0114 247 1452
This 750-acre country park offers woods and parkland, a visitor centre, craft centre, watersports, café and shop. Cycles for hire. Golf. Nature reserve, working mill, coarse fishing, footpaths, orienteering and cycle routes. Picnic sites.

Factory Outlets & Tours

Freeport Hornsea Retail and Leisure Outlet

Rolston Road Hornsea East Riding of Yorkshire HU18 1UT
Tel: 01964 534211
Freeport Hornsea is an outlet village where you'll find everything at up to 50% off high street prices.

Teapottery, The

Leyburn Business Park Leyburn North Yorkshire DL8 5QA
Tel: 01937 588235
Stroll along a walkway through the pottery, and watch the eccentric hand-crafted teapots being made. Information points provided.

Festivals & Shows

Hull Fair

Walton Street Hull Yorkshire HU3 6HU
Tel: 01482 300300
[Next to the KC Stadium. Local parking is extremely limited. Easily accessed (on foot) from Anlaby Rd and Spring Bank West]
The largest travelling fair in Europe recieves over a million visitors every year and dates back to 1293. Over 250 attractions ranging from children's rides, side stalls, traditional rides, games, palmistry and the latest white-knuckle rides. Enjoy traditional fairground food such as candy floss, fish and chips, toffee apples, pomegranates, waffles, nougat, roast chestnuts, brandy snap and even hog roast.
10-18 October 2008 12.00-00.00 (Closed Sunday)

Admission free, rides charged

JORVIK Viking Festival 2009

York North Yorkshire YO1 9WT
Tel: 01904 543403
www.jorvik-viking-centre.com

[Various venues throughout York city centre.]

The JORVIK Viking Festival attracts thousands of visitors from around the world. Events will include children's activities, famous battle re-enactments, sagas and songs. Please call for full programme of events or check the website for further details.

February 2009 (dates to be confirmed)

Whitby Gothic Weekends

Whitby Spa Pavillion Whitby North Yorkshire
YO21 3EN
Tel: 01947 602124
One of the most popular international gothic
events, attracting attendees from across the UK
and around the world. Bands and associated
events are at the Whitby Spa Pavillion, but
there's usually lots of overspill unofficial events
to enjoy. Although referred to as a "weekend"
events usually take place on Friday too, with
fringe events on the Thursday and Monday.
25-26 April & 31 Oct-1 Nov 2008
Prices vary depending on event

Folk & Local History Museums

Beside the Seaside: The Bridlington Experience

34-35 Queen Street Bridlington East Riding of
Yorkshire YO15 2SP
Tel: 01262 608890
Come and see the famous stars who trod the
boards at Bridlington, watch Punch and Judy,
see the thrills of the switchback railway, go on a
'Trip around the Bay', find out about the crazes
of Bridlington's heyday and much more.
Apr-Sep

Hornsea Museum

Burns Farm 11-15 Newbegin Hornsea East
Riding of Yorkshire HU18 1AB
Tel: 01964 533443
Award-winning museum of North Holderness
village life, with displays of local pottery.
Easter-Oct (Closed Mondays and some Sundays)

Nidderdale Museum

King Street Pateley Bridge Harrogate North
Yorkshire HG3 5LE
Tel: 01423 711225
A fascinating collection of exhibits in 12 rooms
of the original Victorian workhouse, illustrating
all aspects of the Dales life in the past.

Ravenscar Coastal Centre

Ravenscar Scarborough North Yorkshire
YO13 0NE
Tel: 01723 870423
Visit the Coastal Centre at Ravenscar and find
out about the fascinating history and geology of
the Yorkshire Coast.

Thirsk Museum

14/16 Kirkgate Thirsk North Yorkshire YO7 1PQ
Tel: 01845 527707
Set in the 1755 birthplace of Thomas Lord,
founder of the London cricket ground that bears
his name, Thirsk Museum offers eight rooms
that take visitors on a nostalgic trip back
through time.

World of James Herriot

23 Kirkgate Thirsk North Yorkshire YO7 1PL
Tel: 01845 524234
The World of James Herriot combines history,
humour, nostalgia, science and education in a
unique tribute to the author James Herriot.

Yorkshire Museum and Gardens

York North Yorkshire YO1 7FR
Tel: 01904 687687
Set in 10 acres of botanical gardens, the muse-
um displays some of the finest Roman, Anglo-
Saxon, Viking and Medieval treasures.

Murton Park

Murton Park Murton Lane York North Yorkshire
YO19 5UF
Tel: 01904 489966
This 10-acre site offers the Yorkshire Museum of
Farming with tools and machinery of a bygone
age, reconstructions of James Herriot's Surgery,
blacksmith's shop, chapel, hardware shop and
Land Army display. Paddocks and pens hold
rare breeds farm animals and poultry. The repli-
ca Dark Ages and Roman Fort, educational pro-
jects are open to the public at certain times.
Murton Park is home to the Derwent Valley
Light Railway, York Bee Pavilion, Ebor Ruggers
and York District Weavers Spinners and Dyers.
Gift shop, café and picnic/play area.

Food & Drink

Black Bull in Paradise Theakston Brewery Visitor Centre

The Brewery Masham North Yorkshire HG4 4YD
Tel: 01765 680000 Fax: 01765 684330
www.theakstons.co.uk

[Masham can be found in the heart of North Yorkshire, between the towns of Ripon, Thirsk, Bedale and Leyburn]

Visit this famous brewery located in the beautiful Yorkshire Dales town of Masham and home of the legendary Old Peculier! Experience the wonderful aromas of hops and malted barley whilst learning about the traditional brewing techniques still in use today. The visitor centre named 'Black Bull in Paradise' after the original Black Bull Inn where Robert Theakston first began brewing in 1827 and Paradise fields where the present brewery now stands. Within the Black Bull in Paradise you will find the heritage centre with a collection of historical brewery artefacts, a virtual tour of the brewery hosted by Simon Theakston and of special interest is the Cooper's workshop and display of tools. The Brewery Tap is the perfect opportunity to sample the legendary ales fresh from the brewery and the gift shop is stocked full of Peculierly Fine souvenirs, Theakston merchandise and other Yorkshire delights.

Heritage Centre, Brewery Tap & Gift Shop are open daily from 10.30. Regular guided tours of the brewery are available. For-up-to-date information on tour times please call the Visitor Centre

Tours: A£5.25 C£2.95 OAPs£4.50 Students(NUS/USI)£4.75, Family Ticket (A2+C2) £13.95. Prices include complimentary drink. We regret for health and safety reasons, we cannot include children under 10 on brewery tours

Black Sheep Brewery

Wellgarth Masham Ripon North Yorkshire HG4 4EN
Tel: 01765 680101/680100 Fax: 01765 689746
www.blacksheepbrewery.com

[Plenty of on-site parking available]

Situated at the gateway to Wensleydale, Masham is the home of the Black Sheep Brewery. Established in the early nineties by Paul Theakston, 5th generation of Masham's famous brewing family, the brewery now produces a staggering 17 million pints of beer each year. The Black Sheep Visitor Centre is the ideal place for an interesting and alternative day out. Regular 'shepherded' tours of the Brewery allow guests to experience the traditional brewing process from the aroma and taste of English hops and malted barley, through to sampling Black Sheep's award-winning ales in the comfort and relaxation of the Baa...r. The spacious split-level Bistro provides a variety of culinary delights throughout the day and the shop is full of 'ewe-nique' delights for the perfect gift.

Opening times vary, please call 01765 680101 prior to your visit

Prices vary, Please call for details

New Inn and Cropton Brewery

Woolcroft Cropton Pickering YO18 8HH
Tel: 01751 417330

Micro brewery producing award-winning real ale in a rural setting on the edge of the North York Moors National Park and Cropton Forest. Visitor centre and gift shop. Real ale bar and restaurant serving traditional Yorkshire fayre.

Forests & Woods

Chevin Forest Park

Johnny Lane Otley West Yorkshire LS21 3JL
Tel: 01943 465023
A 700-acre wooded escarpment overlooking
Otley, with fabulous views, woodland and crags.

Dalby Forest

Low Dalby Pickering North Yorkshire YO18 7LT
Tel: 01751 472771
9-mile scenic drive with car parks, picnic
places, waymarked walks (up to 4.5 miles)
including a Habitat Trail and an orienteering
course. Visitor centre in Low Dalby village (1
mile along the drive from the Thornton Dale
entrance).

Gardens & Horticulture

Parcevall Hall Gardens

Skyreholme Skipton North Yorkshire BD23 6DE
Tel: 01756 720311
These sixteen acres of formal and woodland
gardens rise up the hillside and command
impressive views. Features include a rock garden with pools, an apple orchard, a herb garden, woodland trails, a rose garden, clifftop
walks and a tea room.
Apr-Oct

RHS Garden Harlow Carr

Crag Lane Beckwithshaw Harrogate
North Yorkshire HG3 1QB
Tel: 01423 565418
Beautiful 58-acre gardens, streamside, scented,
grasses and foliage gardens, woodland and
arboretum, vegetable and flower trials.

Sheffield Botanical Gardens

Clarkehouse Road Sheffield S10 2LN
Tel: 0114 267 6496
The Gardens have been developed with many
themed plantings to provide a place of pleasure
and education for families of all ages.

Tropical World and Roundhay Park

Princes Avenue Roundhay Leeds
West Yorkshire LS8 2ER
Tel: 0113 237 0754
Roundhay Park spans over 700 acres of rolling
parkland, lakes, woodlands and specialist gar-
dens. Tropical World, canel gardens, Coronation
Garden, Monet Garden and Alhambra Garden.

Heritage & Industrial

Bradford Industrial Museum and Horses at Work

Moorside Road Eccleshill Bradford
West Yorkshire BD2 3HP
Tel: 01274 435900
Set in the nineteenth-century Moorside Mills, the
museum has displays of textile machinery,
steam power, engineering and motor vehicles,
along with an exciting exhibitions programme.

Elsecar Heritage Centre

Wath Road Elsecar Barnsley Yorkshire S74 8HJ
Tel: 01226 740203
Set in the attractive conservation village of
Elsecar, the Heritage Centre is located within
former ironworks and colliery workshops.
Restored buildings now house an antique cen-
tre, individual craft workshops, and exhibitions
of Elsecar's past.

Old Penny Memories

2 Marlborough Terrace Bridlington
East Riding of Yorkshire YO15 2PA
Tel: 01262 603341/808400
One of the biggest collection of antique slot
machines in England, dating from the 1920s to
the 1960s.

Historical

Bar Convent

17 Blossom Street York YO24 1AQ
Tel: 01904 643238
The oldest living convent in England, estab-
lished in 1686. It now offers a variety of facilities.

Bolton Castle

Leyburn Yorkshire DL8 4ET
Tel: 01969 623981

A massive fortress that has dominated Wensleydale since 1379. It remains one of the country's best preserved castles, in a beautiful setting in the Yorkshire Dales. Medieval gardens, tea room and gift shop.

Brontë Parsonage Museum

Church Street Haworth Keighley West Yorkshire BD22 8DR
Tel: 01535 642323 Fax: 01535 647131
www.bronte.info

[On A6033 from A629 extensively signposted, Museum is at top of Main St behind Parish Church]

Charlotte, Emily and Anne Brontë were the authors of some of the greatest books in the English language. Haworth Parsonage was their much loved home, and Jane Eyre, Wuthering Heights and The Tenant of Wildfell Hall were all written here. Set between the unique village of Haworth and the wild moorland beyond, this homely Georgian house still retains the atmosphere of the Brontës' time. The rooms they once used daily are filled with the Brontës' furniture, clothes and personal possessions. Here you can marvel at the handwriting in their tiny manuscript books, admire Charlotte's wedding bonnet and imagine meeting Emily's pets from her wonderfully lifelike drawings. Gain an insight into the place and objects that inspired them.

All year daily Apr-Sept 10.00-17.30, Oct-Mar 11.00-17.00. Closed 24-27 Dec & 2-31 Jan
A£6.00 C(5-16)£2.50
OAPs&Students(NUS/USI)£4.00, Family Ticket (A2+C3) £15.00. Group Rates: A£4.50 C(5-16)£2.25 OAPs&Students(NUS/USI)£3.20

Discount Offer: Two for the Price of One (full paying adult).

Burton Agnes Hall

Burton Agnes Driffield East Riding of Yorkshire YO25 4NB
Tel: 01262 490324 Fax: 01262 490513
www.burtonagnes.com

[On A614 between Driffield / Bridlington. Plenty of on site parking available]

A beautiful Elizabethan Hall with award-winning gardens. The same family has lived in the Hall since it was built four hundred years ago. They have filled it with treasures, ranging from magnificent Elizabethan carvings and plasterwork to modern French Impressionist paintings, contemporary furniture and tapestries. Lawns, clipped ewe bushes and beautiful woodland gardens surround the Hall. The old Elizabethan walled garden is a unique wonderland containing over four thousand different plants, a potager (vegetable garden) filled with herbs and vegetables, giant board games, herbaceous borders, a maze, fruit beds, a jungle garden, and a national collection of campanulas. In our courtyard you'll find plants and dried flowers from the walled garden, imaginative gifts, and a children's play area. Our 'Farmers' Food Store' is packed with seasonal Yorkshire produce including our own game, fruit and vegetables. Enjoy freshly prepared meals in the Impressionists' Café and indulgent treats in our ice cream parlour.

All facilities: 1 Apr-31 Oct & 14 Nov-23 Dec daily 11.00-17.00. Café, shops and gardens only: 9 Feb-1 Apr daily 11.00 - 16.00

Hall & Gardens: A£6.00 C£3.00 OAPs£5.50. Gardens only: A£3.00 C£1.50 OAPs£2.75. Group rate (30+): 10% discount

Burton Constable Hall

Burton Constable Hull East Riding of Yorkshire
HU11 4LN
Tel: 01964 562400
A large Elizabethan mansion set in a 300-acre
park with nearly 30 rooms open to the public.

Castle Howard

York North Yorkshire YO60 7DA
Tel: 01653 648333
Magnificent eighteenth-century house with
extensive collections and sweeping parklands.

Clifford's Tower

Tower Street York North Yorkshire YO1 1SA
Tel: 01904 646940
At various points in its history, Clifford's Tower
served as a royal mint, a prison and a court.

Conisbrough Castle

Castle Hill Conisbrough Doncaster DN12 3BU
Tel: 01709 863329
A splendid circular twelfth-century keep, with six
buttresses, surrounded by a curtain wall. The
best preserved in England.

East Riddlesden Hall

Bradford Road Riddlesden Keighley Yorkshire
BD20 5EL
Tel: 01535 607075
Seventeenth-century West Riding manor house
with formal and wild gardens, duckpond and
grounds.
15 Mar-2 Nov: Tue-Wed & Sat-Sun

Forbidden Corner

Tupgill Park Estate Coverham Middleham
Leyburn North Yorkshire DL8 4TJ
Tel: 01969 640638
A unique labyrinth of tunnels, chambers, follies
and surprises created in a four acre garden in
the heart of the Yorkshire Dales. A day out with
a difference which will challenge and delight
adults and children of all ages.

Fort Paull

Battery Road Paull Nr Hull East Riding of
Yorkshire HU12 8FP
Tel: 01482 896236 Fax: 01482 896236
www.fortpaull.com

*[3mi past Hull Docks off A1033 Hull-Hedon Rd.
Plenty of on-site parking available]*

10-acre Napoleonic Fortress with 500 years of
Military History. Underground Tunnels and
Chambers with fantastic exhibits and waxworks
plus the world's only Blackburn Beverley
Transport aircraft. bar and café. Children's play
areas and events throughout the summer.

*Apr-Oct 10.00-18.00, Nov-Mar 11.00-16.00.
Closed Dec & Jan*
A£5.00 Concessions£3.00, Family
Ticket(A2+C2) £14.00
Discount Offer: One Child Free.

Harewood House

Harewood Leeds West Yorkshire LS17 9LG
Tel: 0113 218 1010
This eighteenth-century house features art collections, State Rooms and a 'Below Stairs'
exhibition. It is set in landscaped grounds that
include formal gardens and a bird garden.

Helmsley Castle

Helmsley North Yorkshire YO6 5AB
Tel: 01439 770442
Surrounded by spectacular banks and ditches,
the great medieval castle's impressive ruins
stand beside the attractive town of Helmsley.

JORVIK Viking Centre

Coppergate York North Yorkshire YO1 9WT
Tel: 01904 615505/643211 (24hr)
Fax: 01904 627097
www.jorvik-viking-centre.com

[In centre of York. Can be reached from A1 via A64 or A19 or A1079 Park & Ride service call 01904 613161]

Explore York's Viking history on the very site where archaeologists uncovered remains of the Viking-Age City of 'Jorvik'. Get face-to-face with our expert Viking residents, see over 800 arte-facts, excavated between 1976-1981 magically brought to life by talking Viking Ghosts in our exhibition - 'Artefacts Alive!' and learn what life was really like in our special exhibitions. Our new exhibition, 'Are you a Viking?' brings together bio-scientific and artefact evidence to determine if visitors could have Viking ances-tors. 'Unearthed' tells how the people of York lived - and died - as revealed by real bone material. JORVIK also takes visitors through a reconstruction of the actual Viking-Age streets which stood here 1,000 years ago, faithfully recreated following twenty years of archaeologi-cal and historical research. A programme of special events runs throughout the year, includ-ing the JORVIK Viking Festival every February - check the website for further details.

All year daily, Apr-Oct 10.00-17.00, Nov-Mar 10.00-16.00. Closed 25 Dec. Opening hours may vary over Christmas & New Year, please call to confirm

A£7.95 C(under5)£Free C(5-15)£6.60 OAPs&Students(NUS/USI) £6.60, Family Ticket (A2+C2) £21.95 or (A2+C3) £26.50

Discount Offer: One Child Free.

Newby Hall and Gardens

Newby Hall Ripon North Yorkshire HG4 5AE
Tel: 01423 322583 Fax: 01423 324452
www.newbyhall.com

[2mi off A1(M) at Ripon exit (signposted). 40 min (23mi) from York. 45 min (27mi) NE of Leeds/Bradford Airport. 30 min (15mi) from Harrogate. Plenty of on-site parking available]

Designed under the guidance of Sir Christopher Wren, this graceful country house epitomizes the Georgian 'Age of Elegance'. Its beautifully restored interior presents Robert Adam at his very best. The contents of the house include a rare set of Gobelins tapestries, a renowned gallery of classical statuary and some of Chippendale's finest furniture. The 25 acres of award winning gardens are a haven for both the specialist and amateur gardener alike. They include a miniature railway, an adventure garden for children, a woodland discovery walk and a new contemporary sculpture park. Newby also has an irresistible shop and well stocked plant centre.

21 Mar-28 Sept Tue-Sun plus Bank Hols & Mon in July-Aug 12.00-17.00 (Gardens: 11.00-17.30)
House & Garden: A£10.20 C(under4)£Free C£7.80 OAPs£9.20. Gardens only: A£7.20 C(under4)£Free C£5.80 OAPs£6.20

Discount Offer: Two for the Price of One (full-paying adult).

Pontefract Castle

Castle Chain Pontefract WF8 1QH
Tel: 01977 723440
A royal castle from 1399, Pontefract Castle is Famous for the death of Richard II. The remains of the castle and the underground magazine chamber are open to visitors and an exhibition on the site tells the story of the Castle.

Ripley Castle

Ripley Harrogate North Yorkshire HG3 3AY
Tel: 01423 770152 Fax: 01423 771745
www.ripleycastle.co.uk

[Off A61 3.5mi N of Harrogate. Plenty of on-site parking available]

An extraordinary castle with 700 years of history. It is an amazing place to visit, and it's open all year round. Ripley is one of Yorkshire's great visitor attractions and is something the whole family will enjoy. You will learn of kings and queens, civil war and plagues, secrets concealed in the Knight's Chamber, Oliver Cromwell held at gunpoint in the Library, and the Gunpowder Plot - to name but a few. Tours are enthralling for all ages. There are acres of formal gardens, woodland and parkland to explore. Within the beautiful Walled Gardens in late April you will find the National Hyacinth Collection. The kitchen garden contains a rare collection of fruit and vegetables, herbs and spices. Deer Park and Lakes. Children's Play Trail. Superb facilities including tea rooms and wonderful shops. Boar's Head Hotel serves restaurant and bar meals daily and beer garden is very popular in the summer months.

Castle: Guided Tours only - First Tour 11.00, Last Tour 15.00 June-Sept daily. Oct-Nov & Mar-May Tue, Thur, Sat & Sun, Dec-Feb Sat-Sun, Good Friday, Easter & May Bank Hols. Please call prior to visit as opening times may vary without prior notice. Gardens: Daily 09.00-17.00. Except Christmas Day

Castle & Gardens: A£7.00 C(5-16)£4.50 OAPs&Groups£6.00. Gardens only: A£4.50 C£3.00 OAPs&Groups£4.00

Discount Offer: One Child Free.

Sewerby Hall and Gardens

Church Lane Sewerby Bridlington East Riding of Yorkshire YO15 1EA
Tel: 01262 673769

Set in 50 acres of early nineteenth-century parkland, the Hall contains the magnificent Orangery, art and photographic galleries, period rooms, an Amy Johnson room displaying a collection of her awards, trophies and mementoes. There is also a children's zoo.

Skipton Castle

Skipton North Yorkshire BD23 1AW
Tel: 01756 792442 Fax: 01756 796100
www.skiptoncastle.co.uk

[Located in Skipton centre]

Skipton Castle is one of the best preserved, most complete medieval castles in England. Dating from Norman times with a charming Tudor Courtyard, it withstood a three year siege in the Civil War. Explore this exciting castle and relax in the peaceful grounds. Guided tours for pre-booked groups only.

All year daily Mar-Sept Mon-Sat 10.00-18.00, Sun 12.00-18.00, Oct-Feb Mon-Sat 10.00-16.00, Sun 12.00-16.00. Closed 25 Dec

A£5.80* C(0-4)£Free C(5+)£3.20 OAPs£5.20 Students(NUS/USI)£5.20, Family Ticket (A2+C3) £17.90. Group rate (15+): £4.80. *Cost includes illustrated tour sheet in choice of 9 languages (English, French, German, Dutch, Italian, Spanish, Chinese, Japanese or Esperanto)

Discount Offer: Two for the Price of One (full-paying adult).

Wilberforce House

23-24 High Street Hull East Riding of Yorkshire
HU1 1NE
Tel: 01482 300300
Visitors will be able to explore the history of the
Transatlantic Slave Trade through African narra-
tives, exploring the lives of enslaved people
through human voices and stories.

Living History Museums

York Castle Museum

The Eye of York York North Yorkshire YO1 9RY
Tel: 01904 687687
Venture into the prison cell of notorious highwayman Dick Turpin. Wander through Victorian
and Edwardian streets and experience four hundred years of fascinating social history.

Maritime

Saltburn Smugglers Heritage Centre

Old Saltburn Saltburn-by-the-Sea North
Yorkshire TS12 1HF
Tel: 01287 625252 Fax: 01287 625252
www.redcar-cleveland.gov.uk/leisure

[Next to Ship Inn]

Discover the sights, sounds and smells of
Saltburn Smuggling Heritage. Set in authentic
fishermen's cottages alongside the famous Ship
Inn public house, the Saltburn Smugglers
Heritage Centre recreates an age long past -
gone but not forgotten. Discover the many
secrets of the 'King of the Smugglers' and the
hidden contraband stolen from under the noses
of the excise men. Eavesdrop on tales of secret

tunnels between The Ship Inn and the White
House and glimpse their ill-gotten gains. Re-live
the excitement and danger of those bloodthirsty
nights. Saltburn's hidden treasure will appeal to
all age groups - children, young persons, families, special parties - you'll want to spread the
word...but be sure you get there first.

*21 Mar-31 May Wed-Sun 10.00-18.00, 1 Jun-30
Jun Tues-Sun 10:00-18:00, 1 Jul-31 Aug Daily
10:00-18:00, 1 Sept-30 Sept Wed-Sun 10:00-
18:00, Open Spring and Summer Bank Hols*
A&OAPs£1.95 C£1.45, Family Ticket (A2+C2)
£5.80. Prices due to increase

Discount Offer: One Child Free.

Medical Museums

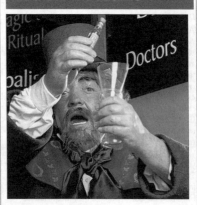

Thackray Museum

Beckett Street Leeds West Yorkshire LS9 7LN
Tel: 0113 244 4343 Fax: 0113 247 0219
www.thackraymuseum.org

*[From M621 follow signs for York, then follow
brown signs. From N, take A58. Next to St
James Hospital. Plenty of on-site parking avail-
able]*

An award winning interactive museum offering a
great day out for all. From a Victorian operating
theatre to the wonders of modern surgery, the
museum's galleries, collections and interactive
displays bring to life the history of medicine.
Experience the sights and sounds of a Victorian
slum, discover the incredible lotions and potions
once offered as treatments. Experience preg-
nancy by trying on an empathy belly and have
fun exploring the workings of the human body
in the Life Zone. Please call the information line

on 0113 245 7084 for further details on school holiday activities.

All year daily 10.00-17.00. Closed 24-26, 31 Dec & 1 Jan

A£5.50 C£4.00 OAPs&Concessions£4.50, Family Ticket £18.00. Group rates available on request

Discount Offer: Two for the Price of One (full-paying adult).

Military & Defence Museums

Eden Camp

Eden Camp Old Malton Malton North Yorkshire YO17 0SD

Tel: 01653 697777

A former winner of the Museum of the Year Award, Eden Camp recreates the experience of life in WWII Britain. Built in original prisoner of war huts.

Royal Armouries Museum

Armouries Drive Leeds West Yorkshire LS10 1LT

Tel: 08700 344 344
www.royalarmouries.org

[Off J4 M621. Follow brown signs to Royal Armouries Museum. A privately operated multi-storey car park is located 100m from Museum entrance plus coach parking spaces. 15 min walk from Leeds City Centre]

The stage is set at the Royal Armouries Leeds

for a legendary day out, with horse shows and falconry displays, action-packed drama and a whole museum of treasures to explore. Discover five stunning galleries - War, Tournament, Oriental, Self Defence and Hunting with over 8,000 exhibits to see - and some you can touch. Find out what it was like to hold a fifteenth-century pollaxe or a powder-firing musket and get up close and personal with the armour Henry VIII actually wore. Experience moments in history through the eyes of real-life heroes thanks to gripping performances from our team of professional interpreters. Join the ranks in the English Civil Wars; listen to tales from the Front in World War I or even cross the Wild West with the American Pioneers. We bring history to life through dramatic performances and hand-to-hand combat displays. From international medieval jousting tournaments to thrilling live horse shows and stunning falconry displays - our live performances put you in the midst of the action. There are special events throughout the year so prepare to be 'dangerously entertained'. See www.royalarmouries.org for more details.

All year daily 10.00-17.00. Closed 24-25 Dec

Museum Admission Free. Some activities/events charged for

Discount Offer: Two for the Price of One (full-paying adult).

South Yorkshire Aircraft Museum

Aeroventure Dakota Way, Airbourne Road Doncaster Leisure Park Doncaster South Yorkshire DN4 5EN

Tel: 01302 761616

The Museum, is based at Aeroventure in original 1940 RAF buildings to give an authentic flavour to the exhibits.

Yorkshire Air Museum

Halifax Way Elvington York YO41 4AU

Tel: 01904 608595

Restored Control Tower, Air Gunners Museum, Archives, Airborne Forces Display, Squadron Memorial Rooms and Gardens.

Mining

National Coal Mining Museum For England

Caphouse Colliery New Road Overton Wakefield West Yorkshire WF4 4RH
Tel: 01924 848806 Fax: 01924 844567
www.ncm.org.uk
[On A642 between Wakefield / Huddersfield. Plenty of on-site parking available]

A great day out for all the family. Don't miss the unique opportunity to travel 140 metres underground down one of Britain's oldest working mines, where models and machinery depict methods and conditions of mining from the early 1800's to the present. An experienced local miner will guide you around the underground workings. Above ground there's a full compliment of restored colliery surface buildings including the steam winding house and the pit head baths. Visit the pit ponies and follow the nature trail. Take a train ride to the recently restored Hope Pit site and experience the science of mining through interactive exhibitions. Visit the Museum's well-stocked shop where you can get your very own mining memorabilia. Children under 5 are not allowed underground, however there is an under 5s indoor play area. Disabled facilities include level parking, ramp and disabled toilets. Underground tours for the disabled are available with prior arrangement.

All year daily 10.00-17.00. Closed 24-26 Dec & 1 Jan. During Bank Hols we recommend you arrive early to ensure a place on an underground tour

Admission Free

Nature & Conservation Parks

Aysgarth Falls

Wensleydale North Yorkshire
Tel: 01969 662910
Aysgarth Falls are a triple flight of waterfalls, carved out by the River Ure over an almost a one-mile stretch on its descent to Wensleydale. The Upper-Falls featured in the film, 'Robin Hood, Prince of Thieves.'

On the Water

Flamborough Head Heritage Coast

Bridlington East Riding of Yorkshire
Tel: 01482 391721
[Off B1255 Bridlington - Flamborough road]
Flamborough Head Heritage Coast boasts spectacular chalk cliffs with nestling seabirds during the summer months. There is access to the foreshore and beach plus a headland walk with wonderful views.

Places of Worship

York Minster

Deangate York North Yorkshire YO1 2JN
Tel: 01904 557216
The second-largest Gothic cathedral in northern Europe, York Minster is the seat of the Archbishop of York (the second-highest office of the Church of England) and the cathedral for the Diocese of York.

Police, Prisons & Dungeons

Prison and Police Museum

St Marygate Ripon North Yorkshire HG4 1LX
Tel: 01765 690799
This grim building dating from 1816 serves as a splendid backdrop to illustrate the harsh conditions of prison life. In the punishment yard medieval stocks, pillory and whipping post contrast with the twentieth-century police call boxes.

Railways

Keighley and Worth Valley Railway

Station Road Haworth Keighley BD22 8NJ
Tel: 01535 645214/647777
Every weekend and daily in the summer you can take steam train journey back in time on the Keighley and Worth Valley Railway.

Kirklees Light Railway

Park Mill Way Clayton West Huddersfield
West Yorkshire HD8 9XJ
Tel: 01484 865727
Steam along on Hawk, Owl, Fox or Badger our four friendly steam engines.

North Yorkshire Moors Railway

Pickering Station Pickering North Yorkshire
YO18 7AJ
Tel: 01751 472508 Fax: 01751 476970
www.nymr.co.uk

[In Pickering off A170]

Operating through the heart of the North York Moors National Park between Pickering and Grosmont, and now with many services extended to Whitby, steam trains cover a distance of 21 miles linking moors and coast. Visit the history display and the artist in residence at his studio at Levisham Station. Beautiful Newtondale Halt gives walkers easy access to forest and moorland. Visit Goathland, otherwise known as "Aidensfield" in the popular TV series "Heartbeat" as well as "Hogsmeade Station" in the Harry Potter film. Or see the locomotive sheds at Grosmont where restoration takes place. Enjoy a day out at the seaside in Whitby with its many attractions. Special events are held through the year to add to the sparkle.

Mar-Nov daily plus some further winter dates, please call for details

All line return (inc Whitby) A£20.00 C£12.00; All line return (Grosmont) A£14.50 C£7.30, Family Ticket (Whitby) (A2+C4) £45.00; Family Ticket (Grosmont) £31.00. Please telephone for additional fares and travel info. Group rates available on request

Science - Earth & Planetary

Eureka! The Museum for Children

Discovery Road Halifax West Yorkshire
HX1 2NE
Tel: 01422 330069 Fax: 01422 330275
www.eureka.org.uk

[M62 J24, follow A629 to Halifax. Plenty of on-site parking available]

Eureka! The Museum for Children is the first and foremost hands-on children's museum in the UK designed especially for under 12s. With more than 400 must touch exhibits and a full programme of events and activities, you'll be amazed at the fun things you can do! Find out how your body and senses work, discover the realities of daily life, explore the science behind sound, rhythm and performance and travel from your backyard to some amazing, faraway places across the globe.

All year daily 10.00-17.00. Closed 24-26 Dec
A£7.25 C(3+)£7.25 C(1-2)£2.25 C(under1)£Free
Donation inclusive prices

Discount Offer: Two for the Price of One (full-paying adult).

Sealife Centres & Aquariums

Scarborough Sea Life and Marine Sanctuary

Scalby Mills Road Scarborough North Yorkshire YO12 6RP
Tel: 01723 376125 Fax: 01723 376285
www.sealifeeurope.com

[Scarborough North Bay]

The three white pyramids housing the Scarborough Sea Life and Marine Sanctuary dominate the North Bay skyline. The Sanctuary houses a vast indoor aquarium with native and tropical sea creatures. The centrepiece is an ocean display with a Great Barrier Reef theme, complete with tropical sharks and our sea turtle, Antiopi. Outdoors there is an otter enclosure and a penguin colony. This year, the Sanctuary's busy seal rescue operation is being expanded and improved. Indoors, the special 'Seal Academy' will serve as introduction to the 'Seal Hospital' (separate to the main building) and from the 'Seal Hospital,' visitors can make their way to the spacious outdoor convalescence pools that house both resident and recuperating seals.

All year daily from 10.00. Closed Christmas Day
Please call for admission prices

Discount Offer: One Child Free.

The Deep - The World's Only Submarium

Hull East Riding of Yorkshire HU1 4DP
Tel: 01482 381000 Fax: 01482 381018
www.thedeep.co.uk

[From N take A1/M, M62/A63. From S take A1/M, A15/A63. From P&O North Sea Ferry Terminal take A1033/A63 for 2mi. Rail: Hull, 4 direct trains from London daily, regular services from Manchester, Sheffield, York & East Coast. 15 min walk or taxi ride from station. Regular local buses run to The Deep]

Encounter the ocean's greatest predator at The Deep. This unique award winning attraction tells the amazing story of the world's oceans using a blend of stunning aquaria and the latest interactives. It is home to 40 sharks and over 3,500 fish. Featuring Slime! - Meet the animals that ooze stick and slide to survive. See the deadly Blue Poison Arrow frogs and Giant African Land snails; discover which fish eats its prey from the inside out and why the anemone will never find Nemo! You've seen 3D films - new for 2008 The Deep goes one better with the ultimate shark movie in 4D! Great whites, Whalesharks and Giant Hammerheads are all brought to life in this free 20-minute spectacular with added theatrical effects.

All year daily 10.00-18.00. Closed 24-25 Dec
A£8.75 C(under 3)Free C£6.75 OAPs£7.25 Student£7.25. Family ticket (A2+C2) £28.00, (A2+C3) £33.25. Group rates (for 10+ or schools) available on request

Discount Offer: One Child Free.

Social History Museums

Hands on History

South Church Side Market Place Hull East
Riding of Yorkshire HU1 1RR
Tel: 01482 300300
Housed in the old Grammar School 'Hands on
History' is a curriculum resource centre for
schools.

Workhouse Museum of Poor Law

Allhallowgate Ripon North Yorkshire HG4 1LE
Tel: 01765 690799
Britain's first workhouse museum is situated in
the men's casual wards of the former Ripon
Union workhouse, which has been refurbished
to portray the treatment of vagrants one hundred years ago.

Spectator Sports

Doncaster Racecourse

The Grandstand Leger Way Doncaster South
Yorkshire DN2 6BB
Tel: 01302 304200 Fax: 01302 323271
www.doncaster-racecourse.com

*[M1 (J32), M18 (J3 or J4), A1M (J36) & M62.
Plenty of on-site parking available]*

At the home of the world's oldest Classic (the
Ladbrokes St Leger), the festivities are sure to
be more colourful than ever before. A £34m
redevelopment enables race-goers to enjoy a
whole new experience at one of the UK's most
prestigious racecourses. At the heart of the new
development is the impressive five storey urban-
i stand, which includes a wide range of excellent catering outlets, bars and luxury dining
areas - all with spectacular views over the racecourse. For a day out with family and friends,
the new-look Doncaster racecourse has it all -
colour, excitement, comfort and convenience,
with race meetings throughout the year.

2 hours before 1st race of the day

A£5.00-£50.00 depending on enclosure and
raceday, C(under16)£Free. Group discounts
available on request. Coach drivers have free
entry to the family enclosure

Ripon Races

Boroughbridge Road Ripon North Yorkshire
HG4 1UG
Tel: 01765 602156 Fax: 01765 690018
www.ripon-races.co.uk

[Plenty of on-site parking available]

Known as the 'Garden Racecourse', Ripon
Racecourse is a family friendly place to experience racing from as little as £15 per car with
four occupants in the course enclosure. With
children's playgrounds, giant screen showing
the racing and a cross section of catering facilities it's a great family day out. Fixtures run from
April to August. Please see events section for
more fixtures.

Apr-Aug. Course opens 2 hrs before first race

£15.00 for car plus 4 occupants in the course
enclosure, accompanied children under 16 Free

Thirsk Racecourse

Station Road Thirsk North Yorkshire YO7 1QL
Tel: 01845 522276 Fax: 01845 525353
www.thirskracecourse.net

[A61 Thirsk/Ripon Road, 0.5mi W of Thirsk. Rail: Thirsk. Helicopter landing by prior arrangement. Plenty of on-site parking available]

Thirsk is one of Yorkshire's most beautiful country courses, set between the North Yorkshire Moors and the Dales with easy access from road or rail. Thirsk is a friendly racecourse with compact, well maintained enclosures. Facilities for entertainment have continuously been improved and upgraded in recent years. Hospitality options are available for all sizes of party in either viewing boxes overlooking the winning post or private banqueting suites. Marquees are also an option. Facilities available on non racedays for private functions.

Race meetings Apr-Sept

Club£19.00 Paddock£13.00 Family Ring £5.00 Cars(+4 people)£16.00. Party booking rates available

Sport & Recreation

Bridlington Leisure World

The Promenade Bridlington
East Riding of Yorkshire YO15 2QO
Tel: 01262 606715
Leisure complex featuring a swimming pool, an entertainment centre, indoor bowls and fitness suite.

Cleethorpes Leisure Centre

Kingsway Cleethorpes East Yorkshire
DN35 0BY
Tel: 01472 323200
Visit the region's most exciting heated indoor water attraction. The centre provides leisure pool, toddlers pool and spectators' area.

Xscape: Castleford

Colorado Way Glasshoughton Castleford West Yorkshire WF10 4TA
Tel: 0871 200 3221 Fax: 01977 523201
www.xscape.co.uk

[Rail: Xscape Castleford or Glasshoughton J32 off M62. Free Parking]

Xscape Castleford offers the ultimate in shopping, relaxing, eating and drinking, plus the thrill of extreme sports and activities all under one roof. With an unrivalled choice of 20 cafés, restaurants, bars and late night dancing, Xscape offers the ideal place to relax over a chilled drink, a delicious meal - or to party and dance the night away. You can also get kitted out with clothing, footwear, accessories and equipment from 100's of extreme and urban sportswear brands available in the exclusive shops at Xscape. And don't forget Xscape's not all about relaxing! There's plenty on offer to keep you active if you want including the UK's premier indoor snow slope with REAL snow, rock climbing walls, aerial assault courses, pro simulation golf, laserzone arena, bowling, cinema, dodgems and a health/fitness centre with spa! For slope enquiries and booking only please call: 0871 222 5671.

All year daily. Snow Slope: All year daily. 09.00 - late (closed 25 Dec)

Please call or visit our website for prices

Theme & Adventure Parks

Diggerland (Yorkshire)
Willowbridge Lane Whitwood Castleford
Yorkshire WF10 5NW
Tel: 08700 344437 Fax: 09012 010300
www.diggerland.com

*[M62 J31. Take A655 towards Castleford &
Diggerland 0.5mi on L, immediately before the Jet
petrol station. Rail: Castleford (not Glasshoughton)
short walk to Bus Station. Bus: MC2 (runs hourly
but less frequently on Sundays) to Whitwood. 1mi
from Railway Station & Bus Station]*

Diggerland are pleased to announce the opening of their 4th Adventure Park in the UK, based
in Castleford West Yorkshire. The ultimate
adventure park, Diggerland allows children and
adults of all ages the chance to experience driving and riding in real JCB's and lots more, all
under the supervision of instructors. The parks
attractions include 'Spin Dizzy', where up to
eight people can ride in the JCB's giant bucket
and are spun around and lifted 25 feet up in the
air. Riders get some time to catch their breath
as they spin over the ground, but it's not long
before you're back in the air. Belt up it's not for
the feint hearted! With other rides such as The
JCB Robots, Land Rover Safari, Diggerland
Dumpers, Mini JCB Challenges, Sky Shuttle and
the Diggerland Train, Diggerland can offer even
the most experienced of theme park adventur-
ers a new thrill.

*9 Feb-2 Nov Weekends & Bank Hols plus daily
during half-term & school hols 10.00-17.00*
A&C£15.00 C(under3)£Free OAPs£7.50. Group
rates: (10+) 10% discount, (50+) 25% discount

**Discount Offer: 10% off Admission
Prices (A&C£13.50).**

Flamingo Land
The Rectory Kirby Misperton Malton
North Yorkshire YO17 6UX
Tel: 0871 9118000
The UK's only theme park, zoo and holiday vil-
lage complex, set in over 375 acres of parkland.

Go Ape! High Wire Forest Adventure (Dalby Forest, Yorkshire)
Dalby Forest Visitor Centre Nr Thornton-le-Dale
North Yorkshire YO18 7LT
Tel: 0845 643 9245
www.goape.co.uk

*[Adjacent to Low Dalby. Access is via Thornton-
le-Dale on A170. Follow brown tourist signs.
Plenty of on-site parking available]*

Take to the trees and experience an exhilarating
course of rope bridges, Tarzan swings and zip-
slides up to 40 feet above the ground! Share
approximately three exciting hours of fun and
adventure, which you'll be talking about for
days. Book online and watch people Go Ape! at
www.goape.co.uk. Minimum height 1.4m.
Maximum weight 130 kg (20.5 stone). Under-
18s must be accompanied by a participating
adult. One adult can supervise either two children (where one or both of them is under 16
years old) or up to five 16-17 year olds. Pre-
booking is essential to avoid disappointment.
Book online or by telephone (there is a £1.00
booking fee on all telephone bookings).

*16-17 & 23-24 Feb, 14 Mar-31 Oct daily, Nov
Sat-Sun. Dec Sat-Sun TBC please visit
www.goape.co.uk. Closed Jan*
Gorillas (18yrs+) £25.00, Baboons (10-17yrs)
£20.00

Discount Offer: £5.00 off per person.

For great hotel deals call Superbreak on 01904 679999 or visit www.superbreak.com

Lightwater Valley Theme Park

North Stanley Ripon North Yorkshire HG4 3HT
Tel: 0871 720 0011 Fax: 0871 721 0011
www.lightwatervalley.co.uk

[Lighwater is well signposted, turn off A1 onto A61 towards Ripon, then take A6108 for 2.5mi. Manchester approx 2hr drive, Preston approx 90 min drive, Hull approx 90 min drive. Plenty of on-site parking available]

Set in 175 acres of gorgeous North Yorkshire Parkland - just North of Ripon - Lightwater Valley Theme Park, Shopping Village and Birds of Prey Centre is renowned for its friendly and welcoming atmosphere. The theme park line-up includes Europe's longest rollercoaster - The Ultimate, and the stomach churning, mighty Eagle's Claw. Located in the grounds of the Theme Park, you'll find our Birds of Prey Centre. As well as seeing possibly the largest Golden Eagle in England, you can see our dramatic flying shows at 2:00pm and 4:00pm every day. Within the Bird of Prey Centre is the Creepy Crawly Cave - with snakes, a tarantula and Australian bearded dragons. Don't forget our shopping village that has over 30,000 square feet of inspired shopping, where you can stroll through our indoor village or have lunch in our Granary restaurant. Click on www.lightwatervalley.co.uk or ring 0871 720 0011 to check opening times and for your guide to the Ultimate family day out!

Gates open at 10.00. Rides & attractions open at 10.30. Park closes from 16.30, depending on time of year. Please see our website or call 0871 720 0011 for further details

Pay once and ride all day: Over 1.3m £16.95, Under 1.3m £14.95, Under 1m £Free OAPS/Disabled£8.50. Family Ticket (3 people) £45.00. Family Ticket (4 people) £60.00, (5 people) £75.00, (6 people) £90.00, Family Ticket (7 people) £105.00, Family Ticket (8 people) £120.00. Single Season Ticket £55.00, Family Season Ticket (4 people) £180.00. Family tickets for up to 6 people admits max of 2 adults, for 7 people admits max of 3 adults, for 8 people admits max of 4 adults. Group rates available on request.

Discount Offer: £6.00 Off Full-Price Entry.

Magna Science Adventure Centre

Sheffield Road Templeborough Rotherham South Yorkshire S60 1DX
Tel: 01709 720002 Fax: 01709 820092
www.visitmagna.co.uk

[M1, J33/ J34, close to Meadowhall shopping centre. Plenty of on-site parking available]

Magna, the UK's first Science Adventure Centre explores the elements earth, air, fire and water. Inside you can have fun firing a giant water cannon, launching rockets, exploding rock faces, working real JCBs and experience the roar of the Big Melt show. Explore Sci-Tek (Europe's largest high-tech playground) and Aqua-Tek (an outdoor water play area).

All year daily 10.00-17.00. Closed 24-27 Dec & 1 Jan

A£9.95 C£(4-15)£7.95 Concessions£7.95, Family Ticket (A2+C2)£31.50, (A2+C3)£35.00. Group rates and annual Centre & Sci-Tek passes available

Discount Offer: One Child Free (with 2 full-paying adults).

York Dungeon

12 Clifford Street York North Yorkshire YO1 9RD
Tel: 01904 632599 Fax: 01904 612602
www.thedungeons.com
[York Centre]

The York Dungeon invites you to a unique feast of fun with history's horrible bits. Live actors, shows and special effects transport you back to those black, bleak times. Are you brave enough to delve into the darkest chapters of history? You know you'll love it! Meet the notorious Viking leader Erik Bloodaxe, wander through Plague-ravaged streets, and face the seventeenth-century judge who knows exactly what you have been up to… The court isn't impressed and the punishment will be harsh! New for 2008: 'Dick Turpin, Highwayman from Hell!' Travel to the dark depths of the dungeons of Knavesmire Prison, where murderer, thief and torturer Dick Turpin is incarcerated as he waits for death at the gallows. Suddenly confusion hits as you enter your worst nightmare; a pitch-dark cell, a murdered guard and a sadistic killer who wants his revenge… in blood!

All year daily. Closed 25 Dec
Please call for admission prices

Discount Offer: One Child Free.

Transport Museums

Ingrow Museum of Rail Travel

Ingrow Railway Centre Keighley West Yorkshire
BD21 5AX
Tel: 01535 680425
Award-winning museum that has provided restored Victorian and Edwardian carriages for over 50 film and television productions.

National Railway Museum

Leeman Road York North Yorkshire YO26 4XJ
Tel: 0844 8153139
www.nrm.org.uk

[A64 from Scarborough, Malton & Pickering. A64 from Tadcaster, Leeds, M62, M1 & A1. A19 from Selby. A19 from Teesside & Thirsk. A59 from Harrogate. A1079 from Hull. Outer ring rd A1237. On Leeman Rd, just outside City Centre, behind Railway Station. Limited on-site parking available]

Nowhere tells the story of the train better than the World's largest railway museum. From Stephenson's Rocket and giant steam engines to Eurostar, the Bullet Train and the Flying Scotsman*, rail travel is brought dramatically to life with interactive displays and lavish exhibitions. Discover it all in one fun-packed family day out where everyone gets in free (excludes certain special events). Picnic facilities available both in and outdoors. Also located at the museum, is York's newest landmark 'must see' attraction, The Yorkshire Wheel. Ride the wheel, rise 60 metres into the sky and be amazed at the beautiful city of York and some of the best views in the county. It's an unforgettable experience for all the family (charges apply).*Please ring to check the whereabouts of the Flying Scotsman*.

All year daily 10.00-18.00. Pre-booked guided tours (prices on application)

Admission Free (excludes certain special events)

Ireland

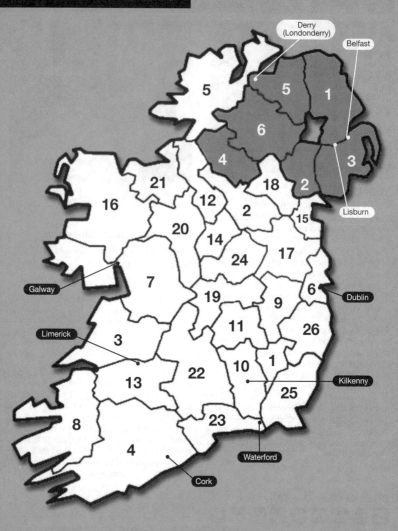

Abbeys

Dunbrody Abbey and Visitor Centre

Campile New Ross County Wexford Ireland
Tel: 00 353 51 388603
Founded in 1170, Dunbrody Abbey is one of the finest examples of a Cistercian Monastery in Ireland. Attractions include the abbey, the Maze with Pitch & Putt, craft shop and tea room.

Kylemore Abbey and Gardens

Kylemore Connemara County Galway Ireland
Tel: 00 353 95 41146
The Monastic home of the Benedictine Order of Nuns in Ireland. With visitor centre, pottery studio, craft and retail shop, and restaurant.

Agriculture / Working Farms

Johnstown Castle Gardens and the Irish Agricultural Museum

Wexford County Wexford Ireland
Tel: 00 353 53 9171200
Formal and wild gardens set against a nineteenth-century fairytale castle and manmade lake. The Irish Agricultural Museum is housed in an olde-worlde former farmyard.

Yola Farmstead Folk Park

Tagoat County Wexford Ireland
Tel: 00 353 53 32611
A 5-acre complex of thatched farm buildings, including a church, forge, windmill, playground and country walks. There's an array of bygone farm machinery and rare species of animals.

Animal Attractions

Ballykeenan Pet Farm And Aviary

Myshall County Carlow Ireland
Tel: 00 353 59 915 7665
Once a working farm, Ballykeenan is now home to a range of animals, from horses to goats, sheep to dogs and from hedgehogs to birds. A tour is provided by the owner.

Nore Valley Park Open Farm

Bennetsbridge County Kilkenny Ireland
Tel: 00 353 56 772 7229
Open farm with a variety of animals and an American-style fort at its centre. Children's playground, crazy golf, go-karts, trailer rides, indoor maze and tea room.

Shrule Deer Farm

Shrule Ballygarrett Gorey County Wexford Ireland
Tel: 00 353 55 27277
The only commercial deer herd open to the public in Wexford. With red deer, goats, pigs, lambs, poultry, rabbits and many more animals. Also features a playground and a gift shop.

Archaeology

National Museum of Ireland: Archaeology and History

Kildare Street Dublin 2 Ireland
Tel: 00 353 1 677 7444
The national repository for all archaeological objects found in Ireland. This museum houses over 2,000,000 artefacts which range in date between 7000BC and the late medieval period.

Art Galleries

Hugh Lane Municipal Gallery of Modern Art

Charlemont House Parnell Square Dublin 1 Ireland
Tel: 00 353 1 874 1903
Situated in Charlemont House, the gallery houses a collection contemporary art. It features around 2000 artworks, which includes work by Manet, Monet, Renoir and Degas.

Irish Museum of Modern Art

Royal Hospital Military Road Kilmainham Dublin 8 Ireland
Tel: 00 353 1 612 9900
The Irish Museum of Modern Art opened in 1991 in the magnificent Royal Hospital building and grounds.

Butler Gallery

Kilkenny Castle Castle Yard Kilkenny
County Kilkenny Ireland
Tel: 00 353 56 776 1106
Located in the basement of Kilkenny Castle, the gallery is a contemporary art space that exhibits emerging and established artists, both Irish and international. It also has a collection of twenti-eth-century art.

National Gallery of Ireland

Merrion Square West Dublin 2 Ireland
Tel: 00 353 1 661 5133
In addition to the national collection of Irish art, the Gallery houses a fine collection of European 'Old Master' paintings.

Arts, Crafts & Textiles

Claypipe Visitor Centre

Knockcroghery Roscommon County
Roscommon Ireland
Tel: 00 353 90 666 1923
The tiny village of Knockcroghery is famous for its claypipes, or 'dúidíns.' This visitor centre is located on the original site of the last ever pipe factory and today, Ethel Kelly makes claypipes using the same skills employed by artisans centuries ago.

Garter Lane Arts Centre

22a O'Connell Street Waterford County
Waterford Ireland
Tel: 00 353 51 55038
Theatre, dance, comedy, music, film, literature, visual art and children's art. There's a vibrant and exciting year-round programme at Garter Lane Arts Centre in the heart of Waterford city.

Glebe House and Gallery

Churchill Letterkenny County Donegal Ireland
Tel: 00 353 74 913 7071
Located in a Regency house, the gallery features William Morris Wallpaper and textiles, Islamic and Japanese art, plus around 300 artworks by twentieth-century artists such as Picasso and Kokosha.

Hunt Museum

The Custom House Rutland Street Limerick
County Limerick Ireland
Tel: 00 353 61 312833
Exhibits one of Ireland's greatest private collections of art and antiquities, dating from Neolithic times to the twentieth century, including works by Renoir, Picasso and Yeats.

National Museum of Ireland: Decorative Arts and History

Collins Barracks Benburb Street Dublin 7
Dublin Region Ireland
Tel: 0 353 1 677 7444
Home to a wide range of objects which include weaponry, furniture, silver, ceramics and glassware, plus examples of folklife and costume.

Orchard Pottery

Center Street Castleconnell County Limerick
Ireland
Tel: 00 353 61 377181
Richard Ferris works alone to produce an ever changing variety of Irish pottery. Whether you are looking for a special gift or just want to watch the work in progress, all visitors are welcome.

Tir Saile - North Mayo Sculpture Trail

Meitheal Mhuigheo Main Street Foxford
County Mayo Ireland
Tel: 00 353 94 925 6811
The largest public arts project ever undertaken in Ireland. It entailed the putting in place of fourteen site specific Sculptures along the North Mayo Coast. The trail is supplemented by an exhibition site at which temporary exhibitions are accommodated.

Triona Design

Ardara County Donegal Ireland
Tel: 00 353 74 4954 1422
Visitors can learn about the traditional art of weaving as well as browsing the displays of beautifully finished clothing, unusual crafts, paintings and jewellery.

Wexford Arts Centre
Cornmarket Wexford County Wexford Ireland
Tel: 00 353 53 23764
A vibrant contemporary multi arts centre putting on top quality theatre, music and literary events as well as exhibiting visual art from traditional to installation in it's two galleries.

Birds, Butterflies & Bees

Straffan Butterfly Farm
Ovidstown Straffan County Kildare Ireland
Tel: 00 353 16 271109
Ireland's first live tropical butterfly exhibition. With a tropical all-weather centre that provides an oppurtunity to see some of the worlds most exotic creatures and observe their interesting life cycles.
1 Jun-31 Aug

Caverns & Caves

Aillwee Cave
Ballyvaughan County Clare Ireland
Tel: 00 353 65 707 7036/707 7067
There is a whole labyrinth of caves, pot holes, underground lakes and streams beneath the surface of The Burren.

Crag Cave
Castleisland County Kerry Ireland
Tel: 00 353 66 714 1244
An ancient fossil cave system, within which can be seen the natural forces that created the complex and beautiful passages.
Mar-Nov daily

Country Parks & Estates

Millstreet Country Park
Millstreet County Cork Ireland
Tel: 00 353 29 70810
Experience the wetlands, herb rich meadow, the upper arboretum, on past our native red deer and on up to the Mushera Ravine.

Exhibition & Visitor Centres

Blasket Centre, Ionad an Bhlascaoid Mhoir
Dún Chaoin Trá Lí County Chiarraí Ireland
Tel: 00 353 66 915 6444/915 6371
The Blasket Centre in Dún Chaoin, on the tip of the Dingle Peninsula, celebrates the story of the Blasket Islanders.

Cashel Heritage Centre
Main Street Cashel County Tipperary
Tel: 00 353 62 62511/ 61333
Award-winning heritage centre with large-scale model of Cashel in the 1640s, audio commentary, tourist information and craft shop stocking stocking local crafts including pottery, textiles, clothing food and books.

National 1798 Visitor Centre
Millpark Road Enniscorthy County Wrexford Ireland
Tel: 00 353 54 37596/7
This visitor centre was specially designed and constructed to mark the bicentennial of the 1798 rebellion. Tells the story using multi-media and interactive computers, and features an audio-visual presentation.

Reginalds Tower
The Quay Waterford City County Waterford Ireland
Tel: 00 353 51 30 4220
The tower dates from the twelfth century and is the oldest urban civic building in the country. It's been restored and now houses an exhibition.

Waterways Visitor Centre
Grand Canal Quay Dublin 2 Ireland
Tel: 00 353 1 677 7510
The newly-refurbished centre houses an exhibition which explores Ireland's inland waterways, their historical background and their modern amenity uses.

Factory Outlets & Tours

Waterford Crystal Visitor Centre
Kilbarry Waterford County Waterford
Tel: 00 353 51 332500
From the factory tour to the restaurant and retail stores, you can experience the magic and spirit that lies behind Waterford crystal.

Festivals & Shows

Wicklow Gardens Festival
Wicklow County Tourism Ltd Clermont Rathnew County Wicklow
Tel: 00 353 404 20070 Fax: 00 353 404 20072
www.visitwicklow.ie

[Throughout the county. 40 min S of Dublin]

The Wicklow Gardens Festival is a great opportunity for visitors to discover the beauty of the gardens throughout County Wicklow. Wicklow has been blessed with an abundance of marvellous gardens ranging from the seventeenth century to the recently created ones, from the grand scale to the small cottage type. While many of the larger gardens are open throughout the season, most of the smaller ones are only open on certain days during the festival. It is an ideal time to experience these wonderful creations where your guide is invariably the garden owner. You will find each garden to be different-from the grand landscape of the great gardens to the intimate personal detail found in the smaller ones. Visit and Enjoy!

1 May-14 August 2008
Charges vary - many go to charity

Folk & Local History Museums

Adare Heritage Centre
Main Street Adare Co. Limerick Ireland
Tel: 00 353 61 396 666
Historical exhibition giving the history of Adare back to the 1200's. Also houses craft shops, Tourist Information Office and a 70 seater restaurant.

Cashel Folk Village
Dominic Street Cashel County Tipperary Ireland
Tel: 00 353 62 62525
A delightful series of informal reconstructions of various traditional thatched village shops, a forge, and other businesses, together with a penal Chapel. There is also an old IRA museum and audio-visual presentation.

Donegal County Museum
High Road Letterkenny County Donegal Ireland
Tel: 00 353 74 912 4613
The museum is based in a old stone building, which was once part of a Letterkenny workhouse. It houses a fascinating range of artefacts covering all aspects of life in Donegal, and temporary exhibitions.

Galway City Museum
Spanish Arch Galway City Ireland
Tel: 00 353 91 532460
This award-winning museum is located behind the Spanish Arch and has three floors of relating the story of Galway from medieval times to the modern day. With changing exhibitions.

Kerry County Museum
Ashe Memorial Hall Denny Street Tralee County Kerry Ireland
Tel: 00 353 66 712 7777
Explores the archaeology and history of the county, with 'Medieval Experience' and award-winning Antarctica Exhibition.

National Museum of Ireland: Country Life
Turlough Park Castlebar County Mayo Ireland

Tel: 00 353   949031773 / 16486392
Exhibitions portray the lives of ordinary people who lived in rural Ireland between 1850-1950. Emphasis is placed on the continuity of lifestyles, which were established for several hundred years and lasted well into the twentieth century.

Number Twenty Nine
29 Lower Fitzwilliam Street Dublin Ireland
Tel: 00 353 1 702 6165
An exhibition of the homelife of a middle-class merchant family in late eighteenth-century Dublin. Houses a unique collection of artifacts and works of art. With tea room and gift shop.

South Tipperary County Museum
Mick Delahunty Square Emmet Street Clonmel County Tipperary Ireland
Tel: 00 353 52 34550
The museum houses two galleries, one that traces the history and heritage of the county and one that hosts a programme of exhibitions.

Tullow Museum
Bridge Street Tullow County Carlow Ireland
Tel: 00 353 59 9151286
Housed in a former Methodist church, the museum houses a splendid collection that documents the region's history.

Valentia Heritage Centre
School Road Knightstown Valentia Island Kerry County Kerry Ireland
Tel: 00 353 66 947 6411
The Centre is housed in the former Knightstown National School. There are three main display rooms: 'The School-Room,' 'Island and Harbour,' and 'The Transatlantic Telegraph.'

Wexford County Museum
Enniscorthy Castle County Wexford Ireland
Tel: 00 353 54 35926
The museum is located in a mediaeval castle. It illustrates the storied past of the county in its varied aspects, ecclesiastical, military, maritime, agricultural and industrial.

Food & Drink

Guinness Storehouse
St James Gate Dublin 8 Ireland
Tel: 00 353 1 408 4800
This hi-tech home of the Black Stuff offers a fascinating insight into 250 years of brewing history. The tour ends with a complimentary pint in the 360° Gravity Bar.

Forests & Woods

Phoenix Park Visitor Centre
Phoenix Park Dublin 8 Ireland
Tel: 00 353 1 677 0095
One of the largest city parks in Europe, with a lively exhibition on display in the visitor centre. Temporary exhibitions are also on display. Adjoining the visitor centre is the fully-restored Ashtown Castle.

Gardens & Horticulture

Celtic Theme Park and Gardens
Kilcornan County Limerick Ireland
Tel: 00 353 61 394243
Situated on an original Celtic settlement, this beautiful park helps to interpret Ireland's past with exhibits of structures associated with ancient Ireland. It also features an extensive range of native plants and a coffee shop.

Celtic Plantarum Dundrum
Dundrum County Tipperary Ireland
Tel: 00 353 62 71303
A magical combination of plants, shrubs and trees (some quite rare), with quaint water features. Also features a range of reconstructions of ancient field monuments.

Glanleam Gardens
Glanleam Estate Valentia Island County Kerry
Tel: 00 353 66 947 6176
A subtropical paradise, a rain forest and a jungle all at the same time. Glanleam is famous for Southern Hemisphere and Asian plants thriving in the mild climate of Valentia Island.

Irish National Stud, Japanese Gardens and St Fiachras Garden

Tully Kildare County Kildare Ireland
Tel: 00 353 45 521617 / 522963
1,000-acre farm (that's home to some of Ireland's finest thoroughbreds) and a horse museum. The Japanese Gardens are situated in the grounds of the Stud Farm and were created between 1906-1910. Also features St. Fiachra's Garden, which has 4 acres of woodland.

John F Kennedy Arboretum

New Ross County Wexford Ireland
Tel: 00 353 51 388171
Arboretum with a massive collection of plants, forest plots, visitor centre, parkland walks, miniature railway, shop and café.

Kilfane Glen And Waterfall

Thomastown County Kilkenny Ireland
Tel: 00 353 56 772 7105
Kilfane is a pristine example of a Romantic-era garden dating from the 1790s. Features a 30-foot waterfall, woodland paths, displayed art-work, lily pond and orchard.

Kilmacurragh Arboretum

Rathdrum County Wicklow Ireland
Tel: 00 353 1 837 0909
This is an arboretum particularly famous for its conifers and calcifuges, planted during the nineteenth century by Thomas Acton.

Kilmokea Gardens

Great Island Campile County Wexford Ireland
Tel: 00 353 51 388109
Seven acres of formal walled gardens, with hundreds of different plant species and a café.

National Botanic Gardens

Glasnevin Dublin 9 Ireland
Tel: 00 353 1 837 4388/7596
These colourful gardens cover a total area of 19.5 hectares, part of which is the natural flood plain of the River Tolka.

Heritage & Industrial

Brú na Bóinne Visitor Centre

Newgrange and Knowth Donore County Meath Ireland
Tel: 00 353 41 988 0300
Interprets the Neolithic monuments of Newgrange, Knowth and Dowth.

Cobh: The Queenstown Story

Cobh Railway Station Cobh County Cork Ireland
Tel: 00 353 21 481 3591
Housed in a restored Victorian railway station, the museum houses an exhibition of the origins, history and legacy of Cobh. Retrace the steps of the 2.5 million adults and children who emigrated from Ireland via Cobh on coffin ships, early steamers and finally on the great ocean liners.

Connemara Heritage and History Centre and Dan O'Hara's Homestead

Lettershea Clifden County Galway
Tel: 00 353 95 21246/21808
Fax: 00 353 95 22098
www.connemaraheritage.com

[Approx. 10 min from Clifden or 1h from Galway City on N59. Plenty of on-site parking available]

Nestling beneath the Twelve Bens mountain range is an award-winning heritage centre that offers a unique insight into nineteenth century Connemara life and the hardship endured by tenant farmers. Enjoy our presentation, 'Connemara through the ages,' which is available in both Irish and English. Experience our authentic reconstructions of a pre-Famine farm, a crannóg (an island used as a settlement), a ringfort (a fortified settlement from the Early Medieval Period) and a clochaun (an Early Christian place of prayer). See the restored homestead of Dan O'Hara (a man made famous in song and story). Guided tours with turf-cutting and sheep-shearing demonstrations are available for groups by prior arrangement. Visit our craft shop with its large selection of knitwear, marble, jewellery and other high-quality gifts. Our restaurant serves delicious fresh seafood. Farmhouse and self-catering accommodation is also available (please call or visit our website for more information).

Apr-Oct daily
A€7.50 C€4.00

Discount Offer: Two for the Price of One (full-paying adult).

Jameson Experience, The

The Old Distillery Midleton County Cork
Tel: 00 353 21 461 3594
Fax: 00 353 21 461 3704
www.jamesonwhiskey.com

[Midleton town is off N25, Cork to Waterford route. Plenty of free on-site parking available]

A tour of the Jameson Experience, Midleton consists of a 15 minute audio-visual presentation, a 35 minute guided tour of the Old Distillery and then back to the Jameson Bar for a whiskey tasting - minerals are available for children. Visitors can see the largest Pot Still in the world with a capacity of 32,000 gallons and the Old Waterwheel manufactured in 1825 to provide motive power prior to the days of electricity and still turning today. The guided tour and audio-visual aids are available in seven languages. After the tour why not relax in the Malt House Restaurant specialising in country farmhouse fare or perhaps browse through the Jameson Gift Shop.

All year daily 10.00-18.00, Closed Good Fri, 24-27 Dec. Tours: Nov-Feb 11.30, 13.15, 14.30 & 16.00, Mar-Oct On demand, last at 17.00
A€12.50 C€6.00 OAPs€9.00, Family Ticket (A2+C3) €25.00. Group rate: €9.00

Kenmare Heritage Centre

The Square Kenmare County Kerry Ireland
Tel: 00 353 64 31633
The centre covers various themes including Kenmare's history and historical sites, effects of the famine on Kenmare and the landlords of Kenmare. It also has the Kenmare Lace Exhibition.

For great hotel deals call Superbreak on 01904 679999 or visit www.superbreak.com

Mayo North Heritage Centre and Enniscoe Gardens

Enniscoe Castlehill Ballina County Mayo Ireland
Tel: 00 353 96 31809
Museum is stocked with local history items and geneology information. Gift shop, working blacksmith, tearoom, organic vegetable garden and Victiorian walled garden.

Roscrea Castle and Damer House

Castle Street Roscrea County Tipperary Ireland
Tel: 00 353 505 21850
Roscrea Castle features a gate tower, curtain walls and corner towers dating from the 1280's. Damer House is a fine example of pre-Palladian architecture. Its rooms house temporary exhibitions.

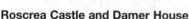

Historical

Athlone Castle

St Peter's Square Athlone Co. Westmeath Ireland
Tel: 00 353 90 647 2107 / 649 2912
This Norman Castle with exhibitions and audio visual presentations on the siege of Athlone. Tearooms and Tourist Information Office on site.

Belvedere House, Gardens and Park

Mullingar Co. Westmeath Ireland
Tel: 00 353 44 49060
160-acre estate with parkland, woodland and lakeshore walks. Belvedere House is an eighteenth-century hunting lodge that has been restored. Features include walled garden, stable block (with modern visitor centre), licensed café, children's play areas and tram rides.

Blarney Castle

Blarney County Cork
Tel: 00 353 21 38525 / 385669
A partial ruin (with battlements and some accessible rooms) that dates back to 1446. At the top of the castle lies the Stone of Eloquence, also called the Blarney Stone. Surrounding the castle are beautiful and extensive gardens.

Bunratty Castle and Folk Park

Bunratty County Clare
Tel: 00 353 61 360788 Fax: 00 353 61 361020
www.shannonheritage.com

[Just off N18 Limerick-Ennis rd (10 min from Shannon Airport). Plenty of on-site parking available]

Bunratty Castle is the most complete and authentic medieval fortress in Ireland. This magnificently restored castle contains fifteenth and sixteenth-century furnishings and tapestries. Within its grounds is Bunratty Folk Park where nineteenth-century Irish Life is tellingly recreated. The Folk Park, set on 26 acres, features a watermill, a church, a village street, a magical walled garden, a playground and various farm animals. By night, Bunratty Castle hosts unique Medieval Castle Banquets which feature music and song by the Bunratty Castle entertainers and the evening is complemented by a delicious 4 course meal with wine (reservations necessary). The Corn Barn venue within the Folk Park hosts an Irish night from April to October and this is also complemented by delicious home cooked food and wine, (reservations necessary).

Jan-Mar & Nov-Dec 09.30-17.30 (last admission 16.15), Apr-May & Sept-Oct 09.00-17.30 (last admission 16.15), June-Aug 09.00-18.00 (last admission 17.15). Closed Good Friday & 24-26 Dec. Medieval Banquets nightly (reservations necessary). Bunratty Folk Park Traditional Irish Night Apr-Oct (reservations necessary)

A€15.00 C€9.00 OAPs€9.00 Students(NUS/USI)€10.00, Family Ticket (A2+C2) €32.00 or (A2+C4) €34.25 or (A2+C6) €35.25

Cahir Castle

Castle Street Cahir County Tipperary Ireland
Tel: 00 353 52 41011
Dating from the twelfth century, Cahir is one of
Ireland's largest and best-preserved castles.
Attractions include a guided tour and several
exhibitions.

Casino Marino

Cherrymount Crescent Marino Dublin 3
Dublin Region Ireland
Tel: 00 353 1 833 1618
The Casino was designed by Sir William
Chambers as a pleasure house for James
Caulfeild, First Earl of Charlemont. It is one of
the finest eighteenth-century neo-classical build-
ings in Europe.

Castletown

Celbridge County Kildare Ireland
Tel: 00 353 1 628 8252
Castletown is the largest and most significant
Palladian style country house in Ireland.

Charles Fort

Summer Cove Kinsale County Cork Ireland
Tel: 00 353 21 477 2263
Constructed in the late seventeenth century on
the site of an earlier coastal fortification, Charles
Fort is a classic example of a star-shaped fort.

Clonmacnoise

Athlone County Offaly Ireland
Tel: 00 353 90 967 4195
An early Christian site founded by Saint Ciaran
in the sixth century on the banks of the River
Shannon.

Cork City Gaol and Radio Museum Experience

Convent Avenue Sunday's Well Cork City
County Cork Ireland
Tel: 00 353 21 430 5022
Step back in time to see what nineteenth-century life was like in Cork - inside and outside
prison walls. Situated in the unlikely setting of
the former Governor's House, the Radio
Museum Experience deals with the early days of
radio broadcasting and its iinpact on our lives.

Craggaunowen - The Living Past

Kilmurry Sixmilebridge Nr Quin County Clare
Tel: 00 353 61 360788 Fax: 00 353 61 361020
www.shannonheritage.com

[Located off R469, nr Quin, Co.Clare]

Visit Ireland's original award winning pre-historic
park. Situated on 50 acres of wooded grounds,
the park interprets Ireland's pre-historic and
early Christian eras. It features a stunning recreation of some of the homesteads, animals and
artefacts that existed in Ireland over 1,000 years
ago. Explore the Crannog (lake dwelling), the
Ring Fort, the Medieval Castle and the 'Brendan
Boat' - a leather hulled boat built by Tim Severin
who sailed across mid-Atlantic and thus re-
enacted the voyage of St. Brendan and the
early Christian monks reputed to have discovered America centuries before Columbus. Visit
Craggaunowen Castle, built in 1550 standing
defiantly on a crag overlooking the lake. See
rare animal breeds - specimens of the pre-historic era. Enjoy the fresh air and lake walks in a
most enjoyable rural setting. Savour the wonderful home-made fare in the charming farmhouse tea room.

Early Apr-Sep 10.00-18.00

A€8.95 C€5.25 OAPs€6.50, Family Ticket
(A2+C2) €20.50 or (A2+C4) €21.50 or (A2+C6)
€22.65

Curraghmore House and Gardens

Portlaw County Waterford Ireland
Tel: 00 353 51 387102
The interior of the house contains exceptionally fine plasterwork. The grounds include an outstanding Arboretum, shell grotto.

Derrynane House, National Historic Park

Caherdaniel County Kerry Ireland
Tel: 00 353 66 947 5113
120 hectares of the lands of Derrynane, together with Derrynane House, make up Derrynane National Historic Park.

Desmond Castle (French Prison)

Cork Street Kinsale County Cork Ireland
Tel: 00 353 21 477 4855 / 2263
A good example of an urban tower house, the castle consists of a keep with storehouses to the rear and domestic offices.

Donegal Castle

Donegal Town County Donegal Ireland
Tel: 00 353 74 972 2405
Built by the O'Donnell chieftain in the fifteenth century, the castle is furnished throughout and includes Persian rugs and French Tapestries. Information panels chronicle the history of the castle owners.

Dublin Castle, State Apartments

Dame Street Dublin 2 Dublin Region Ireland
Tel: 00 353 1 677 7129
Dublin Castle is used for State receptions and Presidential Inaugurations. The State Apartments, Undercroft, Chapel Royal, craft shop, heritage centre and restaurant are open to visitors.

Dún Aonghasa

Kilmurvey Inishmore Aran Islands County Galway Ireland
Tel: 00 353 99 61008
Perched spectacularly on a cliff overlooking the Atlantic Ocean, this is the largest of the prehistoric stone forts of the Aran Islands.

Emo Court Estate

Emo Court Emo Portlaoise County Laois Ireland
Tel: 00 353 502 26573
A magnificent example of the neo-classical style, the house is surrounded by beautiful gardens and parkland. Access to house by guided tour only. Guided tours available hourly. Excellent restaurant and tea room.

Glendalough Visitor Centre

Glendalough Bray County Wicklow Ireland
Tel: 00 353 404 45325/45352
This early Christian Monastic site is et in a glaciated valley with two lakes and includes a superb round tower, stone churches and decorated crosses. The Visitor Centre has an interesting exhibition.

Huntington Castle and Gardens

Clonegal County Carlow Ireland
Tel: 00 353 54 77552
The present castellated house ifeatures a tower house, an ancient vine in the conservatory and a Temple to the Goddess Isis in the basement. Woodland and riverside walks.

Killruddery House and Gardens

Bray County Wicklow Ireland
Tel: 00 353 44 0 44 6024
Killruddery House has been home to the Brabazon family (the Earls of Meath) since 1618. Features include an Orangery and seventeenth-century landscape gardens.

King House Interpretative Galleries and Museum

Boyle County Roscommon Ireland
Tel: 00 353 71 966 3242
A magnificently restored Georgian mansion built in the eighteenth century. Exhibitions tell the story of the house, its people and the surrounding locality. Adventure playground, public park and catering facilities..

King John's Castle

Nicholas Street King's Island Limerick County
Limerick
Tel: 00 353 61 360788 Fax: 00 353 61 361020
www.shannonheritage.com

[Situated on King's Island in Limerick City]

King John's Castle is situated in the heart of
Limerick's Medieval Heritage Precinct, "Kings
Island". The Castle was built between 1200 and
1210 and was repaired and extended many
times in the following centuries. King John's
Castle remains a most impressive Anglo-
Norman Fortification. It retains many of the pioneering features which made its construction
unique for its day. Its massive gatehouse, battlements and corner tower await exploration!
Features include; an imaginative historical exhibition on the history of the castle featuring two-
multi vision shows and archaeological excavations featuring amongst other things the earliest
evidence of settled life in Limerick. Enjoy scenic
battlement walks and views of the surrounding
hinterland.

*Jan-Feb & Nov-Dec 10.00-16.30, Mar-Apr & Oct
09.30-17.00. May-Sept 09.30-17.30. Closed
Good Friday & 24-26 Dec*

A€8.50 C€4.95 OAPs€6.25
Students(NUS/USI)€6.25, Family Ticket
(A2+C2) €19.45 or (A2+C4) €20.45 or (A2+C6)
€21.50

Malahide Castle

Malahide Castle Demesne Malahide
County Dublin
Tel: 00 353 1 846 2184
The house is an interesting mix of architectural
styles. Furnished with beautiful period furniture,
it is home to an extensive collection of Irish
paintings, mainly from the National Gallery.

Muckross House, Gardens and Traditional Farm

Killarney National Park Muckross Killarney
County Kerry Ireland
Tel: 00 353 64 31440
A magnificent Victorian mansion situated in
Killarney National Park. Gives an insight into
upstairs/downstairs lifestyles and is home to a
number of skilled craftworkers. Outside, there
are exotic trees, azaleas, and a rock garden.
The traditional farms are an authentic outdoor
interpretation of rural life in Kerry in the 1930's
and 1940's.

Ormond Castle

Castle Park off Castle Street Carrick-on-Suir
County Tipperary Ireland
Tel: 00 353 51 640787/56 772 4623
Ormond Castle is the best example of an
Elizabethan manor house in Ireland and features
fine decorative plasterwork.

Pearse Museum

St Enda's Park Grange Road Rathfarnham
Dublin 16 Ireland
Tel: 00 353 1 493 4208
Museum with exhibitions, a nature study room
and an audio-visual show. St. Enda's Park features riverside walks, waterfall and walled garden.

Rock of Cashel

Cashel County Tipperary Ireland
Tel: 00 353 62 61437
A spectacular group of Medieval buildings set
on an outcrop of limestone in the Golden Vale.

Shaw Birthplace

33 Synge Street Dublin 8 County Dublin
Tel: 00 353 1 475 0854/872 2077
The neat terraced house is as much a celebration of Victorian Dublin domestic life as of the
early years of one of Dublin's Nobel prize-win-
ners for literature.

Literature & Libraries

Dublin Writers Museum
18 Parnell Square Dublin 1 County Dublin
Tel: 00 353 1 872 2077
Situated in a magnificent eighteenth century
mansion in the north city centre, the collection
features the lives and works of Dublin's literary
celebrities over the past three hundred years.

James Joyce Museum
Joyce Tower Sandycove County Dublin
Tel: 00 353 1 280 9265/872 2077
Joyce Tower is the perfect setting for a museum
dedicated to Joyce, a writer of international
renown who remains the writer most associated
with Dublin.

National Library of Ireland
Kildare Street Dublin 2 Ireland
Tel: 00 353 1 603 0200
The National Library of Ireland, which was
founded in 1877, has many associations with
famous figures in Irish history.

Trinity College Library and the Book of Kells
Trinity College Library College Street Dublin 2
Dublin Region Ireland
Tel: 00 353 1 608 2320
The 'Old Library' and the 'Long Room' at the
Trinity College Library are amongst Ireland's
biggest tourist attractions. The Old Library
houses the famous Book of Kells - an ornately
illustrated manuscript produced by Celtic monks
around AD 800.

Living History Museums

Dublinia
St Michael's Hill Christ Church Dublin 8 Ireland
Tel: 00 353 1 679 4611
Dublinia recreates the sights and sounds of the
medieval city to offer visitors a fascinating
glimpse of Dublin 800 years ago. Detailed
reconstruction of the streets, houses and even
the citizens of the time.

Maritime

Mizen Head Signal Station
Harbour Road Goleen County Cork
Tel: 00 353 28 35115/35225
Fax: 00 353 28 35422
www.mizenhead.ie

*[Leave N71 at Ballydehob, through Schull &
Goleen to Mizen Head or leave N71 at Bantry,
through Durrus on R591 to Goleen & Mizen
Head. Plenty of on-site parking available]*

Mizen Head Signal Station is open to the public
for the first time since it was completed in 1910.
The award winning Mizen Head Visitor Centre in
the Keeper's House and the Engine Room, the
famous Arched Bridge, the 99 Steps, the
Fastnet Hall Navigational Aids Simulator and the
views up the South and West Coasts guarantee
a unique and authentic experience.
Shop@theMizen and Mizen Café. A different
experience every time you visit.

*Mid Mar-May & Oct daily 10.30-17.00, June-end
Sept 10.00-18.00, Nov-mid Mar Sat & Sun
11.00-16.00*

A€6.00 C(0-4)€Free C(5-11)€3.50
OAPs&Students(NUS/USI)€4.50, Family Ticket
(A2+C3) €18.00. Group rate: 10% discount

Mills - Water & Wind

Blennerville Windmill
Windmill Street Blennerville County Kerry Ireland
Tel: 00 353 66 7121064
The largest working windmill in Britain features a
visitor centre with an audio-visual presentation,
exhibition gallery, craft shop and restaurant.

Model Towns & Villages

West Cork Model Railway Village
Inchydoney Road Clonakilty Co. Cork Ireland
Tel: 00 353 2 333224
Here you can see exhibitions of the railways and industries which once linked six Cork towns.

Natural History Museums

National Museum of Ireland: Natural History
Merrion Street Dublin 2 Dublin Region Ireland
Tel: 00 353 1 677 7444
This zoological museum has outstanding examples of wildlife from Ireland and the four corners of the globe. Some animals can still be seen today and some animals are long extinct.

Nature & Conservation Parks

Cliffs of Moher and O'Brien's Tower
Liscannor County Clare Ireland
Tel: 00 353 61 360788
Situated in County Clare and bordering the Burren Area, the Cliffs of Moher are one of Ireland's most spectacular sights.

Connemara National Park
Letterfrack Galway County Galway Ireland
Tel: 00 353 95 41054/41006
The Park covers some 2,000 hectares (4,942 acres) of scenic countryside, rich in wildlife on the slopes of the Twelve Bens.

Glenveagh National Park and Castle
Churchill Letterkenny County Donegal Ireland
Tel: 00 353 74 91 37090
A nineteenth-century castellated mansion set in some 16,500 hectares of mountains, lakes, glens and woods with a large heard of red deer. The central feature is a nineteenth-century castle surrounded by Glenveagh Gardens.

Wicklow Mountains National Park
Upper Lake Glendalough Co Wicklow Ireland
Tel: 00 353 404 45425
20,000 hectares of mountain blanket bogs and Glendalough Wood Nature Reserve. Education Centre providing a range of courses and tours for schoolchildren, students and other groups.

Places of Worship

St Patrick's Cathedral
Saint Patrick's Close Dublin 8 Dublin Region reland
Tel: 00 353 1 453 9472
St. Patrick's Cathedral is the the largest church in Ireland and was built between 1191 and 1270. It is considered the National Cathedral for the whole island.

Police, Prisons & Dungeons

Kilmainham Gaol
Inchicore Road Kilmainham Dublin 8 Dublin Region Ireland
Tel: 00 353 1 453 5984
One of the largest unoccupied gaols in Europe, covering some of the most heroic and tragic events in Ireland's emergence as a modern nation from the 1780s to the 1920s.

Wicklow's Historic Gaol
Kilmantin Hill Wicklow County Wicklow Ireland
Tel: 00 353 404 61599
Wicklow's Historic Gaol tells the story of eighteenth and nineteenth-century social and political history through various forms of interpretation.

Railways

Donegal Railway Heritage Centre
The Old Station Donegal Town County Donegal Ireland
Tel: 00 353 74 972 2655
Find out what it was like to travel on the narrow gauge railways of County Donegal. Includes a historical presentation, artefacts and shop.

Fry Model Railway

Malahide Castle Demesne Malahide
County Dublin
Tel: 00 353 1 846 3779
Situated in the beautiful grounds surrounding
Malahide Castle, this delightful collection is a
treat for railway enthusiasts, children and adults
alike.

Science - Earth & Planetary

Birr Castle Demesne and Ireland's Historic Science Centre

Birr County Offaly Ireland
Tel: 00 353 509 20336
Home to Ireland's largest gardens, offering a
Winter Garden, Formal Garden, Terrace Garden
a River Garden. Parkland with rivers, lakes and
waterfalls. The Great Telescope is fully restored
and looks and moves just as it did 150 years
ago. Ireland's Historic Science Centre features
pioneering achievements in fields of astronomy,
photography engineering and horticulture.

Sealife Centres & Aquariums

National Sea Life Centre (Bray)

Strand Road Bray County Wicklow
Tel: 00 353 1 286 6939
Fax: 00 353 1 286 0562
www.sealife.ie

[Rail: Bray. Bus: 45, 84 & 145]

Dive into a magical marine world at the National
Sea Life Centre, Bray, where you will encounter
strange and beautiful creatures from around the
globe. Also see the mesmerising effects of
beautifully coloured shoals of tropical fish swimming around our mythical sea god, and be
enchanted by our majestic black-tipped reef
sharks. There are also many creatures on display around our own coastline. Informative talks
and feeding presentations throughout the day
provide a deeper insight into the world beneath

the waves and help us to understand why it is
so important to protect these wonderful creatures. Ireland's leading marine conservation
experience has something for the whole family.
Guided tours by prior arrangement.

All year daily from 10.00. Closed 25 & 26 Dec
Please call for admission prices

Discount Offer: One Child Free.

Toy & Childhood Museums

Berkeley Costume and Toy Museum

New Ross County Wexford Ireland
Tel: 00 353 51 21361
Large private collection of eighteenth and nineteenth-century toys, dolls and costumes, suit-
ably displayed in a drawing room.

Wildlife & Safari Parks

Fota Wildlife Park

Fota Estate Carrigtwohill County Cork Ireland
Tel: 00 353 21 812678
Modern wildlife park with more than 70 species
of exotic wildlife (including cheetahs, lemurs,
giraffes and monkeys) in open, natural surroundings. There is also an internationally
renowned arboretum.

Zoos

Dublin Zoo

Phoenix Park Dublin 8 Ireland
Tel: 00 353 1 474 8900
Covering a 70-acre site at Phoenix Park, Dublin
Zoo houses a wide variety of animals, including
red panda, Arctic fox, otter, elephants, and even
a pack of grey wolves. Another popular attraction within the zoo is City Farm, which has a
special children's corner and a flock of Galway
sheep, and the Californian sea lion pool where
audiences watch the animals train at regular
intervals throughout the day.

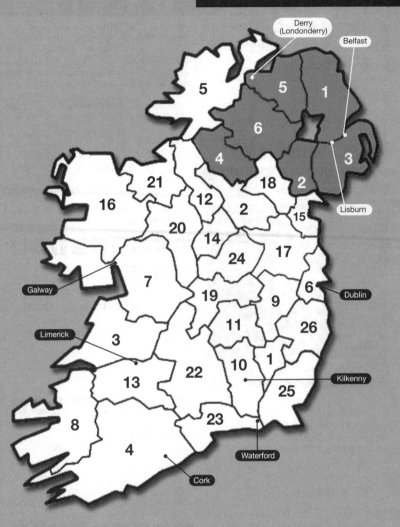

Northern Ireland

Derry (Londonderry)
Belfast
Lisburn
Galway
Limerick
Dublin
Kilkenny
Cork
Waterford

Animal Attractions

Leslie Hill Open Farm

Leslie Hill Macfin Road Ballymoney
County Antrim BT53 6QL
Tel: 028 2766 6803/2766 3109
A Georgian house, magnificent period farm
buildings, and fine grounds with paths, lakes
and trees.

Arts, Crafts & Textiles

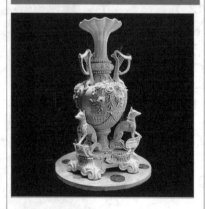

Belleek Pottery

Main Street Rathmore Belleek Enniskillen
County Fermanagh BT93 3FY
Tel: 028 6865 9300 Fax: 028 6865 8625
www.belleek.ie

*[A46 from Enniskillen, follow signs to Belleek.
Pottery is signposted. Plenty of on-site parking
available]*

After celebrating its 150th Anniversary Year with
a range of exciting events and high profile visitors, Belleek Pottery is looking forward to another successful year as one of Ireland's leading
tourist attractions in 2008. In 2008, visitors can
expect to discover the secrets that have made
Belleek Pottery one of the most enduring success stories of Irish craftsmanship. Personally
guided tours take visitors 'behind the scenes' at
the pottery allowing them to marvel at the craft
techniques and attention to detail that make
each piece of Belleek a unique item to cherish.
The Belleek museum boasts an impressive display of priceless Belleek and its audio visual
centre enables visitors to find out more about
the history behind Ireland's oldest pottery. At the
Belleek Showroom, visitors can purchase their

very own piece of pottery with a full range of
traditional Belleek and contemporary Belleek
Living pieces available. Many items are exclusive to the Belleek Visitor Centre. The award
winning Belleek Tea room allows visitors to relax
with refreshments served on Belleek China
tableware. For further information on Belleek
Pottery please contact the Visitor Centre on: Tel:
+44 (0)28 9023 355.

*Mon-Fri 09.00-17.30, Sat 10.00-18.00, Sun
14.00-18.00. Tours Mon-Fri every 30min 09.30-
12.15 & 13.45-15.30 last tour on Fri leaving at
15.00. Please check for Centre opening times in
winter*

Guided tours (every 30min): £4.00

**Discount Offer: Two for the Price of
One (full-paying adult).**

Irish Linen Centre and Lisburn Museum

Market Square Lisburn County Antrim
BT28 1AG
Tel: 028 9266 3377
The Irish Linen Centre and Lisburn Museum is
established in the town's 17th century market
house.

Island Arts Centre

Lagan Valley Island The Island Lisburn
County Antrim BT27 4RL
Tel: 028 92 509509
Nestled by the banks of the River Lagan at
Lagan Valley Island, Island Arts Centre is
Lisburn City Council's visually stunning new arts
base.

Birds, Butterflies & Bees

WWT Castle Espie Wildfowl and Wetland Centre

78 Ballydrain Road Comber Newtownards
County Down BT23 6EA
Tel: 028 9187 4146
Located on the shores of Strangford Lough,
Castle Espie is home to the largest collection of
wildfowl in Ireland.

Country Parks & Estates

Carnfunnock Country Park

Drains Bay Coast Road Larne County Antrim
BT40 2QG
Tel: 028 2827 0541
A maze in the shape of Northern Ireland! Walled
garden, BBQ, picnic sites and golf.

Cavehill Country Park

Antrim Road / Innisfayle Park Belfast
County Antrim
Tel: 07802 301860
Based on the slopes of a 1,200-foot basalt cliff,
the park offers panoramic views, walking trails,
and archaeological/ historical sights. With visitor
centre and adventure playground.

Colin Glen Forest Park

163 Stewartstown Road Dunmurry Belfast
County Antrim BT17 0HW
Tel: 028 9061 4115
Beautiful wooded glen at the foot of Black
Mountain.

Crawfordsburn Country Park

Bridge Road South Helen's Bay County Down
BT19 1LD
Tel: 028 9185 3621
Beaches, wooded glens, waterfalls and flowery
meadows, a wartime fort, a Country Centre with
an exhibition and a restaurant.

Delamont Country Park

Downpatrick County Down
Tel: 028 4482 8333
Boat trips, playground, tearoom/gardens, class-
room, visitor centre, woodlands/parkland,
wildlife, miniature railway and events.

Roe Valley Country Park

nr Limavady Derry County Londonderry
Tel: 028 7772 2074
Forest areas, riverside walk, history trail and bio-
diversity trail. Site of O'Cahan Castle, O'Cahans
Rock and the Dog Leap.

Exhibition & Visitor Centres

Palace Stables Heritage Centre

The Palace Demense Armagh County Armagh
BT60 4EL
Tel: 028 3752 1801 Fax: 028 3751 0180
www.visitarmagh.com

[Armagh City. Plenty of on-site parking available]

The Palace Stables Heritage Centre is a
restored Georgian stable block located on the
Palace Demesne situated next to the impressive
Primate's Palace, formerly the home of the
Archbishops of the Church of Ireland from 1770
until the 1970s. Guided tours are available that
tell the story of the Demesne and through Living
History costumed interpreters recreate both the
grandeur and the squalor of the Georgian peri-
od. These tours also give you access to the
Chapel, School Room, Withdrawing Room,
Tack Room Coachman's Kitchen, Servant's tun-
nel, Ice House and at weekends into the
Demesne.

*Apr, May & Sept Sat 10.00-17.00 Sun 12.00-
17.00, June-Aug Mon-Sat 10.00-17.00 Sun
12.00-17.00. Grounds open all year*

A£5.00 C£3.25 OAPs£4.00, Family Ticket
£15.00

**Discount Offer: Two for the Price of
One (full-paying adult).**

Saint Patrick's Trian Visitor Complex

40 English Street Armagh County Armagh
BT61 7BA
Tel: 028 3752 1801 Fax: 028 3751 0180
www.visitarmagh.com
[City Centre. Plenty of on-site parking available]

An exciting visitor complex located in the heart of Armagh City, Saint Patrick's Trian, (pronounced Tree-an) derives its name from the ancient division of Armagh City into three distinct districts, or 'Trians'. The complex features three major exhibitions: Armagh Story - Step back in time and visit historic Armagh - from the massive stone monuments of pre-history, with its myths and legends, to the coming of Saint Patrick and Celtic Christianity. Francis Johnston, the renowned Armagh architect relates the history of Georgian buildings in the city in a most unusual manner. A thought provoking audio-visual presentation portrays 'belief' throughout the world, with particular emphasis on Armagh, as the Ecclesiastical Capital of Ireland. Saint Patrick's Testament takes its title from Saint Patrick's Confession, and examines the life and work of our patron Saint and his connections with Armagh as found in the ancient manuscript - the 'Book of Armagh'. The Land of Lilliput. - Jonathan Swift, author and clergyman spent time in the district, and his most famous work 'Gullivers Travels' is encapsulated in the fantasy 'Land of Lilliput' where the adventures of Gulliver are narrated with the help of a 20 foot giant.
All year Mon-Sat 10.00-17.00, Sun 14.00-17.00
A£5.00 C£3.25 OAPs£4.00, Family Ticket £15.00

Discount Offer: Two for the Price of One (full-paying adult).

Armagh County Museum

The Mall East Armagh County Armagh
BT61 9BE
Tel: 028 3752 3070 Fax: 028 3752 2631
www.armaghcountymuseum.org.uk
Located near the centre of St Patrick's cathedral city, a visit to Armagh County Museum is an ideal way to experience a flavour of the orchard country. Discover a rich and varied legacy revealed in objects ranging from prehistoric artefacts to household items from a bygone age. An impressive collection of paintings includes works by many well known Irish artists. With a range of changing exhibitions throughout the year, the Museum is an ideal place to see and explore the fair county of Armagh.
All year Mon-Fri 10.00-17.00, Sat 10.00-13.00 & 14.00-17.00
Admission Free

Down County Museum

The Mall English Street Downpatrick
County Down BT30 6AH
Tel: 028 4461 5218
This restored eighteenth-century gaol presents exhibitions on the history of County Down.

Ford Farm Park and Museum

8 Low Road Islandmagee Co. Antrim BT40 3RD
Tel: 028 9335 3264
Situated beside Larne Lough, the museum is housed in a former farm outhouse with over 600 items on display. Enjoy farm animals, birdwatching, shoreline walks, buttermaking and spinning demonstrations (on request).

Ulster Folk and Transport Museum

Bangor Road Cultra Holywood County Down BT18 0EU

Tel: 028 9042 8428 Fax: 028 9042 8728
www.uftm.org.uk

[On A2 at Cultra, 7mi E of Belfast. On main Belfast to Bangor Rd, close to Belfast City Airport & Belfast Harbour. Ample on-site parking]

The Ulster Folk and Transport Museum, is one of Ireland's foremost visitor attractions, illustrating the way of life and the traditions of the people of the north of Ireland. At the open air Folk Museum, 60 acres are devoted to illustrating the way of life of people in the early 1900s. Costumed visitor guides, working buildings and exhibits all bring our stories to life. Indoors the Folk Gallery features a number of interesting exhibitions including Farming and Food and Meet the Victorians. The Transport Museum boasts the most comprehensive transport collection on Ireland. The Irish Railway Collection is displayed in an award-winning gallery. Alongside the Irish Railway Collection are the Road Transport Galleries. These Galleries house a fine collection of vehicles ranging from cycles, motorcycles, trams, buses, fire engines and cars. Also, the 'Titanic' exhibition and the two new, exciting and interactive x2 'Flight' exhibitions located in the General Transport Galleries. The Museum also has a full programme of major seasonal events.,

All year Mar-June Mon-Fri 10.00-17.00, Sat 10.00-18.00, Sun 11.00-18.00, July-Sept Mon-Sat 10.00-18.00, Sun 11.00-18.00, Oct-Feb Mon-Fri 10.00-16.00, Sat 10.00-17.00, Sun 11.00-17.00. Please call for Xmas opening times
Folk or Transport: A£5.50 C£3.50, Family Ticket (A2+C3) £15.50, Family Ticket (A1+C3) £11.00 Group rate (15+): 10% discount

Discount Offer: Two for the Price of One (full-paying adult).

Ulster American Folk Park

2 Mellon Road Castletown Omagh County Tyrone BT78 5QY

Tel: 028 8224 3292 Fax: 028 8224 2241
www.folkpark.com

[N of Omagh on A5 Omagh to Strabane rd. Plenty of free on-site parking available]

The Ulster American Folk Park is an outdoor museum of emigration which tells the story of millions of people who emigrated from these shores throughout the eighteenth and nineteenth centuries. The Old World and New World layout of the park illustrates the various aspects of emigrant life on both sides of the Atlantic. Traditional thatched buildings, American log houses and a full-scale replica emigrant ship and dockside gallery help to bring a bygone era back to life. Costumed demonstrators go about their everyday tasks including spinning, open hearth cookery, printing and textiles. The museum also includes an indoor Emigrants Exhibition and a Centre for Migration Studies / library that is accessible to all visitors if they wish to find further information on the history of emigration and the place of their families in it. A full programme of special events is organised throughout the year.

Apr-Oct Mon-Sat 10.30-18.00, Sun & Bank Hols 11.00-18.30, Nov-Mar Mon-Fri 10.30-17.00. Closed Weekends & Bank Hols
A£5.00 C(5-16)£3.00 Concessions£3.00, Family Ticket (A2+C4)£14.00, (A1+C3)£10.00 Group rates available on request

Discount Offer: Two for the Price of One (full-paying adult).

Food & Drink

Tayto Castle Factory
Tayto Castle Tandragee Craigavon
County Armagh BT62 2AB
Tel: 028 3884 0249
The Factory is inside the castle grounds which
belonged at one time to the Duke of
Manchester. Potato storage techniques and the
process that turns potatoes into crisps.

Gardens & Horticulture

Botanic Gardens
Palm House Botanic Avenue Belfast
County Antrim BT7 1JP
Tel: 028 9032 4902
Twenty eight acres of Victorian Botanic Gardens
established in 1828.

Historical

Belfast Castle
Antrim Road Belfast County Antrim BT15 5GR
Tel: 028 9077 6925
Magnificent nineteenth-century sandstone castle
with superb views of Belfast and Belfast Lough.
Refurbished visitor centre, guided tours and
adventure playground.

Carrickfergus Castle
Marine Highway Carrickfergus County Antrim
BT38 7BG
Tel: 028 9335 1273
One of Ireland's finest Medieval castles. A strik-
ing feature of the landscape from land, sea and
air. Exhibition on the castle's history, audio-visu-
als and shop.

City Walls of Derry
Derry County Londonderry BT48 6TE
Tel: 028 7126 7284
Dating back to the seventeenth century, Derry's
walls are the finest and most complete city walls
to be found in Ireland. Visitors can walk round
the city ramparts - a circuit of one mile.

Crown Liquor Saloon
46 Great Victoria Street Belfast County Antrim
BT2 7BA
Tel: 028 9027 9901
The most famous pub in Belfast and one of the
finest examples of a High Victorian public house
in Europe.

Dunluce Castle
87 Dunluce Road Bushmills County Antrim
BT57 8UY
Tel: 028 2073 1938
This late-medieval and seventeenth-century
castle is dramatically sited, on a headland drop-
ping sheer into the sea on the north Antrim
Coast.

Florence Court
Florence Court Demesne Enniskillen
County Fermanagh BT92 1DB
Tel: 028 6634 8249
Florence Court is one of Ulster's most important
eighteenth-century houses, and is surrounded
by a large area of parkland, garden and wood-
land.

Malone House
Barnett Demesne Upper Malone Road Belfast
County Antrim BT9 5PB
Tel: 028 9068 1246
An elegant, early nineteenth-century Georgian
mansion set in the beautiful parkland of Barnett
Demesne. It houses the Higgin Art Gallery and
restaurant.

Mount Stewart House and Garden
Portaferry Road Newtownards County Down
BT22 2AD
Tel: 028 4278 8387
Neo-classical house and landscaped park, with
dramatic views across Strangford Lough.
Features guided tours, famous formal gardens,
lake, woodland and a new garden shop.

Navan Centre and Fort

81 Killylea Road Armagh County Armagh
BT60 4LD
Tel: 028 3752 1801 Fax: 028 3751 0180
www.visitarmagh.com
[A28 2.5mi from Armagh City. Plenty of on-site parking available]

Visit the Navan Centre, which interprets one of Ireland's most important ancient monuments, Navan Fort! This was the royal seat of the Kings of Ulster and the Province's ancient capital. Start your tour in the 'Vanished World' of lost myths, travel into the 'Real World' of archaeology and then enter the 'Other World' to hear the legends of the Ulster Cycle. Visit the Iron Age/Early Christian period dwelling and through Living History interpretation, learn about that way of life. Multi-Lingual facilities available. Finally, walk the path of history to the great Ancient Seat of Kings, Navan Fort.
June-Aug Mon-Sat 10.00-17.00, Sun 12.00-17.00, Apr, May & Sept (Weekends only) Sat 10.00-17.00, Sun 12.00-17.00. Closed 12 July. Other times by arrangement for Tour Groups or Educational visits
A£5.00 C£3.25 OAPs£4.00, Family Ticket £15.00

Discount Offer: Two for the Price of One (full-paying adult).

Scrabo Country Park

Newtownards County Down BT23 4SJ
Tel: 028 9181 1491
The park is centred around a tower on the summit of Scrabo Hill. It includes the woodlands of Killynether, disused quarries, a pond and a prehistoric hill fort.

Giant's Causeway and Visitor Centre

60 Causeway Road Bushmills County Antrim
BT57 8SU
Tel: 028 2073 1582/2972
This famous geological phenomenon renowned for its polygonal columns of layered basalt is the only World Heritage Site in Ireland.

Carrick-a-Rede Rope Bridge and Larrybane

119a Whitepark Road Carrick-A-Rede
County Antrim BT54 6LS
Tel: 028 2073 1582
One of the most popular visit attractions in Northern Ireland, the Carrick-a-Rede Rope Bridge connects the village of Ballintoy to Carrick Island. It is thought that salmon fishermen have been erecting bridges here for over 300 years. Excellent bird-watching opportunities and stunning views. The surrounding area is known as Larrybane.

Lough Neagh Discovery Centre and Oxford Island

Oxford Island Lurgan Craigavon County Armagh
BT66 6NJ
Tel: 028 3832 2205
Four miles of footpaths, five birdwatching hides, woodland, ponds, wildflower meadows, picnic and play areas. The Discovery Centre is fully accessible and has a craft and gift shop. There is also a cafe with views of the Lough. Varying events programme.

Down Cathedral

Downpatrick County Down BT30 6AB
Tel: 028 4461 4922
Cathedral Hill in Down has been a focus of Christian worship since the twelfth century. In the Cathedral grounds is the reputed burial place of St Patrick, thought to have died in 461.

Sealife Centres & Aquariums

Exploris

Exploris Aquarium The Rope Walk Castle Street Portaferry Newtownards County Down BT22 1NZ

Tel: 028 4272 8062 Fax: 028 4272 8396
www.exploris.org.uk

[From Belfast take A20 through Newtownards to Portaferry. From Downpatrick take A25 following signs for Strangford Ferries (ferries every 30min). Exploris is well signposted. Plenty of on-site parking available]

Exploris - The Northern Ireland Aquarium and seal sanctuary is ideally sited on the shores of a marine nature reserve and area of specific scientific interest - Strangford Lough. A visit to Exploris enables the visitor to learn about the species indigenous to Strangord Lough and the coastline of the island. The seal sanctuary lets visitors view the valuable work carried with rehabilitating sick and injured seal pups. A rolling programme of events, guided tours and demonstrations make Exploris fun for all the family.

Peak: Apr-Sept Mon-Fri 10.00-18-00, Sat 11.00-18.00, Sun 12.00-18.00. Off Peak: Oct-Mar Mon-Fri 10.00-17.00, Sat 11.00 17.00, Sun 13.00-17.00

A£6.90 Concessions£4.00. (subject to change)

Sport & Recreation

Lagan Valley Regional Park

Belvoir Park Forest Belfast County Antrim BT8 4QT

Tel: 028 9049 1922

A tranquil piece of countryside on Belfast's doorstep. Grazed pastures and hay meadows adjoin wetland, marsh and woodland in a rich patchwork of habitats next to the river Lagan.

Portstewart Strand

Portstewart County Londonderry

Tel: 028 7083 6396

Magnificent two mile stretch of dunes and a sandy beach, popular with holidaymakers in summer and walkers throughout the year. The Strand is backed by an important dune system which has a way-marked nature trail through the marram grassland rich with wild flowers and many butterfly species. Dogs must be kept on leads during summer months.

W5

Odyssey 2 Queens Quay Belfast County Antrim BT3 9QQ

Tel: 028 9046 7700

W5 is Ireland's first and only purpose-built inter-active discovery centre and offers an entertaining day out that will appeal to visitors of all ages.

Zoos

Belfast Zoological Gardens

Antrim Road Newtownabbey County Antrim BT36 7PN

Tel: 028 9077 6277

Attractions include the award-winning primate house (gorillas and chimpanzees), penguin enclosure, free-flight aviary, African enclosure and underwater viewing of sea-lions and penguins.

Scotland

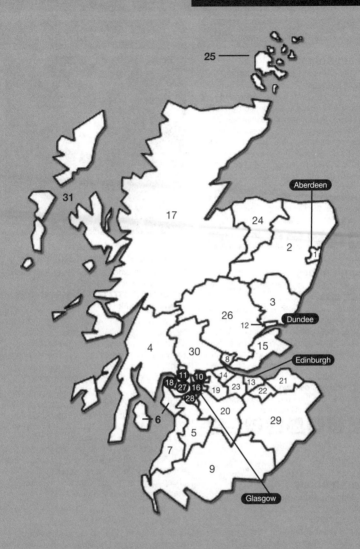

Key to Scottish Subdivisions:

1 Aberdeen
2 Aberdeenshire
3 Angus
4 Argyll and Bute
5 Ayrshire (East)
6 Ayrshire (North)
7 Ayrshire (South)
8 Clackmannanshire
9 Dumfries and Galloway
10 Dunbartonshire (East)
11 Dunbartonshire (West)
12 Dundee
13 Edinburgh
14 Falkirk
15 Fife

16 Glasgow
17 Highland
18 Inverclyde
19 Lanarkshire (North)
20 Lanarkshire (South)
21 Lothian (East)
22 Lothian (Midlothian)
23 Lothian (West)
24 Moray
25 Orkney Isles
26 Perth and Kinross
27 Renfrewshire
28 Renfrewshire (East)
29 Scottish Borders
30 Stirling
31 Western Isles (Na h-Eileanan Siar)

Abbeys

Arbroath Abbey

Abbey Street Arbroath Angus DD11 1EG
Tel: 01241 878756

Arbroath Abbey consists of the substantial ruins of a Tironensian monastery, founded by William the Lion in 1178 and intended as his own burial place. Parts of the abbey church and domestic buildings remain, notably the gatehouse range and the abbot's house. This was the scene of the signing of the Declaration of Arbroath of 1320, which asserted Scotland's independence from England. A visitor centre provides an insight into the abbey's history, which includes an exhibition on the Declaration. The shop features a range of local products made in Tayside.

Dryburgh Abbey

St Boswells Melrose Scottish Borders TD6 0RQ
Tel: 01835 822381

Dryburgh sits by the Tweed River. Its remarkably complete medieval ruins makes it easy to appreciate the attractions of monastic life. The abbey buildings were destroyed by fire three times and ravaged by war on four occasions but fine examples of ecclesiastic architecture and masonry remain, and its chapter house reveals plaster and paintwork dating back to its inception. Also the burial place of Sir Walter Scott and Field Marshall Earl Haig.

Jedburgh Abbey

Abbey Bridgend Jedburgh Scottish Borders TD8 6JQ
Tel: 01835 863925

One of the border abbeys, founded by David I around 1138 for Augustinian canons. The church is built in the Romanesque and early Gothic styles and is remarkably complete. Remains of the cloister buildings have been uncovered and finds from the excavations, (including the twelfth-century 'Jedburgh comb') are on display. Today, there is a cloister and herb garden to explore, and a visitor centre containing eighth-century carvings and artefacts excavated from the abbey grounds. Visitors can also enjoy the interactive play area within the carved stone display.

Agriculture / Working Farms

National Museum of Rural Life

Wester Kittochside Philipshill Road East Kilbride South Lanarkshire G76 9HR
Tel: 0131 247 4377 Fax: 01355 571290
www.nms.ac.uk

[By car: just off A727, approx 10mi S of Glasgow. Plenty of on-site parking available. For detailed directions, please visit our website. By bus: First Bus Service 31 from Glasgow to East Kilbride. By train: The nearest station is East Kilbride (approx. 3mi from the Museum), then by taxi or bus]

A change of scenery? Get a healthy dose of fresh country air! Take in the sights, sounds and smells as you explore Wester Kittochside Farm. Discover what life was like for country people in the past and how this has shaped Scotland's countryside today. Would you cope working on a 1950s farm? Try milking cows by hand! Hitch a ride on our tractor-trailer. Meet the horse, sheep, cows and hens. Get back to nature at the National Museum of Rural Life.

All year daily 10.00-17.00. Closed 25-26 Dec & 1 Jan

A£5.00 C(under12)£Free Concessions£4.00. National Museums Scotland Members free. The National Trust for Scotland Members receive free admission although there may be a charge for some special events

Discount Offer: Two for the Price of One (full-paying adult).

Airfields / Flight Centres

National Museum of Flight Scotland

East Fortune Airfield North Berwick East Lothian EH39 5LF
Tel: 01620 897240 Fax: 01620 880355
www.nms.ac.uk

[By car: 20mi E of Edinburgh, off B1347. For detailed directions, please visit our website. Bus: First Bus service 121, between Haddington & North Berwick, stops at Museum. Plenty of on-site parking available]

Ready for take off? Our historic airfield is home to a collection of key aircraft that chronicle the story of flight, from the daunting early days to the sleek sophistication of Concorde. How difficult were each of them to fly? What speeds did they reach? What would it have been like to actually build and fly them? Seek out the answers at the National Museum of Flight Scotland.

Apr-Oct daily 10.00-17.00, July & Aug 10.00-18.00, Nov-Mar Sat & Sun 10.00-16.00

Museum including The Concorde Experience: A£5.50 C(under12)£Free Concessions£4.50. Museum including Concorde Experience and Concorde Boarding Pass: A£8.50 C(under12)£2.00 Concessions£6.50. Telephone 0870 421 4299 to book your Concorde Booking Pass or book online. Members receive free or reduced entry to all five National Museums Scotland

Discount Offer: Two for the Price of One (full-paying adult).

Animal Attractions

Amazonia

Strathclyde County Park Motherwell North Lanarkshire ML1 3RT
Tel: 0870 112 3777 Fax: 01698 338733
www.discoveramazonia.co.uk

[Plenty of on-site parking available]

Amazonia is Scotland's only tropical indoor rainforest attraction, packed full of exotic animals. This offers a new fun and educational experience for all ages. It's a unique place to learn and explore, giving insight into the life in a tropical forest. Learn about the secret life of some of our rainforest inhabitants. Our reptiles, rare birds, insects, monkeys, amphibians and fish. Marvel at our rare tropical plants, waterfalls and ponds. Amazonia is packed full of exotic animals including, poison dart frogs, tarantulas, pythons, fruit bats, assassin, beetles, geckos, chameleons, marmoset monkeys, toucans, parrots, leaf cutter ants and tropical fish. Visitors are given the opportunity to take part in our daily animal handling sessions, where we try to dispel some of the 'Hollywood myths' surrounding creatures such as tarantulas and pythons. Keep up to date by visiting our new web site.

All year daily 10.00-18.00

A(16+)£5.25 C£4.25

Discount Offer: One Child Free.

Edinburgh Butterfly and Insect World

Dobbies Garden World Melville Nursery
Lasswade Midlothian EH18 1AZ
Tel: 0131 663 4932 Fax: 0131 654 2774
www.edinburgh-butterfly-world.co.uk

*[Located at Dobbies Gardening World off
Edinburgh City Bypass at Gilmerton exit or from
Sheriffhall Roundabout - just follow signs. Bus:
Lothian Region Transport 3 or 29 from Princes
Street (Shops Side) Mon-Sun. Plenty of free on-
site parking available]*

Walk through a tropical paradise and observe
stunning exotic butterflies flying around you.
Iguanas roam free and quail and caterpillars can
be spotted darting through the jungle flora.
There are tarantulas, stick insects, leaf-cutting
ants, scorpions and frogs! You can get up close
and personal at twice daily 'Meet the Beasties'
handling sessions. We can even help cure your
phobias! In the Reptile Room you'll find lizards,
a chameleon, giant pythons and yellow anacon-
das! The nocturnal zone displays bugs and
beasties that can be seen going about their
night time activities, with the leaf cutter ants
nest and glow in the dark scorpions! Every
Friday afternoon you can view the Snake Pit,
where our royal pythons will be fed! With
monthly themes throughout the year, there will
always be a new weird and wonderful creature
to come and see!

*All year daily, summer 09.30-17.30, winter 10.00-
17.00*
A£5.95 C£3.95, Family Tickets from £18.50.
Group rates (for 10+) available on request,
please call for details

Discount Offer: One Child Free.

ILPH Belwade Farm

Aboyne Aberdeenshire AB34 5DJ
Tel: 01339 887186
www.ilph.org/belwadefarm

*[Signposted off A93 between Aboyne &
Kincardine Oneil. Plenty of on-site parking avail-
able]*

When you follow the signs off the A93, down
the mile-long wooded road, no one expects to
find the haven that is the Scottish home of the
ILPH. Belwade Farm has around 65 horses and
ponies at any one time - from Shetland ponies
to Clydesdales and Shires - which came into
our care for many different reasons. Many of the
horses have been through hard times and it is
at the ILPH that they receive the attention they
so rightly deserve. Some just need TLC whilst
others are undergoing intensive rehabilitation to
restore their quality of life. You will be able to
see and meet the horses in work or out in their
fields, while enjoying the views that Belwade
has to offer. Take an enjoyable walk around our
picturesque Centre to take in the wonderful
scenery and watch the wildlife in the natural
habitats. ILPH Belwade Farm has so much to
offer so why not come and see for yourself.

*All year Weds, Weekends & Bank Hols 14.00-
16.00. Closed 25 Dec-1 Jan*
Admission Free

Scottish Wool Centre

Off Main Street Aberfoyle Stirling FK8 3UQ
Tel: 01877 382850
In the heart of the Trossachs, you'll find the
Scottish Wool Centre where you can discover
the story of Scottish wool.

Art Galleries

Gallery of Modern Art
Queen Street Glasgow G1 3AZ
Tel: 0141 229 1996
A new gallery right in the heart of the city, four floor spaces, each with its own distinct style.

Kelvingrove Art Gallery and Museum
Kelvingrove Argyle Street Glasgow G3 8AG
Tel: 0141 287 2699
Kelvingrove reopens its doors on 11 July 2006 after an exciting £28M restoration project. Now with more space, there will be over 8000 objects on display. Masterpieces by Dali, Van Gogh, Monet and Botticelli will be showcased in inspiring new settings, and a new gallery will feature the work of Charles Rennie Mackintosh.

National Gallery Complex
The Mound Edinburgh EH2 2EL
Tel: 0131 624 6200
One of three magnificent galleries in Edinburgh, each home to special exhibitions and different parts of the national collection of fine art. The National Gallery Complex houses the national collection of fine art.

National Modern Art Galleries
73-75 Belford Road Edinburgh EH4 3DR
Tel: 0131 624 6200
One of three magnificent galleries in Edinburgh, each home to special exhibitions and different parts of the national collection of fine art. The Modern Art Galleries comprise the Gallery of Modern Art and the nearby Dean Gallery.

National Portrait Gallery (Edinburgh)
1 Queen Street Edinburgh EH2 1JD
Tel: 0131 624 6200
One of three magnificent galleries in Edinburgh, each home to special exhibitions and different parts of the national collection of fine art. The National Portrait Gallery provides a visual history of Scotland through its portraits.

Arts, Crafts & Textiles

Burrell Collection
2060 Pollokshaws Road Glasgow G41 1AT
Tel: 0141 287 2550
Here you will find a world famous collection of textiles, furniture, ceramics, stained glass, silver, art objects and pictures.

Centre for Contemporary Arts
350 Sauchiehall Street Glasgow G2 3JD
Tel: 0141 352 4900
CCA is recognised as one of Europe's leading contemporary galleries, and in addition works with a range of artforms including visual arts, performance, dance, music, talks and events.

Dundee Contemporary Arts (DCA)
152 Nethergate Dundee DD1 4DY
Tel: 01382 909900/909252
Outstanding exhibitions from British and international artists, the best of world cinema, shop, print studio and café bar.

House for an Art Lover
10 Dumbreck Road Glasgow G41 5BW
Tel: 0141 353 4770
Designed by (and dedicated to) Rennie Mackintosh. Offers hospitality and events. Features a café and Mackintosh gift shop.

Johnstons of Elgin Cashmere Visitor Centre
Newmill Elgin Moray IV30 4AF
Tel: 01343 554099
Free exhibition, audio-visual presentation and guided tour. Mill shop and coffee shop.

Lighthouse, The
11 Mitchell Lane Glasgow G1 3NU
Tel: 0141 221 6362
Spanning six floors, The Lighthouse provides an unrivalled opportunity to experience Architecture and Design through a changing programme of exhibitions, education and life long learning, networking, events and initiatives.

Pier Arts Centre, The

Victoria Street Stromness Orkney Mainland
Orkney Isles KW16 3AA
Tel: 01856 850209
The Pier Arts Centre recently re-opened following a £4.5 million redevelopment project. It houses a remarkable collection of twentieth-century British art. The collection charts the development of modern art in Britain and includes key works by Barbara Hepworth and Ben Nicholson.

Communication Museums

Orkney Wireless Museum

Kiln Corner Kirkwall Mainland Orkney
Orkney Isles KW15 1LB
Tel: 01856 871400
A fascinating collection tracing the history of early domestic radio and wartime communications in Orkney. Rare exhibits, wartime memorabilia and photographs.

Costume & Jewellery Museums

National Museum of Costume Scotland

Shambellie House New Abbey Dumfries
Dumfries and Galloway DG2 8HQ
Tel: 01387 850375 Fax: 01387 850461
www.nms.ac.uk

[7mi S of Dumfries on A710. Bus: 372 from Whitesands. Plenty of on-site parking available]

Dressed for success? Clothes have always defined a period in history or even a time of day. From strait-laced Victorian dress to wartime Utility wear, put yourself in the shoes of those who wore the trends of their time. What was it like wearing a corset? Try one on for size! Enjoy a fitting tribute to past fashions at the National Museum of Costume Scotland.

Apr-Oct daily 10.00-17.00

A£3.00 C(under12)£Free Concessions £2.00.
Members receive free or reduced entry to all five National Museums Scotland

Discount Offer: Two for the Price of One (full-paying adult).

Country Parks & Estates

Chatelherault Country Park

Ferniegair Hamilton South Lanarkshire ML3 7UE
Tel: 01698 426213
Chatelherault was designed in 1732 and includes a Georgian hunting lodge, a visitor centre, a gallery, a shop, a cafe, gardens, river and woodland walks, white cattle, an adventure playground and a Ranger Service.

Duff House

Banff Aberdeenshire AB45 3SX
Tel: 01261 818181
Duff House is a Treasure House with an extraordinary history containing masterpieces from the National Galleries of Scotland. The outstanding collections consist of furniture including chairs by Chippendale, tapestries and paintings by artists such as El Greco. With extensive grounds and woodland walks by the River Deveron you will find plenty to do in the area.

Exhibition & Visitor Centres

3D Loch Ness Experience

1 Parliament Square Royal Mile Edinburgh
EH1 1RE
Tel: 0131 225 2290
The legendary Loch Ness Monster is the World's most famous mystery. In this 3D audio-visual experience you can discover the truth about 'Nessie' right here in Edinburgh. Experience photos, illusions, hoaxes and hear real eye-witness accounts.

Loch Lomond Shores

Ben Lomond Way Balloch West Dunbartonshire
G83 8QL
Tel: 0845 4580 885
A multi-million pound visitor complex housing
shops, cafes, restaurants, the Loch Lomond
National Park Gateway Centre, the Sealife
Aquarium, a children's fun park, Loch Lomond
trains and an outdoor activity centre. Events are
also held here like monthly continental markets.
It opened to visitors in 2002 and attracts over a
million visitors each year.

Loch Ness Exhibition Centre

Drumnadrochit Loch Ness Highland IV63 6TU
Tel: 01456 450573
This award-winning, multi-media interpretation
centre boasts a variety of activities, presentations and displays that give interesting insight
into one of the most famous lakes in the world.
There is also a variety of shops and places to
eat.

National Park Gateway Centre

Ben Lomond Way Balloch West Dunbartonshire
G83 8QL
Tel: 0845 3454978 / 01389 722199
The National Park Gateway Centre is park of
the Loch Lomond Shores visitor complex.
Staffed jointly by Park Rangers and
VisitScotland staff, the centre contains all the
information and tools you need to discover
Scotland's first National Park - Loch Lomond
and the Trossachs.

On the Water

Falkirk Wheel, The

Lime Road Tamfourhill Falkirk FK1 4RS
Tel: 08700 500208
The Falkirk Wheel is world's first rotating boatlift.
This 35-metre high engineering marvel attracts
visitors from all over the world and features a
visitor centre, boardwalk, restaurant, gift shop,
boat trips, children's play areas and a restaurant.

Real Mary King's Close

2 Warriston's Close Writers' Court The Royal
Mile Edinburgh EH1 1PG
Tel: 08702 430160
Beneath the City Chambers on the Royal Mile
lies Edinburgh's deepest secret - a warren of
hidden streets where real people lived, worked
and died between the seventeenth and nineteenth centuries. Now visitors can step back in
time and walk through these underground closes and witness some of the dramatic episodes
and extraordinary apparitions from this sites fascinating and historically rich past. Visit the workshop of Andrew Chesney, the last resident of
Mary King's Close. Witness the highs and lows
of living in the sixteenth and seventeenth centuries. Visit the home of a gravedigger's family
to discover the truth about living with the
plague.

Scapa Flow Visitor Centre and Museum

Lyness Isle of Hoy Orkney Isles KW17
Tel: 01856 791300
Scapa Flow is a body of water in the Orkney
Islands, sheltered by the islands of Mainland,
Graemsay, Burray, South Ronaldsay and Hoy. It
is one of the great natural harbours/anchorages
of the world, with sufficient space to hold a
number of navies. Viking ships anchored in
Scapa Flow more than 1000 years ago, but it is
best known as the site of the United Kingdom's
chief naval base during the First and Second
World Wars. A visitor centre and museum tells
the story of Scapa Flow. Audio-visual display,
cafe and gift shop.

Factory Outlets & Tours

Glenmorangie Distillery and Visitor Centre

Coy Tain Highland IV19 1PZ
Tel: 01862 892477
Half a mile north of Tain in a tranquil glen, overlooking the Dornoch Firth lies the home of
Glenmorangie Single Highland Malt Scotch
Whisky - Scotland's favourite. Tour the Distillery
with one of the guides who will explain the
whisky-making process and introduce you to
the Sixteen Men of Tain.

Festivals & Shows

Braemar Gathering

The Princess Royal and Duke of Fife Memorial
Park Braemar Aberdeenshire AB35 5YX
Tel: 013397 55377
www.braemargathering.org

*[On the A93, 50mi from Perth, 60mi from
Aberdeen. All outside car parking is free, with
exception of the reserved area on Chapel Brae for
buses. Limited on-site parking available]*

The Gathering is a must for tourists; there is
Highland dancing, solo piping events, tug of
war, running and jumping events, a hill race,
and all the heavy events. Pipe bands play in the
arena individually and three times as a massed
band - a tremendous spectacle.

6 September 2008 (09.30-17.00)
A£8.00 C£2.00. Seats bookable in advance,
standing room available on the day

Edinburgh Festival Fringe

Various Venues Edinburgh EH1 1QS
Tel: 0131 226 0016
*[Events take place at various locations throughout
Edinburgh]*
The Edinburgh Festival Fringe is the world's
greatest celebration of live art and performance.
With up to 1,000 different shows a day includ-
ing theatre, music, circus, dance, comedy, chil-
dren's shows and street entertainment, for just
over three weeks in August.
3-25 August 2008
Prices vary depending on event

Edinburgh International Festival

Various Venues Edinburgh EH1 2NE
Tel: 0131 473 2000
*[Events take place at various locations throughout
Edinburgh]*
The Edinburgh International Festival is one of
the most thrilling celebrations of the arts in the
world - for three weeks every summer you'll find
a dizzying array of some of the greatest and
most innovative artists and companies from
around the world.
8-31 August 2008
Prices vary depending on event

Edinburgh Military Tattoo

Edinburgh Castle Esplanade Castle Hill
Edinburgh EH1 2NG
Tel: 08707 555 1188
[At the top of the Royal Mile]
The 2008 Edinburgh Military Tattoo celebrates
over 50 years of music and spectacle set
against the world famous backdrop of
Edinburgh Castle. It is the most spectacular
show in the world and is enjoyed by an international television audience of 100 million.
*The Tattoo in 2008 will take place over the period
1-23 August with performances on Monday to
Friday at 9.00pm and on Saturday at 7.30pm and
10.30pm. There is no performance on Sunday*
£7.50-£44.00

Scottish Traditional Boat Festival

Various venues Portsoy Aberdeenshire
Tel: 01261 842951
www.scottishtraditionalboatfestival.co.uk

*[Portsoy Harbour lies in middle of southern shore
of Moray Firth. It sits N of A98, about 50mi W of
Aberdeen & about 60mi E of Inverness]*

Now well established as the venue for the largest meeting of traditional sailing craft in Scotland, the Festival has also established a reputation for a splendid weekend of maritime activities; live music, song and dance; a wide range of craft demonstrations, an excellent Food Fayre featuring all that's best from the region's producers and an exciting Adventure Land with fun for all ages from 9 to 90. 2008 will also see the restoration and opening of Portsoy's historic Salmon House or Salmon Bothy as it will be called. In addition to housing an exhibition on Scotland's salmon fishing industry, the Bothy will also be a centre for ancestral tourism and for the further development of the Festival's outreach programme including traditional music, visual art and boat building and sailing. The opening of the Salmon Bothy will form the central part of the Festival and its theme of "Saumon Cobles and Silver Darlings". With something for everyone, the Festival promises to be yet again a great weekend for all the family and a showcase event for all that best in the great traditions of the region.

21-22 June 2008

Prices vary according to event

Discount Offer: Two for the Price of One (full-paying adult).

Folk & Local History Museums

Blackhouse Museum

Arnol Isle of Lewis Western Isles HS2 9DB
Tel: 01851 710395
A black house is a traditional type of dry-stone house that used to be common in Highland Scotland, the Hebrides, Ireland and areas of Gaelic settlement in Nova Scotia. The Blackhouse Museum is part of a fascinating complex that comprises the blackhouse itself and an equally interesting "white house", the cottage opposite, furnished as it was in the 1950s and representing the world into which blackhouse residents moved. Next to the white house are the walls of another series of blackhouses, showing an alternative layout to the restored Number 42. Completing the complex is an excellent visitor centre in another nearby converted cottage. This provides background information and has a very helpful cutaway model of the blackhouse.

Breadalbane Folklore Centre

The Falls of Dochart Killin Perth and Kinross FK21 8XE
Tel: 01567 820254 Fax: 01567 820764
www.breadalbanefolklorecentre.com

[Off A85. At western end of Killin, on A827]

Come and find out what makes this part of Scotland so fascinating. Here's the perfect place to stop during your day in the country - The Breadalbane Folklore Centre. At The Falls of Dochart, the river splashes and tumbles past a beautiful old waterside mill. Spend a while in this enchanting spot - and you'll find out what makes Scotland's 'High Country' so special. Trace the story of famous Highland clans, and admire their treasures. Listen to the story of St. Fillan, see his famous healing stones, and discover some of the mythical tales and legends of The Scottish Highlands. Souvenir, gift and book shop. Also see the 'Living Legends' presentations with Scotty Wilson, revealing the secrets of Breadalbane - regular performances from June to September.

Easter-Oct daily 10.00-17.00. Closed Nov-Mar

A£2.95 C£1.95 OAPs£2.50, Family Ticket £7.85

Corrigall Farm Museum

Midhouse Corrigall Harray
Orkney Mainland Orkney Isles KW17
Tel: 01856 771411
Tells the story of Orkney farming from the late eighteenth century to the early twentieth century. Peat fires, livestock, a range of horse powered implements. Activities, gift shop and toilets.

Low Parks Museum

129 Muir Street Hamilton South Lanarkshire
ML3 6BJ
Tel: 01698 328232 Fax: 01698 328412
www.southlanarkshire.gov.uk
*[J6 M74 Nr Hamilton's Palace Grounds Retail
Park Nr Asda Superstore. Plenty of on-site parking available]*
A visit to Low Parks will make you look again at
this unique part of the Clyde Valley. Entertaining
and informative displays will take you on a fascinating journey around South Lanarkshire.
Interesting objects tell their own tales of local life
and industries, which have shaped the land and
people. We are also the home of the
Cameronians (Scottish Rifles) Regimental
Museum. The Cameronians were unique as the
only Scottish rifle regiment. We tell their colourful story from their covenanting origins in 1689
to their defiant disbandment in 1968.
*All year daily Mon-Sat 10.00-17.00, Sun 12.00-
17.00*
Admission Free

Museum of Edinburgh

142 Canongate Royal Mile Edinburgh EH8 8DD
Tel: 0131 529 4143
The Museum is home to important collections
relating to the history of Edinburgh, from prehistoric times to the present day.

Orkney Museum

Tankerness House Broad Street Kirkwall
Mainland Orkney Orkney Isles KW15 1DH
Tel: 01856 873535
Tells the story of Orkney from the Stone Age
through the Vikings to the present day.

Orkneyinga Viking Saga Centre

Earl's Bu Orphir Mainland Orkney Orkney Isles
Tel: 01856 873191
Small unmanned visitor centre with a 20-seater
audio-visual presentation introducing the
Orkneyinga Saga (one of the great Norse
sagas). This is backed up by a text and graphics display. Adjacent to the Earl's Bu (hall) and
the round church of St Nicholas.

People's Palace and Winter Gardens

Glasgow Green Glasgow G40 1AT
Tel: 0141 271 2951
This magnificent musuem is home to the
restored Doultan Fountain, which is the best
surviving example of a terracotta structure in
Britain. The Winter Gardens and Museum has
displays on horticulture and Glasgow's history.

Rob Roy and Trossachs Visitor Centre

Ancaster Square Callander Stirling FK17 8ED
Tel: 01877 330342
Rob Roy's Highland cottage. Cinematic
Trossachs Tour. Gift shop.

Shetland Museum and Archives

Hay's Dock Lerwick Shetland Mainland
Shetland Isles ZE1 0EL
Tel: 01595 695057
From folklore to fine lace, boats to bones,
underwater creatures to Up Helly Aa and ponies
to Pictish art, the Shetland Museum and
Archives is the place to discover Shetland's
story, from its geological beginnings to the present day.

Smailholm Tower

Smailholm Kelso Scottish Borders TD5 7PH
Tel: 01573 460365
Sited high on a rocky outcrop, Smailholm is a
small rectangular tower set within a stone
barmkin wall. Inside the tower is a model of this
Pringle residence and a charming collection of
costume figures and tapestries relating to Sir
Walter Scott's Minstrelsy of the Scottish
Borders.

Stirling Old Town Jail

St John Street Stirling FK8 1EA
Tel: 01786 450050 Fax: 01786 471301
www.oldtownjail.com

[On St John St (main route to Stirling Castle).
Plenty of on-site parking available]

Can you imagine what it was like to be locked up in prison - 150 years ago? Come and find out! Are you ready to explore the historic heart of Stirling? Then get your day off to a great start by visiting an authentic Victorian jail! Step inside for a fascinating live prison tour - the warden himself will welcome you, and the hangman just can't wait to meet you! Who knows who else you'll encounter - perhaps a convict desperately trying to escape? When you reach the Rooftop Viewpoint you'll get a totally different view of the old city and the countryside stretched out beneath you, and make sure you visit the exhibition area for a chilling reminder of the life faced by today's prisoners in Scotland. Especially for children - join the Prison Beastie Hunt! Audio tour, souvenir and gift shop.

All year daily 10.30-16.00, extended opening
Mar-Sept. Closed 25-26 Dec & 1 Jan
A£5.00-£5.95 C&OAPs£3.20-£4.50, Family Ticket £13.25-£15.70

Verdant Works

West Henderson's Wynd Dundee DD1 5BT
Tel: 01382 225282
Take a step back into a Time Capsule of yesteryear and discover how the people of Dundee lived, worked and played over 100 years ago.

Westray Heritage Centre

Pierowall Isle of Westray Orkney Isles
KW17 2BZ
Tel: 01857 677414
Uniquely artistic natural history permanent display. Annual historic exhibition, hands-on children's models, crafts and light refreshments.

World Famous Old Blacksmith's Shop Centre

Gretna Green Dumfries & Galloway DG16 5EA
Tel: 01461 338441
Runaway couples have raced here to marry under Scottish law since 1754. See the world-famous marriage anvil and enjoy the excellent shopping and great places to eat.

Food & Drink

Aberlour Distillery

High Street Aberlour Moray AB38 9PJ
Tel: 01340 881249
Following an overview of the whisky process and a guided tour of the distillery, guests can taste six different whiskies.

Bowmore Distillery

School Street Bowmore Isle of Islay
Argyll and Bute PA43 7JS
Tel: 01496 810671
Take a tour, have a wee dram, and visit our interesting shop.

Cardhu Distillery Visitor Centre

Knockando Aberlour Moray AB38 7RY
Tel: 01340 872555
Share with us the story of Cardhu Distillery the only malt distillery pioneered by a woman.

Dewars World of Whisky

Aberfeldy Perth and Kinross PH15 2EB
Tel: 01887 822010
The visitor centre combines tradition with innovative use of the latest interactive technology to tell the story of the Dewar family.

Famous Grouse Experience

Glenturret Distillery The Hosh Crieff
Perth and Kinross PH7 4HA
Tel: 01764 656565
Join us at The Famous Grouse Experience and we'll show you the secrets that make Scotland's favourite whisky so special. But be warned, when you visit us at Glenturret, Scotland's oldest distillery and our spiritual home, you should expect a few surprises.

Glen Grant Distillery and Garden

Elgin Road Rothes Aberlour Moray AB38 7BS
Tel: 01340 832118
Tour the distillery with traditional wooden vats and large copper stills; then, in Major Grant's Study the adventures of the distillerie's most famous guardian come to life in the most surprising way.

Glenfiddich Distillery

Dufftown Keith Moray AB55 4DH
Tel: 01340 820373
World famous working distillery. On Christmas Day in 1887 William Grant watched proudly as the first spirit ran from the stills at Glenfiddich Distillery. Five generations later the distillery is still owned and managed by the Grant family. Glenfiddich is unique in the fact that it is the only Highland Single Malt that is distilled, matured and bottled at its own distillery.

Glenkinchie Distillery

Pencaitland Tranent East Lothian EH34 5ET
Tel: 01875 342004
The home of 'The Edinburgh Malt' is located in the rolling farmland of East Lothian and houses an exhibition in the listed red brick buildings.

Glenlivet Distillery

Glenlivet Ballindalloch Moray AB37 9DB
Tel: 01340 821720
Explore the turbulent history of the whisky smugglers, delve into the intriguing mysteries of distilling - and of course, sample the Glenlivet.

Highland Park Distillery and Visitor Centre

Holm Road Kirkwall Orkney Mainland
Orkney Isles KW15 1SU
Tel: 01856 874619 / 876091
Founded in 1798 by notorious smuggler Magnus Eunson, the distillery is one of only six remaining in Scotland which malts its own barley. Visitors have the opportunity to see the entire process at the distillery from malting to distillation.

Oban Distillery

Stafford Street Oban Argyll and Bute PA34 5NH
Tel: 01631 572011
Visit Oban Distillery, meet our knowledgeable guides and learn about the ancient art of distilling, then enjoy a complimentary dram of the Oban 14 year-old West Highland Malt.

Royal Lochnagar Distillery

Crathie Ballater Aberdeenshire AB35 5TB
Tel: 01339 742700
Take a guided tour of our traditional working distillery, where you can see the distillers tending to the traditional mash tun and gleaming copper stills. Here you will see the age old traditions and craftsmanship in practice to produce of Scotland's most exlusive whiskies.

Shortbread Visitor Centre

Deans of Huntly Ltd Huntly Aberdeenshire
AB54 8JX
Tel: 01466 792086
Visit the Viewing Gallery and learn about the history of shortbread. Watch staff at work in the purpose-built bakery and see how Dean's shortbread is made.

Strathisla Distillery

Seafield Avenue Keith Moray AB55 3BS
Tel: 01542 783044
With its distinctive pagodas, cobbled courtyard and picturesque buildings, Strathisla Distillery is arguably the most beautiful distillery in Scotland. Founded in 1786, it is also the oldest operating distillery in the Scottish Highlands.
Apr-Oct daily

Gardens & Horticulture

Castle Kennedy Gardens

Stair Estates Rephad Stranraer Dumfries and Galloway DG9 8BX
Tel: 01581 400225 Fax: 01776 706248
www.castlekennedygardens.co.uk

[5mi E of Stranraer on A75 opposite Castle Kennedy Village]

World famous gardens, set in 75 acres of land-scaped terraces and mounds between two lochs, containing a walled garden, the romantic ruined Castle Kennedy, as well as charming tea room and gift shop.

10.00-17.00
A£4.00 C£1.00 OAPs£3.00
Discount Offer: Two for the Price of One (full-paying adult).

David Welch Winter Gardens

Duthie Park Polmuir Road Aberdeen AB11 7TH
Tel: 01224 585310
Visit the Temperate House, Corridor of Perfumes, Fern House, Victorian Corridor, Japanese Garden, Tropical House and the Arid House.

Royal Botanic Garden, Edinburgh

20a Inverleith Row Edinburgh EH3 5LR
Tel: 0131 552 7171
Home to over 6% of all known plants. Discover some of the world's oldest plants, plus other the well known and economically important plants.

Heritage & Industrial

Cruachan: The Hollow Mountain Power Station

Loch Awe Dalmally Argyll and Bute PA33 1AN
Tel: 01866 822618
A vast cavern hidden 1km inside Ben Cruachan houses a hydro power station. With exhibition.

Motherwell Heritage Centre

High Road Motherwell North Lanarkshire ML1 3HU
Tel: 01698 251000 Fax: 01698 268867
http://motherwellheritage.freeservers.com

[From S J6 M74 from N J6 M74. Limited on-site parking available]

Motherwell Heritage Centre is situated in High Road, just off the top of the A723 Hamilton Road. It has a Visit Scotland '4 Star' award. The centre's main feature is the multi-media 'Technopolis' interactive facility. This takes the visitor from the arrival of the Romans, through the rise and fall of heavy industry to the present day regeneration of the district. The use of 'hands on' technology with recreated streets and foundry scenes really brings history of the area to life. The centre also has an exhibition gallery, the focus of many fascinating displays and community projects. There is also a family history research room, with staff available to advise on tracing family and local histories. A fifth floor viewing platform gives an outlook over the Clyde Valley and, on the ground floor, a small shop sells books, postcards and gifts with local heritage flavour.

All year Mon-Sat 10.00-17.00, Sun 12.00-17.00
Admission Free

Museum on the Mound

HBOS Headquarters The Mound Edinburgh
EH1 1YZ
Tel: 0131 243 5464
Want to see a million pounds? See Scotland's
oldest banknote? Explore the changing face of
Edinburgh? Build a model home? Crack open a
safe? Then come to the Museum on the
Mound.

Scotch Whisky Experience

354 Castlehill The Royal Mile Edinburgh
EH1 2NE
Tel: 0131 220 0441
The Scotch Experience, beside Edinburgh
Castle, reveals the history, mystery and
romance of Scotch Whisky making.

Scottish Mining Museum

Lady Victoria Colliery Newtongrange Edinburgh
EH22 4QN
Tel: 0131 663 7519 Fax: 0131 654 1618
www.scottishminingmuseum.com

*[In Newtongrange, 9mi S of Edinburgh on A7.
Regular bus services connect museum with central Edinburgh. Plenty of on-site parking available]*

Set in the Lady Victoria Colliery on the A7 this '5
Star' visitor attraction houses the story of coal
for Scotland. This vital way of life can be discovered through exhibitions, interactivities, film theatres, a recreated underground and coalface
and the Magic Helmet Tour. Also, on
Wednesdays and Sundays take our Big Stuff
Tour - see the huge pieces of machinery and
transportation which were used underground!
As well as our tours we also have a gift shop,
licensed coffee shop serving hot meals and cold
snacks, a picnic and play area and a large free

car park. Credit cards not accepted in restaurant.

*All year daily Mar-Oct 10.00-17.00, Nov-Feb
10.00-16.00. Closed 24-26, 31 Dec & 1-2 Jan*
A£5.95 C&Concessions£3.95. Group rates:
A£4.95 C&Concessions£3.50

Discount Offer: One Child Free.

Summerlee Industrial Museum

Heritage Way Coatbridge North Lanarkshire
ML5 1QD
Tel: 01236 638460 Fax: 01236 638454
www.northlan.gov.uk

*[J8 M8 Eastbound A8 Westbound. Just to W of
town centre, by Central Station. Plenty of on-site
parking available]*

Summerlee Industrial Museum is a Visit
Scotland '4 Star' visitor attraction and a 'Best
Working Attraction' award-winner. Its 22 acres
are based around the site of the nineteenth-
century Summerlee Ironworks and its branch of
Monklands Canal. Please note that Summerlee
is closed mid-summer 2008. This is to allow a
major Heritage Lottery Fund redevelopment of
the main exhibition hall. On reopening there will
be a totally new permanent exhibition on industrial life in Lanarkshire, including interactive
exhibits, a Discovery Zone for kids and a new
café and meeting rooms. If planning a visit
around summer 2008 please call for reopening
details.

Closed until Summer 2008

Historical

Balmoral Castle
Ballater Aberdeenshire AB35 5TB
Tel: 013397 42534
Best known as a royal residence, Balmoral Castle is a spectacular fifteenth-century castle set in a 65,000-acre working estate. The grounds, garden and castle ballroom are open to the public when the Royal family are not in residence.
Apr-Jul

Bishop's Palace and Earl's Palace
Watergate Kirkwall Orkney Mainland
Orkney Isles KW15 1PD
Tel: 01856 875461
The Bishop & Earl's Palace is a hall-house of twelfth-century date, later much altered, with a round tower built by Bishop Reid in 1541-1548.

Broch of Gurness
Evie Orkney Mainland Orkney Isles
Tel: 01856 751414
The remains of an Iron Age village, probably dating to the first century AD. Gurness broch gives a fascinating insight into Orcadian village life around 2,000 years ago.

Castle and Gardens of Mey
Mey Thurso Highland KW14 8XH
Tel: 01847 851473
A sixteenth-century castle with fantastic views over the Pentland Firth. The castle was bought by H.M. Queen Mother in 1952, who commissioned extensive renovation work and used it as a holiday home.
1 May-30 Jul & 13 Aug-30 Sep

Cawdor Castle
Nairn Highland IV12 5RD
Tel: 01667 404401
A fairytale castle that has been the home of the Thanes of Cawdor since its construction in 1370. Superb gardens, nature trails, golf course, restaurant, gift shops, snackbar and picnic area.

Culzean Castle and Country Park
Maybole South Ayrshire KA19 8LE
Tel: 01655 884455
This stunning eighteenth-century castle stands proudly on the edge of the cliff overlooking the Isle of Arran within 500 acres of country park. Attractions include swan pond, adventure playground, camellia house, walled garden, visitor centre and restaurant.
Apr-Oct

Edinburgh Castle
Castle Hill Edinburgh EH1 2NG
Tel: 0131 225 9846
The castle houses the Honours (Crown Jewels) of Scotland, the Stone of Destiny, the famous fifteenth-century gun Mons Meg, the One O' Clock Gun and the National War Museum of Scotland.

Eilean Donan Castle
Dornie by Kyle of Lochalsh Highland IV40 8DX
Tel: 01599 555202
Discover the history, see the stunning views, walk on the ramparts and catch whispers in the wind; they carry a myriad of tales of MacRaes, MacKenzies and much more.
Easter-Oct

Glamis Castle
Glamis Forfar Angus DD8 1RJ
Tel: 01307 840393
Family home of the Earls of Strathmore and Kinghorne. Setting for Shakespeare's 'Macbeth' and childhood home of the Queen Mother.
Mar-Oct daily

Maeshowe Chambered Cairn
Stennes Orkney Mainland Orkney Isles
KW16 3HA
Tel: 01856 761606
[Approx. 9mi W of Kirkwall on A965]
The finest megalithic tomb in the British Isles, with a large mound covering a stone-built passage and a large burial chamber with cells in the walls. Part of the 'Heart of Neolithic Orkney' World Heritage Site.
Visits must be pre-booked by calling 01856 761606

National Wallace Monument

Abbey Craig Hillfoots Road Stirling FK9 5LF
Tel: 01786 472140
www.nationalwallacemonument.com

[Off A907. Plenty of on-site parking available]

A national hero - a national landmark. Come and discover one of Scotland's most magnificent sights, packed with fascinating exhibits and displays, including the magnificent battle sword once wielded by Sir William Wallace. You will come face to face with the martyr and patriot whose victory at The Battle of Stirling Bridge in 1297 inspired generations of Scots the world over. Listen in on a recreation of the trial 700 years ago in London which led to his brutal execution, and visit The Hall of Heroes. Trace the story of Building The Monument, and then when you reach The Crown enjoy one of the most stunning views in Scotland - across those same fields which witnessed so many fearsome encounters, to the beautiful scenery of The Ochil Hills and The Trossachs. Audio tour in 5 languages, picnic area, coffee shop, souvenir and gift shops.

All year daily 10.30-16.00, extended opening Mar-Oct. Closed 25-26 Dec & 1 Jan

A£6.50 C&OAPs£4.00-£4.90, Family Ticket £17.00

Newhailes

Newhailes Road Musselburgh Midlothian EH21 6RY
Tel: 0131 653 5599

Newhailes is a fine late seventeenth-century house with impressive eighteenth-century additions and interiors, set in a fascinating eighteenth-century designed landscape.

Noltland Castle

Pierowall Isle of Westray Orkney Isles
Tel: 01856 841815

[On the island of Westray, 1mi W of Pierowall. Ferry: from Kirkwall]

A fine, ruined Z-plan tower built between 1560 and 1573 but never completed. Remarkable for its large number of gun loops and impressive staircase.

Jun-Sep Daily

Paxton House and Country Park

Paxton Berwick-upon-Tweed Northumberland TD15 1SZ
Tel: 01289 386291 Fax: 01289 386660
www.paxtonhouse.com

[Signposted 3mi from A1 Berwick upon Tweed bypass on B6461. Rail: Berwick upon Tweed (5mi). Plenty of on-site parking available]

Scottish Tourist Board 5 star Visitor Attraction. Built in 1758 to the design of John Adam, Paxton House is among Britain's finest eighteenth century country houses. The twelve period rooms hold one of the finest collections of Chippendale and Trotter furniture in Britain. The restored Regency Picture Gallery, the largest in any Scottish country house, acts as an outstation of the National Galleries of Scotland with over 70 paintings from its collection. Set within 80 acres of beautiful gardens, woodland and riverside, Paxton House is home to a variety of walks and trails. Enjoy rare shrubs, rhododendrons and herbaceous borders, a fountain and well garden as well as a putting green, croquet lawn and excellent wildlife viewing hides for red squirrels, riverside and woodland birds. Two adventure playgrounds, picnic areas, house trails and nature detective trails together with Paxton Teds Super Fundays (every Tuesday, July and August) make Paxton a great place for children. Visit the restored working Georgian kitchen, complete with active charcoal stoves and baking oven. The Rod Fishing Museum tells the story of The Ellem Fishing Club, the world's oldest club, using interactive displays and full scale models comparing traditional and contemporary costume. With all this plus our gift shop, licensed tea room and an exciting program of events and exhibitions, Paxton House is an essential day out for everyone! Please note photography is restricted to outdoor only.

Open daily 21 Mar-31 Oct. House: daily 11.00-17.00 (last tour 16.00) Grounds & Gardens: daily 10.00-sunset. Shop & Tea room: 10.00-17.00

House, Gardens & Grounds: A£6.50 C£3.30, Family Ticket £17.50. Gardens & Grounds only: A£3.00 C£1.50, Family Ticket £8.00

Discount Offer: One Child Free.

Ring of Brodgar, Stone Circle and Henge

Nr Stromness Orkney Mainland Orkney Isles
Tel: 01856 841815
[5mi NE of Stromness, on B9055]
A magnificent circle of upright stones with an enclosing ditch spanned by causeways, dating to late Neolithic period. Part of the 'Heart of Neolithic Orkney' World Heritage Site.

Scottish Crannog Centre

Kenmore South Loch Tay Perth and Kinross
PH15 2HY
Tel: 01887 830583
Find living history from discoveries underwater at Scotland's only authentic recreation of a Celtic loch-dwelling. Artefacts, wet-tanks, video, ancient crafts, friendly staff and personal attention bring the past to life.

Skara Brae Prehistoric Village

Stromness Orkney Mainland Orkney Isles
KW16 3LR
Tel: 01856 841815
[19mi NW of Kirkwall on B9056]
Skara Brae is the best preserved prehistoric village in northern Europe. The houses contain stone furniture, hearths and drains and give a remarkable picture of life in Neolithic times.

Replica house, visitor centre, gift shop and café. Part of the 'Heart of Neolithic Orkney' World Heritage Site.

Skara Brae & Skaill House: 1 Apr-30 Sep, daily 09.30-17.30

St Andrews Castle and Visitor Centre

The Scores St. Andrews Fife KY16 9AR
Tel: 01334 477196
The ruins of the castle of the Archbishops of St Andrews, dating (in part) from the thirteenth century. Notable features include 'bottle-dungeon,' mine and counter-mine. A fascinating exhibition in the visitor centre brings the history of the castle and cathedral to life.

Standing Stones of Stenness

Stenness Orkney Mainland Orkney Isles
Tel: 0131 668 8800
[3m SW off A965 5m NE of Stromness]
Dating back to the second millenium BC, the remains of this stone circle are near the Ring of Brogar - a splendid circle of upright stones surrounded by a ditch. Part of the 'Heart of Neolithic Orkney' World Heritage Site.

Stirling Castle

Castle Wynd Stirling FK8 1EJ
Tel: 01786 450000
Without doubt one of the grandest of all Scottish castles, both in its situation on a commanding rock outcrop and in its architecture. The Great Hall and the Gatehouse of James IV, the marvellous Palace of James V, the Chapel Royal of James VI and the artillery fortifications of the sixteenth to eighteenth centuries are all of interest. The views from the castle rock are spectacular. The Great Hall has recently been restored to how it would have looked around 1500. Displays on castle's history, medieval kitchen and attractive café.

Traquair House

Innerleithen Scottish Borders EH44 6PW
Tel: 01896 830323 Fax: 01896 830639
www.traquair.co.uk

[On B709 off A72 at Peebles. Plenty of on-site parking available]

Visit romantic Traquair where Alexander I signed a charter over 800 years ago and where the 'modern wings' were completed in 1680. Once a pleasure ground for Scottish kings in times of peace, then a refuge for Catholic priests in times of terror, the Stuarts of Traquair supported Mary, Queen of Scots and the Jacobite cause without counting the cost. Imprisoned, fined and isolated for their beliefs, their home, untouched by time, reflects the tranquillity of their family life. Enjoy the unique atmosphere and history. See the secret stairs, spooky cellars, books, embroideries and letters from former times. Visit the ancient brewery and inhale the delicious aroma, then sample the potent liquor in the brewery museum. Browse through the gift shop and then enjoy a relaxed lunch in the Old Walled Garden. Finally, search for the centre of the maze, explore the enchanted woods and look out for the Grey Lady... a truly magical day out for all the family.

Mar 21-24 (Easter) 12.00-17.00, May 12.00-17.00, June-Aug 10.30-17.00, Sept 12.00-17.00, Oct 11.00-15.00. Guided Tours Apr & outside opening hours (please book in advance). Also open Nov & Apr Sat-Sun 11.00-15.00 (for guided tours only)

House & Grounds: A£6.50 C£3.50 OAPs£6.00, Family Ticket (A2+C3) £18.00. Grounds only: A£3.50 C£2.50. Group rates available on request. Guided tours (book in advance, minimum 20 people) £8.00 per-person. Personal guided tour by Catherine Maxwell Stuart (21st Lady of Traquair): £20.00 per-person

Discount Offer: Two for the Price of One (full-paying adult).

Urquhart Castle

Drumnadrochit Inverness Highland IV63 6XJ
Tel: 01456 450551
Magnificently sited castle, overlooking Loch Ness. Urquhart is one of the largest castles in Scotland, with a long and colourful history, built in the 1230s and seized by the English in 1296. The visitor centre contains retail, interpretation area, AV presentation and tearoom and toilets on one level. Stunning views of the loch can be obtained from visitor centre veranda

Literature & Libraries

Burns National Heritage Park

Murdoch's Lone Alloway Ayr South Ayrshire KA7 4PQ
Tel: 01292 443700
The birthplace of Scotland's national poet, Robert Burns, set in the heart of romantic Alloway. Explore Burns Cottage and museum, Burns Monument, the Brig o'Doon and the haunted Kirk Alloway. Relax at the Tam O' Shanter Experience visitor centre.

Hugh Miller's Cottage

Church Street Cromarty Highland IV11 8XA
Tel: 01381 600245
Here in this thatched cottage built c1698 by his great-grandfather was born Hugh Miller, on 10 October, 1802. Miller rose to international acclaim as a geologist, editor and writer. This furnished cottage contains an exhibition and video on his life and work. To the rear is a Scottish wild garden of colourful native plants, redesigned to reflect Millers own love of nature. A reading room has been opened, offering visitors the chance to browse at leisure among Millers works. New artworks on display include a tapestry, sculpture and silver medallion.

Innerpeffray Library

Crieff Perth and Kinross PH7 3RF
Tel: 01764 652819
http://innerpeffraylibrary.co.uk

[5mi from A9 at Gleneagles/Auchterarder on B8062 via Kinkell Bridge. 4mi from A85 at Crieff on B8062. Tourist Board sign on main rd, look for flag. On most road atlas. Plenty of on-site parking available]

Innerpeffray: Early complete, very important group of religious and educational buildings, built by the Drummond family of Strathearn, in continuous use for 500 years. Pre 1680 David Drummond, 3rd Lord Madertie, built and endowed his school and library. All the Knowledge of his world in 400 books in English, Latin, French, German, and Italian etc. Library: 1762, built Bishop Robert Hay Drummond re-opened 1763 - Scotland's oldest free public lending library, continuous borrowing record 1747 - 1969. Bishop's collection on law, history/geography, maths (Newton), the Enlightenment and social comment added similar breadth. Chapel: rebuilt by John 1st Lord Drummond 1508,renaissance triple cube, paintings, hatchments, medieval altar, upper room for library. Free access. Weddings etc. Historic Scotland. Events - Schools and Library friends. School: (rebuilt 1847) six sash windows, bell-cote, and passed 1889 inspection with 29 pupils. Innerpeffray Castle: private, built 1st Lord Madertie, admirable from a distance (countryside access code)- beautiful, if roofless, fortalice.

Mar-Oct Wed-Sat 10.00-12.45 & 14.00-16.45, Sun 14.00-16.00. Closed Sun am. Nov-Feb Closed. Groups are welcome anytime by arrangement.

A£5.00 C£Free, Group rates available on request. Special rates for researchers, school parties: charge for worksheets etc

Writers Museum

Lady Stair's Close Lawnmarket (Royal Mile)
Edinburgh EH1 2PA
Tel: 0131 529 4901
Dedicated to the lives and work of Scotland's great literary figures, in particular Robert Burns (1759-1796), Sir Walter Scott (1771-1832), and Robert Louis Stevenson (1850-1894).

Living History Museums

Callendar House

Callendar Park Falkirk FK1 1YR
Tel: 01324 503770 Fax: 01324 503771
www.falkirk.gov.uk/cultural/museums/call-ho.htm
[E of Falkirk Town Centre on A803. Rail: Falkirk High / Grahamstone. Ample on-site parking]
Imposing mansion within attractive parkland. Facilities include a working kitchen of 1825, where costumed interpreters carry out daily chores including cooking based on 1820s recipes. Exhibition area and 'Story of Callendar House' plus two temporary galleries, regularly changing exhibitions, a history research centre, gift shop and Georgian tea shop at the Stables. Major permanent exhibition 'William Forbes Falkirk' also the new Antonine wall exhibition.

All year Mon-Sat 10.00-17.00, Apr-Sept Sun 14.00-17.00
Admission Free

Discount Offer: 10% discount on all gift shop purchases (when you spend £10.00 or more).

Maritime

Aberdeen Maritime Museum
Shiprow Aberdeen AB11 5BY
Tel: 01224 337700
The City's award-winning Maritime Museum
brings the history of the North Sea to life.

Britannia - The Royal Yacht
Ocean Terminal Leith Edinburgh EH6 6JJ
Tel: 0131 555 5566 Fax: 0131 555 8835
www.royalyachtbritannia.co.uk
*[10min drive from Edinburgh City Centre in Leith,
signposted, or No. 22 bus from Princes St. Plenty
of free on-site parking available]*
"Scotland's leading visitor-friendly attraction"
BBC News. Visit The Royal Yacht Britannia,
now in Edinburgh's historic port of Leith. The
experience starts in the Visitor Centre where
you can discover Britannia's fascinating story.
Then step aboard for your complimentary self-
led audio handset tour (available in 21 languages, children's handset available in English)
which takes you around five decks giving you a
unique insight into what life was like for the
Royal Family, Officers and Yachtsmen.
Highlights include the State Dining Room, the
Drawing Room, the Sun Lounge, the Wardroom
and the Chief Petty Officers' Mess. Good
access for pushchairs and wheelchairs.
Britannia is berthed alongside Ocean Terminal
which has over 65 shops, as well as Cafés and
restaurants.
*All year daily Sept-Jun 10.00, Jul-Aug 9.30.
Closed 25 Dec & 1 Jan*
A£9.75 C(under5)£Free C(5-17)£5.75
OAPs£7.75 Family Ticket (A2+C3) £27.75

Discount Offer: One Child Free.

Discovery Point and RRS Discovery
Discovery Quay Dundee DD1 4XA
Tel: 01382 201245
Follow in the footsteps of Captain Scott and
Ernest Shackleton aboard the Royal Research
Ship Discovery at the multi-award winning
Discovery Point and experience one of the
greatest stories ever told. Come face to face
with the Heroes of the Ice at Discovery Point, an
award winning attraction and museum that tells
the story of RRS Discovery.

Scottish Maritime Museum: Clydebuilt at Braehead
Braehead Shopping Centre Kings Inch Road
Glasgow G51 4BN
Tel: 0141 8861013
The story of the River Clyde and the contribution it made to the development of West Central
Scotland is brought vividly to life at Clydebuilt,
the Scottish Maritime Museum at Braehead.As
you journey through a fascinating period of
Scottish history you cannot help but associate
with the triumphs and tribulations of the men
and women who made the word " Clydebuilt"
synonymous with quality and majesty.

Scottish Maritime Museum: Denny Ship Model Experiment Tank
Castle Street Dumbarton West Dunbartonshire
G82 1QS
Tel: 01389 763444
A visit to the Denny Ship Model Experiment
Tank is a unique chance to step back into the
world of the Victorian ship designer. Built in
1882 the Denny Tank was the first commercial
ship model testing tank built in the world and it
retains many original features today.

Scottish Maritime Museum: Irvine
Laird Forge Gottries Road Irvine North Ayrshire
KA12 8QE
Tel: 01294 278283
The Museum Boatshop is situated on Irvine's
harbourside, where you will find exhibitions,
maritime artwork, ship models and the museum
shop. Guided tours start here throughout the
day.

Stromness Museum

52 Alfred Street Stromness Orkney Mainland
Orkney Isles KW16 3DF
Tel: 01856 850025 Fax: 01856 871560
www.orkneyheritage.com

*[0.5mi walk (or drive) S from Stromness Pier
Head]*

If you want a glimpse into Orkney's Natural
History and Maritime Past, or to study it in more
detail, Stromness Museum is a must. Since
1837 the museum has amassed a unique and
fascinating collection which has something for
everyone. Learn how to survive in the arctic
through displays about Dr John Rae, Sir John
Franklin and the Arctic Whalers. Find out about
local connections with The Hudson Bay
Company and the Canadian Fur Trade. On
show are artefacts salvaged from the German
fleet which was scuttled in Scapa Flow in 1919,
in sight of Stromness. The recently refurbished
Victorian Natural History Gallery has a magnificent bird collection complemented by displays
of eggs, fossils, sea creatures, mammals, butterflies and moths. Also available are kids activities and a photographic archive. You will enjoy
your visit, all you have to do is get here!
Changing summer exhibition: Hands Across the
Sea and Orkney's History Links with Canada.

*Apr-Sept daily 10.00-17.00, Oct-Mar Mon-Sat
11.00-15.30. Closed mid Feb-mid Mar*

A£3.50 C(school age)£1.00 Concessions£2.50,
Family Ticket (A2+C2) £7.00, Entry ticket is valid
for 1 week

**Discount Offer: 10% discount on all
gift shop purchases (when you spend
£10.00 or more).**

Military & Defence Museums

Gordon Highlanders Museum

St Luke's Viewfield Road Aberdeen AB15 7XH
Tel: 01224 311200
At the Gordon Highlanders Museum, you can
re-live the compelling and dramatic story of one
of the British Army's most famous regiments.

National War Museum Scotland

Edinburgh Castle Edinburgh EH1 2NG
Tel: 0131 247 4413 Fax: 0131 225 3848
www.nms.ac.uk

*[Follow signs for Edinburgh Castle throughout
central Edinburgh]*

A force to be reckoned with? War and military
service have touched the lives of countless
Scots, leaving their mark on Scotland's history,
image and reputation abroad. Here, in the magnificent setting of Edinburgh Castle, explore
over 400 years of the Scottish military experience. Uncover stories of courage and determination, victory and defeat, heroics and heart-
break.

*All year daily, Nov-Mar 09.45-16.45, Apr-Oct
09.45-17.45. Closed 25 & 26 Dec*

Entry to the museum is free with admission to
Edinburgh Castle. Please see Edinburgh Castle
website www.edinburghcastle.gov.uk for further
details

Multicultural Museums

National Museum of Scotland

Chambers Street Edinburgh EH1 1JF
Tel: 0131 247 4422 Fax: 0131 220 4819
www.nms.ac.uk

[In heart of Old Town, a few min walk from Princes St & Royal Mile. By bus: Number of buses go via city & stop at George IV Bridge or South Bridge. Rail: nearest Edinburgh Waverley, few min walk. Road: Follow signs for city centre. Pay & display parking on Chambers St with off-street car parking nearby]

Our collections cover life, the universe and everything in it. From science and art to nature and outer space. What influence has the rest of the world had on Scotland and Scotland on it? How has the face of the nation changed over the centuries? Find the answers to all the big questions (and some tricky little ones as well) at the National Museum of Scotland. You can also enjoy special exhibitions, free tours and events for all ages, throughout the year.

All year daily 10.00-17.00. Closed 25 Dec

Admission Free. There may be a charge for special exhibitions/events. Members receive free or reduced entry to all five National Museums Scotland and some charging exhibitions

Nature & Conservation Parks

Scottish Seabird Centre

The Harbour North Berwick East Lothian
EH39 4SS
Tel: 01620 890202 Fax: 01620 890222
www.seabird.org

[From Edinburgh follow A1 to North Berwick, follow tourist signs to Scottish Seabird Centre]

Escape to another world at this stunning five star wildlife visitor attraction! Exhilarating sea air and breathtaking panoramic views over the sea and beautiful sandy beaches. See wildlife really close up with the amazing live interactive cameras. Puffins spring cleaning their burrows, gannets with fluffy white chicks, seals sunning themselves and sometimes even dolphins and whales. Wildlife theatre, new Kids Zone and Saltwater Aquarium, Environment Zone and Migration Flyway, films, talks and a packed programme of festivals and events. A great day out - whatever the weather. Licensed cafe/bistro with deck overlooking the sea. Boat trips to the islands. Well-stocked shop. Full disabled facilities including on-site parking.

All year daily: Apr-Sep 10.00-18.00; Feb-Mar & Oct Mon-Fri 10.00-17.00, Sat & Sun 10.00-17.30; Nov-Jan Mon-Fri 10.00-16.00, Sat & Sun 10.00-17.30. Closed 25 Dec

A£7.95 C£4.50 Concessions£5.95. Group rates available on request

Discount Offer: One Child Free.

On the Water

Falkirk Wheel, The
Lime Road Tamfourhill Falkirk FK1 4RS
Tel: 08700 500208
The world's first rotating boatlift attracts visitors from all over the world and features a visitor centre, boardwalk, restaurant, gift shop, boat trips, play areas and a restaurant.

Loch Katrine
Trossachs Pier Loch Katrine By Callander Stirling FK17 8HZ
Tel: 01877 332000
www.lochkatrine.com
Welcome to Loch Katrine - a special experience for everyone to enjoy. Cruise Loch Katrine on the 'Lady of the Lake,' or experience a classic steamship cruise on the 'Sir Walter Scott,' which has sailed these waters since 1900. Hire a bike from 'Katrinewheelz,' or enjoy a stroll by the shores of the loch. Watch out for wildlife or find a quiet spot for a picnic. Listen to 'Legends of the Loch' as a real Highlander retells the story of Rob Roy McGregor. There are presentations every Saturday and Sunday (Easter to September). Browse through 'Katrine Gifts' for a souvenir of your visit, and then relax in 'The Anchor's Rest.' Stop for a coffee and Danish, or enjoy an evening meal as the sun sets behind the hills of The Trossachs. Plan your visit at www.lochkatrine.com, or call (01877) 332000 for information and advance bookings. Cruises depart every day from 10:30am.
Cruises depart every day from 10:30am. Scenic Cruises (45 mins) and Sailings to Stronachlachar (Return journey: 2 hrs)
45-min Scenic Cruise: A£8.00 C£6.00 Concessions£7.00. Sailings to Stronachlachar: A£8.00 (Single), A£9.50 (Return); C£6.00 (Single), C£7.00 (Return); Concessions£7.00 (Single), Concessions£8.50 (Return)

Palaces

Scone Palace
Scone Perth and Kinross PH2 6BD
Tel: 01738 552300 Fax: 01738 552588
www.scone-palace.co.uk

[2mi N of Perth on A93.Ample on-site parking]

Family home of the Earl of Mansfield, Scone Palace houses a magnificent and varied collection of works of art. Scone Palace is set in mature and historic grounds, with an adventure playground and the Murray Star Maze. Once the crowning place of the Kings of Scots, Scone offers a fascinating day out for all the family. Also features 'I' Spy for children. Exterior photography permitted.

21 Mar-31 Oct daily 09.30-17.30. Grounds close at 17.45. Saturday 09.30-16.45, Grounds close at 17.00

Palace & Grounds: A£8.00 C£5.00 Concessions£7.00. Grounds only: A£4.50 C£3.00 Concessions£4.00. Group rates available on request.

Discount Offer: Two for the Price of One (full-paying adult).

Police, Prisons & Dungeons

Inveraray Jail
Church Square Inveraray Argyll and Bute PA32 8TX
Tel: 01499 302381
An award-winning living nineteenth-century jail and museum.

Railways

Bo'ness and Kinneil Railway

Bo'ness Station Union Street Bo'ness West Lothian EH51 9AQ
Tel: 01506 822298 Fax: 01506 828766
www.srps.org.uk/railway/

[Rail: Linlithgow, Falkirk Grahamston]

Welcome to the living museum of Scotland's Railways! There's so much to see and do, but one of the highlights of your visit must be the thrill of travelling in a train behind a lovingly restored historic locomotive from the collection of listed buildings that make up Bo'ness Station. This is a journey that runs along the shores of the Forth and delivers you to Birkhill, with its lovely woodlands and fascinating fireclay mine. When you get back to Bo'ness, why not visit the Scottish Railway Exhibition? It contains a large selection from our collection of locomotives, carriages and wagons, as well as models and displays that tell the history of railways in Scotland. There are a few surprises too - particularly the signs that encourage you to climb onto and explore some of the exhibits! Throughout the season we have special events for all the family - please see our website for details.

15 Mar- 26 Oct Sat-Sun, 1 July-25 Aug daily - see website for further details

A£5.00 C£2.50 Concessions£4.00, Family Ticket (A2+C2) £13.00

Discount Offer: One Free Child Fare.

CairnGorm Mountain Railway

Aviemore Highland PH22 1RB
Tel: 01479 861261
The CairnGorm Funicular is the country's highest and fastest mountain railway. Panoramic views, exhibition and shop.

Keith and Dufftown Railway

Dufftown Station Dufftown Moray AB55 4BA
Tel: 01340 821181
Eleven-mile heritage line operating in the summer months. The line passes through some of Scotland's most picturesque scenery, with forest and farmland, lochs and glens, castles and distilleries.

Royal

Palace of Holyroodhouse

Edinburgh EH8 8DX
Tel: 0131 556 5100
The official residence of Her Majesty The Queen in Scotland. Hosts a programme of changing exhibitions from the Royal Collection.

Science - Earth & Planetary

Glasgow Science Centre

50 Pacific Quay Glasgow G51 1EA
Tel: 0141 420 5010
With hundreds of interactive exhibits based over 3 floors, the Science Mall also offers live science shows, workshops and demonstrations.

Our Dynamic Earth

Holyrood Road Edinburgh EH8 8AS
Tel: 0131 550 7800
Our Dynamic Earth - it's the Mother Earth of all adventures! Explore our planet's past present and future. You'll be shaken by volcanoes, fly over glaciers, feel the chill of polar ice, and even get caught in a tropical rainstorm.

Sealife Centres & Aquariums

Deep Sea World, Scotland's Shark Capital

Forthside Terrace North Queensferry Fife
KY11 1JR
Tel: 01383 411880
[J1 M90]
Come face to face with one of Europe's largest collections of sharks in one of the world's longest underwater tunnels. Touch live exhibits in the rock pools, see piranha and visit our resident seals.

Macduff Marine Aquarium

11 High Shore Macduff Aberdeenshire
AB44 1SL
Tel: 01261 833369 Fax: 01261 831052
www.macduff-aquarium.org.uk
[1hr N Aberdeen on A947, 90min E of Inverness on A98. Plenty of on-site parking available]
Situated on Aberdeenshire's scenic north coast, Macduff Marine Aquarium offers a fascinating view into the underwater world of the Moray Firth. The aquarium's central exhibit contains a living community of seaweeds, fish and invertebrates normally only seen by scuba divers. Visitors come face to face with hundreds of local fishy characters, from fearsome wolf fish to ancient lobsters, and can watch them from several viewing windows. Several times a week divers hand feed the fish in the main tank. Other innovative displays include a ray pool, rock pools, a splash tank, estuary and deep reef displays. Visitors get a chance to get a feel for seashore life at the touch pools. There are also special talks, videos and feeding shows throughout the week, and quizzes for kids. New jellyfish display in 2008. Tickets valid all day.
All year daily 10.00-17.00. Closed 25-26 & 31 Dec, 1-2 Jan
A£5.40 C£2.70 OAP£3.35, Family Ticket £14.85

Discount Offer: One Child Free.

Loch Lomond Aquarium

Loch Lomond Shores Ben Lomond Way
Balloch West Dunbartonshire G83 8QL
Tel: 01389 721500
www.sealifeeurope.com
This magical attraction takes visitors on a journey from highland stream, via the depths of the loch, to the North Sea and onward to the Caribbean. It houses a trio of otters (Rona, Shona and Mona), countless freshwater and native marine species and it climaxes with a voyage under the sea through the ocean tank, teeming with colourful reef fish and tropical sharks. A special new feature entitled 'Predators' will lead visitors on a guided terror trail to encounter the deadliest hunters of each different habitat… from the Highland loch to the clear blue waters of the Caribbean.

All year daily from 10.00. Closed Christmas Day
Please call for admission prices

Orkney Marine Life Aquarium

Pool Farmhouse Grimness
Isle of South Ronaldsay Orkney Isles KW17 2TH
Tel: 01856 831700
Fascinating aquarium, rock pool, fishing and topical exhibits provide a great family visit. Nautical souvenirs.

Scottish Sea Life Sanctuary

Barcaldine Oban Argyll and Bute PA37 1SE
Tel: 01631 720386 Fax: 01631 720529
www.sealsanctuary.co.uk

[On A828. Plenty of on-site parking available]

The Scottish Sea Life Sanctuary is a real national treasure… a marine wonderland perched on the shores of beautiful Loch Creran. It houses a host of spectacular aquarium displays which open a window beneath the waves, revealing the private lives of everything from shrimps and starfish to seahorses, sharks and rays. It is also a busy working Seal Rescue Centre, and its rescue operation and facilities are receiving a major boost this year. A special redevelopment and re-focus will both enhance the Sanctuary's rescue work, and enable visitors to get a much deeper insight into the whole process… from initial rescue right through to release. Some may even be invited to have a go at feeding a seal pup, but luckily for them, not the real snarling and biting variety, but a plastic model. Feeding time for the resident common seals in the outdoor seal pools is also a spectacle not to be missed, and a chance to learn much about the biology of these endearing marine mammals. Nearby you may be able to catch sight of Fingal, the playful North American otter. The Sanctuary also boasts a fascinating woodland trail, a rustic children's play area, a souvenir shop and a restaurant overlooking the loch.

All year daily from 10.00, 12.00 on New Years Day. Closed Christmas Day

Please call for admission prices

Discount Offer: One Child Free.

Spectator Sports

Perth Racecourse

Scone Palace Park Perth Perth and Kinross PH2 6BB
Tel: 01738 551597 Fax: 01738 553021
www.perth-races.co.uk

[2mi from City Centre off A93. Rail: Perth. Nearest airports are Glasgow or Edinburgh. Plenty of free on-site parking available]

Get your heart racing... Race days at Perth are more than just great horse racing, Perth Races are a great day out for all the family. The new Nelson Stand opened in April 2005 with a unique dining experience overlooking the course. Perth is one of the most beautiful racecourses in the UK. Horses have been racing at Scone Palace Park since 1908. Come and experience the special atmosphere at Perth and be part of it's future. Superb hospitality packages and a wide range of restaurant and licensed bar facilities make the racecourse a perfect venue for group entertainment. Additional pre race entertainment features on major racedays. Best small racecourse in Scotland and North East 2006.

Race meetings Apr-Sept every year. The Drifters playing live after racing on 29th July 2008

Grandstand Enclosure £15.00. Centre Course £10.00. C(under16)£Free. Discounts available for advance bookings of 15+, please call for more details at least one week before race date. Book tickets on the website for any race meeting in 2008

Sport & Recreation

Nevis Range

Torlundy Fort William Highland PH33 6SW
Tel: 01397 705825 / 705855
Scotland 's highest ski area is a winter wonderland for snowsport enthusiasts and sightseers alike.

XScape: Braehead

Kings Inch Road Braehead Renfrew
Renfrewshire PA4 8XQ
Tel: 0871 200 3222
www.xscape.co.uk
[off J26 of M8. Free parking]

Xscape in Braehead offers the ultimate action packed day out with loads of exciting activities, shops, bars and restaurants all under one roof. Whether you're looking for non-stop fun or a place to relax and enjoy quality time with friends and family, Xscape is the place to come. Ski or snowboard at the UK's premier indoor ski slope on REAL snow; get the adrenaline pumping on our indoor rock climbing wall, aerial assault courses and fan drop! Strap yourself into the Robocoaster, take on your friends at mini golf on the world's largest indoor adventure golf complex and with a few games of 10-pin bowling, or learn new football skills at the soccer circus. Catch all the latest movies at our cinema or do some shopping at our great onsite outlets. When its time to relax we have plenty of great restaurants, bars and cafés the ideal way to spend your evening. For slope enquiries and booking only please call: 0871 222 5672.

All year daily 09.00 - late (Closed 25 Dec)

Please call or visit our website for prices

Theme & Adventure Parks

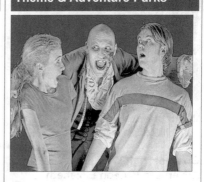

Edinburgh Dungeon

31 Market Street Edinburgh EH1 1QB
Tel: 0131 240 1000 Fax: 0131 240 1002
www.thedungeons.com

[Next to Waverley Bridge]

The Edinburgh Dungeon invites you to a unique feast of fun with history's horrible bits. Live actors, an eerie ride, shows and special effects transport you back to those black, bleak times. Are you brave enough? You'll be exposed to torture, grave robbing, the Plague, cannibalism and (of course) murder! Your journey into the Dungeon begins in a seventeenth-century court of law where an eccentric judge knows exactly what you have been up to. The verdict is always 'guilty' and the punishment is always harsh. Next, travel onboard the spine-chilling boat ride into the lair of cannibal Sawney Bean where you face your fears head on. New for 2008: 'William Wallace.' Freedom! Feel the passion of Scotland's warrior hero Sir William Wallace as you experience the glory of victory against the English at the Battle of Stirling Bridge. A thrilling and fun experience that will leave your family screaming for more! Are you brave enough?

Nov-Mid Mar 11.00-16.00, Sat & Sun 10.30-16.30, Mid Mar-Jun 10.00-17.00, Jul-Aug 10.00-19.00, Sep-Oct 10.00-17.00

Please call for admission prices

Discount Offer: One Child Free.

Go Ape! High Wire Forest Adventure (Queen Elizabeth Forest, Stirling)

Queen Elizabeth Forest Park Aberfoyle Stirling FK8 3SY
Tel: 0845 643 9245
www.goape.co.uk

[From Glasgow follow signs on M8 for Aberfoyle. From Stirling/Callander follow A81 to Aberfoyle via Dukes Pass. Plenty of on-site parking available]

Take to the trees and experience an exhilarating course of rope bridges, Tarzan swings and zip-slides up to 40 feet above the ground! Share approximately three exciting hours of fun and adventure, which you'll be talking about for days. Book online and watch people Go Ape! at www.goape.co.uk. Minimum height 1.4m. Maximum weight 130 kg (20.5 stone). Under-18s must be accompanied by a participating adult. One adult can supervise either two children (where one or both of them is under 16 years old) or up to five 16-17 year olds. Pre-booking is essential to avoid disappointment. Book online or by telephone (there is a £1.00 booking fee on all telephone bookings).

9-12 Feb, 16-17 Feb, 14 Mar-31 Oct daily. Nov Sat-Sun. Dec Sat-Sun TBC please visit www.goape.co.uk. Closed Jan

Gorillas (18yrs+) £25.00, Baboons (10-17yrs) £20.00

Discount Offer: £5.00 off per person.

M and D's Scotland's Theme Park

Strathclyde Country Park Motherwell North Lanarkshire ML1 3RT
Tel: 0870 112 3777 Fax: 01698 303034/338733
www.scotlandsthemepark.com

[Plenty of on-site parking available]

At Scotland's biggest and best value Theme Park there is something for everyone. With over 40 major rides and attractions it really is "Too much fun for just one day". This season M&D's is home to the roller coaster, with white knuckle coasters, the Tsunami and the Tornado and the kids get their very own coaster too the Big Apple. If that's not enough this season M&D's have invested millions of pound in a brand new coaster, The Run Away Mine Train! There are also the old favorites, The Wave Swinger, Flying Carpet, White Water Rapids, three in one water slide, Moby's Revenge and much much more. There are loads for our younger visitors too including, the Crazy Boot, Seastorm, pony express, dropzone, flying bees and many more. There's also our 18 hole mini adventure golf, fun for all the family. Don't forget our multi million pound indoor complex including, indoor bowling, softplay, Amazonia, tropical rainforest, American Pools hall, bars, restaurants, coffee shop and the list goes on. Keep up to date with our new website.

Admission Free. Unlimited Ride Band: Over 1.35m £15.45, Under 1.35m £11.45

Discount Offer: £5.00 off One Unlimited Ride Wristband (for a family of 4).

Toy & Childhood Museums

Hamilton Toy Collection
111 Main Street Callander Stirling FK17 8BQ
Tel: 01877 330 004
Situated in Callander at the gateway to the National Park, the Hamilton Toy Collection is a family affair that features a Doll Room, a 1900 Nursery, a Sci-Fi Room, a Car Room and a Soldier Room.
Easter-Oct, 12.00-16.30

Museum of Childhood
42 High Street Edinburgh EH1 1TG
Tel: 0131 529 4142
Described as 'the noisiest museum in the world,' the museum is a favourite with adults and children alike. It is a treasure house crammed full of objects telling stories of childhood, past and present.

Transport Museums

Bo'ness Motor Museum
Bo'ness Enterprises Ltd Bridgness Road
Bo'ness Falkirk EH51 9JR
Tel: 01506 827007 Fax: 0141 8894757
www.motor-museum.bo-ness.org.uk

[Bo'ness, Scotland]

This 'Visit Scotland' 4-star attraction was conceived by Colin Anderson in 1999. It displays his personal collection of cars and James Bond memorabilia. After much planning and renovation work the museum was officially opened at Easter 2004 following a massive renovation project. Bo'ness Motor Museum is more that just a museum. It features a wide range of James Bond memorabilia including cars and props, plus 'The Little Monster's Fun Factory' (a soft-play area themed on the film 'Monster's Inc'), where parents can let the kids play while they enjoy a drink in 'The Double "O" Bar' (a stylish Bond-themed bar area). There's also the 'Miss Moneypenny's Café/Diner' where you can enjoy a delicious range of light meals and snacks. Colin (and his wife, Fiona) ensure the museum's facilities are of the highest standard and as a result, it boasts a friendly and relaxed atmosphere, which is excellent for families. From kiddies' parties to club and corporate meetings, the Bo'ness Motor Museum really does have something for everyone!

All year daily 10:00-17:00. Other times by prior arrangement.

A£5.50, Concessions£4.00 (Includes 1hr in Soft Play), Family Ticket (A2+C2) £16.00, Soft Play only C£3.50 per 1 hr 30 min

Discount Offer: 20% off all admissions.

Museum of Transport
1 Bunhouse Road Kelvin Hall Glasgow G3 8DP
Tel: 0141 287 2720
The Museum of Transport uses its collection of vehicles and models to tell the story of transport by land and sea.

Victorian Era

Camera Obscura and World of Illusions
Castlehill Royal Mile Edinburgh EH1 2LZ
Tel: 0131 226 3709
A magical 1850s 'cinema' giving a unique experience of Edinburgh. As the panorama unfolds the guide tells the story of the city's historic past.

Wildlife & Safari Parks

Blair Drummond Safari and Adventure Park

Blair Drummond Stirling FK9 4UR
Tel: 01786 841456 Fax: 01786 841491
www.blairdrummond.com

[J10 M9 4mi along A84 towards Callander signposted on M9 & A84. Ample on-site parking]

Drive through our wild animal reserves; see rhinos, giraffes, elephants, lions, tigers, bears, zebras, bison and much more. Sit back, relax, and enjoy our Sea lion Shows and Bird of Prey displays. Wander through Pets' Farm and see donkeys, llamas, ponies, pigs, penguins, lemurs, otters and meerkats. Take a boat trip to visit the chimps on their island and walk through Lemur Land. Enjoy a meal in our restaurant or cafés or if you prefer bring your own food as we have many picnic many areas around the park. Barbecues are available on request with undercover area if required. The children will enjoy the Adventure Play Area which includes a pirate ship with buried treasure!! Finish off your day with a souvenir from one of our gift shops. Facilities are available for Special Needs and visitors with young children.

15 Mar-20 Oct daily 10.00-17.30
A£10.50 C(under3)£Free C/OAPs&Special Needs £7.00 Carers £7.00 (ID required) Free kennels at entrance for dogs

Discount Offer: One Child Free.

Galloway Wildlife Conservation Park

Lochfergus Plantation Kirkcudbright
Dumfries and Galloway DG6 4XX
Tel: 01557 331645 Fax: 01557 331645
www.gallowaywildlife.co.uk

[1mi from Kirkcudbright on B727. Turn up hill at Royal Hotel. Signposted from A75. Plenty of on-site parking available]

A varied collection of over 120 animals from all over the world can be seen within the peaceful and natural settings in the woodlands. Endangered species to be seen at the park including red pandas, maned wolves, otters, lemurs and, of course, our famous Scottish wildcats! Woodland walk and close animal encounters.

Dec-Jan Closed, Feb-Nov daily 10.00-18.00
A£5.50 C(4-16)£3.50 C(under4)£Free
OAPs£4.50

Discount Offer: One Child Free.

Zoos

Edinburgh Zoo

Corstorphine Road Edinburgh EH12 6TS
Tel: 0131 334 9171
The wildest visitor attraction in Scotland, this leading zoo is home to over 1,000 rare and beautiful animals from around the world. Children's play areas, animal-handling sessions, restaurants and gift shop.

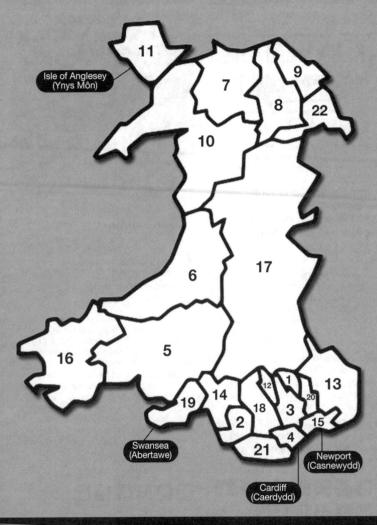

Wales

Isle of Anglesey (Ynys Môn)

11

9

7

8

22

10

6

17

16

5

19

14

12

1

13

18

3

20

2

21

4

15

Swansea (Abertawe)

Newport (Casnewydd)

Cardiff (Caerdydd)

Agriculture / Working Farms

Greenmeadow Community Farm

Greenforge Way Cwmbran Torfaen NP44 5AJ
Tel: 01633 647662 Fax: 01633 647671
www.greenmeadowcommunityfarm.org.uk

[1mi W of Cwmbran town centre. Bus: Nos 5 or 63. Plenty of on-site parking available]

Just four miles from the M4, this is one of Wales' leading farm attractions - milking demonstrations, tractor and trailer rides, adventure play area, farm trail, nature trail and lots more. Phone for details of lambing weekends, shearing, country fair and agricultural shows, Halloween and Christmas events.

All year daily, summer 10.00-18.00, winter 10.00-16.30. Closed 23 Dec-1 Feb

A£4.50 C&Concessions£3.50, Family Ticket (A2+C3) £16.00. Group rates available on request

Discount Offer: One Child Free (with a full-paying adult). Conditions: not valid on Bank Holidays or for group rates.

Animal Attractions

Haulfre Stables

Haulfre Gardens Llangoed Beaumaris
Isle of Anglesey LL58 8RY
Tel: 01248 490709 / 724444
Fax: 01248 750282
www.angleseyheritage.org.uk

[Plenty of on-site parking available]

Haulfre is a small equestrian museum and restored stables. This modest but fascinating museum has an interesting collection of Victorian harness and saddlery, carts and carriages and other equestrian and transport material dating from an earlier age when horses were vital for transport, for agriculture and for haulage of heavy goods. Haulfre also offers an insight into the work of the grooms, coachmen and stable boys, who cared for the horses and the leisure pursuits of a country gentleman. Everything is housed in a historic stable block.

Easter-September (by appointment only)
Please telephone for admission prices

Welsh Mountain Zoo

Colwyn Bay Conwy LL28 5UY
Tel: 01492 532938 Fax: 01492 530498
A wide variety of amazing animals, including snow leopards, brown bears, sumatran tigers, red pandas, camels and penguins.

Arts, Crafts & Textiles

Makers' Guild: Craft in the Bay
Cardiff Bay Cardiff CF10 4QH
Tel: 029 2048 4611
A unique Victorian dockside building showcasing and selling fine contemporary craft. Gallery, retail area, exhibition space, workshops, café and conference room.

National Wool Museum
Carmarthenshire SA44 5UP
Tel: 01559 370929
The museum is housed in the former Cambrian Mills and has a comprehensive display tracing the evolution of the industry.

Newport Museum and Art Gallery
John Frost Square Newport NP9 1PA
Tel: 01633 656656
www.newport.gov.uk/museum
[Newport City Centre]
Natural science displays including geology; fine and applied art, specialising in early English watercolours, teapots and contemporary crafts; prehistoric finds from Gwent and Romano-British remains from Caerwent; local history including the Chartist movement. Regular exhibitions and associated activities. For more information please visit our website www.newport.gov.uk/museum and www.newport.gov.uk/artgallery.
All year Mon-Thur 09.30-17.00, Fri 09.30-16.30, Sat 09.30-16.00
Admission Free

Oriel Ynys Môn History and Art Gallery
Rhosmeirch Llangefni Isle of Anglesey LL77 7TQ
Tel: 01248 724444 Fax: 01248 750282
www.angleseyheritage.org.uk
[Plenty of on-site parking available]
Anglesey's premier purpose built museum and art gallery. HISTORY GALLERY: a fascinating insight into the island's culture, history and environment. One section of the History Gallery is dedicated to a collection of paintings by one of the foremost wildlife artists of his day, Charles. F. Tunnicliffe. ART GALLERY: a dynamic and changing programme of exhibitions, encompassing art, craft, drama and sculpture. ORIEL KYFFIN WILLIAMS opening in the Summer of 2008 will be a permanent and fitting tribute to one of Wales' most celebrated and respected artists with dynamic and changing programme of exhibitions displaying the artists' work. Shop and café.
Mon-Sun & Bank Hol Mon 10.30-17.00
Admission Free

Welsh Royal Crystal
5 Brynberth Industrial Estate East Street Rhayader Powys LD6 5EN
Tel: 01597 811005
The Welsh Royal Crystal glass-making factory uses handcrafting skills going back centuries.

Wrexham Arts Centre
Rhosddu Road Wrexham LL11 1AU
Tel: 01978 292093
A centre for excellence for contemporary visual arts. Programme of temporary exhibitions.

Birds, Butterflies & Bees

Felinwynt Rainforest Centre
Felinwynt Cardigan Ceredigion SA43 1RT

Tel: 01239 810250/810882
Fax: 01239 810465
www.butterflycentre.co.uk
[From A487 (Cardigan-Aberystwth) turn onto B4333 at Airfield, follow Rainforest signposts. Plenty of on-site parking available]

Felinwynt Rainforest Centre has become one of Ceredigion's chief attractions with thousands of visitors every year. The highlight of any visit is the mini-rainforest created by owner John Devereux. Wander through a jungle among tropical plants, exotic butterflies, waterfalls, pools and fish and watch the leafcutter ants with the soothing sounds of the Peruvian Rainforest. The video room shows films of rainforests and butterflies and is free to all customers. The visitor centre houses the gift shop with an extensive range of gifts for everyone, the café where you can have freshly cooked meals and snacks all day, including Dorothy's homemade cakes, and the exhibition based on the Tambopata region of Peru. All facilities are suitable for disabled visitors. Entrance charge applies to Tropical House only. A warm welcome awaits at this Visit Wales Quality Assured visitor attraction. National Winner of Loo of the Year 2005/2006.
Easter-31 Oct daily 10.30-17.00 (11.00-16.00 Oct)
A£4.00 C(3-14)£2.00 C(under 3)£Free OAPs£3.75

Discount Offer: Two for the Price of One (full-paying adult).

WWT National Wetland Centre Wales
Llwynhendy Llanelli Carmarthenshire SA14 9SH
Tel: 01554 741087 Fax: 01554 744101
www.wwt.org.uk
[Off A484 10min from J47 or J48 - M4 follow brown-duck signs. Ample on-site parking]
The award-winning National Wetland Centre Wales (one of the world-famous WWT centres) is situated on the northern shore of the Bury Inlet, with stunning views over the estuary and Gower. Whether you're a serious bird-watcher or just looking for family fun and relaxation, you can enjoy a day of discovery all year round, whatever the weather. Bring your own binoculars or hire them at the centre - you'll want a closer look at the amazing wildlife that inhabits this important national site. The landscaped grounds with acres of pond, lakes, streams and reed-beds provide a picturesque home for hundreds of the world's most spectacular ducks, geese, swans and flamingos - many of which are so tame, they'll feed from your hand. During summertime be sure to see lots of ducklings, cygnets, goslings and flamingo chicks. There's also a hands-on 'Discovery Centre' and outdoor play areas for the children, as well as our new canoe safari and bike trail.
All year daily 9.30-17.00. Closed 24-25 Dec. Centre closes 17.00, Grounds close 18.00 in Summer
Gift Aid Prices: A£6.95 C(under16)£3.85 Concessions£5.20, Family Ticket £19.45.
Standard Prices: A£6.31 C(under16)£3.49 Concessions£4.72, Family Ticket £17.64.
Group Prices: (12+) A£5.90 C(under16)£3.30 Concession£4.40

Discount Offer: Two for the Price of One (full-paying adult).

Caverns & Caves

King Arthur's Labyrinth

Corris Craft Centre Corris Machynlleth Powys
SY20 9RF
Tel: 01654 761584 Fax: 01654 761575
www.kingarthurslabyrinth.com
[Off A487, between Machynlleth & Dolgellau.
Plenty of free on-site parking available]
Your adventure begins with an underground
boat ride, through the great waterfall, deep
inside the spectacular caverns of the Labyrinth
and far into the past... As you explore this dramatic underground setting Welsh tales of King
Arthur and other ancient Welsh legends unfold.
Stories of dragons, of giants, of battles and
much more... fascinating for all ages. Back
above ground, join the Bards' Quest to search
for ancient legends lost in the maze of time.
Corris Craft Centre is the starting point for the
King Arthur's Labyrinth underground adventure
and home to ten craft workshops. See talented
crafts people at work and buy unique hand-
crafted items. Try your hand - have a go at
making your own crafts, is now available at the
centre. An excellent cafe using locally sourced
ingredients serves an interesting menu with a
Welsh twist.
17 Mar-2 Nov daily 10.00-17.00
A£6.50 C£4.65 OAPs£5.85

**Discount Offer: 20% off Adult
Admissions.**

Llechwedd Slate Caverns

Blaenau Ffestiniog Gwynedd LL41 3NB
Tel: 01766 830306
Llechwedd offers two underground rides and
free surface attractions.

Country Parks & Estates

Margam Country Park

Margam Neath Port Talbot SA13 2TJ
Tel: 01639 881635
850-acre country park with extensive grounds
containing several renovated gardens and historic buildings. There is a narrow gauge railway
and adventure playground. The Visitor Centre in
the Castle Courtyard houses a Riverside Pond
Exhibition.

Pembrey Country Park

Burry Port Pembrey Carmarthenshire SA16 0EJ
Tel: 01554 833913
202 hectares of parkland with one of the
longest beaches in Wales. Offers a host of family attractions including horse riding, dry ski
slope, toboggan run, train ride, pitch and putt,
adventure playground, picnic areas, walks,
restaurants and a visitor centre.

Portmeirion

Penrhyndeudraeth Gwynedd LL48 6ET
Tel: 01766 770000
Italianate, candy-coloured resort village built by
Welsh architect Sir Clough Williams-Ellis
between 1926 and 1976.

Exhibition & Visitor Centres

Cardiff Bay Visitor Centre

Britannia Quay Cardiff Bay Cardiff CF10 4PA
Tel: 029 2046 3833
Known locally as "The Tube" because of its
award-winning design, the Visitors Centre houses informative exhibitions as well as tourist information, maps of the area, souvenir shop and
presentations on the on-going development of
the bay area.

Dylan Thomas Centre

Somerset Place Swansea SA1 1RR
Tel: 01792 463980
A permanent exhibition on Dylan and his life,
with an excellent restaurant, and facilities for
conferences and functions.

Gower Heritage Centre

Parkmill Gower Swansea SA3 2EH
Tel: 01792 371206 Fax: 01792 371471
www.gowerheritagecentre.co.uk

[In village of Parkmill, 8mi W of Swansea on A4118, South Gower Rd. Ample on-site parking]
Last year the Gower celebrated its 50th year as the first designated Area of Outstanding Natural Beauty. Still with breath taking unspoilt scenery what better place to come and see its Heritage than at the Gower Heritage Centre, a working water powered corn and saw mill museum, with its superb range of activities and events. In addition to the normal weekend and holiday time heritage tours, we have our outstanding fun days, inspirational crafts, mystical ghost nights and we host a variety of musical events. New for 2007 is our fully operational woollen mill, making authentic Gower shawls and blankets. Also this year we will have a selection of talks by local historians. Recently nominated as the 2nd most important place to visit on the Gower after Worms Head. For further information please call or visit our website.

10.00-17.00
A£4.10 C£3.10, Family Ticket £13.50
Discount Offer: One Child Free.

Fishguard Harbour Ocean Lab

Goodwick Fishguard Pembrokeshire SA64 0DE
Tel: 01348 874737
Ocean Lab in Goodwick features an exhibition gallery with displays of fossils. Other facilities include tourist information, a cyber cafe, soft play area for under 5's, and coffee shop.

Festivals & Shows

Fishguard Folk Festival / Gwyl Werin Abergwaun

Royal Oak Fishguard Various Venues Fishguard Pembrokeshire SA64

Tel: 01348 875183

www.pembrokeshire-folk-music.co.uk

[In & around historic town of Fishguard, scene of the last ever invasion of Britain]

Make a date in your diary for this friendly festival, now extended to four days. Hear live music at its very best, featuring Niamh Ni Charra with Mike Galvin, Ember, Beverly Smith & Carl Jones, Sild, Nick Wyke & Becki Driscoll, Pat Smith & Ned Clamp, Toreth, George Whitfield & Helen Adam, Mike Chant and Joe Latter, plus many more (please see website). There will also be concerts, sessions, workshops, 'meet the artists,' open mic slots, street performers and a guided walk around the historic town of Fishguard (located on the Pembrokeshire coastal path). Based mainly in The Royal Oak, the festival is town-wide.

23-26 May 2008

Prices to be confirmed

Gwyl Ifan 2008

Various venues Cardiff
Tel: 029 2056 3989
www.gwylifan.org
[Central Cardiff, M4-A48(M)-A470. Plenty of on-site parking available]

Gwyl Ifan is the festival of Welsh folk dancing to celebrate summer, and 2008 will be the 32nd festival. It is held at various locations throughout the city and surrounding area, such as Cardiff Bay, with evening activities being held in the Angel Hotel and the historic Coal Exchange in the Bay. Dance teams come to the festival from all over Wales and beyond. This year we will be joined by a group of dancers from Trebeurden Brittany. Come to Cardiff and see a folk dance procession, displays on the streets, 'taplas' (feast and festivities), barn dance and various workshops.
20-22 June 2008

Llangollen International Musical Eisteddfod

Royal International Pavillion Abbey Road
Llangollen Denbighshire LL20 8SW
Tel: 01978 862000 Fax: 01978 862005
www.international-eisteddfod.co.uk
[From Shrewsbury follow A5 signs from Chester A483 onto A529. Plenty of on-site parking available. Disabled parking available]

Beautiful North Wales hosts the International Music festival in Llangollen with International choirs, folk dancers, folk groups and much more. 3 Outdoor stages- for live entertainment and non-stop colourful costume and competition in the Royal Pavilion. Themed days with Wednesday-folk song and dance, Thursday-Youth Day, Friday - Celtic Day and Saturday-International Family Day with international folk performers, entertainers and crafts. Enjoy shopping for souvenirs and the wide range of food and drink from around the world. All you have to do is soak up the atmosphere and enjoy the experience. Celebrity concerts every evening. Visit our website for details.
9-13 July 2008 Wed - Sat, 09.00-17.00. Sunday evening outdoor concert from 18.00, Celebrity concerts every evening from 19.45
Day Ground Admission: A£8.00 C£5.00 (Sat C£2.00). Pavilion Prices: Seats from £12.00

RHS Spring Flower Show, Cardiff

Bute Park Cardiff
Tel: 08700 667799
www.rhs.org.uk/flowershows
Now in its fourth year, this spring show brings gardening designs and astounding floral displays. Talk to the experts, gain tips on the best way to care for your plants and get practical advice on growing your own produce at the Interactive Allotment. To round off your day, visit the Experience Wales marquee, packed with the best of Welsh craft and cuisine.
18-20 April 2008 Fri & Sat 10.00-17.30, Sun 10.00-16.30
A£10.00 (A£9.00 if booked in advance)
C(under16)£Free with accompanying adult

Royal Welsh Agricultural Winter Fair

Royal Welsh Agricultural Society Ltd Llanelwedd
Builth Wells Powys LD2 3SY
Tel: 01982 553683 Fax: 01982 553563
www.rwas.co.uk
[Rail: Builth Rd or Llandrindod Wells station. Plenty of on-site parking available]

The Royal Welsh Agricultural Winter Fair a prime stock show for cattle, sheep, pigs and carcases also features horses, hounds, poultry, tradestands and crafts. Over 24,000 visitors attend.

1st & 2nd December 2008. Please call 01982 553683 for futher information
Please call for prices

Royal Welsh Show

Royal Welsh Agricultural Society Ltd Llanelwedd
Builth Wells Powys LD2 3SY
Tel: 01982 553683 Fax: 01982 553563
www.rwas.co.uk
[Rail: Builth Rd or Llandrindod Wells station]
The Royal Welsh Show provides a prime shop

window for farming in Wales. It attracts more than 200,000 visitors, up to 8,000 entries of livestock and over 1,000 tradestands together with sections covering the whole of farming and rural life in Wales.

21-24 July 2008 Please call RWAS office for further information 01982 553683

Gate: Mon-Wed A£19.00, Thur A£17.00. Gate: C(under16)£4.00 Gate: OAP rate available

Royal Welsh Smallholder and Garden Festival

Royal Welsh Agricultural Society Ltd Llanelwedd
Builth Wells Powys LD2 3SY
Tel: 01982 553683 Fax: 01982 553563
www.rwas.co.uk

[Rail: Builth Rd or Llandrindod Wells station. Plenty of on-site parking available]

The Royal Welsh Smallholder and Garden Festival features livestock, crafts, lectures and advice on countryside issues; displays and auctions of poultry and vintage machinery, display gardens, trade-stands and farmers markets. Over 25,000 visitors attend.

17-18 May 2008. Please call 01982 554408/09 for further information

A£8.00 C(under16)£3.00 OAPs£7.00 Family Ticket-1 day-£20.00, Family Ticket-2 day-£35.00, Weekend caravan & camping £25.00

Tenby Arts Festival
Tenby Pembrokeshire
Tel: 01834 875341
www.tenbyartsfest.co.uk

[Festival held at various venues]

Visit this picturesque walled town when it is enlivened by a splendid feast of music, dance, poetry, film, drama, talks, art, and family fun at the seaside. Tenby Arts Festival presents performances by local, national and international artistes packed into a delightful eight days of entertainment, culture, information, education and relaxation. There will be something for everyone from the beach bum to the culture vulture and all those in between. The Festival opens with a vibrant and colourful procession of street entertainers at the harbour followed by activities on south beach which will occupy and amuse children of all ages. The remainder of the week will provide a cultural repast.

20-27 September 2008
Prices vary according to event attended, range from £Free-£12.00

Folk & Local History Museums

National Museum Cardiff
Cathays Park Cardiff CF10 3NP
Tel: 029 2039 7951
Discover art, archaeology, natural history and geology. With a busy programme of exhibitions and events, there is something for everyone.

Swansea Museum
Victoria Road Maritime Quarter Swansea SA1 1SN
Tel: 01792 653763
With archaeology, natural history and local history exhibits on show.

W H Smith Museum
24 High Street Newtown Powys SY16 2NP
Tel: 01686 626280
The museum is on the first floor of the Newtown branch of W H Smith. It displays models and memorabilia depicting the history of W H Smith from its beginnings to the present day.

Forests & Woods

Cwmcarn Forest Drive, Visitor Centre and Campsite
Cwmcarn Crosskeys Newport NP11 7FA
Tel: 01495 272001
This 7-mile forest drive offers seven car parks where visitors can enjoy cycling and walking.

Gardens & Horticulture

Bodnant Garden
Tal-y-Cafn Colwyn Bay Conwy LL28 5RE
Tel: 01492 650460 Fax: 01492 650448
www.bodnant-garden.co.uk
[Off A470. Rail: Tal-y-Cafn]
Situated above the River Conwy, with spectacular views of the Snowdonia Range, Bodnant Garden is one of the finest in the world and the holder of four National Plant Collections. The rhododendrons, magnolias and camellias are a truly magnificent sight throughout the spring, whilst the world-famous original Laburnum Arch (a 55m long golden tunnel) is spectacular from mid May to early June. These are followed by stunning displays of herbaceous borders, scented roses, water lilies and hydrangeas in the summer, followed by glorious colours in the autumn. Bodnant Garden has many impressive features including a series of five Italianate-style terraces: Upper Rose Terrace, Croquet Terrace, Lily Terrace, Lower Rose Terrace and the Canal Terrace featuring the Pin Mill. The Dell, formed by the valley of the River Hireathlyn, contains the Pinetum and Wild Garden and features 200-year-old native trees together with the tallest Giant Redwood in the UK.
8 Mar-2 Nov daily 10.00-17.00
A£7.20 C£3.60

National Botanic Garden of Wales
Llanarthne Carmarthenshire SA32 8HG
Tel: 01558 668768 Fax: 01558 668933
www.gardenofwales.org.uk
[Off A48 dual carriageway nr Carmarthen, less than 1h from Cardiff. Ample on-site parking]
The No. 1 'Modern Wonder of Wales' boasts the largest single-span glasshouse in the world and is set in more than 500 acres of fantastic, unspoilt, rolling Welsh countryside. The Great Glasshouse is home to some of the most endangered plants on the planet from six Mediterranean climate regions: Western Australia, Chile, the Canaries, California, southern Africa, and the Mediterranean basin. The new Tropical House is bursting with palms, pineapples, coconuts, cardamon…. and hundreds of orchids. There is a unique and historic double-walled garden, lakes, ponds and walks, a theatre, licensed restaurant, shop, gallery, bog garden and bee garden, Physicians of Myddfai Exhibition and Apothecaries' Garden, children's farm, children's play area and discovery centre. Whatever your age, there is something for you at the most visited garden in Wales. Whatever time of year it is, the stunning views and remarkable sights and smells have to be experienced to be believed. But, be warned, you may not be able to see and do it all in a day. A stunning newTropical Glasshouse has opened within the double-walled garden.
All year daily Summer 10.00-18.00, Winter 10.00-16.30. Closed Christmas Day
A£8.00 C(5-16)£3.00 C(under5)£Free Concessions£6.00, Family Ticket (A2+C4) £17.00

Discount Offer: Two for the Price of One (full-paying adult).

Heritage & Industrial

Electric Mountain
Llanberis Caernarfon Gwynedd LL55 4UR
Tel: 01286 870636
Between 1976 and 1982, the heart of a mountain was tunnelled away and a pumped storage power station was built inside.

Inigo Jones and Co Ltd
Tudor Slate Works Y Groeslon Caernarfon Gwynedd LL54 7UE
Tel: 01286 830242
Witness the various processes as craftsmen use age old skills and working machinery to cut, shape and polish raw slate slabs into a multitude of craft items.

National Slate Museum
Gilfach Ddu Padarn Country Park Llanberis Gwynedd LL55 4TY
Tel: 01286 870630
Features a close-up exploration of the largest working waterwheel in mainland Britain, slate-splitting demonstrations, a fascinating tour of the workshops, iron and brass foundry, forges, loco shed and the waterpowered machinery, plus a well-stocked gift shop and inviting cafe.

National Waterfront Museum
Oystermouth Road Swansea SA1 3RD
Tel: 01792 638950
Tells the story of how industry and innovation have affected the lives of people in Wales over the last three hundred years.

Historical

Beaumaris Castle
Beaumaris Isle of Anglesey LL58 8AP
Tel: 01248 810361
Begun in 1295, this unfinished castle is the last and largest of King Edward I's Welsh fortifications. World Heritage Site. Guidebook available, on-site exhibition, plus a small selection of gifts and souvenirs.

Bodelwyddan Castle

Bodelwyddan Denbighshire LL18 5YA
Tel: 01745 584060 Fax: 01745 584563
www.bodelwyddan-castle.co.uk

[Close to seaside resorts Rhyl, Prestatyn & Llandudno. Just off J25 of A55 Express Way. Follow brown tourist signs]

Bodelwyddan Castle's magnificently restored rooms are the perfect setting for nineteenth-century collections from 3 national galleries. Bodelwyddan Castle has something for everyone, regardless of age, interests or abilities. Enjoy a varied programme of temporary exhibitions and events, formal gardens, woodland trail, bird hide, aviary, World War One practice trenches, adventure playground, interactive exhibits, Victorian toys and games room and a free audio guide. The estate has been used as a family residence, an army recuperation hospital and officers' mess, army training facility and a private girls' school, Lowether College. Evidence of this can be seen as you tour the house and grounds. On site facilities include Caffi Castell (specialising in traditional home baking and freshly prepared snacks) 'Craft & Design' (exclusive works by North Wales based artists) and the Castle gift shop (wide range of gifts suited to all pockets). Disabled access is to the ground and first floor only.

Please telephone for current opening times
A£5.00 C(under5)£Free C(5-16)£2.00 Concessions£4.50 Disabled £3.00 Family Ticket (A2+C2) £12.00 or (A1+C3) £10.00 Season Tickets from £5.00

Discount Offer: Two for the Price of One (full-paying adult).

Caernarfon Castle

Castle Ditch Caernarfon Gwynedd LL55 2AY
Tel: 01286 677617
King Edward I intended this castle to be a royal residence and seat of government for north Wales. World Heritage Site. Guidebook available, on-site exhibition and gift shop. The castle also houses the Regimental Museum of the Royal Welch Fusiliers (Wales's oldest regiment).

Caerphilly Castle

Caerphilly CF83 1JD
Tel: 029 2088 3143
One of the largest medieval fortresses in Britain, begun in 1268. Famous for its 'leaning tower'. Guidebook available, gift shop, two exhibitions and an audio-visual display

Cardiff Castle

Castle Street Cardiff CF10 3RB
Tel: 029 2087 8100
A medieval castle and Victorian revival mansion, transformed from a Norman keep that was erected over a Roman fort. Spectacular interiors and grounds, tea rooms and gift shop.

Chepstow Castle

Chepstow Monmouthshire NP6 5EZ
Tel: 01291 624065
Substantial remains of one of the earliest stone-built castles in Britain. Guidebook available, gift shop and on-site exhibition.

Conwy Castle

Rosehill Street Conwy LL32 8LD
Tel: 01492 592358
The castle and town walls were built by Edward I between 1283 and 1289. World Heritage Site. Guidebook, site exhibition and gift shop.

Erddig Hall

Erddig Wrexham LL13 0YT
Tel: 01978 315151
Atmospheric house and estate that vividly evoking its family and servants. With extensive parkland, restored historic machines and horse-drawn carriage rides.

For great hotel deals call Superbreak on 01904 679999 or visit www.superbreak.com

Harlech Castle

Castle Square Harlech Gwynedd LL46 2YH
Tel: 01766 780552
Built between 1283 and 1289 by Edward I, The
castle is designed on a concentric plan with a
small but powerful inner ward dominated by a
twin-towered gatehouse. World Heritage Site.
Guidebook, giftshop and exhibition.

Llanfairpwllgwyngyllgogerychwyr ndrobwllllantysiliogogogoch

Isle of Anglesey
Tel: 01248 750057
*[(From the South) use the A5/A55 to cross the
Britannia Bridge then follow the signs]*
The world-famous tiny village with the big name.

Pembroke Castle

Main Street Pembroke Pembrokeshire
SA71 4LA
Tel: 01646 684585/681510

[10mi W of Tenby]

This early Norman castle houses many fascinating displays and exhibitions. Enjoy a picnic, in
the beautifully kept grounds, or on the roof of
St. Anne's Bastion and take in the views along
the estuary. As the birthplace of Henry VII,
Pembroke can be seen as a pivotal place in history. Henry was the founder of the Tudor
dynasty, and the Crown of England has
remained ever since in the line of his heirs.
Pembroke Castle occupies a strong position
high on a ridge between two tidal inlets. Its fortifications were continually extended throughout
its history and it displays stonework from many
periods.

All year daily. Closed 24-26 Dec and 1 Jan

Penrhyn Castle

Bangor Gwynedd LL57 4HN
Tel: 01248 353084/371337
Nineteenth-century fantasy castle with spectacular contents and grounds. Includes a doll
museum, Victorian kitchens, a railway museum
and an adventure playground.

Powis Castle and Gardens

Welshpool Powys SY21 8RF
Tel: 01938 551929 Fax: 01938 554336
www.nationaltrust.org.uk
*[1mi S of Welshpool off A483. Bus: Arriva North
Midlands 71. Rail: Welshpool 1.75mi. Plenty of
on-site parking available]*
The world-famous garden, overhung with enormous clipped yews, shelters rare and tender
plants. Laid out under the influence of Italian
and French styles, the garden retains its original
lead statues, an orangery and an aviary on the
terraces. In the eighteenth century an informal
woodland wilderness was created on the
opposing ridge. Perched on a rock above the
garden terraces, the medieval castle contains
one of the finest collections in Wales. It was
originally built c.1200 by Welsh princes and was
subsequently adapted and embellished by generations of Herberts and Clives, who furnished
the castle with a wealth of fine paintings and
furniture. A beautiful collection of treasures from
India is displayed in the Clive Museum.
*Garden: 1, 2, 8 & 9 Mar. Castle & Gardens: 13
Mar-2 Nov Thu-Mon, July-Aug Wed-Mon. Please
phone for more details*
Castle & Garden: A£10.50 C(under5)£Free
C(under17)£5.25, Family Ticket (A2+C3)
£26.25. Garden only: A£7.50 C(under5)£Free
C(under17)£3.75, Family Ticket (A2+C3)
£18.75. NT Members £Free

Smallest House in Great Britain
Quay Conwy LL32 8DE
Tel: 01492 593484
[Take Conway rd off A55, signposted in town]
The 'Guinness Book of Records' lists this as the smallest house in Britain. Just 6ft wide by 10ft high, it is furnished in the style of a mid-Victorian Welsh cottage.
Apr-Oct 10.00-18.00
A£1.00 C£0.50 C(under5)£Free

Discount Offer: One Child Free.

Tredegar House and Park
Coedkernew Newport NP10 8YW
Tel: 01633 815880 Fax: 01633 815895
www.newport.gov.uk/tredegarhouse

[2mi W signposted from A48/M4 J28. Rail: Newport. Bus: local services 15 & 30 stop nearby. Plenty of on-site parking available]

Set in ninety acres of award winning gardens and parkland, Tredegar House is one of the finest examples of Restoration Architecture in Wales, and was the ancestral home of the Morgans for over five hundred years. Visitors today can discover what life was like for those who lived 'above and below' stairs. A stunning sequence of Staterooms, elaborately decorated with carvings, gilding, and fine paintings contrast with the fascinating and extensive domestic quarters. Lakeside walks, beautiful walled gardens, orangery and spectacular stable block complete the 'Country House' picture. Gift shop, tea room, craft workshops together with special events in the house and park throughout the year.

Good Fri-end Sept Wed-Sun & Bank Hol 11.30-16.00. Special Christmas & Halloween opening. Group visits at other times

Please call 01633 815880 for admission prices, info on weddings and Victorian school tours

Literature & Libraries

Dylan Thomas Boat House
Dylan's Walk Laugharne Carmarthenshire SA33 4SD
Tel: 01994 427420 Fax: 01994 427420
www.dylanthomasboathouse.com
[14mi W of Carmarthen A40-A4066]
The waterside house, set on the heron priested shore of the Taf estuary, contains much original furniture, family photographs, an art gallery and displays on the life and works of Dylan Thomas.
May-Oct & Easter weekend 10.00-17.30, Nov-Apr 10.30-15.30
A£3.50 C(under 7)Free C(Over 7)£1.75
OAPs£2.95

Discount Offer: One Child Free.

National Library of Wales

Penglais Hill Aberystwyth Ceredigion SY23 3BU
Tel: 01970 632800
The huge library is one of Britain's six copyright libraries, and specialises in Welsh and Celtic literature. It has maps, manuscripts, prints and drawings, as well as books in all languages.

Living History Museums

Llancaiach Fawr Manor

Nelson Treharris Merthyr Tydfil CF46 6ER
Tel: 01443 412248
Step back in time to 1645 to meet Colonel Prichard's servants of the household. Listen to the tales, customs and gossip of the seventeenth-century as you tour the Manor. Period gardens, conservatory restaurant and gift shop.

Maritime

Moelfre Seawatch

Moelfre Isle of Anglesey LL72 8LG
Tel: 01248 410277
www.angleseyheritage.org.uk

[Plenty of on-site parking available]

The Seawatch Centre in the small, picturesque harbour village of Moelfre is a reminder of the island's rich maritime history and importance of the ever present sea for the people of Anglesey. Learn about the wonderful array of marine wildlife to be found in the coastal waters. Learn about the bravery of Coxswain Richard Evans who was awarded two gold medals for saving

the lives of the crew of two ships.

Easter-Sept Tues-Sun & Bank Hol Mon 11.00-17.00. Other times by appointment

Admission free

South Stack

Holyhead Isle of Anglesey
Tel: 01407 769543
www.angleseyheritage.org.uk
[Plenty of on-site parking available]
One of Wales' most spectacular lighthouses. On the way down over 400 steps you will be able to view the geology of the surrounding vertical cliff faces. Once on the island you will be able to see exhibitions on the bird life and the natural environment.

Easter-Sept Mon-Sun & Bank Hol Mon 10.30-17.30. At other times by appointment

Please telephone for admission prices

Military & Defence Museums

Welch Regiment Museum of The Royal Regiment of Wales

Cardiff Castle Grounds Cardiff CF10 2RB
Tel: 029 2022 9367
The Welch Regiment Museum (41st/69th Foot) of The Royal Regiment of Wales (24th/41st Foot) houses Colours, uniform and appointments of the 41st and 69th Foot.

Mills - Water & Wind

Llynnon Mill
Llanddeusant Isle of Anglesey LL65 4AB
Tel: 01407 730797 / 730407
www.angleseyheritage.org.uk

[Plenty of on-site parking available]

The only working windmill in Wales. The mill produces stoneground wholemeal flour for sale using organic wheat. See also a reconstructed settlement, typical of the kind existing on Anglesey about 3,000 years ago providing a unique impression of life in the distant past. Shop, tearoom (offering traditional home-cooking), workshops, traditional events and the Anglesey Mills Trail.

Easter-Sept Mon-Sun & Bank Hol Mon 11.00-17.00. At other times by appointment
Please telephone for admission prices

Mining

Big Pit: National Coal Museum
Blaenafon Torfaen NP4 9XP
Tel: 01495 790311
'Big Pit' closed as a working coalmine in 1980, but today visitors can don safety helmets and lamps, and go 300ft underground to experience a different world.
Mar-Nov daily

Natural History Museums

St Fagans National History Museum
St Fagans Cardiff CF5 6XB
Tel: 029 2057 3500
St Fagans: National History Museum is one of Europe's foremost open-air museums representing the life and culture of Wales and situated in 100 acres of parkland. The museum features 40 original buildings from different historical periods, re-erected in 100 acres of parkland. There are also workshops where craftsmen still demonstrate their traditional skills. Their produce is usually on sale. Native breeds of livestock can be seen in the fields and farmyards, and demonstrations of farming tasks take place daily. There are also galleries with exhibitions of costume, daily life and farming implements. Special exhibitions are also held regularly.

Nature & Conservation Parks

National Park Visitor Centre (Mountain Centre)
Libanus Brecon Powys LD3 8ER
Tel: 01874 623366
The Mountain Centre is run by the Brecon Beacons National Park Authority and features a refreshment lounge and a National Park information section with books, maps and souvenirs. An excellent exhibition offers an introduction to help visitors appreciate and explore this pristine protected landscape.

Welsh Wildlife Centre
Teifi Marshes Nature Reserve Cilgerran Cardigan Ceredigion SA43 2TB
Tel: 01239 621600
The Welsh Wildlife Centre is located just outside the town of Cardigan and sits in the heart of a 264-acre wildlife nature reserve of national and international conservation importance. A series of nature trails guide visitors through the natural habitats of otters, badgers, water voles, and other mammals. The award-winning visitor centre houses informative displays and exhibitions provides a full range of refreshments for visitors to enjoy whilst taking in the relaxing views from the Nuthatch Tea Rooms. Souvenirs of your visit are on sale in the Otters' Holt Gift Shop.

On the Water

Horse Drawn Boats and Narrowboat Aqueduct Trips

The Wharf Wharf Hill Llangollen Denbighshire LL20 8TA
Tel: 01978 860702 Fax: 01978 860702
www.horsedrawnboats.co.uk

[From Llangollen town centre, cross river & continue up hill]

Llangollen Wharf is home to the famous horse-drawn boats. Enjoy the peace and tranquillity of the Llangollen Canal on a 45-minute boat trip (pulled by one of our gorgeous heavy horses). Boats are covered and are therefore suitable for all-weather trips. Enjoy a 2-hour cruise (on our fully weatherproofed, centrally-heated boat) over the Pontcysllte Aqueduct. Commentary, licensed bar and snacks available. You can also enjoy home-cooked food in the Wharf Tearooms (famous for delicious cakes!), where you can watch our beautiful boats pass by, or admire views of Llangollen from the terrace.

Mid Mar-end of Oct daily 9.30-17.00

Horse-Drawn Boat Trips: A£5.00 C£2.50, Family Ticket £12.50. Aqueduct Cruises: A£10.00 C£8.00. Group rates available on request

Places of Worship

Llandaff Cathedral

The Cathedral Green Cardiff CF5 2LA
Tel: 029 2056 4554
Situated on one of the oldest Christian sites in the British Isles, the cathedral was begun in the 12th century but rebuilt and modified over and over again throughout its history. It features significant artworks by a range of artists.

St Davids Cathedral

The Close St Davids Pembrokeshire SA62 6RH
Tel: 01437 720199 Fax: 01437 721885
www.stdavidscathedral.org.uk
[A487]
Begun in 1181 on the site reputed to be where St David founded a monastic settlement in the sixth century. The present building was altered during the twelfth to the fourteenth centuries and again in the sixteenth. It also has an extension added in 1993, so the architecture is varied. The ceilings - oak, painted wood and stone vaulting are of considerable interest. The floor of the nave slopes a metre over its length while over the entire length of the cathedral the difference is four metres. In addition to services there are organ recitals on Wednesdays from late July through to early September. Last year a splendid new refectory opened offering fresh local food.

All year daily 08.30-18.00

Suggested donation of £3.00

Discount Offer: 5% off in the gift shop when you spend £10.00 or more.

Police, Prisons & Dungeons

Beaumaris Courthouse

Castle Street Beaumaris Isle of Anglesey
LL58 8BP
Tel: 01248 811691 / 724444
www.angleseyheritage.org.uk
Beaumaris Courthouse is one of Anglesey's
most fascinating buildings. Now restored and
refurbished to its past splendour, it is a place
that to this day almost orders you to get up and
proclaim out loud '...Not Guilty' Prisoners of all
descriptions have faced trial in this unique
courtroom since it was built in 1614. For many
of them the outcome of their case was a matter
of life or death.

*Easter-Sept Mon-Sun & Bank Hol Mon 10.30-
17.00. At other times by appointment*

Please telephone for admission prices

Beaumaris Gaol

Steeple Lane Beaumaris Isle of Anglesey
LL58 8EP
Tel: 01248 810921 Fax: 01248 750282

www.angleseyheritage.org.uk
This building is full of sad memories and
secrets. Bars and locks. Dark and dusty corridors. Darkness. Cold and despair. Beaumaris
Gaol will live in your memory for a long time.
Not for the faint hearted; call and see for yourself. It will give you a fascinating insight into the
world of the prisoner in Victorian times.

*Easter-Sept Mon-Sun & Bank Hol Mon 10.30-
17.00. At other times by appointment*

Please call for admission prices.

Railways

Ffestiniog Railway

Harbour Station Porthmadog Gwynedd
LL49 9NF
Tel: 01766 516000 Fax: 01766 516006
www.festrail.co.uk

*[Porthmadog: A487 station well signposted.
Blaenau Ffestiniog: A470 - station signposted.]*

The Ffestiniog Railway is the oldest independent
railway company in the world. We have been
operating steam trains for over 140 years. It
was founded in 1823 to carry slate to the harbour at Porthmadog from the quarries of
Blaenau Ffestiniog and was an important part of
the social and industrial culture of the area.
Nowadays, the little steam trains climb over 700
feet from sea level, carrying visitors through the
stunning scenery of the Snowdonia National
Park. There is much to see and do along the
line and a day rover ticket gives you the opportunity to make the most of your day, perhaps
with a walk through the woodlands at Tan-y-
Bwlch station or a visit to Portmeirion village
only a mile away. Trains run daily between
Easter and the end of October with limited services during the winter months. Please phone
or visit our website for details of services. Public

car parks are available in Porthmadog and Blaenau Ffestiniog. For car users we suggest starting your journey from Blaenau Ffestiniog during the summer. Alternatively take advantage of combined Rail / Bus Rover tickets, some of which give discounts on the Ffestiniog Railway.
Trains run daily from 15 Mar-2 Nov plus on other dates. See timetable for details
A£17.50 C£8.75 OAPs£15.75, Family Ticket (A2+C2) £35.00

Llanberis Lake Railway

Padarn Country Park Gilfach Ddu Llanberis Caernarfon Gwynedd LL55 4TY
Tel: 01286 870549 Fax: 01286 870549
www.lake-railway.co.uk
[Off A4086 in Llanberis. 15min from A55 J11 follow Llanberis tourist signs. Plenty of on-site parking available]
Sit back and enjoy a more leisurely way to travel. Let our little steam trains take you on a journey through spectacular scenery right in the heart of Snowdonia. The journey takes you past the thirteenth-century Dolbadarn Castle, across rivers and streams and along part of the old slate railway route following the shores of beautiful Lake Padarn. Enjoy magnificent views of Snowdon and the surrounding high peaks from the comfort of your carriage. The five-mile return journey takes around 60 minutes, and the trains stop briefly at Cei Llydan (midway along the lake). Here we have a very pleasant lakeside picnic site, and there's an independently operated children's play area nearby. All our trains are scheduled to be hauled by one of our historic narrow-gauge steam engines that spent their earlier career working the nearby slate quarries. Souvenir shop and café at Gilfach Ddu Station.
Easter-late Oct: trains run frequently Sun-Fri. June-Aug: daily

Return Fares: A£6.50 C£4.50, Family discounts available

Discount Offer: One Child Free.

Welsh Highland Railway (Caernarfon)

St Helen's Road Caernarfon Gwynedd LL55 2YD
Tel: 01766 516000 Fax: 01766 516006
www.festrail.co.uk
[From A55 follow signs to Caernarfon, then 'brown signs' to station. Plenty of on-site parking]
The Welsh Highland Railway is Snowdonia's newest railway offering you the best of narrow gauge steam and beautiful scenery. This exciting project to restore the old railway line that linked the towns of Porthmadog and Caernarfon has been backed by the Millennium Commission and the Welsh Assembly Government. At the moment, trains run between Caernarfon, right beside the famous castle, and Rhyd Ddu, at the foot of Snowdon, a distance of 13 miles. However, there is much to be seen as work on the extension is in full swing. Why not catch an open top bus onwards to Beddgelert or Porthmadog? It makes a great day out. Ideal as well for using as your transport into the Snowdonia National Park with excellent walks from the line and places to eat along the way. Trains run daily between Easter and October with limited services during the winter months. Please phone or visit our website for details of services.
Trains run daily from 15 Mar-31 Oct, plus other dates. See timetable for details
A£17.50 C£8.75 OAPs£15.75, Family Ticket (A2+C2) £35.00

Science - Earth & Planetary

Techniquest

Stuart Street Cardiff CF10 5BW
Tel: 029 2047 5475
There are over 150 hands-on exhibits that will keep the whole family entertained and the ever-changing programme of special events means that there is always something new to discover.

Sealife Centres & Aquariums

Anglesey Sea Zoo

Brynsiencyn Llanfair Isle of Anglesey LL01 6TQ
Tel: 01248 430411
A fascinating encounter with local marine life in an undercover, underwater attraction.

Spectator Sports

Millennium Stadium Tours

Gate 4 Westgate Street Cardiff CF10 1NS
Tel: 029 2082 2228 Fax: 029 2023 2678
www.cardiffstadium.com
Walk in the footsteps of Ryan Giggs. Stand where Madonna stood. Lift the trophy like one of your heroes. Explore the magnificent facets and features that make Millennium Stadium one of the most impressive icons of modern Wales. See the dressing rooms, hear the roar of the crowd, walk down the players' tunnel and raise the rafters like millions of others who have gone before you at Millennium Stadium Tours.

Mon-Sat 10.00-17.00 Sun 10.00-16.00
A£5.50 C£3.00 Concessions £4.00, Family Ticket(A2+C3) £17.00

Theme & Adventure Parks

GreenWood Forest Park

Y Felinheli Gwynedd LL56 4QN
Tel: 01248 670076 Fax: 01248 670069
www.greenwoodforestpark.co.uk
[Rail: Bangor. Plenty of on-site parking available]
Family adventure and forest fun! Ride our eco-friendly Green Dragon Rollercoaster, zoom down our 70 metre sledge slide, scramble through Tunnel Warren - tunnels, slides, ropes and towers for the under 7s, plus the Giant Jumper - the Biggest Bouncing Pillow ever and the first one in Wales! Enjoy the Jungle Boat Adventure, drive mini-tractors, shoot traditional Longbows and build dens in the woods. Tackle the challenge of our Treetop Towers and find a crocodile in our Maze, Adventure Playgrounds, Puzzle Barn and Toddlers Village, indoor inter-active exhibition in the Great Hall. Gift shop, café and snack bars. New for 2008: Moon Karts - Formula One Fun! Award winning attraction with lots to do, whatever the weather. Plus fantastic entertainment - see website for our events details.

9 Feb-23 Feb daily 11.00-17.00, 12 Mar-1 Sept daily 10.00-17.30, 1 Sept-1 Nov daily 11.00-17.00

Please call or see our website

Oakwood Theme Park

Canaston Bridge Narberth Pembrokeshire SA67 8DE
Tel: 01834 861889
Features over 30 rides and attractions set in 80 acres of beautiful Pembrokeshire countryside.

Amazonia

Strathclyde County Park Motherwell North Lanarkshire ML1 3RT

One Child Free

with a full-paying adult

Cannot be used in conjunction with other offers. One voucher per party. Not valid on Bank Hols or special event days.

Expires end **Valid for 2008 season only**

DISCOUNT VOUCHER

Anglesey Abbey, Gardens and Lode Mill

Quy Road Lode Cambridge Cambridgeshire CB25 9EJ

One Child Free

with full-paying adult

Cannot be used in conjunction with other offers. One voucher per party. Not valid on Bank Hols or special event days.

Expires end Feb 2009 (unless otherwise specified)

DISCOUNT VOUCHER

Anne Hathaway's Cottage

Cottage Lane Shottery Stratford-Upon-Avon Warwickshire CV37 9HH

See Shakespeare's Birthplace voucher for details

Cannot be used in conjunction with other offers. One voucher per party. Not valid on Bank Hols or special event days.

Expires end Feb 2009 (unless otherwise specified)

DISCOUNT VOUCHER

Anne of Cleves House Museum

52 Southover High Street Lewes East Sussex BN7 1JA

Buy One Full-Priced Adult, Senior or Student Ticket and Get Another Ticket Half-Price

(The half-price ticket must be of equal or lesser value, not valid on any special event days, please see website for dates of events)

Cannot be used in conjunction with other offers. One voucher per party. Not valid on Bank Hols or special event days.

Expires end Feb 2009 (unless otherwise specified)

DISCOUNT VOUCHER

Ascot Racecourse

High Street Ascot Berkshire SL5 7JX

£5.00 off per ticket

on all Family Days

Cannot be used in conjunction with other offers. One voucher per party. Not valid on Bank Hols or special event days.

Expires end Feb 2009 (unless otherwise specified)

DISCOUNT VOUCHER

Battersea Park Children's Zoo

Battersea Park London SW11 4NJ

One Free Child

with two full-paying adults

Cannot be used in conjunction with other offers. One voucher per party. Not valid on Bank Hols or special event days.

Expires end Feb 2009 (unless otherwise specified)

DISCOUNT VOUCHER

1. Each voucher entitles the holder to the discount specified by the selected attraction.
2. Valid for use until 28/02/09 (unless otherwise specified, or if attraction season finishes prior to this). Vouchers are subject to the terms, conditions and restrictions of the selected attraction.
3. One voucher per party will be accepted, cannot be used in conjunction with any other offer, photocopies will not be accepted.
4. All attractions offering a discount have confirmed their willingness to participate. All information is subject to change without notice and should any attraction close or decline to accept a voucher for any reason, Days Out UK are not liable and cannot be held responsible.
5. Days Out UK shall not accept liability for any loss, accident or injury that may occur at a participating attraction and any dispute arising must be settled direct with the attraction concerned.
6. Cash redemption value of each voucher is 0.001p.
7. You are advised to check all relevant information with your chosen attraction before commencing your journey.

Days Out UK, PO Box 427, Northampton NN1 3YN. Tel: 01604 622445

1. Each voucher entitles the holder to the discount specified by the selected attraction.
2. Valid for use until 28/02/09 (unless otherwise specified. or if attraction season finishes prior to this). Vouchers are subject to the terms, conditions and restrictions of the selected attraction.
3. One voucher per party will be accepted, cannot be used in conjunction with any other offer, photocopies will not be accepted.
4. All attractions offering a discount have confirmed their willingness to participate. All information is subject to change without notice and should any attraction close or decline to accept a voucher for any reason, Days Out UK are not liable and cannot be held responsible.
5. Days Out UK shall not accept liability for any loss, accident or injury that may occur at a participating attraction and any dispute arising must be settled direct with the attraction concerned.
6. Cash redemption value of each voucher is 0.001p.
7. You are advised to check all relevant information with your chosen attraction before commencing your journey.

Days Out UK, PO Box 427, Northampton NN1 3YN. Tel: 01604 622445

1. Each voucher entitles the holder to the discount specified by the selected attraction.
2. Valid for use until 28/02/09 (unless otherwise specified, or if attraction season finishes prior to this). Vouchers are subject to the terms, conditions and restrictions of the selected attraction.
3. One voucher per party will be accepted, cannot be used in conjunction with any other offer, photocopies will not be accepted.
4. All attractions offering a discount have confirmed their willingness to participate. All information is subject to change without notice and should any attraction close or decline to accept a voucher for any reason, Days Out UK are not liable and cannot be held responsible.
5. Days Out UK shall not accept liability for any loss, accident or injury that may occur at a participating attraction and any dispute arising must be settled direct with the attraction concerned.
6. Cash redemption value of each voucher is 0.001p.
7. You are advised to check all relevant information with your chosen attraction before commencing your journey.

Days Out UK, PO Box 427, Northampton NN1 3YN. Tel: 01604 622445

1. Each voucher entitles the holder to the discount specified by the selected attraction.
2. Valid for use until 28/02/09 (unless otherwise specified, or if attraction season finishes prior to this). Vouchers are subject to the terms, conditions and restrictions of the selected attraction.
3. One voucher per party will be accepted, cannot be used in conjunction with any other offer, photocopies will not be accepted.
4. All attractions offering a discount have confirmed their willingness to participate. All information is subject to change without notice and should any attraction close or decline to accept a voucher for any reason, Days Out UK are not liable and cannot be held responsible.
5. Days Out UK shall not accept liability for any loss, accident or injury that may occur at a participating attraction and any dispute arising must be settled direct with the attraction concerned.
6. Cash redemption value of each voucher is 0.001p.
7. You are advised to check all relevant information with your chosen attraction before commencing your journey.

Days Out UK, PO Box 427, Northampton NN1 3YN. Tel: 01604 622445

1. Each voucher entitles the holder to the discount specified by the selected attraction.
2. Valid for use until 28/02/09 (unless otherwise specified, or if attraction season finishes prior to this). Vouchers are subject to the terms, conditions and restrictions of the selected attraction.
3. One voucher per party will be accepted, cannot be used in conjunction with any other offer, photocopies will not be accepted.
4. All attractions offering a discount have confirmed their willingness to participate. All information is subject to change without notice and should any attraction close or decline to accept a voucher for any reason, Days Out UK are not liable and cannot be held responsible.
5. Days Out UK shall not accept liability for any loss, accident or injury that may occur at a participating attraction and any dispute arising must be settled direct with the attraction concerned.
6. Cash redemption value of each voucher is 0.001p.
7. You are advised to check all relevant information with your chosen attraction before commencing your journey.

Days Out UK, PO Box 427, Northampton NN1 3YN. Tel: 01604 622445

Beale Park
Lower Basildon Reading Berkshire RG8 9NH
One Child Free
with one full-paying adult
Cannot be used in conjunction with other offers. One voucher per party. Not valid on Bank Hols or special event days.
Expires end Feb 2009 (unless otherwise specified)

DISCOUNT VOUCHER

Beatles Story
Britannia Vaults Albert Dock Liverpool L3 4AD
One Child Free
with one full-paying adult
(not to be used with family tickets)
Cannot be used in conjunction with other offers. One voucher per party. Not valid on Bank Hols or special event days.
Valid until 31 Mar 2009

DISCOUNT VOUCHER

Bekonscot Model Village and Railway
Warwick Road Beaconsfield Buckinghamshire HP9 2PL
One Child Free Per Family
with one full-paying adult
Cannot be used in conjunction with other offers. One voucher per party. Not valid on Bank Hols or special event days.
Expires end Feb 2009 (unless otherwise specified)

DISCOUNT VOUCHER

Belleek Pottery
Main Street Rathmore Belleek Enniskillen County Fermanagh
BT93 3FY
Two for the Price of One
with a full-paying adult
Cannot be used in conjunction with other offers. One voucher per party. Not valid on Bank Hols or special event days.
Expires end Feb 2009 (unless otherwise specified)

DISCOUNT VOUCHER

Berkeley Castle
Berkeley Gloucestershire GL13 9BQ
One Child Free
with a full-paying adult
(cannot used on special event days)
Cannot be used in conjunction with other offers. One voucher per party. Not valid on Bank Hols or special event days.
Expires end Feb 2009 (unless otherwise specified)

DISCOUNT VOUCHER

Bewdley Museum
The Shambles Load St. Bewdley Worcestershire DY12 2AE
10% discount
on any purchase in the Museum Tea Shop
Cannot be used in conjunction with other offers. One voucher per party. Not valid on Bank Hols or special event days.
Expires end Feb 2009 (unless otherwise specified)

DISCOUNT VOUCHER

1. Each voucher entitles the holder to the discount specified by the selected attraction.
2. Valid for use until 28/02/09 (unless otherwise specified, or if attraction season finishes prior to this). Vouchers are subject to the terms, conditions and restrictions of the selected attraction.
3. One voucher per party will be accepted, cannot be used in conjunction with any other offer, photocopies will not be accepted.
4. All attractions offering a discount have confirmed their willingness to participate. All information is subject to change without notice and should any attraction close or decline to accept a voucher for any reason, Days Out UK are not liable and cannot be held responsible.
5. Days Out UK shall not accept liability for any loss, accident or injury that may occur at a participating attraction and any dispute arising must be settled direct with the attraction concerned.
6. Cash redemption value of each voucher is 0.001p.
7. You are advised to check all relevant information with your chosen attraction before commencing your journey.

Days Out UK, PO Box 427, Northampton NN1 3YN. Tel: 01604 622445

1. Each voucher entitles the holder to the discount specified by the selected attraction.
2. Valid for use until 28/02/09 (unless otherwise specified, or if attraction season finishes prior to this). Vouchers are subject to the terms, conditions and restrictions of the selected attraction.
3. One voucher per party will be accepted, cannot be used in conjunction with any other offer, photocopies will not be accepted.
4. All attractions offering a discount have confirmed their willingness to participate. All information is subject to change without notice and should any attraction close or decline to accept a voucher for any reason, Days Out UK are not liable and cannot be held responsible.
5. Days Out UK shall not accept liability for any loss, accident or injury that may occur at a participating attraction and any dispute arising must be settled direct with the attraction concerned.
6. Cash redemption value of each voucher is 0.001p.
7. You are advised to check all relevant information with your chosen attraction before commencing your journey.

Days Out UK, PO Box 427, Northampton NN1 3YN. Tel: 01604 622445

1. Each voucher entitles the holder to the discount specified by the selected attraction.
2. Valid for use until 28/02/09 (unless otherwise specified, or if attraction season finishes prior to this). Vouchers are subject to the terms, conditions and restrictions of the selected attraction.
3. One voucher per party will be accepted, cannot be used in conjunction with any other offer, photocopies will not be accepted.
4. All attractions offering a discount have confirmed their willingness to participate. All information is subject to change without notice and should any attraction close or decline to accept a voucher for any reason, Days Out UK are not liable and cannot be held responsible.
5. Days Out UK shall not accept liability for any loss, accident or injury that may occur at a participating attraction and any dispute arising must be settled direct with the attraction concerned.
6. Cash redemption value of each voucher is 0.001p.
7. You are advised to check all relevant information with your chosen attraction before commencing your journey.

Days Out UK, PO Box 427, Northampton NN1 3YN. Tel: 01604 622445

1. Each voucher entitles the holder to the discount specified by the selected attraction.
2. Valid for use until 28/02/09 (unless otherwise specified, or if attraction season finishes prior to this). Vouchers are subject to the terms, conditions and restrictions of the selected attraction.
3. One voucher per party will be accepted, cannot be used in conjunction with any other offer, photocopies will not be accepted.
4. All attractions offering a discount have confirmed their willingness to participate. All information is subject to change without notice and should any attraction close or decline to accept a voucher for any reason, Days Out UK are not liable and cannot be held responsible.
5. Days Out UK shall not accept liability for any loss, accident or injury that may occur at a participating attraction and any dispute arising must be settled direct with the attraction concerned.
6. Cash redemption value of each voucher is 0.001p.
7. You are advised to check all relevant information with your chosen attraction before commencing your journey.

Days Out UK, PO Box 427, Northampton NN1 3YN. Tel: 01604 622445

1. Each voucher entitles the holder to the discount specified by the selected attraction.
2. Valid for use until 28/02/09 (unless otherwise specified, or if attraction season finishes prior to this). Vouchers are subject to the terms, conditions and restrictions of the selected attraction.
3. One voucher per party will be accepted, cannot be used in conjunction with any other offer, photocopies will not be accepted.
4. All attractions offering a discount have confirmed their willingness to participate. All information is subject to change without notice and should any attraction close or decline to accept a voucher for any reason, Days Out UK are not liable and cannot be held responsible.
5. Days Out UK shall not accept liability for any loss, accident or injury that may occur at a participating attraction and any dispute arising must be settled direct with the attraction concerned.
6. Cash redemption value of each voucher is 0.001p.
7. You are advised to check all relevant information with your chosen attraction before commencing your journey.

Days Out UK, PO Box 427, Northampton NN1 3YN. Tel: 01604 622445

1. Each voucher entitles the holder to the discount specified by the selected attraction.
2. Valid for use until 28/02/09 (unless otherwise specified, or if attraction season finishes prior to this). Vouchers are subject to the terms, conditions and restrictions of the selected attraction.
3. One voucher per party will be accepted, cannot be used in conjunction with any other offer, photocopies will not be accepted.
4. All attractions offering a discount have confirmed their willingness to participate. All information is subject to change without notice and should any attraction close or decline to accept a voucher for any reason, Days Out UK are not liable and cannot be held responsible.
5. Days Out UK shall not accept liability for any loss, accident or injury that may occur at a participating attraction and any dispute arising must be settled direct with the attraction concerned.
6. Cash redemption value of each voucher is 0.001p.
7. You are advised to check all relevant information with your chosen attraction before commencing your journey.

Days Out UK, PO Box 427, Northampton NN1 3YN. Tel: 01604 622445

Biddenden Vineyards and Cider Works
Gribble Bridge Lane Biddenden Kent TN27 8DF
One Free Cup of Tea or Coffee in the Café

Cannot be used in conjunction with other offers. One voucher per party. 1 free beverage per voucher & per transaction

Expires end Feb 2009 (unless otherwise specified)

DISCOUNT VOUCHER

Birdland
Rissington Road Bourton on the Water Cheltenham
Gloucestershire GL54 2BN
One Child Free
with a full-paying adult

Cannot be used in conjunction with other offers. One voucher per party. Not valid on Bank Hols or special event days.

Expires end Feb 2009 (unless otherwise specified)

DISCOUNT VOUCHER

Birdworld, Underwater World and Jenny Wren Farm
Farnham Road Holt Pound Farnham Surrey GU10 4LD
Two for the Price of One
with a full-paying adult
(not valid for Santa events, not valid for groups)

Cannot be used in conjunction with other offers. One voucher per party. Not valid on Bank Hols or special event days.

Valid until 31 Oct 2008

DISCOUNT VOUCHER

Birmingham Botanical Gardens and Glasshouses
Westbourne Road Edgbaston Birmingham B15 3TR
One Concession Free
with a full-paying adult

Cannot be used in conjunction with other offers. One voucher per party. Not valid on Bank Hols or special event days.

Expires end Feb 2009 (unless otherwise specified)

DISCOUNT VOUCHER

Blackpool Sea Life Centre
Golden Mile Centre Promenade Blackpool Lancashire FY1 5AA
One Child Free with one full paying adult

1. This voucher entitles free admission to the Blackpool Sea Life Centre for one child when accompanied by one full paying adult.
2. Offer expires 28 February 2009.
3. Cannot be used in conjunction with any other offer.
4. A "child" is classed as a person aged 3-14 inclusive (under 3s go free anyway).
5. No cash alternative, non-refundable; and non-exchangeable.
6. All children must be accompanied by an adult.
7. Only one voucher per party and per transaction.
8. Photocopies not accepted.
9. SEA LIFE/Sanctuaries reserve the right to alter, close or remove details/exhibits without prior notice for technical, operational or other reasons, and no refunds can be given in these circumstances.
10. SEA LIFE/Sanctuaries reserve the right to refuse entry without explanation.
Voucher Ref: DOUK.

Cannot be used in conjunction with other offers. One voucher per party. Not valid on Bank Hols or special event days.

Expires end Feb 2009 (unless otherwise specified)

DISCOUNT VOUCHER

1. Each voucher entitles the holder to the discount specified by the selected attraction.
2. Valid for use until 28/02/09 (unless otherwise specified, or if attraction season finishes prior to this). Vouchers are subject to the terms, conditions and restrictions of the selected attraction.
3. One voucher per party will be accepted, cannot be used in conjunction with any other offer, photocopies will not be accepted.
4. All attractions offering a discount have confirmed their willingness to participate. All information is subject to change without notice and should any attraction close or decline to accept a voucher for any reason, Days Out UK are not liable and cannot be held responsible.
5. Days Out UK shall not accept liability for any loss, accident or injury that may occur at a participating attraction and any dispute arising must be settled direct with the attraction concerned.
6. Cash redemption value of each voucher is 0.001p.
7. You are advised to check all relevant information with your chosen attraction before commencing your journey.

Days Out UK, PO Box 427, Northampton NN1 3YN. Tel: 01604 622445

1. Each voucher entitles the holder to the discount specified by the selected attraction.
2. Valid for use until 28/02/09 (unless otherwise specified, or if attraction season finishes prior to this). Vouchers are subject to the terms, conditions and restrictions of the selected attraction.
3. One voucher per party will be accepted, cannot be used in conjunction with any other offer, photocopies will not be accepted.
4. All attractions offering a discount have confirmed their willingness to participate. All information is subject to change without notice and should any attraction close or decline to accept a voucher for any reason, Days Out UK are not liable and cannot be held responsible.
5. Days Out UK shall not accept liability for any loss, accident or injury that may occur at a participating attraction and any dispute arising must be settled direct with the attraction concerned.
6. Cash redemption value of each voucher is 0.001p.
7. You are advised to check all relevant information with your chosen attraction before commencing your journey.

Days Out UK, PO Box 427, Northampton NN1 3YN. Tel: 01604 622445

1. Each voucher entitles the holder to the discount specified by the selected attraction.
2. Valid for use until 28/02/09 (unless otherwise specified, or if attraction season finishes prior to this). Vouchers are subject to the terms, conditions and restrictions of the selected attraction.
3. One voucher per party will be accepted, cannot be used in conjunction with any other offer, photocopies will not be accepted.
4. All attractions offering a discount have confirmed their willingness to participate. All information is subject to change without notice and should any attraction close or decline to accept a voucher for any reason, Days Out UK are not liable and cannot be held responsible.
5. Days Out UK shall not accept liability for any loss, accident or injury that may occur at a participating attraction and any dispute arising must be settled direct with the attraction concerned.
6. Cash redemption value of each voucher is 0.001p.
7. You are advised to check all relevant information with your chosen attraction before commencing your journey.

Days Out UK, PO Box 427, Northampton NN1 3YN. Tel: 01604 622445

1. Each voucher entitles the holder to the discount specified by the selected attraction.
2. Valid for use until 28/02/09 (unless otherwise specified, or if attraction season finishes prior to this). Vouchers are subject to the terms, conditions and restrictions of the selected attraction.
3. One voucher per party will be accepted, cannot be used in conjunction with any other offer, photocopies will not be accepted.
4. All attractions offering a discount have confirmed their willingness to participate. All information is subject to change without notice and should any attraction close or decline to accept a voucher for any reason, Days Out UK are not liable and cannot be held responsible.
5. Days Out UK shall not accept liability for any loss, accident or injury that may occur at a participating attraction and any dispute arising must be settled direct with the attraction concerned.
6. Cash redemption value of each voucher is 0.001p.
7. You are advised to check all relevant information with your chosen attraction before commencing your journey.

Days Out UK, PO Box 427, Northampton NN1 3YN. Tel: 01604 622445

1. Each voucher entitles the holder to the discount specified by the selected attraction.

2. Valid for use until 28/02/09 (unless otherwise specified, or if attraction season finishes prior to this). Vouchers are subject to the terms, conditions and restrictions of the selected attraction.

3. One voucher per party will be accepted, cannot be used in conjunction with any other offer, photocopies will not be accepted.

4. All attractions offering a discount have confirmed their willingness to participate. All information is subject to change without notice and should any attraction close or decline to accept a voucher for any reason, Days Out UK are not liable and cannot be held responsible.

5. Days Out UK shall not accept liability for any loss, accident or injury that may occur at a participating attraction and any dispute arising must be settled direct with the attraction concerned.

6. Cash redemption value of each voucher is 0.001p.

7. You are advised to check all relevant information with your chosen attraction before commencing your journey.

Days Out UK, PO Box 427, Northampton NN1 3YN. Tel: 01604 622445

Blair Drummond Safari and Adventure Park
Blair Drummond Stirling FK9 4UR
One Child Free
per vehicle

Cannot be used in conjunction with other offers. One voucher per party. Not valid on Bank Hols or special event days.

Valid 15 Mar - 20 Oct 2008

DISCOUNT VOUCHER

Blickling Hall, Gardens and Park
Blickling Norwich Norfolk NR11 6NF
One Child Free
with full-paying adult

Cannot be used in conjunction with other offers. One voucher per party. Not valid on Bank Hols or special event days.

Expires end Feb 2009 (unless otherwise specified)

DISCOUNT VOUCHER

Blue Ice, Solihull Rink
Hobs Moat Road Solihull West Midlands B92 8JN
Save up to £5.00!
Family Ticket (A2+C2) or (A1+C3) for just £17.60
(Not valid Saturdays (all day or evening) or Friday evenings)

Cannot be used in conjunction with other offers. One voucher per party. Not valid on Bank Hols or special event days.

Valid until 1 Nov 2008

DISCOUNT VOUCHER

Blue Reef Aquarium
Clarence Esplanade Southsea Portsmouth Hampshire PO5 3PB
One Child Free
with one full-paying adult
(Not to be used in conjunction with family tickets)

Cannot be used in conjunction with other offers. One voucher per party. Not valid on Bank Hols or special event days.

Valid until 31 Mar 2009

DISCOUNT VOUCHER

Blue Reef Aquarium
Grand Parade Tynemouth Tyne & Wear NE30 4JF
One Child Free
with one full-paying adult
(Not to be used in conjunction with family tickets)

Cannot be used in conjunction with other offers. One voucher per party. Not valid on Bank Hols or special event days.

Valid until 31 Mar 2009

DISCOUNT VOUCHER

Blue Reef Aquarium
Towan Promenade Newquay Cornwall TR7 1DU
One Child Free
with one full-paying adult
(Not to be used in conjunction with family tickets)

Cannot be used in conjunction with other offers. One voucher per party. Not valid on Bank Hols or special event days.

Valid until 31 Mar 2009

DISCOUNT VOUCHER

1. Each voucher entitles the holder to the discount specified by the selected attraction.
2. Valid for use until 28/02/09 (unless otherwise specified, or if attraction season finishes prior to this). Vouchers are subject to the terms, conditions and restrictions of the selected attraction.
3. One voucher per party will be accepted, cannot be used in conjunction with any other offer, photocopies will not be accepted.
4. All attractions offering a discount have confirmed their willingness to participate. All information is subject to change without notice and should any attraction close or decline to accept a voucher for any reason, Days Out UK are not liable and cannot be held responsible.
5. Days Out UK shall not accept liability for any loss, accident or injury that may occur at a participating attraction and any dispute arising must be settled direct with the attraction concerned.
6. Cash redemption value of each voucher is 0.001p.
7. You are advised to check all relevant information with your chosen attraction before commencing your journey.

Days Out UK, PO Box 427, Northampton NN1 3YN. Tel: 01604 622445

1. Each voucher entitles the holder to the discount specified by the selected attraction.
2. Valid for use until 28/02/09 (unless otherwise specified. or if attraction season finishes prior to this). Vouchers are subject to the terms, conditions and restrictions of the selected attraction.
3. One voucher per party will be accepted, cannot be used in conjunction with any other offer, photocopies will not be accepted.
4. All attractions offering a discount have confirmed their willingness to participate. All information is subject to change without notice and should any attraction close or decline to accept a voucher for any reason, Days Out UK are not liable and cannot be held responsible.
5. Days Out UK shall not accept liability for any loss, accident or injury that may occur at a participating attraction and any dispute arising must be settled direct with the attraction concerned.
6. Cash redemption value of each voucher is 0.001p.
7. You are advised to check all relevant information with your chosen attraction before commencing your journey.

Days Out UK, PO Box 427, Northampton NN1 3YN. Tel: 01604 622445

1. Each voucher entitles the holder to the discount specified by the selected attraction.
2. Valid for use until 28/02/09 (unless otherwise specified, or if attraction season finishes prior to this). Vouchers are subject to the terms, conditions and restrictions of the selected attraction.
3. One voucher per party will be accepted, cannot be used in conjunction with any other offer, photocopies will not be accepted.
4. All attractions offering a discount have confirmed their willingness to participate. All information is subject to change without notice and should any attraction close or decline to accept a voucher for any reason, Days Out UK are not liable and cannot be held responsible.
5. Days Out UK shall not accept liability for any loss, accident or injury that may occur at a participating attraction and any dispute arising must be settled direct with the attraction concerned.
6. Cash redemption value of each voucher is 0.001p.
7. You are advised to check all relevant information with your chosen attraction before commencing your journey.

Days Out UK, PO Box 427, Northampton NN1 3YN. Tel: 01604 622445

1. Each voucher entitles the holder to the discount specified by the selected attraction.
2. Valid for use until 28/02/09 (unless otherwise specified, or if attraction season finishes prior to this). Vouchers are subject to the terms, conditions and restrictions of the selected attraction.
3. One voucher per party will be accepted, cannot be used in conjunction with any other offer, photocopies will not be accepted.
4. All attractions offering a discount have confirmed their willingness to participate. All information is subject to change without notice and should any attraction close or decline to accept a voucher for any reason, Days Out UK are not liable and cannot be held responsible.
5. Days Out UK shall not accept liability for any loss, accident or injury that may occur at a participating attraction and any dispute arising must be settled direct with the attraction concerned.
6. Cash redemption value of each voucher is 0.001p.
7. You are advised to check all relevant information with your chosen attraction before commencing your journey.

Days Out UK, PO Box 427, Northampton NN1 3YN. Tel: 01604 622445

1. Each voucher entitles the holder to the discount specified by the selected attraction.
2. Valid for use until 28/02/09 (unless otherwise specified, or if attraction season finishes prior to this). Vouchers are subject to the terms, conditions and restrictions of the selected attraction.
3. One voucher per party will be accepted, cannot be used in conjunction with any other offer, photocopies will not be accepted.
4. All attractions offering a discount have confirmed their willingness to participate. All information is subject to change without notice and should any attraction close or decline to accept a voucher for any reason, Days Out UK are not liable and cannot be held responsible.
5. Days Out UK shall not accept liability for any loss, accident or injury that may occur at a participating attraction and any dispute arising must be settled direct with the attraction concerned.
6. Cash redemption value of each voucher is 0.001p.
7. You are advised to check all relevant information with your chosen attraction before commencing your journey.

Days Out UK, PO Box 427, Northampton NN1 3YN. Tel: 01604 622445

Bo'ness and Kinneil Railway
Bo'ness Station Union Street Bo'ness West Lothian EH51 9AQ
One Free Child Fare
with a full-paying adult or concession
(Not valid on 'Days Out with Thomas' or 'Santa Special' trains)

Cannot be used in conjunction with other offers. One voucher per party. Not valid on Bank Hols or special event days.
Expires end Feb 2009 (unless otherwise specified)

DISCOUNT VOUCHER

Bo'ness Motor Museum
Bridgness Road Bo'ness Falkirk EH51 9JR
20% off all admissions

Cannot be used in conjunction with other offers. One voucher per party. Not valid on Bank Hols or special event days.
Expires end Feb 2009 (unless otherwise specified)

DISCOUNT VOUCHER

Bodelwyddan Castle
Bodelwyddan Denbighshire LL18 5YA
Two for the Price of One
with a full-paying adult
Conditions:
*Cheapest entrant goes free
*Voucher entitles the holder to free like-for-like entry for the individual
invoking the cheapest entry charge
*Offer only valid if one accompanying adult is paying the full entry-price
*Holder may incurr additional charges to obtain entry to special events
*Voucher has no monetary value and cannot be exchanged for any
other goods or services
*Voucher is valid until 28 February 2009
*Bodelwyddan Castle reserves the right to declare damaged or defaced
vouchers null and void.

Cannot be used in conjunction with other offers. One voucher per party. Not valid on Bank Hols or special event days.
Expires end Feb 2009 (unless otherwise specified)

DISCOUNT VOUCHER

Bowes Museum (The)
Barnard Castle County Durham DL12 8NP
Two for the Price of One
with a full-paying adult
(lowest priced ticket goes free)

Cannot be used in conjunction with other offers. One voucher per party. Not valid on Bank Hols or special event days.
Expires end Feb 2009 (unless otherwise specified)

DISCOUNT VOUCHER

Bramall Hall
Bramhall Park Bramhall Cheshire SK7 3NX
Two for the Price of One
with one full-paying adult
(One free adult or child with one full-paying adult)

Cannot be used in conjunction with other offers. One voucher per party. Not valid on Bank Hols or special event days.
Expires end Feb 2009 (unless otherwise specified)

DISCOUNT VOUCHER

485

1. Each voucher entitles the holder to the discount specified by the selected attraction.
2. Valid for use until 28/02/09 (unless otherwise specified, or if attraction season finishes prior to this). Vouchers are subject to the terms, conditions and restrictions of the selected attraction.
3. One voucher per party will be accepted, cannot be used in conjunction with any other offer, photocopies will not be accepted.
4. All attractions offering a discount have confirmed their willingness to participate. All information is subject to change without notice and should any attraction close or decline to accept a voucher for any reason, Days Out UK are not liable and cannot be held responsible.
5. Days Out UK shall not accept liability for any loss, accident or injury that may occur at a participating attraction and any dispute arising must be settled direct with the attraction concerned.
6. Cash redemption value of each voucher is 0.001p.
7. You are advised to check all relevant information with your chosen attraction before commencing your journey.

Days Out UK, PO Box 427, Northampton NN1 3YN. Tel: 01604 622445

1. Each voucher entitles the holder to the discount specified by the selected attraction.

2. Valid for use until 28/02/09 (unless otherwise specified, or if attraction season finishes prior to this). Vouchers are subject to the terms, conditions and restrictions of the selected attraction.

3. One voucher per party will be accepted, cannot be used in conjunction with any other offer, photocopies will not be accepted.

4. All attractions offering a discount have confirmed their willingness to participate. All information is subject to change without notice and should any attraction close or decline to accept a voucher for any reason, Days Out UK are not liable and cannot be held responsible.

5. Days Out UK shall not accept liability for any loss, accident or injury that may occur at a participating attraction and any dispute arising must be settled direct with the attraction concerned.

6. Cash redemption value of each voucher is 0.001p.

7. You are advised to check all relevant information with your chosen attraction before commencing your journey.

Days Out UK, PO Box 427, Northampton NN1 3YN. Tel: 01604 622445

1. Each voucher entitles the holder to the discount specified by the selected attraction.
2. Valid for use until 28/02/09 (unless otherwise specified, or if attraction season finishes prior to this). Vouchers are subject to the terms, conditions and restrictions of the selected attraction.
3. One voucher per party will be accepted, cannot be used in conjunction with any other offer, photocopies will not be accepted.
4. All attractions offering a discount have confirmed their willingness to participate. All information is subject to change without notice and should any attraction close or decline to accept a voucher for any reason, Days Out UK are not liable and cannot be held responsible.
5. Days Out UK shall not accept liability for any loss, accident or injury that may occur at a participating attraction and any dispute arising must be settled direct with the attraction concerned.
6. Cash redemption value of each voucher is 0.001p.
7. You are advised to check all relevant information with your chosen attraction before commencing your journey.

Days Out UK, PO Box 427, Northampton NN1 3YN. Tel: 01604 622445

1. Each voucher entitles the holder to the discount specified by the selected attraction.
2. Valid for use until 28/02/09 (unless otherwise specified, or if attraction season finishes prior to this). Vouchers are subject to the terms, conditions and restrictions of the selected attraction.
3. One voucher per party will be accepted, cannot be used in conjunction with any other offer, photocopies will not be accepted.
4. All attractions offering a discount have confirmed their willingness to participate. All information is subject to change without notice and should any attraction close or decline to accept a voucher for any reason, Days Out UK are not liable and cannot be held responsible.
5. Days Out UK shall not accept liability for any loss, accident or injury that may occur at a participating attraction and any dispute arising must be settled direct with the attraction concerned.
6. Cash redemption value of each voucher is 0.001p.
7. You are advised to check all relevant information with your chosen attraction before commencing your journey.

Days Out UK, PO Box 427, Northampton NN1 3YN. Tel: 01604 622445

Brean Leisure Park
Coast Road Brean Sands Somerset TA8 2QY
Three for the Price of Two
full-paying adults
(Not valid on Bank Holiday weekends (Sun & Mon))

Cannot be used in conjunction with other offers. One voucher per party. Not valid on Bank Hols or special event days.
Expires end Feb 2009 (unless otherwise specified)

DISCOUNT VOUCHER

Bressingham Steam Museum and Gardens
Bressingham Nr Diss Norfolk IP22 2AB
One Child Free
with a full-paying adult
(ref 8150)

Cannot be used in conjunction with other offers. One voucher per party. Not valid on Bank Hols or special event days.
Expires end Feb 2009 (unless otherwise specified)

DISCOUNT VOUCHER

Brighton Sea Life Centre
Marine Parade Brighton East Sussex BN2 1TB
One Child Free with a full-paying adult

1. This voucher entitles free admission to the Brighton Sea Life Centre for one child when accompanied by one full paying adult.
2. Offer expires 28 February 2009.
3. Cannot be used in conjunction with any other offer.
4. A "child" is classed as a person aged 3-14 inclusive (under 3s go free anyway).
5. No cash alternative, non-refundable; and non-exchangeable.
6. All children must be accompanied by an adult.
7. Only one voucher per party and per transaction.
8. Photocopies not accepted.
9. SEA LIFE/Sanctuaries reserve the right to alter, close or remove details/exhibits without prior notice for technical, operational or other reasons, and no refunds can be given in these circumstances.
10. SEA LIFE/Sanctuaries reserve the right to refuse entry without explanation.
Voucher Ref: DOUK.

Cannot be used in conjunction with other offers. One voucher per party. Not valid on Bank Hols or special event days.
Expires end Feb 2009 (unless otherwise specified)

DISCOUNT VOUCHER

Bristol Zoo Gardens
Clifton Bristol BS8 3HA
One Child Free
with a full-paying adult

Cannot be used in conjunction with other offers. One voucher per party. Not valid on Bank Hols or special event days.
Expires end Feb 2009 (unless otherwise specified)

DISCOUNT VOUCHER

Britannia - The Royal Yacht
Ocean Terminal Leith Edinburgh EH6 6JJ
One Child Free
with a full-paying adult or senior

Cannot be used in conjunction with other offers. One voucher per party. Not valid on Bank Hols or special event days.
Expires end Feb 2009 (unless otherwise specified)

DISCOUNT VOUCHER

1. Each voucher entitles the holder to the discount specified by the selected attraction.
2. Valid for use until 28/02/09 (unless otherwise specified, or if attraction season finishes prior to this). Vouchers are subject to the terms, conditions and restrictions of the selected attraction.
3. One voucher per party will be accepted, cannot be used in conjunction with any other offer, photocopies will not be accepted.
4. All attractions offering a discount have confirmed their willingness to participate. All information is subject to change without notice and should any attraction close or decline to accept a voucher for any reason, Days Out UK are not liable and cannot be held responsible.
5. Days Out UK shall not accept liability for any loss, accident or injury that may occur at a participating attraction and any dispute arising must be settled direct with the attraction concerned.
6. Cash redemption value of each voucher is 0.001p.
7. You are advised to check all relevant information with your chosen attraction before commencing your journey.

Days Out UK, PO Box 427, Northampton NN1 3YN. Tel: 01604 622445

1. Each voucher entitles the holder to the discount specified by the selected attraction.

2. Valid for use until 28/02/09 (unless otherwise specified, or if attraction season finishes prior to this). Vouchers are subject to the terms, conditions and restrictions of the selected attraction.

3. One voucher per party will be accepted, cannot be used in conjunction with any other offer, photocopies will not be accepted.

4. All attractions offering a discount have confirmed their willingness to participate. All information is subject to change without notice and should any attraction close or decline to accept a voucher for any reason, Days Out UK are not liable and cannot be held responsible.

5. Days Out UK shall not accept liability for any loss, accident or injury that may occur at a participating attraction and any dispute arising must be settled direct with the attraction concerned.

6. Cash redemption value of each voucher is 0.001p.

7. You are advised to check all relevant information with your chosen attraction before commencing your journey.

Days Out UK, PO Box 427, Northampton NN1 3YN. Tel: 01604 622445

1. Each voucher entitles the holder to the discount specified by the selected attraction.
2. Valid for use until 28/02/09 (unless otherwise specified, or if attraction season finishes prior to this). Vouchers are subject to the terms, conditions and restrictions of the selected attraction.
3. One voucher per party will be accepted, cannot be used in conjunction with any other offer, photocopies will not be accepted.
4. All attractions offering a discount have confirmed their willingness to participate. All information is subject to change without notice and should any attraction close or decline to accept a voucher for any reason, Days Out UK are not liable and cannot be held responsible.
5. Days Out UK shall not accept liability for any loss, accident or injury that may occur at a participating attraction and any dispute arising must be settled direct with the attraction concerned.
6. Cash redemption value of each voucher is 0.001p.
7. You are advised to check all relevant information with your chosen attraction before commencing your journey.

Days Out UK, PO Box 427, Northampton NN1 3YN. Tel: 01604 622445

1. Each voucher entitles the holder to the discount specified by the selected attraction.
2. Valid for use until 28/02/09 (unless otherwise specified, or if attraction season finishes prior to this). Vouchers are subject to the terms, conditions and restrictions of the selected attraction.
3. One voucher per party will be accepted, cannot be used in conjunction with any other offer, photocopies will not be accepted.
4. All attractions offering a discount have confirmed their willingness to participate. All information is subject to change without notice and should any attraction close or decline to accept a voucher for any reason, Days Out UK are not liable and cannot be held responsible.
5. Days Out UK shall not accept liability for any loss, accident or injury that may occur at a participating attraction and any dispute arising must be settled direct with the attraction concerned.
6. Cash redemption value of each voucher is 0.001p.
7. You are advised to check all relevant information with your chosen attraction before commencing your journey.

Days Out UK, PO Box 427, Northampton NN1 3YN. Tel: 01604 622445

Brontë Parsonage Museum
Church Street Haworth Keighley West Yorkshire BD22 8DR
Two for the Price of One
with a full-paying adult

Cannot be used in conjunction with other offers. One voucher per party. Not valid on Bank Hols or special event days.

Expires end Feb 2009 (unless otherwise specified)

DISCOUNT VOUCHER

Broughton Castle
Banbury Oxfordshire OX15 5EB
Two for the Price of One
with a full-paying adult

Cannot be used in conjunction with other offers. One voucher per party. Not valid on Bank Hols or special event days.

Expires end Feb 2009 (unless otherwise specified)

DISCOUNT VOUCHER

Buckinghamshire Railway Centre
Quainton Road Station Quainton Aylesbury Bucks HP22 4BY
Two for the Price of One
with a full-paying adult
(Not valid for 'Days Out with Thomas' or 'Steaming Santa' events)

Cannot be used in conjunction with other offers. One voucher per party. Not valid on Bank Hols or special event days.

Expires end Feb 2009 (unless otherwise specified)

DISCOUNT VOUCHER

Bure Valley Railway
Aylsham Station Norwich Road Aylsham Norfolk NR11 6BW
50p off per Adult
on Standard Fares
(Excludes combined Train/Boat trips, 'Santa Specials' and 'Day Out with Thomas)

Cannot be used in conjunction with other offers. One voucher per party. Not valid on Bank Hols or special event days.

Expires end Feb 2009 (unless otherwise specified)

DISCOUNT VOUCHER

Bush Farm Bison Centre
West Knoyle Mere Wiltshire BA12 6AE
One Child Free
with a full-paying adult

Cannot be used in conjunction with other offers. One voucher per party. Not valid on Bank Hols or special event days.

Expires end Feb 2009 (unless otherwise specified)

DISCOUNT VOUCHER

Butlins Minehead
Warren Road Minehead Somerset TA24 5SH
Kid For A Quid
One child enters for just £1.00
when accompanied by a full-paying adult

Cannot be used in conjunction with other offers. One voucher per party. Not valid on Bank Hols or special event days.

Expires end Feb 2009 (unless otherwise specified)

DISCOUNT VOUCHER

1. Each voucher entitles the holder to the discount specified by the selected attraction.
2. Valid for use until 28/02/09 (unless otherwise specified, or if attraction season finishes prior to this). Vouchers are subject to the terms, conditions and restrictions of the selected attraction.
3. One voucher per party will be accepted, cannot be used in conjunction with any other offer, photocopies will not be accepted.
4. All attractions offering a discount have confirmed their willingness to participate. All information is subject to change without notice and should any attraction close or decline to accept a voucher for any reason, Days Out UK are not liable and cannot be held responsible.
5. Days Out UK shall not accept liability for any loss, accident or injury that may occur at a participating attraction and any dispute arising must be settled direct with the attraction concerned.
6. Cash redemption value of each voucher is 0.001p.
7. You are advised to check all relevant information with your chosen attraction before commencing your journey.

Days Out UK, PO Box 427, Northampton NN1 3YN. Tel: 01604 622445

1. Each voucher entitles the holder to the discount specified by the selected attraction.
2. Valid for use until 28/02/09 (unless otherwise specified. or if attraction season finishes prior to this). Vouchers are subject to the terms, conditions and restrictions of the selected attraction.
3. One voucher per party will be accepted, cannot be used in conjunction with any other offer, photocopies will not be accepted.
4. All attractions offering a discount have confirmed their willingness to participate. All information is subject to change without notice and should any attraction close or decline to accept a voucher for any reason, Days Out UK are not liable and cannot be held responsible.
5. Days Out UK shall not accept liability for any loss, accident or injury that may occur at a participating attraction and any dispute arising must be settled direct with the attraction concerned.
6. Cash redemption value of each voucher is 0.001p.
7. You are advised to check all relevant information with your chosen attraction before commencing your journey.

Days Out UK, PO Box 427, Northampton NN1 3YN. Tel: 01604 622445

1. Each voucher entitles the holder to the discount specified by the selected attraction.
2. Valid for use until 28/02/09 (unless otherwise specified, or if attraction season finishes prior to this). Vouchers are subject to the terms, conditions and restrictions of the selected attraction.
3. One voucher per party will be accepted, cannot be used in conjunction with any other offer, photocopies will not be accepted.
4. All attractions offering a discount have confirmed their willingness to participate. All information is subject to change without notice and should any attraction close or decline to accept a voucher for any reason, Days Out UK are not liable and cannot be held responsible.
5. Days Out UK shall not accept liability for any loss, accident or injury that may occur at a participating attraction and any dispute arising must be settled direct with the attraction concerned.
6. Cash redemption value of each voucher is 0.001p.
7. You are advised to check all relevant information with your chosen attraction before commencing your journey.

Days Out UK, PO Box 427, Northampton NN1 3YN. Tel: 01604 622445

1. Each voucher entitles the holder to the discount specified by the selected attraction.
2. Valid for use until 28/02/09 (unless otherwise specified, or if attraction season finishes prior to this). Vouchers are subject to the terms, conditions and restrictions of the selected attraction.
3. One voucher per party will be accepted, cannot be used in conjunction with any other offer, photocopies will not be accepted.
4. All attractions offering a discount have confirmed their willingness to participate. All information is subject to change without notice and should any attraction close or decline to accept a voucher for any reason, Days Out UK are not liable and cannot be held responsible.
5. Days Out UK shall not accept liability for any loss, accident or injury that may occur at a participating attraction and any dispute arising must be settled direct with the attraction concerned.
6. Cash redemption value of each voucher is 0.001p.
7. You are advised to check all relevant information with your chosen attraction before commencing your journey.

Days Out UK, PO Box 427, Northampton NN1 3YN. Tel: 01604 622445

1. Each voucher entitles the holder to the discount specified by the selected attraction.
2. Valid for use until 28/02/09 (unless otherwise specified, or if attraction season finishes prior to this). Vouchers are subject to the terms, conditions and restrictions of the selected attraction.
3. One voucher per party will be accepted, cannot be used in conjunction with any other offer, photocopies will not be accepted.
4. All attractions offering a discount have confirmed their willingness to participate. All information is subject to change without notice and should any attraction close or decline to accept a voucher for any reason, Days Out UK are not liable and cannot be held responsible.
5. Days Out UK shall not accept liability for any loss, accident or injury that may occur at a participating attraction and any dispute arising must be settled direct with the attraction concerned.
6. Cash redemption value of each voucher is 0.001p.
7. You are advised to check all relevant information with your chosen attraction before commencing your journey.

Days Out UK, PO Box 427, Northampton NN1 3YN. Tel: 01604 622445

Cadbury World

Linden Road Bournville Birmingham West Midlands B30 2LU

£10.00 off One Family Ticket
(A2+C2) or (A2+C3)

Cannot be used in conjunction with other offers. One voucher per party. Not valid on Bank Hols or special event days.

Expires end Feb 2009 (unless otherwise specified)

DISCOUNT VOUCHER

Callendar House

Callendar Park Falkirk FK1 1YR

10% discount on all gift shop purchases
when you spend £10.00 or more

Cannot be used in conjunction with other offers. One voucher per party. Not valid on Bank Hols or special event days.

Expires end Feb 2009 (unless otherwise specified)

DISCOUNT VOUCHER

Camelot Theme Park

Park Hall Road Charnock Richard Chorley Lancs PR7 5LP

Two for the Price of One
with a full-paying adult

Cannot be used in conjunction with other offers. One voucher per party. Not valid on Bank Hols or special event days.

Expires end Feb 2009 (unless otherwise specified)

DISCOUNT VOUCHER

Campaign Paintball Park

Old Lane Cobham Surrey KT11 1NH

100 Free Paintballs
(when you pay for a full game)

Cannot be used in conjunction with other offers. One voucher per party. Not valid on Bank Hols or special event days.

Expires end Feb 2009 (unless otherwise specified)

DISCOUNT VOUCHER

Castle Kennedy Gardens

Stair Estates Rephad Stranraer Dumfries and Galloway DG9 8BX

Two for the Price of One
with a full-paying adult

Cannot be used in conjunction with other offers. One voucher per party. Not valid on Bank Hols or special event days.

Valid until 30 Sept 2008.

DISCOUNT VOUCHER

Catalyst: Science Discovery Centre

Mersey Road Widnes Cheshire WA8 0DF

One Child Free
with a full-paying adult

Cannot be used in conjunction with other offers. One voucher per party. Not valid on Bank Hols or special event days.

Expires end Feb 2009 (unless otherwise specified)

DISCOUNT VOUCHER

1. Each voucher entitles the holder to the discount specified by the selected attraction.
2. Valid for use until 28/02/09 (unless otherwise specified, or if attraction season finishes prior to this). Vouchers are subject to the terms, conditions and restrictions of the selected attraction.
3. One voucher per party will be accepted, cannot be used in conjunction with any other offer, photocopies will not be accepted.
4. All attractions offering a discount have confirmed their willingness to participate. All information is subject to change without notice and should any attraction close or decline to accept a voucher for any reason, Days Out UK are not liable and cannot be held responsible.
5. Days Out UK shall not accept liability for any loss, accident or injury that may occur at a participating attraction and any dispute arising must be settled direct with the attraction concerned.
6. Cash redemption value of each voucher is 0.001p.
7. You are advised to check all relevant information with your chosen attraction before commencing your journey.

Days Out UK, PO Box 427, Northampton NN1 3YN. Tel: 01604 622445

1. Each voucher entitles the holder to the discount specified by the selected attraction.
2. Valid for use until 28/02/09 (unless otherwise specified. or if attraction season finishes prior to this). Vouchers are subject to the terms, conditions and restrictions of the selected attraction.
3. One voucher per party will be accepted, cannot be used in conjunction with any other offer, photocopies will not be accepted.
4. All attractions offering a discount have confirmed their willingness to participate. All information is subject to change without notice and should any attraction close or decline to accept a voucher for any reason, Days Out UK are not liable and cannot be held responsible.
5. Days Out UK shall not accept liability for any loss, accident or injury that may occur at a participating attraction and any dispute arising must be settled direct with the attraction concerned.
6. Cash redemption value of each voucher is 0.001p.
7. You are advised to check all relevant information with your chosen attraction before commencing your journey.

Days Out UK, PO Box 427, Northampton NN1 3YN. Tel: 01604 622445

1. Each voucher entitles the holder to the discount specified by the selected attraction.
2. Valid for use until 28/02/09 (unless otherwise specified, or if attraction season finishes prior to this). Vouchers are subject to the terms, conditions and restrictions of the selected attraction.
3. One voucher per party will be accepted, cannot be used in conjunction with any other offer, photocopies will not be accepted.
4. All attractions offering a discount have confirmed their willingness to participate. All information is subject to change without notice and should any attraction close or decline to accept a voucher for any reason, Days Out UK are not liable and cannot be held responsible.
5. Days Out UK shall not accept liability for any loss, accident or injury that may occur at a participating attraction and any dispute arising must be settled direct with the attraction concerned.
6. Cash redemption value of each voucher is 0.001p.
7. You are advised to check all relevant information with your chosen attraction before commencing your journey.

Days Out UK, PO Box 427, Northampton NN1 3YN. Tel: 01604 622445

1. Each voucher entitles the holder to the discount specified by the selected attraction.
2. Valid for use until 28/02/09 (unless otherwise specified, or if attraction season finishes prior to this). Vouchers are subject to the terms, conditions and restrictions of the selected attraction.
3. One voucher per party will be accepted, cannot be used in conjunction with any other offer, photocopies will not be accepted.
4. All attractions offering a discount have confirmed their willingness to participate. All information is subject to change without notice and should any attraction close or decline to accept a voucher for any reason, Days Out UK are not liable and cannot be held responsible.
5. Days Out UK shall not accept liability for any loss, accident or injury that may occur at a participating attraction and any dispute arising must be settled direct with the attraction concerned.
6. Cash redemption value of each voucher is 0.001p.
7. You are advised to check all relevant information with your chosen attraction before commencing your journey.

Days Out UK, PO Box 427, Northampton NN1 3YN. Tel: 01604 622445

1. Each voucher entitles the holder to the discount specified by the selected attraction.
2. Valid for use until 28/02/09 (unless otherwise specified, or if attraction season finishes prior to this). Vouchers are subject to the terms, conditions and restrictions of the selected attraction.
3. One voucher per party will be accepted, cannot be used in conjunction with any other offer, photocopies will not be accepted.
4. All attractions offering a discount have confirmed their willingness to participate. All information is subject to change without notice and should any attraction close or decline to accept a voucher for any reason, Days Out UK are not liable and cannot be held responsible.
5. Days Out UK shall not accept liability for any loss, accident or injury that may occur at a participating attraction and any dispute arising must be settled direct with the attraction concerned.
6. Cash redemption value of each voucher is 0.001p.
7. You are advised to check all relevant information with your chosen attraction before commencing your journey.

Days Out UK, PO Box 427, Northampton NN1 3YN. Tel: 01604 622445

Charles Dickens' Birthplace
393 Old Commercial Road Portsmouth Hampshire PO1 4QL

20% off Adult Admissions (A£2.80)

(Not valid on events days, maximum 2 discounted adults per transaction)

Cannot be used in conjunction with other offers. One voucher per party. Not valid on Bank Hols or special event days.

Expires end Feb 2009 (unless otherwise specified)

DISCOUNT VOUCHER

Chelsea Football Club Stadium Tours
Stamford Bridge Ground Fulham Road London SW6 1HS

One Child Free
with one full-paying adult

Cannot be used for pre-bookings, voucher must be presented on admission

Cannot be used in conjunction with other offers. One voucher per party. Not valid on Bank Hols or special event days.

Valid until 31 Dec 2008

DISCOUNT VOUCHER

City Cruises
Cherry Garden Pier Cherry Garden Street London SE16 4TU

One Child Free
with a full-paying adult

Cannot be used in conjunction with other offers. One voucher per party. Not valid on Bank Hols or special event days.

Expires end Feb 2009 (unless otherwise specified)

DISCOUNT VOUCHER

City of Caves
Upper Level Broad Marsh Shopping Centre Nottingham Nottinghamshire NG1 7LS

One Child Free
with a full-paying adult

Cannot be used in conjunction with other offers. One voucher per party. Not valid on Bank Hols or special event days.

Expires end Feb 2009 (unless otherwise specified)

DISCOUNT VOUCHER

Clearwell Caves Ancient Iron Mines
Royal Forest of Dean Coleford Gloucestershire GL16 8JR

One Child Free
with a full-paying adult

(Not valid for 'Christmas Fantasy' event)

Cannot be used in conjunction with other offers. One voucher per party. Not valid on Bank Hols or special event days.

Expires end Feb 2009 (unless otherwise specified)

DISCOUNT VOUCHER

Combe Martin Wildlife and Dinosaur Park
Combe Martin Ilfracombe Devon EX34 0NG

One Child Free
with every two full-paying adults

Cannot be used in conjunction with other offers. One voucher per party. Not valid on Bank Hols or special event days.

Expires end Feb 2009 (unless otherwise specified)

DISCOUNT VOUCHER

Compton Acres Gardens

164 Canford Cliffs Road Poole Dorset BH13 7ES

Two for the Price of One

with a full-paying adult

(Not valid on Bank Hols or pre-booked events)

Cannot be used in conjunction with other offers. One voucher per party. Not valid on Bank Hols or special event days.

Valid 1 Mar-31 Oct 2008

DISCOUNT VOUCHER

Compton Verney

Compton Verney Warwickshire CV35 9HZ

Get One Family Ticket Half-Price

Family ticket admits two adults and up to four children

Cannot be used in conjunction with other offers. One voucher per party. Not valid on Bank Hols or special event days.

Valid until 14th Dec 2008.

DISCOUNT VOUCHER

Connemara Heritage and History Centre and Dan O'Hara's Homestead

Lettershea Clifden County Galway Ireland

Two for the Price of One

with a full-paying adult

Cannot be used in conjunction with other offers. One voucher per party. Not valid on Bank Hols or special event days.

Expires end Feb 2009 (unless otherwise specified)

DISCOUNT VOUCHER

Coral Reef Water World

Nine Mile Ride Bracknell Berkshire RG12 7JQ

£5.00 off

One Full-Priced Family Ticket

Cannot be used in conjunction with other offers. One voucher per party. Not valid on Bank Hols or special event days.

Expires end Feb 2009 (unless otherwise specified)

DISCOUNT VOUCHER

Cornwall's Crealy Great Adventure Park

Tredinnick Newquay Cornwall PL27 7RA

One FREE tub of Candy Floss

(one voucher per party and per transaction Code: douk-08c)

Cannot be used in conjunction with other offers. One voucher per party. Not valid on Bank Hols or special event days.

Valid until 31st Aug 2008

DISCOUNT VOUCHER

Cotswold Farm Park

Guiting Power Stow on the Wold Cheltenham Gloucestershire GL54 5UG

One Child Free

with a full-paying adult

Cannot be used in conjunction with other offers. One voucher per party. Not valid on Bank Hols or special event days.

Expires end Feb 2009 (unless otherwise specified)

DISCOUNT VOUCHER

Coventry Transport Museum
Millennium Place Hales St Coventry Warwickshire CV1 1JD
10% discount on all gift shop purchases
when you spend £10.00 or more

Cannot be used in conjunction with other offers. One voucher per party. Not valid on Bank Hols or special event days.
Expires end Feb 2009 (unless otherwise specified)

DISCOUNT VOUCHER

Cowper and Newton Museum
Orchard Side Market Place Olney Bucks MK46 4AJ
Two for the Price of One
with a full-paying adult

Cannot be used in conjunction with other offers. One voucher per party. Not valid on Bank Hols or special event days.
Expires end Feb 2009 (unless otherwise specified)

DISCOUNT VOUCHER

Crabble Corn Mill
Lower Road River Dover Kent CT17 0UY
One Child Free
With A Paying Adult on Guided Tours of The Mill

Cannot be used in conjunction with other offers. One voucher per party. Not valid on Bank Hols or special event days.
Expires end Feb 2009 (unless otherwise specified)

DISCOUNT VOUCHER

Crich Tramway Village
Crich Matlock Derbyshire DE4 5DP
One Child Free
with every full-paying adult

Cannot be used in conjunction with other offers. One voucher per party. Not valid on Bank Hols or special event days.
Expires end Feb 2009 (unless otherwise specified)

DISCOUNT VOUCHER

D-Day Museum and Overlord Embroidery
Clarence Esplanade Southsea Hampshire PO5 3NT
20% off Adult Admissions (A£4.80)
(Not valid on event days, maximum 4 discounted adults per transaction)

Cannot be used in conjunction with other offers. One voucher per party. Not valid on Bank Hols or special event days.
Expires end Feb 2009 (unless otherwise specified)

DISCOUNT VOUCHER

Darlington Railway Centre and Museum
North Road Station Station Road Darlington County Durham DL3 6ST
Two for the Price of One
with a full-paying adult

Cannot be used in conjunction with other offers. One voucher per party. Not valid on Bank Hols or special event days.
Expires end Feb 2009 (unless otherwise specified)

DISCOUNT VOUCHER

DISCOUNT VOUCHER

Dartington Crystal
Linden Close Torrington Devon EX38 7AN
Two for the Price of One
with a full-paying adult
Cannot be used in conjunction with other offers. One voucher per party. Not valid on Bank Hols or special event days.
Expires end Feb 2009 (unless otherwise specified)

DISCOUNT VOUCHER

Dean Forest Railway
Norchard Station Forest Rd Lydney Gloucestershire GL15 4ET
One Child Free
with a full-paying adult
Cannot be used in conjunction with other offers. One voucher per party. Not valid on Bank Hols or special event days.
Valid until 31st Oct 2008

DISCOUNT VOUCHER

Denby Pottery Visitor Centre
Derby Road Denby Ripley Derbyshire DE5 8NX
Two for the Price of One
with a full-paying adult
(Applies to Factory Tours, lowest priced ticket goes free, one per party)
Cannot be used in conjunction with other offers. One voucher per party. Not valid on Bank Hols or special event days.
Expires end Feb 2009 (unless otherwise specified)

DISCOUNT VOUCHER

Denmans Garden
Denmans Garden Fontwell West Sussex BN18 0SU
Two for the Price of One
with a full-paying adult
(Excluding weekends and Bank Holidays, no cash alternative)
Cannot be used in conjunction with other offers. One voucher per party. Not valid on Bank Hols or special event days.
Expires end Feb 2009 (unless otherwise specified)

DISCOUNT VOUCHER

Devon's Crealy Great Adventure Park
Sidmouth Road Clyst St Mary Exeter Devon EX5 1DR
One FREE Go-Kart Ride
Code: douk-08d
Cannot be used in conjunction with other offers. One voucher per party. Not valid on Bank Hols or special event days.
Valid until 31st Aug 08

DISCOUNT VOUCHER

Didcot Railway Centre
Didcot Oxfordshire OX11 7NJ
Two for the Price of One
with a full-paying adult
(Not valid for 'Days Out with Thomas' or 'Santa Specials')
Cannot be used in conjunction with other offers. One voucher per party. Not valid on Bank Hols or special event days.
Expires end Feb 2009 (unless otherwise specified)

1. Each voucher entitles the holder to the discount specified by the selected attraction.
2. Valid for use until 28/02/09 (unless otherwise specified, or if attraction season finishes prior to this). Vouchers are subject to the terms, conditions and restrictions of the selected attraction.
3. One voucher per party will be accepted, cannot be used in conjunction with any other offer, photocopies will not be accepted.
4. All attractions offering a discount have confirmed their willingness to participate. All information is subject to change without notice and should any attraction close or decline to accept a voucher for any reason, Days Out UK are not liable and cannot be held responsible.
5. Days Out UK shall not accept liability for any loss, accident or injury that may occur at a participating attraction and any dispute arising must be settled direct with the attraction concerned.
6. Cash redemption value of each voucher is 0.001p.
7. You are advised to check all relevant information with your chosen attraction before commencing your journey.

Days Out UK, PO Box 427, Northampton NN1 3YN. Tel: 01604 622445

1. Each voucher entitles the holder to the discount specified by the selected attraction.
2. Valid for use until 28/02/09 (unless otherwise specified. or if attraction season finishes prior to this). Vouchers are subject to the terms, conditions and restrictions of the selected attraction.
3. One voucher per party will be accepted, cannot be used in conjunction with any other offer, photocopies will not be accepted.
4. All attractions offering a discount have confirmed their willingness to participate. All information is subject to change without notice and should any attraction close or decline to accept a voucher for any reason, Days Out UK are not liable and cannot be held responsible.
5. Days Out UK shall not accept liability for any loss, accident or injury that may occur at a participating attraction and any dispute arising must be settled direct with the attraction concerned.
6. Cash redemption value of each voucher is 0.001p.
7. You are advised to check all relevant information with your chosen attraction before commencing your journey.

Days Out UK, PO Box 427, Northampton NN1 3YN. Tel: 01604 622445

1. Each voucher entitles the holder to the discount specified by the selected attraction.
2. Valid for use until 28/02/09 (unless otherwise specified, or if attraction season finishes prior to this). Vouchers are subject to the terms, conditions and restrictions of the selected attraction.
3. One voucher per party will be accepted, cannot be used in conjunction with any other offer, photocopies will not be accepted.
4. All attractions offering a discount have confirmed their willingness to participate. All information is subject to change without notice and should any attraction close or decline to accept a voucher for any reason, Days Out UK are not liable and cannot be held responsible.
5. Days Out UK shall not accept liability for any loss, accident or injury that may occur at a participating attraction and any dispute arising must be settled direct with the attraction concerned.
6. Cash redemption value of each voucher is 0.001p.
7. You are advised to check all relevant information with your chosen attraction before commencing your journey.

Days Out UK, PO Box 427, Northampton NN1 3YN. Tel: 01604 622445

1. Each voucher entitles the holder to the discount specified by the selected attraction.
2. Valid for use until 28/02/09 (unless otherwise specified, or if attraction season finishes prior to this). Vouchers are subject to the terms, conditions and restrictions of the selected attraction.
3. One voucher per party will be accepted, cannot be used in conjunction with any other offer, photocopies will not be accepted.
4. All attractions offering a discount have confirmed their willingness to participate. All information is subject to change without notice and should any attraction close or decline to accept a voucher for any reason, Days Out UK are not liable and cannot be held responsible.
5. Days Out UK shall not accept liability for any loss, accident or injury that may occur at a participating attraction and any dispute arising must be settled direct with the attraction concerned.
6. Cash redemption value of each voucher is 0.001p.
7. You are advised to check all relevant information with your chosen attraction before commencing your journey.

Days Out UK, PO Box 427, Northampton NN1 3YN. Tel: 01604 622445

1. Each voucher entitles the holder to the discount specified by the selected attraction.
2. Valid for use until 28/02/09 (unless otherwise specified, or if attraction season finishes prior to this). Vouchers are subject to the terms, conditions and restrictions of the selected attraction.
3. One voucher per party will be accepted, cannot be used in conjunction with any other offer, photocopies will not be accepted.
4. All attractions offering a discount have confirmed their willingness to participate. All information is subject to change without notice and should any attraction close or decline to accept a voucher for any reason, Days Out UK are not liable and cannot be held responsible.
5. Days Out UK shall not accept liability for any loss, accident or injury that may occur at a participating attraction and any dispute arising must be settled direct with the attraction concerned.
6. Cash redemption value of each voucher is 0.001p.
7. You are advised to check all relevant information with your chosen attraction before commencing your journey.

Days Out UK, PO Box 427, Northampton NN1 3YN. Tel: 01604 622445

DIG - An Archaeological Adventure
St Saviour's Church St. Saviourgate York North Yorkshire YO1 8NN
One Child Free
with two full-paying adults
(Valid Mon-Fri 10.00-15.30)

Cannot be used in conjunction with other offers. One voucher per party. Not valid on Bank Hols or special event days.
Expires end Feb 2009 (unless otherwise specified)

DISCOUNT VOUCHER

Diggerland
Medway Valley Leisure Park Roman Way Strood Kent ME2 2NU
10% off Admission Prices (A&C£13.50)
(Maximum six discounted people per party, not valid on Bank Holidays)

Cannot be used in conjunction with other offers. One voucher per party. Not valid on Bank Hols or special event days.
Expires end Feb 2009 (unless otherwise specified)

DISCOUNT VOUCHER

Diggerland
Langley Park County Durham DH7 9TT
10% off Admission Prices (A&C£13.50)
(Maximum six discounted people per party, not valid on Bank Holidays)

Cannot be used in conjunction with other offers. One voucher per party. Not valid on Bank Hols or special event days.
Expires end Feb 2009 (unless otherwise specified)

DISCOUNT VOUCHER

Diggerland
Verbeer Manor Cullompton Devon EX15 2PE
10% off Admission Prices (A&C£13.50)
(Maximum six discounted people per party, not valid on Bank Holidays)

Cannot be used in conjunction with other offers. One voucher per party. Not valid on Bank Hols or special event days.
Expires end Feb 2009 (unless otherwise specified)

DISCOUNT VOUCHER

Diggerland
Willowbridge Lane Whitwood Castleford Yorkshire WF10 5NW
10% off Admission Prices (A&C£13.50)
(Maximum six discounted people per party, not valid on Bank Holidays)

Cannot be used in conjunction with other offers. One voucher per party. Not valid on Bank Hols or special event days.
Expires end Feb 2009 (unless otherwise specified)

DISCOUNT VOUCHER

Dinosaur Isle
Culver Parade Sandown Isle of Wight PO36 8QA
One Child Free
with every full-paying adult

Cannot be used in conjunction with other offers. One voucher per party. Not valid on Bank Hols or special event days.
Expires end Feb 2009 (unless otherwise specified)

DISCOUNT VOUCHER

1. Each voucher entitles the holder to the discount specified by the selected attraction.
2. Valid for use until 28/02/09 (unless otherwise specified, or if attraction season finishes prior to this). Vouchers are subject to the terms, conditions and restrictions of the selected attraction.
3. One voucher per party will be accepted, cannot be used in conjunction with any other offer, photocopies will not be accepted.
4. All attractions offering a discount have confirmed their willingness to participate. All information is subject to change without notice and should any attraction close or decline to accept a voucher for any reason, Days Out UK are not liable and cannot be held responsible.
5. Days Out UK shall not accept liability for any loss, accident or injury that may occur at a participating attraction and any dispute arising must be settled direct with the attraction concerned.
6. Cash redemption value of each voucher is 0.001p.
7. You are advised to check all relevant information with your chosen attraction before commencing your journey.

Days Out UK, PO Box 427, Northampton NN1 3YN. Tel: 01604 622445

1. Each voucher entitles the holder to the discount specified by the selected attraction.
2. Valid for use until 28/02/09 (unless otherwise specified, or if attraction season finishes prior to this). Vouchers are subject to the terms, conditions and restrictions of the selected attraction.
3. One voucher per party will be accepted, cannot be used in conjunction with any other offer, photocopies will not be accepted.
4. All attractions offering a discount have confirmed their willingness to participate. All information is subject to change without notice and should any attraction close or decline to accept a voucher for any reason, Days Out UK are not liable and cannot be held responsible.
5. Days Out UK shall not accept liability for any loss, accident or injury that may occur at a participating attraction and any dispute arising must be settled direct with the attraction concerned.
6. Cash redemption value of each voucher is 0.001p.
7. You are advised to check all relevant information with your chosen attraction before commencing your journey.

Days Out UK, PO Box 427, Northampton NN1 3YN. Tel: 01604 622445

1. Each voucher entitles the holder to the discount specified by the selected attraction.
2. Valid for use until 28/02/09 (unless otherwise specified, or if attraction season finishes prior to this). Vouchers are subject to the terms, conditions and restrictions of the selected attraction.
3. One voucher per party will be accepted, cannot be used in conjunction with any other offer, photocopies will not be accepted.
4. All attractions offering a discount have confirmed their willingness to participate. All information is subject to change without notice and should any attraction close or decline to accept a voucher for any reason, Days Out UK are not liable and cannot be held responsible.
5. Days Out UK shall not accept liability for any loss, accident or injury that may occur at a participating attraction and any dispute arising must be settled direct with the attraction concerned.
6. Cash redemption value of each voucher is 0.001p.
7. You are advised to check all relevant information with your chosen attraction before commencing your journey.

Days Out UK, PO Box 427, Northampton NN1 3YN. Tel: 01604 622445

1. Each voucher entitles the holder to the discount specified by the selected attraction.
2. Valid for use until 28/02/09 (unless otherwise specified, or if attraction season finishes prior to this). Vouchers are subject to the terms, conditions and restrictions of the selected attraction.
3. One voucher per party will be accepted, cannot be used in conjunction with any other offer, photocopies will not be accepted.
4. All attractions offering a discount have confirmed their willingness to participate. All information is subject to change without notice and should any attraction close or decline to accept a voucher for any reason, Days Out UK are not liable and cannot be held responsible.
5. Days Out UK shall not accept liability for any loss, accident or injury that may occur at a participating attraction and any dispute arising must be settled direct with the attraction concerned.
6. Cash redemption value of each voucher is 0.001p.
7. You are advised to check all relevant information with your chosen attraction before commencing your journey.

Days Out UK, PO Box 427, Northampton NN1 3YN. Tel: 01604 622445

1. Each voucher entitles the holder to the discount specified by the selected attraction.
2. Valid for use until 28/02/09 (unless otherwise specified, or if attraction season finishes prior to this). Vouchers are subject to the terms, conditions and restrictions of the selected attraction.
3. One voucher per party will be accepted, cannot be used in conjunction with any other offer, photocopies will not be accepted.
4. All attractions offering a discount have confirmed their willingness to participate. All information is subject to change without notice and should any attraction close or decline to accept a voucher for any reason, Days Out UK are not liable and cannot be held responsible.
5. Days Out UK shall not accept liability for any loss, accident or injury that may occur at a participating attraction and any dispute arising must be settled direct with the attraction concerned.
6. Cash redemption value of each voucher is 0.001p.
7. You are advised to check all relevant information with your chosen attraction before commencing your journey.

Days Out UK, PO Box 427, Northampton NN1 3YN. Tel: 01604 622445

Dudley Zoological Gardens

2 The Broadway Dudley West Midlands DY1 4QB

One Child Free

with a full-paying adult

Cannot be used in conjunction with other offers. One voucher per party. Not valid on Bank Hols or special event days.

Expires end Feb 2009 (unless otherwise specified)

Dulwich Picture Gallery

Gallery Road Dulwich London SE21 7AD

Two for the Price of One

with a full-paying adult

Cannot be used in conjunction with other offers. One voucher per party. Not valid on Bank Hols or special event days.

Expires end Feb 2009 (unless otherwise specified)

Dylan Thomas Boat House

Dylan's Walk Laugharne Carmarthenshire SA33 4SD

One Child Free

with a full-paying adult

Cannot be used in conjunction with other offers. One voucher per party. Not valid on Bank Hols or special event days.

Expires end Feb 2009 (unless otherwise specified)

East Lancashire Railway

Bolton Street Station Bolton Street Bury Greater Manchester BL9 0EY

Two for the Price of One

with a full-paying adult

Cannot be used in conjunction with other offers. One voucher per party. Not valid on Bank Hols or special event days.

Expires end Feb 2009 (unless otherwise specified)

Eastbourne Beer Festival

Winter Garden Compton Street Eastbourne East Sussex BN21 4JJ

£1.00 off individual admissions

(Quote 'Days Out UK' when booking, valid for evening session on the 9th & lunchtime session on the 11th Oct, not valid on the 10th Oct 2008, voucher to be presented at time of purchase)

Cannot be used in conjunction with other offers. One voucher per party. Not valid on Bank Hols or special event days.

Expires end Feb 2009 (unless otherwise specified)

Eastnor Castle

Eastnor Ledbury Herefordshire HR8 1RL

Two for the Price of One

with full-paying adult

Cannot be used in conjunction with other offers. One voucher per party. Not valid on Bank Hols or special event days.

Expires end Feb 2009 (unless otherwise specified)

1. Each voucher entitles the holder to the discount specified by the selected attraction.
2. Valid for use until 28/02/09 (unless otherwise specified, or if attraction season finishes prior to this). Vouchers are subject to the terms, conditions and restrictions of the selected attraction.
3. One voucher per party will be accepted, cannot be used in conjunction with any other offer, photocopies will not be accepted.
4. All attractions offering a discount have confirmed their willingness to participate. All information is subject to change without notice and should any attraction close or decline to accept a voucher for any reason, Days Out UK are not liable and cannot be held responsible.
5. Days Out UK shall not accept liability for any loss, accident or injury that may occur at a participating attraction and any dispute arising must be settled direct with the attraction concerned.
6. Cash redemption value of each voucher is 0.001p.
7. You are advised to check all relevant information with your chosen attraction before commencing your journey.

Days Out UK, PO Box 427, Northampton NN1 3YN. Tel: 01604 622445

1. Each voucher entitles the holder to the discount specified by the selected attraction.
2. Valid for use until 28/02/09 (unless otherwise specified. or if attraction season finishes prior to this). Vouchers are subject to the terms, conditions and restrictions of the selected attraction.
3. One voucher per party will be accepted, cannot be used in conjunction with any other offer, photocopies will not be accepted.
4. All attractions offering a discount have confirmed their willingness to participate. All information is subject to change without notice and should any attraction close or decline to accept a voucher for any reason, Days Out UK are not liable and cannot be held responsible.
5. Days Out UK shall not accept liability for any loss, accident or injury that may occur at a participating attraction and any dispute arising must be settled direct with the attraction concerned.
6. Cash redemption value of each voucher is 0.001p.
7. You are advised to check all relevant information with your chosen attraction before commencing your journey.

Days Out UK, PO Box 427, Northampton NN1 3YN. Tel: 01604 622445

1. Each voucher entitles the holder to the discount specified by the selected attraction.
2. Valid for use until 28/02/09 (unless otherwise specified, or if attraction season finishes prior to this). Vouchers are subject to the terms, conditions and restrictions of the selected attraction.
3. One voucher per party will be accepted, cannot be used in conjunction with any other offer, photocopies will not be accepted.
4. All attractions offering a discount have confirmed their willingness to participate. All information is subject to change without notice and should any attraction close or decline to accept a voucher for any reason, Days Out UK are not liable and cannot be held responsible.
5. Days Out UK shall not accept liability for any loss, accident or injury that may occur at a participating attraction and any dispute arising must be settled direct with the attraction concerned.
6. Cash redemption value of each voucher is 0.001p.
7. You are advised to check all relevant information with your chosen attraction before commencing your journey.

Days Out UK, PO Box 427, Northampton NN1 3YN. Tel: 01604 622445

1. Each voucher entitles the holder to the discount specified by the selected attraction.
2. Valid for use until 28/02/09 (unless otherwise specified, or if attraction season finishes prior to this). Vouchers are subject to the terms, conditions and restrictions of the selected attraction.
3. One voucher per party will be accepted, cannot be used in conjunction with any other offer, photocopies will not be accepted.
4. All attractions offering a discount have confirmed their willingness to participate. All information is subject to change without notice and should any attraction close or decline to accept a voucher for any reason, Days Out UK are not liable and cannot be held responsible.
5. Days Out UK shall not accept liability for any loss, accident or injury that may occur at a participating attraction and any dispute arising must be settled direct with the attraction concerned.
6. Cash redemption value of each voucher is 0.001p.
7. You are advised to check all relevant information with your chosen attraction before commencing your journey.

Days Out UK, PO Box 427, Northampton NN1 3YN. Tel: 01604 622445

1. Each voucher entitles the holder to the discount specified by the selected attraction.
2. Valid for use until 28/02/09 (unless otherwise specified, or if attraction season finishes prior to this). Vouchers are subject to the terms, conditions and restrictions of the selected attraction.
3. One voucher per party will be accepted, cannot be used in conjunction with any other offer, photocopies will not be accepted.
4. All attractions offering a discount have confirmed their willingness to participate. All information is subject to change without notice and should any attraction close or decline to accept a voucher for any reason, Days Out UK are not liable and cannot be held responsible.
5. Days Out UK shall not accept liability for any loss, accident or injury that may occur at a participating attraction and any dispute arising must be settled direct with the attraction concerned.
6. Cash redemption value of each voucher is 0.001p.
7. You are advised to check all relevant information with your chosen attraction before commencing your journey.

Days Out UK, PO Box 427, Northampton NN1 3YN. Tel: 01604 622445

Edinburgh Butterfly and Insect World
Dobbies Garden World Melville Nursery Lasswade Midlothian
EH18 1AZ
One Child Free
with a full-paying adult

Cannot be used in conjunction with other offers. One voucher per party. Not valid on Bank Hols or special event days.
Expires end Feb 2009 (unless otherwise specified)

DISCOUNT VOUCHER

Edinburgh Dungeon
31 Market Street Edinburgh EH1 1QB
One Child Free
with every full-paying adult

Cannot be used in conjunction with other offers. One voucher per party. Not valid on Bank Hols or special event days.
Expires end Feb 2009 (unless otherwise specified)

DISCOUNT VOUCHER

Escot Gardens, Maze and Fantasy Woodland
Escot Fairmile Nr Ottery St Mary Devon EX11 1LU
One Child Free
with a full-paying adult

Cannot be used in conjunction with other offers. One voucher per party. Not valid on Bank Hols or special event days.
Expires end Feb 2009 (unless otherwise specified)

DISCOUNT VOUCHER

Eureka! The Museum for Children
Discovery Road Halifax West Yorkshire HX1 2NE
Two for the Price of One
with a full-paying adult

(One discount per transaction, cheapest ticket goes free, Code 437)

Cannot be used in conjunction with other offers. One voucher per party. Not valid on Bank Hols or special event days.
Expires end Feb 2009 (unless otherwise specified)

DISCOUNT VOUCHER

Explosion! The Museum of Naval Firepower
Priddy's Hard Heritage Way Gosport Hampshire PO12 4LE
Two for the Price of One
with a full-paying adult

Cannot be used in conjunction with other offers. One voucher per party. Not valid on Bank Hols or special event days.
Expires end Feb 2009 (unless otherwise specified)

DISCOUNT VOUCHER

Fairhaven Woodland and Water Garden
School Road South Walsham Norwich Norfolk NR13 6DZ
Two for the Price of One
with a full-paying adult

(Cannot be used on special event days, voucher must be produced on admission)

Cannot be used in conjunction with other offers. One voucher per party. Not valid on Bank Hols or special event days.
Expires end Feb 2009 (unless otherwise specified)

DISCOUNT VOUCHER

1. Each voucher entitles the holder to the discount specified by the selected attraction.
2. Valid for use until 28/02/09 (unless otherwise specified, or if attraction season finishes prior to this). Vouchers are subject to the terms, conditions and restrictions of the selected attraction.
3. One voucher per party will be accepted, cannot be used in conjunction with any other offer, photocopies will not be accepted.
4. All attractions offering a discount have confirmed their willingness to participate. All information is subject to change without notice and should any attraction close or decline to accept a voucher for any reason, Days Out UK are not liable and cannot be held responsible.
5. Days Out UK shall not accept liability for any loss, accident or injury that may occur at a participating attraction and any dispute arising must be settled direct with the attraction concerned.
6. Cash redemption value of each voucher is 0.001p.
7. You are advised to check all relevant information with your chosen attraction before commencing your journey.

Days Out UK, PO Box 427, Northampton NN1 3YN. Tel: 01604 622445

1. Each voucher entitles the holder to the discount specified by the selected attraction.
2. Valid for use until 28/02/09 (unless otherwise specified, or if attraction season finishes prior to this). Vouchers are subject to the terms, conditions and restrictions of the selected attraction.
3. One voucher per party will be accepted, cannot be used in conjunction with any other offer, photocopies will not be accepted.
4. All attractions offering a discount have confirmed their willingness to participate. All information is subject to change without notice and should any attraction close or decline to accept a voucher for any reason, Days Out UK are not liable and cannot be held responsible.
5. Days Out UK shall not accept liability for any loss, accident or injury that may occur at a participating attraction and any dispute arising must be settled direct with the attraction concerned.
6. Cash redemption value of each voucher is 0.001p.
7. You are advised to check all relevant information with your chosen attraction before commencing your journey.

Days Out UK, PO Box 427, Northampton NN1 3YN. Tel: 01604 622445

1. Each voucher entitles the holder to the discount specified by the selected attraction.
2. Valid for use until 28/02/09 (unless otherwise specified. or if attraction season finishes prior to this). Vouchers are subject to the terms, conditions and restrictions of the selected attraction.
3. One voucher per party will be accepted, cannot be used in conjunction with any other offer, photocopies will not be accepted.
4. All attractions offering a discount have confirmed their willingness to participate. All information is subject to change without notice and should any attraction close or decline to accept a voucher for any reason, Days Out UK are not liable and cannot be held responsible.
5. Days Out UK shall not accept liability for any loss, accident or injury that may occur at a participating attraction and any dispute arising must be settled direct with the attraction concerned.
6. Cash redemption value of each voucher is 0.001p.
7. You are advised to check all relevant information with your chosen attraction before commencing your journey.

Days Out UK, PO Box 427, Northampton NN1 3YN. Tel: 01604 622445

1. Each voucher entitles the holder to the discount specified by the selected attraction.
2. Valid for use until 28/02/09 (unless otherwise specified, or if attraction season finishes prior to this). Vouchers are subject to the terms, conditions and restrictions of the selected attraction.
3. One voucher per party will be accepted, cannot be used in conjunction with any other offer, photocopies will not be accepted.
4. All attractions offering a discount have confirmed their willingness to participate. All information is subject to change without notice and should any attraction close or decline to accept a voucher for any reason, Days Out UK are not liable and cannot be held responsible.
5. Days Out UK shall not accept liability for any loss, accident or injury that may occur at a participating attraction and any dispute arising must be settled direct with the attraction concerned.
6. Cash redemption value of each voucher is 0.001p.
7. You are advised to check all relevant information with your chosen attraction before commencing your journey.

Days Out UK, PO Box 427, Northampton NN1 3YN. Tel: 01604 622445

1. Each voucher entitles the holder to the discount specified by the selected attraction.
2. Valid for use until 28/02/09 (unless otherwise specified, or if attraction season finishes prior to this). Vouchers are subject to the terms, conditions and restrictions of the selected attraction.
3. One voucher per party will be accepted, cannot be used in conjunction with any other offer, photocopies will not be accepted.
4. All attractions offering a discount have confirmed their willingness to participate. All information is subject to change without notice and should any attraction close or decline to accept a voucher for any reason, Days Out UK are not liable and cannot be held responsible.
5. Days Out UK shall not accept liability for any loss, accident or injury that may occur at a participating attraction and any dispute arising must be settled direct with the attraction concerned.
6. Cash redemption value of each voucher is 0.001p.
7. You are advised to check all relevant information with your chosen attraction before commencing your journey.

Days Out UK, PO Box 427, Northampton NN1 3YN. Tel: 01604 622445

1. Each voucher entitles the holder to the discount specified by the selected attraction.
2. Valid for use until 28/02/09 (unless otherwise specified, or if attraction season finishes prior to this). Vouchers are subject to the terms, conditions and restrictions of the selected attraction.
3. One voucher per party will be accepted, cannot be used in conjunction with any other offer, photocopies will not be accepted.
4. All attractions offering a discount have confirmed their willingness to participate. All information is subject to change without notice and should any attraction close or decline to accept a voucher for any reason, Days Out UK are not liable and cannot be held responsible.
5. Days Out UK shall not accept liability for any loss, accident or injury that may occur at a participating attraction and any dispute arising must be settled direct with the attraction concerned.
6. Cash redemption value of each voucher is 0.001p.
7. You are advised to check all relevant information with your chosen attraction before commencing your journey.

Days Out UK, PO Box 427, Northampton NN1 3YN. Tel: 01604 622445

Felbrigg Hall

Felbrigg Norwich Norfolk NR11 8PR

One Child Free

with a full-paying adult

Cannot be used in conjunction with other offers. One voucher per party. Not valid on Bank Hols or special event days.

Expires end Feb 2009 (unless otherwise specified)

Felinwynt Rainforest Centre

Felinwynt Cardigan Ceredigion SA43 1RT

Two for the Price of One

with a full-paying adult

Cannot be used in conjunction with other offers. One voucher per party. Not valid on Bank Hols or special event days.

Expires end Feb 2009 (unless otherwise specified)

Fishbourne Roman Palace

Salthill Road Fishbourne Chichester West Sussex PO19 3QR

Buy One Full-Priced Adult, Senior or Student Ticket and Get Another Ticket Half-Price

(The half-price ticket must be of equal or lesser value,
not valid on any special event days, please see website for dates of events)

Cannot be used in conjunction with other offers. One voucher per party. Not valid on Bank Hols or special event days.

Expires end Feb 2009 (unless otherwise specified)

Flambards Experience

Helston Cornwall TR13 0QA

One Child Free

when accompanied by a full-paying adult

(Maximum 2 children per transaction, not valid 29 Oct 2008)

Cannot be used in conjunction with other offers. One voucher per party. Not valid on Bank Hols or special event days.

Valid 18 Mar-1 Nov 2008

Fleet Air Arm Museum

Royal Naval Air Station Yeovilton Yeovil Somerset BA22 8HT

One Child Free

with every full-paying adult

Cannot be used in conjunction with other offers. One voucher per party. Not valid on Bank Hols or special event days.

Expires end Feb 2009 (unless otherwise specified)

Ford Green Hall

Ford Green Rd Smallthorne Stoke-on-Trent Staffs ST6 1NG

Two for the Price of One

with a full-paying adult

(Excludes evening events and children's activities)

Cannot be used in conjunction with other offers. One voucher per party. Not valid on Bank Hols or special event days.

Expires end Feb 2009 (unless otherwise specified)

1. Each voucher entitles the holder to the discount specified by the selected attraction.
2. Valid for use until 28/02/09 (unless otherwise specified, or if attraction season finishes prior to this). Vouchers are subject to the terms, conditions and restrictions of the selected attraction.
3. One voucher per party will be accepted, cannot be used in conjunction with any other offer, photocopies will not be accepted.
4. All attractions offering a discount have confirmed their willingness to participate. All information is subject to change without notice and should any attraction close or decline to accept a voucher for any reason, Days Out UK are not liable and cannot be held responsible.
5. Days Out UK shall not accept liability for any loss, accident or injury that may occur at a participating attraction and any dispute arising must be settled direct with the attraction concerned.
6. Cash redemption value of each voucher is 0.001p.
7. You are advised to check all relevant information with your chosen attraction before commencing your journey.

Days Out UK, PO Box 427, Northampton NN1 3YN. Tel: 01604 622445

1. Each voucher entitles the holder to the discount specified by the selected attraction.
2. Valid for use until 28/02/09 (unless otherwise specified, or if attraction season finishes prior to this). Vouchers are subject to the terms, conditions and restrictions of the selected attraction.
3. One voucher per party will be accepted, cannot be used in conjunction with any other offer, photocopies will not be accepted.
4. All attractions offering a discount have confirmed their willingness to participate. All information is subject to change without notice and should any attraction close or decline to accept a voucher for any reason, Days Out UK are not liable and cannot be held responsible.
5. Days Out UK shall not accept liability for any loss, accident or injury that may occur at a participating attraction and any dispute arising must be settled direct with the attraction concerned.
6. Cash redemption value of each voucher is 0.001p.
7. You are advised to check all relevant information with your chosen attraction before commencing your journey.

Days Out UK, PO Box 427, Northampton NN1 3YN. Tel: 01604 622445

1. Each voucher entitles the holder to the discount specified by the selected attraction.
2. Valid for use until 28/02/09 (unless otherwise specified, or if attraction season finishes prior to this). Vouchers are subject to the terms, conditions and restrictions of the selected attraction.
3. One voucher per party will be accepted, cannot be used in conjunction with any other offer, photocopies will not be accepted.
4. All attractions offering a discount have confirmed their willingness to participate. All information is subject to change without notice and should any attraction close or decline to accept a voucher for any reason, Days Out UK are not liable and cannot be held responsible.
5. Days Out UK shall not accept liability for any loss, accident or injury that may occur at a participating attraction and any dispute arising must be settled direct with the attraction concerned.
6. Cash redemption value of each voucher is 0.001p.
7. You are advised to check all relevant information with your chosen attraction before commencing your journey.

Days Out UK, PO Box 427, Northampton NN1 3YN. Tel: 01604 622445

1. Each voucher entitles the holder to the discount specified by the selected attraction.
2. Valid for use until 28/02/09 (unless otherwise specified, or if attraction season finishes prior to this). Vouchers are subject to the terms, conditions and restrictions of the selected attraction.
3. One voucher per party will be accepted, cannot be used in conjunction with any other offer, photocopies will not be accepted.
4. All attractions offering a discount have confirmed their willingness to participate. All information is subject to change without notice and should any attraction close or decline to accept a voucher for any reason, Days Out UK are not liable and cannot be held responsible.
5. Days Out UK shall not accept liability for any loss, accident or injury that may occur at a participating attraction and any dispute arising must be settled direct with the attraction concerned.
6. Cash redemption value of each voucher is 0.001p.
7. You are advised to check all relevant information with your chosen attraction before commencing your journey.

Days Out UK, PO Box 427, Northampton NN1 3YN. Tel: 01604 622445

1. Each voucher entitles the holder to the discount specified by the selected attraction.
2. Valid for use until 28/02/09 (unless otherwise specified, or if attraction season finishes prior to this). Vouchers are subject to the terms, conditions and restrictions of the selected attraction.
3. One voucher per party will be accepted, cannot be used in conjunction with any other offer, photocopies will not be accepted.
4. All attractions offering a discount have confirmed their willingness to participate. All information is subject to change without notice and should any attraction close or decline to accept a voucher for any reason, Days Out UK are not liable and cannot be held responsible.
5. Days Out UK shall not accept liability for any loss, accident or injury that may occur at a participating attraction and any dispute arising must be settled direct with the attraction concerned.
6. Cash redemption value of each voucher is 0.001p.
7. You are advised to check all relevant information with your chosen attraction before commencing your journey.

Days Out UK, PO Box 427, Northampton NN1 3YN. Tel: 01604 622445

Forge Mill Needle Museum and Bordesley Abbey Visitor Centre
Needle Mill Lane Riverside Redditch Worcestershire B98 8HY

Two for the Price of One
with a full-paying adult

Cannot be used in conjunction with other offers. One voucher per party. Not valid on Bank Hols or special event days.

Expires end Feb 2009 (unless otherwise specified)

DISCOUNT VOUCHER

Fort Paull
Battery Road Paull Nr Hull East Riding of Yorkshire HU12 8FP

One Child Free
with a full-paying adult

Cannot be used in conjunction with other offers. One voucher per party. Not valid on Bank Hols or special event days.

Expires end Feb 2009 (unless otherwise specified)

DISCOUNT VOUCHER

Galloway Wildlife Conservation Park
Lochfergus Plantation Kirkcudbright Dumfries and Galloway DG6 4XX

One Child Free
with every full paying adult
(Not valid on Easter weekend or Bank Holidays)

Cannot be used in conjunction with other offers. One voucher per party. Not valid on Bank Hols or special event days.

Expires end Feb 2009 (unless otherwise specified)

DISCOUNT VOUCHER

Gardens and Grounds of Herstmonceux Castle
Herstmonceux Hailsham East Sussex BN27 1RN

One Child Free
with every full-paying adult

(Cannot be used on special event days, valid for Gardens & Grounds only)
Cannot be used in conjunction with other offers. One voucher per party. Not valid on Bank Hols or special event days.

Expires end Feb 2009 (unless otherwise specified)

DISCOUNT VOUCHER

Gladstone Pottery Museum
Uttoxeter Road Longton Stoke-On-Trent Staffs ST3 1PQ

Two for the Price of One
with a full-paying adult

Cannot be used in conjunction with other offers. One voucher per party. Not valid on Bank Hols or special event days.

Expires end Feb 2009 (unless otherwise specified)

DISCOUNT VOUCHER

Gloucestershire Warwickshire Railway
The Railway Station Toddington Cheltenham Gloucestershire GL54 5DT

Two for the Price of One
with a full-paying adult

Cannot be used in conjunction with other offers. One voucher per party. Not valid on Bank Hols or special event days.

Valid until 1 Jan 2009

DISCOUNT VOUCHER

1. Each voucher entitles the holder to the discount specified by the selected attraction.
2. Valid for use until 28/02/09 (unless otherwise specified, or if attraction season finishes prior to this). Vouchers are subject to the terms, conditions and restrictions of the selected attraction.
3. One voucher per party will be accepted, cannot be used in conjunction with any other offer, photocopies will not be accepted.
4. All attractions offering a discount have confirmed their willingness to participate. All information is subject to change without notice and should any attraction close or decline to accept a voucher for any reason, Days Out UK are not liable and cannot be held responsible.
5. Days Out UK shall not accept liability for any loss, accident or injury that may occur at a participating attraction and any dispute arising must be settled direct with the attraction concerned.
6. Cash redemption value of each voucher is 0.001p.
7. You are advised to check all relevant information with your chosen attraction before commencing your journey.

Days Out UK, PO Box 427, Northampton NN1 3YN. Tel: 01604 622445

1. Each voucher entitles the holder to the discount specified by the selected attraction.
2. Valid for use until 28/02/09 (unless otherwise specified. or if attraction season finishes prior to this). Vouchers are subject to the terms, conditions and restrictions of the selected attraction.
3. One voucher per party will be accepted, cannot be used in conjunction with any other offer, photocopies will not be accepted.
4. All attractions offering a discount have confirmed their willingness to participate. All information is subject to change without notice and should any attraction close or decline to accept a voucher for any reason, Days Out UK are not liable and cannot be held responsible.
5. Days Out UK shall not accept liability for any loss, accident or injury that may occur at a participating attraction and any dispute arising must be settled direct with the attraction concerned.
6. Cash redemption value of each voucher is 0.001p.
7. You are advised to check all relevant information with your chosen attraction before commencing your journey.

Days Out UK, PO Box 427, Northampton NN1 3YN. Tel: 01604 622445

1. Each voucher entitles the holder to the discount specified by the selected attraction.
2. Valid for use until 28/02/09 (unless otherwise specified, or if attraction season finishes prior to this). Vouchers are subject to the terms, conditions and restrictions of the selected attraction.
3. One voucher per party will be accepted, cannot be used in conjunction with any other offer, photocopies will not be accepted.
4. All attractions offering a discount have confirmed their willingness to participate. All information is subject to change without notice and should any attraction close or decline to accept a voucher for any reason, Days Out UK are not liable and cannot be held responsible.
5. Days Out UK shall not accept liability for any loss, accident or injury that may occur at a participating attraction and any dispute arising must be settled direct with the attraction concerned.
6. Cash redemption value of each voucher is 0.001p.
7. You are advised to check all relevant information with your chosen attraction before commencing your journey.

Days Out UK, PO Box 427, Northampton NN1 3YN. Tel: 01604 622445

1. Each voucher entitles the holder to the discount specified by the selected attraction.
2. Valid for use until 28/02/09 (unless otherwise specified, or if attraction season finishes prior to this). Vouchers are subject to the terms, conditions and restrictions of the selected attraction.
3. One voucher per party will be accepted, cannot be used in conjunction with any other offer, photocopies will not be accepted.
4. All attractions offering a discount have confirmed their willingness to participate. All information is subject to change without notice and should any attraction close or decline to accept a voucher for any reason, Days Out UK are not liable and cannot be held responsible.
5. Days Out UK shall not accept liability for any loss, accident or injury that may occur at a participating attraction and any dispute arising must be settled direct with the attraction concerned.
6. Cash redemption value of each voucher is 0.001p.
7. You are advised to check all relevant information with your chosen attraction before commencing your journey.

Days Out UK, PO Box 427, Northampton NN1 3YN. Tel: 01604 622445

1. Each voucher entitles the holder to the discount specified by the selected attraction.
2. Valid for use until 28/02/09 (unless otherwise specified, or if attraction season finishes prior to this). Vouchers are subject to the terms, conditions and restrictions of the selected attraction.
3. One voucher per party will be accepted, cannot be used in conjunction with any other offer, photocopies will not be accepted.
4. All attractions offering a discount have confirmed their willingness to participate. All information is subject to change without notice and should any attraction close or decline to accept a voucher for any reason, Days Out UK are not liable and cannot be held responsible.
5. Days Out UK shall not accept liability for any loss, accident or injury that may occur at a participating attraction and any dispute arising must be settled direct with the attraction concerned.
6. Cash redemption value of each voucher is 0.001p.
7. You are advised to check all relevant information with your chosen attraction before commencing your journey.

Days Out UK, PO Box 427, Northampton NN1 3YN. Tel: 01604 622445

Go Ape! High Wire Forest Adventure
High Lodge Forest Visitor Centre Thetford Forest Nr. Brandon Suffolk IP27 0AF
£5.00 off per person
(Offer valid Mon-Fri excluding Bank Holidays, book online using promotional code THR001 or call 0845 643 9245 quoting "Days Out UK", voucher must be produced on admission)

Cannot be used in conjunction with other offers. One voucher per party. Not valid on Bank Hols or special event days.
Expires end Feb 2009 (unless otherwise specified)

DISCOUNT VOUCHER

Go Ape! High Wire Forest Adventure
Grizedale Forest Visitor Centre Grizedale Hawkshead Cumbria LA22 0QJ
£5.00 off per person
(Offer valid Mon-Fri excluding school holidays and Bank Holidays, book online using promotional code GRB001 or call 0845 643 9245 quoting "Days Out UK", voucher must be produced on admission)

Cannot be used in conjunction with other offers. One voucher per party. Not valid on Bank Hols or special event days.
Expires end Feb 2009 (unless otherwise specified)

DISCOUNT VOUCHER

Go Ape! High Wire Forest Adventure
Sherwood Pines Visitor Centre Sherwood Pines Forest Park Nr. Edwinstowe Mansfield Nottinghamshire NG21 9JH
£5.00 off per person
(Offer valid Mon-Fri excluding Bank Holidays, book online using promotional code SHE001 or call 0845 643 9245 quoting "Days Out UK", voucher must be produced on admission)

Cannot be used in conjunction with other offers. One voucher per party. Not valid on Bank Hols or special event days.
Expires end Feb 2009 (unless otherwise specified)

DISCOUNT VOUCHER

Go Ape! High Wire Forest Adventure
Moors Valley Country Park Horton Road Ashley Heath Nr. Ringwood Dorset BH24 2ET
£5.00 off per person
(Offer valid Mon-Fri excluding Bank Holidays, book online using promotional code MVE001 or call 0845 643 9245 quoting "Days Out UK", voucher must be produced on admission)

Cannot be used in conjunction with other offers. One voucher per party. Not valid on Bank Hols or special event days.
Expires end Feb 2009 (unless otherwise specified)

DISCOUNT VOUCHER

Go Ape! High Wire Forest Adventure
The Look Out Nine Mile Ride Swinley Forest Bracknell Berkshire RG12 7QW
£5.00 off per person
(Offer valid Mon-Fri excluding Bank Holidays, book online using promotional code BRF001 or call 0845 643 9245 quoting "Days Out UK", voucher must be produced on admission)

Cannot be used in conjunction with other offers. One voucher per party. Not valid on Bank Hols or special event days.
Expires end Feb 2009 (unless otherwise specified)

DISCOUNT VOUCHER

Go Ape! High Wire Forest Adventure
Mallards Pike Lake Forest of Dean Lydney Gloucestershire GL15 4HD
£5.00 off per person
(Offer valid Mon-Fri excluding Bank Holidays, book online using promotional code FDG001 or call 0845 643 9245 quoting "Days Out UK", voucher must be produced on admission)

Cannot be used in conjunction with other offers. One voucher per party. Not valid on Bank Hols or special event days.
Expires end Feb 2009 (unless otherwise specified)

DISCOUNT VOUCHER

1. Each voucher entitles the holder to the discount specified by the selected attraction.
2. Valid for use until 28/02/09 (unless otherwise specified, or if attraction season finishes prior to this). Vouchers are subject to the terms, conditions and restrictions of the selected attraction.
3. One voucher per party will be accepted, cannot be used in conjunction with any other offer, photocopies will not be accepted.
4. All attractions offering a discount have confirmed their willingness to participate. All information is subject to change without notice and should any attraction close or decline to accept a voucher for any reason, Days Out UK are not liable and cannot be held responsible.
5. Days Out UK shall not accept liability for any loss, accident or injury that may occur at a participating attraction and any dispute arising must be settled direct with the attraction concerned.
6. Cash redemption value of each voucher is 0.001p.
7. You are advised to check all relevant information with your chosen attraction before commencing your journey.

Days Out UK, PO Box 427, Northampton NN1 3YN. Tel: 01604 622445

1. Each voucher entitles the holder to the discount specified by the selected attraction.
2. Valid for use until 28/02/09 (unless otherwise specified, or if attraction season finishes prior to this). Vouchers are subject to the terms, conditions and restrictions of the selected attraction.
3. One voucher per party will be accepted, cannot be used in conjunction with any other offer, photocopies will not be accepted.
4. All attractions offering a discount have confirmed their willingness to participate. All information is subject to change without notice and should any attraction close or decline to accept a voucher for any reason, Days Out UK are not liable and cannot be held responsible.
5. Days Out UK shall not accept liability for any loss, accident or injury that may occur at a participating attraction and any dispute arising must be settled direct with the attraction concerned.
6. Cash redemption value of each voucher is 0.001p.
7. You are advised to check all relevant information with your chosen attraction before commencing your journey.

Days Out UK, PO Box 427, Northampton NN1 3YN. Tel: 01604 622445

1. Each voucher entitles the holder to the discount specified by the selected attraction.
2. Valid for use until 28/02/09 (unless otherwise specified. or if attraction season finishes prior to this). Vouchers are subject to the terms, conditions and restrictions of the selected attraction.
3. One voucher per party will be accepted, cannot be used in conjunction with any other offer, photocopies will not be accepted.
4. All attractions offering a discount have confirmed their willingness to participate. All information is subject to change without notice and should any attraction close or decline to accept a voucher for any reason, Days Out UK are not liable and cannot be held responsible.
5. Days Out UK shall not accept liability for any loss, accident or injury that may occur at a participating attraction and any dispute arising must be settled direct with the attraction concerned.
6. Cash redemption value of each voucher is 0.001p.
7. You are advised to check all relevant information with your chosen attraction before commencing your journey.

Days Out UK, PO Box 427, Northampton NN1 3YN. Tel: 01604 622445

1. Each voucher entitles the holder to the discount specified by the selected attraction.
2. Valid for use until 28/02/09 (unless otherwise specified, or if attraction season finishes prior to this). Vouchers are subject to the terms, conditions and restrictions of the selected attraction.
3. One voucher per party will be accepted, cannot be used in conjunction with any other offer, photocopies will not be accepted.
4. All attractions offering a discount have confirmed their willingness to participate. All information is subject to change without notice and should any attraction close or decline to accept a voucher for any reason, Days Out UK are not liable and cannot be held responsible.
5. Days Out UK shall not accept liability for any loss, accident or injury that may occur at a participating attraction and any dispute arising must be settled direct with the attraction concerned.
6. Cash redemption value of each voucher is 0.001p.
7. You are advised to check all relevant information with your chosen attraction before commencing your journey.

Days Out UK, PO Box 427, Northampton NN1 3YN. Tel: 01604 622445

1. Each voucher entitles the holder to the discount specified by the selected attraction.
2. Valid for use until 28/02/09 (unless otherwise specified, or if attraction season finishes prior to this). Vouchers are subject to the terms, conditions and restrictions of the selected attraction.
3. One voucher per party will be accepted, cannot be used in conjunction with any other offer, photocopies will not be accepted.
4. All attractions offering a discount have confirmed their willingness to participate. All information is subject to change without notice and should any attraction close or decline to accept a voucher for any reason, Days Out UK are not liable and cannot be held responsible.
5. Days Out UK shall not accept liability for any loss, accident or injury that may occur at a participating attraction and any dispute arising must be settled direct with the attraction concerned.
6. Cash redemption value of each voucher is 0.001p.
7. You are advised to check all relevant information with your chosen attraction before commencing your journey.

Days Out UK, PO Box 427, Northampton NN1 3YN. Tel: 01604 622445

1. Each voucher entitles the holder to the discount specified by the selected attraction.
2. Valid for use until 28/02/09 (unless otherwise specified, or if attraction season finishes prior to this). Vouchers are subject to the terms, conditions and restrictions of the selected attraction.
3. One voucher per party will be accepted, cannot be used in conjunction with any other offer, photocopies will not be accepted.
4. All attractions offering a discount have confirmed their willingness to participate. All information is subject to change without notice and should any attraction close or decline to accept a voucher for any reason, Days Out UK are not liable and cannot be held responsible.
5. Days Out UK shall not accept liability for any loss, accident or injury that may occur at a participating attraction and any dispute arising must be settled direct with the attraction concerned.
6. Cash redemption value of each voucher is 0.001p.
7. You are advised to check all relevant information with your chosen attraction before commencing your journey.

Days Out UK, PO Box 427, Northampton NN1 3YN. Tel: 01604 622445

1. Each voucher entitles the holder to the discount specified by the selected attraction.
2. Valid for use until 28/02/09 (unless otherwise specified, or if attraction season finishes prior to this). Vouchers are subject to the terms, conditions and restrictions of the selected attraction.
3. One voucher per party will be accepted, cannot be used in conjunction with any other offer, photocopies will not be accepted.
4. All attractions offering a discount have confirmed their willingness to participate. All information is subject to change without notice and should any attraction close or decline to accept a voucher for any reason, Days Out UK are not liable and cannot be held responsible.
5. Days Out UK shall not accept liability for any loss, accident or injury that may occur at a participating attraction and any dispute arising must be settled direct with the attraction concerned.
6. Cash redemption value of each voucher is 0.001p.
7. You are advised to check all relevant information with your chosen attraction before commencing your journey.

Days Out UK, PO Box 427, Northampton NN1 3YN. Tel: 01604 622445

1. Each voucher entitles the holder to the discount specified by the selected attraction.
2. Valid for use until 28/02/09 (unless otherwise specified, or if attraction season finishes prior to this). Vouchers are subject to the terms, conditions and restrictions of the selected attraction.
3. One voucher per party will be accepted, cannot be used in conjunction with any other offer, photocopies will not be accepted.
4. All attractions offering a discount have confirmed their willingness to participate. All information is subject to change without notice and should any attraction close or decline to accept a voucher for any reason, Days Out UK are not liable and cannot be held responsible.
5. Days Out UK shall not accept liability for any loss, accident or injury that may occur at a participating attraction and any dispute arising must be settled direct with the attraction concerned.
6. Cash redemption value of each voucher is 0.001p.
7. You are advised to check all relevant information with your chosen attraction before commencing your journey.

Days Out UK, PO Box 427, Northampton NN1 3YN. Tel: 01604 622445

1. Each voucher entitles the holder to the discount specified by the selected attraction.
2. Valid for use until 28/02/09 (unless otherwise specified, or if attraction season finishes prior to this). Vouchers are subject to the terms, conditions and restrictions of the selected attraction.
3. One voucher per party will be accepted, cannot be used in conjunction with any other offer, photocopies will not be accepted.
4. All attractions offering a discount have confirmed their willingness to participate. All information is subject to change without notice and should any attraction close or decline to accept a voucher for any reason, Days Out UK are not liable and cannot be held responsible.
5. Days Out UK shall not accept liability for any loss, accident or injury that may occur at a participating attraction and any dispute arising must be settled direct with the attraction concerned.
6. Cash redemption value of each voucher is 0.001p.
7. You are advised to check all relevant information with your chosen attraction before commencing your journey.

Days Out UK, PO Box 427, Northampton NN1 3YN. Tel: 01604 622445

1. Each voucher entitles the holder to the discount specified by the selected attraction.
2. Valid for use until 28/02/09 (unless otherwise specified, or if attraction season finishes prior to this). Vouchers are subject to the terms, conditions and restrictions of the selected attraction.
3. One voucher per party will be accepted, cannot be used in conjunction with any other offer, photocopies will not be accepted.
4. All attractions offering a discount have confirmed their willingness to participate. All information is subject to change without notice and should any attraction close or decline to accept a voucher for any reason, Days Out UK are not liable and cannot be held responsible.
5. Days Out UK shall not accept liability for any loss, accident or injury that may occur at a participating attraction and any dispute arising must be settled direct with the attraction concerned.
6. Cash redemption value of each voucher is 0.001p.
7. You are advised to check all relevant information with your chosen attraction before commencing your journey.

Days Out UK, PO Box 427, Northampton NN1 3YN. Tel: 01604 622445

1. Each voucher entitles the holder to the discount specified by the selected attraction.
2. Valid for use until 28/02/09 (unless otherwise specified, or if attraction season finishes prior to this). Vouchers are subject to the terms, conditions and restrictions of the selected attraction.
3. One voucher per party will be accepted, cannot be used in conjunction with any other offer, photocopies will not be accepted.
4. All attractions offering a discount have confirmed their willingness to participate. All information is subject to change without notice and should any attraction close or decline to accept a voucher for any reason, Days Out UK are not liable and cannot be held responsible.
5. Days Out UK shall not accept liability for any loss, accident or injury that may occur at a participating attraction and any dispute arising must be settled direct with the attraction concerned.
6. Cash redemption value of each voucher is 0.001p.
7. You are advised to check all relevant information with your chosen attraction before commencing your journey.

Days Out UK, PO Box 427, Northampton NN1 3YN. Tel: 01604 622445

1. Each voucher entitles the holder to the discount specified by the selected attraction.
2. Valid for use until 28/02/09 (unless otherwise specified, or if attraction season finishes prior to this). Vouchers are subject to the terms, conditions and restrictions of the selected attraction.
3. One voucher per party will be accepted, cannot be used in conjunction with any other offer, photocopies will not be accepted.
4. All attractions offering a discount have confirmed their willingness to participate. All information is subject to change without notice and should any attraction close or decline to accept a voucher for any reason, Days Out UK are not liable and cannot be held responsible.
5. Days Out UK shall not accept liability for any loss, accident or injury that may occur at a participating attraction and any dispute arising must be settled direct with the attraction concerned.
6. Cash redemption value of each voucher is 0.001p.
7. You are advised to check all relevant information with your chosen attraction before commencing your journey.

Days Out UK, PO Box 427, Northampton NN1 3YN. Tel: 01604 622445

1. Each voucher entitles the holder to the discount specified by the selected attraction.
2. Valid for use until 28/02/09 (unless otherwise specified, or if attraction season finishes prior to this). Vouchers are subject to the terms, conditions and restrictions of the selected attraction.
3. One voucher per party will be accepted, cannot be used in conjunction with any other offer, photocopies will not be accepted.
4. All attractions offering a discount have confirmed their willingness to participate. All information is subject to change without notice and should any attraction close or decline to accept a voucher for any reason, Days Out UK are not liable and cannot be held responsible.
5. Days Out UK shall not accept liability for any loss, accident or injury that may occur at a participating attraction and any dispute arising must be settled direct with the attraction concerned.
6. Cash redemption value of each voucher is 0.001p.
7. You are advised to check all relevant information with your chosen attraction before commencing your journey.

Days Out UK, PO Box 427, Northampton NN1 3YN. Tel: 01604 622445

1. Each voucher entitles the holder to the discount specified by the selected attraction.
2. Valid for use until 28/02/09 (unless otherwise specified. or if attraction season finishes prior to this). Vouchers are subject to the terms, conditions and restrictions of the selected attraction.
3. One voucher per party will be accepted, cannot be used in conjunction with any other offer, photocopies will not be accepted.
4. All attractions offering a discount have confirmed their willingness to participate. All information is subject to change without notice and should any attraction close or decline to accept a voucher for any reason, Days Out UK are not liable and cannot be held responsible.
5. Days Out UK shall not accept liability for any loss, accident or injury that may occur at a participating attraction and any dispute arising must be settled direct with the attraction concerned.
6. Cash redemption value of each voucher is 0.001p.
7. You are advised to check all relevant information with your chosen attraction before commencing your journey.

Days Out UK, PO Box 427, Northampton NN1 3YN. Tel: 01604 622445

1. Each voucher entitles the holder to the discount specified by the selected attraction.
2. Valid for use until 28/02/09 (unless otherwise specified, or if attraction season finishes prior to this). Vouchers are subject to the terms, conditions and restrictions of the selected attraction.
3. One voucher per party will be accepted, cannot be used in conjunction with any other offer, photocopies will not be accepted.
4. All attractions offering a discount have confirmed their willingness to participate. All information is subject to change without notice and should any attraction close or decline to accept a voucher for any reason, Days Out UK are not liable and cannot be held responsible.
5. Days Out UK shall not accept liability for any loss, accident or injury that may occur at a participating attraction and any dispute arising must be settled direct with the attraction concerned.
6. Cash redemption value of each voucher is 0.001p.
7. You are advised to check all relevant information with your chosen attraction before commencing your journey.

Days Out UK, PO Box 427, Northampton NN1 3YN. Tel: 01604 622445

1. Each voucher entitles the holder to the discount specified by the selected attraction.
2. Valid for use until 28/02/09 (unless otherwise specified, or if attraction season finishes prior to this). Vouchers are subject to the terms, conditions and restrictions of the selected attraction.
3. One voucher per party will be accepted, cannot be used in conjunction with any other offer, photocopies will not be accepted.
4. All attractions offering a discount have confirmed their willingness to participate. All information is subject to change without notice and should any attraction close or decline to accept a voucher for any reason, Days Out UK are not liable and cannot be held responsible.
5. Days Out UK shall not accept liability for any loss, accident or injury that may occur at a participating attraction and any dispute arising must be settled direct with the attraction concerned.
6. Cash redemption value of each voucher is 0.001p.
7. You are advised to check all relevant information with your chosen attraction before commencing your journey.

Days Out UK, PO Box 427, Northampton NN1 3YN. Tel: 01604 622445

Days Out UK, PO Box 427, Northampton NN1 3YN. Tel: 01604 622445

517

1. Each voucher entitles the holder to the discount specified by the selected attraction.

2. Valid for use until 28/02/09 (unless otherwise specified, or if attraction season finishes prior to this). Vouchers are subject to the terms, conditions and restrictions of the selected attraction.

3. One voucher per party will be accepted, cannot be used in conjunction with any other offer, photocopies will not be accepted.

4. All attractions offering a discount have confirmed their willingness to participate. All information is subject to change without notice and should any attraction close or decline to accept a voucher for any reason, Days Out UK are not liable and cannot be held responsible.

5. Days Out UK shall not accept liability for any loss, accident or injury that may occur at a participating attraction and any dispute arising must be settled direct with the attraction concerned.

6. Cash redemption value of each voucher is 0.001p.

7. You are advised to check all relevant information with your chosen attraction before commencing your journey.

Days Out UK, PO Box 427, Northampton NN1 3YN. Tel: 01604 622445

1. Each voucher entitles the holder to the discount specified by the selected attraction.
2. Valid for use until 28/02/09 (unless otherwise specified. or if attraction season finishes prior to this). Vouchers are subject to the terms, conditions and restrictions of the selected attraction.
3. One voucher per party will be accepted, cannot be used in conjunction with any other offer, photocopies will not be accepted.
4. All attractions offering a discount have confirmed their willingness to participate. All information is subject to change without notice and should any attraction close or decline to accept a voucher for any reason, Days Out UK are not liable and cannot be held responsible.
5. Days Out UK shall not accept liability for any loss, accident or injury that may occur at a participating attraction and any dispute arising must be settled direct with the attraction concerned.
6. Cash redemption value of each voucher is 0.001p.
7. You are advised to check all relevant information with your chosen attraction before commencing your journey.

Days Out UK, PO Box 427, Northampton NN1 3YN. Tel: 01604 622445

1. Each voucher entitles the holder to the discount specified by the selected attraction.
2. Valid for use until 28/02/09 (unless otherwise specified, or if attraction season finishes prior to this). Vouchers are subject to the terms, conditions and restrictions of the selected attraction.
3. One voucher per party will be accepted, cannot be used in conjunction with any other offer, photocopies will not be accepted.
4. All attractions offering a discount have confirmed their willingness to participate. All information is subject to change without notice and should any attraction close or decline to accept a voucher for any reason, Days Out UK are not liable and cannot be held responsible.
5. Days Out UK shall not accept liability for any loss, accident or injury that may occur at a participating attraction and any dispute arising must be settled direct with the attraction concerned.
6. Cash redemption value of each voucher is 0.001p.
7. You are advised to check all relevant information with your chosen attraction before commencing your journey.

Days Out UK, PO Box 427, Northampton NN1 3YN. Tel: 01604 622445

1. Each voucher entitles the holder to the discount specified by the selected attraction.
2. Valid for use until 28/02/09 (unless otherwise specified, or if attraction season finishes prior to this). Vouchers are subject to the terms, conditions and restrictions of the selected attraction.
3. One voucher per party will be accepted, cannot be used in conjunction with any other offer, photocopies will not be accepted.
4. All attractions offering a discount have confirmed their willingness to participate. All information is subject to change without notice and should any attraction close or decline to accept a voucher for any reason, Days Out UK are not liable and cannot be held responsible.
5. Days Out UK shall not accept liability for any loss, accident or injury that may occur at a participating attraction and any dispute arising must be settled direct with the attraction concerned.
6. Cash redemption value of each voucher is 0.001p.
7. You are advised to check all relevant information with your chosen attraction before commencing your journey.

Days Out UK, PO Box 427, Northampton NN1 3YN. Tel: 01604 622445

1. Each voucher entitles the holder to the discount specified by the selected attraction.
2. Valid for use until 28/02/09 (unless otherwise specified, or if attraction season finishes prior to this). Vouchers are subject to the terms, conditions and restrictions of the selected attraction.
3. One voucher per party will be accepted, cannot be used in conjunction with any other offer, photocopies will not be accepted.
4. All attractions offering a discount have confirmed their willingness to participate. All information is subject to change without notice and should any attraction close or decline to accept a voucher for any reason, Days Out UK are not liable and cannot be held responsible.
5. Days Out UK shall not accept liability for any loss, accident or injury that may occur at a participating attraction and any dispute arising must be settled direct with the attraction concerned.
6. Cash redemption value of each voucher is 0.001p.
7. You are advised to check all relevant information with your chosen attraction before commencing your journey.

Days Out UK, PO Box 427, Northampton NN1 3YN. Tel: 01604 622445

Hartlepool's Maritime Experience
Maritime Avenue Hartlepool Tees Valley TS24 0XZ
One Child Free
with a full-paying adult
Cannot be used in conjunction with other offers. One voucher per party. Not valid on Bank Hols or special event days.
Valid until 31 Dec 2008

Hawk Conservancy Trust
Sarson Lane Weyhill Andover Hampshire SP11 8DY
£1.00 off Child Admission
Cannot be used in conjunction with other offers. One voucher per party. Not valid on Bank Hols or special event days.
Expires end Feb 2009 (unless otherwise specified)

Hedingham Castle
Bayley Street Castle Hedingham Halstead Essex CO9 3DJ
One Child Free
with one full-paying adult
(Sun-Thu only, not valid for special events or Bank Holidays)
Cannot be used in conjunction with other offers. One voucher per party. Not valid on Bank Hols or special event days.
Valid until 28th Sept 2008

Henry Moore Institute
74 The Headrow Leeds West Yorkshire LS1 3AH
15% discount on all publications
plus one free poster of your choice
Cannot be used in conjunction with other offers. One voucher per party. Not valid on Bank Hols or special event days.
Expires end Feb 2009 (unless otherwise specified)

Heritage Motor Centre
Banbury Road Gaydon Warwickshire CV35 0BJ
Two for the Price of One
with a full-paying adult
Cannot be used in conjunction with other offers. One voucher per party. Not valid on Bank Hols or special event days.
Expires end Feb 2009 (unless otherwise specified)

Hollycombe Steam Collection
Midhurst Road Liphook Hampshire GU30 7LP
One Child Free
with a full-paying adult
Cannot be used in conjunction with other offers. One voucher per party. Not valid on Bank Hols or special event days.
Expires end Feb 2009 (unless otherwise specified)

519

1. Each voucher entitles the holder to the discount specified by the selected attraction.
2. Valid for use until 28/02/09 (unless otherwise specified, or if attraction season finishes prior to this). Vouchers are subject to the terms, conditions and restrictions of the selected attraction.
3. One voucher per party will be accepted, cannot be used in conjunction with any other offer, photocopies will not be accepted.
4. All attractions offering a discount have confirmed their willingness to participate. All information is subject to change without notice and should any attraction close or decline to accept a voucher for any reason, Days Out UK are not liable and cannot be held responsible.
5. Days Out UK shall not accept liability for any loss, accident or injury that may occur at a participating attraction and any dispute arising must be settled direct with the attraction concerned.
6. Cash redemption value of each voucher is 0.001p.
7. You are advised to check all relevant information with your chosen attraction before commencing your journey.

Days Out UK, PO Box 427, Northampton NN1 3YN. Tel: 01604 622445

1. Each voucher entitles the holder to the discount specified by the selected attraction.
2. Valid for use until 28/02/09 (unless otherwise specified, or if attraction season finishes prior to this). Vouchers are subject to the terms, conditions and restrictions of the selected attraction.
3. One voucher per party will be accepted, cannot be used in conjunction with any other offer, photocopies will not be accepted.
4. All attractions offering a discount have confirmed their willingness to participate. All information is subject to change without notice and should any attraction close or decline to accept a voucher for any reason, Days Out UK are not liable and cannot be held responsible.
5. Days Out UK shall not accept liability for any loss, accident or injury that may occur at a participating attraction and any dispute arising must be settled direct with the attraction concerned.
6. Cash redemption value of each voucher is 0.001p.
7. You are advised to check all relevant information with your chosen attraction before commencing your journey.

Days Out UK, PO Box 427, Northampton NN1 3YN. Tel: 01604 622445

1. Each voucher entitles the holder to the discount specified by the selected attraction.
2. Valid for use until 28/02/09 (unless otherwise specified, or if attraction season finishes prior to this). Vouchers are subject to the terms, conditions and restrictions of the selected attraction.
3. One voucher per party will be accepted, cannot be used in conjunction with any other offer, photocopies will not be accepted.
4. All attractions offering a discount have confirmed their willingness to participate. All information is subject to change without notice and should any attraction close or decline to accept a voucher for any reason, Days Out UK are not liable and cannot be held responsible.
5. Days Out UK shall not accept liability for any loss, accident or injury that may occur at a participating attraction and any dispute arising must be settled direct with the attraction concerned.
6. Cash redemption value of each voucher is 0.001p.
7. You are advised to check all relevant information with your chosen attraction before commencing your journey.

Days Out UK, PO Box 427, Northampton NN1 3YN. Tel: 01604 622445

1. Each voucher entitles the holder to the discount specified by the selected attraction.
2. Valid for use until 28/02/09 (unless otherwise specified, or if attraction season finishes prior to this). Vouchers are subject to the terms, conditions and restrictions of the selected attraction.
3. One voucher per party will be accepted, cannot be used in conjunction with any other offer, photocopies will not be accepted.
4. All attractions offering a discount have confirmed their willingness to participate. All information is subject to change without notice and should any attraction close or decline to accept a voucher for any reason, Days Out UK are not liable and cannot be held responsible.
5. Days Out UK shall not accept liability for any loss, accident or injury that may occur at a participating attraction and any dispute arising must be settled direct with the attraction concerned.
6. Cash redemption value of each voucher is 0.001p.
7. You are advised to check all relevant information with your chosen attraction before commencing your journey.

Days Out UK, PO Box 427, Northampton NN1 3YN. Tel: 01604 622445

1. Each voucher entitles the holder to the discount specified by the selected attraction.
2. Valid for use until 28/02/09 (unless otherwise specified, or if attraction season finishes prior to this). Vouchers are subject to the terms, conditions and restrictions of the selected attraction.
3. One voucher per party will be accepted, cannot be used in conjunction with any other offer, photocopies will not be accepted.
4. All attractions offering a discount have confirmed their willingness to participate. All information is subject to change without notice and should any attraction close or decline to accept a voucher for any reason, Days Out UK are not liable and cannot be held responsible.
5. Days Out UK shall not accept liability for any loss, accident or injury that may occur at a participating attraction and any dispute arising must be settled direct with the attraction concerned.
6. Cash redemption value of each voucher is 0.001p.
7. You are advised to check all relevant information with your chosen attraction before commencing your journey.

Days Out UK, PO Box 427, Northampton NN1 3YN. Tel: 01604 622445

Hop Farm at the Kentish Oast Village

Beltring Maidstone Road Paddock Wood Tonbridge Kent TN12 6PY

One Child Free

with one full-paying adult

(Excludes 'War & Peace,' 'Monster Mania' and music events, no cash alternative)

Cannot be used in conjunction with other offers. One voucher per party. Not valid on Bank Hols or special event days.

Valid until 31 Dec 2008

DISCOUNT VOUCHER

Houghton Mill

Houghton nr Huntingdon Cambridgeshire PE28 2AZ

One Child Free

with full-paying adult

Cannot be used in conjunction with other offers. One voucher per party. Not valid on Bank Hols or special event days.

Expires end Feb 2009 (unless otherwise specified)

DISCOUNT VOUCHER

Howletts Wild Animal Park

Bekesbourne Lane Bekesbourne Canterbury Kent CT4 5EL

Kid for a Quid

(Each child must be accompanied by a full-paying adult)

Cannot be used in conjunction with other offers. One voucher per party. Not valid on Bank Hols or special event days.

Valid until 31 Dec 2008

DISCOUNT VOUCHER

Hunstanton Sea Life Sanctuary

Southern Promenade Hunstanton Norfolk PE36 5BH

One Child Free with a full-paying adult

1. This voucher entitles free admission to the Hunstanton Sea Life Sanctuary for one child when accompanied by one full paying adult.
2. Offer expires 28 February 2009.
3. Cannot be used in conjunction with any other offer.
4. A "child" is classed as a person aged 3-14 inclusive (under 3s go free anyway).
5. No cash alternative, non-refundable; and non-exchangeable.
6. All children must be accompanied by an adult.
7. Only one voucher per party and per transaction.
8. Photocopies not accepted.
9. SEA LIFE/Sanctuaries reserve the right to alter, close or remove details/exhibits without prior notice for technical, operational or other reasons, and no refunds can be given in these circumstances.
10. SEA LIFE/Sanctuaries reserve the right to refuse entry without explanation.
Voucher Ref: DOUK.

annot be used in conjunction with other offers. One voucher per party. Not valid on Bank Hols or special event days.

Expires end Feb 2009 (unless otherwise specified)

DISCOUNT VOUCHER

Hylands House

Hylands Park London Road Chelmsford Essex CM2 8WQ

Two for the Price of One

with a full-paying adult

(Valid Sundays and Mondays only)

Cannot be used in conjunction with other offers. One voucher per party. Not valid on Bank Hols or special event days.

Expires end Feb 2009 (unless otherwise specified)

DISCOUNT VOUCHER

1. Each voucher entitles the holder to the discount specified by the selected attraction.
2. Valid for use until 28/02/09 (unless otherwise specified, or if attraction season finishes prior to this). Vouchers are subject to the terms, conditions and restrictions of the selected attraction.
3. One voucher per party will be accepted, cannot be used in conjunction with any other offer, photocopies will not be accepted.
4. All attractions offering a discount have confirmed their willingness to participate. All information is subject to change without notice and should any attraction close or decline to accept a voucher for any reason, Days Out UK are not liable and cannot be held responsible.
5. Days Out UK shall not accept liability for any loss, accident or injury that may occur at a participating attraction and any dispute arising must be settled direct with the attraction concerned.
6. Cash redemption value of each voucher is 0.001p.
7. You are advised to check all relevant information with your chosen attraction before commencing your journey.

Days Out UK, PO Box 427, Northampton NN1 3YN. Tel: 01604 622445

1. Each voucher entitles the holder to the discount specified by the selected attraction.
2. Valid for use until 28/02/09 (unless otherwise specified. or if attraction season finishes prior to this). Vouchers are subject to the terms, conditions and restrictions of the selected attraction.
3. One voucher per party will be accepted, cannot be used in conjunction with any other offer, photocopies will not be accepted.
4. All attractions offering a discount have confirmed their willingness to participate. All information is subject to change without notice and should any attraction close or decline to accept a voucher for any reason, Days Out UK are not liable and cannot be held responsible.
5. Days Out UK shall not accept liability for any loss, accident or injury that may occur at a participating attraction and any dispute arising must be settled direct with the attraction concerned.
6. Cash redemption value of each voucher is 0.001p.
7. You are advised to check all relevant information with your chosen attraction before commencing your journey.

Days Out UK, PO Box 427, Northampton NN1 3YN. Tel: 01604 622445

1. Each voucher entitles the holder to the discount specified by the selected attraction.

2. Valid for use until 28/02/09 (unless otherwise specified, or if attraction season finishes prior to this). Vouchers are subject to the terms, conditions and restrictions of the selected attraction.

3. One voucher per party will be accepted, cannot be used in conjunction with any other offer, photocopies will not be accepted.

4. All attractions offering a discount have confirmed their willingness to participate. All information is subject to change without notice and should any attraction close or decline to accept a voucher for any reason, Days Out UK are not liable and cannot be held responsible.

5. Days Out UK shall not accept liability for any loss, accident or injury that may occur at a participating attraction and any dispute arising must be settled direct with the attraction concerned.

6. Cash redemption value of each voucher is 0.001p.

7. You are advised to check all relevant information with your chosen attraction before commencing your journey.

Days Out UK, PO Box 427, Northampton NN1 3YN. Tel: 01604 622445

1. Each voucher entitles the holder to the discount specified by the selected attraction.
2. Valid for use until 28/02/09 (unless otherwise specified, or if attraction season finishes prior to this). Vouchers are subject to the terms, conditions and restrictions of the selected attraction.
3. One voucher per party will be accepted, cannot be used in conjunction with any other offer, photocopies will not be accepted.
4. All attractions offering a discount have confirmed their willingness to participate. All information is subject to change without notice and should any attraction close or decline to accept a voucher for any reason, Days Out UK are not liable and cannot be held responsible.
5. Days Out UK shall not accept liability for any loss, accident or injury that may occur at a participating attraction and any dispute arising must be settled direct with the attraction concerned.
6. Cash redemption value of each voucher is 0.001p.
7. You are advised to check all relevant information with your chosen attraction before commencing your journey.

Days Out UK, PO Box 427, Northampton NN1 3YN. Tel: 01604 622445

Ickworth House Park and Gardens

The Rotunda Ickworth Bury St Edmunds Suffolk IP29 5QE

One Child Free
with a full-paying adult

Cannot be used in conjunction with other offers. One voucher per party. Not valid on Bank Hols or special event days.

Expires end Feb 2009 (unless otherwise specified)

Intech Science Centre

Telegraph Way Morn Hill Winchester Hampshire SO21 1HX

One Child Free
with full-paying adult

(Offer applies to Science Centre only - it does not include the Planetarium)

Cannot be used in conjunction with other offers. One voucher per party. Not valid on Bank Hols or special event days.

Expires end Feb 2009 (unless otherwise specified)

International Women's Tennis Open

Devonshire Park Eastbourne East Sussex BN21 4JJ

Save up to £2.00 off any full rate price

(Simply call our booking line: 01323 412000 and quote "Days Out UK" to claim your discount when ordering. Conditions: no cash alternative, cannot be used in conjunction with any other offer, one discount per transaction)

Cannot be used in conjunction with other offers. One voucher per party. Not valid on Bank Hols or special event days.

Expires end Feb 2009 (unless otherwise specified)

Jodrell Bank Visitor Centre

Jodrell Bank Lower Withington Macclesfield Cheshire SK11 9DL

Two for the Price of One
with a full-paying adult

Cannot be used in conjunction with other offers. One voucher per party. Not valid on Bank Hols or special event days.

Expires end Feb 2009 (unless otherwise specified)

JORVIK Viking Centre

Coppergate York North Yorkshire YO1 9WT

One Child Free
with a full-paying adult

Cannot be used in conjunction with other offers. One voucher per party. Not valid on Bank Hols or special event days.

Expires end Feb 2009 (unless otherwise specified)

Kempt Tower Visitor Centre

Five Mile Road St Ouen Jersey Channel Islands JE3 2FN

Two for the Price of One
with a full-paying adult

Cannot be used in conjunction with other offers. One voucher per party. Not valid on Bank Hols or special event days.

Expires end Feb 2009 (unless otherwise specified)

1. Each voucher entitles the holder to the discount specified by the selected attraction.
2. Valid for use until 28/02/09 (unless otherwise specified, or if attraction season finishes prior to this). Vouchers are subject to the terms, conditions and restrictions of the selected attraction.
3. One voucher per party will be accepted, cannot be used in conjunction with any other offer, photocopies will not be accepted.
4. All attractions offering a discount have confirmed their willingness to participate. All information is subject to change without notice and should any attraction close or decline to accept a voucher for any reason, Days Out UK are not liable and cannot be held responsible.
5. Days Out UK shall not accept liability for any loss, accident or injury that may occur at a participating attraction and any dispute arising must be settled direct with the attraction concerned.
6. Cash redemption value of each voucher is 0.001p.
7. You are advised to check all relevant information with your chosen attraction before commencing your journey.

Days Out UK, PO Box 427, Northampton NN1 3YN. Tel: 01604 622445

1. Each voucher entitles the holder to the discount specified by the selected attraction.
2. Valid for use until 28/02/09 (unless otherwise specified. or if attraction season finishes prior to this). Vouchers are subject to the terms, conditions and restrictions of the selected attraction.
3. One voucher per party will be accepted, cannot be used in conjunction with any other offer, photocopies will not be accepted.
4. All attractions offering a discount have confirmed their willingness to participate. All information is subject to change without notice and should any attraction close or decline to accept a voucher for any reason, Days Out UK are not liable and cannot be held responsible.
5. Days Out UK shall not accept liability for any loss, accident or injury that may occur at a participating attraction and any dispute arising must be settled direct with the attraction concerned.
6. Cash redemption value of each voucher is 0.001p.
7. You are advised to check all relevant information with your chosen attraction before commencing your journey.

Days Out UK, PO Box 427, Northampton NN1 3YN. Tel: 01604 622445

1. Each voucher entitles the holder to the discount specified by the selected attraction.
2. Valid for use until 28/02/09 (unless otherwise specified, or if attraction season finishes prior to this). Vouchers are subject to the terms, conditions and restrictions of the selected attraction.
3. One voucher per party will be accepted, cannot be used in conjunction with any other offer, photocopies will not be accepted.
4. All attractions offering a discount have confirmed their willingness to participate. All information is subject to change without notice and should any attraction close or decline to accept a voucher for any reason, Days Out UK are not liable and cannot be held responsible.
5. Days Out UK shall not accept liability for any loss, accident or injury that may occur at a participating attraction and any dispute arising must be settled direct with the attraction concerned.
6. Cash redemption value of each voucher is 0.001p.
7. You are advised to check all relevant information with your chosen attraction before commencing your journey.

Days Out UK, PO Box 427, Northampton NN1 3YN. Tel: 01604 622445

1. Each voucher entitles the holder to the discount specified by the selected attraction.
2. Valid for use until 28/02/09 (unless otherwise specified, or if attraction season finishes prior to this). Vouchers are subject to the terms, conditions and restrictions of the selected attraction.
3. One voucher per party will be accepted, cannot be used in conjunction with any other offer, photocopies will not be accepted.
4. All attractions offering a discount have confirmed their willingness to participate. All information is subject to change without notice and should any attraction close or decline to accept a voucher for any reason, Days Out UK are not liable and cannot be held responsible.
5. Days Out UK shall not accept liability for any loss, accident or injury that may occur at a participating attraction and any dispute arising must be settled direct with the attraction concerned.
6. Cash redemption value of each voucher is 0.001p.
7. You are advised to check all relevant information with your chosen attraction before commencing your journey.

Days Out UK, PO Box 427, Northampton NN1 3YN. Tel: 01604 622445

1. Each voucher entitles the holder to the discount specified by the selected attraction.
2. Valid for use until 28/02/09 (unless otherwise specified, or if attraction season finishes prior to this). Vouchers are subject to the terms, conditions and restrictions of the selected attraction.
3. One voucher per party will be accepted, cannot be used in conjunction with any other offer, photocopies will not be accepted.
4. All attractions offering a discount have confirmed their willingness to participate. All information is subject to change without notice and should any attraction close or decline to accept a voucher for any reason, Days Out UK are not liable and cannot be held responsible.
5. Days Out UK shall not accept liability for any loss, accident or injury that may occur at a participating attraction and any dispute arising must be settled direct with the attraction concerned.
6. Cash redemption value of each voucher is 0.001p.
7. You are advised to check all relevant information with your chosen attraction before commencing your journey.

Days Out UK, PO Box 427, Northampton NN1 3YN. Tel: 01604 622445

DAYSOUTUK
The place to look for places to go

Kentwell Hall and Gardens
Long Melford Sudbury Suffolk CO10 9BA
One Child Free
with two full-paying adults
(Voucher must be presented at time of purchase, excludes special events)
Cannot be used in conjunction with other offers. One voucher per party. Not valid on Bank Hols or special event days.
Expires end Feb 2009 (unless otherwise specified)

DISCOUNT VOUCHER

DAYSOUTUK
The place to look for places to go

Kettering Museum and Art Gallery
The Coach House Sheep St Kettering Northamptonshire NN16 0AN
10% off in the Museum gift shop
with any purchase
Cannot be used in conjunction with other offers. One voucher per party. Not valid on Bank Hols or special event days.
Expires end Feb 2009 (unless otherwise specified)

DISCOUNT VOUCHER

DAYSOUTUK
The place to look for places to go

King Arthur's Labyrinth
Corris Craft Centre Corris Machynlleth Powys SY20 9RF
20% off Adult Admissions to the Labyrinth
(Makes adult admissions £5.20, offer applies to full-priced admissions only, cannot be used during the month of August)
Cannot be used in conjunction with other offers. One voucher per party. Not valid on Bank Hols or special event days.
Expires end Feb 2009 (unless otherwise specified)

DISCOUNT VOUCHER

DAYSOUTUK
The place to look for places to go

Knebworth Gardens, Adventure Playground and Park
Knebworth Hertfordshire SG3 6PY
Two for the Price of One
with a full-paying adult
(Valid Mon-Fri, not valid Bank Holiday weekends and special event days)
Cannot be used in conjunction with other offers. One voucher per party. Not valid on Bank Hols or special event days.
Expires end Feb 2009 (unless otherwise specified)

DISCOUNT VOUCHER

DAYSOUTUK
The place to look for places to go

Knockhatch Adventure Park
Hempstead Lane Hailsham East Sussex BN27 3PR
One Child Free
with every full-paying adult
(Applies to Park entry only)
Cannot be used in conjunction with other offers. One voucher per party. Not valid on Bank Hols or special event days.
Expires end Feb 2009 (unless otherwise specified)

DISCOUNT VOUCHER

DAYSOUTUK
The place to look for places to go

Lavenham Guildhall of Corpus Christi
Market Place Lavenham Sudbury Suffolk CO10 9QZ
One Child Free
with full-paying adult
Cannot be used in conjunction with other offers. One voucher per party. Not valid on Bank Hols or special event days.
Expires end Feb 2009 (unless otherwise specified)

DISCOUNT VOUCHER

Lee Valley Park Farms
Stubbins Hall Lane, Waltham Abbey, Essex, EN9 2EF
Save £3.50! One Child Free
with one full-paying adult
(No cash alternative, one voucher per party)

Cannot be used in conjunction with other offers. One voucher per party. Not valid on Bank Hols or special event days.

Valid 1 Mar - 31 Oct 2008

DISCOUNT VOUCHER

LEGOLAND Windsor
Winkfield Road Windsor Berkshire SL4 4AY
Save up to £25.00!
(Voucher entitles a maximum of 5 people to £5.00 off full admission price per person at LEGOLAND Windsor)

Terms & Conditions: 1.Voucher must be presented upon entrance into LEGOLAND Windsor and surrendered to the ticket booth operator. Discount vouchers cannot be used for pre-bookings. 2. Not to be used in conjunction with any other offer, reward/loyalty program, 2 Day Pass, Annual Pass, group booking, on-line tickets or rail inclusive offers. 3.Guests are advised that not all attractions and shows may be operational on the day of their visit. 4. Height, age and weight restrictions apply on some rides. Some rides will require guests who only just meet the minimum height requirements to be accompanied by a person aged 16 years or over. 5. Guests under the age of 14 must be accompanied by a person aged 16 or over. 6. This voucher is not for re-sale, is non-refundable and non-transferable. 7. The park opens for the 2008 season on 15 March and closes on 2 November. 8.This voucher is valid for admissions from 15 March to 2 November, 2008 excluding the month of August and selected dates - please check www.LEGOLAND.co.uk in advance to confirm excluded dates. 9. This offer is limited to one per household. 10. This offer will apply irrespective of the entrance price at the time of use. 11. LEGOLAND Windsor will be closed on selected weekdays in April, May, September, October and November. 12. PLEASE visit www.LEGOLAND.co.uk in advance to confirm dates and prices. For great hotel offers go to www.LEGOLANDhotels.co.uk

Cannot be used in conjunction with other offers. One voucher per party. Not valid on Bank Hols or special event days.

15 Mar- 2 Nov 2008 (excludes August)

DISCOUNT VOUCHER

Leighton Buzzard Railway
Page's Park Station Billington Road Leighton Buzzard Beds LU7 4TN
Two for the Price of One
adult paying full-fare
(Not valid on Christmas services in December)

Cannot be used in conjunction with other offers. One voucher per party. Not valid on Bank Hols or special event days.

Expires end Feb 2009 (unless otherwise specified)

DISCOUNT VOUCHER

Leighton Hall
Carnforth Lancashire LA5 9ST
Two for the Price of One
with a full-paying adult

Cannot be used in conjunction with other offers. One voucher per party. Not valid on Bank Hols or special event days.

Expires end Feb 2009 (unless otherwise specified)

DISCOUNT VOUCHER

Lewes Castle and Barbican House Museum
169 High Street Lewes East Sussex BN7 1YE
Buy One Full-Priced Adult, Senior or Student Ticket and Get Another Ticket Half-Price
(The half-price ticket must be of equal or lesser value, not valid on any special event days, please see website for dates of events)

Cannot be used in conjunction with other offers. One voucher per party. Not valid on Bank Hols or special event days.

Expires end Feb 2009 (unless otherwise specified)

DISCOUNT VOUCHER

1. Each voucher entitles the holder to the discount specified by the selected attraction.

2. Valid for use until 28/02/09 (unless otherwise specified. or if attraction season finishes prior to this). Vouchers are subject to the terms, conditions and restrictions of the selected attraction.

3. One voucher per party will be accepted, cannot be used in conjunction with any other offer, photocopies will not be accepted.

4. All attractions offering a discount have confirmed their willingness to participate. All information is subject to change without notice and should any attraction close or decline to accept a voucher for any reason, Days Out UK are not liable and cannot be held responsible.

5. Days Out UK shall not accept liability for any loss, accident or injury that may occur at a participating attraction and any dispute arising must be settled direct with the attraction concerned.

6. Cash redemption value of each voucher is 0.001p.

7. You are advised to check all relevant information with your chosen attraction before commencing your journey.

Days Out UK, PO Box 427, Northampton NN1 3YN. Tel: 01604 622445

1. Each voucher entitles the holder to the discount specified by the selected attraction.
2. Valid for use until 28/02/09 (unless otherwise specified, or if attraction season finishes prior to this). Vouchers are subject to the terms, conditions and restrictions of the selected attraction.
3. One voucher per party will be accepted, cannot be used in conjunction with any other offer, photocopies will not be accepted.
4. All attractions offering a discount have confirmed their willingness to participate. All information is subject to change without notice and should any attraction close or decline to accept a voucher for any reason, Days Out UK are not liable and cannot be held responsible.
5. Days Out UK shall not accept liability for any loss, accident or injury that may occur at a participating attraction and any dispute arising must be settled direct with the attraction concerned.
6. Cash redemption value of each voucher is 0.001p.
7. You are advised to check all relevant information with your chosen attraction before commencing your journey.

Days Out UK, PO Box 427, Northampton NN1 3YN. Tel: 01604 622445

1. Each voucher entitles the holder to the discount specified by the selected attraction.
2. Valid for use until 28/02/09 (unless otherwise specified, or if attraction season finishes prior to this). Vouchers are subject to the terms, conditions and restrictions of the selected attraction.
3. One voucher per party will be accepted, cannot be used in conjunction with any other offer, photocopies will not be accepted.
4. All attractions offering a discount have confirmed their willingness to participate. All information is subject to change without notice and should any attraction close or decline to accept a voucher for any reason, Days Out UK are not liable and cannot be held responsible.
5. Days Out UK shall not accept liability for any loss, accident or injury that may occur at a participating attraction and any dispute arising must be settled direct with the attraction concerned.
6. Cash redemption value of each voucher is 0.001p.
7. You are advised to check all relevant information with your chosen attraction before commencing your journey.

Days Out UK, PO Box 427, Northampton NN1 3YN. Tel: 01604 622445

1. Each voucher entitles the holder to the discount specified by the selected attraction.
2. Valid for use until 28/02/09 (unless otherwise specified, or if attraction season finishes prior to this). Vouchers are subject to the terms, conditions and restrictions of the selected attraction.
3. One voucher per party will be accepted, cannot be used in conjunction with any other offer, photocopies will not be accepted.
4. All attractions offering a discount have confirmed their willingness to participate. All information is subject to change without notice and should any attraction close or decline to accept a voucher for any reason, Days Out UK are not liable and cannot be held responsible.
5. Days Out UK shall not accept liability for any loss, accident or injury that may occur at a participating attraction and any dispute arising must be settled direct with the attraction concerned.
6. Cash redemption value of each voucher is 0.001p.
7. You are advised to check all relevant information with your chosen attraction before commencing your journey.

Days Out UK, PO Box 427, Northampton NN1 3YN. Tel: 01604 622445

Liberty's Raptor and Reptile Centre
Crow Lane Ringwood Hampshire BH24 3EA
One Child Free
with a full-paying adult

Cannot be used in conjunction with other offers. One voucher per party. Not valid on Bank Hols or special event days.

Expires end Feb 2009 (unless otherwise specified)

DISCOUNT VOUCHER

Lightwater Valley Theme Park
North Stainley Ripon North Yorkshire HG4 3HT
£10.95 entry to Lightwater Valley
£6.00 Off Full Price Entry of £16.95
(Max 6 people per voucher. Park open from 15 Mar until 2 Nov. Please phone or check website for exact dates.)

Cannot be used in conjunction with other offers. One voucher per party. Not valid on Bank Hols or special event days.

Valid throughout 2008 season

DISCOUNT VOUCHER

Liverpool Football Club Museum and Tour Centre
Anfield Road Liverpool Merseyside L4 0TH
One Child Free
with a full-paying adult

Cannot be used in conjunction with other offers. One voucher per party. Not valid on Bank Hols or special event days.

Expires end Feb 2009 (unless otherwise specified)

DISCOUNT VOUCHER

Llanberis Lake Railway
Padarn Country Park Gilfach Ddu Llanberis Caernarfon Gwynedd LL55 4TY
One Child Free
with a full-paying adult
(Not valid on special event days or Santa Trains)

Cannot be used in conjunction with other offers. One voucher per party. Not valid on Bank Hols or special event days.

Valid 10 Feb - 10 Dec 2008

DISCOUNT VOUCHER

London Dungeon
28-34 Tooley Street London SE1 2SZ
One Child Free
with every full-paying adult

Cannot be used in conjunction with other offers. One voucher per party. Not valid on Bank Hols or special event days.

Expires end Feb 2009 (unless otherwise specified)

DISCOUNT VOUCHER

London Waterbus Company
London NW1 8AF
80p off Adult Fares
one-way or return tickets to Camden Lock or Little Venice
(Present voucher on board, not valid for fares to or from London Zoo, one voucher per person, not for use with any other offer, seats subject to availability)

Cannot be used in conjunction with other offers. One voucher per party. Not valid on Bank Hols or special event days.

Valid until 31 Oct 2008

DISCOUNT VOUCHER

1. Each voucher entitles the holder to the discount specified by the selected attraction.
2. Valid for use until 28/02/09 (unless otherwise specified, or if attraction season finishes prior to this). Vouchers are subject to the terms, conditions and restrictions of the selected attraction.
3. One voucher per party will be accepted, cannot be used in conjunction with any other offer, photocopies will not be accepted.
4. All attractions offering a discount have confirmed their willingness to participate. All information is subject to change without notice and should any attraction close or decline to accept a voucher for any reason, Days Out UK are not liable and cannot be held responsible.
5. Days Out UK shall not accept liability for any loss, accident or injury that may occur at a participating attraction and any dispute arising must be settled direct with the attraction concerned.
6. Cash redemption value of each voucher is 0.001p.
7. You are advised to check all relevant information with your chosen attraction before commencing your journey.

Days Out UK, PO Box 427, Northampton NN1 3YN. Tel: 01604 622445

1. Each voucher entitles the holder to the discount specified by the selected attraction.
2. Valid for use until 28/02/09 (unless otherwise specified. or if attraction season finishes prior to this). Vouchers are subject to the terms, conditions and restrictions of the selected attraction.
3. One voucher per party will be accepted, cannot be used in conjunction with any other offer, photocopies will not be accepted.
4. All attractions offering a discount have confirmed their willingness to participate. All information is subject to change without notice and should any attraction close or decline to accept a voucher for any reason, Days Out UK are not liable and cannot be held responsible.
5. Days Out UK shall not accept liability for any loss, accident or injury that may occur at a participating attraction and any dispute arising must be settled direct with the attraction concerned.
6. Cash redemption value of each voucher is 0.001p.
7. You are advised to check all relevant information with your chosen attraction before commencing your journey.

Days Out UK, PO Box 427, Northampton NN1 3YN. Tel: 01604 622445

1. Each voucher entitles the holder to the discount specified by the selected attraction.
2. Valid for use until 28/02/09 (unless otherwise specified, or if attraction season finishes prior to this). Vouchers are subject to the terms, conditions and restrictions of the selected attraction.
3. One voucher per party will be accepted, cannot be used in conjunction with any other offer, photocopies will not be accepted.
4. All attractions offering a discount have confirmed their willingness to participate. All information is subject to change without notice and should any attraction close or decline to accept a voucher for any reason, Days Out UK are not liable and cannot be held responsible.
5. Days Out UK shall not accept liability for any loss, accident or injury that may occur at a participating attraction and any dispute arising must be settled direct with the attraction concerned.
6. Cash redemption value of each voucher is 0.001p.
7. You are advised to check all relevant information with your chosen attraction before commencing your journey.

Days Out UK, PO Box 427, Northampton NN1 3YN. Tel: 01604 622445

1. Each voucher entitles the holder to the discount specified by the selected attraction.
2. Valid for use until 28/02/09 (unless otherwise specified, or if attraction season finishes prior to this). Vouchers are subject to the terms, conditions and restrictions of the selected attraction.
3. One voucher per party will be accepted, cannot be used in conjunction with any other offer, photocopies will not be accepted.
4. All attractions offering a discount have confirmed their willingness to participate. All information is subject to change without notice and should any attraction close or decline to accept a voucher for any reason, Days Out UK are not liable and cannot be held responsible.
5. Days Out UK shall not accept liability for any loss, accident or injury that may occur at a participating attraction and any dispute arising must be settled direct with the attraction concerned.
6. Cash redemption value of each voucher is 0.001p.
7. You are advised to check all relevant information with your chosen attraction before commencing your journey.

Days Out UK, PO Box 427, Northampton NN1 3YN. Tel: 01604 622445

1. Each voucher entitles the holder to the discount specified by the selected attraction.
2. Valid for use until 28/02/09 (unless otherwise specified, or if attraction season finishes prior to this). Vouchers are subject to the terms, conditions and restrictions of the selected attraction.
3. One voucher per party will be accepted, cannot be used in conjunction with any other offer, photocopies will not be accepted.
4. All attractions offering a discount have confirmed their willingness to participate. All information is subject to change without notice and should any attraction close or decline to accept a voucher for any reason, Days Out UK are not liable and cannot be held responsible.
5. Days Out UK shall not accept liability for any loss, accident or injury that may occur at a participating attraction and any dispute arising must be settled direct with the attraction concerned.
6. Cash redemption value of each voucher is 0.001p.
7. You are advised to check all relevant information with your chosen attraction before commencing your journey.

Days Out UK, PO Box 427, Northampton NN1 3YN. Tel: 01604 622445

Longdown Activity Farm
Longdown Ashurst Southampton Hampshire SO40 7EH
One Child Free
with one full-paying adult
(Not valid Bank Holidays or Easter Half-Term or special event days, cannot be used in conjunction with family tickets or any other offer)
Cannot be used in conjunction with other offers. One voucher per party. Not valid on Bank Hols or special event days.
Expires end Feb 2009 (unless otherwise specified)

DISCOUNT VOUCHER

Look Out Discovery Centre, The
Nine Mile Ride Bracknell Berkshire RG12 7QW
One Child Free
with a full paying adult
Cannot be used in conjunction with other offers. One voucher per party. Not valid on Bank Hols or special event days.
Expires end Feb 2009 (unless otherwise specified)

DISCOUNT VOUCHER

Lord's Tour and MCC Museum
Lord's Ground St John's Wood London NW8 8QN
One Child Free
with one full-paying adult
(Valid on all public tours, not valid on match tickets)
Cannot be used in conjunction with other offers. One voucher per party. Not valid on Bank Hols or special event days.
Expires end Feb 2009 (unless otherwise specified)

DISCOUNT VOUCHER

Lulworth Castle and Park
East Lulworth Wareham Dorset BH20 5QS
One Child Free
with every full-paying adult
Cannot be used in conjunction with other offers. One voucher per party. Not valid on Bank Hols or special event days.
Expires end Feb 2009 (unless otherwise specified)

DISCOUNT VOUCHER

M and D's Scotland's Theme Park
Strathclyde Country Park Motherwell North Lanarkshire ML1 3RT
£5.00 off One Unlimited Ride Wristband
for a family of 4
Cannot be used in conjunction with other offers. One voucher per party. Not valid on Bank Hols or special event days.
Valid for 2008 season only

DISCOUNT VOUCHER

Macduff Marine Aquarium
11 High Shore Macduff Aberdeenshire AB44 1SL
One Child Free
with a full-paying adult
Cannot be used in conjunction with other offers. One voucher per party. Not valid on Bank Hols or special event days.
Expires end Feb 2009 (unless otherwise specified)

DISCOUNT VOUCHER

1. Each voucher entitles the holder to the discount specified by the selected attraction.
2. Valid for use until 28/02/09 (unless otherwise specified, or if attraction season finishes prior to this). Vouchers are subject to the terms, conditions and restrictions of the selected attraction.
3. One voucher per party will be accepted, cannot be used in conjunction with any other offer, photocopies will not be accepted.
4. All attractions offering a discount have confirmed their willingness to participate. All information is subject to change without notice and should any attraction close or decline to accept a voucher for any reason, Days Out UK are not liable and cannot be held responsible.
5. Days Out UK shall not accept liability for any loss, accident or injury that may occur at a participating attraction and any dispute arising must be settled direct with the attraction concerned.
6. Cash redemption value of each voucher is 0.001p.
7. You are advised to check all relevant information with your chosen attraction before commencing your journey.

Days Out UK, PO Box 427, Northampton NN1 3YN. Tel: 01604 622445

1. Each voucher entitles the holder to the discount specified by the selected attraction.
2. Valid for use until 28/02/09 (unless otherwise specified, or if attraction season finishes prior to this). Vouchers are subject to the terms, conditions and restrictions of the selected attraction.
3. One voucher per party will be accepted, cannot be used in conjunction with any other offer, photocopies will not be accepted.
4. All attractions offering a discount have confirmed their willingness to participate. All information is subject to change without notice and should any attraction close or decline to accept a voucher for any reason, Days Out UK are not liable and cannot be held responsible.
5. Days Out UK shall not accept liability for any loss, accident or injury that may occur at a participating attraction and any dispute arising must be settled direct with the attraction concerned.
6. Cash redemption value of each voucher is 0.001p.
7. You are advised to check all relevant information with your chosen attraction before commencing your journey.

Days Out UK, PO Box 427, Northampton NN1 3YN. Tel: 01604 622445

1. Each voucher entitles the holder to the discount specified by the selected attraction.
2. Valid for use until 28/02/09 (unless otherwise specified, or if attraction season finishes prior to this). Vouchers are subject to the terms, conditions and restrictions of the selected attraction.
3. One voucher per party will be accepted, cannot be used in conjunction with any other offer, photocopies will not be accepted.
4. All attractions offering a discount have confirmed their willingness to participate. All information is subject to change without notice and should any attraction close or decline to accept a voucher for any reason, Days Out UK are not liable and cannot be held responsible.
5. Days Out UK shall not accept liability for any loss, accident or injury that may occur at a participating attraction and any dispute arising must be settled direct with the attraction concerned.
6. Cash redemption value of each voucher is 0.001p.
7. You are advised to check all relevant information with your chosen attraction before commencing your journey.

Days Out UK, PO Box 427, Northampton NN1 3YN. Tel: 01604 622445

1. Each voucher entitles the holder to the discount specified by the selected attraction.
2. Valid for use until 28/02/09 (unless otherwise specified, or if attraction season finishes prior to this). Vouchers are subject to the terms, conditions and restrictions of the selected attraction.
3. One voucher per party will be accepted, cannot be used in conjunction with any other offer, photocopies will not be accepted.
4. All attractions offering a discount have confirmed their willingness to participate. All information is subject to change without notice and should any attraction close or decline to accept a voucher for any reason, Days Out UK are not liable and cannot be held responsible.
5. Days Out UK shall not accept liability for any loss, accident or injury that may occur at a participating attraction and any dispute arising must be settled direct with the attraction concerned.
6. Cash redemption value of each voucher is 0.001p.
7. You are advised to check all relevant information with your chosen attraction before commencing your journey.

Days Out UK, PO Box 427, Northampton NN1 3YN. Tel: 01604 622445

1. Each voucher entitles the holder to the discount specified by the selected attraction.
2. Valid for use until 28/02/09 (unless otherwise specified, or if attraction season finishes prior to this). Vouchers are subject to the terms, conditions and restrictions of the selected attraction.
3. One voucher per party will be accepted, cannot be used in conjunction with any other offer, photocopies will not be accepted.
4. All attractions offering a discount have confirmed their willingness to participate. All information is subject to change without notice and should any attraction close or decline to accept a voucher for any reason, Days Out UK are not liable and cannot be held responsible.
5. Days Out UK shall not accept liability for any loss, accident or injury that may occur at a participating attraction and any dispute arising must be settled direct with the attraction concerned.
6. Cash redemption value of each voucher is 0.001p.
7. You are advised to check all relevant information with your chosen attraction before commencing your journey.

Days Out UK, PO Box 427, Northampton NN1 3YN. Tel: 01604 622445

533

1. Each voucher entitles the holder to the discount specified by the selected attraction.
2. Valid for use until 28/02/09 (unless otherwise specified, or if attraction season finishes prior to this). Vouchers are subject to the terms, conditions and restrictions of the selected attraction.
3. One voucher per party will be accepted, cannot be used in conjunction with any other offer, photocopies will not be accepted.
4. All attractions offering a discount have confirmed their willingness to participate. All information is subject to change without notice and should any attraction close or decline to accept a voucher for any reason, Days Out UK are not liable and cannot be held responsible.
5. Days Out UK shall not accept liability for any loss, accident or injury that may occur at a participating attraction and any dispute arising must be settled direct with the attraction concerned.
6. Cash redemption value of each voucher is 0.001p.
7. You are advised to check all relevant information with your chosen attraction before commencing your journey.

Days Out UK, PO Box 427, Northampton NN1 3YN. Tel: 01604 622445

1. Each voucher entitles the holder to the discount specified by the selected attraction.
2. Valid for use until 28/02/09 (unless otherwise specified. or if attraction season finishes prior to this). Vouchers are subject to the terms, conditions and restrictions of the selected attraction.
3. One voucher per party will be accepted, cannot be used in conjunction with any other offer, photocopies will not be accepted.
4. All attractions offering a discount have confirmed their willingness to participate. All information is subject to change without notice and should any attraction close or decline to accept a voucher for any reason, Days Out UK are not liable and cannot be held responsible.
5. Days Out UK shall not accept liability for any loss, accident or injury that may occur at a participating attraction and any dispute arising must be settled direct with the attraction concerned.
6. Cash redemption value of each voucher is 0.001p.
7. You are advised to check all relevant information with your chosen attraction before commencing your journey.

Days Out UK, PO Box 427, Northampton NN1 3YN. Tel: 01604 622445

1. Each voucher entitles the holder to the discount specified by the selected attraction.
2. Valid for use until 28/02/09 (unless otherwise specified, or if attraction season finishes prior to this). Vouchers are subject to the terms, conditions and restrictions of the selected attraction.
3. One voucher per party will be accepted, cannot be used in conjunction with any other offer, photocopies will not be accepted.
4. All attractions offering a discount have confirmed their willingness to participate. All information is subject to change without notice and should any attraction close or decline to accept a voucher for any reason, Days Out UK are not liable and cannot be held responsible.
5. Days Out UK shall not accept liability for any loss, accident or injury that may occur at a participating attraction and any dispute arising must be settled direct with the attraction concerned.
6. Cash redemption value of each voucher is 0.001p.
7. You are advised to check all relevant information with your chosen attraction before commencing your journey.

Days Out UK, PO Box 427, Northampton NN1 3YN. Tel: 01604 622445

1. Each voucher entitles the holder to the discount specified by the selected attraction.
2. Valid for use until 28/02/09 (unless otherwise specified, or if attraction season finishes prior to this). Vouchers are subject to the terms, conditions and restrictions of the selected attraction.
3. One voucher per party will be accepted, cannot be used in conjunction with any other offer, photocopies will not be accepted.
4. All attractions offering a discount have confirmed their willingness to participate. All information is subject to change without notice and should any attraction close or decline to accept a voucher for any reason, Days Out UK are not liable and cannot be held responsible.
5. Days Out UK shall not accept liability for any loss, accident or injury that may occur at a participating attraction and any dispute arising must be settled direct with the attraction concerned.
6. Cash redemption value of each voucher is 0.001p.
7. You are advised to check all relevant information with your chosen attraction before commencing your journey.

Days Out UK, PO Box 427, Northampton NN1 3YN. Tel: 01604 622445

1. Each voucher entitles the holder to the discount specified by the selected attraction.
2. Valid for use until 28/02/09 (unless otherwise specified, or if attraction season finishes prior to this). Vouchers are subject to the terms, conditions and restrictions of the selected attraction.
3. One voucher per party will be accepted, cannot be used in conjunction with any other offer, photocopies will not be accepted.
4. All attractions offering a discount have confirmed their willingness to participate. All information is subject to change without notice and should any attraction close or decline to accept a voucher for any reason, Days Out UK are not liable and cannot be held responsible.
5. Days Out UK shall not accept liability for any loss, accident or injury that may occur at a participating attraction and any dispute arising must be settled direct with the attraction concerned.
6. Cash redemption value of each voucher is 0.001p.
7. You are advised to check all relevant information with your chosen attraction before commencing your journey.

Days Out UK, PO Box 427, Northampton NN1 3YN. Tel: 01604 622445

Melford Hall
Long Melford Sudbury Suffolk CO10 9AA
One Child Free
with a full-paying adult

Cannot be used in conjunction with other offers. One voucher per party. Not valid on Bank Hols or special event days.
Expires end Feb 2009 (unless otherwise specified)

DISCOUNT VOUCHER

Mersey Ferries Ltd
Victoria Place Wallasey Merseyside CH44 6QY
Save up to £1.00 off your journey
(£1.00 off a return ferry adult ticket or 50p off a return ferry child ticket)

Cannot be used in conjunction with other offers. One voucher per party. Not valid on Bank Hols or special event days.
Expires end Feb 2009 (unless otherwise specified)

DISCOUNT VOUCHER

Michelham Priory
Upper Dicker Nr Hailsham East Sussex BN27 3QS
£1.00 off each full-priced adult, senior or student ticket
(Not valid for child tickets, cannot be used on weekends, not valid on any special event days, please see website for dates of events)

Cannot be used in conjunction with other offers. One voucher per party. Not valid on Bank Hols or special event days.
Valid 1 Mar - 31 Oct 2008

DISCOUNT VOUCHER

Middle Farm
Firle Lewes East Sussex BN8 6LJ
Two for the Price of One
with a full-paying adult

Cannot be used in conjunction with other offers. One voucher per party. Not valid on Bank Hols or special event days.
Expires end Feb 2009 (unless otherwise specified)

DISCOUNT VOUCHER

Milestones, Hampshire's Living History Museum
Leisure Park Churchill Way West Basingstoke Hampshire
Two for the Price of One
full-paying adult
(Not valid for groups, joint ticket events or Christmas Gala evenings)

Cannot be used in conjunction with other offers. One voucher per party. Not valid on Bank Hols or special event days.
Expires end Feb 2009 (unless otherwise specified)

DISCOUNT VOUCHER

Moggerhanger Park
Park Road Moggerhanger Bedford Bedfordshire MK44 3RW
Two for the Price of One
with a full-paying adult
(Can be used for guided tours of Moggerhanger House)

Cannot be used in conjunction with other offers. One voucher per party. Not valid on Bank Hols or special event days.
Valid 14 Jun - 12 Sept 2008

DISCOUNT VOUCHER

535

1. Each voucher entitles the holder to the discount specified by the selected attraction.
2. Valid for use until 28/02/09 (unless otherwise specified, or if attraction season finishes prior to this). Vouchers are subject to the terms, conditions and restrictions of the selected attraction.
3. One voucher per party will be accepted, cannot be used in conjunction with any other offer, photocopies will not be accepted.
4. All attractions offering a discount have confirmed their willingness to participate. All information is subject to change without notice and should any attraction close or decline to accept a voucher for any reason, Days Out UK are not liable and cannot be held responsible.
5. Days Out UK shall not accept liability for any loss, accident or injury that may occur at a participating attraction and any dispute arising must be settled direct with the attraction concerned.
6. Cash redemption value of each voucher is 0.001p.
7. You are advised to check all relevant information with your chosen attraction before commencing your journey.

Days Out UK, PO Box 427, Northampton NN1 3YN. Tel: 01604 622445

1. Each voucher entitles the holder to the discount specified by the selected attraction.
2. Valid for use until 28/02/09 (unless otherwise specified. or if attraction season finishes prior to this). Vouchers are subject to the terms, conditions and restrictions of the selected attraction.
3. One voucher per party will be accepted, cannot be used in conjunction with any other offer, photocopies will not be accepted.
4. All attractions offering a discount have confirmed their willingness to participate. All information is subject to change without notice and should any attraction close or decline to accept a voucher for any reason, Days Out UK are not liable and cannot be held responsible.
5. Days Out UK shall not accept liability for any loss, accident or injury that may occur at a participating attraction and any dispute arising must be settled direct with the attraction concerned.
6. Cash redemption value of each voucher is 0.001p.
7. You are advised to check all relevant information with your chosen attraction before commencing your journey.

Days Out UK, PO Box 427, Northampton NN1 3YN. Tel: 01604 622445

1. Each voucher entitles the holder to the discount specified by the selected attraction.
2. Valid for use until 28/02/09 (unless otherwise specified, or if attraction season finishes prior to this). Vouchers are subject to the terms, conditions and restrictions of the selected attraction.
3. One voucher per party will be accepted, cannot be used in conjunction with any other offer, photocopies will not be accepted.
4. All attractions offering a discount have confirmed their willingness to participate. All information is subject to change without notice and should any attraction close or decline to accept a voucher for any reason, Days Out UK are not liable and cannot be held responsible.
5. Days Out UK shall not accept liability for any loss, accident or injury that may occur at a participating attraction and any dispute arising must be settled direct with the attraction concerned.
6. Cash redemption value of each voucher is 0.001p.
7. You are advised to check all relevant information with your chosen attraction before commencing your journey.

Days Out UK, PO Box 427, Northampton NN1 3YN. Tel: 01604 622445

1. Each voucher entitles the holder to the discount specified by the selected attraction.
2. Valid for use until 28/02/09 (unless otherwise specified, or if attraction season finishes prior to this). Vouchers are subject to the terms, conditions and restrictions of the selected attraction.
3. One voucher per party will be accepted, cannot be used in conjunction with any other offer, photocopies will not be accepted.
4. All attractions offering a discount have confirmed their willingness to participate. All information is subject to change without notice and should any attraction close or decline to accept a voucher for any reason, Days Out UK are not liable and cannot be held responsible.
5. Days Out UK shall not accept liability for any loss, accident or injury that may occur at a participating attraction and any dispute arising must be settled direct with the attraction concerned.
6. Cash redemption value of each voucher is 0.001p.
7. You are advised to check all relevant information with your chosen attraction before commencing your journey.

Days Out UK, PO Box 427, Northampton NN1 3YN. Tel: 01604 622445

1. Each voucher entitles the holder to the discount specified by the selected attraction.
2. Valid for use until 28/02/09 (unless otherwise specified, or if attraction season finishes prior to this). Vouchers are subject to the terms, conditions and restrictions of the selected attraction.
3. One voucher per party will be accepted, cannot be used in conjunction with any other offer, photocopies will not be accepted.
4. All attractions offering a discount have confirmed their willingness to participate. All information is subject to change without notice and should any attraction close or decline to accept a voucher for any reason, Days Out UK are not liable and cannot be held responsible.
5. Days Out UK shall not accept liability for any loss, accident or injury that may occur at a participating attraction and any dispute arising must be settled direct with the attraction concerned.
6. Cash redemption value of each voucher is 0.001p.
7. You are advised to check all relevant information with your chosen attraction before commencing your journey.

Days Out UK, PO Box 427, Northampton NN1 3YN. Tel: 01604 622445

Mr Hardman's Photographic Studio

59 Rodney Street Liverpool Merseyside L1 9EX

One Child Free

with a full-paying adult

Cannot be used in conjunction with other offers. One voucher per party. Not valid on Bank Hols or special event days.

Expires end Feb 2009 (unless otherwise specified)

DAYSOUTUK
The place to look for places to go

Museum in Docklands

No 1 Warehouse West India Quay Hertsmere Road London E14 4AL

Two for the Price of One
with a full-paying adult

Cannot be used in conjunction with other offers. One voucher per party. Not valid on Bank Hols or special event days.

Expires end Feb 2009 (unless otherwise specified)

DAYSOUTUK
The place to look for places to go

Nash's House and New Place

Chapel Street Stratford-Upon-Avon Warwickshire CV37 6EP

See Shakespeare's Birthplace voucher
for details

Cannot be used in conjunction with other offers. One voucher per party. Not valid on Bank Hols or special event days.

Expires end Feb 2009 (unless otherwise specified)

DAYSOUTUK
The place to look for places to go

National Botanic Garden of Wales

Llanarthne Carmarthenshire SA32 8HG

Two for the Price of One
with a full-paying adult

(Garden closed on Christmas Day only, cannot be used for groups or in conjunction with any other offer, voucher to be used once only, not valid on special event days, concert days or Bank Holidays, photocopies are not acceptable, no cash alternative)

Cannot be used in conjunction with other offers. One voucher per party. Not valid on Bank Hols or special event days.

Valid until 31 Dec 2008

DAYSOUTUK
The place to look for places to go

National Horseracing Museum and Tours

99 High Street Newmarket Suffolk CB8 8JH

Two for the Price of One

with a full-paying adult

Cannot be used in conjunction with other offers. One voucher per party. Not valid on Bank Hols or special event days.

Expires end Feb 2009 (unless otherwise specified)

DAYSOUTUK
The place to look for places to go

National Maritime Museum

Romney Road Greenwich London SE10 9NF

20% Off Peter Harrison Planetarium Ticket
(A£4.80, C£3.20)

(No cash alternative. This voucher cannot be resold. Discount is not valid for Family Ticket. Not to be used in conjunction with any other offer. Hand in at Planetarium ticket desk to receive discount)

Cannot be used in conjunction with other offers. One voucher per party. Not valid on Bank Hols or special event days.

Valid from 28 Feb 2008 - 18 Jul 2008

DAYSOUTUK
The place to look for places to go

1. Each voucher entitles the holder to the discount specified by the selected attraction.
2. Valid for use until 28/02/09 (unless otherwise specified, or if attraction season finishes prior to this). Vouchers are subject to the terms, conditions and restrictions of the selected attraction.
3. One voucher per party will be accepted, cannot be used in conjunction with any other offer, photocopies will not be accepted.
4. All attractions offering a discount have confirmed their willingness to participate. All information is subject to change without notice and should any attraction close or decline to accept a voucher for any reason, Days Out UK are not liable and cannot be held responsible.
5. Days Out UK shall not accept liability for any loss, accident or injury that may occur at a participating attraction and any dispute arising must be settled direct with the attraction concerned.
6. Cash redemption value of each voucher is 0.001p.
7. You are advised to check all relevant information with your chosen attraction before commencing your journey.

Days Out UK, PO Box 427, Northampton NN1 3YN. Tel: 01604 622445

1. Each voucher entitles the holder to the discount specified by the selected attraction.
2. Valid for use until 28/02/09 (unless otherwise specified. or if attraction season finishes prior to this). Vouchers are subject to the terms, conditions and restrictions of the selected attraction.
3. One voucher per party will be accepted, cannot be used in conjunction with any other offer, photocopies will not be accepted.
4. All attractions offering a discount have confirmed their willingness to participate. All information is subject to change without notice and should any attraction close or decline to accept a voucher for any reason, Days Out UK are not liable and cannot be held responsible.
5. Days Out UK shall not accept liability for any loss, accident or injury that may occur at a participating attraction and any dispute arising must be settled direct with the attraction concerned.
6. Cash redemption value of each voucher is 0.001p.
7. You are advised to check all relevant information with your chosen attraction before commencing your journey.

Days Out UK, PO Box 427, Northampton NN1 3YN. Tel: 01604 622445

1. Each voucher entitles the holder to the discount specified by the selected attraction.
2. Valid for use until 28/02/09 (unless otherwise specified, or if attraction season finishes prior to this). Vouchers are subject to the terms, conditions and restrictions of the selected attraction.
3. One voucher per party will be accepted, cannot be used in conjunction with any other offer, photocopies will not be accepted.
4. All attractions offering a discount have confirmed their willingness to participate. All information is subject to change without notice and should any attraction close or decline to accept a voucher for any reason, Days Out UK are not liable and cannot be held responsible.
5. Days Out UK shall not accept liability for any loss, accident or injury that may occur at a participating attraction and any dispute arising must be settled direct with the attraction concerned.
6. Cash redemption value of each voucher is 0.001p.
7. You are advised to check all relevant information with your chosen attraction before commencing your journey.

Days Out UK, PO Box 427, Northampton NN1 3YN. Tel: 01604 622445

1. Each voucher entitles the holder to the discount specified by the selected attraction.
2. Valid for use until 28/02/09 (unless otherwise specified, or if attraction season finishes prior to this). Vouchers are subject to the terms, conditions and restrictions of the selected attraction.
3. One voucher per party will be accepted, cannot be used in conjunction with any other offer, photocopies will not be accepted.
4. All attractions offering a discount have confirmed their willingness to participate. All information is subject to change without notice and should any attraction close or decline to accept a voucher for any reason, Days Out UK are not liable and cannot be held responsible.
5. Days Out UK shall not accept liability for any loss, accident or injury that may occur at a participating attraction and any dispute arising must be settled direct with the attraction concerned.
6. Cash redemption value of each voucher is 0.001p.
7. You are advised to check all relevant information with your chosen attraction before commencing your journey.

Days Out UK, PO Box 427, Northampton NN1 3YN. Tel: 01604 622445

1. Each voucher entitles the holder to the discount specified by the selected attraction.
2. Valid for use until 28/02/09 (unless otherwise specified, or if attraction season finishes prior to this). Vouchers are subject to the terms, conditions and restrictions of the selected attraction.
3. One voucher per party will be accepted, cannot be used in conjunction with any other offer, photocopies will not be accepted.
4. All attractions offering a discount have confirmed their willingness to participate. All information is subject to change without notice and should any attraction close or decline to accept a voucher for any reason, Days Out UK are not liable and cannot be held responsible.
5. Days Out UK shall not accept liability for any loss, accident or injury that may occur at a participating attraction and any dispute arising must be settled direct with the attraction concerned.
6. Cash redemption value of each voucher is 0.001p.
7. You are advised to check all relevant information with your chosen attraction before commencing your journey.

Days Out UK, PO Box 427, Northampton NN1 3YN. Tel: 01604 622445

National Maritime Museum Cornwall

Discovery Quay Falmouth Cornwall TR11 3QY

One Child Free
with a full-paying adult

Cannot be used in conjunction with other offers. One voucher per party. Not valid on Bank Hols or special event days.

Expires end Feb 2009 (unless otherwise specified)

DISCOUNT VOUCHER

National Museum of Costume Scotland

Shambellie House New Abbey Dumfries Dumfries & Galloway DG2 8HQ

Two for the Price of One
with a full-paying adult

(Offer does not include entry to special events, Cannot be used November-March when the
National Museum of Costume Scotland is closed)

Cannot be used in conjunction with other offers. One voucher per party. Not valid on Bank Hols or special event days.

Expires end Feb 2009 (unless otherwise specified)

DISCOUNT VOUCHER

National Museum of Flight Scotland

East Fortune Airfield North Berwick East Lothian EH39 5LF

Two for the Price of One
with a full-paying adult

(Valid April-October 08 (daily), plus weekends during November 08 - March 09; offer applies
to adult and concession tickets; offer includes the Concorde Experience, offer excludes
Concorde boarding passes; not valid for special events)

Cannot be used in conjunction with other offers. One voucher per party. Not valid on Bank Hols or special event days.

Expires end Feb 2009 (unless otherwise specified)

DISCOUNT VOUCHER

National Museum of Rural Life

Wester Kittochside Philipshill Road East Kilbride South Lanarkshire
G76 9HR

Two for the Price of One
with a full-paying adult

(Excludes special events)

Cannot be used in conjunction with other offers. One voucher per party. Not valid on Bank Hols or special event days.

Expires end Feb 2009 (unless otherwise specified)

DISCOUNT VOUCHER

National Sea Life Centre

The Waters Edge Brindleyplace Birmingham B1 2HL

One Child Free with a full-paying adult

Conditions:
1. This voucher entitles free admission to the National Sea Life Centre for one child
when accompanied by one full paying adult.
2. Offer expires 28 February 2009.
3. Cannot be used in conjunction with any other offer.
4. A "child" is classed as a person aged 3-14 inclusive (under 3s go free anyway).
5. No cash alternative, non-refundable; and non-exchangeable.
6. All children must be accompanied by an adult.
7. Only one voucher per party and per transaction.
8. Photocopies not accepted.
9. SEA LIFE/Sanctuaries reserve the right to alter, close or remove details/exhibits
without prior notice for technical, operational or other reasons, and no refunds can
be given in these circumstances.
10. SEA LIFE/Sanctuaries reserve the right to refuse entry without explanation.
Voucher Ref: DOUK.

Cannot be used in conjunction with other offers. One voucher per party. Not valid on Bank Hols or special event days.

Expires end Feb 2009 (unless otherwise specified)

DISCOUNT VOUCHER

1. Each voucher entitles the holder to the discount specified by the selected attraction.
2. Valid for use until 28/02/09 (unless otherwise specified, or if attraction season finishes prior to this). Vouchers are subject to the terms, conditions and restrictions of the selected attraction.
3. One voucher per party will be accepted, cannot be used in conjunction with any other offer, photocopies will not be accepted.
4. All attractions offering a discount have confirmed their willingness to participate. All information is subject to change without notice and should any attraction close or decline to accept a voucher for any reason, Days Out UK are not liable and cannot be held responsible.
5. Days Out UK shall not accept liability for any loss, accident or injury that may occur at a participating attraction and any dispute arising must be settled direct with the attraction concerned.
6. Cash redemption value of each voucher is 0.001p.
7. You are advised to check all relevant information with your chosen attraction before commencing your journey.

Days Out UK, PO Box 427, Northampton NN1 3YN. Tel: 01604 622445

1. Each voucher entitles the holder to the discount specified by the selected attraction.
2. Valid for use until 28/02/09 (unless otherwise specified, or if attraction season finishes prior to this). Vouchers are subject to the terms, conditions and restrictions of the selected attraction.
3. One voucher per party will be accepted, cannot be used in conjunction with any other offer, photocopies will not be accepted.
4. All attractions offering a discount have confirmed their willingness to participate. All information is subject to change without notice and should any attraction close or decline to accept a voucher for any reason, Days Out UK are not liable and cannot be held responsible.
5. Days Out UK shall not accept liability for any loss, accident or injury that may occur at a participating attraction and any dispute arising must be settled direct with the attraction concerned.
6. Cash redemption value of each voucher is 0.001p.
7. You are advised to check all relevant information with your chosen attraction before commencing your journey.

Days Out UK, PO Box 427, Northampton NN1 3YN. Tel: 01604 622445

1. Each voucher entitles the holder to the discount specified by the selected attraction.
2. Valid for use until 28/02/09 (unless otherwise specified, or if attraction season finishes prior to this). Vouchers are subject to the terms, conditions and restrictions of the selected attraction.
3. One voucher per party will be accepted, cannot be used in conjunction with any other offer, photocopies will not be accepted.
4. All attractions offering a discount have confirmed their willingness to participate. All information is subject to change without notice and should any attraction close or decline to accept a voucher for any reason, Days Out UK are not liable and cannot be held responsible.
5. Days Out UK shall not accept liability for any loss, accident or injury that may occur at a participating attraction and any dispute arising must be settled direct with the attraction concerned.
6. Cash redemption value of each voucher is 0.001p.
7. You are advised to check all relevant information with your chosen attraction before commencing your journey.

Days Out UK, PO Box 427, Northampton NN1 3YN. Tel: 01604 622445

1. Each voucher entitles the holder to the discount specified by the selected attraction.
2. Valid for use until 28/02/09 (unless otherwise specified, or if attraction season finishes prior to this). Vouchers are subject to the terms, conditions and restrictions of the selected attraction.
3. One voucher per party will be accepted, cannot be used in conjunction with any other offer, photocopies will not be accepted.
4. All attractions offering a discount have confirmed their willingness to participate. All information is subject to change without notice and should any attraction close or decline to accept a voucher for any reason, Days Out UK are not liable and cannot be held responsible.
5. Days Out UK shall not accept liability for any loss, accident or injury that may occur at a participating attraction and any dispute arising must be settled direct with the attraction concerned.
6. Cash redemption value of each voucher is 0.001p.
7. You are advised to check all relevant information with your chosen attraction before commencing your journey.

Days Out UK, PO Box 427, Northampton NN1 3YN. Tel: 01604 622445

1. Each voucher entitles the holder to the discount specified by the selected attraction.

2. Valid for use until 28/02/09 (unless otherwise specified, or if attraction season finishes prior to this). Vouchers are subject to the terms, conditions and restrictions of the selected attraction.

3. One voucher per party will be accepted, cannot be used in conjunction with any other offer, photocopies will not be accepted.

4. All attractions offering a discount have confirmed their willingness to participate. All information is subject to change without notice and should any attraction close or decline to accept a voucher for any reason, Days Out UK are not liable and cannot be held responsible.

5. Days Out UK shall not accept liability for any loss, accident or injury that may occur at a participating attraction and any dispute arising must be settled direct with the attraction concerned.

6. Cash redemption value of each voucher is 0.001p.

7. You are advised to check all relevant information with your chosen attraction before commencing your journey.

Days Out UK, PO Box 427, Northampton NN1 3YN. Tel: 01604 622445

National Sea Life Centre

Strand Road Bray County Wicklow Ireland

One Child Free with a full-paying adult

Conditions:

1. This voucher entitles free admission to the National Sea Life Centre for one child when accompanied by one full paying adult.
2. Offer expires 28 February 2009.
3. Cannot be used in conjunction with any other offer.
4. A "child" is classed as a person aged 3-14 inclusive (under 3s go free anyway).
5. No cash alternative, non-refundable; and non-exchangeable.
6. All children must be accompanied by an adult.
7. Only one voucher per party and per transaction.
8. Photocopies not accepted.
9. SEA LIFE/Sanctuaries reserve the right to alter, close or remove details/exhibits without prior notice for technical, operational or other reasons, and no refunds can be given in these circumstances.
10. SEA LIFE/Sanctuaries reserve the right to refuse entry without explanation.

Voucher Ref: DOUK.

Cannot be used in conjunction with other offers. One voucher per party. Not valid on Bank Hols or special event days.

Expires end Feb 2009 (unless otherwise specified)

DISCOUNT VOUCHER

National Seal Sanctuary

Gweek Helston Cornwall TR12 6UG

One Child Free with a full-paying adult

Conditions:

1. This voucher entitles free admission to the National Seal Sanctuary for one child when accompanied by one full paying adult.
2. Offer expires 28 February 2009.
3. Cannot be used in conjunction with any other offer.
4. A "child" is classed as a person aged 3-14 inclusive (under 3s go free anyway).
5. No cash alternative, non-refundable; and non-exchangeable.
6. All children must be accompanied by an adult.
7. Only one voucher per party and per transaction.
8. Photocopies not accepted.
9. SEA LIFE/Sanctuaries reserve the right to alter, close or remove details/exhibits without prior notice for technical, operational or other reasons, and no refunds can be given in these circumstances.
10. SEA LIFE/Sanctuaries reserve the right to refuse entry without explanation.

Voucher Ref: DOUK.

Cannot be used in conjunction with other offers. One voucher per party. Not valid on Bank Hols or special event days.

Expires end Feb 2009 (unless otherwise specified)

DISCOUNT VOUCHER

National Wildflower Centre

Court Hey Park Roby Road Liverpool Merseyside L16 3NA

Two for the Price of One
with a full-paying adult

Cannot be used in conjunction with other offers. One voucher per party. Not valid on Bank Hols or special event days.

Valid Mar - Sept 2008 only

DISCOUNT VOUCHER

Nature in Art

Wallsworth Hall Twigworth Gloucester
Gloucestershire GL2 9PA

Two for the Price of One
with a full-paying adult

Cannot be used in conjunction with other offers. One voucher per party. Not valid on Bank Hols or special event days.

Expires end Feb 2009 (unless otherwise specified)

DISCOUNT VOUCHER

1. Each voucher entitles the holder to the discount specified by the selected attraction.

2. Valid for use until 28/02/09 (unless otherwise specified, or if attraction season finishes prior to this). Vouchers are subject to the terms, conditions and restrictions of the selected attraction.

3. One voucher per party will be accepted, cannot be used in conjunction with any other offer, photocopies will not be accepted.

4. All attractions offering a discount have confirmed their willingness to participate. All information is subject to change without notice and should any attraction close or decline to accept a voucher for any reason, Days Out UK are not liable and cannot be held responsible.

5. Days Out UK shall not accept liability for any loss, accident or injury that may occur at a participating attraction and any dispute arising must be settled direct with the attraction concerned.

6. Cash redemption value of each voucher is 0.001p.

7. You are advised to check all relevant information with your chosen attraction before commencing your journey.

Days Out UK, PO Box 427, Northampton NN1 3YN. Tel: 01604 622445

1. Each voucher entitles the holder to the discount specified by the selected attraction.
2. Valid for use until 28/02/09 (unless otherwise specified, or if attraction season finishes prior to this). Vouchers are subject to the terms, conditions and restrictions of the selected attraction.
3. One voucher per party will be accepted, cannot be used in conjunction with any other offer, photocopies will not be accepted.
4. All attractions offering a discount have confirmed their willingness to participate. All information is subject to change without notice and should any attraction close or decline to accept a voucher for any reason, Days Out UK are not liable and cannot be held responsible.
5. Days Out UK shall not accept liability for any loss, accident or injury that may occur at a participating attraction and any dispute arising must be settled direct with the attraction concerned.
6. Cash redemption value of each voucher is 0.001p.
7. You are advised to check all relevant information with your chosen attraction before commencing your journey.

Days Out UK, PO Box 427, Northampton NN1 3YN. Tel: 01604 622445

1. Each voucher entitles the holder to the discount specified by the selected attraction.
2. Valid for use until 28/02/09 (unless otherwise specified, or if attraction season finishes prior to this). Vouchers are subject to the terms, conditions and restrictions of the selected attraction.
3. One voucher per party will be accepted, cannot be used in conjunction with any other offer, photocopies will not be accepted.
4. All attractions offering a discount have confirmed their willingness to participate. All information is subject to change without notice and should any attraction close or decline to accept a voucher for any reason, Days Out UK are not liable and cannot be held responsible.
5. Days Out UK shall not accept liability for any loss, accident or injury that may occur at a participating attraction and any dispute arising must be settled direct with the attraction concerned.
6. Cash redemption value of each voucher is 0.001p.
7. You are advised to check all relevant information with your chosen attraction before commencing your journey.

Days Out UK, PO Box 427, Northampton NN1 3YN. Tel: 01604 622445

Navan Centre and Fort

81 Killylea Road Armagh County Armagh BT60 4LD

Two for the Price of One

with a full-paying adult

Cannot be used in conjunction with other offers. One voucher per party. Not valid on Bank Hols or special event days.

Expires end Feb 2009 (unless otherwise specified)

DISCOUNT VOUCHER

NCCL Galleries of Justice

Shire Hall High Pavement Lace Market Nottingham NG1 1HN

One Child Free

with a full-paying adult

Cannot be used in conjunction with other offers. One voucher per party. Not valid on Bank Hols or special event days.

Expires end Feb 2009 (unless otherwise specified)

DISCOUNT VOUCHER

Needles Park

Alum Bay Isle of Wight PO39 0JD

Three for the Price of Two

(Super-Saver ticket books)
(ride restrictions may apply
please check www.theneedles.co.uk for more info)

Cannot be used in conjunction with other offers. One voucher per party. Not valid on Bank Hols or special event days.

Valid until 31 Oct 2008

DISCOUNT VOUCHER

New Forest Otter, Owl & Wildlife Conservation Park

Deerleap Lane Longdown Nr Ashhurst Southampton Hants SO40 4UH

One Child Free

with a full-paying adult

Cannot be used in conjunction with other offers. One voucher per party. Not valid on Bank Hols or special event days.

Expires end Feb 2009 (unless otherwise specified)

DISCOUNT VOUCHER

Newby Hall and Gardens

Newby Hall Ripon North Yorkshire HG4 5AE

Two for the Price of One

with a full-paying adult

Cannot be used in conjunction with other offers. One voucher per party. Not valid on Bank Hols or special event days.

Expires end Feb 2009 (unless otherwise specified)

DISCOUNT VOUCHER

Newquay Zoo

Trenance Gardens Newquay Cornwall TR7 2LZ

One Child Free

with two full-paying adults

(Cannot be used in conjunction with family tickets)

Cannot be used in conjunction with other offers. One voucher per party. Not valid on Bank Hols or special event days.

Valid until 31 Dec 2008

DISCOUNT VOUCHER

1. Each voucher entitles the holder to the discount specified by the selected attraction.
2. Valid for use until 28/02/09 (unless otherwise specified, or if attraction season finishes prior to this). Vouchers are subject to the terms, conditions and restrictions of the selected attraction.
3. One voucher per party will be accepted, cannot be used in conjunction with any other offer, photocopies will not be accepted.
4. All attractions offering a discount have confirmed their willingness to participate. All information is subject to change without notice and should any attraction close or decline to accept a voucher for any reason, Days Out UK are not liable and cannot be held responsible.
5. Days Out UK shall not accept liability for any loss, accident or injury that may occur at a participating attraction and any dispute arising must be settled direct with the attraction concerned.
6. Cash redemption value of each voucher is 0.001p.
7. You are advised to check all relevant information with your chosen attraction before commencing your journey.

Days Out UK, PO Box 427, Northampton NN1 3YN. Tel: 01604 622445

1. Each voucher entitles the holder to the discount specified by the selected attraction.
2. Valid for use until 28/02/09 (unless otherwise specified. or if attraction season finishes prior to this). Vouchers are subject to the terms, conditions and restrictions of the selected attraction.
3. One voucher per party will be accepted, cannot be used in conjunction with any other offer, photocopies will not be accepted.
4. All attractions offering a discount have confirmed their willingness to participate. All information is subject to change without notice and should any attraction close or decline to accept a voucher for any reason, Days Out UK are not liable and cannot be held responsible.
5. Days Out UK shall not accept liability for any loss, accident or injury that may occur at a participating attraction and any dispute arising must be settled direct with the attraction concerned.
6. Cash redemption value of each voucher is 0.001p.
7. You are advised to check all relevant information with your chosen attraction before commencing your journey.

Days Out UK, PO Box 427, Northampton NN1 3YN. Tel: 01604 622445

1. Each voucher entitles the holder to the discount specified by the selected attraction.
2. Valid for use until 28/02/09 (unless otherwise specified, or if attraction season finishes prior to this). Vouchers are subject to the terms, conditions and restrictions of the selected attraction.
3. One voucher per party will be accepted, cannot be used in conjunction with any other offer, photocopies will not be accepted.
4. All attractions offering a discount have confirmed their willingness to participate. All information is subject to change without notice and should any attraction close or decline to accept a voucher for any reason, Days Out UK are not liable and cannot be held responsible.
5. Days Out UK shall not accept liability for any loss, accident or injury that may occur at a participating attraction and any dispute arising must be settled direct with the attraction concerned.
6. Cash redemption value of each voucher is 0.001p.
7. You are advised to check all relevant information with your chosen attraction before commencing your journey.

Days Out UK, PO Box 427, Northampton NN1 3YN. Tel: 01604 622445

1. Each voucher entitles the holder to the discount specified by the selected attraction.
2. Valid for use until 28/02/09 (unless otherwise specified, or if attraction season finishes prior to this). Vouchers are subject to the terms, conditions and restrictions of the selected attraction.
3. One voucher per party will be accepted, cannot be used in conjunction with any other offer, photocopies will not be accepted.
4. All attractions offering a discount have confirmed their willingness to participate. All information is subject to change without notice and should any attraction close or decline to accept a voucher for any reason, Days Out UK are not liable and cannot be held responsible.
5. Days Out UK shall not accept liability for any loss, accident or injury that may occur at a participating attraction and any dispute arising must be settled direct with the attraction concerned.
6. Cash redemption value of each voucher is 0.001p.
7. You are advised to check all relevant information with your chosen attraction before commencing your journey.

Days Out UK, PO Box 427, Northampton NN1 3YN. Tel: 01604 622445

1. Each voucher entitles the holder to the discount specified by the selected attraction.
2. Valid for use until 28/02/09 (unless otherwise specified, or if attraction season finishes prior to this). Vouchers are subject to the terms, conditions and restrictions of the selected attraction.
3. One voucher per party will be accepted, cannot be used in conjunction with any other offer, photocopies will not be accepted.
4. All attractions offering a discount have confirmed their willingness to participate. All information is subject to change without notice and should any attraction close or decline to accept a voucher for any reason, Days Out UK are not liable and cannot be held responsible.
5. Days Out UK shall not accept liability for any loss, accident or injury that may occur at a participating attraction and any dispute arising must be settled direct with the attraction concerned.
6. Cash redemption value of each voucher is 0.001p.
7. You are advised to check all relevant information with your chosen attraction before commencing your journey.

Days Out UK, PO Box 427, Northampton NN1 3YN. Tel: 01604 622445

DAYSOUTUK
The place to look for places to go

Ocean Beach Pleasure Park
23 The Foreshore Sea Rd South Shields Tyne & Wear NE33 2LD
Save £10.00!
Get £25.00 worth of tokens for just £15.00
(single tokens cost 50p)

Cannot be used in conjunction with other offers. One voucher per party. Not valid on Bank Hols or special event days.
Expires end Feb 2009 (unless otherwise specified)

DISCOUNT VOUCHER

DAYSOUTUK
The place to look for places to go

Orford Ness National Nature Reserve
Orford Quay Orford Woodbridge Suffolk IP12 2NU
One Child Free
with a full-paying adult

Cannot be used in conjunction with other offers. One voucher per party. Not valid on Bank Hols or special event days.
Expires end Feb 2009 (unless otherwise specified)

DISCOUNT VOUCHER

DAYSOUTUK
The place to look for places to go

Original Great Maze
Blake House Craft Centre Blake End Rayne Nr. Braintree
Essex CM77 6RA
One Child Free
with two full-paying adults

Cannot be used in conjunction with other offers. One voucher per party. Not valid on Bank Hols or special event days.
Expires end Feb 2009 (unless otherwise specified)

DISCOUNT VOUCHER

DAYSOUTUK
The place to look for places to go

Oxburgh Hall, Garden and Estate
Oxborough King's Lynn Norfolk PE33 9PS
One Child Free
with a full-paying adult

Cannot be used in conjunction with other offers. One voucher per party. Not valid on Bank Hols or special event days.
Expires end Feb 2009 (unless otherwise specified)

DISCOUNT VOUCHER

DAYSOUTUK
The place to look for places to go

Palace Stables Heritage Centre
The Palace Demense Armagh County Armagh BT60 4EL
Two for the Price of One
with a full-paying adult

Cannot be used in conjunction with other offers. One voucher per party. Not valid on Bank Hols or special event days.
Expires end Feb 2009 (unless otherwise specified)

DISCOUNT VOUCHER

DAYSOUTUK
The place to look for places to go

Paradise Park
Avis Road Newhaven East Sussex BN9 0DH
One Child Free
with a full-paying adult

Cannot be used in conjunction with other offers. One voucher per party. Not valid on Bank Hols or special event days.
Expires end Feb 2009 (unless otherwise specified)

DISCOUNT VOUCHER

1. Each voucher entitles the holder to the discount specified by the selected attraction.
2. Valid for use until 28/02/09 (unless otherwise specified, or if attraction season finishes prior to this). Vouchers are subject to the terms, conditions and restrictions of the selected attraction.
3. One voucher per party will be accepted, cannot be used in conjunction with any other offer, photocopies will not be accepted.
4. All attractions offering a discount have confirmed their willingness to participate. All information is subject to change without notice and should any attraction close or decline to accept a voucher for any reason, Days Out UK are not liable and cannot be held responsible.
5. Days Out UK shall not accept liability for any loss, accident or injury that may occur at a participating attraction and any dispute arising must be settled direct with the attraction concerned.
6. Cash redemption value of each voucher is 0.001p.
7. You are advised to check all relevant information with your chosen attraction before commencing your journey.

Days Out UK, PO Box 427, Northampton NN1 3YN. Tel: 01604 622445

1. Each voucher entitles the holder to the discount specified by the selected attraction.
2. Valid for use until 28/02/09 (unless otherwise specified, or if attraction season finishes prior to this). Vouchers are subject to the terms, conditions and restrictions of the selected attraction.
3. One voucher per party will be accepted, cannot be used in conjunction with any other offer, photocopies will not be accepted.
4. All attractions offering a discount have confirmed their willingness to participate. All information is subject to change without notice and should any attraction close or decline to accept a voucher for any reason, Days Out UK are not liable and cannot be held responsible.
5. Days Out UK shall not accept liability for any loss, accident or injury that may occur at a participating attraction and any dispute arising must be settled direct with the attraction concerned.
6. Cash redemption value of each voucher is 0.001p.
7. You are advised to check all relevant information with your chosen attraction before commencing your journey.

Days Out UK, PO Box 427, Northampton NN1 3YN. Tel: 01604 622445

1. Each voucher entitles the holder to the discount specified by the selected attraction.
2. Valid for use until 28/02/09 (unless otherwise specified, or if attraction season finishes prior to this). Vouchers are subject to the terms, conditions and restrictions of the selected attraction.
3. One voucher per party will be accepted, cannot be used in conjunction with any other offer, photocopies will not be accepted.
4. All attractions offering a discount have confirmed their willingness to participate. All information is subject to change without notice and should any attraction close or decline to accept a voucher for any reason, Days Out UK are not liable and cannot be held responsible.
5. Days Out UK shall not accept liability for any loss, accident or injury that may occur at a participating attraction and any dispute arising must be settled direct with the attraction concerned.
6. Cash redemption value of each voucher is 0.001p.
7. You are advised to check all relevant information with your chosen attraction before commencing your journey.

Days Out UK, PO Box 427, Northampton NN1 3YN. Tel: 01604 622445

1. Each voucher entitles the holder to the discount specified by the selected attraction.
2. Valid for use until 28/02/09 (unless otherwise specified, or if attraction season finishes prior to this). Vouchers are subject to the terms, conditions and restrictions of the selected attraction.
3. One voucher per party will be accepted, cannot be used in conjunction with any other offer, photocopies will not be accepted.
4. All attractions offering a discount have confirmed their willingness to participate. All information is subject to change without notice and should any attraction close or decline to accept a voucher for any reason, Days Out UK are not liable and cannot be held responsible.
5. Days Out UK shall not accept liability for any loss, accident or injury that may occur at a participating attraction and any dispute arising must be settled direct with the attraction concerned.
6. Cash redemption value of each voucher is 0.001p.
7. You are advised to check all relevant information with your chosen attraction before commencing your journey.

Days Out UK, PO Box 427, Northampton NN1 3YN. Tel: 01604 622445

1. Each voucher entitles the holder to the discount specified by the selected attraction.
2. Valid for use until 28/02/09 (unless otherwise specified, or if attraction season finishes prior to this). Vouchers are subject to the terms, conditions and restrictions of the selected attraction.
3. One voucher per party will be accepted, cannot be used in conjunction with any other offer, photocopies will not be accepted.
4. All attractions offering a discount have confirmed their willingness to participate. All information is subject to change without notice and should any attraction close or decline to accept a voucher for any reason, Days Out UK are not liable and cannot be held responsible.
5. Days Out UK shall not accept liability for any loss, accident or injury that may occur at a participating attraction and any dispute arising must be settled direct with the attraction concerned.
6. Cash redemption value of each voucher is 0.001p.
7. You are advised to check all relevant information with your chosen attraction before commencing your journey.

Days Out UK, PO Box 427, Northampton NN1 3YN. Tel: 01604 622445

Days out UK
The place to look for places to go

Paxton House and Country Park

Paxton Berwick-upon-Tweed Northumberland TD15 1SZ

One Child Free

with a full-paying adult

Cannot be used in conjunction with other offers. One voucher per party. Not valid on Bank Hols or special event days.

Expires end Feb 2009 (unless otherwise specified)

DISCOUNT VOUCHER

Days out UK
The place to look for places to go

Peckover House and Garden

North Brink Wisbech Cambridgeshire PE13 1JR

One Child Free

with a full-paying adult

Cannot be used in conjunction with other offers. One voucher per party. Not valid on Bank Hols or special event days.

Expires end Feb 2009 (unless otherwise specified)

DISCOUNT VOUCHER

Days out UK
The place to look for places to go

Penshurst Place and Gardens

Penshurst Tonbridge Kent TN11 8DG

One Child Free

with a full-paying adult

Cannot be used in conjunction with other offers. One voucher per party. Not valid on Bank Hols or special event days.

Expires end Feb 2009 (unless otherwise specified)

DISCOUNT VOUCHER

Days out UK
The place to look for places to go

Pettitts Animal Adventure Park

Camphill Church Road Reedham Norfolk NR13 3UA

Two for the Price of One

with a full-paying adult

Cannot be used in conjunction with other offers. One voucher per party. Not valid on Bank Hols or special event days.

Expires end Feb 2009 (unless otherwise specified)

DISCOUNT VOUCHER

Days out UK
The place to look for places to go

Pleasure Beach, Blackpool

Blackpool Lancashire FY4 1EZ

Three Wristbands for the Price of Two Wristbands

(Not valid on any UK Public Holidays or Sat-Mon during Bank Hol weekends, offer only applies to full priced Wristbands, cheapest priced wristband goes free. Height restrictions apply. Code: 8004)

Cannot be used in conjunction with other offers. One voucher per party. Not valid on Bank Hols or special event days.

Expires end Feb 2009 (unless otherwise specified)

DISCOUNT VOUCHER

Days out UK
The place to look for places to go

Pleasure Island Theme Park

Kings Road Cleethorpes Lincolnshire DN35 0PL

Two for the Price of One

with a full-paying adult

Cannot be used in conjunction with other offers. One voucher per party. Not valid on Bank Hols or special event days.

Expires end Feb 2009 (unless otherwise specified)

DISCOUNT VOUCHER

Pleasurewood Hills Theme Park
Leisure Way Corton Lowestoft Suffolk NR32 5DZ
Three for the Price of Two
full-paying adults
(Cannot be used in conjunction with an other offer, discount or family tickets, one voucher per group, no photocopies accepted)
Cannot be used in conjunction with other offers. One voucher per party. Not valid on Bank Hols or special event days.

Valid until 28th Sept 2008

DISCOUNT VOUCHER

Pooh Corner
High Street Hartfield East Sussex TN7 4AE
5% discount on all gift shop purchases
(When you spend £10.00 or more)
Cannot be used in conjunction with other offers. One voucher per party. Not valid on Bank Hols or special event days.

Expires end Feb 2009 (unless otherwise specified)

DISCOUNT VOUCHER

Poole's Cavern and Buxton Country Park
Green Lane Buxton Derbyshire SK17 9DH
20% off Adult Admissions
(A£5.40)
Cannot be used in conjunction with other offers. One voucher per party. Not valid on Bank Hols or special event days.

Expires end Feb 2009 (unless otherwise specified)

DISCOUNT VOUCHER

Port Lympne Wild Animal Park
Aldington Road Lympne nr Ashford Kent CT21 4PD
Kid for a Quid
(Each child must be accompanied by a full-paying adult)
Cannot be used in conjunction with other offers. One voucher per party. Not valid on Bank Hols or special event days.

Valid 1 Apr - 31 Dec 2008

DISCOUNT VOUCHER

Portsmouth Historic Dockyard
Visitor Centre Victory Gate Portsmouth Hampshire PO1 3LJ
20% off all Annual Admission
(Tickets A£18.50 C£14.00 OAPs£16.50
Family Ticket(A2+C3) £51.50)
Conditions:
This ticket gives one entry to each of the ships, museums and other attractions at Portsmouth Historic Dockyard including HMS Victory, HMS Warrior 1860, Mary Rose Ship Hall and Museum, Action Stations and a Harbour Tour (subject to availability). The ticket is valid for one year from redemption so you can return within 12 months to see any attractions you may have missed. Cannot be used with any special rate, event tickets or any other offer. Voucher must be redeemed and no photocopies will be accepted. One voucher per person.
Cannot be used in conjunction with other offers. One voucher per party. Not valid on Bank Hols or special event days.

Valid until 31 Dec 2008

DISCOUNT VOUCHER

1. Each voucher entitles the holder to the discount specified by the selected attraction.
2. Valid for use until 28/02/09 (unless otherwise specified, or if attraction season finishes prior to this). Vouchers are subject to the terms, conditions and restrictions of the selected attraction.
3. One voucher per party will be accepted, cannot be used in conjunction with any other offer, photocopies will not be accepted.
4. All attractions offering a discount have confirmed their willingness to participate. All information is subject to change without notice and should any attraction close or decline to accept a voucher for any reason, Days Out UK are not liable and cannot be held responsible.
5. Days Out UK shall not accept liability for any loss, accident or injury that may occur at a participating attraction and any dispute arising must be settled direct with the attraction concerned.
6. Cash redemption value of each voucher is 0.001p.
7. You are advised to check all relevant information with your chosen attraction before commencing your journey.

Days Out UK, PO Box 427, Northampton NN1 3YN. Tel: 01604 622445

1. Each voucher entitles the holder to the discount specified by the selected attraction.
2. Valid for use until 28/02/09 (unless otherwise specified. or if attraction season finishes prior to this). Vouchers are subject to the terms, conditions and restrictions of the selected attraction.
3. One voucher per party will be accepted, cannot be used in conjunction with any other offer, photocopies will not be accepted.
4. All attractions offering a discount have confirmed their willingness to participate. All information is subject to change without notice and should any attraction close or decline to accept a voucher for any reason, Days Out UK are not liable and cannot be held responsible.
5. Days Out UK shall not accept liability for any loss, accident or injury that may occur at a participating attraction and any dispute arising must be settled direct with the attraction concerned.
6. Cash redemption value of each voucher is 0.001p.
7. You are advised to check all relevant information with your chosen attraction before commencing your journey.

Days Out UK, PO Box 427, Northampton NN1 3YN. Tel: 01604 622445

1. Each voucher entitles the holder to the discount specified by the selected attraction.
2. Valid for use until 28/02/09 (unless otherwise specified, or if attraction season finishes prior to this). Vouchers are subject to the terms, conditions and restrictions of the selected attraction.
3. One voucher per party will be accepted, cannot be used in conjunction with any other offer, photocopies will not be accepted.
4. All attractions offering a discount have confirmed their willingness to participate. All information is subject to change without notice and should any attraction close or decline to accept a voucher for any reason, Days Out UK are not liable and cannot be held responsible.
5. Days Out UK shall not accept liability for any loss, accident or injury that may occur at a participating attraction and any dispute arising must be settled direct with the attraction concerned.
6. Cash redemption value of each voucher is 0.001p.
7. You are advised to check all relevant information with your chosen attraction before commencing your journey.

Days Out UK, PO Box 427, Northampton NN1 3YN. Tel: 01604 622445

1. Each voucher entitles the holder to the discount specified by the selected attraction.

2. Valid for use until 28/02/09 (unless otherwise specified, or if attraction season finishes prior to this). Vouchers are subject to the terms, conditions and restrictions of the selected attraction.

3. One voucher per party will be accepted, cannot be used in conjunction with any other offer, photocopies will not be accepted.

4. All attractions offering a discount have confirmed their willingness to participate. All information is subject to change without notice and should any attraction close or decline to accept a voucher for any reason, Days Out UK are not liable and cannot be held responsible.

5. Days Out UK shall not accept liability for any loss, accident or injury that may occur at a participating attraction and any dispute arising must be settled direct with the attraction concerned.

6. Cash redemption value of each voucher is 0.001p.

7. You are advised to check all relevant information with your chosen attraction before commencing your journey.

Days Out UK, PO Box 427, Northampton NN1 3YN. Tel: 01604 622445

DAYS OUT UK
The place to look for places to go

Preston Hall Museum and Park
Preston Park Yarm Rd Stockton-On-Tees Tees Valley TS18 3RH
Two for the Price of One
with a full-paying adult
Cannot be used in conjunction with other offers. One voucher per party. Not valid on Bank Hols or special event days.
Expires end Feb 2009 (unless otherwise specified)

DISCOUNT VOUCHER

DAYS OUT UK
The place to look for places to go

Priest House
North Lane West Hoathly nr East Grinstead West Sussex RH19 4PP
£1.00 off each full-priced adult, senior or student ticket
(Not valid for child tickets, cannot be used in conjunction with any other offer, not valid on any special event days (please see website for dates of events))
Cannot be used in conjunction with other offers. One voucher per party. Not valid on Bank Hols or special event days.
Expires end Feb 2009 (unless otherwise specified)

DISCOUNT VOUCHER

DAYS OUT UK
The place to look for places to go

Pulborough Brooks RSPB Nature Reserve
Wiggonholt Pulborough West Sussex RH20 2EL
50% off One Family Ticket
(A2+C4 £3.50)
Cannot be used in conjunction with other offers. One voucher per party. Not valid on Bank Hols or special event days.
Expires end Feb 2009 (unless otherwise specified)

DISCOUNT VOUCHER

DAYS OUT UK
The place to look for places to go

Ramsgate Maritime Museum
Clock House Pier Yard Royal Harbour Ramsgate Kent CT11 8LS
Two for the Price of One
with a full-paying adult
Cannot be used in conjunction with other offers. One voucher per party. Not valid on Bank Hols or special event days.
Expires end Feb 2009 (unless otherwise specified)

DISCOUNT VOUCHER

DAYS OUT UK
The place to look for places to go

Raptor Foundation
The Heath St Ives Rd Woodhurst Cambridgeshire PE28 3BT
Two for the Price of One
with a full-paying adult
Cannot be used in conjunction with other offers. One voucher per party. Not valid on Bank Hols or special event days.
Expires end Feb 2009 (unless otherwise specified)

DISCOUNT VOUCHER

DAYS OUT UK
The place to look for places to go

Redwings Ada Cole Rescue Stables
Broadlands Epping Road Broadley Common Waltham Abbey Essex EN9 2DH
Free Poster
Cannot be used in conjunction with other offers. One voucher per party. Not valid on Bank Hols or special event days.
Expires end Feb 2009 (unless otherwise specified)

DISCOUNT VOUCHER

1. Each voucher entitles the holder to the discount specified by the selected attraction.
2. Valid for use until 28/02/09 (unless otherwise specified, or if attraction season finishes prior to this). Vouchers are subject to the terms, conditions and restrictions of the selected attraction.
3. One voucher per party will be accepted, cannot be used in conjunction with any other offer, photocopies will not be accepted.
4. All attractions offering a discount have confirmed their willingness to participate. All information is subject to change without notice and should any attraction close or decline to accept a voucher for any reason, Days Out UK are not liable and cannot be held responsible.
5. Days Out UK shall not accept liability for any loss, accident or injury that may occur at a participating attraction and any dispute arising must be settled direct with the attraction concerned.
6. Cash redemption value of each voucher is 0.001p.
7. You are advised to check all relevant information with your chosen attraction before commencing your journey.

Days Out UK, PO Box 427, Northampton NN1 3YN. Tel: 01604 622445

1. Each voucher entitles the holder to the discount specified by the selected attraction.
2. Valid for use until 28/02/09 (unless otherwise specified, or if attraction season finishes prior to this). Vouchers are subject to the terms, conditions and restrictions of the selected attraction.
3. One voucher per party will be accepted, cannot be used in conjunction with any other offer, photocopies will not be accepted.
4. All attractions offering a discount have confirmed their willingness to participate. All information is subject to change without notice and should any attraction close or decline to accept a voucher for any reason, Days Out UK are not liable and cannot be held responsible.
5. Days Out UK shall not accept liability for any loss, accident or injury that may occur at a participating attraction and any dispute arising must be settled direct with the attraction concerned.
6. Cash redemption value of each voucher is 0.001p.
7. You are advised to check all relevant information with your chosen attraction before commencing your journey.

Days Out UK, PO Box 427, Northampton NN1 3YN. Tel: 01604 622445

1. Each voucher entitles the holder to the discount specified by the selected attraction.
2. Valid for use until 28/02/09 (unless otherwise specified, or if attraction season finishes prior to this). Vouchers are subject to the terms, conditions and restrictions of the selected attraction.
3. One voucher per party will be accepted, cannot be used in conjunction with any other offer, photocopies will not be accepted.
4. All attractions offering a discount have confirmed their willingness to participate. All information is subject to change without notice and should any attraction close or decline to accept a voucher for any reason, Days Out UK are not liable and cannot be held responsible.
5. Days Out UK shall not accept liability for any loss, accident or injury that may occur at a participating attraction and any dispute arising must be settled direct with the attraction concerned.
6. Cash redemption value of each voucher is 0.001p.
7. You are advised to check all relevant information with your chosen attraction before commencing your journey.

Days Out UK, PO Box 427, Northampton NN1 3YN. Tel: 01604 622445

1. Each voucher entitles the holder to the discount specified by the selected attraction.
2. Valid for use until 28/02/09 (unless otherwise specified, or if attraction season finishes prior to this). Vouchers are subject to the terms, conditions and restrictions of the selected attraction.
3. One voucher per party will be accepted, cannot be used in conjunction with any other offer, photocopies will not be accepted.
4. All attractions offering a discount have confirmed their willingness to participate. All information is subject to change without notice and should any attraction close or decline to accept a voucher for any reason, Days Out UK are not liable and cannot be held responsible.
5. Days Out UK shall not accept liability for any loss, accident or injury that may occur at a participating attraction and any dispute arising must be settled direct with the attraction concerned.
6. Cash redemption value of each voucher is 0.001p.
7. You are advised to check all relevant information with your chosen attraction before commencing your journey.

Days Out UK, PO Box 427, Northampton NN1 3YN. Tel: 01604 622445

1. Each voucher entitles the holder to the discount specified by the selected attraction.
2. Valid for use until 28/02/09 (unless otherwise specified, or if attraction season finishes prior to this). Vouchers are subject to the terms, conditions and restrictions of the selected attraction.
3. One voucher per party will be accepted, cannot be used in conjunction with any other offer, photocopies will not be accepted.
4. All attractions offering a discount have confirmed their willingness to participate. All information is subject to change without notice and should any attraction close or decline to accept a voucher for any reason, Days Out UK are not liable and cannot be held responsible.
5. Days Out UK shall not accept liability for any loss, accident or injury that may occur at a participating attraction and any dispute arising must be settled direct with the attraction concerned.
6. Cash redemption value of each voucher is 0.001p.
7. You are advised to check all relevant information with your chosen attraction before commencing your journey.

Days Out UK, PO Box 427, Northampton NN1 3YN. Tel: 01604 622445

1. Each voucher entitles the holder to the discount specified by the selected attraction.
2. Valid for use until 28/02/09 (unless otherwise specified, or if attraction season finishes prior to this). Vouchers are subject to the terms, conditions and restrictions of the selected attraction.
3. One voucher per party will be accepted, cannot be used in conjunction with any other offer, photocopies will not be accepted.
4. All attractions offering a discount have confirmed their willingness to participate. All information is subject to change without notice and should any attraction close or decline to accept a voucher for any reason, Days Out UK are not liable and cannot be held responsible.
5. Days Out UK shall not accept liability for any loss, accident or injury that may occur at a participating attraction and any dispute arising must be settled direct with the attraction concerned.
6. Cash redemption value of each voucher is 0.001p.
7. You are advised to check all relevant information with your chosen attraction before commencing your journey.

Days Out UK, PO Box 427, Northampton NN1 3YN. Tel: 01604 622445

DISCOUNT VOUCHER

Redwings Caldecott Visitor Centre
Caldecott Hall Beccles Road Fritton Great Yarmouth
Norfolk NR31 9EY

Free Poster

Cannot be used in conjunction with other offers. One voucher per party. Not valid on Bank Hols or special event days.

Expires end Feb 2009 (unless otherwise specified)

DISCOUNT VOUCHER

Redwings Oxhill Rescue Centre
Banbury Road Oxhill Warwickshire CV35 0RP

Free Poster

Cannot be used in conjunction with other offers. One voucher per party. Not valid on Bank Hols or special event days.

Expires end Feb 2009 (unless otherwise specified)

DISCOUNT VOUCHER

RHS Garden Hyde Hall
Buckhatch Lane Rettendon Chelmsford Essex CM3 8ET

Two for the Price of One
with a full-paying adult

Cannot be used in conjunction with other offers. One voucher per party. Not valid on Bank Hols or special event days.

Valid until 31 Dec 2008

DISCOUNT VOUCHER

RHS Garden Rosemoor
Great Torrington Devon EX38 8PH

One Child Free
with one full-paying adult

(Cannot be used in conjunction with any other offer,
not valid for groups or in conjunction with group offers)

Cannot be used in conjunction with other offers. One voucher per party. Not valid on Bank Hols or special event days.

Expires end Feb 2009 (unless otherwise specified)

DISCOUNT VOUCHER

RHS Garden Wisley
RHS Garden Wisley Woking Surrey GU23 6QB

Two for the Price of One
with a full-paying adult

(Mon-Sat only, not valid Bank Holiday weekends, not to be used in conjunction with any other offer)

Cannot be used in conjunction with other offers. One voucher per party. Not valid on Bank Hols or special event days.

Expires end Feb 2009 (unless otherwise specified)

DISCOUNT VOUCHER

Ripley Castle
Ripley Harrogate North Yorkshire HG3 3AY

One Child Free
with one full-paying adult

Cannot be used in conjunction with other offers. One voucher per party. Not valid on Bank Hols or special event days.

Expires end Feb 2009 (unless otherwise specified)

1. Each voucher entitles the holder to the discount specified by the selected attraction.
2. Valid for use until 28/02/09 (unless otherwise specified, or if attraction season finishes prior to this). Vouchers are subject to the terms, conditions and restrictions of the selected attraction.
3. One voucher per party will be accepted, cannot be used in conjunction with any other offer, photocopies will not be accepted.
4. All attractions offering a discount have confirmed their willingness to participate. All information is subject to change without notice and should any attraction close or decline to accept a voucher for any reason, Days Out UK are not liable and cannot be held responsible.
5. Days Out UK shall not accept liability for any loss, accident or injury that may occur at a participating attraction and any dispute arising must be settled direct with the attraction concerned.
6. Cash redemption value of each voucher is 0.001p.
7. You are advised to check all relevant information with your chosen attraction before commencing your journey.

Days Out UK, PO Box 427, Northampton NN1 3YN. Tel: 01604 622445

1. Each voucher entitles the holder to the discount specified by the selected attraction.
2. Valid for use until 28/02/09 (unless otherwise specified. or if attraction season finishes prior to this). Vouchers are subject to the terms, conditions and restrictions of the selected attraction.
3. One voucher per party will be accepted, cannot be used in conjunction with any other offer, photocopies will not be accepted.
4. All attractions offering a discount have confirmed their willingness to participate. All information is subject to change without notice and should any attraction close or decline to accept a voucher for any reason, Days Out UK are not liable and cannot be held responsible.
5. Days Out UK shall not accept liability for any loss, accident or injury that may occur at a participating attraction and any dispute arising must be settled direct with the attraction concerned.
6. Cash redemption value of each voucher is 0.001p.
7. You are advised to check all relevant information with your chosen attraction before commencing your journey.

Days Out UK, PO Box 427, Northampton NN1 3YN. Tel: 01604 622445

1. Each voucher entitles the holder to the discount specified by the selected attraction.
2. Valid for use until 28/02/09 (unless otherwise specified, or if attraction season finishes prior to this). Vouchers are subject to the terms, conditions and restrictions of the selected attraction.
3. One voucher per party will be accepted, cannot be used in conjunction with any other offer, photocopies will not be accepted.
4. All attractions offering a discount have confirmed their willingness to participate. All information is subject to change without notice and should any attraction close or decline to accept a voucher for any reason, Days Out UK are not liable and cannot be held responsible.
5. Days Out UK shall not accept liability for any loss, accident or injury that may occur at a participating attraction and any dispute arising must be settled direct with the attraction concerned.
6. Cash redemption value of each voucher is 0.001p.
7. You are advised to check all relevant information with your chosen attraction before commencing your journey.

Days Out UK, PO Box 427, Northampton NN1 3YN. Tel: 01604 622445

1. Each voucher entitles the holder to the discount specified by the selected attraction.
2. Valid for use until 28/02/09 (unless otherwise specified, or if attraction season finishes prior to this). Vouchers are subject to the terms, conditions and restrictions of the selected attraction.
3. One voucher per party will be accepted, cannot be used in conjunction with any other offer, photocopies will not be accepted.
4. All attractions offering a discount have confirmed their willingness to participate. All information is subject to change without notice and should any attraction close or decline to accept a voucher for any reason, Days Out UK are not liable and cannot be held responsible.
5. Days Out UK shall not accept liability for any loss, accident or injury that may occur at a participating attraction and any dispute arising must be settled direct with the attraction concerned.
6. Cash redemption value of each voucher is 0.001p.
7. You are advised to check all relevant information with your chosen attraction before commencing your journey.

Days Out UK, PO Box 427, Northampton NN1 3YN. Tel: 01604 622445

1. Each voucher entitles the holder to the discount specified by the selected attraction.
2. Valid for use until 28/02/09 (unless otherwise specified, or if attraction season finishes prior to this). Vouchers are subject to the terms, conditions and restrictions of the selected attraction.
3. One voucher per party will be accepted, cannot be used in conjunction with any other offer, photocopies will not be accepted.
4. All attractions offering a discount have confirmed their willingness to participate. All information is subject to change without notice and should any attraction close or decline to accept a voucher for any reason, Days Out UK are not liable and cannot be held responsible.
5. Days Out UK shall not accept liability for any loss, accident or injury that may occur at a participating attraction and any dispute arising must be settled direct with the attraction concerned.
6. Cash redemption value of each voucher is 0.001p.
7. You are advised to check all relevant information with your chosen attraction before commencing your journey.

Days Out UK, PO Box 427, Northampton NN1 3YN. Tel: 01604 622445

Romney Hythe and Dymchurch Railway
New Romney Station Littlestone Road New Romney Kent
TN28 8PL
One Child Free
with a full-paying adult

Cannot be used in conjunction with other offers. One voucher per party. Not valid on Bank Hols or special event days.

Expires end Feb 2009 (unless otherwise specified)

DISCOUNT VOUCHER

Royal Armouries Museum
Armouries Drive Leeds West Yorkshire LS10 1LT
Two for the Price of One
with a full-paying adult

(One free ticket issued on the purchase of another full priced ticket, one free ticket issued per voucher, not valid with any other offers or discount, subject to availability, vouchers have no monetary value, excludes Easter & Aug bank holiday tournaments & themed jousts)

Cannot be used in conjunction with other offers. One voucher per party. Not valid on Bank Hols or special event days.

Expires end Feb 2009 (unless otherwise specified)

DISCOUNT VOUCHER

Royal Marines Museum
Eastney Esplanade Southsea Hampshire PO4 9PX
Two for the Price of One
with a full-paying adult

Cannot be used in conjunction with other offers. One voucher per party. Not valid on Bank Hols or special event days.

Expires end Feb 2009 (unless otherwise specified)

DISCOUNT VOUCHER

Royal Navy Submarine Museum
Haslar Jetty Road Gosport Hampshire PO12 2AS
Two for the Price of One
full-paying adult

Cannot be used in conjunction with other offers. One voucher per party. Not valid on Bank Hols or special event days.

Valid until 31 Mar 2009

DISCOUNT VOUCHER

Royal Worcester Visitor Centre
Severn Street Worcester Worcestershire WR1 2NE
Two for the Price of One
with a full-paying adult

(Offer applies to guided tour, film, handpainting demonstration, museum and audio tour package)

Cannot be used in conjunction with other offers. One voucher per party. Not valid on Bank Hols or special event days.

Expires end Feb 2009 (unless otherwise specified)

DISCOUNT VOUCHER

Rural Life Centre
The Reeds Tilford Farnham Surrey GU10 2DL
Two for the Price of One
with a full-paying adult

Cannot be used in conjunction with other offers. One voucher per party. Not valid on Bank Hols or special event days.

Expires end Feb 2009 (unless otherwise specified)

DISCOUNT VOUCHER

Sacrewell Farm and Country Centre
Thornhaugh Peterborough Cambridgeshire PE8 6HJ
One Child Free
with every full-paying adult
(Additional charges may apply for special events)

Cannot be used in conjunction with other offers. One voucher per party. Not valid on Bank Hols or special event days.

Expires end Feb 2009 (unless otherwise specified)

DISCOUNT VOUCHER

Saint Patrick's Trian Visitor Complex
40 English Street Armagh County Armagh Northern Ireland BT61 7BA
Two for the Price of One
with a full-paying adult
(Not valid for special events or in conjunction with any other offers)

Cannot be used in conjunction with other offers. One voucher per party. Not valid on Bank Hols or special event days.

Expires end Feb 2009 (unless otherwise specified)

DISCOUNT VOUCHER

Saltburn Smugglers Heritage Centre
Old Saltburn Saltburn-by-the-Sea North Yorkshire TS12 1HF
One Child Free
with a full-paying adult

Cannot be used in conjunction with other offers. One voucher per party. Not valid on Bank Hols or special event days.

Expires end Feb 2009 (unless otherwise specified)

DISCOUNT VOUCHER

Scarborough Sea Life and Marine Sanctuary
Scalby Mills Road Scarborough North Yorkshire YO12 6RP
One Child Free with a full-paying adult
Conditions:

1. This voucher entitles free admission to the Scarborough Sea Life and Marine Sanctuary for one child when accompanied by one full paying adult.
2. Offer expires 28 February 2009.
3. Cannot be used in conjunction with any other offer.
4. A "child" is classed as a person aged 3-14 inclusive (under 3s go free anyway).
5. No cash alternative, non-refundable; and non-exchangeable.
6. All children must be accompanied by an adult.
7. Only one voucher per party and per transaction.
8. Photocopies not accepted.
9. SEA LIFE/Sanctuaries reserve the right to alter, close or remove details/exhibits without prior notice for technical, operational or other reasons, and no refunds can be given in these circumstances.
10. SEA LIFE/Sanctuaries reserve the right to refuse entry without explanation.
Voucher Ref: DOUK.

Cannot be used in conjunction with other offers. One voucher per party. Not valid on Bank Hols or special event days.

Expires end Feb 2009 (unless otherwise specified)

DISCOUNT VOUCHER

Scone Palace
Scone Perth Perth and Kinross PH2 6BD
Two for the Price of One
with a full-paying adult

Cannot be used in conjunction with other offers. One voucher per party. Not valid on Bank Hols or special event days.

Expires end Feb 2009 (unless otherwise specified)

DISCOUNT VOUCHER

1. Each voucher entitles the holder to the discount specified by the selected attraction.
2. Valid for use until 28/02/09 (unless otherwise specified, or if attraction season finishes prior to this). Vouchers are subject to the terms, conditions and restrictions of the selected attraction.
3. One voucher per party will be accepted, cannot be used in conjunction with any other offer, photocopies will not be accepted.
4. All attractions offering a discount have confirmed their willingness to participate. All information is subject to change without notice and should any attraction close or decline to accept a voucher for any reason, Days Out UK are not liable and cannot be held responsible.
5. Days Out UK shall not accept liability for any loss, accident or injury that may occur at a participating attraction and any dispute arising must be settled direct with the attraction concerned.
6. Cash redemption value of each voucher is 0.001p.
7. You are advised to check all relevant information with your chosen attraction before commencing your journey.

Days Out UK, PO Box 427, Northampton NN1 3YN. Tel: 01604 622445

1. Each voucher entitles the holder to the discount specified by the selected attraction.
2. Valid for use until 28/02/09 (unless otherwise specified. or if attraction season finishes prior to this). Vouchers are subject to the terms, conditions and restrictions of the selected attraction.
3. One voucher per party will be accepted, cannot be used in conjunction with any other offer, photocopies will not be accepted.
4. All attractions offering a discount have confirmed their willingness to participate. All information is subject to change without notice and should any attraction close or decline to accept a voucher for any reason, Days Out UK are not liable and cannot be held responsible.
5. Days Out UK shall not accept liability for any loss, accident or injury that may occur at a participating attraction and any dispute arising must be settled direct with the attraction concerned.
6. Cash redemption value of each voucher is 0.001p.
7. You are advised to check all relevant information with your chosen attraction before commencing your journey.

Days Out UK, PO Box 427, Northampton NN1 3YN. Tel: 01604 622445

1. Each voucher entitles the holder to the discount specified by the selected attraction.

2. Valid for use until 28/02/09 (unless otherwise specified, or if attraction season finishes prior to this). Vouchers are subject to the terms, conditions and restrictions of the selected attraction.

3. One voucher per party will be accepted, cannot be used in conjunction with any other offer, photocopies will not be accepted.

4. All attractions offering a discount have confirmed their willingness to participate. All information is subject to change without notice and should any attraction close or decline to accept a voucher for any reason, Days Out UK are not liable and cannot be held responsible.

5. Days Out UK shall not accept liability for any loss, accident or injury that may occur at a participating attraction and any dispute arising must be settled direct with the attraction concerned.

6. Cash redemption value of each voucher is 0.001p.

7. You are advised to check all relevant information with your chosen attraction before commencing your journey.

Days Out UK, PO Box 427, Northampton NN1 3YN. Tel: 01604 622445

1. Each voucher entitles the holder to the discount specified by the selected attraction.
2. Valid for use until 28/02/09 (unless otherwise specified, or if attraction season finishes prior to this). Vouchers are subject to the terms, conditions and restrictions of the selected attraction.
3. One voucher per party will be accepted, cannot be used in conjunction with any other offer, photocopies will not be accepted.
4. All attractions offering a discount have confirmed their willingness to participate. All information is subject to change without notice and should any attraction close or decline to accept a voucher for any reason, Days Out UK are not liable and cannot be held responsible.
5. Days Out UK shall not accept liability for any loss, accident or injury that may occur at a participating attraction and any dispute arising must be settled direct with the attraction concerned.
6. Cash redemption value of each voucher is 0.001p.
7. You are advised to check all relevant information with your chosen attraction before commencing your journey.

Days Out UK, PO Box 427, Northampton NN1 3YN. Tel: 01604 622445

Scottish Mining Museum

Lady Victoria Colliery Newtongrange Edinburgh Scotland
EH22 4QN

One Child Free
with every full-paying adult

Cannot be used in conjunction with other offers. One voucher per party. Not valid on Bank Hols or special event days.

Expires end Feb 2009 (unless otherwise specified)

Scottish Sea Life Sanctuary

Barcaldine Oban Argyll and Bute PA37 1SE

One Child Free with a full-paying adult

Conditions:

1. This voucher entitles free admission to the Scottish Sea Life Sanctuary for one child when accompanied by one full paying adult.
2. Offer expires 28 February 2009.
3. Cannot be used in conjunction with any other offer.
4. A "child" is classed as a person aged 3-14 inclusive (under 3s go free anyway).
5. No cash alternative, non-refundable; and non-exchangeable.
6. All children must be accompanied by an adult.
7. Only one voucher per party and per transaction.
8. Photocopies not accepted.
9. SEA LIFE/Sanctuaries reserve the right to alter, close or remove details/exhibits without prior notice for technical, operational or other reasons, and no refunds can be given in these circumstances.
10. SEA LIFE/Sanctuaries reserve the right to refuse entry without explanation.
Voucher Ref: DOUK.

Cannot be used in conjunction with other offers. One voucher per party. Not valid on Bank Hols or special event days.

Expires end Feb 2009 (unless otherwise specified)

Scottish Seabird Centre

The Harbour North Berwick East Lothian EH39 4SS

One Child Free
with a full-paying adult

Cannot be used in conjunction with other offers. One voucher per party. Not valid on Bank Hols or special event days.

Expires end Feb 2009 (unless otherwise specified)

Scottish Traditional Boat Festival

Various venues Portsoy Aberdeenshire

Two for the Price of One
with a full-paying adult

Cannot be used in conjunction with other offers. One voucher per party. Not valid on Bank Hols or special event days.

Valid 21 - 22 Jun 2008

Sealife Adventure

Eastern Esplanade Southend-On-Sea Essex SS1 2ER

Two for the Price of One
with a full-paying adult
(Free ticket to be of equal or lesser value, cannot be used in conjunction with any other offer)

Cannot be used in conjunction with other offers. One voucher per party. Not valid on Bank Hols or special event days.

Valid until 31 Dec 2008

1. Each voucher entitles the holder to the discount specified by the selected attraction.
2. Valid for use until 28/02/09 (unless otherwise specified, or if attraction season finishes prior to this). Vouchers are subject to the terms, conditions and restrictions of the selected attraction.
3. One voucher per party will be accepted, cannot be used in conjunction with any other offer, photocopies will not be accepted.
4. All attractions offering a discount have confirmed their willingness to participate. All information is subject to change without notice and should any attraction close or decline to accept a voucher for any reason, Days Out UK are not liable and cannot be held responsible.
5. Days Out UK shall not accept liability for any loss, accident or injury that may occur at a participating attraction and any dispute arising must be settled direct with the attraction concerned.
6. Cash redemption value of each voucher is 0.001p.
7. You are advised to check all relevant information with your chosen attraction before commencing your journey.

Days Out UK, PO Box 427, Northampton NN1 3YN. Tel: 01604 622445

1. Each voucher entitles the holder to the discount specified by the selected attraction.
2. Valid for use until 28/02/09 (unless otherwise specified, or if attraction season finishes prior to this). Vouchers are subject to the terms, conditions and restrictions of the selected attraction.
3. One voucher per party will be accepted, cannot be used in conjunction with any other offer, photocopies will not be accepted.
4. All attractions offering a discount have confirmed their willingness to participate. All information is subject to change without notice and should any attraction close or decline to accept a voucher for any reason, Days Out UK are not liable and cannot be held responsible.
5. Days Out UK shall not accept liability for any loss, accident or injury that may occur at a participating attraction and any dispute arising must be settled direct with the attraction concerned.
6. Cash redemption value of each voucher is 0.001p.
7. You are advised to check all relevant information with your chosen attraction before commencing your journey.

Days Out UK, PO Box 427, Northampton NN1 3YN. Tel: 01604 622445

1. Each voucher entitles the holder to the discount specified by the selected attraction.
2. Valid for use until 28/02/09 (unless otherwise specified, or if attraction season finishes prior to this). Vouchers are subject to the terms, conditions and restrictions of the selected attraction.
3. One voucher per party will be accepted, cannot be used in conjunction with any other offer, photocopies will not be accepted.
4. All attractions offering a discount have confirmed their willingness to participate. All information is subject to change without notice and should any attraction close or decline to accept a voucher for any reason, Days Out UK are not liable and cannot be held responsible.
5. Days Out UK shall not accept liability for any loss, accident or injury that may occur at a participating attraction and any dispute arising must be settled direct with the attraction concerned.
6. Cash redemption value of each voucher is 0.001p.
7. You are advised to check all relevant information with your chosen attraction before commencing your journey.

Days Out UK, PO Box 427, Northampton NN1 3YN. Tel: 01604 622445

SeaQuarium Ltd
Marine Parade Weston-Super-Mare Somerset BS23 1BE
One Child Free
with every full-paying adult
Cannot be used in conjunction with other offers. One voucher per party. Not valid on Bank Hols or special event days.
Valid until 31 Mar 2009

DISCOUNT VOUCHER

Seaton Tramway
Harbour Road Seaton Devon EX12 2NQ
One Child Free
with every full-paying adult
(Excludes the month of August, Bank Holidays, special events, birdwatching trips and santa specials)
Cannot be used in conjunction with other offers. One voucher per party. Not valid on Bank Hols or special event days.
Expires end Feb 2009 (unless otherwise specified)

DISCOUNT VOUCHER

Secret Hills - The Shropshire Hills Discovery Centre
School Lane Craven Arms Shropshire SY7 9RS
Two for the Price of One
with a full-paying adult
Cannot be used in conjunction with other offers. One voucher per party. Not valid on Bank Hols or special event days.
Expires end Feb 2009 (unless otherwise specified)

DISCOUNT VOUCHER

Seven Stories
30 Lime Street Newcastle-upon-Tyne Tyne & Wear NE1 2PQ
One Child Free
with a full-paying adult
Cannot be used in conjunction with other offers. One voucher per party. Not valid on Bank Hols or special event days.
Expires end Feb 2009 (unless otherwise specified)

DISCOUNT VOUCHER

Shakespeare's Birthplace
The Shakespeare Centre Henley St Stratford-Upon-Avon
Warwickshire CV37 6QW
Two for the Price of One
with a full-paying adult
Conditions:

Voucher entitles one adult or one child to be admitted free of charge when accompanied by a full-paying adult to one of the following venues:
Shakespeare's Birthplace, Hall's Croft, Mary Arden's Farm, Nash's House and New Place or Anne Hathaway's Cottage.
Cannot be used in conjunction with other offers. One voucher per party. Not valid on Bank Hols or special event days.
Expires end Feb 2009 (unless otherwise specified)

DISCOUNT VOUCHER

561

Shakespeare's Globe Theatre Tour and Exhibition

21 New Globe Walk Bankside London SE1 9DT

One Child Free

with a full-paying adult

Cannot be used in conjunction with other offers. One voucher per party. Not valid on Bank Hols or special event days.

Expires end Feb 2009 (unless otherwise specified)

DISCOUNT VOUCHER

Shaw's Corner

Ayot St. Lawrence Welwyn Hertfordshire AL6 9BX

One Child Free

with a full-paying adult

Cannot be used in conjunction with other offers. One voucher per party. Not valid on Bank Hols or special event days.

Expires end Feb 2009 (unless otherwise specified)

DISCOUNT VOUCHER

Shepreth Wildlife Park

Willersmill Station Road Shepreth Nr Royston Hertfordshire SG8 6PZ

Free guide map with voucher

Cannot be used in conjunction with other offers. One voucher per party. Not valid on Bank Hols or special event days.

Expires end Feb 2009 (unless otherwise specified)

DISCOUNT VOUCHER

Sir Richard Arkwright's Masson Mills

Working Textile Museum Derby Road Matlock Bath Derbyshire DE4 3PY

Two for the Price of One

with a full-paying adult

Cannot be used in conjunction with other offers. One voucher per party. Not valid on Bank Hols or special event days.

Expires end Feb 2009 (unless otherwise specified)

DISCOUNT VOUCHER

Skipton Castle

Skipton North Yorkshire BD23 1AW

Two for the Price of One

with a full-paying adult

(Offer applies to full-priced adult tickets only)

Cannot be used in conjunction with other offers. One voucher per party. Not valid on Bank Hols or special event days.

Expires end Feb 2009 (unless otherwise specified)

DISCOUNT VOUCHER

Smallest House in Great Britain

Quay Conwy LL32 8DE

One Child Free

with a full-paying adult

Cannot be used in conjunction with other offers. One voucher per party. Not valid on Bank Hols or special event days.

Expires end Feb 2009 (unless otherwise specified)

DISCOUNT VOUCHER

1. Each voucher entitles the holder to the discount specified by the selected attraction.
2. Valid for use until 28/02/09 (unless otherwise specified, or if attraction season finishes prior to this). Vouchers are subject to the terms, conditions and restrictions of the selected attraction.
3. One voucher per party will be accepted, cannot be used in conjunction with any other offer, photocopies will not be accepted.
4. All attractions offering a discount have confirmed their willingness to participate. All information is subject to change without notice and should any attraction close or decline to accept a voucher for any reason, Days Out UK are not liable and cannot be held responsible.
5. Days Out UK shall not accept liability for any loss, accident or injury that may occur at a participating attraction and any dispute arising must be settled direct with the attraction concerned.
6. Cash redemption value of each voucher is 0.001p.
7. You are advised to check all relevant information with your chosen attraction before commencing your journey.

Days Out UK, PO Box 427, Northampton NN1 3YN. Tel: 01604 622445

1. Each voucher entitles the holder to the discount specified by the selected attraction.
2. Valid for use until 28/02/09 (unless otherwise specified. or if attraction season finishes prior to this). Vouchers are subject to the terms, conditions and restrictions of the selected attraction.
3. One voucher per party will be accepted, cannot be used in conjunction with any other offer, photocopies will not be accepted.
4. All attractions offering a discount have confirmed their willingness to participate. All information is subject to change without notice and should any attraction close or decline to accept a voucher for any reason, Days Out UK are not liable and cannot be held responsible.
5. Days Out UK shall not accept liability for any loss, accident or injury that may occur at a participating attraction and any dispute arising must be settled direct with the attraction concerned.
6. Cash redemption value of each voucher is 0.001p.
7. You are advised to check all relevant information with your chosen attraction before commencing your journey.

Days Out UK, PO Box 427, Northampton NN1 3YN. Tel: 01604 622445

1. Each voucher entitles the holder to the discount specified by the selected attraction.
2. Valid for use until 28/02/09 (unless otherwise specified, or if attraction season finishes prior to this). Vouchers are subject to the terms, conditions and restrictions of the selected attraction.
3. One voucher per party will be accepted, cannot be used in conjunction with any other offer, photocopies will not be accepted.
4. All attractions offering a discount have confirmed their willingness to participate. All information is subject to change without notice and should any attraction close or decline to accept a voucher for any reason, Days Out UK are not liable and cannot be held responsible.
5. Days Out UK shall not accept liability for any loss, accident or injury that may occur at a participating attraction and any dispute arising must be settled direct with the attraction concerned.
6. Cash redemption value of each voucher is 0.001p.
7. You are advised to check all relevant information with your chosen attraction before commencing your journey.

Days Out UK, PO Box 427, Northampton NN1 3YN. Tel: 01604 622445

1. Each voucher entitles the holder to the discount specified by the selected attraction.
2. Valid for use until 28/02/09 (unless otherwise specified, or if attraction season finishes prior to this). Vouchers are subject to the terms, conditions and restrictions of the selected attraction.
3. One voucher per party will be accepted, cannot be used in conjunction with any other offer, photocopies will not be accepted.
4. All attractions offering a discount have confirmed their willingness to participate. All information is subject to change without notice and should any attraction close or decline to accept a voucher for any reason, Days Out UK are not liable and cannot be held responsible.
5. Days Out UK shall not accept liability for any loss, accident or injury that may occur at a participating attraction and any dispute arising must be settled direct with the attraction concerned.
6. Cash redemption value of each voucher is 0.001p.
7. You are advised to check all relevant information with your chosen attraction before commencing your journey.

Days Out UK, PO Box 427, Northampton NN1 3YN. Tel: 01604 622445

1. Each voucher entitles the holder to the discount specified by the selected attraction.
2. Valid for use until 28/02/09 (unless otherwise specified, or if attraction season finishes prior to this). Vouchers are subject to the terms, conditions and restrictions of the selected attraction.
3. One voucher per party will be accepted, cannot be used in conjunction with any other offer, photocopies will not be accepted.
4. All attractions offering a discount have confirmed their willingness to participate. All information is subject to change without notice and should any attraction close or decline to accept a voucher for any reason, Days Out UK are not liable and cannot be held responsible.
5. Days Out UK shall not accept liability for any loss, accident or injury that may occur at a participating attraction and any dispute arising must be settled direct with the attraction concerned.
6. Cash redemption value of each voucher is 0.001p.
7. You are advised to check all relevant information with your chosen attraction before commencing your journey.

Days Out UK, PO Box 427, Northampton NN1 3YN. Tel: 01604 622445

Snibston
Ashby Road Coalville Leicestershire LE67 3LN
One Child Free
with a full-paying adult
Cannot be used in conjunction with other offers. One voucher per party. Not valid on Bank Hols or special event days.
Expires end Feb 2009 (unless otherwise specified)

DISCOUNT VOUCHER

SnowDome
Leisure Island River Drive Tamworth Staffordshire B79 7ND
Two for the Price of One
Purchase either a single tobogganing, tubing, ice skating, snow-play or swimming session, a group ski or snowboard lesson or a one-hour recreational pass for one person and another person goes free. Age and height restrictions may apply, valid for one person only, not to be used with any other offer/promotion, voucher has no cash value and cannot be resold, all sessions should be pre-booked by calling 08705 000011, please quote **'Day Out UK offer.'**
Cannot be used in conjunction with other offers. One voucher per party. Not valid on Bank Hols or special event days.
Valid from 1st Apr 2008 until 30 Sept 2008

DISCOUNT VOUCHER

Southsea Castle
Clarence Esplanade Southsea Hampshire PO5 3PA
20% off Adult Admissions
(A£2.80)
(Not valid on events days, maximum 2 discounted adults per transaction)
Cannot be used in conjunction with other offers. One voucher per party. Not valid on Bank Hols or special event days.
Expires end Feb 2009 (unless otherwise specified)

DISCOUNT VOUCHER

Speke Hall
The Walk Speke Liverpool Merseyside L24 1XD
One Child Free
with a full-paying adult
Cannot be used in conjunction with other offers. One voucher per party. Not valid on Bank Hols or special event days.
Expires end Feb 2009 (unless otherwise specified)

DISCOUNT VOUCHER

Spetchley Park Gardens
Spetchley Worcester Worcestershire WR5 1RS
Two for the Price of One
with a full-paying adult
Cannot be used in conjunction with other offers. One voucher per party. Not valid on Bank Hols or special event days.
Expires end Feb 2009 (unless otherwise specified)

DISCOUNT VOUCHER

1. Each voucher entitles the holder to the discount specified by the selected attraction.
2. Valid for use until 28/02/09 (unless otherwise specified, or if attraction season finishes prior to this). Vouchers are subject to the terms, conditions and restrictions of the selected attraction.
3. One voucher per party will be accepted, cannot be used in conjunction with any other offer, photocopies will not be accepted.
4. All attractions offering a discount have confirmed their willingness to participate. All information is subject to change without notice and should any attraction close or decline to accept a voucher for any reason, Days Out UK are not liable and cannot be held responsible.
5. Days Out UK shall not accept liability for any loss, accident or injury that may occur at a participating attraction and any dispute arising must be settled direct with the attraction concerned.
6. Cash redemption value of each voucher is 0.001p.
7. You are advised to check all relevant information with your chosen attraction before commencing your journey.

Days Out UK, PO Box 427, Northampton NN1 3YN. Tel: 01604 622445

1. Each voucher entitles the holder to the discount specified by the selected attraction.
2. Valid for use until 28/02/09 (unless otherwise specified, or if attraction season finishes prior to this). Vouchers are subject to the terms, conditions and restrictions of the selected attraction.
3. One voucher per party will be accepted, cannot be used in conjunction with any other offer, photocopies will not be accepted.
4. All attractions offering a discount have confirmed their willingness to participate. All information is subject to change without notice and should any attraction close or decline to accept a voucher for any reason, Days Out UK are not liable and cannot be held responsible.
5. Days Out UK shall not accept liability for any loss, accident or injury that may occur at a participating attraction and any dispute arising must be settled direct with the attraction concerned.
6. Cash redemption value of each voucher is 0.001p.
7. You are advised to check all relevant information with your chosen attraction before commencing your journey.

Days Out UK, PO Box 427, Northampton NN1 3YN. Tel: 01604 622445

1. Each voucher entitles the holder to the discount specified by the selected attraction.
2. Valid for use until 28/02/09 (unless otherwise specified, or if attraction season finishes prior to this). Vouchers are subject to the terms, conditions and restrictions of the selected attraction.
3. One voucher per party will be accepted, cannot be used in conjunction with any other offer, photocopies will not be accepted.
4. All attractions offering a discount have confirmed their willingness to participate. All information is subject to change without notice and should any attraction close or decline to accept a voucher for any reason, Days Out UK are not liable and cannot be held responsible.
5. Days Out UK shall not accept liability for any loss, accident or injury that may occur at a participating attraction and any dispute arising must be settled direct with the attraction concerned.
6. Cash redemption value of each voucher is 0.001p.
7. You are advised to check all relevant information with your chosen attraction before commencing your journey.

Days Out UK, PO Box 427, Northampton NN1 3YN. Tel: 01604 622445

DAYSOUTUK
The place to look for places to go

Spode Visitor Centre
Church Street Stoke-On-Trent Staffordshire ST4 1BX

Two for the Price of One
with a full-paying adult on the Combined Tour

Cannot be used in conjunction with other offers. One voucher per party. Not valid on Bank Hols or special event days.
Expires end Feb 2009 (unless otherwise specified)

DAYSOUTUK
The place to look for places to go

St Davids Cathedral
The Close St Davids Pembrokeshire SA62 6RH

5% off in the gift shop
when you spend £10.00 or more

Cannot be used in conjunction with other offers. One voucher per party. Not valid on Bank Hols or special event days.
Expires end Feb 2009 (unless otherwise specified)

DAYSOUTUK
The place to look for places to go

Stapeley Water Gardens and The Palms Tropical Oasis
London Road Stapeley Nantwich Cheshire CW5 7LH

One Child Free
with one full-paying adult

Cannot be used in conjunction with other offers. One voucher per party. Not valid on Bank Hols or special event days.
Expires end Feb 2009 (unless otherwise specified)

DAYSOUTUK
The place to look for places to go

Stratford-upon-Avon Butterfly Farm
Swan's Nest Lane Stratford-upon-Avon Warwickshire CV37 7LS

Two for the Price of One
with a full-paying adult

Cannot be used in conjunction with other offers. One voucher per party. Not valid on Bank Hols or special event days.
Expires end Feb 2009 (unless otherwise specified)

DAYSOUTUK
The place to look for places to go

Stromness Museum
Alfred St Stromness Orkney Mainland Orkney Isles KW16 3DF

10% discount
on all gift shop purchases
(when you spend £10.00 or more)

Cannot be used in conjunction with other offers. One voucher per party. Not valid on Bank Hols or special event days.
Expires end Feb 2009 (unless otherwise specified)

DAYSOUTUK
The place to look for places to go

Strutt's North Mill Museum & Visitor Centre
Derwent Valley Visitor Centre North Mill Bridgefoot Belper Derbyshire DE56 1YD

Two for the Price of One
with a full-paying adult

Cannot be used in conjunction with other offers. One voucher per party. Not valid on Bank Hols or special event days.
Expires end Feb 2009 (unless otherwise specified)

1. Each voucher entitles the holder to the discount specified by the selected attraction.
2. Valid for use until 28/02/09 (unless otherwise specified, or if attraction season finishes prior to this). Vouchers are subject to the terms, conditions and restrictions of the selected attraction.
3. One voucher per party will be accepted, cannot be used in conjunction with any other offer, photocopies will not be accepted.
4. All attractions offering a discount have confirmed their willingness to participate. All information is subject to change without notice and should any attraction close or decline to accept a voucher for any reason, Days Out UK are not liable and cannot be held responsible.
5. Days Out UK shall not accept liability for any loss, accident or injury that may occur at a participating attraction and any dispute arising must be settled direct with the attraction concerned.
6. Cash redemption value of each voucher is 0.001p.
7. You are advised to check all relevant information with your chosen attraction before commencing your journey.

Days Out UK, PO Box 427, Northampton NN1 3YN. Tel: 01604 622445

1. Each voucher entitles the holder to the discount specified by the selected attraction.
2. Valid for use until 28/02/09 (unless otherwise specified, or if attraction season finishes prior to this). Vouchers are subject to the terms, conditions and restrictions of the selected attraction.
3. One voucher per party will be accepted, cannot be used in conjunction with any other offer, photocopies will not be accepted.
4. All attractions offering a discount have confirmed their willingness to participate. All information is subject to change without notice and should any attraction close or decline to accept a voucher for any reason, Days Out UK are not liable and cannot be held responsible.
5. Days Out UK shall not accept liability for any loss, accident or injury that may occur at a participating attraction and any dispute arising must be settled direct with the attraction concerned.
6. Cash redemption value of each voucher is 0.001p.
7. You are advised to check all relevant information with your chosen attraction before commencing your journey.

Days Out UK, PO Box 427, Northampton NN1 3YN. Tel: 01604 622445

1. Each voucher entitles the holder to the discount specified by the selected attraction.
2. Valid for use until 28/02/09 (unless otherwise specified, or if attraction season finishes prior to this). Vouchers are subject to the terms, conditions and restrictions of the selected attraction.
3. One voucher per party will be accepted, cannot be used in conjunction with any other offer, photocopies will not be accepted.
4. All attractions offering a discount have confirmed their willingness to participate. All information is subject to change without notice and should any attraction close or decline to accept a voucher for any reason, Days Out UK are not liable and cannot be held responsible.
5. Days Out UK shall not accept liability for any loss, accident or injury that may occur at a participating attraction and any dispute arising must be settled direct with the attraction concerned.
6. Cash redemption value of each voucher is 0.001p.
7. You are advised to check all relevant information with your chosen attraction before commencing your journey.

Days Out UK, PO Box 427, Northampton NN1 3YN. Tel: 01604 622445

1. Each voucher entitles the holder to the discount specified by the selected attraction.
2. Valid for use until 28/02/09 (unless otherwise specified, or if attraction season finishes prior to this). Vouchers are subject to the terms, conditions and restrictions of the selected attraction.
3. One voucher per party will be accepted, cannot be used in conjunction with any other offer, photocopies will not be accepted.
4. All attractions offering a discount have confirmed their willingness to participate. All information is subject to change without notice and should any attraction close or decline to accept a voucher for any reason, Days Out UK are not liable and cannot be held responsible.
5. Days Out UK shall not accept liability for any loss, accident or injury that may occur at a participating attraction and any dispute arising must be settled direct with the attraction concerned.
6. Cash redemption value of each voucher is 0.001p.
7. You are advised to check all relevant information with your chosen attraction before commencing your journey.

Days Out UK, PO Box 427, Northampton NN1 3YN. Tel: 01604 622445

1. Each voucher entitles the holder to the discount specified by the selected attraction.
2. Valid for use until 28/02/09 (unless otherwise specified, or if attraction season finishes prior to this). Vouchers are subject to the terms, conditions and restrictions of the selected attraction.
3. One voucher per party will be accepted, cannot be used in conjunction with any other offer, photocopies will not be accepted.
4. All attractions offering a discount have confirmed their willingness to participate. All information is subject to change without notice and should any attraction close or decline to accept a voucher for any reason, Days Out UK are not liable and cannot be held responsible.
5. Days Out UK shall not accept liability for any loss, accident or injury that may occur at a participating attraction and any dispute arising must be settled direct with the attraction concerned.
6. Cash redemption value of each voucher is 0.001p.
7. You are advised to check all relevant information with your chosen attraction before commencing your journey.

Days Out UK, PO Box 427, Northampton NN1 3YN. Tel: 01604 622445

Sudeley Castle, Gardens and Exhibitions
Winchcombe Cheltenham Gloucestershire GL54 5JD
One Child Free
with every full-paying adult
Cannot be used in conjunction with other offers. One voucher per party. Not valid on Bank Hols or special event days.
Expires end Feb 2009 (unless otherwise specified)

DISCOUNT VOUCHER

Sutton Hoo
Tranmer House Woodbridge Suffolk IP12 3DJ
One Child Free
with a full-paying adult
Cannot be used in conjunction with other offers. One voucher per party. Not valid on Bank Hols or special event days.
Expires end Feb 2009 (unless otherwise specified)

DISCOUNT VOUCHER

Tales of Robin Hood
30-38 Maid Marian Way Nottingham Notts NG1 6GF
One Child Free
with a full paying adult
Cannot be used in conjunction with other offers. One voucher per party. Not valid on Bank Hols or special event days.
Expires end Feb 2009 (unless otherwise specified)

DISCOUNT VOUCHER

Tamworth Castle
The Holloway Ladybank Tamworth Staffordshire B79 7NA
Two for the Price of One
with a full-paying adult
Cannot be used in conjunction with other offers. One voucher per party. Not valid on Bank Hols or special event days.
Expires end Feb 2009 (unless otherwise specified)

DISCOUNT VOUCHER

Tanfield Railway
Old Marley Hill Nr Stanley Newcastle Upon Tyne
Tyne & Wear NE16 5ET
Two for the Price of One
with a full-paying adult
Cannot be used in conjunction with other offers. One voucher per party. Not valid on Bank Hols or special event days.
Expires end Feb 2009 (unless otherwise specified)

DISCOUNT VOUCHER

Thackray Museum
Beckett Street Leeds West Yorkshire LS9 7LN
Two for the Price of One
with a full-paying adult
Cannot be used in conjunction with other offers. One voucher per party. Not valid on Bank Hols or special event days.
Expires end Feb 2009 (unless otherwise specified)

DISCOUNT VOUCHER

1. Each voucher entitles the holder to the discount specified by the selected attraction.
2. Valid for use until 28/02/09 (unless otherwise specified, or if attraction season finishes prior to this). Vouchers are subject to the terms, conditions and restrictions of the selected attraction.
3. One voucher per party will be accepted, cannot be used in conjunction with any other offer, photocopies will not be accepted.
4. All attractions offering a discount have confirmed their willingness to participate. All information is subject to change without notice and should any attraction close or decline to accept a voucher for any reason, Days Out UK are not liable and cannot be held responsible.
5. Days Out UK shall not accept liability for any loss, accident or injury that may occur at a participating attraction and any dispute arising must be settled direct with the attraction concerned.
6. Cash redemption value of each voucher is 0.001p.
7. You are advised to check all relevant information with your chosen attraction before commencing your journey.

Days Out UK, PO Box 427, Northampton NN1 3YN. Tel: 01604 622445

1. Each voucher entitles the holder to the discount specified by the selected attraction.
2. Valid for use until 28/02/09 (unless otherwise specified, or if attraction season finishes prior to this). Vouchers are subject to the terms, conditions and restrictions of the selected attraction.
3. One voucher per party will be accepted, cannot be used in conjunction with any other offer, photocopies will not be accepted.
4. All attractions offering a discount have confirmed their willingness to participate. All information is subject to change without notice and should any attraction close or decline to accept a voucher for any reason, Days Out UK are not liable and cannot be held responsible.
5. Days Out UK shall not accept liability for any loss, accident or injury that may occur at a participating attraction and any dispute arising must be settled direct with the attraction concerned.
6. Cash redemption value of each voucher is 0.001p.
7. You are advised to check all relevant information with your chosen attraction before commencing your journey.

Days Out UK, PO Box 427, Northampton NN1 3YN. Tel: 01604 622445

1. Each voucher entitles the holder to the discount specified by the selected attraction.
2. Valid for use until 28/02/09 (unless otherwise specified. or if attraction season finishes prior to this). Vouchers are subject to the terms, conditions and restrictions of the selected attraction.
3. One voucher per party will be accepted, cannot be used in conjunction with any other offer, photocopies will not be accepted.
4. All attractions offering a discount have confirmed their willingness to participate. All information is subject to change without notice and should any attraction close or decline to accept a voucher for any reason, Days Out UK are not liable and cannot be held responsible.
5. Days Out UK shall not accept liability for any loss, accident or injury that may occur at a participating attraction and any dispute arising must be settled direct with the attraction concerned.
6. Cash redemption value of each voucher is 0.001p.
7. You are advised to check all relevant information with your chosen attraction before commencing your journey.

Days Out UK, PO Box 427, Northampton NN1 3YN. Tel: 01604 622445

1. Each voucher entitles the holder to the discount specified by the selected attraction.
2. Valid for use until 28/02/09 (unless otherwise specified, or if attraction season finishes prior to this). Vouchers are subject to the terms, conditions and restrictions of the selected attraction.
3. One voucher per party will be accepted, cannot be used in conjunction with any other offer, photocopies will not be accepted.
4. All attractions offering a discount have confirmed their willingness to participate. All information is subject to change without notice and should any attraction close or decline to accept a voucher for any reason, Days Out UK are not liable and cannot be held responsible.
5. Days Out UK shall not accept liability for any loss, accident or injury that may occur at a participating attraction and any dispute arising must be settled direct with the attraction concerned.
6. Cash redemption value of each voucher is 0.001p.
7. You are advised to check all relevant information with your chosen attraction before commencing your journey.

Days Out UK, PO Box 427, Northampton NN1 3YN. Tel: 01604 622445

1. Each voucher entitles the holder to the discount specified by the selected attraction.
2. Valid for use until 28/02/09 (unless otherwise specified, or if attraction season finishes prior to this). Vouchers are subject to the terms, conditions and restrictions of the selected attraction.
3. One voucher per party will be accepted, cannot be used in conjunction with any other offer, photocopies will not be accepted.
4. All attractions offering a discount have confirmed their willingness to participate. All information is subject to change without notice and should any attraction close or decline to accept a voucher for any reason, Days Out UK are not liable and cannot be held responsible.
5. Days Out UK shall not accept liability for any loss, accident or injury that may occur at a participating attraction and any dispute arising must be settled direct with the attraction concerned.
6. Cash redemption value of each voucher is 0.001p.
7. You are advised to check all relevant information with your chosen attraction before commencing your journey.

Days Out UK, PO Box 427, Northampton NN1 3YN. Tel: 01604 622445

1. Each voucher entitles the holder to the discount specified by the selected attraction.
2. Valid for use until 28/02/09 (unless otherwise specified, or if attraction season finishes prior to this). Vouchers are subject to the terms, conditions and restrictions of the selected attraction.
3. One voucher per party will be accepted, cannot be used in conjunction with any other offer, photocopies will not be accepted.
4. All attractions offering a discount have confirmed their willingness to participate. All information is subject to change without notice and should any attraction close or decline to accept a voucher for any reason, Days Out UK are not liable and cannot be held responsible.
5. Days Out UK shall not accept liability for any loss, accident or injury that may occur at a participating attraction and any dispute arising must be settled direct with the attraction concerned.
6. Cash redemption value of each voucher is 0.001p.
7. You are advised to check all relevant information with your chosen attraction before commencing your journey.

Days Out UK, PO Box 427, Northampton NN1 3YN. Tel: 01604 622445

The Deep - The World's Only Submarium
Hull East Riding of Yorkshire HU1 4DP
One Child Free
with every two full-paying adults
(code DAYS280209)

Cannot be used in conjunction with other offers. One voucher per party. Not valid on Bank Hols or special event days.

Expires end Feb 2009 (unless otherwise specified)

DISCOUNT VOUCHER

The Original Tour - London Sightseeing
Jews Row Wandsworth London SW18 1TB
Save Money
Book in advance through www.theoriginaltour.com entering promotional code daysoutuk08. Alternatively, call and quote on telephone number 020 8877 2120

Cannot be used in conjunction with other offers. One voucher per party. Not valid on Bank Hols or special event days.

Expires end Feb 2009 (unless otherwise specified)

DISCOUNT VOUCHER

Thursford Collection
Thursford Fakenham Norfolk NR21 OAS
Two for the Price of One
with a full-paying adult

Cannot be used in conjunction with other offers. One voucher per party. Not valid on Bank Hols or special event days.

Expires end Feb 2009 (unless otherwise specified)

DISCOUNT VOUCHER

Torquay Museum
529 Babbacombe Road Torquay Devon TQ1 1HG
Two for the Price of One
with a full-paying adult
(No cash value or alternative, Torquay Museum reserves the right to change or amend this offer at any time for any reason)

Cannot be used in conjunction with other offers. One voucher per party. Not valid on Bank Hols or special event days.

Expires end Feb 2009 (unless otherwise specified)

DISCOUNT VOUCHER

Traquair House
Innerleithen Scottish Borders EH44 6PW
Two for the Price of One
with a full-paying adult
(Not valid for special events or Bank Holidays)

Cannot be used in conjunction with other offers. One voucher per party. Not valid on Bank Hols or special event days.

Expires end Feb 2009 (unless otherwise specified)

DISCOUNT VOUCHER

Treak Cliff Cavern
Buxton Road Castleton Hope Valley Derbyshire S33 8WP
10% off Adult Admissions
(A£6.30)

Cannot be used in conjunction with other offers. One voucher per party. Not valid on Bank Hols or special event days.

Expires end Feb 2009 (unless otherwise specified)

DISCOUNT VOUCHER

1. Each voucher entitles the holder to the discount specified by the selected attraction.
2. Valid for use until 28/02/09 (unless otherwise specified, or if attraction season finishes prior to this). Vouchers are subject to the terms, conditions and restrictions of the selected attraction.
3. One voucher per party will be accepted, cannot be used in conjunction with any other offer, photocopies will not be accepted.
4. All attractions offering a discount have confirmed their willingness to participate. All information is subject to change without notice and should any attraction close or decline to accept a voucher for any reason, Days Out UK are not liable and cannot be held responsible.
5. Days Out UK shall not accept liability for any loss, accident or injury that may occur at a participating attraction and any dispute arising must be settled direct with the attraction concerned.
6. Cash redemption value of each voucher is 0.001p.
7. You are advised to check all relevant information with your chosen attraction before commencing your journey.

Days Out UK, PO Box 427, Northampton NN1 3YN. Tel: 01604 622445

1. Each voucher entitles the holder to the discount specified by the selected attraction.
2. Valid for use until 28/02/09 (unless otherwise specified. or if attraction season finishes prior to this). Vouchers are subject to the terms, conditions and restrictions of the selected attraction.
3. One voucher per party will be accepted, cannot be used in conjunction with any other offer, photocopies will not be accepted.
4. All attractions offering a discount have confirmed their willingness to participate. All information is subject to change without notice and should any attraction close or decline to accept a voucher for any reason, Days Out UK are not liable and cannot be held responsible.
5. Days Out UK shall not accept liability for any loss, accident or injury that may occur at a participating attraction and any dispute arising must be settled direct with the attraction concerned.
6. Cash redemption value of each voucher is 0.001p.
7. You are advised to check all relevant information with your chosen attraction before commencing your journey.

Days Out UK, PO Box 427, Northampton NN1 3YN. Tel: 01604 622445

1. Each voucher entitles the holder to the discount specified by the selected attraction.
2. Valid for use until 28/02/09 (unless otherwise specified, or if attraction season finishes prior to this). Vouchers are subject to the terms, conditions and restrictions of the selected attraction.
3. One voucher per party will be accepted, cannot be used in conjunction with any other offer, photocopies will not be accepted.
4. All attractions offering a discount have confirmed their willingness to participate. All information is subject to change without notice and should any attraction close or decline to accept a voucher for any reason, Days Out UK are not liable and cannot be held responsible.
5. Days Out UK shall not accept liability for any loss, accident or injury that may occur at a participating attraction and any dispute arising must be settled direct with the attraction concerned.
6. Cash redemption value of each voucher is 0.001p.
7. You are advised to check all relevant information with your chosen attraction before commencing your journey.

Days Out UK, PO Box 427, Northampton NN1 3YN. Tel: 01604 622445

1. Each voucher entitles the holder to the discount specified by the selected attraction.
2. Valid for use until 28/02/09 (unless otherwise specified, or if attraction season finishes prior to this). Vouchers are subject to the terms, conditions and restrictions of the selected attraction.
3. One voucher per party will be accepted, cannot be used in conjunction with any other offer, photocopies will not be accepted.
4. All attractions offering a discount have confirmed their willingness to participate. All information is subject to change without notice and should any attraction close or decline to accept a voucher for any reason, Days Out UK are not liable and cannot be held responsible.
5. Days Out UK shall not accept liability for any loss, accident or injury that may occur at a participating attraction and any dispute arising must be settled direct with the attraction concerned.
6. Cash redemption value of each voucher is 0.001p.
7. You are advised to check all relevant information with your chosen attraction before commencing your journey.

Days Out UK, PO Box 427, Northampton NN1 3YN. Tel: 01604 622445

1. Each voucher entitles the holder to the discount specified by the selected attraction.
2. Valid for use until 28/02/09 (unless otherwise specified, or if attraction season finishes prior to this). Vouchers are subject to the terms, conditions and restrictions of the selected attraction.
3. One voucher per party will be accepted, cannot be used in conjunction with any other offer, photocopies will not be accepted.
4. All attractions offering a discount have confirmed their willingness to participate. All information is subject to change without notice and should any attraction close or decline to accept a voucher for any reason, Days Out UK are not liable and cannot be held responsible.
5. Days Out UK shall not accept liability for any loss, accident or injury that may occur at a participating attraction and any dispute arising must be settled direct with the attraction concerned.
6. Cash redemption value of each voucher is 0.001p.
7. You are advised to check all relevant information with your chosen attraction before commencing your journey.

Days Out UK, PO Box 427, Northampton NN1 3YN. Tel: 01604 622445

Trolleybus Museum at Sandtoft

Belton Road Sandtoft Doncaster North Lincolnshire DN8 5SX

One Adult Admitted at the Concession Rate

Cannot be used in conjunction with other offers. One voucher per party. Not valid on Bank Hols or special event days.

Expires end Feb 2009 (unless otherwise specified)

DAYSOUTUK
The place to look for places to go

Tropical Butterfly House, Wildlife and Falconry Centre

Woodsetts Rd North Anston Nr Sheffield South Yorks S25 4EQ

One Child Free
with a full-paying adult
(Not valid on Bank Holiday weekends)

Cannot be used in conjunction with other offers. One voucher per party. Not valid on Bank Hols or special event days.

Expires end Feb 2009 (unless otherwise specified)

DAYSOUTUK
The place to look for places to go

Twycross Zoo

Burton Road Atherstone Warwickshire CV9 3PX

One Child Free
with two full-paying adults

(Not valid on Bank Holiday weekends. TWPROM/11/2/08)

Cannot be used in conjunction with other offers. One voucher per party. Not valid on Bank Hols or special event days.

Expires end Feb 2009 (unless otherwise specified)

DAYSOUTUK
The place to look for places to go

Ulster American Folk Park

2 Mellon Road Castletown Omagh County Tyrone
Northern Ireland BT78 5QY

Two for the Price of One
with a full-paying adult
(Not valid on Bank Holidays, for special events or school groups)

Cannot be used in conjunction with other offers. One voucher per party. Not valid on Bank Hols or special event days.

Expires end Feb 2009 (unless otherwise specified)

DAYSOUTUK
The place to look for places to go

Ulster Folk and Transport Museum

Bangor Road Cultra Holywood County Down
Northern Ireland BT18 0EU

Two for the Price of One

with a full-paying adult

Cannot be used in conjunction with other offers. One voucher per party. Not valid on Bank Hols or special event days.

Expires end Feb 2009 (unless otherwise specified)

DAYSOUTUK
The place to look for places to go

Walsingham Abbey Grounds and Shirehall Museum

Estate Office Common Place Walsingham Norfolk NR22 6BP

Two for the Price of One
with a full-paying adult

Cannot be used in conjunction with other offers. One voucher per party. Not valid on Bank Hols or special event days.

Not valid during February 2009

DAYSOUTUK
The place to look for places to go

1. Each voucher entitles the holder to the discount specified by the selected attraction.
2. Valid for use until 28/02/09 (unless otherwise specified, or if attraction season finishes prior to this). Vouchers are subject to the terms, conditions and restrictions of the selected attraction.
3. One voucher per party will be accepted, cannot be used in conjunction with any other offer, photocopies will not be accepted.
4. All attractions offering a discount have confirmed their willingness to participate. All information is subject to change without notice and should any attraction close or decline to accept a voucher for any reason, Days Out UK are not liable and cannot be held responsible.
5. Days Out UK shall not accept liability for any loss, accident or injury that may occur at a participating attraction and any dispute arising must be settled direct with the attraction concerned.
6. Cash redemption value of each voucher is 0.001p.
7. You are advised to check all relevant information with your chosen attraction before commencing your journey.

Days Out UK, PO Box 427, Northampton NN1 3YN. Tel: 01604 622445

1. Each voucher entitles the holder to the discount specified by the selected attraction.
2. Valid for use until 28/02/09 (unless otherwise specified. or if attraction season finishes prior to this). Vouchers are subject to the terms, conditions and restrictions of the selected attraction.
3. One voucher per party will be accepted, cannot be used in conjunction with any other offer, photocopies will not be accepted.
4. All attractions offering a discount have confirmed their willingness to participate. All information is subject to change without notice and should any attraction close or decline to accept a voucher for any reason, Days Out UK are not liable and cannot be held responsible.
5. Days Out UK shall not accept liability for any loss, accident or injury that may occur at a participating attraction and any dispute arising must be settled direct with the attraction concerned.
6. Cash redemption value of each voucher is 0.001p.
7. You are advised to check all relevant information with your chosen attraction before commencing your journey.

Days Out UK, PO Box 427, Northampton NN1 3YN. Tel: 01604 622445

1. Each voucher entitles the holder to the discount specified by the selected attraction.
2. Valid for use until 28/02/09 (unless otherwise specified, or if attraction season finishes prior to this). Vouchers are subject to the terms, conditions and restrictions of the selected attraction.
3. One voucher per party will be accepted, cannot be used in conjunction with any other offer, photocopies will not be accepted.
4. All attractions offering a discount have confirmed their willingness to participate. All information is subject to change without notice and should any attraction close or decline to accept a voucher for any reason, Days Out UK are not liable and cannot be held responsible.
5. Days Out UK shall not accept liability for any loss, accident or injury that may occur at a participating attraction and any dispute arising must be settled direct with the attraction concerned.
6. Cash redemption value of each voucher is 0.001p.
7. You are advised to check all relevant information with your chosen attraction before commencing your journey.

Days Out UK, PO Box 427, Northampton NN1 3YN. Tel: 01604 622445

1. Each voucher entitles the holder to the discount specified by the selected attraction.
2. Valid for use until 28/02/09 (unless otherwise specified, or if attraction season finishes prior to this). Vouchers are subject to the terms, conditions and restrictions of the selected attraction.
3. One voucher per party will be accepted, cannot be used in conjunction with any other offer, photocopies will not be accepted.
4. All attractions offering a discount have confirmed their willingness to participate. All information is subject to change without notice and should any attraction close or decline to accept a voucher for any reason, Days Out UK are not liable and cannot be held responsible.
5. Days Out UK shall not accept liability for any loss, accident or injury that may occur at a participating attraction and any dispute arising must be settled direct with the attraction concerned.
6. Cash redemption value of each voucher is 0.001p.
7. You are advised to check all relevant information with your chosen attraction before commencing your journey.

Days Out UK, PO Box 427, Northampton NN1 3YN. Tel: 01604 622445

1. Each voucher entitles the holder to the discount specified by the selected attraction.
2. Valid for use until 28/02/09 (unless otherwise specified, or if attraction season finishes prior to this). Vouchers are subject to the terms, conditions and restrictions of the selected attraction.
3. One voucher per party will be accepted, cannot be used in conjunction with any other offer, photocopies will not be accepted.
4. All attractions offering a discount have confirmed their willingness to participate. All information is subject to change without notice and should any attraction close or decline to accept a voucher for any reason, Days Out UK are not liable and cannot be held responsible.
5. Days Out UK shall not accept liability for any loss, accident or injury that may occur at a participating attraction and any dispute arising must be settled direct with the attraction concerned.
6. Cash redemption value of each voucher is 0.001p.
7. You are advised to check all relevant information with your chosen attraction before commencing your journey.

Days Out UK, PO Box 427, Northampton NN1 3YN. Tel: 01604 622445

DAYSOUTUK
The place to look for places to go

Watercress Line
The Railway Station Alresford Hampshire SO24 9JG
Two for the Price of One
with a full-paying adult
(Not valid for special events, luxury dining, real ale trains, driving experiences or
footplate rides, cannot be used in conjunction with any other offer)
Cannot be used in conjunction with other offers. One voucher per party. Not valid on Bank Hols or special event days.
Expires end Feb 2009 (unless otherwise specified)

DISCOUNT VOUCHER

DAYSOUTUK
The place to look for places to go

Weald and Downland Open Air Museum
Singleton Chichester West Sussex PO18 0EU
One Child Free
with every full-paying adult
(Not to be used in conjunction with any other offer, not valid with group bookings, photo-
copies cannot be accepted, no cash alternative)
Cannot be used in conjunction with other offers. One voucher per party. Not valid on Bank Hols or special event days.
Expires end Feb 2009 (unless otherwise specified)

DISCOUNT VOUCHER

DAYSOUTUK
The place to look for places to go

Wedgwood Visitor Centre
Barlaston Stoke-On-Trent Staffordshire ST12 9ES
Two for the Price of One
with a full-paying adult or concession
(One person admitted free when accompanied by one full-paying adult or concession,
no cash alternative, voucher must be presented at time of purchase, no photocopies,
not to be used in conjunction with any other offer/promotion/discount, Wedgwood
Visitor Centre reserved the right to alter details without notice, subject to availablity)
Cannot be used in conjunction with other offers. One voucher per party. Not valid on Bank Hols or special event days.
Expires end Feb 2009 (unless otherwise specified)

DISCOUNT VOUCHER

DAYSOUTUK
The place to look for places to go

Wellington Country Park
Odiham Road Riseley Reading Berkshire RG7 1SP
Two for the Price of One with a full-paying adult
Cannot be used in conjunction with other offers. One voucher per party. Not valid on Bank Hols or special event days.
Valid 21 Apr - 20 Jul 2008

DISCOUNT VOUCHER

DAYSOUTUK
The place to look for places to go

West Dean Gardens
West Dean Chichester West Sussex PO18 0QZ
One Child Free
with a paying adult
Cannot be used in conjunction with other offers. One voucher per party. Not valid on Bank Hols or special event days.
Expires end Feb 2009 (unless otherwise specified)

DISCOUNT VOUCHER

DAYSOUTUK
The place to look for places to go

West Garden at Hatfield House
Hatfield Hertfordshire AL9 5NQ
Two for the Price of One
with a full-paying adult
(Applies to Park and West Garden only, not valid for major events, cannot
be used in conjunction with any other offer)
Cannot be used in conjunction with other offers. One voucher per party. Not valid on Bank Hols or special event days.
Valid 22 Mar - end of Sept 2008

DISCOUNT VOUCHER

1. Each voucher entitles the holder to the discount specified by the selected attraction.
2. Valid for use until 28/02/09 (unless otherwise specified, or if attraction season finishes prior to this). Vouchers are subject to the terms, conditions and restrictions of the selected attraction.
3. One voucher per party will be accepted, cannot be used in conjunction with any other offer, photocopies will not be accepted.
4. All attractions offering a discount have confirmed their willingness to participate. All information is subject to change without notice and should any attraction close or decline to accept a voucher for any reason, Days Out UK are not liable and cannot be held responsible.
5. Days Out UK shall not accept liability for any loss, accident or injury that may occur at a participating attraction and any dispute arising must be settled direct with the attraction concerned.
6. Cash redemption value of each voucher is 0.001p.
7. You are advised to check all relevant information with your chosen attraction before commencing your journey.

Days Out UK, PO Box 427, Northampton NN1 3YN. Tel: 01604 622445

1. Each voucher entitles the holder to the discount specified by the selected attraction.
2. Valid for use until 28/02/09 (unless otherwise specified, or if attraction season finishes prior to this). Vouchers are subject to the terms, conditions and restrictions of the selected attraction.
3. One voucher per party will be accepted, cannot be used in conjunction with any other offer, photocopies will not be accepted.
4. All attractions offering a discount have confirmed their willingness to participate. All information is subject to change without notice and should any attraction close or decline to accept a voucher for any reason, Days Out UK are not liable and cannot be held responsible.
5. Days Out UK shall not accept liability for any loss, accident or injury that may occur at a participating attraction and any dispute arising must be settled direct with the attraction concerned.
6. Cash redemption value of each voucher is 0.001p.
7. You are advised to check all relevant information with your chosen attraction before commencing your journey.

Days Out UK, PO Box 427, Northampton NN1 3YN. Tel: 01604 622445

1. Each voucher entitles the holder to the discount specified by the selected attraction.
2. Valid for use until 28/02/09 (unless otherwise specified, or if attraction season finishes prior to this). Vouchers are subject to the terms, conditions and restrictions of the selected attraction.
3. One voucher per party will be accepted, cannot be used in conjunction with any other offer, photocopies will not be accepted.
4. All attractions offering a discount have confirmed their willingness to participate. All information is subject to change without notice and should any attraction close or decline to accept a voucher for any reason, Days Out UK are not liable and cannot be held responsible.
5. Days Out UK shall not accept liability for any loss, accident or injury that may occur at a participating attraction and any dispute arising must be settled direct with the attraction concerned.
6. Cash redemption value of each voucher is 0.001p.
7. You are advised to check all relevant information with your chosen attraction before commencing your journey.

Days Out UK, PO Box 427, Northampton NN1 3YN. Tel: 01604 622445

Wicksteed Park
Barton Road Kettering Northamptonshire NN15 6NJ
Three Wristbands for the Price of Two
(cheapest wristband free)
(Maximum saving £15.00, Not valid on Bank Holiday weekends, cannot be used in conjunction with any other offer, management reserve the right to withdraw this offer at any time)

Cannot be used in conjunction with other offers. One voucher per party. Not valid on Bank Hols or special event days.

Expires end Feb 2009 (unless otherwise specified)

DISCOUNT VOUCHER

Wild Britain
Bedford Butterfly Park 65a Renhold Rd Wilden Bedford
Bedfordshire MK44 2PX
One Child Free
with a full-paying adult

Cannot be used in conjunction with other offers. One voucher per party. Not valid on Bank Hols or special event days.

Expires end Feb 2009 (unless otherwise specified)

DISCOUNT VOUCHER

Wimpole Hall
Arrington Royston Cambridgeshire SG8 0BW
One Child Free
with full-paying adult

Cannot be used in conjunction with other offers. One voucher per party. Not valid on Bank Hols or special event days.

Expires end Feb 2009 (unless otherwise specified)

DISCOUNT VOUCHER

Wimpole Home Farm
Arrington Royston Cambridgeshire SG8 0BW
One Child Free
with a full-paying adult

Cannot be used in conjunction with other offers. One voucher per party. Not valid on Bank Hols or special event days.

Expires end Feb 2009 (unless otherwise specified)

DISCOUNT VOUCHER

Winston Churchill's Britain at War Experience
64-66 Tooley Street London SE1 2TF
Two for the Price of One
with a full-paying adult

Cannot be used in conjunction with other offers. One voucher per party. Not valid on Bank Hols or special event days.

Expires end Feb 2009 (unless otherwise specified)

DISCOUNT VOUCHER

Wolterton Park
Wolterton Hall Erpingham Aylsham Norfolk NR11 7LY
Two for the Price of One
with a full-paying adult
(Offer applies to Hall admission only, not valid on charity days)

Cannot be used in conjunction with other offers. One voucher per party. Not valid on Bank Hols or special event days.

Expires end Feb 2009 (unless otherwise specified)

DISCOUNT VOUCHER

Woodlands Leisure Park
Blackawton Dartmouth Devon TQ9 7DQ
12% off Individual Admissions
(makes admissions £8.58)
(Maximum of four people per voucher, cannot be used in conjunction with
any other offer, no photocopies, no cash alternative)

Cannot be used in conjunction with other offers. One voucher per party. Not valid on Bank Hols or special event days.

Valid until 2 Nov 2008

Wookey Hole Caves
Wookey Hole Wells Somerset BA5 1BB
Two for the Price of One
with a full-paying adult

Cannot be used in conjunction with other offers. One voucher per party. Not valid on Bank Hols or special event days.

Expires end Feb 2009 (unless otherwise specified)

WWT Arundel, The Wildfowl and Wetlands Trust
Mill Road Arundel West Sussex BN18 9PB
Two for the Price of One
with a full-paying adult
(lowest entry fee goes free)

Cannot be used in conjunction with other offers. One voucher per party. Not valid on Bank Hols or special event days.

Expires end Feb 2009 (unless otherwise specified)

WWT National Wetland Centre Wales
Llwynhendy Llanelli Carmarthenshire Wales SA14 9SH
Two for the Price of One
with a full-paying adult

Cannot be used in conjunction with other offers. One voucher per party. Not valid on Bank Hols or special event days.

Expires end Feb 2009 (unless otherwise specified)

York Dungeon
12 Clifford Street York North Yorkshire YO1 9RD
One Child Free
with every full-paying adult

Cannot be used in conjunction with other offers. One voucher per party. Not valid on Bank Hols or special event days.

Expires end Feb 2009 (unless otherwise specified)

Yorkshire Dales Falconry and Conservation Centre
Crows Nest Austwick via Lancaster North Yorkshire LA2 8AS
One Child Free
with two full-paying adults

Cannot be used in conjunction with other offers. One voucher per party. Not valid on Bank Hols or special event days.

Expires end Feb 2009 (unless otherwise specified)

1. Each voucher entitles the holder to the discount specified by the selected attraction.
2. Valid for use until 28/02/09 (unless otherwise specified, or if attraction season finishes prior to this). Vouchers are subject to the terms, conditions and restrictions of the selected attraction.
3. One voucher per party will be accepted, cannot be used in conjunction with any other offer, photocopies will not be accepted.
4. All attractions offering a discount have confirmed their willingness to participate. All information is subject to change without notice and should any attraction close or decline to accept a voucher for any reason, Days Out UK are not liable and cannot be held responsible.
5. Days Out UK shall not accept liability for any loss, accident or injury that may occur at a participating attraction and any dispute arising must be settled direct with the attraction concerned.
6. Cash redemption value of each voucher is 0.001p.
7. You are advised to check all relevant information with your chosen attraction before commencing your journey.

Days Out UK, PO Box 427, Northampton NN1 3YN. Tel: 01604 622445

1. Each voucher entitles the holder to the discount specified by the selected attraction.
2. Valid for use until 28/02/09 (unless otherwise specified. or if attraction season finishes prior to this). Vouchers are subject to the terms, conditions and restrictions of the selected attraction.
3. One voucher per party will be accepted, cannot be used in conjunction with any other offer, photocopies will not be accepted.
4. All attractions offering a discount have confirmed their willingness to participate. All information is subject to change without notice and should any attraction close or decline to accept a voucher for any reason, Days Out UK are not liable and cannot be held responsible.
5. Days Out UK shall not accept liability for any loss, accident or injury that may occur at a participating attraction and any dispute arising must be settled direct with the attraction concerned.
6. Cash redemption value of each voucher is 0.001p.
7. You are advised to check all relevant information with your chosen attraction before commencing your journey.

Days Out UK, PO Box 427, Northampton NN1 3YN. Tel: 01604 622445

1. Each voucher entitles the holder to the discount specified by the selected attraction.
2. Valid for use until 28/02/09 (unless otherwise specified, or if attraction season finishes prior to this). Vouchers are subject to the terms, conditions and restrictions of the selected attraction.
3. One voucher per party will be accepted, cannot be used in conjunction with any other offer, photocopies will not be accepted.
4. All attractions offering a discount have confirmed their willingness to participate. All information is subject to change without notice and should any attraction close or decline to accept a voucher for any reason, Days Out UK are not liable and cannot be held responsible.
5. Days Out UK shall not accept liability for any loss, accident or injury that may occur at a participating attraction and any dispute arising must be settled direct with the attraction concerned.
6. Cash redemption value of each voucher is 0.001p.
7. You are advised to check all relevant information with your chosen attraction before commencing your journey.

Days Out UK, PO Box 427, Northampton NN1 3YN. Tel: 01604 622445

1. Each voucher entitles the holder to the discount specified by the selected attraction.
2. Valid for use until 28/02/09 (unless otherwise specified, or if attraction season finishes prior to this). Vouchers are subject to the terms, conditions and restrictions of the selected attraction.
3. One voucher per party will be accepted, cannot be used in conjunction with any other offer, photocopies will not be accepted.
4. All attractions offering a discount have confirmed their willingness to participate. All information is subject to change without notice and should any attraction close or decline to accept a voucher for any reason, Days Out UK are not liable and cannot be held responsible.
5. Days Out UK shall not accept liability for any loss, accident or injury that may occur at a participating attraction and any dispute arising must be settled direct with the attraction concerned.
6. Cash redemption value of each voucher is 0.001p.
7. You are advised to check all relevant information with your chosen attraction before commencing your journey.

Days Out UK, PO Box 427, Northampton NN1 3YN. Tel: 01604 622445

1. Each voucher entitles the holder to the discount specified by the selected attraction.
2. Valid for use until 28/02/09 (unless otherwise specified, or if attraction season finishes prior to this). Vouchers are subject to the terms, conditions and restrictions of the selected attraction.
3. One voucher per party will be accepted, cannot be used in conjunction with any other offer, photocopies will not be accepted.
4. All attractions offering a discount have confirmed their willingness to participate. All information is subject to change without notice and should any attraction close or decline to accept a voucher for any reason, Days Out UK are not liable and cannot be held responsible.
5. Days Out UK shall not accept liability for any loss, accident or injury that may occur at a participating attraction and any dispute arising must be settled direct with the attraction concerned.
6. Cash redemption value of each voucher is 0.001p.
7. You are advised to check all relevant information with your chosen attraction before commencing your journey.

Days Out UK, PO Box 427, Northampton NN1 3YN. Tel: 01604 622445

<u>SAVE £20 OFF</u> a Blackpool Mini Break!

To claim your discount, please call **0870 043 7633**
and quote "*Days Out UK Blackpool Reward*"
(lines are open 08.00-23.00, 7 days a week).

To request a free *Superbreak* brochure, please call **08705 499 499**
or simply visit **www.superbreak.com** for more information.

Offer Ends 28th February 2009

DISCOUNT VOUCHER

<u>SAVE £20 OFF</u> a Brighton Mini Break!

To claim your discount, please call **0870 043 7633**
and quote "*Days Out UK Brighton Reward*"
(lines are open 08.00-23.00, 7 days a week)

To request a free *Superbreak* brochure, please call **08705 499 499**
or simply visit **www.superbreak.com** for more information.

Offer Ends 28th February 2009

DISCOUNT VOUCHER

<u>SAVE £20 OFF</u> a Edinburgh Mini Break!

To claim your discount, please call **0870 043 7633**
and quote "*Days Out UK Edinburgh Reward*"
(lines are open 08.00-23.00, 7 days a week)

To request a free *Superbreak* brochure, please call **08705 499 499**
or simply visit **www.superbreak.com** for more information.

Offer Ends 28th February 2009

DISCOUNT VOUCHER

<u>SAVE £20 OFF</u> a Glasgow Mini Break!

To claim your discount, please call **0870 043 7633**
and quote "*Days Out UK Glasgow Reward*"
(lines are open 08.00-23.00, 7 days a week)

To request a free *Superbreak* brochure, please call **08705 499 499**
or simply visit **www.superbreak.com** for more information.

Offer Ends 28th February 2009

DISCOUNT VOUCHER

<u>SAVE £30 OFF</u> a Golf Break!

To claim your discount, please call **0870 043 7633**
and quote "*Days Out UK Golf Reward*"
(lines are open 08.00-23.00, 7 days a week)

To request a free *Superbreak* brochure, please call **08705 499 499**
or simply visit **www.superbreak.com** for more information.

Offer Ends 28th February 2009

DISCOUNT VOUCHER

<u>SAVE £20 OFF</u> a London Mini Break!

To claim your discount, please call **0870 043 7633**
and quote "*Days Out UK London Reward*"
(lines are open 08.00-23.00, 7 days a week)

To request a free *Superbreak* brochure, please call **08705 499 499**
or simply visit **www.superbreak.com** for more information.

Offer Ends 28th February 2009

DISCOUNT VOUCHER

1. Valid for use until 28/02/09 (unless chosen break becomes unavailable prior to this). Offer is subject to the terms, conditions and restrictions of Superbreak Mini-Holidays
2. Offer cannot be used in conjunction with any other offer.
3. All information is subject to change without notice and should offer become unavailble for any reason, Days Out UK are not liable and cannot be held responsible.
4. Days Out UK shall not accept liability for any loss, accident or injury that may occur, and any dispute arising must be settled direct with Superbreak Mini Holidays.
5. Offer valid for bookings for 2 persons for 2 nights or more.
6. Minimum spend before offer becomes valid: £100.00.
7. Only one discount per booking.

Superbreak Mini-Holidays 60 Piccadilly, York, YO1 9WX www.superbreak.com

1. Valid for use until 28/02/09 (unless chosen break becomes unavailable prior to this). Offer is subject to the terms, conditions and restrictions of Superbreak Mini-Holidays
2. Offer cannot be used in conjunction with any other offer.
3. All information is subject to change without notice and should offer become unavailble for any reason, Days Out UK are not liable and cannot be held responsible.
4. Days Out UK shall not accept liability for any loss, accident or injury that may occur, and any dispute arising must be settled direct with Superbreak Mini Holidays.
5. Offer valid for bookings for 2 persons for 2 nights or more.
6. Minimum spend before offer becomes valid: £100.00.
7. Only one discount per booking.

Superbreak Mini-Holidays 60 Piccadilly, York, YO1 9WX www.superbreak.com

1. Valid for use until 28/02/09 (unless chosen break becomes unavailable prior to this). Offer is subject to the terms, conditions and restrictions of Superbreak Mini-Holidays
2. Offer cannot be used in conjunction with any other offer.
3. All information is subject to change without notice and should offer become unavailble for any reason, Days Out UK are not liable and cannot be held responsible.
4. Days Out UK shall not accept liability for any loss, accident or injury that may occur, and any dispute arising must be settled direct with Superbreak Mini Holidays.
5. Offer valid for bookings for 2 persons for 2 nights or more.
6. Minimum spend before offer becomes valid: £100.00.
7. Only one discount per booking.

Superbreak Mini-Holidays 60 Piccadilly, York, YO1 9WX www.superbreak.com

1. Valid for use until 28/02/09 (unless chosen break becomes unavailable prior to this). Offer is subject to the terms, conditions and restrictions of Superbreak Mini-Holidays
2. Offer cannot be used in conjunction with any other offer.
3. All information is subject to change without notice and should offer become unavailble for any reason, Days Out UK are not liable and cannot be held responsible.
4. Days Out UK shall not accept liability for any loss, accident or injury that may occur, and any dispute arising must be settled direct with Superbreak Mini Holidays.
5. Offer valid for bookings for 2 persons for 2 nights or more.
6. Minimum spend before offer becomes valid: £100.00.
7. Only one discount per booking.

Superbreak Mini-Holidays 60 Piccadilly, York, YO1 9WX www.superbreak.com

1. Valid for use until 28/02/09 (unless chosen break becomes unavailable prior to this). Offer is subject to the terms, conditions and restrictions of Superbreak Mini-Holidays
2. Offer cannot be used in conjunction with any other offer.
3. All information is subject to change without notice and should offer become unavailble for any reason, Days Out UK are not liable and cannot be held responsible.
4. Days Out UK shall not accept liability for any loss, accident or injury that may occur, and any dispute arising must be settled direct with Superbreak Mini Holidays.
5. Offer valid for bookings for 2 persons for 2 nights or more.
6. Minimum spend before offer becomes valid: £100.00.
7. Only one discount per booking.

Superbreak Mini-Holidays 60 Piccadilly, York, YO1 9WX www.superbreak.com

1. Valid for use until 28/02/09 (unless chosen break becomes unavailable prior to this). Offer is subject to the terms, conditions and restrictions of Superbreak Mini-Holidays
2. Offer cannot be used in conjunction with any other offer.
3. All information is subject to change without notice and should offer become unavailble for any reason, Days Out UK are not liable and cannot be held responsible.
4. Days Out UK shall not accept liability for any loss, accident or injury that may occur, and any dispute arising must be settled direct with Superbreak Mini Holidays.
5. Offer valid for bookings for 2 persons for 2 nights or more.
6. Minimum spend before offer becomes valid: £100.00.
7. Only one discount per booking.

Superbreak Mini-Holidays 60 Piccadilly, York, YO1 9WX www.superbreak.com

SAVE £30 OFF a London Theatre Break!

To claim your discount, please call **0870 043 7633**
and quote "*Days Out UK Theatre Break Reward*"
(lines are open 08.00-23.00, 7 days a week)

To request a free *Superbreak* brochure, please call **08705 499 499**
or simply visit **www.superbreak.com** for more information.

Offer Ends 28th February 2009

DISCOUNT VOUCHER

SAVE £20 OFF a Manchester Mini Break!

To claim your discount, please call **0870 043 7633**
and quote "*Days Out UK Manchester Reward*"
(lines are open 08.00-23.00, 7 days a week)

To request a free *Superbreak* brochure, please call **08705 499 499**
or simply visit **www.superbreak.com** for more information.

Offer Ends 28th February 2009

DISCOUNT VOUCHER

SAVE £20 OFF a Stratford Mini Break!

To claim your discount, please call **0870 043 7633**
and quote "*Days Out UK Stratford Reward*"
(lines are open 08.00-23.00, 7 days a week)

To request a free *Superbreak* brochure, please call **08705 499 499**
or simply visit **www.superbreak.com** for more information.

Offer Ends 28th February 2009

DISCOUNT VOUCHER

SAVE £20 OFF a Wales Mini Break!

To claim your discount, please call **0870 043 7633**
and quote "*Days Out UK Wales Reward*"
(lines are open 08.00-23.00, 7 days a week)

To request a free *Superbreak* brochure, please call **08705 499 499**
or simply visit **www.superbreak.com** for more information.

Offer Ends 28th February 2009

DISCOUNT VOUCHER

SAVE £20 OFF a West Country Mini Break!

To claim your discount, please call **0870 043 7633**
and quote "*Days Out UK West Country Reward*"
(lines are open 08.00-23.00, 7 days a week)

To request a free *Superbreak* brochure, please call **08705 499 499**
or simply visit **www.superbreak.com** for more information.

Offer Ends 28th February 2009

DISCOUNT VOUCHER

SAVE £20 OFF a York Mini Break!

To claim your discount, please call **0870 043 7633**
and quote "*Days Out UK York Reward*"
(lines are open 08.00-23.00, 7 days a week)

To request a free *Superbreak* brochure, please call **08705 499 499**
or simply visit **www.superbreak.com** for more information.

Offer Ends 28th February 2009

DISCOUNT VOUCHER

1. Valid for use until 28/02/09 (unless chosen break becomes unavailable prior to this). Offer is subject to the terms, conditions and restrictions of Superbreak Mini-Holidays
2. Offer cannot be used in conjunction with any other offer.
3. All information is subject to change without notice and should offer become unavailble for any reason, Days Out UK are not liable and cannot be held responsible.
4. Days Out UK shall not accept liability for any loss, accident or injury that may occur, and any dispute arising must be settled direct with Superbreak Mini Holidays.
5. Offer valid for bookings for 2 persons for 2 nights or more.
6. Minimum spend before offer becomes valid: £100.00.
7. Only one discount per booking.

Superbreak Mini-Holidays 60 Piccadilly, York, YO1 9WX www.superbreak.com

1. Valid for use until 28/02/09 (unless chosen break becomes unavailable prior to this). Offer is subject to the terms, conditions and restrictions of Superbreak Mini-Holidays
2. Offer cannot be used in conjunction with any other offer.
3. All information is subject to change without notice and should offer become unavailble for any reason, Days Out UK are not liable and cannot be held responsible.
4. Days Out UK shall not accept liability for any loss, accident or injury that may occur, and any dispute arising must be settled direct with Superbreak Mini Holidays.
5. Offer valid for bookings for 2 persons for 2 nights or more.
6. Minimum spend before offer becomes valid: £100.00.
7. Only one discount per booking.

Superbreak Mini-Holidays 60 Piccadilly, York, YO1 9WX www.superbreak.com

1. Valid for use until 28/02/09 (unless chosen break becomes unavailable prior to this). Offer is subject to the terms, conditions and restrictions of Superbreak Mini-Holidays
2. Offer cannot be used in conjunction with any other offer.
3. All information is subject to change without notice and should offer become unavailble for any reason, Days Out UK are not liable and cannot be held responsible.
4. Days Out UK shall not accept liability for any loss, accident or injury that may occur, and any dispute arising must be settled direct with Superbreak Mini Holidays.
5. Offer valid for bookings for 2 persons for 2 nights or more.
6. Minimum spend before offer becomes valid: £100.00.
7. Only one discount per booking.

Superbreak Mini-Holidays 60 Piccadilly, York, YO1 9WX www.superbreak.com

1. Valid for use until 28/02/09 (unless chosen break becomes unavailable prior to this). Offer is subject to the terms, conditions and restrictions of Superbreak Mini-Holidays
2. Offer cannot be used in conjunction with any other offer.
3. All information is subject to change without notice and should offer become unavailble for any reason, Days Out UK are not liable and cannot be held responsible.
4. Days Out UK shall not accept liability for any loss, accident or injury that may occur, and any dispute arising must be settled direct with Superbreak Mini Holidays.
5. Offer valid for bookings for 2 persons for 2 nights or more.
6. Minimum spend before offer becomes valid: £100.00.
7. Only one discount per booking.

Superbreak Mini-Holidays 60 Piccadilly, York, YO1 9WX www.superbreak.com

1. Valid for use until 28/02/09 (unless chosen break becomes unavailable prior to this). Offer is subject to the terms, conditions and restrictions of Superbreak Mini-Holidays
2. Offer cannot be used in conjunction with any other offer.
3. All information is subject to change without notice and should offer become unavailble for any reason, Days Out UK are not liable and cannot be held responsible.
4. Days Out UK shall not accept liability for any loss, accident or injury that may occur, and any dispute arising must be settled direct with Superbreak Mini Holidays.
5. Offer valid for bookings for 2 persons for 2 nights or more.
6. Minimum spend before offer becomes valid: £100.00.
7. Only one discount per booking.

Superbreak Mini-Holidays 60 Piccadilly, York, YO1 9WX www.superbreak.com

1. Valid for use until 28/02/09 (unless chosen break becomes unavailable prior to this). Offer is subject to the terms, conditions and restrictions of Superbreak Mini-Holidays
2. Offer cannot be used in conjunction with any other offer.
3. All information is subject to change without notice and should offer become unavailble for any reason, Days Out UK are not liable and cannot be held responsible.
4. Days Out UK shall not accept liability for any loss, accident or injury that may occur, and any dispute arising must be settled direct with Superbreak Mini Holidays.
5. Offer valid for bookings for 2 persons for 2 nights or more.
6. Minimum spend before offer becomes valid: £100.00.
7. Only one discount per booking.

Superbreak Mini-Holidays 60 Piccadilly, York, YO1 9WX www.superbreak.com

Notes

Notes

Notes